KT-458-711

MODULE OPENERS

BRIEF CONTENTS

[Exploring Management]

Second Edition

John R. Schermerhorn, Jr.

John Wiley & Sons, Inc.

VICE PRESIDENT & PUBLISHER	George Hoffman
EXECUTIVE EDITOR	Lisé Johnson
DEVELOPMENTAL EDITOR	Susan McLaughlin
ASSISTANT EDITOR	Carissa Marker Doshi
ASSOCIATE DIRECTOR OF MARKETING	Amy Scholz
ASSISTANT MARKETING MANAGER	Diane Mars
MARKETING ASSISTANT	Luella Finley
CREATIVE DIRECTOR	Harry Nolan
INTERIOR DESIGNER	Brian Salisbury
PRODUCTION MANAGER	Dorothy Sinclair
SENIOR DESIGNER	Maddy Lesure
SENIOR PRODUCTION EDITOR	Sandra Dumas
EXECUTIVE MEDIA EDITOR	Allison Morris
ASSOCIATE MEDIA EDITOR	Elena Santa Maria
PHOTO DEPARTMENT MANAGER	Hilary Newman
PHOTO RESEARCHER	Teri Stratford
SENIOR EDITORIAL ASSISTANT	Sarah Vernon
ILLUSTRATION EDITOR	Anna Melhorn
PRODUCTION MANAGEMENT SERVICES	Ingrao Associates
COVER PHOTO	©Marina Filipovic Marinshe, www.marinshe.com

This book was typeset in 10/12 Sabon Regular at Aptara®, Inc. and printed and bound by Courier/ Kendallville. The cover was printed by Courier/Kendallville.

The paper in this book was manufactured by a mill whose forest management programs include sustained yield harvesting of its timberlands. Sustained yield harvesting principles ensure that the number of trees cut each year does not exceed the amount of new growth.

This book is printed on acid-free paper.

Copyright © 2010, 2007 by John Wiley & Sons, Inc. All rights reserved. No part of this publication may be reproduced, stored in a retrieval system or transmitted in any form or by any means, electronic, mechanical, photocopying recording, scanning or otherwise, except as permitted under Sections 107 or 108 of the 1976 United States Copyright Act, without either the prior written permission of the Publisher or authorization through payment of the appropriate per-copy fee to the Copyright Clearance Center, 222 Rosewood Drive, Danvers, MA 01923, (978) 750-8400, fax (978) 646-8600. Requests to the Publisher for permission should be addressed to the Permissions Department, John Wiley & Sons, Inc., 111 River Street, Hoboken, NJ 07030-5774, (201) 748-6011, fax (201) 748-6008.

Evaluation copies are provided to qualified academics and professionals for review purposes only, for use in their courses during the next academic year. These copies are licensed and may not be sold or transferred to a third party. Upon completion of the review period, please return the evaluation copy to Wiley. Return instructions and a free of charge return shipping label are available at **www.wiley.com/go/returnlabel**. Outside of the United States, please contact your local representative.

ISBN 13 978-0470-16964-3
ISBN 13 978-0470-55671-9

Printed in the United States of America.

SOUTHAMPTON SOLENT
UNIVERSITY LIBRARY
SUPPLIER   BLACKW
ORDER No
DATE 08 / 03 / 10

I once again dedicate this book to the person who lovingly helps
me explore and appreciate life's wonders: My wife, Ann.

About the Author

Dr. John R. Schermerhorn Jr. is the Charles G. O'Bleness Professor Emeritus of Management in the College of Business at Ohio University where he teaches undergraduate and MBA courses in management, organizational behavior, and Asian business. He also serves the university as Director of the Center for Southeast Asian Studies. He earned a PhD degree in organizational behavior from Northwestern University, after receiving an MBA degree (with distinction) in management and international business from New York University, and a BS degree in business administration from the State University of New York at Buffalo.

Highly dedicated to instructional excellence and serving the needs of practicing managers, Dr. Schermerhorn continually focuses on bridging the gap between the theory and practice of management both in the classroom and in his textbooks. He has won awards for teaching excellence at Tulane University, The University of Vermont, and Ohio University, where he was named a *University Professor*, the university's leading campus-wide award for undergraduate teaching. He also received the excellence in leadership award for his service as Chair of the Management Education and Development Division of the Academy of Management.

Dr. Schermerhorn's international experience adds a unique global dimension to his teaching and textbooks. He holds an honorary doctorate from the University of Pécs in Hungary, awarded for his international scholarly contributions to management research and education. He has also served as a Visiting Professor of Management at the Chinese University of Hong Kong, as on-site Coordinator of the Ohio University MBA and Executive MBA programs in Malaysia, and as Kohei Miura visiting professor at the Chubu University of Japan. Presently he is Adjunct Professor at the National University of Ireland at Galway, a member of the graduate faculty at Bangkok University in Thailand, Permanent Lecturer in the PhD program at the University of Pécs in Hungary, and advisor to the Lao-American College in Vientiane, Laos.

An enthusiastic scholar, Dr. Schermerhorn is a member of the Academy of Management, where he served as chairperson of the Management Education and Development Division. Educators and students alike know him as author of *Management 10e* (Wiley, 2010) and senior co-author of *Organizational Behavior 10e* (Wiley, 2009). His many books are available in Chinese, Dutch, French, Indonesian, Portuguese, Russian, and Spanish language editions. Dr. Schermerhorn has also published numerous articles in publications such as the *Academy of Management Journal, Academy of Management Review, Academy of Management Executive, Organizational Dynamics, Journal of Management Education*, and the *Journal of Management Development*.

Dr. Schermerhorn is a popular guest speaker at colleges and universities. His recent student and faculty workshop topics include innovations in business education, teaching the millennial generation, global perspectives in management, and textbook writing and scholarly manuscript development.

Dear Reader:

My career as a management educator began many years ago. The journey has evolved into one of continuous exploration and tremendous learning, as I benefit from my work both in the classroom and with students and colleagues around the world.

I believe the study of management is also an exploration, a daily one, whether we are instructors or students. After all, management is part of our everyday lives—at work, at school, at home, and even at leisure. It is ever present as we sort through the challenges of multiple responsibilities, distant horizons, constantly changing opportunities, great potential, and the wonders of a diverse global community.

Perhaps these words from T. S. Eliot's poem *Little Gidding* best describe the quest we all share:

> *We shall not cease from exploration*
> *And the end of all our exploring*
> *Will be to arrive where we started*
> *And know the place for the first time.*

The study of management is an ongoing journey, one full of enrichment and exploration. But in the end we return to application, trying to use what we have learned through experience to better our lives and those of others. This is really what this book, *Exploring Management, Second Edition*, is all about.

Take a minute to look at the book's cover, browse through the book's overall design, and just flip through some of the pages. Does the art inspire you and the design attract you to consider not only what's ahead in the book and in your management course, but also in your own life? I hope so. Because after all, how well we manage our lives, careers, and organizations can make a big difference in our increasingly complex world.

Please join me in using *Exploring Management, Second Edition,* and your management course as great learning opportunities, ones that can have life-long career and personal benefits. I believe you'll find the experience rich with the potential for lasting personal and professional value.

Have a great course and learning experience.

Sincerely,

John Schermerhorn

What makes *Exploring Management, Second Edition,* different?

I have written *Exploring Management, Second Edition,* to help students embrace management in the context of their everyday lives, career aspirations, and personal experiences. It is designed to meet and engage the new generation of students in their personal spaces, using lots of examples, applications, visual highlights, thought-provoking questions, and learning aids to convey the essentials of management. My hope is that this book with its special approach and underlying pedagogy will be a useful asset to committed management educators as they work in many unique and innovative ways to enrich the learning experiences of their students.

• *Exploring Management* offers a more flexible, topic-specific presentation.

The first thing you'll notice is that *Exploring Management* presents material in a way that meets student preferences for reading and studying "chunks" of material that can be digested in relatively short time periods, much like Internet news reports. This is in response to my classroom experiences where I, and my students, find the typical book chapters increasingly cumbersome and awkward to handle in the context of our course designs. In *Exploring Management* students never read more than several pages before hitting a "Study Guide" section that asks and allows them to bring closure to what they have just read in a meaningful way. And as users of the first edition confirm, when students can read and achieve closure on a "module" of material they tend to study it better, remember it better, and achieve better on tests and assignments dealing with it.

What a modular approach means for the instructor is that topics in the book are easily assignable and sized just right for a class session or a class discussion. The book covers the traditional planning, organizing, leading, and controlling framework, but everything can be used in any order based on instructor preferences. There are many options available for courses of different types, lengths, and meeting schedules, including online and distance learning formats. It all depends on what fits best with your course design, learning approaches, and class session objectives.

• *Exploring Management* presents an integrated learning design.

Exploring Management offers an integrated pedagogy. Every module opens with a clear visual presentation that helps students understand material right from the beginning. An **Opening Example** highlights an issue or issues relevant to the module and its subtitle, while presenting a brief report on real organizations and people. The two-page opening layout includes a **Learning Outline** presenting major headings as questions and answers. This helps students frame their reading and also prepares them for reinforcement provided in the integrated **Study Guide** at the end of each major section. This one-page checkpoint for learning and test preparation allows students to pause, consolidate, and check learning before moving on to the next section. The study guide elements include

- *Rapid Review*—bullet-list summary of concepts and points,
- *Terms to Define*—glossary quiz for vocabulary development,

- *Be Sure You Can*—checkpoint of major learning outcomes for mastery,
- *Questions for Discussion*—questions to stimulate inquiry and prompt class discussions.

How will *Exploring Management, Second Edition,* motivate students to learn about management?

The fact is that today's students continuously deal with a wide variety of conflicting demands and distractions. As I explore and learn about their world, I find that my teaching methods and instructional materials must constantly evolve. That's why I have taken special care to complement the modular approach of this book with a student-friendly writing style, emphasis on visual learning, inclusion of lots of timely features and examples, and an appealing design to the book's pages. I hope you'll agree that I am writing and presenting material in ways that come closer to meeting our students in their spaces—rich, varied, colorful, spontaneous and digital.

• *Exploring Management* relates concepts to students' experiences and interests.

I want students to embrace management in the context of their everyday lives, career aspirations, and personal experiences, and I constantly read and find materials that can do this when presented as part of a textbook discussion. To make this connection easier and highly visible, *Exploring Management* includes a number of special features that present additional and timely content reference points in a visually appealing and meaningful way. If you flip through the pages of the book, you will find that these features are not only interesting and meaningful to the reader. But don't forget they are also prompts and frames that can be used as opportunities for class and online discussions as well as follow-up individual and team assignments. Each chapter includes

- **Trendsetters**–introducing a real person's experience with the issues being discussed. Examples include Ursula Burns, CEO of Xerox and the first African American woman to head a *Fortune* 500 firm; Evan Williams and Biz Stone, founders of Twitter; and Patricia Karter, founder and head of the small and socially responsible Dancing Deer Baking Co.
- **News Feed**–highlighting an actual news story and posing questions in reaction to it. Topic examples include "Good and Bad News for Middle Managers," "Millennials May Need Special Handling," "Recession a Great Time for Prioritizing," and "Internet Censorship Spurs Cultural Debate."
- **Tips to Remember**–offering short reminders and suggestions for how to apply the module content to one's life and career. The tips cover useful and relevant issues such as a "Checklist for Dealing with Ethical Dilemmas," "How to Succeed in a Telephone Interview," and "Ins and Outs of Negotiating Salaries."
- **Stay Tuned**–brief summary of data and facts that stimulate critical inquiry and offer fuel for class discussions and debates. Examples include "Diversity Contradictions in Employment Trends," "Office Romance Policies Vary Widely," and "Corruption and Bribes Haunt International Business."

• *Exploring Management* uses a conversational and interactive writing style.

When writing *Exploring Management* I knew that to engage today's students I needed to break away from the textbook norm of communicating as the "sage on stage." So, I have tried to speak with students the way I do in the classroom—conversationally, interactively, and in a nondidactic fashion. User experiences with the first edition confirmed that this is the right approach.

You will notice this writing style right from the opening examples, through the content presentation, and in all of the in-text examples and special features offered for student enrichment. Although it may seem unusual to have an author speaking directly to his audience, just as with this preface, my goal is to be a real person and to approach the student readers in the spirit of what Ellen Langer calls *mindful learning*.[1] She describes this as engaging students from a perspective of active inquiry rather than as consumers of facts and prescriptions. I view it as a way of trying to move textbook writing in the same direction we are moving our teaching—being less didactic and more interactive, trying to involve students in a dialog around meaningful topics, questions, examples, and even dilemmas.

In short, I want students to actively question and engage the world around them; I want them to be informed; I want them to take ownership of the principles and insights of our discipline. Don't you want the same, and more?

• *Exploring Management* visually enhances the content presentation to appeal to visual learners.

I am convinced today, more than ever, that our students are very visual in their attention to information; this is a reflection of trends in popular culture. They watch movies, play video games, read and work online, chat, and Tweet—often all at once! This has to make a difference in how they approach their courses, and it is why I visually enhance the presentation of text content in two significant ways.

First, in *major figures* that have some complexity the figure title or caption is posed as a question. I then answer that question both in the figure drawing and in a short narrative summary below the figure. I call these "talking figures" in that the narrative speaks to the reader as he or she visualizes the topic being discussed.

Second, I periodically supplement the running text presentation with visual highlights. Whether it is a *table* that briefly lists important points, a *boxed highlight* that summarizes a key point or theory, or a *mini-figure* that schematically summarizes a concept under discussion, everything is designed to fit into and flow naturally with the text. These visual accents and reminders are designed as informative parts of a holistic reading experience, much as we engage when reading magazines, newspapers, and Internet content.

How will *Exploring Management, Second Edition,* ensure that students understand and apply management concepts and practices?

It is my belief that good things, like the field of management itself, grow from strong foundations. As instructors we need to help our students not only gain those foundations, but also see the connections to the real-world of management applications and practices. We need to help them develop intellectual capital that is supported by personal capacities for growth, continuous learning, and good old-fashioned hard work.

• *Exploring Management* includes a carefully selected set of end-of-module learning activities.

The end-of-module activities are designed to keep students moving in the direction of active learning. Keeping in mind what often matters most to students—

[1]Ellen J. Langer, *The Power of Mindful Learning* (Reading, MA: Perseus, 1997).

grades—my first priority is to help them prepare for quizzes and tests and to earn the best possible grades in their course. **Test Prep** asks students to answer multiple choice, short response, and integration and application questions to provide a good starting point for testing success. When coupled with the additional interactive test versions available on the *Exploring Management* student companion Web site, Test Prep becomes a substantial learning resource.

Of course we want students to move beyond pure test readiness, don't we? Don't we want them to understand that there are no "one best ways" or guaranteed solutions out there, and to realize that we need to craft much of what we do in work and with our lives to fit the moment? Don't we want them to willingly seek out problems and opportunities, search for answers, gather information, and work cooperatively with others, just as they will likely have to do in the workplace? To pursue these personal development directions, *Exploring Management* is fully loaded with opportunities for reflection and application.

Each module offers a **Self-Assessment** chosen to complement the subject matter. Examples include Learning Tendencies, Internal/External Locus of Control, and Managerial Assumptions. Students score and interpret the assessments to encourage greater self-reflection and personal exploration. A **Case Snapshot** introduces the recommended case study using a "tag line" and magazine format to interest the student reader and focus him or her on key issues and themes relevant to material being studied. Further, the **Online Interactive Learning Resources** section includes recommended active-learning activities (located online and in WileyPLUS). These include **More Self-Assessments**—to help students to further explore their managerial skills, tendencies, and personal characteristics; **Experiential Exercises**—for class activities and teamwork relating to the module content; and at least one **Team Project**—an active-learning group assignment that requires research, writing, and presentation on a current topic or issue.

• *Exploring Management* provides a portfolio of timely and comprehensive cases.

The cases for *Exploring Management* are more than just the standard set of textbook cases. Instead, we carefully developed these cases to help fulfill this book's goals and objectives as a comprehensive learning instrument. The cases actively engage students through their content, writing style, and visual presentation, while being timely, compelling, and representative of the range of organizations and people that are in today's news. They offer high versatility and will fit a variety of course applications and uses.

To provide maximum flexibility and to stimulate involvement, the cases appear in the format of a magazine article. And as with many magazine articles, some cases have internal sidebars. These sidebars not only focus on a person or organization that relates to the subject for the longer case, they also become "short cases" of their own. For example, the case on *Electronic Arts* contains a sidebar on *Take2Interactive*, the case on *Dunkin Donuts* contains a sidebar on *Starbucks*, and the case on *Trader Joe's* contains a sidebar on *Whole Foods*.

[Student and Instructor Resources]

What additional special materials does *Exploring Management, Second Edition,* offer to both instructors and students?

When it comes to support packages, it's always helpful to have a lot of useful material available. With that in mind, I worked closely with Wiley and my colleagues in designing materials for instructors and students that extend the goals of this book. The next two pages are just a sampler of the additional resources that can enrich your course.

- **Companion Web Site** The Companion Web site for *Exploring Management* at http://www.wiley.com/college/schermerhorn, contains a myriad of tools and links to aid both teaching and learning, including nearly all of the resources described in this section.

- **Instructor's Resource Guide** Prepared by Susan Verhulst, Des Moines Area Community College, the Instructor's Resource Guide includes a Conversion Guide, for moving from a chapter format to a modular format; Module Outlines; Module Objectives; Teaching Notes on how to integrate and assign special features; and suggested answers for all quiz and test questions found in the text. A series of Lecture Notes are included to help integrate the various resources available. The Instructor's Resource Guide also includes additional discussion questions and assignments that relate specifically to the cases, as well as case notes, self-assessments, and team exercises.

- **Test Bank** This Test Bank consists of over 40 true/false, multiple-choice, and short-answer questions per module. Vince Lutheran, University of North Carolina, Wilmington, specifically designed the questions to vary in degree of difficulty, from straightforward recall to challenging, to offer instructors the most flexibility when designing their exams. Adding more flexibility is the *Computerized Test Bank*, which requires a PC running Windows. The Computerized Test Bank, which contains all the questions from the manual version, includes a test-generating program that allows instructors to customize their exams.

- **PowerPoint Slides** Prepared by Susan Verhulst, Des Moines Area Community College, this set of interactive PowerPoint slides includes lecture notes to accompany each slide. This resource provides another visual enhancement and learning aid for students, as well as additional talking points for instructors. Instructors can access the PowerPoint slides and lecture notes on the instructor portion of the book's Web site.

- **Personal Response System** Vince Lutheran designed this set of Personal Response System questions (PRS or "Clicker" content) for each module, to spark additional discussion and debate in the classroom. For more information on PRS, please contact your local Wiley sales representative.

- **Web Quizzes** This resource, available on the student portion of the *Exploring Management* companion Web site, offers online quizzes, with questions varying in level of difficulty, designed to help students evaluate their individual progress through a module. Each module's quiz includes 10 questions. These review questions, developed by the Test Bank author, were created to provide the most effective and efficient testing system. Within this system, students have the opportunity to "practice" the type of knowledge they'll be expected to demonstrate on the exam.

- **Pre- and Post-Lecture Quizzes** Prepared by Gail Fraser, Kean University, the Pre- and Post-Lecture Quizzes, found in WileyPLUS, consist of

10–15 questions (multiple choice and true/false) per module, varying in level of detail and difficulty, but all focusing on that module's key terms and concepts. This resource allows instructors to quickly and easily evaluate their students' progress, by monitoring their comprehension of the material from before the lecture to after it.

- **Videos and Video Teaching Guide** were prepared by Kasey Sheehan Madara. This set of short video clips provides an excellent starting point for lectures or for general classroom discussion. Please contact your local Wiley representative for more information about the Management Video Program.

- **Movies and Music** Interested in integrating pop culture into your management course? Looking for ways to integrate the humanities through movies and music into your classroom? Robert L. Holbrook, Ohio University, provides *Art Imitates Life*, a supplement rich with innovative teaching ideas for integrating these ideas into your classroom experience. This instructor's supplement is available exclusively for adopters. Please contact your local Wiley representative.

- **MP3 downloads** These mini-lectures, one for each module, cover the main concepts and key points of each module. Each 2–4 minute audio file is a perfect tool for student review and can be downloaded to student computers or personal mp3 players.

- **Cases** This resource, available in the book and on WileyPLUS, contains cases linked to each module of the text. Ranging in length, these featured companies, selected specifically to appeal to students, include Zara International, Nike, Apple, and MySpace. Longer cases include sidebar discussions to illustrate different viewpoints. A set of discussion questions accompanies each case, with suggested answers found in the Instructor's Resource Guide.

- **Business Extra Select** Wiley has launched this online program, found at http://www.wiley.com/college/bxs, to provide instructors with millions of content resources, including an extensive database of cases, journals, periodicals, newspapers, and supplemental readings. This courseware system lends itself extremely well to integrating real-world content within the management course, thereby enabling instructors to convey the relevance of the course to their students.

WileyPLUS

WileyPLUS is a powerful online tool that provides instructors and students with an integrated suite of teaching and learning resources, including an online version of the text, in one easy-to-use Web site. To learn more about WileyPLUS, and view a demo, please visit www.wiley.com/college/WileyPLUS.

- **WileyPLUS Tools for Instructors** WileyPLUS enables instructors to:
  - Assign automatically graded homework, practice, and quizzes from the end of chapter and test bank.
  - Track students' progress in an instructor's gradebook.
  - Access all teaching and learning resources including an online version of the text, and student and instructor supplements, in one easy-to-use Web site. These include teaching tips, full color PowerPoint slides, and in-class activities.
  - Create class presentations using Wiley-provided resources, with the ability to customize and add your own materials.
- **WileyPLUS Resources for Students** WileyPLUS provides students with a variety of study tools:
  - mp3 downloads—audio overviews of each module exclusively available with WileyPLUS
  - team evaluation tools
  - experiential exercises
  - self-assessments
  - flashcards of key terms, and more!

[Acknowledgments]

This isn't the typical "book" project that most publishers deal with, one developed from a neat proposal. Instead, *Exploring Management, Second Edition,* is a "concept" book, which began, grew, and found life and form in its first edition over the course of many telephone conversations, conference calls, e-mail exchanges, and face-to-face meetings. It has since matured and been refined in content, style, and direction as a second edition through the useful feedback provided by many satisfied users and reviewers. It has also benefited from the continued commitments and sharp eyes of a most professional staff at John Wiley & Sons.

As always, there wouldn't be an *Exploring Management* without the support, commitment, creativity, and dedication of the following members of the Wiley team. It's a team with which I am most proud to be associated. My thanks travel now to you all: Lisé Johnson, *Executive Editor*; Susan McLaughlin *Developmental Editor,* George Hoffman, *Vice President and Publisher*; Carissa Marker Doshi, *Assistant Editor*; Sarah Vernon, *Senior Editorial Assistant*; Amy Scholz, *Associate Director of Marketing*; Sandra Dumas, *Senior Production Editor*; Harry Nolan, *Creative Director;* Hilary Newman, *Photo Manager*; Teri Stratford, *Photo Researcher*; Anna Melhorn, *Illustration Editor* and Suzanne Ingrao, *Outside Production Service Manager.*

I also want to thank the many individuals who took the time to read and evaluate draft manuscripts prior to production. These reviewers generously provided their expertise to help me ensure the book's accuracy, clarity, and focus on the needs of today's management instruction. Without their many, many helpful comments, the book would not be what it is today. Thank you to all of the following for your invaluable contributions to *Exploring Management.*

Focus Group Participants:
Maria Aria, *Camden County College*
Ellen Benowitz, *Mercer County Community College*
John Brogan, *Monmouth University*
Lawrence J. Danks, *Camden County College*
Matthew DeLuca, *Baruch College*
David Fearon, *Central Connecticut State University*
Stuart Ferguson, *Northwood University*
Eugene Garaventa, *College of Staten Island*
Scott Geiger, *University of South Florida, St. Petersburg*
Larry Grant, *Bucks County Community College*
Fran Green, *Pennsylvania State University, Delaware County*
F. E. Hamilton, *Eckerd College*
Don Jenner, *Borough of Manhattan Community College*
John Podoshen, *Franklin and Marshall College*
Neuman Pollack, *Florida Atlantic University*
David Radosevich, *Montclair State University*
Moira Tolan, *Mount Saint Mary College*

Virtual Focus Group Participants:
George Alexakis, *Nova Southeastern University*
Steven Bradley, *Austin Community College*
Paula Brown, *Northern Illinois University*
Elnora Farmer, *Clayton State University*
Paul Gagnon, *Central Connecticut State University*
Eugene Garaventa, *College of Staten Island*
Larry Garner, *Tarleton State University*

Wayne Grossman, *Hofstra University*
Dee Guillory, *University of South Carolina, Beaufort*
Julie Hays, *University of St. Thomas*
Kathleen Jones, *University of North Dakota*
Marvin Karlins, *University of South Florida*
Al Laich, *University of Northern Virginia*
Vincent Lutheran, *University of North Carolina, Wiilmington*
Douglas L. Micklich, *Illinois State University*
David Oliver, *Edison College*
Jennifer Oyler, *University of Central Arkansas*
Kathleen Reddick, *College of Saint Elizabeth*
Terry L. Riddle, *Central Virginia Community College*
Roy L. Simerly, *East Carolina University*
Frank G. Titlow, *St. Petersburg College*
David Turnipseed, *Indiana University – Purdue University, Fort Wayne*
Michael Wakefield, *Colorado State University, Pueblo*
George A. (Bud) Wynn, *University of Tampa*

Reviewers:
Peter Geoffrey Bowen, *University of Denver*
Kenneth G. Brown, *University of Iowa*
Beverly Bugay, *Tyler Junior College*
Robert Cass, *Virginia Wesleyan College*
Susan Davis, *Claflin University*
Matthew DeLuca, *Baruch College*
Valerie Evans, *Lincoln Memorial University*
Paul Ewell, *Bridgewater College*
Elnora Farmer, *Clayton State University*
Larry Garner, *Tarleton State University*
Dee Guillory, *University of South Carolina, Beaufort*
Debra Hunter, *Troy University*
Gary S. Insch, *West Virginia University*
Robert Klein, *Philadelphia University*
John Knutsen, *Everett Community College*
Al Laich, *University of Northern Virginia*
Susan Looney, *Delaware Technical & Community College*
Vincent Lutheran, *University of North Carolina, Wilmington*
John Markert, *Wells College*
Brenda McAleer, *Colby College*
Gerald McFry, *Coosa Valley Technical College*
Diane Minger, *Cedar Valley College*
Michael Monahan, *Frostburg State University*
Joelle Nisolle, *West Texas A&M University*
Penny Olivi, *York College of Pennsylvania*
Jennifer Oyler, *University of Central Arkansas*
Kathy Pederson, *Hennepin Technical College*
Joseph C. Santora, *Essex County College*
Howard Stanger, *Canisius College*
David Turnipseed, *Indiana University – Purdue University, Fort Wayne*
Robert Turrill, *University of Southern California*
Michael Wakefield, *Colorado State University, Pueblo*
Daniel Wubbena, *Western Iowa Tech Community College*

Second Edition Reviewers
Alan Wright, *Henderson State University*
Howard Stanger, *Canisius College*
Ralph R. Braithwaite, *University of Hartford*
Jeanette Davy, *Wright State University*

Catherine J. Ruggieri, *St. John's University*
M. David Albritton, *Northern Arizona University*
Charles D. White, *James Madison University*
Savannah Clay, *Central Piedmont Community College*
Kathryn Dansky, *Pennsylvania State University*
Vincent Lutheran, *University of North Carolina, Wilmington*
Mitchell Alegre, *Niagara University*
Matt DeLuca, *Baruch College*
Nancy Ray-Mitchell, *McLennan Community College*

Student Focus Group Participants, Baruch College:
Farhana Alam, Laureen Attreed, Sarah Bohsali, Susanna Eng, Dino Genzano, Annie Gustave, Andrew Josefiak, Diana Pang, Vidushi Parmar, Dulari Ramkishun, Vicky Roginskaya, Jessica Scheiber, Ruta Skarbauskaite, Darren Smith, Anita Alickaj, Dana Fleischer, Mandie Gellis, Haider Mehmood, and Dina Shlafman

Brief Contents

Detailed Contents

[Exploring Management]

Second Edition

1 Managers and the Management Process

Everyone Becomes a Manager Someday

Learning Outline

1.1 What Does It Mean to Be a Manager?
- Organizations have different types and levels of managers
- Accountability is a cornerstone of managerial performance
- Effective managers help others achieve high performance and satisfaction
- Managers must meet multiple and changing expectations

1.2 What Do Managers Do?
- Managerial work is often intense and demanding
- Managers plan, organize, lead, and control
- Managers enact informational, interpersonal, and decisional roles
- Managers pursue action agendas and engage in networking
- Managers use a variety of technical, human, and conceptual skills
- Managers learn from experience

1.3 What Issues and Concerns Complicate the New Workplace?
- Recession, globalization, and job migration are changing the world of work
- Failures of ethics and corporate governance are troublesome
- Diversity and discrimination are continuing social priorities
- People and intellectual capital drive high-performance organizations
- Career success requires continuous learning and a capacity for self-management

A Day at Work Should Be an Experience Full of Opportunities and Rewards. What about you? Is your work, or the prospect of working, a source of learning and experience, or just a means to a paycheck? Are you informed about the state of the economy and prospects for jobs, and are you well prepared for a promising future career? What is your ideal job? Do your skills and competencies match well with job requirements, and are they competitive when you stack yourself up against others seeking the same positions? Will you be able to balance career demands with personal responsibilities? What about other people; do you understand their needs and aspirations?

As you ponder these and related questions, take time to browse *Fortune* magazine's online list of "100 Best Companies to Work For." It's an enlightening read and one that should help set your aspirations for employment. The Container Store is one example of a respected company that treats its employees well. It was built with an idea—help people streamline their lives by selling them great containers at good prices, and founded upon a set of values—respect all those who contribute to making the company a success. The Container Store is consistently ranked among America's top employers and was even able to stick with its

Trendsetters
Ursula Burns leads Xerox
with confidence in trying
times.

News Feed
Great internships are a
good way to jump-start
careers.

Case Snapshot
Trader Joe's—Managing
with a cool edge

expansion plans during the recession. Co-founder and CEO Kip Tindell says: "We are so proud to foster a place where people enjoy getting up and coming to work every morning, working alongside great people—truly making a difference every single day."

The Container Store seems to walk the talk. It's known for treating its employees well—training, good pay, equal treatment, and the opportunity for input. The firm's Web site proclaims: ". . . the goal never has been growth for growth's sake. Rather, it is to adhere to a fundamental set of business values, centered around deliberate merchandising, superior customer service and constant employee input. Growth and success have been the natural and inevitable result."

Wouldn't you like to work in the type of environment like the one Tindell and his management team created at The Container Store? In your own career, wouldn't you like to be known as someone who shows a genuine respect for others? And when it comes to that career, would you agree that now is a good time to assess and advance your managerial potential? After all, everyone becomes a manager someday.

1.1 What Does It Mean to Be a Manager?

You find them everywhere, in small and large businesses, voluntary associations, government agencies, schools, hospitals, and wherever people work together for a common cause. Even though the job titles vary from team leader to department head, project leader, president, administrator, and more, the people in these jobs all share a common responsibility—helping others do their best work. We call them **managers**—persons who directly supervise, support, and help activate work efforts to achieve the performance goals of individuals, teams, or even an organization as a whole. In this sense, I think you'll agree with the chapter subtitle; we all are presently, or will be someday be, managers.

A **manager** is a person who supports and is responsible for the work of others.

• Organizations have different types and levels of managers.

"I've just never worked on anything that so visibly, so dramatically changes the quality of someone's life. Some days you wake up, and if you think about all the work you have to do it's so overwhelming, you could be paralyzed." These are the words of Justin Fritz as he described his experiences leading a 12-member team to launch a new product at Medtronic, a large medical products company. About the challenge of managerial work, he says: "You just have to get it done."[1]

Look at **Figure 1.1**. It describes an organization as a series of layers, each of which represents different levels of work and managerial responsibilities.[2] See where Justin would fit as a **first-line manager**—someone who leads a group of people who perform nonmanagerial duties. Common job titles for first-line managers like Justin include department head, team leader, and supervisor.[3]

First-line managers supervise people who perform nonmanagerial duties.

FIGURE 1.1

What Are the Typical Job Titles and Levels of Management in Organizations?

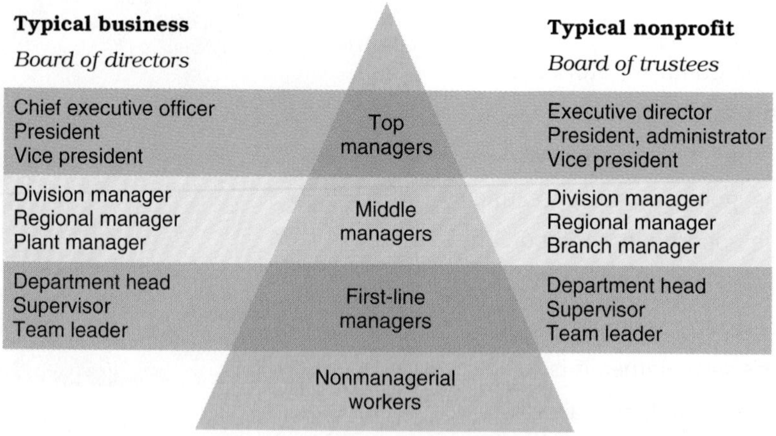

Typical business *Board of directors*		Typical nonprofit *Board of trustees*
Chief executive officer President Vice president	Top managers	Executive director President, administrator Vice president
Division manager Regional manager Plant manager	Middle managers	Division manager Regional manager Branch manager
Department head Supervisor Team leader	First-line managers	Department head Supervisor Team leader
	Nonmanagerial workers	

The traditional organization is structured as a pyramid. The top manager, typically a CEO, president, or executive director, reports to a board of directors (business) or board of trustees (nonprofit organization). Middle managers report to top managers whereas first-line managers report to middle managers. Nonmanagerial workers report to first-line managers.

Look again at Figure 1.1. This time consider where Justin may be headed in his career. At the next level above team leader we find **middle managers**—persons in charge of relatively large departments or divisions consisting of several smaller work units or teams. Middle managers usually supervise several first-line managers.

Middle managers oversee the work of large departments or divisions.

Examples might include clinic directors in hospitals; deans in universities; and division managers, plant managers, and regional sales managers in businesses. Because of their position "in the middle," these managers must be able to work well with people from all parts of the organization—higher, lower, and side-to-side. Obviously, as you or Justin move up the career ladder to middle management there will be more pressure and new challenges to face. But there should also be rewards and satisfaction.

Some middle managers advance still higher in the organization, earning job titles such as chief executive officer (CEO), president, or vice president. These **top managers** are responsible for the performance of an organization as a whole or for one of its larger parts. They are expected to be alert to trends and developments in the external environment, recognize potential problems and opportunities, and lead the organization to long-term success.[4] Procter & Gamble's former Chief Executive Officer, CEO, A. G. Lafley says the job is to "link the external world with the internal organization . . . make sure the voice of the consumer is heard . . . shape values and standards."[5] The best top managers are future-oriented strategic thinkers able to make good decisions under highly competitive and uncertain conditions. As Lafley points out, they should be "balancing the need for performance in the short term with the need to invest for the longer term." And, they should communicate an inspiring vision that motivates and keeps organization members focused on important objectives.[6]

John A. Byrne, now at *Business Week*, provides further insight into the work of a top manager. He was already used to hard work when he first became a top editor, but with every new issue published he admits to the "thrill" of doing a challenging job and the rush of accomplishment from doing it well.[7] He talks about extreme hours—8 AM to 10 PM is the norm. Yet he also points out that "rarely do I leave thinking I've wasted a day doing something that I didn't want to do. More often than not, I walk out feeling immensely proud of the people I work with and of the amazing things we have achieved together." Byrne even jokes that his job sometimes reminds him of being in college and pulling all-nighters on major projects. And in final recognition that being a manager is highly meaningful, Byrne says: "I'm enriched by the learning and personal growth that come from doing a job that I love."

Both A. G. Lafley and John Byrnes seem responsible and successful, but think about those top managers who are just the opposite. You have to admit that some managers slack off, don't live up to expectations, and even take personal advantage of their positions, perhaps to the point of abusing them and committing illegal acts. If CEOs and other senior managers really are at the top of organizations, who or what keeps them focused and high performing?

Figure 1.1 reminds us that even the CEO or president of an organization reports to a higher-level boss. In business corporations this is a **board of directors** whose members are elected by stockholders to represent their ownership interests. In nonprofit organizations, such as a hospital or university, top managers report to a *board of trustees*. These board members may be elected by local citizens, appointed by government bodies, or invited to serve by existing members.

In both business and the public sector, the basic responsibilities of a board are the same. The members are supposed to oversee the affairs of the organization and the performance of its top management. In other words, they are supposed to make sure that the organization is always being run right. This is called **governance**, the oversight of top management by an organization's board of directors or board of trustees.

• Accountability is a cornerstone of managerial performance.

Just one week before she was fired as CEO of Hewlett-Packard, Carly Fiorina, once described as America's most powerful businesswoman, told reporters that her relationship with the HP board was "excellent."[8] But board members soon

Top managers guide the performance of the organization as a whole or of one of its major parts.

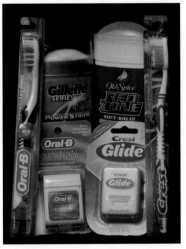

According to A. G. Lafley, Procter & Gamble's former CEO, the top manager's job is to "link the external world with the internal organization" and "make sure the voice of the consumer is heard."

Members of a **board of directors** are elected by stockholders to represent their ownership interests.

Governance is oversight of top management by a board of directors or board of trustees.

acted to exercise governance and hold her accountable for what they considered to be HP's unacceptable performance results.

Throughout the workplace, not just at the top, the term **accountability** describes the requirement of one person to answer to a higher authority for performance achieved in his or her area of work responsibility. This notion of accountability is an important aspect of managerial performance. In the traditional organizational pyramid, accountability flows upward. Team members are accountable to a team leader; the team leader is accountable to a middle manager; the middle manager is accountable to a top manager; and, as in the case of Carly Fiorina at HP, the top manager is accountable to a board of directors.

Of course, it is also important to recognize the unique challenges of accountability and dependency in managerial performance. At the same time that any manager is being held accountable by a higher level for the performance results of her or his area of supervisory responsibility, the manager is dependent on others to do the required work. In fact, we might say that a large part of the study of management is all about learning how to best manage the dynamics of accountability and dependency, as shown in **Figure 1.2**.

Accountability is the requirement to show performance results to a supervisor.

FIGURE 1.2

Accountability and Dependency Are Important Issues in Managerial Work.

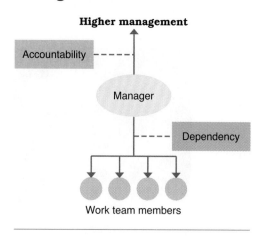

An **effective manager** successfully helps others achieve high performance and satisfaction in their work.

Quality of work life is the overall quality of human experiences in the workplace.

• Effective managers help others achieve high performance and satisfaction.

This discussion of performance accountability and related challenges may make you wonder: What exactly is an effective manager? Most people, perhaps you, would reply that an effective manager is someone who helps people and organizations perform. That's a fine starting point, but I like to go one step further. I define an **effective manager** as someone who successfully helps others achieve both high performance and satisfaction in their work.

This concern for not just performance but also satisfaction is a central theme in the new workplace. It brings to our attention **quality of work life** (QWL) issues. This term describes the overall quality of human experiences in the workplace. Have you experienced a "high QWL" environment? Most people would describe it as a place where they are respected and valued by their employer; a place where they have fair pay, safe work conditions, opportunities to learn and use new skills, room to grow and progress in a career, and protection of individual rights; a place where members take pride in their work and the organization.

Are you willing to work anywhere other than in a high QWL setting? Would you, as a manager, be pleased with anything less than knowing you excel at helping others achieve not just high performance, but also job satisfaction?[9] Sadly, the real world of work doesn't always live up to these expectations. Talk to people at work, your parents, and friends. You might be surprised. Many people today still encounter difficult, sometimes even hostile and unhealthy, work environments—low QWL to be sure![10]

• Managers must meet multiple and changing expectations.

Like everything else in our lives, the work of managers constantly evolves along with changes in our society and organizations. It is common today to hear managers referred to as "coordinators" and "coaches." These labels certainly contrast with the more traditional notion of managers as "order-givers" and "directors." Just their use gives a very different impression of the manager's job. And the fact is that most organizations need more than managers who simply sit back and tell others what to do.

Take a moment to jot down a few notes on the behaviors and characteristics of the *best* managers you've ever had. My students describe theirs as leading by example, willing to do any job, treating others as equals and with respect, acting approachable, being enthusiastic, expecting outstanding performance, and helping others grow. They talk about managers who often work alongside those they supervise, spending most of their time providing advice and support so that others can perform to the best of their abilities, and with satisfaction. How does this listing compare with your experiences?

Figure 1.3 uses the notion of an *upside-down pyramid* to describe a new mindset for managers—a real expression of what it means to act as a coach rather than an order-giver. Prominent at the top of the upside-down pyramid are nonmanagerial workers, people who interact directly with customers and clients, or produce products and services for them. Managers are shown a level below. Their attention is concentrated on supporting these workers so they can best serve the organization's customers.

FIGURE 1.3

How Do Mindsets Change When the Organization Is Viewed as an Upside-Down Pyramid?

Inverting the traditional organizational pyramid offers a valuable perspective on the new emerging roles of managers. In the upside-down pyramid view, managers (at the bottom) are expected to support operating workers (above managers) so that they can best serve the organization's customers (at the top). The appropriate "mindset" of the supportive manager is more "coaching" and "helping" than "directing" and "order giving."

In the upside-down pyramid view there is no doubt that the organization exists to serve its customers. And it is clear that managers are there to help and support the people whose work makes that possible. Doesn't that sound like the way things should be?

Study Guide

1.1
What Does It Mean to Be a Manager?

Rapid review

- Managers support and facilitate the work efforts of other people in organizations.
- Top managers scan the environment and pursue long-term goals; middle managers coordinate activities among large departments or divisions; first-line managers, like team leaders, supervise and support nonmanagerial workers.
- Everyone in organizations is accountable to a higher level manager for his or her performance accomplishments; at the highest level, top managers are held accountable by boards of directors.
- Effective managers help others achieve both high performance and high levels of job satisfaction.
- New directions in managerial work emphasize "coaching" and "supporting," rather than "directing" and "order giving."
- In the upside-down pyramid view of organizations, the role of managers is to support nonmanagerial workers who serve the needs of customers at the top.

Terms to define

Accountability
Board of directors
Effective manager
First-line manager
Governance
Manager
Middle managers
Quality of work life
Top managers

Be sure you can

- explain how managers contribute to organizations
- describe the activities of managers at different levels
- explain how accountability operates in organizations
- describe the goals of an effective manager
- list several ways the work of managers is changing from the past
- explain the role of managers in the upside-down pyramid

Questions for discussion

1. Other than at work, in what situations do you expect to be a manager during your lifetime?
2. Why should a manager be concerned about the quality of work life in an organization?
3. In what ways does the upside-down pyramid view of organizations offer advantages over the traditional view of the top-down pyramid?

1.2 What Do Managers Do?

The managers we have been discussing are indispensable to organizations; their efforts bring together resources, technology, and human talents to get things done. Some are fairly routine tasks that are done day after day. Many others, however, are challenging and novel, often appearing as unexpected problems and opportunities. But regardless of the task at hand, managers are expected to make things happen in ways that best serve the goals of the organization and the interests of its members.

• Managerial work is often intense and demanding.

The manager can never be free to forget the job, and never has the pleasure of knowing, even temporarily, that there is nothing else to do. . . . Managers always carry the nagging suspicion that they might be able to contribute just a little bit more. Hence they assume an unrelenting pace in their work.[11]

Although what managers do may seem straightforward, this quote shows that putting it into practice can be much more complicated. In his classic book, *The Nature of Managerial Work*, Henry Mintzberg describes the daily work of corporate chief executives as: "There was no break in the pace of activity during office hours. The mail . . . telephone calls . . . and meetings . . . accounted for almost every minute from the moment these executives entered their offices in the morning until they departed in the evenings."[12] Today, we might add the Blackberry or iPhone, ever-full e-mail, instant messaging, voice-mail inboxes, and even Twitter to Mintzberg's list of executive preoccupations.[13]

Can you imagine a day filled with these responsibilities? The managers Mintzberg observed had little free time because unexpected problems and continuing requests for meetings consumed almost all the time that was available. Their workdays were intense, hectic, and fast paced; the pressure for continuously improving performance was all-encompassing. Any manager, according to Mintzberg, must be ready to work long hours on fragmented and varied tasks at an intense pace, while getting things done through communication and interpersonal relationships.

Self-Assessment
This is a good point to complete the self-assessment "*Personal Management Foundations*" found on page 24.

• Managers plan, organize, lead, and control.

There is little doubt that managerial work can be busy, demanding, and stressful not just for chief executives in large businesses, but for managers at all levels of responsibility in any organization.[14] If you are ready to perform as a manager or to get better as one, a good starting point is **Figure 1.4**. It shows the four functions in the **management process**—planning, organizing, leading, and controlling. The belief is that all managers, regardless of title, level, and organizational setting, are responsible for doing each of them well.[15]

In management, **planning** is the process of setting performance objectives and determining what actions should be taken to accomplish them. When managers plan, they set goals and objectives, and select ways to achieve them.

There was a time, for example, when Ernst & Young's top management grew concerned about the firm's retention rates for women.[16] Why? Turnover rates at the time were much higher for women than among men, running some 22 percent per year and costing the firm about 150 percent of each person's annual salary to hire and train a replacement. Then Chairman Philip A. Laskawy responded to the situation by setting a planning objective to reduce turnover rates for women.

Even the best plans will fail without strong implementation. Success begins with **organizing**, the process of assigning tasks, allocating resources, and coordinating the activities of individuals and groups. When managers organize they bring people and resources together to put plans into action.

The **management process** is planning, organizing, leading, and controlling the use of resources to accomplish performance goals.

Planning is the process of setting objectives and determining what should be done to accomplish them.

Organizing is the process of assigning tasks, allocating resources, and coordinating work activities.

FIGURE 1.4

What Are the Four Functions That Make Up the Management Process?

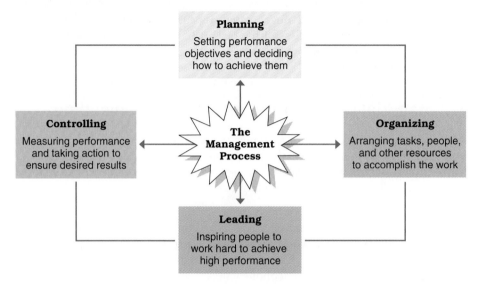

The management process consists of four functions: planning, organizing, leading, and controlling. Planning sets the direction as performance objectives; organizing arranges people and tasks to do the work; leading inspires others to work hard; and controlling measures performance to make sure that plans and objectives are accomplished.

At Ernst & Young, Laskawy organized to meet his planning objective by convening and personally chairing a Diversity Task Force of partners. He also established a new Office of Retention and hired Deborah K. Holmes to head it. As retention problems were identified in various parts of the firm, Holmes created special task forces to tackle them and recommend location-specific solutions.

Leading is the process of arousing enthusiasm and inspiring efforts to achieve goals.

The management function of **leading** is the process of arousing people's enthusiasm to work hard and inspiring their efforts to fulfill plans and accomplish objectives. When managers lead, they build commitments to plans and influence others to do their best work in implementing them.

Deborah K. Holmes actively pursued her leadership responsibilities at Ernst & Young. She noticed that, in addition to the intense work at the firm, women often faced more stress because their spouses also worked. She became a champion of improved work-life balance and pursued it relentlessly. She started "call-free holidays" where professionals did not check voice mail or e-mail on weekends and holidays. She also started a "travel sanity" program that limited staffers' travel to four days a week so that they could get home for weekends. And she started a Woman's Access Program to provide mentoring and career development.

Controlling is the process of measuring performance and taking action to ensure desired results.

Controlling is the process of measuring work performance, comparing results to objectives, and taking corrective action as needed. As you have surely experienced, things don't always go as planned. When managers control, they stay in contact with people as they work, gather and interpret information on performance results, and use this information to make adjustments.

At Ernst & Young, Laskawy and Holmes regularly measured retention rates for women at the firm and compared them to the rate that existed when their new programs were started. By comparing results with plans and objectives, they were able to track changes in work-life balance and retention rates, and pinpoint where they needed to make further adjustments in their programs. Over time, turnover rates for women were reduced at all levels in the firm.[17]

• Managers enact informational, interpersonal, and decisional roles.

When you consider the four management functions, don't be unrealistic. The functions aren't always performed one at a time or step-by-step. Remember the manager's workday as earlier described by Mintzberg—intense, fast-paced, and stressful. The reality is that managers must plan, organize, lead, and control continuously while dealing with the numerous events, situations, and problems of the day.

To describe how managers actually get things done, Mintzberg identified three sets of roles that he believed all good managers enact successfully.[18] As shown in **Figure 1.5**, a manager's *informational roles* focus on the giving, receiving, and analyzing of information. The *interpersonal roles* reflect interactions with people inside and outside the work unit. The *decisional roles* involve using information to make decisions to solve problems or address opportunities.[19] It is through these roles, so to speak, that managers fulfill their planning, organizing, leading, and controlling responsibilities.

FIGURE 1.5
Mintzberg's Description of a Manager's Informational, Interpersonal, and Decisional Roles.

Interpersonal roles	Informational roles	Decisional roles
How a manager interacts with other people • Figurehead • Leader • Liaison	How a manager exchanges and processes information • Monitor • Disseminator • Spokesperson	How a manager uses information in decision making • Entrepreneur • Disturbance handler • Resource allocator • Negotiator

• Managers pursue action agendas and engage in networking.

While we are speaking about realities, consider this description of just one incident from the workday of a general manager.[20]

> On the way to a scheduled meeting, a general manager met a staff member who did not report to him. They exchanged "hellos" and in a two-minute conversation the manager: (a) asked two questions and received helpful information; (b) reinforced his relationship with the staff member by sincerely complimenting her on recent work; and (c) enlisted the staff member's help on another project.

Can you see the pattern here? In just two short minutes, this general manager accomplished a lot. In fact, he demonstrated excellence with two activities that management consultant and scholar John Kotter considers critical to succeeding with the management process—agenda setting and networking.[21]

Through *agenda setting*, managers develop action priorities. These agendas may be incomplete and loosely connected in the beginning. But over time, as the manager utilizes information continually gleaned from many different sources, the agendas become more specific. Kotter believes that the best managers keep their agendas always in mind so they can quickly recognize and take advantage of opportunities to advance them. In the example above, what might have happened if the manager had simply nodded "hello" to the staff member and continued on to his meeting?

Trendsetters

Ursula Burns Leads Xerox with Confidence in Trying Times

"**F**rankness," "sharp humor," "willingness to take risks," "deep industry knowledge," "technical prowess." These are all adjectives used to describe Ursula Burns, the new CEO of Xerox Corporation. Burns' appointment capped a career that began with the company as an intern in 1980 to become the first African-American woman to head a *Fortune* 500 firm as well as the first to succeed another woman in the CEO spot. Her predecessor, Anne Mulcahy, was also a company veteran who had worked her way to the top over a 27-year career. In praising Mulcahy's leadership, Ilene Lang, who heads Catalyst, a nonprofit supporting women in business, said: "Most companies have one woman who might be a possibility to become CEO, Xerox has a range of them."

Burns took over the firm at the height of financial crisis and faced declining sales and profits, as well as a stock price that had lost half its value in a year's time. But reports are very positive that her experience and leadership skills are just what the firm now needs to address competitive challenges. And the challenges are many: less paper being used in offices, less equipment being bought or leased, and falling prices. Yet Burns conveys confidence with a smile, intending to pursue more sales in emerging markets, better efficiencies, and more sales of high margin services.

In her prior role as president, Burns made tough decisions on downsizing, closed Xerox manufacturing operations, and changed the product mix. She also knows how to work well with the firm's board. Director Robert A. McDonald of Procter & Gamble says, "She understands the technology and can communicate it in a way that a director can understand it."

Burns is a working mother and spouse with a teenage daughter and 20-year old stepson. She was raised by a single mom in New York City public housing and eventually earned a master's degree in engineering from Columbia University. Pride in her achievements comes across loud and clear in a speech to the YWCA in Cleveland. "I'm in this job because I believe I earned it through hard work and high performance," she said. "Did I get some opportunities early in my career because of my race and gender? Probably . . . I imagine race and gender got the hiring guys' attention. And then the rest was really up to me."

Through *networking*, managers build and maintain positive relationships with other people, ideally those whose help might be useful someday. These networks create the opportunities through which many agenda items can be fulfilled. Much of what needs to be done is beyond a manager's capabilities alone; the support and contributions of other people often make the difference between success and failure.

In the present example, our manager needed help from someone who did not report directly to him. Although he wasn't in a position to order the staff person to help him out, this wasn't a problem. Because of the working relationship they maintained through networking, she wanted to help when asked.

Most managers maintain extensive networks with peers, members of their work teams, higher-level executives, and people at various points elsewhere in the organization at the very least. Many are expected to network even more broadly, such as with customers, suppliers, and community representatives.

How do you rate your agenda-setting and networking capabilities? Are your To-Do lists too long, filled with minor rather than major things? Do you engage in or avoid opportunities to network with other people whose support and assistance might be helpful someday?

• Managers use a variety of technical, human, and conceptual skills.

The discussion of roles, agendas, and networking is but a starting point for inquiry into your personal portfolio of management skills. Another step forward is available through the work of Harvard scholar Robert L. Katz. He has classified the essential skills of managers into three categories—technical, human, and conceptual. As shown in **Figure 1.6**, the relative importance of each skill varies by level of managerial responsibility.[22]

A **technical skill** is the ability to use expertise to perform a task with proficiency.

A **technical skill** is the ability to use a special proficiency or expertise to perform particular tasks. Accountants, engineers, market researchers, financial planners, and systems analysts, for example, possess obvious technical skills. Other baseline technical skills for any college graduate today include such things as written and oral communication, computer literacy, and math and numeracy.

In Katz's model, technical skills are very important at career entry levels. So how do you get them? Formal education is an initial source for learning these skills, but continued training and job experiences are important in further developing them. Why not take a moment to inventory your technical skills, the ones you have and the ones you still need to learn for your future career? Katz tells us that the technical skills are especially important at job entry and early career

FIGURE 1.6

Three Essential Managerial Skills and How Their Importance Varies Across Levels.

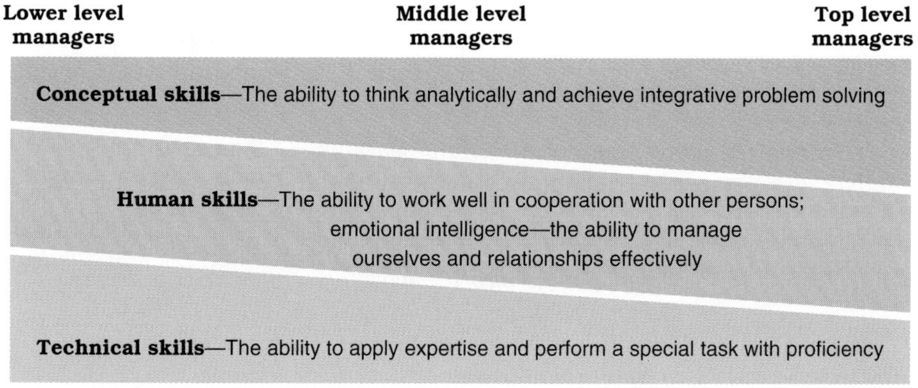

Lower level managers	Middle level managers	Top level managers

Conceptual skills—The ability to think analytically and achieve integrative problem solving

Human skills—The ability to work well in cooperation with other persons; emotional intelligence—the ability to manage ourselves and relationships effectively

Technical skills—The ability to apply expertise and perform a special task with proficiency

points. Surely, you want to be ready the next time a job interviewer asks the bottom-line question: "What can you really do for us?"

The ability to work well with others is a **human skill**, and it is a foundation for managerial success. How can we excel at networking, for example, without an ability and willingness to relate well with other people? A manager with good human skills will have a high degree of self-awareness and a capacity to understand or empathize with the feelings of others. You would most likely observe this person working with others in a spirit of trust, enthusiasm, and genuine involvement.

A manager with good human skills is also likely to be high in **emotional intelligence**. Considered an important leadership attribute, "EI" is defined by scholar and consultant Daniel Goleman as the "ability to manage ourselves and our relationships effectively."[23] He believes that emotional intelligence is built upon the following five foundations.

1. *Self-awareness*—understanding moods and emotions
2. *Self-regulation*—thinking before acting, controlling disruptive impulses
3. *Motivation*—working hard and persevering
4. *Empathy*—understanding emotions of others
5. *Social skills*—gaining rapport and building good relationships

Given the highly interpersonal nature of managerial work, it is easy to see why human skills and emotional intelligence are so helpful. As shown in the previous figure, Katz believes they are consistently important across all the managerial levels.

The ability to think critically and analytically is a **conceptual skill**. It involves the capacity to break down problems into smaller parts, see the relations between the parts, and recognize the implications of any one problem for others. While all managers should have the ability to view situations broadly and to solve problems to the benefit of everyone concerned, Katz believes that the conceptual skills actually grow in importance as people advance to higher management responsibilities. At each higher level, the problems managers face often become more ambiguous and have many complications with longer-term consequences.

• Managers learn from experience.

Functions, roles, agendas, networks, skills! How can anyone develop and be consistently good at all of these things? How can the capacity to do them all well be developed and maintained for long-term career success?

A **human skill** is the ability to work well in cooperation with other people.

Emotional intelligence is the ability to manage ourselves and our relationships effectively.

A **conceptual skill** is the ability to think analytically and solve complex problems.

This book can be a good starting point, a foundation for the future. Take your time and give some thought to answering the questions that I ask as you read. Consider also how you might apply what you are learning to your current situations—school, work, and personal. And then ask what you can learn from these situations in turn. It is well recognized that successful managers do this all the time. We call it learning from experience.

The challenge for all of us is to be good at **lifelong learning**—the process of continuously learning from our daily experiences and opportunities. Consider this point by State Farm CEO Ed Rust.[24]

> *I think the whole concept of lifelong learning is more relevant today than ever before. It's scary to realize that the skill sets we possess today are likely to be inadequate five years from now, just due to the normal pace of change. As more young people come into the workforce, they need a deeper, fundamental understanding of the basic skills—not just to get a job, but to grow with the job as their responsibilities change over their lifetimes.*

Does Rust's assessment sound daunting? Or is it a challenge you are confident in meeting? Do you agree that this is an accurate description of today's career environment? If you do, and I believe you should, you'll also have to admit that learning, learning, and more learning are top priorities in our lives.

Why not use **Table 1.1**, *Six "Must Have" Managerial Skills*, as a preliminary checklist for assessing your managerial learning and career readiness? How do you stack up?

With this list as a starting point, the rest of this book should be even more meaningful for your personal development. And in this regard, another question is worth asking: Given all the hard work and challenges that it involves, why would anyone want to be a manager? Beyond the often-higher salaries, there is one very compelling answer: pride. As pointed out by management theorist Henry Mintzberg, being a manager is an important and socially responsible job[25]:

> *No job is more vital to our society than that of the manager. It is the manager who determines whether our social institutions serve us well or whether they squander our talents and resources. It is time to strip away the folklore about managerial work, and time to study it realistically so that we can begin the difficult task of making significant improvement in its performance.*

Lifelong learning is continuous learning from daily experiences.

[TABLE 1.1]

Six "Must Have" Managerial Skills

Teamwork
Able to work effectively as team member and leader; strong on team contributions, leadership, conflict management, negotiation, consensus building

Self-Management
Able to evaluate self, modify behavior, and meet obligations; strong on ethical reasoning, personal flexibility, tolerance for ambiguity, performance responsibility

Leadership
Able to influence and support others to perform complex and ambiguous tasks; strong on diversity awareness, project management, strategic action

Critical Thinking
Able to gather and analyze information for problem solving; strong on information analysis and interpretation, creativity and innovation, judgment, and decision making

Professionalism
Able to sustain a positive impression and instill confidence in others; strong on personal presence, initiative, and career management

Communication
Able to express self well in communication with others; strong on writing, oral presentation, giving and receiving feedback, technology utilization

Study Guide

1.2
What Do Managers Do?

Rapid review

- The daily work of managers is often intense and stressful, involving long hours and continuous performance pressures.
- In the management process, planning sets the direction, organizing assembles the human and material resources, leading provides the enthusiasm and direction, and controlling ensures results.
- Managers perform interpersonal, informational, and decision-making roles while pursuing high-priority agendas and engaging in successful networking.
- Managers rely on a combination of technical skills (ability to use special expertise), human skills (ability to work well with others), and conceptual skills (ability to analyze and solve complex problems).
- Everyday experience is an important source of continuous lifelong learning for managers.

Terms to define

Conceptual skill
Controlling
Emotional intelligence
Human skill
Leading
Lifelong learning
Management process
Organizing
Planning
Technical skill

Be sure you can

- describe the intensity and pace of a typical workday for a manager
- give examples of each of the four management functions
- list the three managerial roles identified by Mintzberg
- explain how managers use agendas and networks in their work
- give examples of a manager's technical, human, and conceptual skills
- explain how these skills vary in importance across management levels
- explain the importance of experience as a source of managerial learning

Questions for discussion

1. Is Mintzberg's view of the intense and demanding nature of managerial work realistic and, if so, why would you want to do it?
2. If Katz's model of how different levels of management use the essential managerial skills is accurate, what are its career implications for you?
3. Why is emotional intelligence an important component of one's human skills?

Managers gain the trust of others by consistently displaying personal integrity and ethical behavior.

Globalization is the worldwide interdependence of resource flows, product markets, and business competition.

Global outsourcing involves contracting for work that is performed by workers in other countries.

Job migration occurs when global outsourcing shifts from one country to another.

1.3 What Issues and Concerns Complicate the New Workplace?

You might already have noticed that this text may differ from others you've read. I'm going to ask you a lot of questions, and expose you to different viewpoints and possibilities. This process of active inquiry begins with recognition that we live and work at a time of great changes, ones that are not only socially troublesome and personally challenging, but also ones that are likely to increase, not decrease, in number, intensity, and complexity in the future. Are you ready for the challenges ahead? Are you informed about the issues and concerns that complicate our new workplace? Are you willing to admit that this is no time for complacency?

• Recession, globalization, and job migration are changing the world of work.

Look around—there's hardly a person you know who hasn't been touched in some way or another by the global recession. Many have lost jobs, retirement savings, and even homes. Today's students wonder what the future holds for them post graduation; parents worry about how they can help pay for their daughters' and sons' college educations. And at the very time that our domestic economy is suffering, the rest of the world is struggling as well. We're all interconnected now, and the fortunes and misfortunes of one country easily spill over to affect others.

Speaking of the global economy, do you know where your favorite athletic shoes or the parts for your computer and cell phone were manufactured? Can you go to the store and buy a toy or piece of apparel that is really "Made in America"? And whom do you speak with when calling a service center with computer problems, trying to track a missing package, or seeking information on retail store locations? More likely than not, the person serving you is on the phone from India, the Philippines, Ireland, or even Ghana.

Japanese management consultant Kenichi Ohmae calls this a "borderless world," suggesting the disappearance of national boundaries in world business.[26] Take the example of Hewlett-Packard.[27] It operates in 178 countries and most of its 140,000+ employees work outside of the United States. It is the largest technology company in Europe, the Middle East, and Russia. Although headquartered in Palo Alto, California, one has to wonder: is HP truly an American company any more?

What we are talking about is **globalization**, the worldwide interdependence of resource flows, product markets, and business competition.[28] In the global economy, businesses sell goods and services to customers around the world. They also search the world to buy the things they need wherever they can be found at the lowest price. Many businesses actively engage in **global outsourcing** by hiring workers and contracting for supplies and services in other countries. The firms save money and gain efficiency by manufacturing things and getting jobs done in countries with lower costs of labor. When, for example, a shoe that costs $12 to make in the United States can be made in China for 40 cents, doesn't it make perfect business sense for Ohio-based Rocky Boots to shut down its American production line and outsource in China? Or is there more to the story?[29]

One controversial side effect to global outsourcing such as that pursued by Rocky Boots is **job migration**, the shifting of jobs from one country to another. At present, the U.S. economy is a net loser to job migration, with global outsourcing causing many layoffs. By contrast, countries such as China, India, and the Philippines are net gainers. And such countries aren't just sources of unskilled labor anymore; they are now able to offer highly trained workers—engineers, scientists, accountants, health professionals—for as little as one-fifth the cost of an equivalent U.S. worker.

Politicians and policymakers regularly debate how to best deal with the high costs of job migration, as local workers lose their jobs and their communities lose economic vitality. One side looks for new government policies to stop job migration by protecting the jobs of U.S. workers. The other side calls for patience, believing that the national economy will strengthen in the long run as it readjusts and creates new jobs for U.S. workers. Which side are you on?

• Failures of ethics and corporate governance are troublesome.

When Bernard Madoff was sentenced to 150 years in jail for crimes committed during the sensational collapse of his investment company and its 20+billion dollar fraudulent Ponzi scheme, the message was crystal clear.[30] There is no excuse for senior executives in any organization to act illegally and to tolerate management systems that enrich the few while damaging the many.

The harm done by Madoff hurt individuals who lost life-long and retirement savings, charitable foundations that had invested monies with his firm, and the employees of his firm and others that went out of business as a result of the fraud. You could also argue that society at large paid a price, too, as faith in the nation's business system was damaged by the scandal.[31] And worse yet, Madoff is not alone. All too often we learn about more scandals affecting banks and other financial institutions, as well as businesses and organizations of many other types. How would you recover if an employer bankruptcy or major business fraud affected you?

At the end of the day, we depend on individual people, working at all levels of organizations, to act ethically. **Ethics** is a code of moral principles that sets standards of conduct for what is "good" and "right" as opposed to "bad" or "wrong." Given all the scandals, you might be cynical about ethical behavior in organizations. But even though ethical failures get most of the publicity, there is still a lot of good happening in the world of work. Look around. You should find that many people and organizations exemplify a new ethical reawakening, one that places high value on personal integrity and ethical leadership.

In a book entitled *The Transparent Leader*, former CEO of Dial Corporation, Herb Baum, argues that integrity is a major key to ethics in leadership. He also believes that the responsibility to set the tone for leadership integrity begins at the top. He tries to walk the talk—no reserved parking place, straight talking, open door, honest communication, careful listening, and hiring good people.

News Feed

Good and Bad News for Middle Managers

A book by Paul Osterman, *The Truth About Middle Managers: Who They Are, How They Work, Why They Matter*, sets out to "tell the truth" about middle managers. Noting that authors of business books usually focus on executives at the top of the organizational hierarchy, Osterman pays attention to those in the middle. These "all-important" middle managers, he says, amount to about one-fifth of the American workforce.

A main theme in Osterman's book is how the work of middle managers has changed as both organizations and the nature of work itself have moved in new directions. Middle managers are no longer viewed as order-givers who pass directives from those above them to those below. In today's horizontal organizations they are more often called upon to excel as active participants in cross-functional teams where people from different functions come together to work on special tasks and solve complex problems.

There's good news for middle managers in Osterman's analysis. He finds that they have more discretion than their predecessors who worked in more traditional vertical structures. He also finds them using a mix of skills that allow them to develop real pride in what they do. As one manager told him, "I think my job is a nice mix of technical and business. I think I have a lot of autonomy. . . . It's very dynamic. It's always changing."

The bad news is a number of middle managers complained to Osterman about lack of clear career paths for upward advancement and too much hiring of persons from outside the organization when new higher-level positions become available. Given the importance of middle managers to the success of all organizations, Osterman argues that they should be given more attention, and their needs for recognition and advancement should become top management priorities.

Reflect and React

Why not find and talk with middle managers from your family and friendship groups? What do they say about their work? Do their observations mesh with those reported here? Where does Osterman seem to be on track and off in respect to the life of middle managers today?

Ethics set moral standards of what is "good" and "right" behavior in organizations and in our personal lives.

Believing that most CEOs are overpaid, he once gave his annual bonus to the firm's lowest paid workers. He also tells the story of an ethical role model—a rival CEO, Reuben Mark of Colgate Palmolive. Mark called him one day to say that a newly hired executive had brought with him to Colgate a disk containing Dial's new marketing campaign. Rather than read it, he returned the disk to Baum—an act Baum called "the clearest case of leading with honor and transparency I've witnessed in my career."[32]

One positive result from the rash of business ethics failures is renewed attention on the role of **corporate governance**, the active oversight of management decisions, corporate strategy, and financial reporting by a company's board of directors.[33] Typical responsibilities of corporate board members include overseeing decisions on hiring, firing, and compensating senior executives, assessing strategies and their implementation, and verifying financial records.

Corporate governance is oversight of a company's management by a board of directors.

• Diversity and discrimination are continuing social priorities.

Workforce diversity describes differences among workers in gender, race, age, ethnicity, religion, sexual orientation, and able-bodiedness.

The **glass ceiling effect** is an invisible barrier limiting career advancement of women and minorities.

The term **workforce diversity** describes the composition of a workforce in terms of differences among people on gender, age, race, ethnicity, religion, sexual orientation, and physical ability.[34] The diversity trends of changing demographics are well recognized: minorities now constitute more than one-third of the U.S. population and the proportion is growing. The U.S. Census Bureau predicts that by 2050 whites will be in the minority and the combined populations of African American, American Indians, Asians, and Hispanics will be the new majority. Hispanics are presently the largest minority group and the fastest growing. By 2030 more than 20% of the population will be aged 65+ years. And in current economic conditions, more seniors presently at work are deciding to postpone retirement.[35]

Even though our society is diverse, many diversity issues in employment remain as open challenges. Look at the diversity facts in the box and ask how they can be explained. Consider also how we can explain research in which résumés with white-sounding first names, like Brett, received 50% more responses from potential employers than those with black-sounding first names, such as Kareem?[36] The fact that these résumés were created with equal credentials suggests diversity bias.

U.S. laws strictly prohibit the use of demographic characteristics when human resource management decisions such as hiring, promotion, and firing are made. But laws are one thing, actions are yet another. Do you ever wonder why women and minorities hold few top jobs in large companies? One explanation is a subtle form of discrimination known as the **glass ceiling effect**. It occurs when an invisible barrier or "ceiling" prevents

Stay Tuned ℮

Employment Contradictions in Workforce Diversity

The nonprofit research group Catalyst reports regularly on the status of women in leadership. A press release for their recent survey points out that: "Now more than ever, as companies examine how to best weather an economy in crisis, we need talented business leaders, and many of these leaders, yet untapped, are women." But, contradictions still exist regarding women and diversity and the American workforce.

- Women earn some 60% of college degrees, hold 50.6% of managerial jobs, and hold 15.7% of board seats at *Fortune* 500 companies; women of color hold 3.2% of board seats and only 4% of firms have two women of color on their boards.
- For each $1 earned by men, women earn 76 cents; African-American women earn 64 cents, and Hispanic women earn 52 cents.
- The median compensation of female CEOs in North American firms is 85% that of males; in the largest firms it is 61%
- African Americans are 11.5% of the workforce, and hold 8.3% of managerial and professional jobs.
- Asian Americans are 4.7% of the workforce, and hold 6.3% of managerial and professional jobs.
- Hispanics are 11.1% of the workforce, and hold 5% of managerial jobs.

Your Thoughts?

How can these data be explained? What contradictions do you spot and how can they be justified? What are the implications of these data for you and your career aspirations?

members of diverse populations from advancing to high levels of responsibility in organizations.[37]

There is little doubt that women and minorities still face special work and career challenges in our society at large.[38] Although progress is being made—for example 39% of new corporate board seats in early 2009 went to women (up more than 10% from the prior year and about 20% from three years earlier), diversity bias still exists in too many of our work settings.[39] This bias begins with **prejudice**, the holding of negative, irrational attitudes regarding people who are different from us. An example is lingering prejudice against working mothers. The nonprofit Families and Work Institute reports that in 1977 only 49% of men and 71% of women believed that mothers can be good employees; in 2008 the figures had risen to 67% and 80% respectively.[40] However, don't you wonder why the figures fail to show 100% support of working mothers?

Prejudice becomes active **discrimination**, like that revealed in the résumés study, when people in organizations treat minority members unfairly and deny them full membership benefits. It becomes discrimination when a male or female manager refuses to promote a working mother on the belief that "she has too many parenting responsibilities to do a good job at this level." Scholar Judith Rosener suggests that employment discrimination of any form comes at a high cost—not just to the individuals involved, but also to society. The organization's loss for any discriminatory practices, she says, is "undervalued and underutilized human capital."[41]

Many voices call diversity a "business imperative," meaning that today's increasingly diverse and multicultural workforce should be an asset that, if tapped, creates opportunities for performance gains. A female vice president at Avon once posed the diversity challenge this way: "Consciously creating an environment where everyone has an equal shot at contributing, participating, and most of all advancing."[42] But even with such awareness existing, consultant R. Roosevelt Thomas says that too many employers still address diversity with the goal of "making their numbers," rather than truly valuing and managing diversity.[43]

Prejudice is the display of negative, irrational attitudes toward women or minorities.

Discrimination actively denies women and minorities the full benefits of organizational membership.

• People and intellectual capital drive high-performance organizations.

A values statement on the Web site of Herman Miller, the innovative manufacturer of designer furniture, reads: "Our greatest assets as a corporation are the gifts, talents and abilities of our employee-owners. . . . When we as a corporation invest in developing people, we are investing in our future."

We shouldn't expect to find prejudice and discrimination at Herman Miller. Rather, we should find a work environment that respects all employees, raises their confidence, and inspires them to achieve high performance and find self-fulfillment. Hopefully, this also describes the organization in which you work, will work, and, perhaps, even will someday lead.

After studying high-performing companies, management scholars Charles O'Reilly and Jeffrey Pfeffer conclude that they do better because they get extraordinary results from the people working for them. "These companies have won the war for talent," they say, "not just by being great places to work—although they are that—but by figuring out how to get the best out of all of their people, every day."[44]

O'Reilly and Pfeffer are talking about an organization's **intellectual capital**, the collective brainpower or shared knowledge of its workforce.[45] For you, intellectual capital can be a personal asset—a package of brains, skills, and capabilities that differentiates you from others and that makes you valuable to potential employers. And as you think about it, consider this intellectual capital equation: Intellectual Capital = Competency × Commitment.[46]

Intellectual capital is the collective brainpower or shared knowledge of a workforce.

Competency represents our talents or job-relevant capabilities, and commitment represents our willingness to work hard in applying them to important tasks. Obviously both are essential; one without the other is not enough to meet anyone's career needs or any organization's performance requirements. Max DePree, former CEO of Herman Miller, puts it this way: "We talk about the difference between being successful and being exceptional. Being successful is meeting goals in a good way—being exceptional is reaching your potential."[47]

Knowledge workers use their minds and intellects as critical assets to employers.

When it comes to human potential, the new workplace is well into the *information age* dominated by **knowledge workers**. These are persons whose minds, not just their physical capabilities, are critical assets.[48] And things are not standing still. Futurist Daniel Pink says that we are already moving into a new *conceptual age* in which intellectual capital rests with people who are both "high concept"—creative and good with ideas, and "high touch"—joyful and good with relationships.[49] Pink believes the future will belong to those with "whole mind" competencies, ones that combine left-brain analytical thinking with right-brain intuitive thinking.

• Career success requires continuous learning and a capacity for self-management.

In a **free-agent economy,** people change jobs more often, and many work on independent contracts with a shifting mix of employers.

A **shamrock organization** operates with a core group of full-time long-term workers supported by others who work on contracts and part-time.

No matter how you look at it, the future poses a complex setting for career success. And if current trends continue, it will be more and more of a **free-agent economy**. Like professional athletes, many of us will be changing jobs more often and even working on flexible contracts with a shifting mix of employers over time.[50]

British scholar and consultant Charles Handy uses the analogy of the **shamrock organization**, shown in **Figure 1.7**, to describe the implications.[51] Each leaf in the shamrock organization represents a different group of workers.

The first leaf in Handy's shamrock organization is a core group of permanent, full-time employees with critical skills, who follow standard career paths. The second leaf consists of workers hired as "freelancers" and "independent contractors." They provide organizations with specialized skills and talents for specific projects and then change employers when projects are completed. An increasing number of jobs in the new economy fall into this category. Some call this a time of *giganomics* where even well-trained professionals make their livings moving from one "gig" to the next, instead of holding a traditional full-time job.[52] The third leaf is a group of temporary part-timers. Their hours of work increase or decrease as the needs of the

FIGURE 1.7
Today's "Shamrock" Organizations Offer New Career Challenges and Opportunities.

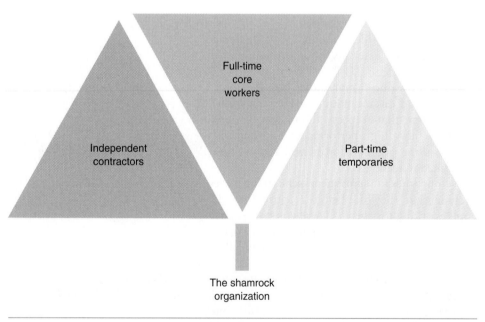

Full-time core workers

Independent contractors

Part-time temporaries

The shamrock organization

business grow or fall. They often work without benefits and are the first to lose their jobs when an employer runs into economic difficulties.

As you might guess, today's college graduates must be prepared to succeed in the second and third leaves of Handy's shamrock organization, not just the first. And to achieve success, Handy advises everyone to maintain a portfolio of skills that is always up-to-date and attractive to potential employers, regardless of where in the shamrock your goals may center. Former IBM CEO Lou Gerstner says we must set a goal of "lifetime employability" and we must accept personal responsibility for its achievement. This places a premium on your capacity for **self-management**, realistically assessing yourself and actively managing your personal development. It means showing emotional intelligence, exercising initiative, accepting responsibility for accomplishments and failures, and continually seeking new learning opportunities and experiences.

The fact is that what happens from this point forward in your career is largely up to you. Would you agree that there is no better time than the present to start taking charge? Picture yourself in an interview situation. The person sitting across the table asks the question, "What can you do for us?" How do you reply?

A good answer to the interviewer's question will describe your "personal brand"—a unique and timely package of skills and capabilities of real value to a potential employer. Management consultant Tom Peters advises that your brand should be "remarkable, measurable, distinguished, and distinctive" relative to the competition—others who want the same career opportunities that you do.[53]

Have you thought about what employers want? Are you clear and confident about the brand called "You?" Does your personal portfolio include new workplace survival skills like those shown in Tips to Remember?[54]

Tips to Remember

How to Survive— and Prosper—in Today's Workplace

- *Task mastery:* You must be good at something, to contribute something of value to your employer.
- *Personal capabilities:* You must be strong in communication, teamwork, ethics and integrity, analysis and problem-solving, and leadership.
- *Entrepreneurship:* You must be willing to take risks, spot opportunities, and step out to engage them.
- *Love of technology:* You must embrace technology, and be willing and able to fully utilize it in all aspects of work.
- *Marketing:* You must create a positive impression, and communicate well your successes and progress.
- *Passion for renewal:* You must be willing and able to learn and change continuously, to update yourself for the future.

Self-management is the ability to understand oneself, exercise initiative, accept responsibility, and learn from experience.

Study Guide

1.3
What Issues and Concerns Complicate the New Workplace?

Rapid review

- Globalization is bringing increased use of global outsourcing by businesses and concern for the adverse effects of job migration.
- Society increasingly expects organizations and their members to perform with high ethical standards and in socially responsible ways.
- Organizations operate with diverse workforces and each member should be respected for her or his talents and capabilities.
- Work in the new economy is increasingly knowledge-based, relying on people with the capacity to bring valuable intellectual capital to the workplace.
- Careers in the new economy are becoming more flexible, requiring personal initiative to build and maintain skill portfolios that are always up-to-date and valued by employers.

Terms to define

Corporate governance
Discrimination
Ethics
Free-agent economy
Glass ceiling effect
Global outsourcing
Globalization
Intellectual capital
Job migration
Knowledge workers
Prejudice
Self-management
Shamrock organization
Workforce diversity

Be sure you can

- describe how corporate governance influences ethics in organizations
- explain how globalization and job migration are changing the economy
- differentiate prejudice, discrimination, and the glass ceiling effect
- state the intellectual capital equation
- discuss career opportunities in the shamrock organization
- explain the importance of self-management to career success in the new economy

Questions for discussion

1. To what extent are current concerns for ethics in business, globalization, and changing careers addressed in your courses and curriculum?
2. How can members of minority groups avoid being hurt by prejudice, discrimination, and the glass ceiling effect in their careers?
3. In what ways can the capacity for self-management help you to prosper in a free-agent economy?

[Test Prep]

1. If a sales department supervisor is held accountable by a middle manager for the department's performance, whom is the department supervisor dependent upon to make this performance possible?

   (a) Board of directors   (b) top management
   (c) customers or clients   (d) department sales persons

2. The management function of _____ is being activated when a bookstore manager measures daily sales in the magazine section and compares them with daily sales targets.

   (a) planning   (b) agenda setting
   (c) controlling   (d) delegating

3. The process of building and maintaining good working relationships with others who may someday help a manager implement his or her work agendas is called _____.

   (a) governance   (b) networking
   (c) emotional intelligence   (d) entrepreneurship

4. According to thinking by Robert Katz, _____ skills are more likely to be emphasized by top managers than by first-line managers.

   (a) human   (b) conceptual
   (c) informational (d) technical

5. An effective manager is someone who helps others to achieve high levels of both _____ and _____.

   (a) pay/satisfaction   (b) performance/satisfaction
   (c) performance/pay   (d) pay/quality work life

6. _____ is the active oversight by boards of directors of top management decisions in such areas as corporate strategy and financial reporting.

   (a) value chain analysis   (b) productivity
   (c) outsourcing   (d) corporate governance

7. When a manager denies promotion to a qualified worker simply because of a personal dislike for the fact that she is Hispanic, this is an example of _____.

   (a) discrimination   (b) workforce diversity
   (c) self-management   (d) a free-agent economy

8. A company buys cloth in one country, has designs made in another country, sews the garments in another country, and sells the finished product in yet other countries. This firm is actively engaging in the practice of _____.

   (a) job migration   (b) performance effectiveness
   (c) value creation (d) global outsourcing

9. The intellectual capital equation states that: Intellectual Capital = _____ × Commitment.

   (a) Diversity   (b) Confidence
   (c) Competency   (d) Communication

10. If the direction in managerial work today is away from command and control, what is it toward?

    (a) coaching and facilitating
    (b) telling and selling
    (c) pushing and pulling
    (d) carrot and stick

11. The manager's role in the "upside-down pyramid" view of organizations is best described as providing _____ so that operating workers can directly serve _____.

    (a) direction, top management
    (b) leadership, organizational goals
    (c) support, customers
    (d) agendas, networking

12. When a team leader clarifies desired work targets and deadlines for a work team, he or she is fulfilling the management function of _____.

    (a) planning   (b) delegating
    (c) controlling (d) supervising

13. The research of Mintzberg and others concludes that managers _____.

    (a) work at a leisurely pace
    (b) have blocks of private time for planning
    (c) always live with the pressures of performance responsibility
    (d) have the advantages of short work weeks

14. The accounting manager for a local newspaper would be considered a _____ manager, whereas the editorial manager would be considered a _____ manager.

    (a) general, functional   (b) middle, top
    (c) staff, line   (d) senior, junior

15. Which of the following is a responsibility that is most associated with the work of a CEO or chief executive officer of a large company?

    (a) link the company with the external environment
    (b) review annual pay raises for all employees
    (c) monitor short-term performance by task forces and committees
    (d) conduct hiring interviews for new college graduates

16. What is the difference between prejudice and workplace discrimination?

17. How is the emergence of a "free-agent economy" changing career and work opportunities?

18. In what ways will the job of a top manager typically differ from that of a first-line manager?

19. How does planning differ from controlling in the management process?

20. Suppose you have been hired as the new supervisor of an audit team for a national accounting firm. With four years of auditing experience, you feel technically well prepared. However, it is your first formal appointment as a manager. The team has 12 members of diverse demographic and cultural backgrounds, and varying work experience. The workload is intense and there is lots of performance pressure.

Questions: In order to be considered *effective* as a manager, what goals will you set for yourself in the new job? What skills will be important to you, and why, as you seek success as the audit team supervisor?

Personal Management Foundations

Instructions

Use this scale to rate yourself on the following list of personal characteristics.[55]

> *S = Strong, I am very confident with this one.*
> *G = Good, but I still have room to grow.*
> *W = Weak, I really need work on this one.*
> *U = Unsure, I just don't know.*

1. *Resistance to stress:*
   The ability to get work done even under stressful conditions.

2. *Tolerance for uncertainty:*
   The ability to get work done even under ambiguous and uncertain conditions.

3. *Social objectivity:*
   The ability to act free of racial, ethnic, gender, and other prejudices or biases.

4. *Inner work standards:*
   The ability to personally set and work to high performance standards.

5. *Stamina:*
   The ability to sustain long work hours.

6. *Adaptability:*
   The ability to be flexible and adapt to changes.

7. *Self-confidence:*
   The ability to be consistently decisive and display one's personal presence.

8. *Self-objectivity:*
   The ability to evaluate personal strengths and weaknesses and to understand one's motives and skills relative to a job.

9. *Introspection:*
   The ability to learn from experience, awareness, and self-study.

10. *Entrepreneurism:*
    The ability to address problems and take advantage of opportunities for constructive change.

Scoring

Give yourself 1 point for each S, and 1/2 point for each G. Do not give yourself points for W and U responses. Total your points and enter the result here [**PMF =** _____].

Interpretation

This assessment offers a self-described *profile of your management foundations* (PMF). Are you a perfect 10, or something less? There shouldn't be too many 10s around.

Ask someone else to also assess you on this instrument. You may be surprised at the results, but the insights are well worth thinking about. The items on the list are skills and personal characteristics that should be nurtured now and throughout your career.

 For further exploration go to WileyPlus

Case Snapshot

Trader Joe's—Managing With a Cool Edge

The average Trader Joe's stocks only a small percentage of the products of local supermarkets in a space little larger than a corner store. How did this neighborhood market grow to earnings of $6.5 billion, garner superior ratings, and become a model of management? Take a walk down the aisles of Trader Joe's and learn how sharp attention to the fundamentals of retail management made this chain more than the average Joe.

Online Interactive Learning Resources

MORE SELF-ASSESSMENTS
- Emotional Intelligence
- Diversity Maturity

EXPERIENTIAL EXERCISES
- The Future Workplace
- Organizational Metaphors

TEAM PROJECT
- Service Learning in Management

2 Management Learning

Great Things Grow from Strong Foundations

You Can Build a Million-Dollar Company Without Sacrificing Values. Imagine! Yes, you can! Go for it! Life is good. Well, make that: life is really good! These are thoughts that turn dreams into realities. They're also part and parcel of the $80 million company named Life Is Good. It began with two brothers, Bert and John Jacobs, making T-shirts, and has grown into a 200+ employee company selling a variety of fun apparel and related products in 14 or more countries. *Inc.* magazine calls it a "fine small business that only wants to make me happy."

Picture a card table set up at a Boston street fair and two young brothers setting out 48 T-shirts printed with a smiling face—Jake, and the words "Life is good." Then picture the cart empty, with all shirts sold for $10 apiece, and two brothers happily realizing they might, just might, have a viable business idea.

From that modest beginning, Bert—Chief Executive Optimist and Jake—Chief Creative Optimist, built a company devoted to humor and humility. John says: "It's important that we're saying 'Life is good,' not 'Life is great' or 'Life is perfect,' there's a big difference. . . . Don't determine that you're going to be happy when you get the new car or the big promotion or meet that special person. You can decide that you're going to be happy today." And that's the message of the Life is Good brand.

Trendsetters
Carol Bartz uses executive experience to create change at Yahoo.

Outliers
THE STORY OF SUCCESS
MALCOLM GLADWELL

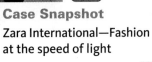

News Feed
Noted author believes practice beats intelligence among super achievers.

Case Snapshot
Zara International—Fashion at the speed of light

So how did brothers Bert and John build a successful firm? Well they didn't start with business degrees or experience, but they do have good instincts combined with creativity and obviously positive views on life. And they've learned as they've progressed, becoming good at things such as marketing, supply chain management and distribution, and brand protection. Each step forward in the business was a chance to capture experience, learn from it, and keep getting better.

Bert and Jake have stuck to their values on this journey to business success. They live the brand, enjoying leisure pursuits such as kayaking and ultimate Frisbee; they support philanthropies such as Camp Sunshine for children with serious illnesses and Project Joy for traumatized children; and the company runs seasonal Life is Good festivals to help raise money for charities. And, of course, they try to keep everyone, from college students to grandparents to toddlers, decked out in Life is Good merchandise. John says: "We don't miss any demographics but we miss one psychographic—people who can't see the positive side of things."

2.1 What Can We Learn from Classical Management Thinking?

Historians trace management as far back as 5000 BC, when ancient Sumerians used written records to assist in governmental and commercial activities.[1] Management contributed to the construction of the Egyptian pyramids, the rise of the Roman Empire, and the commercial success of 14th-century Venice. During the Industrial Revolution in the 1700s, great social changes helped to prompt a leap forward in the manufacture of basic staples and consumer goods. Adam Smith's ideas of efficient production through specialized tasks and the division of labor further accelerated industrial development.

By the turn of the 20th century, Henry Ford and others were making mass production a mainstay of the emerging economy.[2] What we now call the classical school was launching a path of rapid and continuing development in the science and practices of management.[3] Prominent representatives of this school and their major contributions to management thinking are shown in **Figure 2.1**. They include Frederick Taylor—scientific management, Max Weber—bureaucracy, and Henri Fayol—administrative principles.

FIGURE 2.1

Major Branches in the Classical Approach to Management.

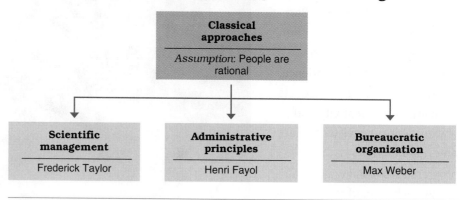

• Taylor's scientific management sought efficiency in job performance.

In 1911, Frederick W. Taylor stated the following in his book *The Principles of Scientific Management:* "The principal object of management should be to secure maximum prosperity for the employer, coupled with the maximum prosperity for the employee."[4] Taylor had noticed that many workers did their jobs in their own way—perhaps haphazard, and without consistent supervision. And it seemed to him that a lack of clear and uniform methods caused workers to lose efficiency and perform below their true capacities. As a result, their organizations also underperformed.

To correct this problem, Taylor believed that jobs should be studied to identify their basic steps and motions, and determine the most efficient ways of doing them. Once this job "science" was defined, workers could be trained to follow it, and supervisors could be trained to best support and encourage workers to perform to the best of their abilities. This approach became known as **scientific management**. Its four core principles are:

1. Develop a "science" for each job—rules of motion, standard work tools, proper work conditions.

Scientific management emphasizes careful selection and training of workers and supervisory support.

2. Hire workers with the right abilities for the job.

3. Train and motivate workers to do their jobs according to the science.

4. Support workers by planning and assisting their work by the job science.

UPS is well known for many efficient operations based on current applications of scientific management principles.

Are you clear about the principles of scientific management? Think about what happens when a top coach trains a group of soccer players. If the coach teaches players the techniques of their positions and how the positions fit into the overall team strategy, the team will probably do better in its games, right? In the same way, Taylor hoped to improve the productivity of workers and organizations. With a stopwatch and notebook in hand, he analyzed tasks and motions to describe the most efficient ways to perform them.[5] He then linked these requirements with job training, monetary incentives for performance success, and better direction and assistance from supervisors.

If you really look, you will find that Taylor's ideas are still influential (see Tips to Remember). For example, calibrated productivity standards carefully guide workers at the United Parcel Service (UPS). After analyzing delivery stops on regular van routes, supervisors generally know within a few minutes how long a driver's pickups and deliveries will take. Industrial engineers devise precise routines for drivers, who save time by knocking on customers' doors rather than looking for the doorbell. Handheld computers further enhance delivery efficiencies. At UPS, savings of seconds on individual stops add up to significant increases in productivity. Wouldn't Taylor be pleased?

Tips to Remember

Scientific Management Lessons for Today's Managers

- Make results-based compensation a performance incentive.
- Carefully design jobs with efficient work methods.
- Carefully select workers with the abilities to do these jobs.
- Train workers to perform jobs to the best of their abilities.
- Train supervisors to support workers to best perform their jobs.

• Weber's bureaucratic organization is supposed to be efficient and fair.

Max Weber was a late-19th-century German intellectual whose insights have made a significant impact on the field of management and the sociology of organizations. Like Taylor, his ideas developed somewhat in reaction to what he considered to be poor performance by the organizations of his day. He was especially concerned that people were in positions of authority not because of their job-related capabilities, but because of their social standing or "privileged" status in German society. Haven't you seen the same problem today—people who rise to positions of major responsibility not because of their competencies but because of whom they know or what families they belong to?

At the heart of Weber's proposal for correcting such problems was a specific form of organization he called a **bureaucracy**.[6] When staffed and structured along the lines listed in **Table 2.1**, *Characteristics of an Ideal Bureaucracy*, he believed organizations could be both highly efficient and very fair in treating their members and clients. In Weber's own words, the bureaucratic organization is described as[7]:

A **bureaucracy** is a rational and efficient form of organization founded on logic, order, and legitimate authority.

. . . capable of attaining the highest degree of efficiency. . . . It is superior to any other form in precision, in stability, in the stringency of its discipline, and in its reliability. It thus makes possible a particularly high degree of calculability of results for the heads of the organization and for those acting in relation to it. It is finally superior both in intensive efficiency and in the scope of its operations and is formally capable of application to all kinds of administrative tasks.

[**TABLE** 2.1]

Characteristics of an Ideal Bureaucracy

Clear Division of Labor

Jobs are well defined, and workers become highly skilled at performing them.

Clear Hierarchy of Authority

Authority and responsibility are well defined, and each position reports to a higher-level one.

Formal Rules and Procedures

Written guidelines describe expected behavior and decisions in jobs; written files are kept for historical record.

Impersonality

Rules and procedures are impartially and uniformly applied; no one gets preferential treatment.

Careers Based on Merit

Workers are selected and promoted on ability and performance; managers are career employees of the organization.

A bureaucracy works well, in theory at least, because of its reliance on logic, order, and legitimate authority, as well as promotions based on competency and demonstrated performance. But if it is so good, why do we so often hear the terms "bureaucracy" and "bureaucrat" used negatively? That's because bureaucracies don't always live up to Weber's expectations.

Think of the last time you were a client of a traditional bureaucracy, perhaps a government agency or the registrar at your school. Would you agree that they are sometimes slow in handling problems, making changes, and adapting to new customer or client needs? As a customer, have you sometimes encountered employees who seem impersonal, resistant to change, even apathetic?

These and other disadvantages are among the reasons why the bureaucratic model isn't always the best choice for organizations; it works well sometimes, but not all of the time. In fact, a major challenge for research on organizational design is to identify when and under what conditions bureaucratic features work well, and what the best alternatives are when they don't. Later in the module we'll call this type of problem solving "contingency thinking."

• Fayol's administrative principles describe managerial duties and practices.

Another branch in the classical approaches to management includes attempts to document and understand the experiences of successful managers. The most prominent writer in this realm is Henri Fayol.

In 1916, after a career in French industry, Henri Fayol published *Administration Industrielle et Générale*.[8] The book outlines his views on the proper management of organizations and the people within them. It identifies five "rules" or "duties" of management in respect to foresight, organization, command, coordination, and control.

- *Foresight*—complete a plan of action for the future.
- *Organization*—provide and mobilize resources to implement plan.
- *Command*—lead, select, and evaluate workers.
- *Coordination*—fit diverse efforts together, ensure information is shared and problems solved.
- *Control*—make sure things happen according to plan, take necessary corrective action.

Look closely at Fayol's duties. Do you see how they resemble the four functions of management that we talk about today—planning, organizing, leading, and controlling?

Study Guide

2.1
What Can We Learn from Classical Management Thinking?

Rapid review

- Taylor's principles of scientific management focused on the need to carefully select, train, support, and reward workers in their jobs.
- Weber considered bureaucracy, with its clear hierarchy, formal rules, well-defined jobs, and competency-based staffing, as a form of organization that is efficient and fair.
- Fayol suggested that managers learn and fulfill duties we now call the management functions of planning, organizing, leading, and controlling.

Terms to define

Bureaucracy
Scientific management

Be sure you can

- list the principles of Taylor's scientific management
- list key characteristics of bureaucracy
- explain why Weber considered bureaucracy an ideal form of organization
- list possible disadvantages of bureaucracy
- describe how Fayol's "duties" overlap with the four functions of management

Questions for discussion

1. How did Taylor and Weber differ in the approaches they took to improving the performance of organizations?
2. Should Weber's concept of the bureaucratic organization be scrapped, or does it still have potential value today?
3. What are the risks of accepting the "lessons of experience" offered by successful executives such as Fayol?

2.2 What Is Unique about the Behavioral Management Approaches?

During the 1920s, emphasis on the human side of the workplace influenced the emergence of behavioral management approaches. As shown in **Figure 2.2**, this new school of thought included Follett's notion of the organization as a community, the famous Hawthorne studies, and Maslow's theory of human needs, as well as theories generated from the work of Douglas McGregor and Chris Argyris. The underlying assumption is that people are social and self-actualizing, and that workers seek satisfying social relationships, respond to group pressures, and search for personal fulfillment. Does that sound like you?

FIGURE 2.2

Foundations of the Behavioral or Human Resource Approaches to Management Thinking.

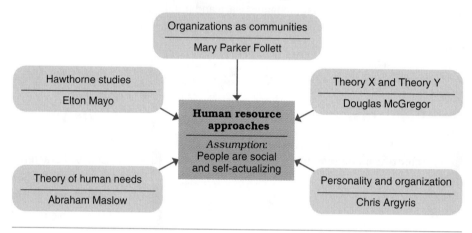

• Follett viewed organizations as communities of cooperative action.

Coming just a bit later than Fayol, Mary Parker Follett made significant contributions to the development of management thinking. In fact, she was eulogized as "one of the most important women America has yet produced in the fields of civics and sociology."[9] Follett has been called a "prophet" of management, and her work is a reminder that good things really do grow from strong foundations.[10]

In Follett's view, groups were important aspects of organizations; they provided the means that allowed individuals to combine their talents for a greater good. She described organizations as "communities" in which managers and workers should labor in harmony, without one party dominating the other and with the freedom to talk over and truly reconcile conflicts and differences. And she believed that managers should help people in organizations cooperate with one another and achieve an integration of interests.

Follett suggested that making every employee an owner in the business would create feelings of collective responsibility. Today, we address the same issues as "employee ownership," "profit sharing," and "gain-sharing plans." Follet believed that business problems involve a wide variety of factors that must be considered in relationship to one another. Today, we talk about "systems" when describing the same phenomenon. Follett viewed businesses as services, organizations that should always consider making profits vis-à-vis the public good. Today, we pursue the same issues as "managerial ethics" and "corporate social responsibility."

Even though Follett's ideas were expressed more than 80 years ago, many would consider them very farsighted indeed.[11] Her ideas still offer the wisdom of history. She advocated social responsibility, respect for workers, and better cooperation throughout organizations; she warned against the dangers of too much hierarchy and called for visionary leadership. Many of these themes are still central to management theory, even though we describe them by terms such as "empowerment," "involvement," "flexibility," "self-management," and "transformational leadership."

And what can be said about executive success today?[12] I wonder what Follett would say? My guess is that Follett would agree that the successful 21st-century executive must be an *inspiring leader* who attracts talented people, and motivates them in a setting where everyone can do his or her best work. She would argue that every manager, regardless of level, should be an *ethical role model*—always acting ethically, setting high ethical standards, and infusing ethics throughout the organization. And she would point out that anyone aspiring to managerial success must be an *active doer*, someone ready to make things happen, focus attention on the right things, and make sure that they really get done.

• The Hawthorne studies focused attention on the human side of organizations.

In 1924, the Western Electric Company commissioned a study of individual productivity at the Hawthorne Works of the firm's Chicago plant.[13] The initial "Hawthorne studies," with a research team headed by Elton Mayo of Harvard University, sought to determine how economic incentives and the physical conditions of the workplace affected the output of workers. But their results were perplexing. After failing to find that better lighting in the manufacturing facilities would improve productivity, they concluded that unforeseen "psychological factors" somehow interfered with their study. Yet, similar results occurred when they conducted further tests.

After isolating six relay-assembly workers in a special room, Mayo and his team measured the effect on outputs of various rest pauses, and lengths of workdays and workweeks. They found no direct relationship between changes in physical working conditions and performance; productivity increased regardless of the changes made. The researchers concluded that these results were caused by the new "social setting" in the test room. The six workers in the test room shared pleasant conversations with one another and received more attention from the researchers than they got from supervisors in their usual jobs. As a result, they tried to do what they thought the researchers wanted them to do—a good job.

Stay Tuned

Employers Grapple with Employee Satisfaction and Retention

Results from Employee Satisfaction and Retention Survey by Salary.com show differences in employer and employee views on job satisfaction and retention issues. The survey reports:

- 65% of employees are at least "somewhat satisfied" with their jobs; employers estimate the level at 77%.
- 65% of employees are actively or passively (surfing job lists, networking, updating résumés, posting résumés) job hunting; employers estimate the level at 37%.
- 40% of employees report no plans for job hunting in coming months; employers estimate the level at 80%.
- Employee satisfaction is higher at higher pay levels; older workers are more satisfied than younger workers; younger workers are most likely to be job hunting.

Your Thoughts?

Are you surprised at the level of satisfaction reported by employees during a time of economic downturn? Would you expect it to be higher or lower? Why are employers underestimating employee interest in finding new jobs? If you were an employer, what concerns would you have about younger workers based on this survey?

The **Hawthorne effect** is the tendency of persons singled out for special attention to perform as expected.

This tendency to try to live up to expectations became known as the **Hawthorne effect**. And one of its major implications is the possibility that people's performance will be affected by the way they are treated by their managers. Have you noticed in your experience that people given special attention will tend to perform as expected? Could the Hawthorne effect explain why some students, perhaps you, do better in smaller classes or for instructors who pay more attention to them in class?

The Hawthorne studies continued until the economic conditions of the Depression forced their termination in 1932. By then, interest in the human factor had broadened to include employee attitudes, interpersonal relations, and group relations. For example, over 21,000 employees were interviewed to learn what they liked and disliked about their work environment. "Complex" and "baffling" results led the researchers to conclude that the same things that satisfied some workers—such as work conditions or wages, led to dissatisfaction for others. And in a final study in the bank wiring room at Western Electric, a "surprise" finding was that people would restrict their output in order to avoid the displeasure of the group, even if it meant sacrificing increased pay. Mayo and his team had recognized first-hand what most of us realize already: that groups can have strong negative, as well as positive, influences on the behaviors of their members.

Scholars have criticized the Hawthorne studies for poor research design, weak empirical support for the conclusions drawn, and overgeneralized findings.[14] And there is no doubt that management research has moved on from this point of departure with greater care in the use of scientific methods. Yet, the Hawthorne studies were significant turning points in the evolution of management thought. They helped shift the attention of managers and management researchers away from just the technical and structural concerns of the classical approaches, and toward social and human concerns as important potential keys to workplace productivity.

• Maslow described a hierarchy of human needs with self-actualization at the top.

The work of psychologist Abraham Maslow in the area of human needs emerged as a key component of the new direction in management thinking.[15] He began with the notion of the human **need**, a physiological or psychological deficiency that a person feels compelled to satisfy. Why, you might ask, is this a significant concept for managers? The answer is because needs create tensions that can influence a person's work attitudes and behaviors.

A **need** is a physiological or psychological deficiency that a person wants to satisfy.

What needs, for example, are important to you? How do they influence your behavior, the way you study and the way you work? Maslow described the five levels of human needs shown in **Figure 2.3**. From lowest to highest in order, they are physiological, safety, social, esteem, and self-actualization needs.

According to Maslow, people try to satisfy the five needs in sequence, moving step by step from lowest up to the highest. He calls this the *progression principle*—a need at any level becomes activated only after the next-lower-level need is satisfied. Once a need is activated, it dominates attention and determines behavior until it is satisfied. Maslow calls this the *deficit principle*—people act to satisfy needs for which a satisfaction deficit exists; a satisfied need doesn't motivate behavior. Only at the highest level of self-actualization do the deficit and progression principles cease to operate. The more this need is satisfied, the stronger it grows.

Maslow's theory can help us to better understand people's needs and help find ways to satisfy them through their work. Of course, this is easier said than done. If it were easy we wouldn't have so many cases of workers going on strike against their employers, complaining about their jobs, or quitting to find better ones. Consider also the case of volunteers working for the local Red Cross,

FIGURE 2.3
How Does Maslow's Hierarchy of Human Needs Operate?

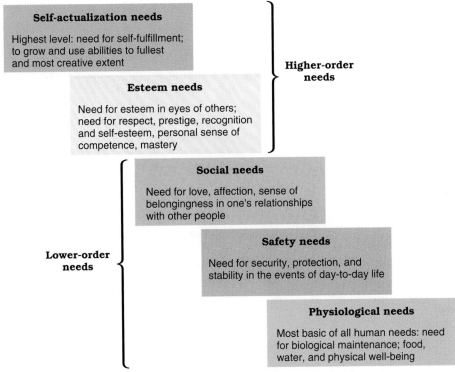

In Abraham Maslow's theory, human needs are satisfied in a step-by-step progression. People first satisfy the lower-order needs: physiological, safety, and social. Once these are satisfied, they focus on the higher-order ego and self-actualization needs. A satisfied need no longer motivates behavior, except at the level of self-actualization. At this top level, the need grows stronger the more it is satisfied.

community hospital, or youth soccer league. Our society needs volunteers; most nonprofit organizations depend on them. But what needs do they pursue? How can one keep volunteers involved and committed in the absence of pay?

• McGregor believed managerial assumptions create self-fulfilling prophecies.

Maslow's work along with the Hawthorne studies surely influenced another prominent management theorist, Douglas McGregor. His classic book, *The Human Side of Enterprise*, suggests that managers should pay more attention to the social and self-actualizing needs of people at work.[16] He framed his argument as a contrast between two opposing views of human nature: a set of negative assumptions he called "Theory X" and a set of positive ones he called "Theory Y."

Managers holding **Theory X** assumptions expect people to generally dislike work, lack ambition, act irresponsibly, resist change, and prefer to follow rather than to lead. McGregor considers such thinking wrong, believing that **Theory Y** assumptions are more appropriate and consistent with human potential. Managers holding Theory Y assumptions expect people to be willing to work, capable of self-control and self-direction, responsible, and creative.

Can you spot differences in how you behave or react when treated in a Theory X way or a Theory Y way? McGregor strongly believed that these assumptions create **self-fulfilling prophecies**. That is, as with the Hawthorne effect, people end up behaving consistent with the assumptions. Managers holding Theory X

Theory X assumes people dislike work, lack ambition, are irresponsible, and prefer to be led.

Theory Y assumes people are willing to work, accept responsibility, are self-directed, and are creative.

A **self-fulfilling prophecy** occurs when a person acts in ways that confirm another's expectations.

assumptions are likely to act in directive "command-and-control" ways, often giving people little say over their work. This in turn often creates passive, dependent, and reluctant subordinates who do only what they are told to do. Have you ever encountered a manager or instructor with a Theory X viewpoint?

Managers with Theory Y assumptions behave quite differently. They are more "participative," likely giving others more control over their work. This creates opportunities to satisfy higher-order esteem and self-actualization needs. In response, the workers are more likely to act with initiative, responsibility, and high performance. The self-fulfilling prophecy occurs again, but this time it is a positive one. You should find Theory Y thinking reflected in a lot of the ideas and developments discussed in this book, such as valuing diversity, employee involvement, job enrichment, empowerment, and self-managing teams.[17]

Self-Assessment

This is a good point to complete the self-assessment "*Managerial Assumptions*" found on page 46.

• **Argyris suggests that workers treated as adults will be more productive.**

Ideas set forth by the well-regarded scholar and consultant Chris Argyris also reflect the belief in human nature advanced by Maslow and McGregor. In his book *Personality and Organization*, Argyris contrasts the management practices found in traditional and hierarchical organizations with the needs and capabilities of mature adults.[18]

Argyris clearly believes that when problems such as employee absenteeism, turnover, apathy, alienation, and low morale plague organizations, they may be caused by a mismatch between management practices and the adult nature of their workforces. His basic point is that no one wants to be treated like a child, but that's just the way many organizations treat their workers. The result, he suggests, is a group of stifled and unhappy workers who perform below their potential.

Does Argyris seem to have a good point? For example, scientific management assumes that people will work more efficiently on better-defined tasks. Argyris would likely disagree, believing that limits opportunities for self-actualization in one's work. In a Weberian bureaucracy, typical of many of our government agencies, people work in a clear hierarchy of authority, with higher levels directing and controlling the work of lower levels.[19] This is supposed to be an efficient way of doing things. Argyris would worry that workers lose initiative and end up being less productive. Also, Fayol's administrative principles assume that efficiency will increase when supervisors plan and direct a person's work. Argyris might suggest that this sets up conditions for psychological failure; psychological success is more likely when people define their own goals.

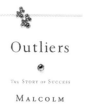

Outliers

THE STORY OF SUCCESS

MALCOLM GLADWELL

News Feed

Noted Author Believes Practice Beats Intelligence Among Super Achievers

When Bill Gates was a kid he attended a school which gave him access to a computer. He learned programming, had thousands of hours to practice and, as we all know, went on to found Microsoft. Was it an abundance of intelligence or the thousands of hours of practice that most accounts for his success? Malcolm Gladwell, author of the popular book *Outliers*, believes the latter. In fact, he offers what he calls the "10,000 hour rule"—you need to spend 10,000 hours of practice to reach the top in any field. Anything less just doesn't cut it.

Gladwell believes his rule applies to all fields of endeavor, from athletics to music to computers. His main theme in the book is that people who have achieved super success in our high technology age—Bill Gates at Microsoft and Steve Jobs at Apple, for example—did so not because of "extraordinary talent" but because they had the "right opportunities at exactly the right time," and were relentless in their commitments to practice, practice, practice. In reviewing *Outliers*, Catherine Arnst asks: "If a million more teens had the same opportunities as Bill Gates, how many more stars might have emerged?" She also points out that Gladwell's work suggests that "timing, persistence and an eye for the main chance" are key determinants of success.

Reflect and React:

In what ways does Gladwell's notion prompt you to think more about yourself and what you can accomplish? Are you going to someday qualify for greatness under the 10,000-hour rule? How can Gladwell's ideas be used by managers to build work environments in which people are able to achieve their full potential?

Study Guide

2.2
What Is Unique about the Behavioral Management Approaches?

Rapid review

- Follett's ideas on groups, human cooperation, and organizations that served social purposes foreshadowed current management themes.
- The Hawthorne studies suggested that social and psychological forces influence work behavior, and that good human relations may gain improved work performance.
- Maslow's hierarchy of human needs suggested the importance of self-actualization and the potential for people to satisfy important needs through their work.
- McGregor criticized negative Theory X assumptions about human nature and advocated positive Theory Y assumptions that view people as independent, responsible, and capable of self-direction in their work.
- Argyris pointed out that people in the workplace are mature adults who may react negatively when management practices treat them as if they were immature.

Terms to define

Hawthorne effect

Need

Self-fulfilling prophecies

Theory X

Theory Y

Be sure you can

- explain why Follett's ideas were quite modern in concept
- summarize findings of the Hawthorne studies
- explain and illustrate the "Hawthorne effect"
- explain Maslow's deficit and progression principles
- distinguish between McGregor's Theory X and Theory Y assumptions
- explain the self-fulfilling prophecies created by Theory X and Theory Y
- explain Argyris's concern that traditional organizational practices are inconsistent with mature adult personalities

Questions for discussion

1. How did insights from the Hawthorne studies bridge the gap between the classical and modern management approaches?
2. If Maslow's hierarchy of needs theory is correct, how can a manager use it to become more effective?
3. Where and how do McGregor's notions of Theory X and Theory Y overlap with Argyris's ideas regarding adult personalities?

2.3 What Are the Foundations of the Modern Management Approaches?

The next step in the timeline of management history sets the stage for a stream of new developments that are continuing to this day. Loosely called the modern management approaches, they share the assumption that people and organizations are complex, growing and changing over time in response to new problems and opportunities in their environments. The many building blocks of modern management include use of quantitative tools and techniques, recognition of the inherent complexity of organizations as systems, contingency thinking that rejects the search for universal management principles, attention to quality management, respect for knowledge management and organizational learning, and the desire to ground management practice in solid scientific evidence.

• Managers use quantitative analysis and tools to solve complex problems.

About the same time that some scholars were developing human resource approaches to management, others were investigating how quantitative techniques could improve managerial decision making. The foundation of these analytical decision sciences approaches is the assumption that mathematical techniques can be used for better problem solving. At Google, for example, a math formula has been developed to aid in talent planning. It pools information from performance reviews and surveys, promotions, and pay histories to identify employees who might feel underutilized and be open to offers from other firms. Human resource management plans are then developed to try and retain them.[20]

Management science and **operations research** apply mathematical techniques to solve management problems.

The terms **management science** and **operations research** are often used interchangeably to describe the scientific applications of mathematical techniques to management problems. A typical quantitative approach proceeds as follows. A problem is encountered, it is systematically analyzed, appropriate mathematical models and computations are applied, and an optimum solution is identified. Consider these examples of management science applications.

Problem A real estate developer wants to control costs and complete building a new apartment complex on time. Quantitative approach: *Network models* like the Gantt Chart pictured in **Figure 2.4** break large tasks into smaller components to track completion of many different activities on the required timetables.

FIGURE 2.4

Sample Gantt Chart for Project Planning and Control.

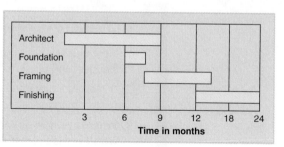

Problem An oil exploration company is worried about future petroleum reserves in various parts of the world. Quantitative approach: *Mathematical forecasting* helps make future projections for reserve sizes and depletion rates that are useful in the planning process.

Problem A "big box" retailer is trying to deal with pressures on profit margins by minimizing costs of inventories while never being "out of stock" for customers. Quantitative approach: *Inventory analysis* helps control inventories by mathematically determining how much to automatically order and when.

Problem A grocery store is getting complaints from customers that waiting times are too long for check outs during certain times of the day. Quantitative approach: *Queuing theory* helps allocate service personnel and workstations based on alternative workload demands and in a way that minimizes both customer waiting times and costs of service workers.

Problem A manufacturer wants to maximize profits for producing three different products on three different machines, each of which can be used for different periods of times and at different costs. Quantitative approach: *Linear programming* is used to calculate how best to allocate production among different machines.

An important counterpart to the management science approaches is **operations management** which focuses on how organizations produce goods and services efficiently and effectively. The emphasis is on the study and improvement of operations, the transformation process through which goods and services are actually created. The applications include such things as business process analysis, workflow designs, facilities layouts and locations, work scheduling and project management, production planning, inventory management, and quality control.

Operations management is the study of how organizations produce goods and services.

• Organizations are open systems that interact with their environments.

The concept of system is a key ingredient of modern management thinking. **Figure 2.5** shows that organizations are **open systems** that interact with their environments to obtain resources—people, technology, information, money, and supplies, that are transformed through work activities into goods and services

An **open system** transforms resource inputs from the environment into product outputs.

FIGURE 2.5

How Do Organizations as Open Systems Interact with Their External Environments?

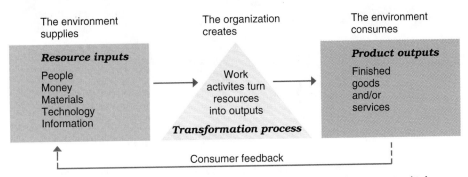

As open systems, organizations continually interact with their external environments to obtain resource inputs, transform those inputs through work activities into goods and services, and deliver finished products to their customers. Feedback from customers indicates how well they are doing.

for their customers and clients. Google, Ben & Jerry's, your college or university, and the local bookstore can all be described in this manner.

The open-systems concept helps explain why there is so much emphasis today on organizations being customer-driven. This means they try hard to focus their resources, energies, and goals on continually satisfying the needs of their customers and clients. Look again at the figure and you should recognize the logic. Can you see how customers hold the keys to the long-term prosperity and survival of a business, like an auto manufacturer? Their willingness to buy products or use services provides the revenues needed to obtain resources and keep the cycle in motion. And as soon as the customers balk or start to complain, someone should be listening. This feedback is a warning that the organization needs to change and do things better in the future.

• Organizations operate as complex networks of cooperating subsystems.

A **subsystem** is a smaller component of a larger system.

Any organization also operates as a complex network of **subsystems** or smaller components whose activities individually and collectively support the work of the larger system.[21] **Figure 2.6** shows the importance of cooperation among organizational subsystems.[22] In the figure, for example, the operations and service management systems serve as a central point. They provide the integration among other subsystems, such as purchasing, accounting, sales, and information, all of which are essential to the work, and the success, of the organization. But the reality is that the cooperation is often imperfect and could be improved upon. Just how organizations achieve this, of course, is a major management challenge.

FIGURE 2.6

How Do Organizations Operate as Complex Networks of Subsystems?

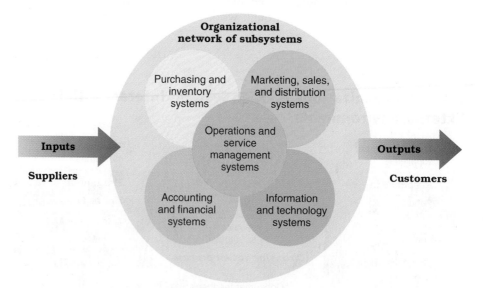

Externally, organizations interact with suppliers and customers in their environments. Internally, many different subsystems must interact and work well together so that high quality inputs are transformed into products satisfying customers' needs. Common subsystems of a business include purchasing, information technology, operations management, marketing and sales, distribution, human resources, and accounting and finance.

• Contingency thinking believes there is no one best way to manage.

Rather than try to find the one best way to manage in all circumstances, modern management adopts **contingency thinking**. That is, it recognizes organizational complexities and attempts to identify practices that best fit with the unique demands of different situations.

Consider again the concept of bureaucracy. Weber offered it as an ideal form of organization. But from a contingency perspective, the strict bureaucratic form is only one possible way of organizing things. What turns out to be the best structure in any given situation will depend on many factors, including environmental uncertainty, available technology, staff competencies, and more. Contingency thinking recognizes that the structure that works well for one organization may not work well for another in different circumstances. Also, what works well at one point in time may not work as well in the future if things have changed.[23]

You should find a lot of contingency thinking in this book. Its implications extend to all of the management functions—from planning and controlling for diverse environmental conditions, to organizing for diverse workforces and multiple tasks, to leading in different performance situations. And this is a good reflection of everyday realities. Don't you use a lot of contingency thinking when solving problems and otherwise going about your personal affairs?

• Quality management focuses attention on continuous improvement.

The work of W. Edwards Deming is a cornerstone of the quality movement in management.[24] His story begins in 1951 when he was invited to Japan to explain quality control techniques that had been developed in the United States. The result was a lifelong relationship epitomized in the Deming Application Prize, which is still awarded annually in Japan for companies achieving extraordinary excellence in quality.

"When Deming spoke," we might say, "the Japanese listened." The principles he taught the Japanese were straightforward and they worked: tally defects, analyze and trace them to the source, make corrections, and keep a record of what happens afterward. Deming's approach to quality emphasizes constant innovation, use of statistical methods, and commitment to training in the fundamentals of quality assurance.[25]

Contingency thinking tries to match management practices with situational demands.

Trendsetters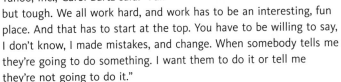

Carol Bartz Uses Executive Experience to Create Change at Yahoo

When Carol Bartz was interviewed by the *Wall Street Journal* regarding her leadership as the new CEO of Yahoo, Inc., Carol Bartz said: "Fair but tough. We all work hard, and work has to be an interesting, fun place. And that has to start at the top. You have to be willing to say, I don't know, I made mistakes, and change. When somebody tells me they're going to do something, I want them to do it or tell me they're not going to do it."

Indeed, Bartz's management style has been described by others as mixing "bluntness" and "humor." One of her former executives at Autodesk points out "she could get the best out of people." Well, that's what the Yahoo board was hoping when Bartz was appointed as the new CEO. The firm had struggled under founder Jerry Yang's leadership and the intense competition from rival Google. She faces low employee morale and shareholder discontent as well as lots of pressure from the financial analysts. But many think Bartz is well-suited to the task.

With plenty of technology experience—14 years as CEO of Autodesk and board appointments with the likes of Intel and Cisco Systems, she is known for being tough and insightful. But through it all she has fought the glass ceiling, making no bones about what she considered discrimination from a business community ruled by men. She cites an incident that occurred in a meeting with U.S. Senators. One turned to Carol Bartz and said: "So, how are we going to start the meeting." Looking back on it she says: "He thought I must be the moderator. It's annoying. I don't have time for these guys, but when it's ridiculous I call them on it."

Bartz has proven herself to be talented and skilled at leading big businesses. And she didn't waste any time digging in to the management challenges at Yahoo. Within six weeks of her being appointed as the new CEO she was "preparing a company-wide reorganization" that reflected her "belief in a more top-down management approach." She calls Yahoo an "important property and such a great name" that needs "structure."

Whatever you might think about Bartz's style, don't you agree that she certainly doesn't lack confidence or decisiveness?

Total quality management is managing with an organization-wide commitment to continuous improvement, product quality, and customer needs.

One outgrowth of Deming's work was the emergence of **total quality management**, or TQM. This is a process that makes quality principles part of the organization's strategic objectives, applying them to all aspects of operations and striving to meet customers' needs by doing things right the first time. Most TQM approaches begin with an insistence that the total quality commitment applies to everyone in an organization, from resource acquisition and supply chain management, through production and into the distribution of finished goods and services, and ultimately to customer relationship management.

Joseph Juran was one of Deming's contemporaries in the quality movement. His long career also included consultations at major companies around the world.[26] He is known for the slogan: "There is always a better way," and for his three guiding principles, "plan, control, improve."[27] This search for and commitment to quality is now tied to the emphasis modern management gives to the notion of **continuous improvement**—always looking for new ways to improve on current performance.[28] The idea is that one can never be satisfied; something always can and should be improved upon.

Continuous improvement involves always searching for new ways to improve work quality and performance.

ISO certification indicates conformance with a rigorous set of international quality standards.

An indicator of just how embedded quality objectives have become in operations management and services is the importance of **ISO certification** by the International Standards Organization in Geneva, Switzerland. It has been adopted by many countries of the world as a quality benchmark. Businesses that want to compete as "world-class companies" are increasingly expected to have ISO certification at various levels. To do so, they must refine and upgrade quality in all operations, and then undergo a rigorous assessment by outside auditors to determine whether they meet ISO requirements.

• Knowledge management and organizational learning provide continuous adaptation.

Knowledge management is the process of using intellectual capital for competitive advantage.

The term **knowledge management** describes the processes through which organizations use information technology to develop, organize, and share knowledge to achieve performance success.[29] You can spot the significance of knowledge management with the presence of an executive job title—chief knowledge officer. The "CKO" is responsible for energizing learning processes and making sure that an organization's portfolio of intellectual assets is well managed and continually enhanced. These assets include such things as patents, intellectual property rights, trade secrets, and special processes and methods, as well as the accumulated knowledge and understanding of the entire workforce.

Google can be considered a knowledge management company. It not only runs a business model based on information searches, but also operates as an organization with an information-rich culture driven by creativity and knowledge. Google morphs and grows and excels, in part because the firm is organized and operates in ways that continually tap the developing knowledge of its members. Its information technologies and management philosophies help and encourage employees located around the world to share information and collaborate to solve problems and explore opportunities. The net result is a firm that seems to keep competitors and the business community at large always guessing what its next steps might be.

Google is a leader in knowledge management and continues to grow and morph into new areas while thriving on learning.

A **learning organization** continuously changes and improves, using the lessons of experience.

Companies that emphasize knowledge management are moving toward what consultant Peter Senge calls a **learning organization**, one that strives to continually learn from and adapt to new circumstances.[30] In his book *The Fifth Discipline*, Senge describes learning organizations as work settings that are exceptionally good at encouraging and helping all of their members to learn continuously. They emphasize information sharing, teamwork, empowerment, and participation as keys to learning. And importantly, the leaders of learning organizations set an example for others by embracing change and communicating enthusiasm for solving problems and growing with new opportunities.

This notion of the learning organization is an ideal concept. But, at the very least, you should be able to find examples that fit parts of the description. And you should notice that some organizations really are better than others at learning from experience.

• Evidence-based management seeks hard facts about what really works.

A book published by Tom Peters and Robert Waterman in 1982, *In Search of Excellence: Lessons from America's Best-Run Companies*, helped kindle interest in the attributes of organizations that achieve performance excellence.[31] Peters and Waterman highlighted things such as "closeness to customers," "bias toward action," "simple form and lean staff," and "productivity through people," all of which seemed to make good sense. Later findings, however, showed that many of the companies deemed to be "excellent" at the time encountered future problems.[32] And in the recent recession, similar problems were noted with firms featured in a popular book published in 2001 by Jim Collins, *Good to Great*.[33]

Today's management scholars are trying to move beyond generalized impressions of excellence to understand more empirically the characteristics of **high-performance organizations**—ones that consistently achieve high-performance results while also creating high quality-of-work-life environments for their employees. Following this line of thinking, Jeffrey Pfeffer and Robert Sutton make the case for **evidence-based management, or EBM.** This is the process of making management decisions on "hard facts"—that is, about what really works, rather than on "dangerous half-truths"—things that sound good but lack empirical substantiation.[34]

A **high-performance organization** consistently achieves excellence while creating a high-quality work environment.

Evidence-based management involves making decisions based on hard facts about what really works.

Using data from a sample of some 1,000 firms, for example, Pfeffer and a colleague found that firms using a mix of selected human resource management practices had more sales and higher profits per employee than those that didn't.[35] Those practices included employment security, selective hiring, self-managed teams, high wages based on performance merit, training and skill development, minimal status differences, and shared information. Examples of other EBM findings include: challenging goals accepted by an employee are likely to result in high performance; unstructured employment interviews are unlikely to result in the best person being hired to fill a vacant position.[36]

Scholars pursue a variety of solid empirical studies in many areas of management research. Some carve out new and innovative territories, while others build upon and extend knowledge that has come down through the history of management thought. By staying abreast of such developments and findings, managers can have more confidence that they are approaching decisions from a solid foundation of evidence rather than mere speculation or hearsay.

Basic scientific methods

- A research question or problem is identified.
- Hypotheses, or possible explanations, are stated.
- A research design is created to systematically test the hypotheses.
- Data gathered in the research are analyzed and interpreted.
- Hypotheses are accepted or rejected based upon the evidence.

Study Guide

2.3
What Are the Foundations of the Modern Management Approaches?

Rapid review

- Advanced quantitative techniques in decision sciences and operations management help managers solve complex problems.
- The systems view depicts organizations as complex networks of subsystems that must interact and cooperate with one another if the organization as a whole is to accomplish its goals.
- Contingency thinking avoids "one best way" arguments, recognizing instead that managers need to understand situational differences and respond appropriately to them.
- Quality management focuses on making continuous improvements in processes and systems.
- In learning organizations the leadership and internal environment encourage continuous learning from experience to improve work methods and processes.
- Evidence-based management uses findings from rigorous scientific research to identify management practices for high performance.

Terms to define

Contingency thinking

Continuous improvement

Evidence-based management

High performance organization

ISO certification

Knowledge management

Learning organization

Open system

Subsystem

Total quality management

Be sure you can

- discuss the importance of quantitative analysis in management decision making
- use the terms open system and subsystem to describe how an organization operates
- explain how contingency thinking might influence a manager's choices of organization structures
- describe the role of continuous improvement in total quality management
- give examples of workplace situations that can benefit from evidence-based management

Questions for discussion

1. Can you use the concepts of open system and subsystem to describe the operations of an organization in your community?
2. In addition to the choice of organization structures, in what other areas of management decision making do you think contingency thinking plays a role?
3. Is a learning organization something that comes about because of the actions of managers, workers, or both?

[Test Prep]

1. A management consultant who advises managers to study jobs, carefully train workers to do those jobs with the most efficient motions, and offer financial incentives tied to job performance would most likely be using ideas from _____.

   (a) scientific management (b) contingency thinking
   (c) Henri Fayol (d) Theory Y

2. The Hawthorne studies were important in management history because they raised awareness about the importance of _____ as possible influences on productivity.

   (a) organization structures (b) human factors
   (c) physical work conditions (d) pay and rewards

3. If Douglas McGregor heard an instructor complaining that her students were lazy, didn't want to come to class, lacked creativity, and were irresponsible, he would worry that she might _____.

   (a) fail to use scientific management
   (b) spend too much time worrying about their need satisfactions
   (c) create a negative self-fulfilling prophecy
   (d) miss the chance to create a bureaucratic class organization

4. If your local bank or credit union is a complex system, then the loan-processing department of the bank would be considered a _____.

   (a) subsystem (b) closed system
   (c) learning organization (d) bureaucracy

5. When a manager puts Kwabena in a customer relations job because he has strong social needs and gives Sherrill lots of daily praise because she has strong ego needs, the manager is displaying _____ in his management approach.

   (a) systems thinking (b) Theory X
   (c) contingency thinking (d) administrative principles

6. In the learning organization, as described by Peter Senge, you would expect to find _____.

   (a) emphasis on following rules and procedures
   (b) promotions based on seniority
   (c) willingness to set aside old thinking and embrace new ways
   (d) a strict hierarchy of authority

7. When the registrar of a university deals with students by an identification number rather than a name, which characteristic of bureaucracy is being displayed and what is its intended benefit?

   (a) division of labor/competency
   (b) merit-based careers/productivity
   (c) rules and procedures/efficiency
   (d) impersonality/fairness

8. One of the conclusions from the Hawthorne studies was that _____.

   (a) motion studies could improve performance
   (b) groups can sometimes restrict productivity of their members
   (c) people respond well to monetary incentives
   (d) supervisors should avoid close relations with their subordinates

9. If an organization was performing poorly and Henri Fayol was called in as a consultant, what would he most likely advise as a way to improve things?

   (a) teach managers to better plan, organize, lead, and control
   (b) teach workers more efficient job methods
   (c) promote to management only the most competent workers
   (d) find ways to increase corporate social responsibility

10. When a worker has a family, makes car payments, has a mortgage, and is active in supporting community organizations, how might Argyris explain her poor performance at work?

    (a) management practices don't treat her as an adult
    (b) managers use too many Theory Y assumptions
    (c) there are inefficient subsystems in the organization
    (d) she doesn't work in a learning organization

11. The assumption that people are complex with widely varying needs is most associated with the _____ management approaches.

    (a) classical (b) neoclassical
    (c) behavioral (d) modern

12. Conflict between the mature adult personality and a rigid organization was a major concern of _____.

    (a) Argyris (b) Follett
    (c) Gantt (d) Fuller

13. When your local bank or credit union is viewed as an open system, the loan-processing department would be considered a _____.

    (a) subsystem (b) closed system
    (c) resource input (d) value center

14. In a learning organization, as described by Peter Senge, one would expect to find _____.

   (a) priority placed on following rules and procedures

   (b) promotions based on seniority

   (c) employees who are willing to set aside old thinking and embrace new ways

   (d) a strict hierarchy of authority

15. When people perform in a situation as they are expected to, this is sometimes called the _____ effect.

   (a) Hawthorne   (b) systems

   (c) contingency   (d) open-systems

Short response

16. Give an example of how principles of scientific management can apply in organizations today.

17. How do the deficit and progression principles operate in Maslow's hierarchy?

18. Compare the Hawthorne effect with McGregor's notion of self-fulfilling prophecies.

19. Explain by example several ways a manager might use contingency thinking in the management process.

Integration & application

20. Enrique Temoltzin is the new manager of your local college bookstore. He wants to do a good job for the owner and therefore decides to operate the store according to Weber's concept of bureaucracy.

Questions: Is the bureaucracy a good management approach for Enrique to follow? What are the potential advantages and disadvantages? How could Enrique use contingency thinking in this situation?

Managerial Assumptions

Instructions

Use the space in the left margin to write "Yes" if you agree with the statement, or "No" if you disagree with it. Force yourself to take a "yes" or "no" position for every statement.

1. Are good pay and a secure job enough to satisfy most workers?

2. Should a manager help and coach subordinates in their work?

3. Do most people like real responsibility in their jobs?

4. Are most people afraid to learn new things in their jobs?

5. Should managers let subordinates control the quality of their work?

6. Do most people dislike work?

7. Are most people creative?

8. Should a manager closely supervise and direct the work of subordinates?

9. Do most people tend to resist change?

10. Do most people work only as hard as they have to?

11. Should workers be allowed to set their own job goals?

12. Are most people happiest off the job?

13. Do most workers really care about the organization they work for?

14. Should a manager help subordinates advance and grow in their jobs?

Scoring

Count the number of "yes" responses to items 1, 4, 6, 8, 9, 10, 12; write that number here as [X = _____]. Count the number of "yes" responses to items 2, 3, 5, 7, 11, 13, 14; write that score here as [Y = _____].

Interpretation

This assessment examines your orientation toward Douglas McGregor's Theory X (your "X" score) and Theory Y (your "Y" score) assumptions. Consider how your X/Y assumptions might influence how you behave toward other people at work. What self-fulfilling prophecies are you likely to create?

 For further exploration go to WileyPlus

Case Snapshot

Zara International—Fashion at the Speed of Light

Fast fashion is an emerging force that sees clothing retailers frequently purchasing small quantities of merchandise that are delivered speedily to stores. This allows them to stay on top of emerging trends while avoiding the great industry pitfalls of "hot today, gauche tomorrow." No company does fast fashion better than Zara International. Shoppers in over 70 countries have taken to Zara's knack for bringing the latest styles from sketchbook to clothing rack in record time.

Online Interactive Learning Resources

SELF-ASSESSMENT
• Self-Awareness

EXPERIENTIAL EXERCISES
• What would the classics say?
• The great management history debate

TEAM PROJECT
• Management in Popular Culture

3 Ethics and Social Responsibility

Character Doesn't Stay Home When We

Social Business Model Joins Fight Against Poverty.
For Muhammad Yunus, Nobel Prize winner and noted social entrepreneur from Bangladesh, a world without poverty may be a dream, but it's a dream that he has long been pursuing. He's CEO of Grameen Bank, an innovator in micro-finance that provides loans to poor people with no collateral. The bank has loaned over $7.5 billion to date and now employs 27,000+ people.

Poverty is, unfortunately, a part of our global environment. You can find it in your local community and it's a national concern. A large proportion of the world's population lives in poverty conditions—at least a billion people live on less than one dollar per day while 94% of world income benefits only 40% of its people. And according to Yunus, two-thirds of the world's population has no access to banks. He says: "The way the banking institutions have been designed and built is based on certain criteria which poor people don't fulfill."

As an economist in Bangladesh, Yunus developed the Grameen Bank to help poor people start and operate small businesses. Recognizing that many poor couldn't get regular bank loans because they didn't have sufficient collateral, Yunus came up with the "micro credit" idea to

Trendsetters
Former Microsoft executive fights illiteracy with Room to Read.

News Feed
Welcome "corporate greens" and the new ECOnomics.

Case Snapshot
Tom's of Maine—where doing business means doing good

Go to Work

lend small amounts of money at very low interest rates with the goal of promoting self-sufficiency through operating small enterprises.

By design, the vast majority of loan recipients, 97%, are women. Yunus says: ". . . we saw real benefits of money going straight to women—children benefited directly and women had long-term vision for escaping poverty." Each loan recipient becomes part of a local group of similar borrowers who agree to support and encourage one another. They pay the loans off in weekly installments and a borrower only gets another loan when the first is paid off successfully. The system works; the repayment rate is 98%.

The Grameen Bank model has been replicated in more than 40 countries, including the United States. Yunus continues to pursue poverty initiatives, including a commitment to "social business." In his book *Creating a World Without Poverty,* Yunus defines a social business as one that accomplishes a social goal and in which profits are reinvested in the business rather than distributed as dividends to the owners.

3.1 How Do Ethics and Ethical Behavior Play Out in the Workplace?

Does learning about bad business behavior shock and dismay you? "Madoff fraud bankrupts charities." "Madoff gets 150 years in prison." "Worldcom CEO sentenced to 25 years in prison." "Former Enron CEO appeals lengthy jail sentence." "Owner of peanut factory refuses to testify at Congressional hearing into *Salmonella* deaths." Such headlines and their underlying scandals are all too frequent in the news. And rather than by incompetence, the stories underlying them are often caused by personal failures such as greed.[1] With bleak reports like these, it's understandable that some people, perhaps a lot of them, are left feeling cynical, pessimistic, and even helpless regarding the state of executive leadership in our society.[2]

So, what can be done? For starters, would you say that it is time to get serious about the moral aspects and social implications of behavior in and by organizations? Can we agree here that, in your career and for any manager, the goal should always be to achieve performance objectives through ethical and socially responsible actions? As you think about these questions, keep in mind this advice from Desmond Tutu, archbishop of Capetown, South Africa, and winner of the Nobel Peace Prize.[3]

You are powerful people. You can make this world a better place where business decisions and methods take account of right and wrong as well as profitability . . . . You must take a stand on important issues: the environment and ecology, affirmative action, sexual harassment, racism and sexism, the arms race, poverty, the obligations of the affluent West to its less-well-off sisters and brothers elsewhere.

• Ethical behavior can always be described as "good" or "right."

It is tempting to say that any behavior that is legal can also be considered ethical. But this is too easy; the "letter of the law" does not always translate into what others would consider as ethical actions.[4] For example, U.S. laws once allowed slavery, permitted only men to vote, and allowed young children to work full-time jobs. Today we consider such actions unethical.

Ethics is defined as the code of moral principles that sets standards of good or bad, or right or wrong, in our conduct.[5] Thus, personal ethics are guides for behavior, helping people make moral choices among alternative courses of action. Most typically, we use the term **ethical behavior** to describe what we accept as "good" and "right" as opposed to "bad" or "wrong."

• Ethical behavior is values driven.

It's one thing to look back and make ethical judgments; it is a bit harder to make them in real time. Is it truly ethical for an employee to take longer than necessary to do a job . . . to make personal telephone calls on company time . . . to call in sick and go on holiday instead? While not strictly illegal, many people would consider any one or more of these acts to be unethical. How about you? How often and in what ways have you committed or observed acts that could be considered unethical in your school or workplace?[6]

Many ethical problems arise at work when people are asked to do something that violates their personal beliefs. For some, if the act is legal, they proceed with confidence and consider their behavior ethical. For others, the ethical test goes beyond legality and extends to personal **values**—the underlying beliefs and judgments regarding what is right or desirable and that influence individual attitudes and behaviors.

Ethics sets standards of good or bad, or right or wrong, in our conduct.

Ethical behavior is "right" or "good" in the context of a governing moral code.

Values are broad beliefs about what is appropriate behavior.

The psychologist Milton Rokeach distinguishes between "terminal" and "instrumental" values.[7] **Terminal values** focus on desired ends, such as the goal of lifelong learning. Examples of terminal values considered important by managers include self-respect, family security, freedom, inner harmony, and happiness. **Instrumental values** concern the means for accomplishing these ends, such as the role of intellectual curiosity in lifelong learning. Instrumental values held important by managers include honesty, ambition, courage, imagination, and self-discipline.

Although terminal and instrumental values tend to be quite enduring for any one individual, they can vary considerably from one person to the next. A contrast of such values might help to explain why different people respond quite differently to the same situation. Although two people might share the terminal value of career success, they might disagree on how to balance the instrumental values of honesty and ambition in accomplishing it.

Test this point. Talk with some of your friends or classmates about terminal values (what you and they want to achieve) and instrumental values (how you and they are willing to do it). Don't be surprised to find values differences, and don't be surprised to find that these differences create conflicts. Some of the disagreements, furthermore, may rest on significant differences in what behaviors are and are not considered ethical. Consider an example. Did you know that about 10% of a recent MBA class at Duke University was caught cheating on a take-home final exam?[8] The "cheaters" averaged 29 years of age and six years of work experience, and they were also part and parcel of the Internet age—big on music downloads, file sharing, open source software, text-messaging, and electronic collaboration. Some say what happened is a good example of "postmodern learning" that one should expect from students who are taught to collaborate and work in teams and utilize the latest communication technologies. For others, there is no doubt—it was an individual exam and they cheated.

Terminal values are preferences about desired end states.

Instrumental values are preferences regarding the means to desired ends.

Self-Assessment
This is a good point to complete the self-assessment "*Terminal Values Survey*" found on page 69.

In the **utilitarian view** ethical behavior delivers the greatest good to the most people.

• What is considered ethical varies among moral reasoning approaches.

Figure 3.1 shows four different philosophical views of ethical behavior, with each representing an alternative approach to moral reasoning.[9] The **utilitarian view** considers ethical behavior as that which delivers the greatest good to the greatest number of people. Founded in the work of 19th-century philosopher John Stuart Mill, this results-oriented view tries to assess the moral implications of our actions in terms of their consequences. Business executives, for example, might use profits, efficiency, and other performance criteria to judge what decision is best for the most people. An example is the manager who decides to cut 30% of a plant's workforce in order to keep the plant profitable and save the remaining jobs, rather than lose them all to business failure.

Stay Tuned

Behavior of Managers Key to Ethical Workplace

Managers make a big difference in ethical behavior at work, according to a survey conducted for Deloitte & Touche USA. Some findings include:

- 42% of workers say the behavior of their managers is a major influence on an ethical workplace.
- Most common unethical acts by managers and supervisors include verbal, sexual, and racial harassment, misuse of company property, and giving preferential treatment.
- 91% of workers are more likely to behave ethically when they have work-life balance; 30% say they suffer from poor work-life balance.
- Top reasons for unethical behavior are lack of personal integrity (80%) and lack of job satisfaction (60%).
- Most workers consider it unacceptable to steal from an employer, cheat on expense reports, take credit for another's accomplishments, and lie on time sheets.
- Most workers consider it acceptable to ask a work colleague for a personal favor, take sick days when not ill, or use company technology for personal affairs.

Your Thoughts?

Are there any surprises in these data? Is this emphasis on manager and direct supervisor behavior justified as the key to an ethical workplace? Would you make any changes to what the workers in this survey report as acceptable and unacceptable work behaviors?

FIGURE 3.1

How Do Alternative Moral Reasoning Approaches View Ethical Behavior?

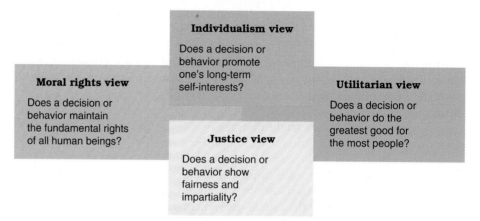

Individualism view

Does a decision or behavior promote one's long-term self-interests?

Moral rights view

Does a decision or behavior maintain the fundamental rights of all human beings?

Utilitarian view

Does a decision or behavior do the greatest good for the most people?

Justice view

Does a decision or behavior show fairness and impartiality?

People often differ in the approaches they take toward moral reasoning, and they may use different approaches at different times and situations. Four ways to reason through the ethics of a course of action are utilitarianism, individualism, moral rights, and justice. Each approach can justify an action as ethical, but the reasoning will differ from that of the other views.

In the **individualism view**, ethical behavior advances long-term self-interests.

In the **justice view**, ethical behavior treats people impartially and fairly.

Procedural justice focuses on the fair application of policies and rules.

Distributive justice focuses on treating people the same regardless of personal characteristics.

Interactional justice is the degree to which others are treated with dignity and respect.

In the **moral rights view**, ethical behavior respects and protects fundamental rights.

In the **utilitarian view** ethical behavior delivers the greatest good to the most people. An appeal to the **individualism view** of ethical behavior would focus on the long-term advancement of self-interests. People supposedly become self-regulating as they strive for individual advantage over time; ethics are maintained in the process. For example, just suppose that you might think about cheating on your next test. But you also realize this quest for short-term gain might lead to a long-term loss if you get caught and expelled. This reasoning should cause a quick rejection of the original idea.

Not everyone, as you might expect, agrees that self-regulation will always promote honesty and integrity. One complaint is that individualism in business practice too often results in a "pecuniary ethic." This has been described by one executive as a tendency to "push the law to its outer limits," and "run rough-shod over other individuals to achieve one's objectives."[10]

The **justice view** of moral reasoning considers a behavior ethical when people are treated impartially and fairly, according to legal rules and standards. It judges the ethical aspects of any decision on the basis of how equitable it is for everyone affected.[11] Researchers now like to speak about three aspects of justice in the workplace—procedural, distributive, and interactional.

Procedural justice involves the fair administration of policies and rules. For example, does a sexual harassment charge levied against a senior executive receive the same full hearing as one made against a first-level supervisor? **Distributive justice** involves the allocation of outcomes without respect to individual characteristics, such as those based on ethnicity, race, gender, or age. For example, does a woman with the same qualifications and experience as a man receive the same consideration for hiring or promotion? **Interactional justice** focuses on the treatment of others with dignity and respect. For example, does a bank loan officer take the time to fully explain to an applicant why he or she was turned down for a loan?[12]

Finally, a **moral rights view** considers behavior as ethical when it respects and protects the fundamental rights of people. Based on the teachings of John Locke and Thomas Jefferson, this view considers inviolate the rights of all people to life, liberty, and fair treatment under the law. In organizations, this translates into protecting the rights of employees to privacy, due process, free speech, free consent, health and safety, and freedom of conscience.

As our nation and others grapple with the complexities of global society, one of the issues we often hear raised and debated is human rights. Even though the United Nations stands by the Universal Declaration of Human Rights passed by the General Assembly in 1948, business executives, representatives of activist groups, and leaders of governments still argue and disagree over human rights issues in various circumstances.[13] And without doubt, one of the areas where human rights can be most controversial is the arena of international business.

• What is considered ethical can vary across cultures.

Situation: A 12-year-old boy is working in a garment factory in Bangladesh. He is the sole income earner for his family. He often works 12-hour days and was once burned quite badly by a hot iron. One day he is told he can't work. His employer was given an ultimatum by his firm's major American customer—"no child workers if you want to keep our contracts." The boy says: "I don't understand. I could do my job very well. I need the money."

The question is "should this child be allowed to work?" And it is but one example among the many ethics challenges faced in international business. Former Levi CEO Robert Haas once said that an ethical problem "becomes even more difficult when you overlay the complexities of different cultures and values systems that exist throughout the world."[14] It would probably be hard to find a corporate leader or business person engaged in international business who would disagree. Put yourself in their positions. How would you deal with an issue such as child labor in a factory owned by one of your major suppliers?

Those who believe that behavior in foreign settings should be guided by the classic rule of "when in Rome, do as the Romans do" reflect an ethical position of **cultural relativism**.[15] This is the belief that there is no one right way to behave, and that ethical behavior is always determined by its cultural context. An American international business executive guided by rules of cultural relativism, for example, would argue that the use of child labor is okay in another country as long as it is consistent with local laws and customs.

Figure 3.2 contrasts cultural relativism with the alternative of **universalism**. This is an absolutist ethical position suggesting that if a behavior or practice is not okay in one's home environment, it is not acceptable practice anywhere else. In other words, ethical standards are universal and should apply absolutely across cultures and national boundaries. In the former example, the American executive would not do business in a setting where child labor was used, since it is unacceptable at home. Critics of such a universal approach claim that it is a form of **ethical imperialism**, or the attempt to externally impose one's ethical standards on others.

Business ethicist Thomas Donaldson finds fault with both cultural relativism and ethical imperialism. He argues instead that certain fundamental rights and ethical standards can be preserved, while values and traditions of a given culture are respected.[16] The core values or "hyper-norms" that should transcend cultural boundaries focus on human dignity, basic rights, and good citizenship. Donaldson believes international business behaviors can be tailored to local and regional cultural contexts while still committing to these core values. In the case of child labor, again, the American executive might ensure that any children working in a factory under contract to his or her business would work in safe conditions and be provided schooling during scheduled hours as well as employment.[17]

Excerpts from the Universal Declaration of Human Rights, United Nations

- Article 1—All human beings are born free and equal in dignity and right.
- Article 18—Everyone has the right to freedom of thought, conscience, and religion.
- Article 19—Everyone has the right to freedom of opinion and expression.
- Article 23—Everyone has the right to work, to free choice of employment, to just and favorable conditions of work.
- Article 26—Everyone has the right to education.

Cultural relativism suggests there is no one right way to behave; cultural context determines ethical behavior.

Universalism suggests ethical standards apply absolutely across all cultures.

Ethical imperialism is an attempt to impose one's ethical standards on other cultures.

FIGURE 3.2

How Do Cultural Relativism and Moral Absolutism Influence International Business Ethics?

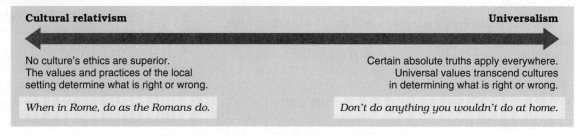

Cultural relativism	Universalism
No culture's ethics are superior. The values and practices of the local setting determine what is right or wrong.	Certain absolute truths apply everywhere. Universal values transcend cultures in determining what is right or wrong.
When in Rome, do as the Romans do.	*Don't do anything you wouldn't do at home.*

The international business world is one of the most challenging settings in respect to ethical decision making. This figure identifies two diametrically opposed extremes. Cultural relativism justifies a decision if it conforms to local values, laws, and practices. Universalism justifies a decision only if it conforms to the ways of the home country.

(*Source*: Developed from Thomas Donaldson, "Values in Tension: Ethics Away from Home," *Harvard Business Review*, vol. 74 (September/October 1996), pp. 48–62.)

• Ethical dilemmas arise as tests of personal ethics and values.

It's all well and good to discuss ethical behavior in theory and in the safety of the college classroom. The real personal test, however, occurs when we encounter a real-life situation that challenges our ethical beliefs and standards. And sooner or later, we all will. Often ambiguous and unexpected, these ethical challenges are inevitable.

Think ahead to your next job search. Suppose you have accepted one job offer, only to get a better one from another employer two weeks later. Should you come up with an excuse to back out of the first job so that you can accept the second one instead?

An **ethical dilemma** is a situation requiring a decision about a course of action that, although offering potential benefits, may be considered unethical. As a further complication, there may be no clear consensus on what is "right" and "wrong." In these circumstances, one's personal values are often the best indicators that something isn't right. An engineering manager speaking from experience sums it up this way: "I define an unethical situation as one in which I have to do something I don't feel good about."[18]

Take a look at the **Table 3.1**—Common Situations for Unethical Behavior at Work.[19] Have you been exposed to anything like this? Are you ready to deal with these situations and any ethical dilemmas that they may create?

In a survey of *Harvard Business Review* subscribers, managers reported that many of their ethical dilemmas arise out of conflicts with superiors, customers, and subordinates.[20] The most frequent issues involve dishonesty in advertising and in communications with top management, clients, and government agencies. Other ethics problems involve dealing with special gifts, entertainment expenses, and kickbacks.

Significantly, managers report that their bosses are often a cause of ethical dilemmas. They complain about bosses who engage in various forms of harassment, misuse organizational resources, and give preferential treatment to certain

An **ethical dilemma** is a situation that although offering potential benefit or gain is also unethical.

[TABLE 3.1]

Common Situations for Unethical Behavior at Work

Discrimination: Denying people a promotion or job because of their race, religion, gender, age, or another reason that is not job-relevant

Sexual harassment: Making a coworker feel uncomfortable because of inappropriate comments or actions regarding sexuality, or by requesting sexual favors in return for favorable job treatment

Conflicts of interest: Taking bribes, kickbacks, or extraordinary gifts in return for making decisions favorable to another person

Customer confidence: Giving someone privileged information regarding the activities of a customer

Organizational resources: Using official stationery or a business e-mail account to communicate personal opinions or to make requests from community organizations

persons.[21] They report feeling pressured at times to support incorrect viewpoints, sign false documents, overlook the boss's wrongdoings, and do business with the boss's friends. A surprising two-thirds of chief financial officers in a *Newsweek* survey, for example, said that they had been asked by their bosses to falsify financial records. Of them, 45% said they refused the directive, while 12% said they complied.[22]

At the top of any list of bad boss behaviors is holding people accountable for unrealistically high performance goals.[23] When individuals feel extreme performance pressures, they sometimes act incorrectly and engage in questionable practices in attempting to meet these expectations. As scholar Archie Carroll says: ". . . otherwise decent people start cutting corners on accuracy or quality, or start covering up incidents, lying or deceiving customers."[24] The lesson is to be realistic and supportive in what you request of others. In Carroll's words again, "Good management means that one has to be sensitive to how pressure to perform might be perceived by those who want to please the boss."[25]

• People have tendencies to rationalize unethical behaviors.

What happens after someone commits an unethical act? Most of us generally view ourselves as "good" people. When we do something that is or might be "wrong," therefore, it leaves us doubtful, uncomfortable, and anxious. A common response is to rationalize the questionable behavior to make it seem acceptable in our minds.

You might observe in yourself and others tendencies toward four rationalizations that are used to justify ethical misconduct.[26] First, a rationalizer might say, *It's not really illegal.* This implies that the behavior is acceptable, especially in ambiguous situations. When dealing with shady or borderline situations, you may not be able to precisely determine right from wrong; in such cases it is important to stop and reconsider things. When in doubt about the ethics of a decision, the best advice is: don't do it.

A rationalizer might also say: *It's in everyone's best interests.* This response suggests that just because someone might benefit from the behavior, it becomes justifiable. To overcome this "ends justify the means" rationalization, we need to look beyond short-run results to address longer-term implications. Sometimes rationalizing uses a third excuse: *No one will ever know about it.* The argument implies that only upon discovery is a crime committed. Lack of accountability, unrealistic pressures to perform, and a boss who prefers "not to know" can all reinforce such thinking. In today's world of great transparency, such thinking seems very hard to justify.

Finally, the rationalizer may proceed with a questionable action because he or she believes that *the organization will stand behind me.* This is misperceived loyalty. The individual believes that the organization's best interests stand above all others. In return, the individual believes that top managers will condone the behavior and protect the individual from harm. But if caught doing something wrong, would you want to count on the organization going to bat for you? And when you read about people who have done wrong and then try to excuse it by saying "I only did what I was ordered to do," how sympathetic are you?

People have tendencies to try and rationalize unethical acts to justify them and reduce anxieties.

Study Guide

3.1
How Do Ethics and Ethical Behavior Play Out in the Workplace?

Rapid review

- Ethical behavior is that which is accepted as "good" or "right" as opposed to "bad" or "wrong."
- The utilitarian, individualism, moral rights, and justice views offer different approaches to moral reasoning; each takes a different perspective of when and how a behavior becomes ethical.
- Cultural relativism argues that no culture is ethically superior to any other; moral absolutism believes there are clear rights and wrongs that apply universally, no matter where in the world one might be.
- An ethical dilemma occurs when one must decide whether to pursue a course of action that, although offering the potential for personal or organizational gain, may be unethical.
- Ethical dilemmas faced by managers often involve conflicts with superiors, customers, and subordinates over requests that involve some form of dishonesty.
- Common rationalizations for unethical behavior include believing the behavior is not illegal, is in everyone's best interests, will never be noticed, or will be supported by the organization.

Terms to define

Cultural relativism
Distributive justice
Ethical behavior
Ethical dilemmas
Ethical imperialism
Ethics
Individualism view
Instrumental values
Interactional justice
Justice view
Moral absolutism
Moral rights view
Procedural justice
Terminal values
Utilitarian view
Values

Be sure you can

- differentiate legal behavior and ethical behavior
- differentiate terminal and instrumental values, and give examples of each
- list and explain four approaches to moral reasoning
- illustrate distributive, procedural, and interactive justice in organizations
- explain the positions of cultural relativism and moral absolutism in international business ethics
- illustrate the types of ethical dilemmas common in the workplace
- explain how bad management can cause ethical dilemmas
- list four common rationalizations for unethical behavior

Questions for discussion

1. For a manager, is any one of the moral reasoning approaches better than the others?
2. Will a belief in cultural relativism create inevitable ethics problems for international business executives?
3. Are ethical dilemmas always problems, or can they be opportunities?

3.2 How Can We Maintain High Standards of Ethical Conduct?

As quick as we are to recognize the bad news and problems about ethical behavior in organizations, we shouldn't forget that there is a lot of good news, too. There are many organizations out there whose leaders and members set high ethics standards for themselves and others, and engage in a variety of methods to encourage consistent ethical behaviors.

The opening example of how Mohammad Yunus fights poverty with his social business model should have started you thinking. Look around; there are other cases of people and organizations operating in ethical and socially responsible ways out there. Some are quite well known now—Tom's of Maine and Burt's Bees are two that are featured in the recommended chapter case study. Surely there are other examples right in your local community of how "profits with principles" can be achieved. But even as you think about organizations that do good things, don't forget that the underlying foundations rest with the people who run them—individuals like you and me.

• Personal factors and moral development influence ethical decision making.

There are many possible influences on our personal ethics and how we apply them at work. One set traces to who we are as a person, what might be called our "character." This is what we represent and stand for in terms of family influences, religious beliefs, personal standards, personal values, and even past experiences.

Character shouldn't stay home when we go to work, but it isn't always easy to stand up for what you believe. This problem grows when we are exposed to extreme pressures, when we get contradictory or just plain bad advice, and when our career is at stake. "Do this or lose your job!" That's a terribly intimidating message. So it may be no surprise that 56% of U.S. workers in one survey reported feeling pressured to act unethically in their jobs.[27] Sadly, the same survey also revealed that 48% of respondents had themselves committed questionable acts within the past year.

Such problems become more manageable when we have solid **ethical frameworks**, or well-thought-out personal rules and strategies for ethical decision making. Taking the time to think through our ethical anchors can help us to act consistently and confidently. By giving high priority to such virtues as honesty, fairness, integrity, and self-respect, the process provides ethical anchors that can help us make correct decisions even under the most difficult conditions.

The many personal influences on ethical decision making come together in the three levels of moral development described by Lawrence Kohlberg and shown in **Figure 3.3**: preconventional, conventional, and postconventional or principled.[28] There are two stages in each phase, and Kohlberg believes that we move step-by-step through the stages as we grow in maturity and education. Not everyone, in fact perhaps only a few of us, reach the postconventional level.

In Kohlberg's *preconventional stage* of moral development, **Figure 3.3** shows that the individual is self-centered.

Ethical frameworks are well-thought-out personal rules and strategies for ethical decision making.

FIGURE 3.3

What Are the Stages in Kohlberg's Three Levels of Moral Development?

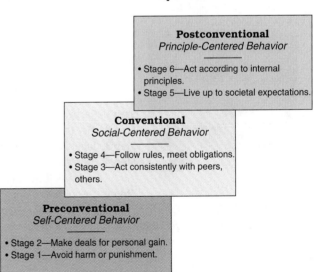

At the preconventional level of moral development the individual focuses on self-interests, avoiding harm and making deals for gain. At the conventional level attention becomes more social-centered, and the individual tries to be consistent and meet obligations to peers. At the postconventional level of moral development, principle-centered behavior results in the individual living up to societal expectations and personal principles.

Moral thinking is largely limited to issues of punishment, obedience, and personal interest. Decisions made in the preconventional stage of moral development are likely to be directed toward personal gain and based on obedience to rules. In the *conventional stage*, by contrast, attention broadens to include more societal concerns. Decisions made in this stage are likely to be based on following social norms, meeting the expectations of others, and living up to agreed upon obligations.

In the *postconventional stage* of moral development, also referred to as the principled stage, the individual is strongly driven by core principles and personal beliefs. This is the stage where a strong ethics framework is evident and the individual can be willing to break with norms and conventions, even laws, to make decisions consistent with personal principles. You might recall that Kohlberg believes that only a small percentage of people progress to this stage of moral development. An example might be the student who passes on an opportunity to cheat on a take-home examination because he or she believes it is just wrong, and even though the consequence will be a lower grade on the test. Another might be someone who refuses to use pirated computer software easily available through the Internet and social networks, preferring to purchase them and maintain one's respect for intellectual property rights.

• Training in ethical decision making can improve ethical conduct.

Ethics training seeks to help people understand the ethical aspects of decision making and to incorporate high ethical standards into their daily behavior.

It would be nice if people had access through their employers to **ethics training** that helps them understand and best deal with ethical aspects of decision making. Although not all will have this opportunity, more and more are getting it, including most college students. Most business schools, for example, now offer required and elective courses on ethics or integrate ethics into courses on other subjects.[29]

In college or in the workplace, however, we should keep ethics training in perspective. It won't work for everyone; it won't provide surefire answers to all ethical dilemmas; it won't guarantee ethical behavior throughout an organization. But it does help. An executive at Chemical Bank once put it this way: "We aren't teaching people right from wrong—we assume they know that. We aren't giving people moral courage to do what is right—they should be able to do that anyhow. We focus on dilemmas."[30]

One of the biggest differences between facing an ethical dilemma in a training seminar or as part of class discussions is pressure. Many times we must, or believe we must, move fast. *Tips to Remember* offers a reminder that it often helps to pause and double-check important decisions before taking action in uncomfortable circumstances. It presents a seven-step checklist that is used in some corporate training workshops. Would you agree that the most powerful is Step 6? This is what some call the test of the **Spotlight Questions**. You might think of this as the risk of public disclosure for your actions. Asking and answering the questions about how you would feel if family, friends, and acquaintances learn of your actions is a powerful way to test whether a decision is consistent with your ethical standards.[31]

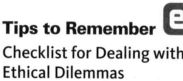

Tips to Remember

Checklist for Dealing with Ethical Dilemmas

Step 1. Recognize the ethical dilemma.
Step 2. Get the facts.
Step 3. Identify your options.
Step 4. Test each option: Is it legal? Is it right? Is it beneficial?
Step 5. Decide which option to follow.
Step 6. Ask *Spotlight Questions* to double check your decision.
   "How would I feel if my family found out about my decision?"
   "How would I feel if my decision is reported in the local newspaper or posted on the Internet?"
   "What would the person I know who has the strongest character and best ethical judgment say about my decision?"
Step 7. Take action.

Spotlight Questions highlight the risks from public disclosure of one's actions.

• Protection of whistleblowers can encourage ethical conduct.

Agnes Connolly pressed her employer to report two toxic chemical accidents.

Dave Jones reported that his company was using unqualified suppliers in constructing a nuclear power plant.

Margaret Newsham revealed that her firm allowed workers to do personal business while on government contracts.

Herman Cohen charged that the ASPCA in New York was mistreating animals.

Barry Adams complained that his hospital followed unsafe practices.

Who are these people? They are **whistleblowers**, persons who expose organizational misdeeds in order to preserve ethical standards and protect against wasteful, harmful, or illegal acts.[32] All were also fired from their jobs.

It shouldn't be too surprising to you that whistleblowers take significant career risks when they expose wrongdoing in organizations. Although there are federal and state laws that offer whistleblowers some defense against "retaliatory discharge," the protection is still inadequate overall. Laws vary from state to state, and the federal laws mainly protect government workers. Furthermore, even with legal protection, there are other reasons why potential whistleblowers might hesitate.

Have you ever encountered a student cheating on an exam or homework assignment? If so, did you blow the whistle by informing the instructor? A survey by the Ethics Resource Center reports that some 44% of U.S. workers fail to report the wrongdoings they observe at work. The top reasons for not reporting are "the belief that no corrective action would be taken, and the fear that reports would not be kept confidential."[33]

The very nature of organizations as power structures creates potential barriers to whistleblowing. A *strict chain of command* can make it hard to bypass the boss if he or she is the one doing something wrong. *Strong work group identities* can discourage whistleblowing and encourage loyalty and self-censorship. And *ambiguous priorities* can make it hard sometimes to distinguish right from wrong.[34]

Whistleblowers expose misconduct of organizations and their members.

• Managers as positive role models can inspire ethical conduct.

While still a college student, Gabrielle Melchionda started Mad Gab's Inc., an all-natural skin-care business in Portland, Maine. Some time after her sales had risen to over $300,000, an exporter offered to sell $2 million of her products abroad. She turned it down. Why? The exporter also sold weapons, which contradicted her values. Melchionda's personal values guide all of her business decisions, from offering an employee profit-sharing plan, to hiring disabled adults, to using only packaging designs that minimize waste.[35]

The way business owners and top managers approach ethics can make a big difference in what happens in their organizations. They have a lot of power to shape an organization's policies and set its moral tone. Some of this power works through the attention given to policies that set high ethics standards, and to their enforcement. Another and significantly large part of this power works through the personal examples top managers set. In order to have a positive impact on ethical conduct throughout an organization, those at the top must walk the talk.

Of course, it's not just managers at the top who have this power and the responsibility to use it well. Managers at all levels in organizations probably have more power than they realize to influence the ethical behavior of others. Again, part of this power is walking the talk, setting the example, and acting as an ethical role model. Another part is just practicing good management, and keeping goals and performance expectations reasonable. Some 64% of 238 executives in one study, for example, reported feeling so stressed to achieve company goals that they considered compromising personal standards. A *Fortune*

Gabrielle Melchionda founded Mad Gab on a set of ethical business principles, and she sticks with them.

FIGURE 3.4
Differences Between Amoral, Immoral, and Moral Managers.

Chooses to behave unethically	Fails to consider ethics	Makes ethical behavior a personal goal
Immoral manager	Amoral manager	Moral manager

An **immoral manager** chooses to behave unethically.

An **amoral manager** fails to consider the ethics of her or his behavior.

A **moral manager** makes ethical behavior a personal goal.

A **code of ethics** is a formal statement of values and ethical standards.

survey also reported that 34% of its respondents felt a company president can help to create an ethical climate by setting reasonable goals "so that subordinates are not pressured into unethical actions."[36]

Management scholar Archie Carroll makes the distinction between amoral, immoral, and moral managers that is shown in **Figure 3.4**.[37] The **immoral manager** chooses to behave unethically. He or she does something purely for personal gain and intentionally disregards the ethics of the action or situation. The **amoral manager** also disregards the ethics of an act or decision, but does so unintentionally. This manager simply fails to consider the ethical consequences of his or her actions. In contrast to both prior types, the **moral manager** considers ethical behavior as a personal goal. He or she makes decisions and acts always in full consideration of ethical issues. In Kohlberg's terms again, this manager is operating at the postconventional or principled stage of moral development.[38]

Think about these three types of managers and how common they might be in the real world of work. Although it may seem surprising, Carroll suggests that most of us act amorally. Although well intentioned, we remain mostly uninformed or undisciplined in considering the ethical aspects of our behavior.

• Formal codes of ethics set standards for ethical conduct.

Many organizations today have a **code of ethics** that formally states the values and ethical principles members are expected to display. Some employers even require new hires to sign and agree to the code as a condition of employment. Don't be surprised if you encounter this someday.

Ethics codes can get specific to the point of offering guidelines on how to behave in situations susceptible to ethical dilemmas—such as how sales representatives and purchasing agents should handle giving and receiving gifts. They might also specify consequences for bribes and kickbacks, dishonesty of books or records, and confidentiality breaches of corporate information. And, ethics codes are common in the complicated world of international business, where dilemmas such as the child labor case introduced earlier are common and perplexing.[39] Corporate executives realize that their customers and society at large hold them accountable for the actions of their foreign suppliers. They have become much stricter in policing their international operations. Leading firms such as the Gap Inc. use codes of conduct to anchor their international business dealings and communicate clear expectations to their business partners.[40]

At Gap Inc., global manufacturing is governed by a formal Code of Vendor Conduct.[41] The document specifically deals with discrimination—"Factories shall employ workers on the basis of their ability to do the job, not on the basis of their personal characteristics or beliefs"; forced labor—"Factories shall not use any prison, indentured or forced labor"; working conditions—"Factories must treat all workers with respect and dignity and provide them with a safe and healthy environment"; and freedom of association—"Factories must not interfere with workers who wish to lawfully and peacefully associate, organize or bargain collectively."

Of course you have to be careful in expecting too much of ethics codes; they set forth nice standards but they can't guarantee the desired conduct. In fact, one of the most notorious corporate scandals of recent memory occurred at a company active in philanthropy, known for social responsibility, and operating with a clear code of ethics—the Enron Corporation. The firm collapsed due to major fraud by senior executives who failed, as we might say, to "walk the ethics talk."[42]

A formal Code of Vendor Conduct helps Gap Inc. stay in control of conditions in its global supply chain.

Study Guide

3.2
How Can We Maintain High Standards of Ethical Conduct?

Rapid review

- Ethical behavior is influenced by an individual's character, represented by core values and beliefs.
- Kohlberg describes three levels of moral development—preconventional, conventional, and postconventional, with each of us moving step-by-step through the levels as we grow ethically over time.
- Ethics training can help people better understand how to make decisions when dealing with ethical dilemmas at work.
- Whistleblowers who expose the unethical acts of others have incomplete protection from the law and can face organizational penalties.
- All managers have responsibility for acting as ethical role models for others.
- Written codes of conduct spell out the basic ethical expectations of employers regarding the behavior of employees and other contractors.
- Immoral managers choose to behave unethically; amoral managers fail to consider ethics; moral managers make ethics a personal goal.

Terms to define

Amoral manager
Code of ethics
Ethical frameworks
Ethics training
Immoral manager
Moral manager
Spotlight questions
Whistleblowers

Be sure you can

- explain how ethical behavior is influenced by personal factors
- list and explain Kohlberg's three levels of moral development
- explain the term whistleblower
- list three organizational barriers to whistleblowing
- compare and contrast ethics training, codes of conduct, and ethics role models for their influence on ethics in the workplace
- state the "Spotlight Questions" for double checking the ethics of a decision
- describe differences between the inclinations of amoral, immoral, and moral managers

Questions for discussion

1. Is it right for organizations to require ethics training of employees?
2. Should whistleblowers have complete protection under the law?
3. Should all managers be evaluated on how well they serve as ethics role models?

3.3 What Should We Know about the Social Responsibilities of Organizations?

The organizations, groups, and persons with whom an organization interacts and conducts business are known as its **stakeholders** because they have a direct "stake" or interest in its performance; they are affected in one way or another by what the organization does and how it performs. As **Figure 3.5** shows, the field of organizational stakeholders can become quite complex. Perhaps the most recognizable among them are the organization's customers, suppliers, competitors, regulators, investors/owners, as well as employees.

> **Stakeholders** are people and institutions most directly affected by an organization's performance.

FIGURE 3.5
Who Are the Stakeholders of Organizations?

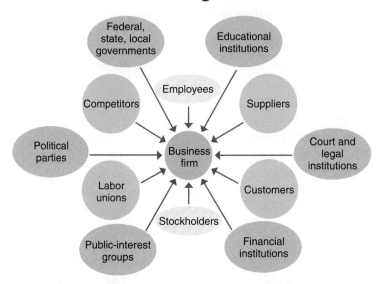

Stakeholders are the individuals, groups, and other organizations that have a direct interest in how well an organization performs. A basic list of stakeholders for any organization would begin with the employees and contractors who work for the organization, customers and clients who consume the goods and services, suppliers of needed resources, owners who invest capital, regulators in the form of government agencies, and special interest groups such as community members and activists.

When it comes to the performance of an organization, stakeholders can have rather different interests. Customers, for example, typically want value prices and quality products; owners are interested in realizing profits as returns on their investments; suppliers are interested in long-term business relationships; communities are interested in corporate citizenship and support for public services; employees are interested in good wages, benefits, security, and satisfaction in their work.

• Social responsibility is an organization's obligation to best serve society.

The way organizations behave in relationship with their many stakeholders is a good indicator of their underlying ethical characters.[5] When we talk about the "good" and the "bad" in business and society relationships, **corporate social responsibility** is at issue. Often called "CSR," it is defined as an obligation of the organization to act in ways that serve both its own interests and the interests of its stakeholders, representing society at large.

> **Corporate social responsibility** is the obligation of an organization to serve its own interests and those of its stakeholders.

Even though corporate "irresponsibility" seems to get most of the media's attention, we can't forget that there is a lot of responsible behavior taking place as well. Increasingly this has become part of what is called the **triple bottom line**—how well an organization performs when measured not only on financial criteria, but also on social and environmental ones. The triple bottom line in business decision making is checked by asking these questions: Is the decision economically sound? Is the decision socially responsible? Is the decision environmentally sound?[43]

Not too long ago, Deloitte & Touche, one of the world's largest accounting firms, all but closed its doors for a day. Instead of working, many of the firm's employees volunteered over 240,000 hours of community service in cities throughout the United States.[44] IBM has a program to help retiring workers with science and math skills to become certified teachers; Google set up a philanthropic foundation to be funded by 1% of its equity and profits; Procter & Gamble invests in venture capital funds for minority businesses.[45] Each of Timberland Company's full-time employees gets 40 hours of paid time per year for community volunteer work. One person who turned down a higher-paying job elsewhere says: "Timberland's motto is 'when you come to work in the morning, don't leave your values at the door.'"[46]

The list of socially responsible examples can go on. And yet you may notice, some firms and organizations seem to act in socially responsible ways out of pure *compliance*—that is, with the desire to avoid adverse consequences. But sometimes, perhaps in the examples just cited, organizations seem to act out of *conviction*—that is, with the desire to create positive impact.[47]

For students at the University of New Hampshire, the institution's conviction to being green is evident; the majority of its heat and electricity is generated from landfill gas, and leftover food goes to compost.[48] Such conviction surely puts UNH higher up on the social responsibility scale than would simple compliance with environmental laws and other conventions. But not all organizations step forward in this way, and this fact leads us to the question: just as with people, shouldn't organizations have ethics, too?

• Scholars argue cases for and against corporate social responsibility.

You may or may not be surprised to learn that not everyone agrees that organizations should make social responsibility a top business goal. Two contrasting views of corporate social responsibility, the classical view and the socioeconomic view, have stimulated quite a bit of debate in academic and public policy circles.[49]

More employers are offering employees time to pursue social service projects.

The **triple bottom line** of organizational performance includes financial, social, and environmental criteria.

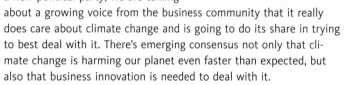

News Feed

Welcome "Corporate Greens" and the New ECOnomics

Get ready—you'll be reading and hearing a lot more about "corporate greens." No, we're not talking about a new political party; we are talking about a growing voice from the business community that it really does care about climate change and is going to do its share in trying to best deal with it. There's emerging consensus not only that climate change is harming our planet even faster than expected, but also that business innovation is needed to deal with it.

The Subaru plant in Indiana defines "green" into all operations. Through continuing process redesign it has reduced waste produced per vehicle by 47% and recycles 99.9% of the waste produced; it sends no garbage to landfills. Whereas Subaru used to recycle Styrofoam packaging, an Associate Kaizen or continual improvement team suggested it be sent back to the supplier and reused. The Styrofoam packaging now makes up to 10 round trips.

Ryan Wright is manager in charge of utility and sustainability at the At Bellisio Foods plant in Jackson, Ohio. You may not think there's a lot that can be done to "green up" a manufacturing facility, but he's found the way. A large treatment plant digests food waste, using bio-organisms to create the methane which becomes fuel to run the factory's boilers. Wright believes the process cuts CO_2 output by 43,000 tons per year by saving on costs of natural gas and transporting waste to a landfill. Although the price of the system was $4.65 million, he says: It's a great project; we're proud of it; it's the right thing to do."

When the *Wall Street Journal* advertises a major executive conference on ECOnomics: Creating Environmental Capital, you know the message has arrived in the executive ranks. The bottom line is that the link between business and the natural environment is no longer being left to chance; there's corporate strategy and image to be addressed at this important boundary.

"Carbon down, profits up," they say. Giving climate change a top business priority can make good financial sense. "Corporate green" is for real; it's no longer an oxymoron.

Green business practices can launch a virtuous circle in which acting responsibly improves financial performance and encourages more social responsibility.

The **classical view of CSR** is that business should focus on the pursuit of profits.

The **socioeconomic view of CSR** is that business should focus on contributions to society and not just making profits.

The **classical view of CSR** holds that management's only responsibility in running a business is to maximize profits, and thereby shareholder value. It puts the focus on the single bottom line of financial performance. In other words: "The business of business is business." This view takes a very narrow stakeholder perspective and is represented in the views of the late Milton Friedman, a respected economist and Nobel Laureate. He says: "Few trends could so thoroughly undermine the very foundations of our free society as the acceptance by corporate officials of social responsibility other than to make as much money for their stockholders as possible."[50]

The arguments against corporate social responsibility include fears that its pursuit will reduce business profits, raise business costs, dilute business purpose, give business too much social power, and do so without business accountability to the public. Although not against corporate social responsibility in its own right, Friedman and other proponents of the classical view believe that society's best interests are always served in the long run by executives who focus on profit maximization by their businesses.

The **socioeconomic view of CSR** holds that management of any organization should be concerned for the broader social welfare, not just corporate profits. This view takes a broad stakeholder perspective and puts the focus on an expanded triple bottom line that includes not just financial performance but also social and environmental performance. It is supported by Paul Samuelson, another distinguished economist and also a Nobel Laureate. He states: "A large corporation these days not only may engage in social responsibility, it had damn well better try to do so."

Among the arguments in favor of corporate social responsibility are that it will add long-run profits for businesses, improve the public image of businesses, and help them avoid government regulation. Furthermore, businesses often have vast resources with the potential to have enormous social impact. Thus, business executives have ethical obligations to ensure that their firms act responsibly in the interests of society at large. There is little doubt today that the public at large wants businesses and other organizations to act with genuine social responsibility. Stakeholder expectations are increasingly well voiced and include demands that organizations integrate social responsibility into their core values and daily activities.

The **virtuous circle** is when corporate social responsibility leads to improved financial performance that leads to more social responsibility.

At the very least, the argument that commitments to social responsibility will hurt the financial bottom line of businesses is getting harder to defend. The worst-case scenario seems to be that social responsibility has no adverse impact.[51] And there is some evidence for the existence of a **virtuous circle** in the social responsibility and performance relationship.[52] This occurs when corporate social responsibility leads to improved financial performance that, in turn, leads to more socially responsible actions in the future. An example might be the Subaru plant in Indiana discussed in the prior *News Feed*. When the plant was opened 20 years ago, executives asked employees to search for ways to conserve energy; they were able to cut energy usage by 14%—a positive impact on the financial bottom line. That led to more efforts to eliminate waste which kept making the plant "greener" over time. And as the plant's environmental impact improved step-by-step, cost savings added to profits.[53]

• Social business and social entrepreneurship point the way in social responsibility.

A **social business** is one in which the underlying business model directly addresses a social problem.

Recall the opening example of Mohammad Yunus and the Grameen Bank. On one level it is a business innovation—micro-credit lending. But at another level it is a **social business** in that the underlying business model directly addresses a social problem—in this case, using micro-credit lending to help fight poverty. And in the domain of social enterprises the Grameen Bank is a very good benchmark. You'll be hearing and reading a lot more about social businesses; they are already being called the new "fourth sector" of our economy—joining private for-profit businesses, public government organizations, and non-profits.[54]

As the late management guru Peter Drucker once said: "Every single social and global issue of our day is a business opportunity in disguise."

Housing and job training for the homeless . . . Bringing technology to poor families. . . . Improving literacy among disadvantaged youth. . . . Making small loans to start minority-owned businesses . . . What do these examples have in common? They are all targets for **social entrepreneurship**, a unique form of entrepreneurship that seeks novel ways to solve pressing social problems at home and abroad.[55] Social entrepreneurs share many characteristics with other entrepreneurs with one unique difference: a social mission drives them.[56] Their personal quests are for innovations that help solve social problems, or at least help make lives better for people who are disadvantaged. A good example is the Trendsetters feature on John Wood and his organization Room to Read.

Social entrepreneurship is risk taking by entrepreneurs striving to solve pressing social problems.

• Failures of ethics and social responsibility prompt calls for stronger governance.

When we admit that organizations and their leaders can have different approaches toward social responsibility, it raises an issue first discussed in Module 1: governance. We have been using the term **corporate governance** to describe oversight of the top management of an organization by its board of directors. Active governance typically involves hiring, firing, and compensating the CEO; assessing business strategy; verifying financial records; and, more generally, making sure that the firm operates in the best interests of the owners and shareholders. One board member describes his governance responsibilities this way: "It's really about setting and maintaining high standards."[57]

Corporate governance is the oversight of top management by a board of directors.

It is tempting to think that corporate governance is a clear-cut way to ensure that organizations behave with social responsibility and that their members always act ethically. But even though its purpose is clear, there is a lot of concern that corporate governance can be inadequate and in some cases ineffectual. Consider, for example, controversies that emerged over "bailout" funding provided to banks and financial institutions by the U.S. government during the economic crisis. Many in Congress and the public at large were irate at CEO compensation, executive bonuses, and perks paid out at times when banks were failing and thousands were losing their jobs.

Where, you might ask, were the boards of directors? What happened to corporate governance in these situations?

When corporate scandals and controversies occur, executive greed and weak governance in controlling it often get blamed. And when they do, you will sometimes see

Trendsetters

Former Microsoft Executive Fights Illiteracy with Room to Read

John Wood is a social entrepreneur. During his successful career as a Microsoft executive, his life changed on a vacation to the Himalayas of Nepal. While there, Wood was shocked at the lack of schools. And he discovered a passion that determines what he calls the "second chapter" in his life: to provide the lifelong benefits of education to poor children.

Wood came home and ended up quitting his Microsoft job to start a nonprofit organization called Room to Read. So far, the organization has built over 100 schools and 1,000 libraries in Cambodia, India, Nepal, Vietnam, and Laos.

Noting that one-seventh of the global population can't read or write, Wood says: "I don't see how we are going to solve the world's problems without literacy." The Room to Read model is so efficient that it can build schools for as little as $6,000. *Time* magazine has honored Wood and his team as "Asian Heroes," and *Fast Company* magazine tapped his organization for a Social Capitalist Award.

government stepping in to try and correct things for the future. Laws are passed and regulating agencies are put in place in an attempt to better control and direct business behavior. An example is the **Sarbanes-Oxley Act**, or SOX. It was passed by Congress to ensure that top managers properly oversee the financial conduct of their organizations, and the law makes it easier for corporate executives to be tried and sentenced to jail for financial misconduct. The act also created the Public Company Accounting Oversight Board and set a new

The **Sarbanes-Oxley Act** requires that top managers properly oversee the financial conduct of their organizations.

standard for auditors to verify reporting processes in the companies they audit. CEOs and CFOs who misstate their firms' financial records can go to jail and pay substantial personal fines.

Indications are that business executives are starting to embrace corporate governance reform. If nothing else, they see its value in terms of enhanced corporate reputations.[58] Of course we often hear business executives complaining about the burdens imposed by the increased regulations. And they do have a point. But the fact is, we wouldn't need the laws and have the regulators if all organizations were socially responsible and all of their leaders were highly ethical in the first place.

Finally, even as one talks about corporate governance at the level of boards and executives, it is important to remember that all managers must accept personal responsibility for doing the "right" things. **Figure 3.6** highlights what might be called the need for ethics self-governance in day-to-day work behavior. It is not enough to fulfill performance accountabilities; they must be fulfilled in an ethical and socially responsible manner. The full weight of this responsibility holds in every organizational setting, from small to large and from private to nonprofit, and at every managerial level from top to bottom. Once again there is no escaping the ultimate reality—being a manager is a very socially responsible job!

FIGURE 3.6
Ethics and Self-Governance in Management and Leadership.

Study Guide

3.3
What Should We Know about the Social Responsibilities of Organizations?

Rapid review

- Corporate social responsibility is an obligation of the organization to act in ways that serve both its own interests and the interests of its stakeholders.
- Criteria for evaluating corporate social performance include how well it meets economic, legal, ethical, and discretionary responsibilities.
- The argument against corporate social responsibility says that businesses should focus on making profits; the argument for corporate social responsibility says that businesses should use their resources to serve broader social concerns.
- Governments sometimes enact laws to regulate business behavior and make up for weak governance; an example is the Sarbanes-Oxley Act.

Terms to define

Corporate governance

Corporate social responsibility

Sarbanes-Oxley Act

Social business

Social entrepreneurship

Triple bottom line

Virtuous circle

Be sure you can

- explain the concept of social responsibility
- summarize arguments for and against corporate social responsibility
- illustrate how the virtuous circle of corporate social responsibility might work
- explain the role of governance in business and nonprofit organizations
- explain a team leader's performance accountability in a way that includes the notion of self-governance

Questions for discussion

1. Choose an organization in your community; what questions would you ask to complete an audit of its social responsibility practices?
2. Is the logic of the virtuous circle a convincing argument in favor of corporate social responsibility?
3. Should government play a stronger role in making up for weak corporate governance?

Multiple choice

1. A business owner makes a decision to reduce a plant's workforce by 10% in order to cut costs and be able to save jobs for the other 90% of employees. This decision could be justified as ethical using the _____ approach to moral reasoning.
   - (a) utilitarian
   - (b) individualism
   - (c) justice
   - (d) moral rights

2. If a manager fails to enforce a late-to-work policy for all workers, that is, by allowing favored employees to arrive late without penalties, this would be considered a violation of _____.
   - (a) human rights
   - (b) personal values
   - (c) distributive justice
   - (d) Sarbanes-Oxley law

3. According to research on ethics in the workplace, _____ is/are often a major and frequent source of pressures that create ethical dilemmas for people in their jobs.
   - (a) declining morals in society
   - (b) long work hours
   - (c) low pay
   - (d) requests or demands from bosses

4. Someone who exposes the ethical misdeeds of others in an organization is usually called a/an _____.
   - (a) whistleblower
   - (b) ethics advocate
   - (c) ombudsman
   - (d) stakeholder

5. Two employees are talking about ethics in their workplaces. Sean says that ethics training and codes of ethical conduct are worthless; Maura says they are the only ways to ensure ethical behavior by all employees. Who is right and why?
   - (a) Sean—no one cares.
   - (b) Maura—only the organization can influence ethical behavior.
   - (c) Neither Sean nor Maura—training and codes can encourage but never guarantee ethical behavior.
   - (d) Neither Sean nor Maura—only the threat of legal punishment will make people act ethically.

6. Which ethical position has been criticized as a source of "ethical imperialism?"
   - (a) individualism
   - (b) absolutism
   - (c) utilitarianism
   - (d) rationalism

7. If a manager takes a lot of time explaining to a subordinate why he did not get a promotion and sincerely listens to his concerns, this is an example of an attempt to act ethically according to _____.
   - (a) utilitarian reasoning
   - (b) individualism
   - (c) interactional justice
   - (d) moral rights

8. Things such as family influences, religious beliefs, and personal values can be the source of strong _____ that can help individuals better deal with the ethical dilemmas they encounter at work.
   - (a) moral quality circles
   - (b) ethical frameworks
   - (c) codes of ethical conduct
   - (d) ethics training

9. In respect to the link between bad management and ethical behavior, research shows that _____.
   - (a) unrealistic goals can cause unethical behavior
   - (b) most whistleblowers just want more pay
   - (c) only top management behavior really makes a difference
   - (d) codes of ethics make up for any management deficiencies

10. A person's desires for a comfortable life and family security represent _____ values, while his or her desires to be honest and hard working represent _____ values.
    - (a) terminal/instrumental
    - (b) instrumental/terminal
    - (c) universal/individual
    - (d) individual/universal

11. A proponent of the classical view of corporate social responsibility would most likely agree with which of these statements?
    - (a) Social responsibility improves the public image of business.
    - (b) The primary responsibility of business is to maximize profits.
    - (c) By acting responsibly, businesses avoid government regulation.
    - (d) Businesses should do good while they are doing business.

12. Which well-known economist is most associated with the case against corporate social responsibility?
    - (a) Paul Samuelson
    - (b) Milton Friedman
    - (c) Alan Greenspan
    - (d) Kofi Annan

13. The "triple bottom line" of organizational performance would include measures of financial, social, and _____ performance.

    (a) philanthropic   (b) environmental
    (c) cost savings   (d) profit maximization

14. An amoral manager _____.

    (a) always acts in consideration of ethical issues
    (b) chooses to behave unethically
    (c) makes ethics a personal goal
    (d) acts unethically but unintentionally

15. A manager supports an organization's attempts at self-governance when he or she always tries to achieve performance objectives in ways that are

    _____.

    (a) performance effective
    (b) cost efficient
    (c) quality oriented
    (d) ethical and socially responsible

Short response

16. How does distributive justice differ from procedural justice?

17. What are the spotlight questions for double-checking the ethics of a decision?

18. If someone commits an unethical act, how can he or she rationalize it to make it seem right?

19. What is the virtuous circle of corporate social responsibility?

Integration & application

20. A small outdoor clothing company in Georgia has just received an attractive proposal from a business in Tanzania to manufacture the work gloves that it sells. Accepting the offer from the Tanzanian firm would allow for substantial cost savings compared to the current supplier. However, the outdoor clothing firm's manager has recently read reports that some businesses in Tanzania are forcing people to work in unsafe conditions in order to keep their costs down. The manager seeks your help in clarifying the ethical aspects of this opportunity.

Questions: How would you describe the manager's alternatives in terms of cultural relativism and absolutism? What would be the major issues and concerns in terms of the cultural relativism position versus the absolutist position?

Self-Assessment

Terminal Values Survey

Instructions

Rate each of the following values in terms of its importance to you.[59] Think about each value in terms of its importance as a guiding principle in your life. As you work, consider each value in relation to all the other values listed in the survey. Use this scale for each item:

1	2	3	4	5	6	7
Of lesser importance				Of greater importance		

Terminal Values

1. A comfortable life	1	2	3	4	5	6	7
2. An exciting life	1	2	3	4	5	6	7
3. A sense of accomplishment	1	2	3	4	5	6	7
4. A world at peace	1	2	3	4	5	6	7
5. A world of beauty	1	2	3	4	5	6	7
6. Equality	1	2	3	4	5	6	7
7. Family security	1	2	3	4	5	6	7
8. Freedom	1	2	3	4	5	6	7
9. Happiness	1	2	3	4	5	6	7
10. Inner harmony	1	2	3	4	5	6	7
11. Mature love	1	2	3	4	5	6	7

12. National security	1	2	3	4	5	6	7
13. Pleasure	1	2	3	4	5	6	7
14. Salvation	1	2	3	4	5	6	7
15. Self-respect	1	2	3	4	5	6	7
16. Social recognition	1	2	3	4	5	6	7
17. True friendship	1	2	3	4	5	6	7
18. Wisdom	1	2	3	4	5	6	7

Interpretation and Scoring

Terminal values reflect a person's preferences concerning the ends to be achieved. They are the goals individuals would like to achieve in their lifetimes. Multiply your score for each item times a "weight"—e.g., (#3 × 5) = your new question 3 score.

1. Calculate your Personal Values Score as:

   (#1 × 5) + (#2 × 4) + (#3 × 4) + (#7) + (#8) + (#9 × 4) + (#10 × 5) + (#11 × 4) + (#13 × 5) + (#14 × 3) + (#15 × 5) + (#16 × 3) + (#17 × 4) + (#18 × 5).

2. Calculate your Social Values Score as:

   (#4 × 5) + (#5 × 3) + (#6 × 5) + (#12 × 5).

3. Calculate your Terminal Values Score as: Personal Values—Social Values.

 For further exploration go to WileyPlus

Case Snapshot

Tom's of Maine—Where Doing Business Means Doing Good

Tom's of Maine, one of the first natural health care companies to distribute outside normal channels, holds fast to the values that got owners Tom and Kate Chappell started more than three decades ago, providing insight into how a small firm can grow while staying true to its founding principles in the midst of competition. Now that Tom's has been sold to Colgate, one wonders if those principles can hold up in a large corporate environment.

Online Interactive Learning Resources

SELF-ASSESSMENT
• Instrumental Values

EXPERIENTIAL EXERCISE
• Confronting Ethical Dilemmas

TEAM PROJECT
• Cheating on Campus

4
Managers as Decision Makers

There Is No Substitute for a Good Decision

Smart people create their own futures. As the leading global online career site, Monster.com represents the growing field of online job placement services available on the Web. Its founder, Jeff Taylor, describes its birth this way: "One morning I woke up at 4 A.M., and wrote an idea down on a pad of paper I keep next to my bed. I had this dream that I created a bulletin board called the Monster Board. That became the original name for the company. When I got up, I went to a coffee shop, and from 5:30 A.M. until about 10:00 A.M. I wrote the user interface for what today is Monster.com."

Monster.com is still a top destination for job seekers and one of the most visited domains on the Internet, but it gets lots of competition from the likes of CareerBuilder.com, Yahoo!, HotJobs, and Indeed.com. Monster also represents itself as a "lifelong career network" that serves everyone from recent college graduates all the way up to seasoned executives. But again, in the new age of multi-media resumes and high tech employment searches, networking sites such as LinkedIn and ZoomInfo offer competitive alternatives.

Trendsetters
Indra Nooyi brings new
style and a sharp eye
to Pepsi.

News Feed
Shareholders push to
regulate executive pay.

Case Snapshot
Amazon.com—One
e-store rules them all.

Like the rest of us, the Monster needs to keep changing with the times.

The new CEO of Monster Worldwide, Inc., Sal Ianuzzi, was hired to reinvigorate "the monster" in the face of tough competition. He says: "Any company that grows as fast as this one was bound to have some problems." Now, there's no complacency at Monster.com, no becoming comfortable with success. The same challenge holds for you—no room for complacency. This book and your management course offer many ways to explore your career skills and capabilities, and to identify and develop new ones. Take good advantage of the opportunity and always remember: What happens is up to you! Thus, there is no better time than the present to commit to learning and personal growth.

You don't need to create your own company like Jeff Taylor did to achieve career success, although you could. What you must do, however, is discover and invigorate the learning "monster" within yourself. Remember: smart people create their own futures!

4.1 How Do Managers Use Information to Make Decisions and Solve Problems?

"The significant problems we face cannot be solved at the same level of thinking we were at when we created them." Albert Einstein

Problem solving involves identifying and taking action to resolve problems.

Information competency is the ability to gather and use information to solve problems.

A **performance threat** is a situation where something is wrong or likely to be wrong.

A **performance opportunity** is a situation that offers the possibility of a better future if the right steps are taken.

The bankruptcy of General Motors shocked the world. But an automobile industry analyst says we should have seen it coming because the firm suffered from "decades of dumb decisions" that created unwarranted concessions to labor unions, poor styling and "look-alike cars, bad acquisitions, and misguided bets on big SUVs."[1] Anyone who studies management knows that decision making is part of the job. They also know that not all decisions are going to be easy ones; some will always have to be made under tough conditions; and not all decisions will turn out right. But we should also admit that the goal is to do a lot better than was the case at GM.

All of those case studies, experiential exercises, class discussions, and even essay exam questions are intended to engage students in the complexities of managerial decision making, the potential problems and pitfalls, and even the pressures of crisis situations. From the classroom forward, however, it's all up to you. Only you can determine whether you step forward and make the best out of very difficult problems, or collapse under pressure.

Problem solving is the process of identifying a discrepancy between an actual and a desired state of affairs, and then taking action to resolve it. The context for managerial problem solving is depicted in **Figure 4.1**. It clearly shows why managers fit our earlier definition of *knowledge workers*, persons whose value to organizations rests with their intellectual, not physical, capabilities.[2] All managers continually solve problems as they gather, give, receive, and process information from many sources.[3] In fact, one of your most critical skills might be described as **information competency**—the ability to locate, retrieve, evaluate, organize, and analyze information to make decisions that solve problems.

FIGURE 4.1

In What Ways Do Managers Serve as Information Nerve Centers in Organizations?

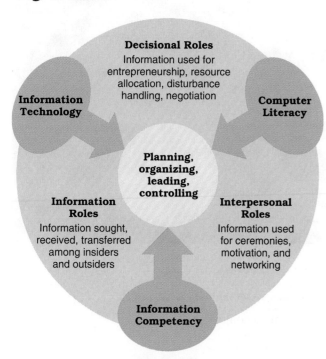

Managers sit at the center of complex networks of information flows; they serve as information-processing hubs or nerve centers. Each of the management functions—planning, organizing, leading, and controlling—requires the gathering, use, and transferring of information in these networks. Managers must have the information competencies needed to perform well in these roles.

• Managers deal with problems posing threats and offering opportunities.

The most obvious problem-solving situation for managers, or anyone for that matter, is a **performance threat**. This occurs as an actual or potential performance deficiency: something is wrong, or is likely to be wrong in the near future. Hurricane Katrina is a ready example. There were lots of warnings, but many underestimated or were either ambivalent or overconfident in preparing for it. They weren't ready when Katrina hit New Orleans, and a high price was paid for their errors.

Let's not forget, however, that problem solving often involves, or should involve, a **performance opportunity**.[4] This is a situation that offers the possibility of a better future, if the right steps are taken now. Suppose that a regional manager notices that sales at one retail store are unusually high. Does she just say "Great," and go on about her business? That's an opportunity missed. If she says, "Wait a minute, there may be something happening here that I could learn from and possibly transfer to other stores; I had better find out what's going on." That's an opportunity gained.

• Managers can be problem avoiders, problem solvers, or problem seekers.

What do you do when you receive a lower grade than expected on an exam or assignment? Do you get the grade, perhaps complain a bit to yourself or friends, and then forget it? Or do you get the grade, recognize that a problem exists, and try to learn from it so that you can do better in the future? Managers are just like you and me. They approach problem solving in different ways, and realize different consequences.

Some managers are *problem avoiders* who ignore information that would otherwise signal the presence of a performance threat or opportunity. They are not active in gathering information, preferring not to make decisions or deal with problems.

Other managers are *problem solvers* who will make decisions and try to solve problems when required. They are reactive, gathering information and responding to problems when they occur, but not before. These managers may deal reasonably well with performance threats, but they are likely to miss many performance opportunities.

Still other managers, perhaps the better ones, are *problem seekers* who are always looking for problems to solve or opportunities to explore. True problem seekers are proactive information gatherers, and they are forward thinking. They anticipate threats and opportunities, and they are eager to take action to gain the advantage in dealing with them.

• Managers display systematic and intuitive thinking in problem-solving.

Again, like you and me, managers also differ in their use of "systematic" and "intuitive" thinking. In **systematic thinking** a person approaches problems in a rational, step-by-step, and analytical fashion. You might recognize this when someone you are working with tries to break a complex problem into smaller components that can be addressed one by one. We might expect systematic managers to make a plan before taking action, and to search for information and proceed with problem solving in a fact-based and step-by-step fashion.

Someone using **intuitive thinking** is more flexible and spontaneous than the systematic thinker; the person may also be quite creative.[5] You might observe this pattern as someone who always seems to come up with an imaginative response to a problem, often based on a quick and broad evaluation of the situation. Intuitive managers often tend to deal with many aspects of a problem at once, jump quickly from one issue to another, and act on hunches from experience or on spontaneous ideas. Amazon.com's Jeff Bezos says that when it's not possible for the firm's top managers to make systematic fact-based decisions, "you have to rely on experienced executives who've honed their instincts" and are able to make good judgments.[6] In other words, there's a place for both systematic and intuitive decision making in management.

Systematic thinking approaches problems in a rational and analytical fashion.

Intuitive thinking approaches problems in a flexible and spontaneous fashion.

Self-Assessment
This is a good point to complete the self-assessment "*Intuitive Thinking*" found on page 92.

• Managers use different cognitive styles to process information for decision making.

When US Airways Flight 1549 took off from LaGuardia airport January 15, all was normal. It was normal, that is, until the plane hit a flock of birds and both engines failed; Flight 1549 was going to crash. Pilot Chesley Sullenberger quickly realized he couldn't get to an airport and decided to land in the Hudson

After a successful emergency landing, Pilot Chesley Sullenberger III said: "I know I speak for the entire crew when I tell you we were simply doing the jobs we were trained to do."

River. But he had both a clear head and a clear sense of what he had been trained to do. The landing was successful and no lives were lost. Called a "hero" for his efforts, Sullenberger described his thinking this way.[7]

I needed to touch down with the wings exactly level. I needed to touch down with the nose slightly up. I needed to touch down at . . . a descent rate that was survivable. And I needed to touch down just above our minimum flying speed but not below it. And I needed to make all these things happen simultaneously.

This example points us toward a discussion of cognitive styles, or the way individuals deal with information while making decisions. If you take the end of chapter self-assessment, it will examine your cognitive style as a contrast of tendencies toward information gathering—sensation vs. intuition, and information evaluation—feeling vs. thinking, in one's approach to problem solving. Most likely, pilot Sullenberger would score high in both sensation and thinking, and that is probably an ideal type for his job. But **Figure 4.2** shows that this is only one of four master cognitive styles. It's helpful to understand the different styles and their characteristics both for yourself and as they are displayed by others.[8]

FIGURE 4.2
Cognitive Styles in Decision Making.

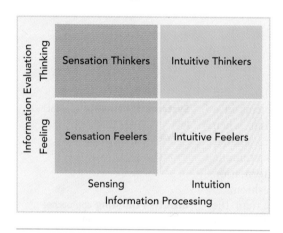

- *Sensation Thinkers*—STs tend to emphasize the impersonal rather than the personal and take a realistic approach to problem solving. They like hard "facts," clear goals, certainty, and situations of high control.
- *Intuitive Thinkers*—ITs are comfortable with abstraction and unstructured situations. They tend to be idealistic, prone toward intellectual and theoretical positions; they are logical and impersonal but also avoid details.
- *Intuitive Feelers*—IFs prefer broad and global issues. They are insightful and tend to avoid details, being comfortable with intangibles; they value flexibility and human relationships.
- *Sensation Feelers*—SFs tend to emphasize both analysis and human relations. They tend to be realistic and prefer facts; they are open communicators and sensitive to feelings and values.

As the descriptions suggest, people with different cognitive styles may approach problems and make decisions in ways quite different from one another. It is important to understand our cognitive styles and tendencies, as well as those of others. In the social context of the workplace, lots of decisions are made by teams, and the more diverse the cognitive styles of team members, the more difficulty we might expect in the decision-making process.

• Managers make decisions under conditions of certainty, risk, and uncertainty.

It's not just personal styles that differ in problem solving; the environment counts, too. **Figure 4.3** shows three different conditions or problem environments in which managers make decisions—certainty, risk, and uncertainty. As you might expect, the levels of risk and uncertainty in problem environments tend to increase the higher one moves in management ranks. You might think about this each time you hear about Coca-Cola or Pepsi launching

FIGURE 4.3
What Are the Differences Between Certain, Risk, and Uncertain Decision-Making Environments?

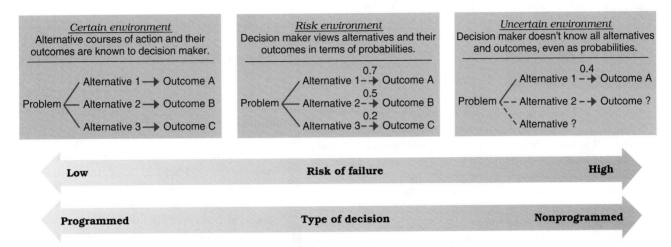

Managers rarely face a problem where they can know all the facts, identify all alternatives and their consequences, and chart a clear course of action. Such *certainty* is more often than not replaced by problem environments involving risk and uncertainty. *Risk* is where alternatives are known but their consequences can be described in terms of probabilities. *Uncertainty* is where all alternatives are not known and their consequences are highly speculative.

a new flavor or product. Are the top executives making these decisions *certain* that the results will be successful; or are they taking *risks* in market situations that are *uncertain* as to whether the new flavor or product will be positively received by customers?

It would be nice if we could all make decisions and solve problems in the relative predictability of a **certain environment**. This is an ideal decision situation where factual information exists for the possible alternative courses of action and their consequences. All a decision maker needs to do is study the alternatives and choose the best solution. It isn't easy to find examples of decision situations with such certain conditions. One possibility is a decision to take out a student loan; at least you can make the decision knowing future interest costs and repayment timetables.

Whereas absolute certainty is the best scenario for decision makers, the reality is that in our personal lives and in management we more often face **risk environments** where information and facts are incomplete. Alternative courses of action and their consequences can be discussed and analyzed only as *probabilities* (e.g., 4 chances out of 10) of occurrence. One way of dealing with risk is by gathering as much information as possible, perhaps in different ways. In the case of a new product, such as Zero Coke or even a college textbook like this, it is unlikely that marketing executives would make go-ahead decisions without getting positive reports from multiple focus groups that tested the product in the sample stage.

When facts are few and information is so poor that managers have a hard time even assigning probabilities to things, an **uncertain environment** exists. This is the most difficult decision condition.[9] Responses to uncertainty depend greatly on intuition, judgment, informed guessing, and hunches—all of which leave considerable room for error. This is one reason why groups are often used for this type of problem solving. By bringing more information, perspectives, and creativity to bear on the situation, the chances for a good decision are often improved.

A **certain environment** offers complete information on possible action alternatives and their consequences.

A **risk environment** lacks complete information but offers probabilities of the likely outcomes for possible action alternatives.

An **uncertain environment** lacks so much information that it is difficult to assign probabilities to the likely outcomes of alternatives.

News Feed

Shareholders Push to Regulate Executive Pay

You should already know how controversial CEO and senior executive pay has become in the aftermath of the financial crisis and recession. The former CEO of Merrill Lynch & Co., John Thain, was called to task by New York Attorney General Andrew Cuomo for paying out "billions of dollars" in executive bonuses on an accelerated timetable before the firm was bought by Bank of America. This occurred at the same time that BofA was seeking $20 billion of bailout monies from the U.S. government's TARP (Troubled Asset Relief Program). Citigroup Inc.'s CEO received $38.2 million in direct compensation for 2008, even though his firm had to accept government bailout monies. Among other top earners in 2008, Motorola's Sanjay K. Jha received $104 million and Walt Disney's Robert A. Iger received $49.7 million.

At a time when hundreds of thousands of workers were losing their jobs and wealth was evaporating due to falling stock and real estate prices, such high executive compensation raised many calls for rebuke of corporate greed. And for some, especially financial institutions, the aftermath includes a growing number of shareholder proposals to limit executive compensation.

Reflect and React:

How can a decision such as Thain's be explained? Is it pure greed, or is it an executive trying to take good care of loyal employees that deserve the bonuses they were being paid? Are you one of those favoring limits on executive pay, either by shareholder resolutions or Congressional legislation? What are the pros and cons of such actions?

A **decision** is a choice among possible alternative courses of action.

A **programmed decision** applies a solution from past experience to a routine problem.

A **nonprogrammed decision** applies a specific solution that has been crafted to address a unique problem.

• Managers make programmed and nonprogrammed decisions when solving problems.

So far in this discussion we have used the word *decision* rather casually. From this point forward, though, let's agree that a **decision** is a choice among possible alternative courses of action. Let's also acknowledge that decisions can be made in different ways, with some approaches working better than others in various circumstances.

Some management problems are routine and repetitive. They can be addressed through **programmed decisions** that apply preplanned solutions based on the lessons of past experience. Such decisions work best for structured problems that are familiar, straightforward, and clear with respect to information needs. In human resource management, for example, decisions always have to be made on things such as vacations and holiday work schedules. Forward-looking managers can use past experience and plan ahead to make these decisions in programmed, not spontaneous, ways.

Other management problems, many in fact, arise as new or unusual situations full of ambiguities and information deficiencies. These problems require **nonprogrammed decisions** that craft novel solutions to meet the unique demands of a situation. In the recent financial crisis, for example, all eyes were on President Obama's choice of Treasury Secretary Timothy Geithner. His task was to solve the problems with billions in bad loans made by the nation's banks and restore stability to the financial markets. But it was uncharted territory; no prepackaged solutions were readily available. Geithner and his team crafted an attempted solution that they believed was the best possible at the time. But under the circumstances, only time would tell if the nonprogrammed decisions they made were the right ones.

Study Guide

4.1
How Do Managers Use Information to Make Decisions and Solve Problems?

Rapid review

- A problem can occur as a threat or an opportunity, and involves an existing or potential discrepancy between an actual and a desired state of affairs.
- Managers deal with problems in different ways, with some being problem avoiders, others being reactive problem solvers, and still others being proactive problem finders.
- Managers using systematic thinking approach problems in a rational step-by-step fashion; managers using intuitive thinking approach them in a more flexible and spontaneous way.
- The problems that managers face occur in environments of certainty, risk, and uncertainty.
- Managers can deal with structured and routine problems using programmed decisions; novel and unique problems require special solutions developed by nonprogrammed decisions.

Terms to define

Certain environment
Decision
Information competency
Intuitive thinking
Nonprogrammed decision
Performance opportunity
Performance threat
Problem solving
Programmed decision
Risk environment
Systematic thinking
Uncertain environment

Be sure you can

- explain the notion of problem solving
- describe different ways managers approach and deal with problems
- discuss the differences between systematic and intuitive thinking
- explain the challenges of decision making under conditions of certainty, risk, and uncertainty environments
- differentiate programmed and nonprogrammed decisions

Questions for discussion

1. Can a manager be justified for acting as a problem avoider in certain situations?
2. Would an organization be better off with mostly systematic or mostly intuitive thinkers?
3. Is it possible to develop programmed decisions for use in conditions of risk and uncertainty?

4.2 What Are the Steps in the Decision-Making Process?

The **decision-making** process begins with identification of a problem and ends with evaluation of implemented solutions.

The **decision-making process** involves a straightforward series of steps shown in **Figure 4.4**: identify and define the problem, generate and evaluate alternative solutions, decide on a preferred course of action and do an ethics double-check, implement the decision, and then evaluate results.[10] When General Motors announced it was closing nine plants in North America and cutting 30,000 jobs, it was a blow to workers, their families, and communities.[11] The following case isn't quite as sensational, but it's equally real. Let's use it to follow how the decision-making steps might apply in real situations.

FIGURE 4.4

Steps in the Decision-Making Process.

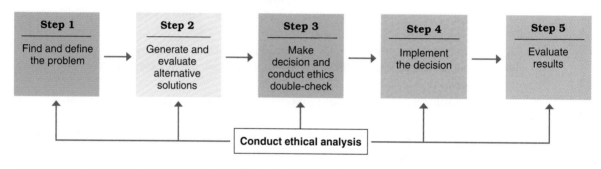

The Ajax case   On December 31, the Ajax Company decided to close down its Murphysboro plant. Market conditions and a recessionary economy were forcing layoffs, and the company hadn't been able to find a buyer for the plant. Of the 172 employees, some had been with the company as long as 18 years, others as little as 6 months. Ajax needed to terminate all of them. Under company policy they would be given severance pay equal to one week's pay per year of service.

This case reflects how competition, changing times, and the forces of globalization can take their toll on organizations, the people that work for them, and the communities in which they operate. How would you feel—as one of the affected employees, as the mayor of this small town, or as a corporate executive having to make the tough decisions?

• Step 1 is to identify and define the problem.

The first step in decision making is to identify and define the problem. This is a stage of information gathering, information processing, and deliberation. It is also where goals are clarified to specify exactly what a decision should accomplish. The more specific the goals, the easier it is to evaluate results after implementing the decision.

Three mistakes are common in this critical first step in decision making. First, we may define the problem too broadly or too narrowly. To take a classic example, instead of stating the problem as "Build a better mousetrap" we define it as "Get rid of the mice." Ideally, problems are defined in ways that give them the best possible range of problem-solving options.

Second, we may focus on symptoms instead of causes. Symptoms only indicate that problems may exist; they aren't the problems themselves. Of course, managers need to be good at spotting problem symptoms (e.g., a drop in performance). But instead of just treating symptoms (such as simply encouraging higher performance), they need to seek out and address their root causes (e.g., discovering the worker's need for training in the use of a complex new computer system).

Third, we may choose the wrong problem to deal with. This can easily happen when we are rushed and time is short, or when there are many things happening at once. Instead of just doing something, it's important to do the right things. This means setting priorities and dealing with the most important problems first.

Common mistakes when identifying problems

1. Defining problem too broadly or too narrowly
2. Dealing with symptoms, not real causes
3. Focusing on wrong problem to begin with

Back to the Ajax case   Closing the plant will result in a loss of jobs for a substantial number of people from the small community of Murphysboro. The unemployment created will negatively impact these individuals, their families, and the community as a whole. The loss of the Ajax tax base will further hurt the community. Ajax management therefore defines the problem as how to minimize the adverse impact of the plant closing on the employees, their families, and the community.

• Step 2 is to generate and evaluate alternative courses of action.

After the problem is defined, the next step in decision making is to assemble the needed facts and information. Here managers must be clear on exactly what they know and what they need to know. Extensive information gathering should identify alternative courses of action, as well as their anticipated consequences. It's a time to identify key stakeholders in the problem and consider the effects of each possible course of action on them. In the case of GM's plant closings and layoffs, for example, a union negotiator said: "While GM's continuing decline in market share isn't the fault of workers or our communities, it is these groups that will suffer."

Most managers use some form of **cost-benefit analysis** to evaluate alternatives. This compares what an alternative will cost with its expected benefits. At a minimum, benefits should exceed costs. In addition, an alternative should be timely, acceptable to as many stakeholders as possible, and ethically sound. But we should not forget that the better the pool of alternatives and the better the analysis, the more likely it is that a good decision will result.

Criteria for evaluating alternatives

- **Cost and benefits:** Are expected benefits greater than costs?
- **Timeliness:** How long before the benefits occur?
- **Acceptability:** Is it acceptable to key stakeholders?
- **Ethical soundness:** Does it satisfy ethical standards?

Cost-benefit analysis involves comparing the costs and benefits of each potential course of action.

Back to the Ajax case   Ajax will definitely close the plant; keeping it open is no longer an option. These alternatives are considered: close the plant on schedule and be done with it; delay the plant closing and try again to sell it to another firm; offer to sell the plant to the employees and/or local interests; close the plant and offer transfers to other Ajax plant locations; close the plant, offer transfers, and help the employees find new jobs in and around Murphysboro.

• Step 3 is to decide on a preferred course of action.

Management theory recognizes two quite different ways that alternatives get explored and decisions get made: the classical and behavioral models shown in **Figure 4.5**. The **classical decision model** views the manager as acting rationally and in a fully informed manner. The problem is clearly defined, all possible action alternatives are known, and their consequences are clear. As a result, he or she makes an **optimizing decision** that gives the absolute best solution to the problem.

Although this sounds ideal, it's a bit too good to be true, at least most of the time. Because there are limits to our information-processing capabilities, something called *cognitive limitations*, it is hard to be fully informed and make

The **classical decision model** describes decision making with complete information.

An **optimizing decision** chooses the alternative giving the absolute best solution to a problem.

FIGURE 4.5

How Does the Classical Model of Managerial Decision Making Differ from the Behavioral Model?

Classical Model

- Structured problem
- Clearly defined
- Certain environment
- Complete information
- All alternatives and consequences known

Optimizing Decision

Choose absolute best among alternatives

Rationality

Acts in perfect world

Manager as decision maker

Bounded rationality

Acts with cognitive limitations

Behavioral Model

- Unstructured problem
- Not clearly defined
- Uncertain environment
- Incomplete information
- Not all alternatives and consequences known

Satisficing Decision

Choose first "satisfactory" alternative

The classical model views decision makers as having complete information and making optimum decisions that are the absolute best choices to resolve problems. The behavioral model views decision makers as having limited information-processing capabilities. They act with incomplete information and make satisficing decisions, choosing the first satisfactory alternative that comes to their attention.

The **behavioral decision model** describes decision making with limited information and bounded rationality.

A **satisficing decision** chooses the first satisfactory alternative that presents itself.

Lack-of-participation error is failure to include the right people in the decision-making process.

perfectly rational decisions in all situations.[12] Recognizing this, the premise of the **behavioral decision model** is that people act only in terms of their perceptions, which are frequently imperfect. Furthermore, armed with only partial knowledge about the available action alternatives and their consequences, decision makers are likely to choose the first alternative that appears satisfactory to them. Herbert Simon, who won a Nobel Prize for his work, calls this the tendency to make **satisficing decisions**. What do you think? Does this seem accurate in describing how we make a lot of decisions?

Back to the Ajax case Ajax executives decide to close the plant, offer employees transfers to company plants in another state, and offer to help displaced employees find new jobs in and around Murphysboro.

• Step 4 is to implement the decision.

Once a preferred course of action is chosen, managers must take action to fully implement it. Until they do, nothing new can or will happen to solve the problem. This not only requires the determination and creativity to arrive at a decision, it also requires the ability and personal willingness to act. And, most likely, it requires the support of many other people. More often than you might realize, it is insufficient support that sabotages the implementation of otherwise perfectly good decisions.

Managers fall prey to **lack-of-participation error** when they don't include in the decision-making process those persons whose support is necessary for implementation. When managers use participation wisely, by contrast, they get the right people involved from the beginning. This not only gains their inputs and insights, it helps build commitments to support the decision and make sure it works as intended. Remember the module subtitle: Decisions, when implemented, solve problems.

Back to the Ajax case Ajax management ran an ad in the local and regional newspapers for several days that announced an "Ajax skill bank" composed of "qualified, dedicated, and well-motivated employees with a variety of skills and experiences." The ad urged interested employers to contact Ajax for further information.

• Step 5 is to evaluate results.

A decision isn't much good if it doesn't achieve the desired results or results in undesired side effects. This is why the decision-making process is not complete until results are evaluated. This is a form of control. It involves gathering data to measure performance results against initial goals, and examining both positive and negative outcomes. If the original decision appears inadequate, it also means reassessing things and perhaps redoing earlier steps in the decision-making process.

Back to the Ajax case How effective was Ajax's decision? Well, we don't know for sure. After Ajax ran the advertisement for 15 days, the plant's industrial relations manager said: "I've been very pleased with the results." However, we really need a lot more information for a true evaluation. How many employees got new jobs locally? How many transferred to other Ajax plants? How did the local economy perform in the following months? Probably you can add questions of your own to this list.

• Ethical reasoning is important at all steps in decision making.

Choices made at each step in the decision-making process often have a moral dimension that might easily be overlooked. For example, should you accept a late job offer from a highly desired employer if you have already made a verbal commitment to accept another one?

If you look back to Figure 4.4 you'll see that each step in the decision-making process is linked with ethical reasoning.[13] Attention to ethical analysis at each step helps to ensure that any underlying moral problems will be identified and dealt with in the best possible ways. One way to handle the responsibility for ethical reasoning is to frame what you are deciding and how you are acting in the context of an ongoing "ethics double check." It is accomplished by asking and answering two sets of questions.

Trendsetters

Indra Nooyi Brings New Style and a Sharp Eye to Pepsi

The best advice she ever got, says Indra Nooyi, Pepsico's Chairman and CEO, came from her father. Calling him "an absolutely wonderful human being," she says: "From him I learned to always assume positive intent. Whatever anybody says or does, assume positive intent. You will be amazed at how your whole approach to a person or problem becomes very different. . . . You are trying to understand and listen because at your basic core you are saying, 'Maybe they are saying something to me that I am not hearing.'"

That advice has carried Nooyi to the top ranks of global business, only the 12th woman to head a *Fortune* 500 firm and a long way from her early years in Chennai, India, and her first university degree in chemistry. After a Masters in Management from Yale she joined the Boston Consulting Group and eventually ended up joining Pepsico, where she moved through a variety of management positions to become CEO in 2006.

Business Week described her "prescient business sense" as behind the firm's moves to spin off its fast food businesses Taco Bell, Pizza Hut, and KFC, a merger with Quaker Oats, and the purchase of Tropicana. All proved successful for the firm and for Nooyi. But through it all she also maintained a personal style that allows her personality to shine. Former CEO Roger Enrico says "Indra can drive as deep and hard as anyone I've ever met, but she can do it with a sense of heart and fun." ABC news described her as a blend of "Indian culture mixed in with the traditional American working mom."

The first set of ethical reasoning questions is based on four ethical criteria described in the work of ethicist Gerald Cavanagh and his associates.[14]

1. *Utility*—Does the decision satisfy all constituents or stakeholders?
2. *Rights*—Does the decision respect the rights and duties of everyone?
3. *Justice*—Is the decision consistent with the canons of justice?
4. *Caring*—Is the decision consistent with my responsibilities to care?

The second set of questions basically exposes a decision to public scrutiny and forces the decision maker to consider it in the context of full transparency and the prospect of shame.[15] These so-called *spotlight questions*, part of our earlier discussion of ethics and social responsibility, are especially powerful when the decision maker comes from a morally scrupulous family or social structure.

1. "How would I feel if my family found out about this decision?"
2. "How would I feel if this decision were published in the local newspaper or posted on the Internet?"
3. "What would the person I know who has the strongest character and best ethical judgment say about my decision?"

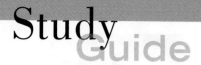

Study Guide

4.2
What Are the Steps in the Decision-Making Process?

Rapid review

The steps in the decision-making process are: (1) identify and define the problem; (2) generate and evaluate alternatives; (3) decide on the preferred course of action; (4) implement the decision; (5) evaluate the results.

- A cost-benefit analysis compares the expected costs of a decision alternative with its expected results.
- In the classical model, an optimizing decision chooses the absolute best solution from a known set of alternatives.
- In the behavioral model, cognitive limitations lead to satisficing decisions that choose the first satisfactory alternative to come to attention.
- The ethics double-check is a way to make sure decisions meet ethical standards.

Terms to define

Behavioral decision model
Classical decision model
Cost-benefit analysis
Decision-making process
Lack-of-participation error
Optimizing decision
Satisficing decision

Be sure you can

- list the steps in the decision-making process
- apply these steps to a sample decision-making situation
- explain cost-benefit analysis
- compare and contrast the classical and behavioral decision models
- illustrate "optimizing" and "satisficing" in your personal decision-making experiences
- list three questions for double-checking the ethics of a decision

Questions for discussion

1. Do the steps in the decision-making process have to be followed in order?
2. Do you see any problems or pitfalls for managers using the behavioral decision model?
3. Can the ethics double-check questions fail to ensure an ethical decision?

4.3 What Are Some Current Issues in Managerial Decision Making?

Once you accept the fact that each of us is likely to make imperfect decisions at least some of the time, it makes sense to probe even further into the how's and why's of decision making in organizations. In addition to the issues of ethical reasoning and analysis already discussed, other practicalities to be considered are possible causes of decision bias and error, advantages and disadvantages of group decision making, and the challenges of decision making under crisis conditions.

• Personal factors help drive creativity in decision making.

Lonnie Johnson is a former U.S. Air Force Captain and a NASA engineer. You probably don't know him, but most likely you are familiar with something he invented—the Super Soaker water gun. Johnson didn't set out to invent the water gun; he was working in his basement on an idea for refrigeration systems that would use water rather than Freon. Something connected in his mind and the Super Soaker was born. Johnson says: "The Super Soaker changed my life." He now heads his own research and development company and, among other things, the Web site says there are some 100 toys in development.[16]

In management we discuss **creativity** as the generation of a novel idea or unique approach to solving performance problems or exploiting performance opportunities.[17] Just imagine what we can accomplish with all the creative potential that exists in an organization's workforce. But how do you turn that potential into actual creativity in decision making—the Lonnie Johnson model so to speak?

Creativity is one of our greatest personal assets, even though it may be too often unrecognized by us and by others. We exercise creativity every day in lots of ways—solving problems at home, building something for the kids, or even finding ways to pack too many things into too small a suitcase. But are we creative when it would really help in solving workplace problems?

One source of insight into personal creativity drivers is the three-component model of task expertise, task motivation, and creativity skills.[18] From a management standpoint the model is helpful because it points us in the direction of actions that can be taken to build creativity drivers into the work setting and thus facilitate more creativity in decision making.

Creative decisions are more likely to occur when the person or team has a lot of task expertise. As in the case of Lonnie Johnson, creativity is an outgrowth of skill and typically extends something one is good at or knows about in new directions. Creativity is also more likely when the people making decisions are highly task motivated. That is, creativity tends to occur in part because people work exceptionally hard to resolve a problem or exploit an opportunity. And, in the course of old-fashioned hard work—Lonnie Johnson spending hours in his home basement, for example—something new and different is accomplished.

Creative decisions are more likely when the people involved have stronger creativity skill sets. In popular conversations you might refer to this as the contrast between "right brain" thinking—imagination, intuition, spontaneity and emotion, and "left brain" thinking—logic, order, method, and analysis. But just what are we talking about here? Is creativity something

Creativity is one of our greatest personal assets, even though it is sometimes untapped.

Creativity is the generation of a novel idea or unique approach that solves a problem or crafts an opportunity.

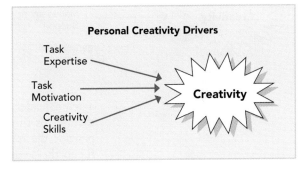

Personal Creativity Drivers

Task Expertise

Task Motivation → Creativity

Creativity Skills

Organizations that value creativity go to great lengths to support people and make it possible for them to create innovations.

that is built into some of us and not built into others? Or is creativity something that one can work to develop along with other personal skills and competencies?

Researchers argue the prior points. But the debate is healthy and they also tend to agree that the following characteristics often describe creative people and that most of us can develop these abilities into creativity skill sets. As you read the list, why not use it as a personal test—a self check of potential strengths and weaknesses in creativity skills?[19]

- Ability to work with high energy
- Ability to identify problems, plan, make decisions
- Ability to hold one's ground in face of criticism
- Ability to accept responsibility for what happens
- Ability to be resourceful even in difficult situations
- Ability to be both systematic and intuitive in problem solving
- Ability to think "outside of the box"—divergent thinking
- Ability to synthesize and find correct answers—convergent thinking
- Ability to use "lateral thinking," looking at diverse ways to solve problems
- Ability to transfer learning from one setting to others
- Ability to "step back," be objective, question assumptions

• Situational factors help drive creativity in decision making.

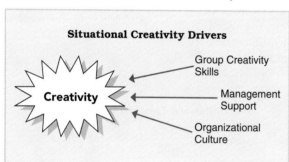

Situational Creativity Drivers

Creativity

Group Creativity Skills

Management Support

Organizational Culture

If you mix creative people and traditional organization and management practices, what will you get? Perhaps not much by way of innovations; it takes more than individual creativity alone to bring creativity to bear on the full multitude of decisions that are made every day. In this sense it is also important to recognize what we might call situational creativity drivers as well.

Of course, managers should try to make sure that their teams and organizations are well staffed with creative members. But in order to unlock the full potential of this creativity, they also need to build strong situational creativity drivers. Important among these are management support and organizational cultures that are as conducive as possible to creativity in decision making. This can involve small things such as a team leader who has the patience to allow for creative processes to work themselves through a decision situation and top management that is willing to provide the resources—time, technology, and space, for example, that are helpful to the creative processes. But it also involves valuing creativity and making it a top priority in the broader work climate and surrounding organizational culture.

Think creative whenever you use or see someone using an Apple iPhone, or when you're captured by some of its latest features. There's a lot of genius behind the products in concept, design, and marketing. But give the company and its leadership credit, too; they built an organizational culture and supportive management environment where great ideas not only happen, they float to the surface and make their ways into attractive new products.

Think creative also the next time you see a young child playing with a really neat toy. It may be from *Fisher-Price Toys*—part of Mattel, Inc. In the firm's headquarters you'll find a special place called the "Cave," and it's not your typical office space. Picture beanbag chairs, soft lighting, casual chairs, and couches. It's a place for brainstorming, where designers, marketers, engineers, and others can meet and join in freewheeling to come up with the next great toy for preschoolers. Consultants recommend that such innovation spaces be separated from the normal workplace and be large enough for no more than 15 to 20 people.[20]

• Group decision making has both advantages and disadvantages.

Sometimes the most important decisions we make involve choosing whether to make them alone or with the participation of others. And it really shouldn't be an either/or question. Effective managers and team leaders typically switch back and forth between individual and group decision making, trying to use the best methods for the problems at hand. To do this well, however, they need to understand the implications of **Table 4.1**—*Potential Advantages and Disadvantages of Group Decision Making*.[21]

In respect to advantages, group decisions can be good because they bring greater amounts of information, knowledge, and expertise to bear on a problem. They often expand the number and even the creativity of action alternatives examined. And, as noted earlier, participation helps group members gain better understanding of any decisions reached. This increases the likelihood that they will both accept and work hard to help implement them.

In respect to disadvantages, we all know that it is sometimes difficult and time consuming for people trying to work together. There may be social pressure to conform in group situations. Some individuals may feel intimidated or compelled to go along with the apparent wishes of others. Minority domination might cause some members to feel forced or railroaded into a decision advocated by one vocal individual or a small coalition. Also, the more people involved, the longer it can take to reach a group decision.

[**TABLE** 4.1]

Potential Advantages and Disadvantages of Group Decision Making

Why group decisions are often good:

More information—More information, expertise, and viewpoints are available to help solve problems.
More alternatives—More alternatives are generated and considered during decision making.
Increased understanding—There is increased understanding and greater acceptance of decision by group members.
Greater commitment—There is increased commitment of group members to work hard and support the decision.

Why group decisions can be bad:

Conformity with social pressures—Some members feel intimidated by others and give in to social pressures to conform.
Domination by a few members—A minority dominates; some members get railroaded by small coalition of others.
Time delays—More time is required to make decisions when many people try to work together.

• Judgmental heuristics and other biases and traps may cause decision-making errors.

Faced with limited information, time, and even energy, people often use simplifying strategies for decision making. But these strategies, known as *heuristics*, can cause decision-making errors.[22]

The **availability heuristic** occurs when people use information "readily available" from memory as a basis for assessing a current event or situation. You may decide, for example, not to buy running shoes from a company if your last pair didn't last long. The potential bias is that the readily available information may be fallible and irrelevant. Even though your present running shoes are worn out, you may have purchased the wrong model for your needs or used them in the wrong conditions.

The **representativeness heuristic** occurs when people assess the likelihood of something occurring based on its similarity to a stereotyped set of occurrences. An example is deciding to hire someone for a job vacancy simply because he or she graduated from the same school attended by your last and most successful new hire. Using the representative stereotype may mask the truly important factors relevant to the decision, the real abilities and career expectations of the new job candidate.

The **anchoring and adjustment heuristic** involves making decisions based on adjustments to a previously existing value, or starting point. For example, a manager may set a new salary level for a current employee by simply raising the prior year's salary by a percentage increment. But this increment is anchored in the existing salary level, and that may be much lower than the

The **availability heuristic** uses readily available information to assess a current situation.

The **representativeness heuristic** assesses the likelihood of an occurrence using a stereotyped set of similar events.

The **anchoring and adjustment heuristic** adjusts a previously existing value or starting point to make a decision.

Stay Tuned 🅱

Greenhouse-Gas Emissions Join List of Executive Priorities

The average national footprint for greenhouse-gas emissions from fossil fuels is 4.68 tons per capita; the United States generates 19 tons and China 4.27 tons. Business executives are taking notice as consumers become more informed about carbon footprints of their favorite products.

- *Car*: Toyota Prius—97,000 pounds (from production through use and ultimate disposal)
- *Fleece jacket*: Patagonia Talus—66 pounds.
- *Six-pack of beer*: Fat Tire Amber Ale—7 pounds
- *Half-gallon of milk*: Aurora Organic Dairy—7.2 pounds
- *Laundry detergent*: Tesco non-biological liquid (1.5 liter)— 31 pounds
- *Hiking boots*: Timberland Winter Park slip-ons—121 pounds

Your Thoughts?

When you look at these numbers, is the glass "half full" or "half empty" when it comes to protection of our natural environment? How much do you worry about the carbon footprints of the products you consume? How high on the list of executive priorities should issues such as sustainability and carbon neutrality be?

Framing error is solving a problem in the context perceived.

Confirmation error is when we attend only to information that confirms a decision already made.

Escalating commitment is the continuation of a course of action even though it is not working.

---

employee's true market value. Rather than being pleased with a raise, the employee may start looking for another, higher-paying job.

In addition to heuristic biases, **framing error** can influence one's decisions. Framing occurs when managers evaluate and resolve a problem in the context in which they perceive it—either positive or negative. Suppose that marketing data show that a new product has a 40% market share. What does this really mean? A negative frame views the product as deficient because it is missing 60% of the market. Discussion and problem solving within this frame would likely focus on: "What are we doing wrong?" If the marketing team used a positive frame and considered a 40% share as a success, the conversation might be quite different: "How can we do even better?" And, by the way, we are constantly exposed to framing in the world of politics; the word used to describe it is "spin".

One of our tendencies after making a decision is to try and find ways to justify it. In the case of unethical acts, for example, we often try to "rationalize" them after the fact with statements such as: "No one will ever find out" or "The boss will protect me." Such thinking causes a decision-making trap known as **confirmation error**. This means that we notice, accept, and even seek out only that information that is confirming or consistent with a decision we have just made. Other and perhaps critical information is downplayed or denied. This is a form of selective perception because the tendency is to focus on problems from our particular reference or vantage points only. In so doing we neglect other points of view or information that might lead us to a different decision.

Another decision-making trap is **escalating commitment**. This is a tendency to increase effort and perhaps apply more resources to pursue a course of action that signals indicate is not working.[23] Perhaps you have experienced an inability to call it quits, even when the facts suggest this is the best decision under the circumstances. Ego and the desire to avoid being associated with a mistake or bad decision can play a big role in escalation. Are you disciplined enough to minimize this risk in the future?

Fortunately, researchers have provided some good ideas on how to avoid getting trapped in escalating commitments. They include:

- Setting advance limits on your involvement and commitment to a particular course of action; stick with these limits.
- Making your own decisions; don't follow the lead of others, since they are also prone to escalation.
- Carefully determining just why you are continuing a course of action; if there are insufficient reasons to continue, don't.
- Reminding yourself of the costs of a course of action; consider saving these costs as a reason to discontinue.

• Managers must be prepared for crisis decision making.

One of the most challenging of all decision situations is the **crisis**. This is an unexpected problem that can lead to disaster if not resolved quickly and appropriately. The ability to handle crises could well be the ultimate test of any manager's decision-making capabilities. But unfortunately, research indicates that we sometimes react to crises by doing exactly the wrong things.

Managers err in crisis situations when they isolate themselves and try to solve the problem alone or in a small, closed group.[24] This denies them access to crucial information at the very time that they need it the most. It not only sets them up for poor decisions, it may create even more problems. This is why many organizations are developing formal crisis management programs. They train managers in crisis decision making, assign people ahead of time to crisis management teams, and develop crisis management plans to deal with various contingencies.

Just as fire and police departments, the Red Cross, and community groups plan ahead and train to best handle civil and natural disasters, and airline crews train for flight emergencies, so, too, can managers and work teams plan ahead and train to best deal with organizational crises.[25] This only makes sense, doesn't it?

A **crisis** is an unexpected problem that can lead to disaster if not resolved quickly and appropriately.

Tips to Remember
Six Rules for Crisis Management

1. *Figure out what is going on*—Take the time to understand what's happening and the conditions under which the crisis must be resolved.
2. *Remember that speed matters*—Attack the crisis as quickly as possible, trying to catch it when it is as small as possible.
3. *Remember that slow counts, too*—Know when to back off and wait for a better opportunity to make progress with the crisis.
4. *Respect the danger of the unfamiliar*—Understand the danger of all-new territory where you and others have never been before.
5. *Value the skeptic*—Don't look for and get too comfortable with agreement; appreciate skeptics and let them help you see things differently.
6. *Be ready to "fight fire with fire"*—When things are going wrong and no one seems to care, you may have to start a crisis to get their attention.

Study Guide

4.3
What Are Some Current Issues in Managerial Decision Making?

Rapid review

- Judgmental heuristics such as availability, anchoring and adjustment, and representativeness can bias decisions by oversimplifying the situation.
- Framing errors influence decisions by placing them in either a negative or a positive situational context.
- Escalating commitment occurs when one sticks with a course of action even though evidence indicates that it is not working.
- Group decisions offer the potential advantages of more information, greater understanding, and expanded commitments; a major disadvantage is that they are often time consuming.
- A crisis problem occurs unexpectedly and can lead to disaster if managers fail to handle it quickly and properly.
- Taking time for the ethics double-check is a useful way for managers to make sure that their decisions always meet ethical standards.

Terms to define

Anchoring and adjustment heuristic

Availability heuristic

Confirmation error

Crisis

Escalating commitment

Framing error

Representativeness heuristic

Be sure you can

- explain the availability, representativeness, and anchoring and adjustment heuristics
- illustrate framing error and escalating commitment in decision making
- explain and give an example of escalating commitment
- list potential advantages and disadvantages of group decision making
- describe what managers can do to prepare for crisis decisions
- list three questions that can be asked to double-check the ethics of a decision

Questions for discussion

1. How can you avoid being hurt by anchoring and adjustment in your annual pay raises?

2. What are some real-world examples of escalating commitment in decision making?

3. How can someone turn a crisis into an opportunity?

[Test Prep]

Multiple choice

1. A manager who is reactive and works hard to address problems after they occur is described as a _____.
   - (a) problem seeker
   - (b) problem solver
   - (c) rational thinker
   - (d) strategic opportunist

2. A problem is a discrepancy between a/an _____ situation and a desired situation.
   - (a) unexpected
   - (b) risk
   - (c) actual
   - (d) uncertain

3. If a manager approaches problems in a rational and analytical way, trying to solve them in step-by-step fashion, he or she is well described as a/an _____.
   - (a) systematic thinker
   - (b) intuitive thinker
   - (c) problem seeker
   - (d) behavioral decision maker

4. The first step in the decision-making process is to _____.
   - (a) generate a list of alternatives
   - (b) assess costs and benefits of each alternative
   - (c) find and define the problem
   - (d) perform the ethics double-check

5. When the members of a special task force are asked to develop a proposal for increasing the international sales of an existing product, this problem most likely requires _____ decisions.
   - (a) routine
   - (b) programmed
   - (c) crisis
   - (d) nonprogrammed

6. Costs, benefits, timeliness, and _____ are among the recommended criteria for evaluating alternative courses of action in the decision-making process.
   - (a) ethical soundness
   - (b) past history
   - (c) availability
   - (d) simplicity

7. The _____ decision model views managers as making optimizing decisions, whereas the _____ decision model views them as making satisficing decisions.
   - (a) behavioral/judgmental heuristics
   - (b) classical/behavioral
   - (c) judgmental heuristics/ethical
   - (d) crisis/routine

8. When a manager makes a decision about someone's annual pay raise only after looking at the person's current salary, the risk is that the decision will be biased because of _____.
   - (a) a framing error
   - (b) escalating commitment

   - (c) anchoring and adjustment
   - (d) strategic opportunism

9. One of the reasons why certainty is the most favorable environment for problem solving is that it can be addressed through _____ decisions.
   - (a) satisficing
   - (b) optimizing
   - (c) programmed
   - (d) intuitive

10. A common mistake by managers facing crisis situations is _____.
    - (a) trying to get too much information before responding
    - (b) relying too much on group decision making
    - (c) isolating themselves to make the decision alone
    - (d) forgetting to use their crisis management plan

11. In which decision environment does a manager deal with probabilities regarding possible courses of action and their consequences?
    - (a) risk
    - (b) certainty
    - (c) uncertainty
    - (d) optimal

12. A manager who decides against hiring a new employee who just graduated from Downstate University because the last person hired from there turned out to be a low performer, is falling prey to _____ error.
    - (a) availability
    - (b) adjustment
    - (c) anchoring
    - (d) representativeness

13. Which decision-making error is most associated with the old adage: "If you don't succeed, try and try again?"
    - (a) satisficing
    - (b) escalating commitment
    - (c) confirmation
    - (d) too late to fail

14. Personal creativity drivers include creativity skills, task expertise, and _____.
    - (a) strategic opportunism
    - (b) management support
    - (c) organizational culture
    - (d) task motivation

15. The last step in the decision-making process is to _____.
    - (a) choose a preferred alternative
    - (b) evaluate results
    - (c) find and define the problem
    - (d) perform the ethics double-check

16. How does an optimizing decision differ from a satisficing decision?

17. What is the difference between a risk environment and an uncertain environment in decision making?

18. How can you tell from people's behavior if they tend to be systematic or intuitive in problem solving?

19. What is escalating commitment and how can it be avoided?

Integration & application

20. As a participant in a new "mentoring" program between your university and a local high school, you have volunteered to give a presentation to a class of sophomores on the topic: "Individual versus group decision making: Is one better than the other?"

Questions: What will you say to them, and why?

Self-Assessment

Intuitive Ability

1. Do you prefer to
   (a) be given a problem and left free to do it?
   (b) get clear instructions how to solve a problem before starting?

2. Do you prefer to work with colleagues who are
   (a) realistic?   (b) imaginative?

3. Do you most admire
   (a) creative people?   (b) careful people?

4. Do your friends tend to be
   (a) serious and hard working?
   (b) exciting and emotional?

5. When you ask for advice on a problem, do you
   (a) seldom or never get upset if your basic assumptions are questioned?
   (b) often get upset with such questions?

6. When you start your day, do you
   (a) seldom make or follow a specific plan?
   (b) usually make and follow a plan?

7. When working with numbers, do you make factual errors
   (a) seldom or never?   (b) often?

8. Do you
   (a) seldom daydream and really don't enjoy it?
   (b) often daydream and enjoy it?

9. When working on a problem, do you
   (a) prefer to follow instructions or rules?
   (b) often enjoy bypassing instructions or rules?

10. When trying to put something together, do you prefer
    (a) step-by-step assemble instructions?
    (b) a picture of the assembled item?

11. Do you find that people who irritate you most appear to be
    (a) disorganized?   (b) organized?

12. When an unexpected crisis comes up, do you
    (a) feel anxious?
    (b) feel excited by the challenge?

Scoring

Total the "a" responses for 1, 3, 5, 6, 11; [A = _____].
Total the "b" responses for 2, 4, 7, 8, 9, 10, 12; [B = _____].
Your *intuitive score* is A + B. The highest score is 12.[26]

Case Snapshot

Amazon.com—One e-store Rules Them All

Amazon.com has soared ahead of other online merchants. What the firm can't carry in its 22 world-wide warehouses, affiliated retailers distribute for it. Not content to rest on past laurels, CEO Jeff Bezos has introduced a number of new services to keep customers glued to the Amazon site. And his latest investments include launching the e-book reader Kindle and purchasing once-rival Zappos.com. But will the investments pay off for the long term? Can Amazon hold its own in a changing economy and in face of upstart competitors?

Online Interactive Learning Resources

SELF-ASSESSMENT
• Cognitive Style

EXPERIENTIAL EXERCISES
• Decision-Making Biases
• Lost at Sea

TEAM PROJECT
• Dealing with Crisis

5

Plans and Planning Techniques

Good Objectives Get You There Faster

Think now and embrace the future. Oprah Winfrey is a well-known media star, corporate executive, popular personality, and the wealthiest woman in the world. Having grown up poor, she is grateful for her good education, calling it "the most vital aspect of my life." With a $40 million donation, she's sharing that experience through the Oprah Winfrey Leadership Academy for young women in South Africa. At the opening ceremony she said: "I wanted to give this opportunity to girls who had a light so bright that not even poverty could dim that light." She also talked about her past as "a poor girl who grew up with my grandmother, like so many of these girls, with no water and electricity."

Oprah's goal is for the new academy to "be the best school in the world." The idea grew out of conversations with Nelson Mandela, first president of non-apartheid South Africa. He also spoke at the opening ceremony and praised her vision. "The key to any country's future is in educating its youth," said Mandela. "Oprah is therefore not only investing in a few young individuals, but in the future of our country." He went on to say, "It is my hope that this school will

Trendsetters
Don Thompson keeps
McDonald's USA on focus.

News Feed
Recession is a good time for
setting priorities.

Case Snapshot
Lands' End—Living by the
golden rule

become the dream of every South African girl and they
will study hard and qualify for the school one day." One
of the first students said, "I would have had a
completely different life if this hadn't happened to me."

The academy selects girls competitively on both
academic excellence and leadership potential. They must
also come from households with limited incomes; many
are from families hurt by HIV/AIDS and from overcrowded
schools with poor facilities and resources. Yet, even with
the best intentions, things don't always go according to
plan. Not long after the academy launched, it was hit by
scandal. One of the dorm matrons was arrested for
physical and sexual abuse. Oprah apologized to the
students and their families, and rededicated herself to the
school. "I think that crisis is there to teach you about life,"
she said. "The school is going to be even better because
that happened." And looking even further ahead, she
hasn't stopped dreaming or planning—her intention is to
build yet another school for both young men and young women.

Oprah's experience in South Africa shows that you can make great things happen with
good insight and the right plans. And even though things don't always go as intended, both
the plans and their implementation can often be adjusted to achieve the goals.

5.1 How and Why Do Managers Plan?.

It can be easy to get so engrossed in the present that we forget about the future. Yet a mad rush to the future can sometimes go off track without solid reference points in the past. The trick is to blend past experiences and lessons with future aspirations and goals, and a willingness to adjust as new circumstances arise. The management process of **planning** helps us do just that. It is a process of setting goals and objectives, and determining how to best accomplish them. Said a bit differently, planning involves looking ahead, identifying exactly what you want to accomplish, and deciding how to best go about it.

Planning is the process of setting objectives and determining how to accomplish them.

• Planning is one of the four functions of management.

Among the four management functions shown in **Figure 5.1**, planning comes first. When done well, it sets the stage for the others: organizing—allocating and arranging resources to accomplish tasks; leading—guiding the efforts of human resources to ensure high levels of task accomplishment; and controlling—monitoring task accomplishments and taking necessary corrective action.

FIGURE 5.1

The Central Role of Planning in the Management Process.

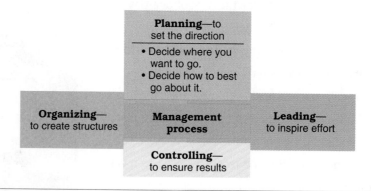

In today's demanding organizational and career environments, effective planning is essential to staying one step ahead of the competition. An Eaton Corporation annual report, for example, once stated: "Planning at Eaton means taking the hard decisions before events force them upon you, and anticipating the future needs of the market before the demand asserts itself."[1]

You really should take these words to heart. But instead of a company, think about your personal situation. What hard decisions do you need to make? Where are the job markets going? Where do you want to be in 5 or 10 years?

• Planning sets objectives and identifies how to achieve them.

From experience alone you are probably familiar with planning and all that it involves. But, it also helps to understand **Table 5.1**—*Steps in the Planning Process* and its action implications.

Step 1 in planning is to define your **objectives**, to identify the specific results or desired goals you hope to achieve. This step is important enough to stop and reflect a moment. Whether you call them goals or objectives, they are targets;

Objectives are specific results that one wishes to achieve.

they point us toward the future and provide a frame of reference for evaluating progress. With them, as the module subtitle suggests, you should get where you want to go and get there faster. But goals and objectives have to be good ones; they should push you to achieve substantial, not trivial, things. Jack Welch, former CEO of GE, believed in what he called **stretch goals**—performance targets that we have to work extra hard and really stretch to reach.[2] Would you agree that stretch goals can add real strength to the planning process, for organizations and for individuals?

Step 2 in planning is to compare where you are at present with the objectives. This establishes a baseline for performance; the present becomes a standard against which future progress can be gauged. *Step 3* is to formulate premises about future conditions. It is where one looks ahead trying to figure out what may happen. *Step 4* is to analyze the alternatives, choose one, and make an actual **plan**. This is a list of actions that must be taken in order to pursue the alternative and accomplish the objectives. *Step 5* is to implement the plan and evaluate results. This is where action takes place and measurement happens. Results are compared with objectives and, if needed, new plans are made to improve things in the future.

Don't consider this planning process just a textbook model; it's real. It is something we do at school, at work, and in our everyday lives. But we probably rarely stop to think about it so systematically. Have you thought about how well you plan and how you might do it better?

Managers should be asking the same question. They rarely get to plan while working alone in quiet rooms, free from distractions, and at regularly scheduled times. Because of the fast pace and complications of the typical workday, managerial planning is ongoing. It takes place even as one deals with a constant flow of problems in a sometimes hectic and demanding work setting.[3] Yet, it's all worth it: planning offers many benefits to people and organizations.[4]

[**TABLE** 5.1]

Steps in the Planning Process

Step 1. Define your objectives
Know where you want to go; be specific enough to know you have arrived when you get there and how far off you are along the way.

Step 2. Determine current status vis-à-vis objectives
Know where you stand in reaching the objectives; identify strengths that work in your favor and weaknesses that can hold you back.

Step 3. Develop premises regarding future conditions
Generate alternative scenarios for what may happen; identify for each scenario things that may help or hinder progress toward your objectives.

Step 4. Make a plan
Choose the action alternative most likely to accomplish your objectives; describe what must be done to implement this course of action.

Step 5. Implement the plan and evaluate results
Take action; measure progress toward objectives as implementation proceeds; take corrective actions and revise plan as needed.

Stretch goals are performance targets that we have to work extra hard and stretch to reach.

A **plan** is a statement of intended means for accomplishing objectives.

• Planning improves focus and action orientation.

Planning can help sharpen focus and increase flexibility, both of which improve performance. An organization with focus knows what it does best and what it needs to do. Individuals with focus know where they want to go in a career or situation, and they keep the focus even when difficulties arise. An organization with flexibility is willing and able to change and adapt to shifting circumstances. An individual with flexibility adjusts career plans to fit new and developing opportunities.

Planning helps us avoid the trap of complacency, becoming lulled into inaction by successes or failures of the moment. Instead, planning keeps us looking toward the future. Management consultant Stephen R. Covey describes this as an action orientation that includes a clear set of priorities.[5] He points out that the most successful executives "zero in on what they do that adds value to an organization." They know what is important and they work first on the things that really count. They don't waste time by working on too many things at once.

Would Covey describe you as focused on priorities, or as always jumping from one thing to another? Could you achieve more by getting your priorities straight and working hard on things that really count?

Good planning makes us:

- *Action oriented*—keeping a results-driven sense of direction
- *Priority oriented*—making sure the most important things get first attention
- *Advantage oriented*—ensuring that all resources are used to best advantage
- *Change oriented*—anticipating problems and opportunities so they can be best dealt with

• Planning improves coordination and control.

In a **hierarchy of objectives**, lower-level objectives help to accomplish higher-level ones.

Organizations consist of many people and subsystems doing many different things at the same time. But even as they pursue specific tasks and objectives, their accomplishments must add together meaningfully if the organization is to succeed. Good planning facilitates this by linking people and subsystems together in a **hierarchy of objectives**. This is a means–ends chain in which lower-level objectives (the means) lead to the accomplishment of higher-level ones (the ends). An example is the total quality management program shown in **Figure 5.2**.

FIGURE 5.2

What Is a Sample Hierarchy of Objectives for a Quality Management Program in a Manufacturing Firm?

Mission and Purpose
Serve the world as the number one supplier of recyclable food containers.

Top Management Objective
Firm
Deliver error-free products meeting customer requirements 100% of the time.

Senior Management Objective
Manufacturing Division
100% on-time production of error-free products.

Middle Management Objective
Plant
Increase error-free product acceptance rate by 16%.

Top Management Objective
Shift Supervisor
Assess machine operator skills and train for error-free production.

A hierarchy of objectives identifies a means-ends chain through which lower-level objectives become the pathways for accomplishing higher-level ones. In the case of total quality management, the top-level objective (delivering error-free products that meet customer needs 100% of the time) moves step-by-step down the hierarchy until the point where a shift supervisor supports TQM with the objective of making sure that machine operators are trained well enough to do error-free work.

Good planning also provides an essential link with controlling in the management process. Without planning objectives it's hard to exercise control; without control, plans may fail because of a lack of follow-through. With both, it's a lot easier to spot when things aren't going well and make the necessary adjustments. For example, two years after launching a costly information technology upgrade, the CEO of McDonald's realized that the system couldn't deliver on its promises. He stopped the project, took a loss of $170 million, and refocused the firm's resources on projects with more direct impact on customers.[6]

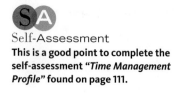
Self-Assessment
This is a good point to complete the self-assessment *"Time Management Profile"* found on page 111.

• Planning improves time management.

Daniel Vasella is CEO of Novartis AG and its 98,000 employees spread across 140 countries. He's also calendar bound. He says: "I'm locked in by meetings, travel and other constraints. . . . I have to put down in priority things I like to do." Kathleen Murphy is CEO of ING US Wealth Management. She's also calendar bound, with conferences and travel booked a year ahead. She books meetings at half-hour intervals, works 12-hour days, and spends 60% of her time traveling. She also makes good use of her time on planes. "No one can reach me by phone and I can get reading and thinking done."[7]

These are common executive stories—tight schedules, little time alone, lots of meetings and phone calls, and not much room for spontaneity. And the keys to success in these classic management scenarios rest, in part at least, with another benefit of good planning—time management. It is an important management skill and competency, and a lot of time management comes down to discipline and priorities. Lewis Platt, former chairman of Hewlett-Packard, once

Tips to Remember
Do's and Don'ts for Managing Your Time

1. *Do* say "No" to requests that divert you from what you really should be doing.
2. *Don't* get bogged down in details that you can address later or leave for others.
3. *Do* have a system for screening telephone calls, e-mails, and requests for meetings.
4. *Don't* let drop-in visitors or instant messages use too much of your time.
5. *Do* prioritize what you will work on in terms of importance and urgency.
6. *Don't* become calendar bound by letting others control your schedule.
7. *Do* follow priorities; work on the most important and urgent tasks first.

said: "Basically, the whole day is a series of choices."[8] These choices have to be made in ways that allocate your time to the most important priorities. Platt says that he was "ruthless about priorities" and that you "have to continually work to optimize your time."

Surely you have experienced difficulties in balancing time-consuming commitments and requests. Indeed, it is all too easy to lose track of time and fall prey to what consultants identify as "time wasters" such as those shown in Tips to Remember.

How often do you allow other people or nonessential activities to dominate your time?[9] Perhaps like many others you use To-Do lists as a way of staying on top of things. But while they can help, they aren't much good unless the lists contain the high-priority things. In daily living and in management we need to distinguish between things that we must do (top priority), should do (high priority), might do (low priority), and really don't need to do (no priority).

Study Guide

5.1
How and Why Do Managers Plan?

Rapid review

- Planning is the process of setting performance objectives and determining how to accomplish them.
- A plan is a set of intended actions for accomplishing important objectives.
- The steps in the planning process are: (1) define your objectives; (2) determine where you stand vis-à-vis objectives; (3) develop your premises regarding future conditions; (4) make a plan to best accomplish objectives; (5) implement the plan, and evaluate results.
- The benefits of planning include better focus and action orientation, better coordination and control, and better time management.
- Planning improves time management by setting priorities and avoiding time wasters.

Terms to define

Hierarchy of objectives
Objectives
Plan
Planning
Stretch goals

Be sure you can

- explain the importance of planning as the first of four management functions
- list the steps in the formal planning process
- illustrate the benefits of planning for a business or an organization familiar to you
- illustrate the benefits of planning for your personal career development
- list at least three things you can do now to improve your time management

Questions for discussion

1. Should all employees plan, or just managers?
2. Which step in the planning process do you think is the hardest to accomplish?
3. How could better planning help in your personal career development?

5.2 What Types of Plans Do Managers Use?

Managers face different planning challenges in the flow and pace of activities in organizations. In some cases, the planning environment is stable and predictable. In others, it is more dynamic and uncertain. To meet these different needs, managers rely on a variety of plans.

• Managers use short-range and long-range plans.

We live and work in a fast-paced world where planning horizons are becoming compressed. We now talk about planning in Internet time, where businesses are continually changing and updating plans. Even most top managers would likely agree that *long*-range planning is becoming shorter and shorter. A reasonable rule of thumb in this context is that **short-range plans** cover a year or less, whereas **long-range plans** look ahead three or more years into the future.[10]

Quite frankly, the advent of Internet time and shorter planning horizons might be an advantage for many of us. Management researcher Elliot Jaques found that very few people have the capacity to think long term.[11] As shown in **Figure 5.3**, he believes that most of us work comfortably with only three-month time spans; some can think about a year into the future; only about one person in several million can handle a 20-year time frame.

Do Jaques's conclusions match your experience? And if we accept his findings, what are their implications for managers and career development? Although a team leader's planning challenges may rest mainly in the weekly or monthly range, a chief executive needs to have a vision extending at least some years into the future. Career progress to higher management levels still requires the conceptual skills to work well with longer-range time frames.[12]

Short-range plans usually cover a year or less.

Long-range plans usually cover three years or more.

FIGURE 5.3

Jaques's Findings on Short-Term versus Long-Term Planning Horizons.

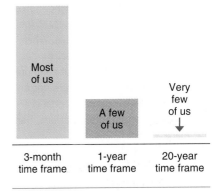

• Managers use strategic and operational plans.

When planning for the organization as a whole or a major component, the focus is on **strategic plans**. They are longer-term plans that set broad and comprehensive directions for an organization, and that create a framework for allocating resources for maximum long-term performance impact. Such planning begins with a **vision** that clarifies the purpose of the organization and expresses what it hopes to be in the future. Strategic planning sets out the ways to turn that vision into reality.

When a sports team enters a game or contest, it typically does so with a "strategy" in hand. Most often this strategy is set by the head coach in conjunction with assistants. The goal is clear and long term—win the game or contest. As the game unfolds, a variety of situations arise that require adjustments and responses to solve problems or exploit opportunities. They call for "tactics" that deal with the situation at hand while advancing the overall strategy for winning against the competition. These tactics are often decided upon by assistant coaches, perhaps in consultation with the head coach.

The same logic holds true for organizations. **Tactical plans**, also called **operational plans**, are developed and deployed to implement all or parts of strategic plans. They tend to be intermediate term and specify step-by-step means for using the organization's resources to put strategies into action. At times they are responses to specific problems or opportunities that arise; other times they are simply smaller pieces put in place to fill out the strategic plan.

A **strategic plan** identifies long-term directions for the organization.

A **vision** clarifies the purpose of the organization and expresses what it hopes to be in the future.

A **tactical plan** or **operational plan** sets out ways to implement a strategic plan.

Trendsetters 👤

Don Thompson Keeps McDonald's USA on Focus

Some call Don Thompson, president of McDonald's USA, the accidental executive. At the age of 44 he's not only one of the youngest top managers in the Fortune 500, he also may have followed the most unusual career path. After graduating from Purdue with a degree in electrical engineering, Johnson went to work for Northrop Grumman, a leading global security company. He did well, rose into engineering management, and one day received a call from a head-hunter. Thompson listened, thinking the job being offered was at McDonnell Douglas Company, another engineering-centric firm. Upon finding out it was at McDonald's he almost turned the opportunity down. But with encouragement he took the interview, and his career, and McDonald's, haven't been the same since.

Thompson hit the ground running at McDonald's and did well, but became frustrated eventually when he failed to win the annual McDonald's President's Award. He decided it might be time to move on. But with the recommendation of the firm's diversity officer he spoke with Raymond Mines, at the time the firm's highest-ranking African American executive. When Thompson confided that he "wanted to have an impact on decisions," Mines told him to move out of engineering and into the operations side of the business. Thompson did and his work not only excelled, it got him the attention he needed to advance to ever-higher responsibilities that spanned restaurant operations, franchisee relations, and strategic management.

From his childhood on Chicago's south side, Don Thompson rose quickly in his career to fill the president's chair at McDonald's world headquarters in Oak Brook, Illinois. He has a corner office, but no door; the building is configured with an open floor plan. And that fits well with Thompson's management style and personality. His former mentor Raymond Mines says: "he has the ability to listen, blend in, analyze, and communicate. People feel at ease with him. A lot of corporate executives have little time for those below them. Don makes everyone a part of the process." As for Thompson, he says "I want to make sure others achieve their goals, just as I have."

In the sports context you might think of tactical plans as involving the use of "special teams" plans or as "special plays" designed to meet a particular threat or opportunity. In business, tactical plans often take the form of **functional plans** that indicate how different components of the enterprise will contribute to the overall strategy. Such functional plans might include the following:

- *Production plans* deal with the methods and technology needed by people in their work.
- *Financial plans* deal with money required to support various operations.
- *Facilities plans* deal with facilities and work layouts.
- *Marketing plans* deal with the requirements of selling and distributing goods or services.
- *Human resource plans* deal with the recruitment, selection, and placement of people into various jobs.

• Organizational policies and procedures are plans.

In addition to strategic and operational plans, organizations also need plans that provide members with day-to-day guidance on such things as attendance, hiring practices, ethical behavior, privacy, trade secrets, and more. This is often provided in the form of organizational policies and procedures.

A **policy** communicates broad guidelines for making decisions and taking action in specific circumstances. Common human resource policies address such matters as employee hiring, termination, performance appraisals, pay increases, promotions, and discipline. Consider also the issue of sexual harassment. How should individual behavior be guided? A sample sexual harassment policy states: "Sexual harassment is specifically prohibited by this organization. Any employee found to have violated the policy against sexual harassment will be subject to immediate and appropriate disciplinary action including but not limited to possible suspension or termination."

Procedures, or *rules,* describe exactly what actions to take in specific situations. They are often found stated in employee handbooks or manuals as SOPs (standard operating procedures). Whereas a policy sets broad guidelines, procedures define specific actions to be taken. A sexual harassment policy, for example, should be backed with procedures that spell out how to file a sexual harassment complaint, as well as the steps through which any complaint will be handled.[13] When Judith Nitsch started her own engineering

A **functional plan** identifies how different parts of an enterprise will contribute to accomplishing strategic plans.

A **policy** is a standing plan that communicates broad guidelines for decisions and action.

A **procedure** or rule precisely describes actions to take in specific situations.

consulting business, for example, she defined a sexual harassment policy, established clear procedures for its enforcement, and designated both a male and a female employee for others to talk with about sexual harassment concerns.[14]

• Budgets are plans that commit resources to activities.

A **budget** is a plan that commits resources to activities, programs, or projects. It is a powerful tool that allocates scarce resources among multiple and often competing uses. Managers typically negotiate with their bosses to obtain budgets that support the needs of their work units or teams. They are also expected to achieve performance objectives while keeping within their budgets.

Managers deal with and use various types of budgets. *Financial budgets* project cash flows and expenditures; *operating budgets* plot anticipated sales or revenues against expenses; *non-monetary* budgets allocate resources such as labor, equipment, and space. A *fixed budget* allocates a fixed amount of resources for a specific purpose, such as $50,000 for equipment purchases in a given year. A *flexible budget* allows resources to vary in proportion with various levels of activity, such as monies to hire temporary workers when work loads exceed certain levels.

All such budgets play important roles in planning by linking planned activities with the resources needed to accomplish them. But budgets can also get out of control when they are allowed to creep higher and higher without sufficient critical attention.

One of the most common problems in some organizations is that resource allocations get rolled over from one time period to the next without any real performance review. A **zero-based budget** deals with this problem by approaching each new budget period as if it were brand new. No guarantee exists for renewing any past funding. Instead, all proposals compete for available funds at the start of each new budget cycle. This helps eliminate waste by making sure scarce resources are not spent on outdated or unimportant activities. Indeed, you might be surprised by how much waste there is in some carryover budgets. In a major division of Campbell Soups, managers using zero-based budgeting once discovered that 10% of the marketing budget was being spent on sales promotions that were totally irrelevant.

A **budget** is a plan that commits resources to projects or activities.

A **zero-based budget** allocates resources as if each budget was brand new.

Stay Tuned

Policies on Office Romances Vary Widely

A former CEO of Boeing was asked to resign by the firm's board after his relationship with a female executive became public. A former CEO of Starwood Hotels and Resorts Worldwide gave up a $35 million severance when asked to leave by his firm's board, even after he denied allegations of improper advances toward female employees. In fact, employer policies on office relationships vary widely as this survey shows.

- 4%—prohibit any relationships between employees.
- 24%—prohibit relationships among persons in the same department.
- 13%—prohibit relationships among persons who have the same supervisor.
- 80%—prohibit relationships between supervisors and subordinates.
- 5%—have no restrictions on office romances.

Your Thoughts?

Do you know anyone that has been involved in an office relationship? What are your thoughts? Is this an area that employers should be regulating, or should office "romance" be left to the best judgments of those involved?

5.2
What Types of Plans Do Managers Use?

Rapid review

- Short-range plans tend to cover a year or less, whereas long-range plans extend out to three years or more.
- Strategic plans set critical long-range directions; operational plans are designed to support and help implement strategic plans.
- Policies, such as a sexual harassment policy, are plans that set guidelines for the behavior of organizational members.
- Procedures are plans that describe actions to take in specific situations, such as how to report a sexual harassment complaint.
- Budgets are plans that allocate resources to activities or projects.
- A zero-based budget allocates resources as if each new budget period is brand new; no "roll over" resource allocations are allowed without new justifications.

Terms to define

Budget
Long-range plan
Operational plan
Policy
Procedures
Project
Short-range plan
Strategic plan
Zero-based budget

Be sure you can

- differentiate short-range and long-range plans
- differentiate strategic and operational plans
- explain how strategic and operational plans complement one another
- differentiate policies and procedures, and give examples of each
- explain the benefits of a zero-based budget

Questions for discussion

1. Is there any need for long-range plans in today's fast-moving environment?
2. What types of policies do you believe are essential for any organization?
3. Are there any possible disadvantages to zero-based budgeting?

5.3 What Are Some Useful Planning Tools and Techniques?

The benefits of planning are best realized when plans are built from strong foundations. The useful planning tools and techniques include forecasting, contingency planning, scenarios, benchmarking, participatory planning, and the use of staff planners.

• Forecasting tries to predict the future.

Who would have predicted even a few years ago that China would now be the second largest car market in the world? Would you believe that by 2025 China will have more cars on the roads than the United States has now? **Forecasting** is the process of predicting what will happen in the future.[15] And most plans involve forecasts of some sort.

Forecasting attempts to predict the future.

Periodicals such as *Business Week, Fortune,* and *The Economist* regularly report forecasts of industry conditions, interest rates, unemployment trends, and national economies, among other issues.[16] Some rely on qualitative forecasting, which uses expert opinions to predict the future. Others involve quantitative forecasting, which uses mathematical models and statistical analysis of historical data and surveys.

Any forecast should be used with caution. They are planning aids, not planning substitutes. It is said that a music agent once told Elvis Presley: "You ought to go back to driving a truck because you ain't going nowhere." That's the problem with forecasts; they always rely on human judgment, and that can be wrong.

• Contingency planning creates back-up plans for when things go wrong.

Things often go wrong, as you well know. It is highly unlikely that any plan will ever be perfect. Picture, for example, this scene. Tiger Woods is striding down the golf course with an iron in each hand. The one in his left hand is "the plan;" the one in his right is the "backup plan." Which club he uses will depend on how the ball lies on the fairway.

One of Tiger Woods's great strengths as a golfer is being able to adjust to the situation by putting the right club to work in the circumstances at hand. Planning in our work and personal affairs is often like that. By definition planning involves thinking ahead. But the more uncertain the environment, the more likely one's original assumptions, forecasts, and intentions may prove inadequate

News Feed

Recession Is a Good Time for Setting Priorities.

"**P**eople want to hunker down and not spend money on anything," said Allstate Corp.'s senior vice president and chief technology officer Catherine Brune as she talked about managing in a recession. But she didn't let that be an excuse to run and hide from the decision-making opportunities that tough times can bring. Instead she recognized that "we're going to come out of this, and as a business you have to be poised to take advantage of that." And that's where planning comes into play.

Brune says that she and her colleagues used the economic crisis to reconsider what projects were most important to be working on and what the firm should do now to best prepare for the better times that would surely be ahead. "We spent a good amount of time prioritizing our projects against our vision," she said. In tough times she advises that you have to get back in touch with the core of your business and focus on the things that really move it forward. At Allstate she operated with this planning rule: ". . . look at every one of your projects and ask, 'Is the end result something that customers are telling us they need . . . ?'" If the answer isn't "yes" to this question, she sees no place for the projects in the firm's future plans.

As to being a woman in a career field largely limited to men, Brune is confident. She believes women are starting to have a high impact in IT. But she would also like to see more women majoring in the discipline at colleges and universities.

Reflect and React:

Why is it that some executives like Catherine Brune will look at a poor economy and see opportunities, not just problems? Does Brune have the right idea when she says a business shouldn't be spending money on projects that don't deliver what customers say they need? Does Brune's example have anything to offer to your career development and job hunting plans?

Even the most successful firms must have contingency plans to deal with unexpected events.

Contingency planning identifies alternative courses of action to take when things go wrong.

Scenario planning identifies alternative future scenarios and makes plans to deal with each.

Benchmarking uses external comparisons to gain insights for planning.

Best practices are methods that lead to superior performance.

Firms such as L.L. Bean, Inc. and The Walt Disney Company are highly regarded as sources of management and best practices benchmarks.

or wrong. And when they do, the best managers and organizations have contingency plans ready to go.

Contingency planning identifies alternative courses of action that can be implemented to meet the needs of changing circumstances. A really good contingency plan will even contain "trigger points" to indicate when to activate preselected alternatives. Given the uncertainties of our day, this is really an indispensable tool for managerial and personal planning.

Coca-Cola and PepsiCo spend hundreds of millions of dollars on advertising as they engage one another in the ongoing "Cola War." It may seem that they have nothing to worry about save each other and a few discounters. But more than 50% of their revenues come internationally. And the world at large is a dynamic place, with new developments continually taking center stage. Contingency planning helps both firms prepare for things such as new competition from Mecca Cola and Qibla Cola. They appeared in European markets during a wave of resentment of U.S. brands and multinationals. The founder of Qibla says: "By choosing to boycott major brands, consumers are sending an important signal: that the exploitation of Muslims cannot continue unchecked."[17]

• Scenario planning crafts plans for alternative future conditions.

A long-term version of contingency planning, called **scenario planning**, involves identifying several alternative future scenarios or states of affairs. Managers then make plans to deal with each, should it actually occur.[18]

Scenario planning began years ago at Royal Dutch/Shell when top managers asked themselves a perplexing question: "What would Shell do after its oil supplies ran out?" Although recognizing that scenario planning can never be inclusive of all future possibilities, a Shell executive once said that it helps "condition the organization to think" and better prepare for "future shocks." For Shell this has meant planning for such issues as climate change, sustainable development, fossil fuel alternatives, human rights, and biodiversity.[19]

• Benchmarking identifies best practices used by others.

All too often managers and planners become too comfortable with the ways things are going. They become trapped by habits and overconfident that the past is a good indicator of the future. Planning helps us deal with such tendencies by challenging the status quo and reminding us not to always accept things as they are. One way to do this is through **benchmarking**, a planning technique that makes use of external comparisons to better evaluate current performance.[20] It is basically a way of learning from the successes of others. There's little doubt that sports stars benchmark one another; scientists and scholars do it; executives and managers do it. Could you be doing it, too?

Managers use benchmarking to find out what other people and organizations are doing well, and plan how to incorporate these ideas into their own operations. They search for **best practices** inside and outside of the organization, and among competitors and non-competitors alike. These are things that others are doing and that help them to achieve superior performance.

Xerox, for example, has benchmarked L.L. Bean's warehousing and distribution methods, Ford's plant layouts, and American Express's billing and collections. In building its "world car," the Fiesta, Ford benchmarked BMW's popular 3 series. James D. Farley, Ford's global marketing head, says: "The ubiquity of the 3 series engenders trust in every part of the world, and its design always has a strong point of view . . ."[21]

• Staff planners provide special expertise in planning.

As organizations grow, they often employ staff planners who are specialists in all steps of the planning process, as well as up to date on the latest planning tools and techniques. These staff planners can help bring focus, expertise, and energy to important planning tasks. But, one of the risks is that a communication gap develops between the planners and the rest of the organization. Plans can end up getting made in a vacuum. Not only might the plans end up off the mark, there might be little commitment in the workforce to their implementation. Even when staff planners are used, therefore, it's important to make sure other members of the organization are actively involved in the planning process.

• Participatory planning improves implementation capacities.

When it comes to implementation, participation can be a very important word in planning. **Participatory planning**, as shown in **Figure 5.4**, includes in all steps of the process those people whose ideas and inputs can benefit the plans and whose support is needed for implementation. It has all the advantages of group decision making as previously discussed in Module 4.3.

Participatory planning includes the persons who will be affected by plans and/or who will be asked to implement them.

FIGURE 5.4
How Do Participation and Involvement Help Build Commitments to Plans?

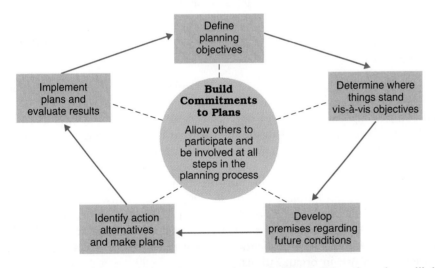

Any plan needs the efforts and support of many people to make it work. It is easier and more likely to get this commitment when the people responsible for implementation have had the opportunity to participate in developing the plans in the first place. When managers use participatory planning and allow others to become involved in the planning process, it leads to better plans, a deeper understanding of the plans, and a strengthened commitment to fully implementing the plans.

Participatory planning can increase the creativity and information available, it can increase understanding and acceptance of plans, and it can build stronger commitments to a plan's success. When 7-Eleven executives planned for new upscale products and services, such as selling fancy meals-to-go, they learned this lesson the hard way. Although their ideas sounded good at the top, franchise owners and managers resisted. The executives learned a hard lesson on the value of taking time to involve them in planning new directions for the stores.[22]

• Goal setting helps align plans and activities throughout an organization.

In the dynamic and highly competitive technology industry, CEO T. J. Rodgers of Cypress Semiconductor Corp. has earned a reputation for valuing both performance goals and accountability. He supports a planning system where employees work with clear and quantified work goals that they help set. He believes the system helps people find problems before they interfere with performance. Says Rodgers: "Managers monitor the goals, look for problems, and expect people who fall behind to ask for help before they lose control of or damage a major project."[23]

Although Rodgers makes us aware of the importance of goal setting in management, he may make it look too easy. Actually, the way goals are set can make a major difference in how well they work in pointing plans in the right directions and helping to ensure that the plans are implemented with the desired results. The following guidelines are starting points in moving from "no goals" and even just everyday run-of-the-mill "average goals" to having really "great goals"—ones that result in plans being successfully implemented. Great goals are:

1. *Specific*—clearly target key results and outcomes to be accomplished.
2. *Timely*—linked to specific timetables and "due dates".
3. *Measurable*—described so results can be measured without ambiguity.
4. *Challenging*—include a stretch factor that moves toward real gains.
5. *Attainable*—although challenging, realistic and possible to achieve.

Specific
Desired outcomes clear to anyone

Attainable
Realistic, possible to accomplish

Timely
Linked to due date and timetable

Great Goals

Challenging
Include "stretch," focused on doing better

Measurable
No doubt when accomplished, or missed

Even when goals are well set as part of a plan, it is quite another challenge to make sure that the goals and plan for one person or work unit are helpful in accomplishing the goals of the organization as a whole. It's always important to align goals from one level to the next so that the right things happen at the right times throughout an organization. Goals set anywhere in the organization should ideally help advance the overall mission or purpose. Strategic goals set by top management to achieve this purpose then cascade down the organization to become goals and objectives for lower levels. Ideally, everything works together in a consistent "means-end" fashion as suggested earlier in Figure 5.2. When a hierarchy of goals and objectives is well defined, through good planning, this helps improve coordination among the multiple tasks, components, and levels of work in organizations.

Study Guide

5.3
What Are Some Useful Planning Tools and Techniques?

Rapid review

- Forecasting, which attempts to predict what might happen in the future, is a planning aid but not a planning substitute.
- Contingency planning identifies alternative courses of action to implement if and when circumstances change and an existing plan fails.
- Scenario planning analyzes the implications of alternative versions of the future.
- Benchmarking utilizes external comparisons to identify best practices and possibly desirable actions.
- Participation and involvement open the planning process to valuable inputs from people whose efforts are essential to the effective implementation of plans.

Terms to define

Benchmarking
Best practices
Contingency planning
Forecasting
Participatory planning
Scenario planning

Be sure you can

- differentiate among forecasting, contingency planning, scenario planning, and benchmarking
- explain the importance of contingency planning
- explain why staff planners sometimes don't succeed
- describe the benefits of participatory planning as a special case of group decision making

Questions for discussion

1. If forecasting is going to be imperfect, why bother with it?
2. Shouldn't all planning provide for contingency plans?
3. Will members of today's workforce like participatory planning?

[Test Prep]

Multiple choice

1. Planning is best described as the process of _____ and _____.

    (a) developing premises about the future/evaluating them
    (b) measuring results/taking corrective action
    (c) measuring past performance/targeting future performance
    (d) setting objectives/deciding how to accomplish them

2. The benefits of planning should include _____.

    (a) improved focus
    (b) lower labor costs
    (c) more accurate forecasts
    (d) increased business profits

3. The first step in the planning process is to _____.

    (a) decide how to get where you want to go
    (b) define your objectives
    (c) identify possible future conditions or scenarios
    (d) act quickly to take advantage of opportunities

4. In order to help implement her firm's strategic plans, the CEO of a business firm would most likely want marketing, manufacturing, and finance executives to develop _____.

    (a) means–ends chains   (b) operational plans
    (c) flexible budgets   (d) project management

5. _____ planning identifies alternative courses of action that can be taken if problems occur with the original plan.

    (a) Benchmark   (b) Participatory
    (c) Staff   (d) Contingency

6. A "No Smoking" rule and a sexual harassment policy are examples of _____ that are types of _____ in organizations.

    (a) long-range plans/policies
    (b) single-use plans/means–ends chains
    (c) policies/standing-use plans
    (d) operational plans/short-range plans

7. When a manager is asked to justify a new budget proposal on the basis of projected activities rather than as an incremental adjustment to the prior year's budget, this is an example of _____.

    (a) zero-based budgeting
    (b) strategic planning
    (c) operational planning
    (d) contingency planning

8. One of the expected benefits of participatory planning is

    (a) faster planning
    (b) less need for forecasting
    (c) greater attention to contingencies
    (d) more commitment to implementation

9. When managers use the benchmarking approach to planning, they usually try to _____.

    (a) use flexible budgets
    (b) identify best practices used by others
    (c) find the most accurate forecasts that are available
    (d) use expert staff planners to set objectives

10. In a hierarchy of objectives, plans at lower levels are supposed to act as _____ for accomplishing higher-level plans.

    (a) means   (b) ends
    (c) scenarios   (d) benchmarks

11. In addition to providing better focus, good planning offers the benefits of _____.

    (a) guaranteed performance success
    (b) eliminating the need to change
    (c) improved action orientation
    (d) less emphasis on coordination and control

12. According to recommended time management tips, which manager is likely to be in best control of his or her time? One who _____.

    (a) tries to never say "no" to requests from others
    (b) works on the most important things first
    (c) immediately responds to instant messages
    (d) always has "an open office door"

13. In a business firm, a marketing plan would most likely deal with _____.

    (a) production methods and technologies
    (b) money and capital investments
    (c) facilities and workforce recruiting
    (d) sales and product distribution

14. Managers often identify "best practices" through a planning approach known as _____.

    (a) goal setting   (b) forecasting
    (c) benchmarking   (d) visioning

15. The planning process isn't complete until _____.

    (a) future conditions have been identified
    (b) stretch goals have been set
    (c) plans are implemented and results evaluated
    (d) budgets commit resources to plans

16. List the five steps in the planning process, and give examples of each.

17. How does planning facilitate controlling?

18. What is the difference between contingency planning and scenario planning?

19. Why is participation good for the planning process?

20. My friends Curt and Rich own a local bookstore. They are very interested in making plans for improving the store and better dealing with competition from the other bookstores that serve college students in our town. I once heard Curt saying to Rich: "We should be benchmarking what some of the successful coffee shops, restaurants, and novelty stores are doing." Rich replied: "I don't see why; we should only be interested in bookstores. Why don't we study the local competition and even look at what the best bookstores are doing in the big cities?"

Questions: Who is right? If you were hired by Curt and Rich as a planning consultant, what would you suggest as the best way to utilize benchmarking as a planning technique to improve their bookstore?

Time Management Profile

Instructions

Indicate "Y" (yes) or "N" (no) for each item. Be frank; let your responses describe an accurate picture of how you tend to respond to these kinds of situations.

1. When confronted with several items of similar urgency and importance, I tend to do the easiest one first.

2. I do the most important things during that part of the day when I know I perform best.

3. Most of the time I don't do things someone else can do; I delegate this type of work to others.

4. Even though meetings without a clear and useful purpose upset me, I put up with them.

5. I skim documents before reading them and don't complete any that offer a low return on my time investment.

6. I don't worry much if I don't accomplish at least one significant task each day.

7. I save the most trivial tasks for that time of day when my creative energy is lowest.

8. My workspace is neat and organized.

9. My office door is always "open"; I never work in complete privacy.

10. I schedule my time completely from start to finish every workday.

11. I don't like "to-do" lists, preferring to respond to daily events as they occur.

12. I "block" a certain amount of time each day or week that is dedicated to high-priority activities.

Scoring and Interpretation

Count the number of "Y" responses to items 2, 3, 5, 7, 8, 12. [Enter that score here _____.] Count the number of "N" responses to items 1, 4, 6, 9, 10, 11. [Enter that score here _____.] Add together the two scores.

The higher the total score, the closer your behavior matches recommended time management guidelines. Reread those items where your response did not match the desired one. Why don't they match? Are there reasons for your action tendencies? Think about what you can do to be more consistent with time management guidelines.

Case Snapshot

Lands' End—Living by the Golden Rule

What's so interesting about a company that just wants to be nice? Longevity and year-after-year success, for starters. From a no-questions-asked return policy to patient, limitless customer support, Lands' End has built a solid business model around treating customers the way they'd like to be treated. See how this former retailer of sailing products turned good manners into healthy profits.

Online Interactive Learning Resources

SELF-ASSESSMENT
• Time Management

EXPERIENTIAL EXERCISE
• Beating the Time Wasters

TEAM PROJECT
• Affirmative Action Directions

6

Controls and Control Systems

What Gets Measured Happens

Well Treated Staff Delivers Consistent Results.
You can get a tasty sandwich at Chick-fil-A, but don't plan on stopping in on a Sunday. All of the chain's 1270 stores are closed. It is a tradition started by 85-year-old founder Truett Cathy, who believes that employees deserve a day of rest. Someone who places "people before profits," Truett has built a successful, and fast growing, fast-food franchise known for consistent quality and great customer service.

Chick-fil-A, headquartered in Atlanta, GA, where its first restaurant was opened, is wholly owned by Truett's family, and is now headed by his son. It has a reputation as a great business, processing about 10,000 inquiries each year for 100 restaurant franchise opportunities. The president of the national Restaurant Association Educational Foundation says: "I don't think there's any chain that creates such a wonderful culture around the way they treat their people and the respect they have for their employees."

Truett asks his employees to always say "my pleasure" when thanked by a customer. He says: "It's important to keep people happy." He also believes in "continuous improvement," continuing to upgrade menus and stores even after 40 years of increasing sales. Woody

Trendsetters

Patricia Karter shows brands with values are really sweet.

News Feed

"Elsewhere Class" struggles to balance work and leisure.

Case Snapshot

Electronic Arts—Inside fantasy sports

Faulk, vice president of brand development, says: "It would be very easy for us to pause after such a successful year, but in doing that, we would be in jeopardy of falling into a trap of complacency." He adds: "Change in the quick-service industry is much like that of the fashion industry. Customer needs are constantly fluctuating, and we have to be intentional about staying ahead of and remaining relevant to those changes."

The results seem to speak for themselves. Chick-fil-A is the 2nd largest chicken restaurant chain in the United States, with 1425 restaurants in 38 states, and reached over $3 billion sales in 2008. Chick-fil-A's turnover among restaurant operators is only 3%, compared to an industry average as high as 50%. It is also a relatively inexpensive franchise, costing $5,000, compared to $50,000 that is typical of its competitors.

Current President Dan T. Cathy believes the Sunday day of rest is a statement about that culture. He says: "If we take care of our team members and operators behind the counter, then they are going to do a better job on Monday. In fact, I say our food tastes better on Monday because we are closed on Sunday." Another statement is the Leadership Scholarship program that supports education by employees. When the 20,000th scholarship was awarded, Truett said: "It has long been my goal to encourage our restaurant employees to strive for excellence . . . so they will have the tools necessary to secure a bright future for themselves and our nation."

6.1 What Is Important to Know about the Control Process?

"Keeping in touch" . . . "Staying informed" . . . "Being in control." These are important responsibilities for every manager. But "control" is a word like "power." If you aren't careful when and how the word is used, it leaves a negative connotation. But control plays a positive and necessary role in the management process. To have things "under control" is good; for things to be "out of control" is generally bad.

Managers understand **controlling** as a process of measuring performance and taking action to ensure desired results. Its purpose is straightforward—to make sure that plans are achieved and that actual performance meets or surpasses objectives. Like any aspect of decision making, the foundation of control is information. Henry Schacht, former CEO of Cummins Engine Company, once discussed control in terms of what he called "friendly facts." He stated, "Facts that reinforce what you are doing . . . are nice, because they help in terms of psychic reward. Facts that raise alarms are equally friendly, because they give you clues about how to respond, how to change, where to spend the resources."[1]

Controlling is the process of measuring performance and taking action to ensure desired results.

• Controlling is one of the four functions of management.

How does control fit in with the other management functions? Planning sets the directions. Organizing arranges people and resources for work. Leading inspires people toward their best efforts. And as shown in **Figure 6.1**, controlling sees to it that the right things happen, in the right way, and at the right time. And if things go wrong, control helps get things back on track.

FIGURE 6.1

The Importance of Controling in the Management Process.

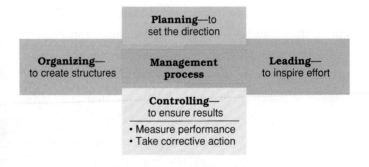

Effective control offers the great opportunity of learning from experience. Consider, for example, the program of **after-action review** pioneered by the U.S. Army and now utilized in many corporate settings. This is a structured review of lessons learned and results accomplished through a completed project, task force assignment, or special operation. Participants are asked to answer questions like: "What was the intent?" "What actually happened?" "What did we learn?"[2] The after-action review encourages everyone involved to take responsibility for his or her performance efforts and accomplishments. The end of chapter self-assessment is modeled on this approach.

An **after-action review** identifies lessons learned from a completed project, task force assignment, or special operation.

Even though improving performance through learning is one of the great opportunities offered by the control process, the potential benefits are realized only when learning is translated into corrective actions. After setting up Diversity Network Groups (DNGs) worldwide, for example, IBM executives learned that male attitudes were major barriers to the success of female managers. They addressed this finding by making male senior executives report annually on the progress of women managers in their divisions. This action is credited with substantially increasing the percentage of women in IBM's senior management ranks.[3]

• Control begins with objectives and standards.

The control process consists of the four steps shown in **Figure 6.2**. The process begins with setting performance objectives along with standards for measuring them. It can't start any other way. This is the planning part: setting the performance objectives against which results can eventually be compared. Measurement standards are important, too. It isn't always easy to set them, but they are essential.

FIGURE 6.2
Four Steps in the Control Process.

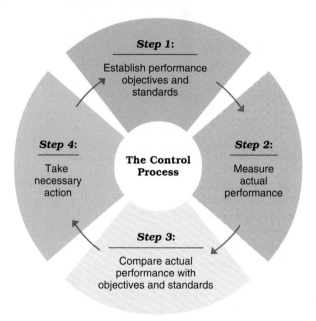

Standards for measuring business performance that we often hear about are things such as earnings per share, sales growth, and market shares. Others include quantity and quality of production, costs incurred, service or delivery time, and error rates. But how about other types of organizations, such as a symphony orchestra? When the Cleveland Orchestra wrestled with performance standards, the members weren't willing to rely on vague generalities like "we played well," "the audience seemed happy," "not too many mistakes were made." Rather, they decided to track standing ovations, invitations to perform in other countries, and how often other orchestras copied their performance styles.[4]

These have all been examples of **output standards** that measure actual outcomes or work results. Businesses use many output standards; we have already discussed a couple. Just based on your experience at work and as a customer you can probably come up with even more examples. When Allstate Corporation launched a new diversity initiative, it created a "diversity index" to quantify performance on diversity issues. The standards included how well employees met

An **output standard** measures performance results in terms of quantity, quality, cost, or time.

Stay Tuned 🅑

Bad Economy Brings Out More Corporate Thieves.

Not all corporate thievery is at the million-dollar level of the Bernard Madoff financial fraud. There's a lot of lower-level crime in the corporate world, and many believe a bad economy tends to bring out the worst in some of us. Consider these results from a survey of 392 U.S. firms.

- 20% say worker theft is a "moderate to very big problem."
- 18% report an increase in money crimes such as stolen cash or fraudulent transactions.
- 24% report an increase in thefts of office supplies and company products.
- 17% have tightened security to prevent employee theft.

Your Thoughts?

Do these data tell the real story: is employee theft mainly a "bad economy" problem? Is it a smaller or larger problem than that indicated here? Have you witnessed such theft and, if so, what did you do about it? And have you been a participant in such bad employee behavior?

the goals of bias-free customer service, and how well managers met the firm's diversity expectations.[5] When GE became concerned about managing ethics in its 320,000-member global workforce, it created measurement standards to track compliance. Each business unit now reports quarterly on how many of its members attended ethics training sessions and what percentage signed the firm's "Spirit and Letter" ethics guide.[6]

The control process also uses **input standards** to measure work efforts. These are often used in situations where outputs are difficult or expensive to measure. Examples of input standards for a college professor might be the existence of an orderly course syllabus, meeting all class sessions, and returning exams and assignments in a timely fashion. Of course, as this example might suggest, measuring inputs doesn't mean that outputs, such as high-quality teaching and learning, are necessarily achieved. Other examples of input standards in the workplace include conformance with rules and procedures, efficiency in the use of resources, and work attendance or punctuality.

• Control measures actual performance.

An **input standard** measures work efforts that go into a performance task.

The second step in the control process is to measure actual performance using agreed-upon standards. Accurate and timely measurement is essential in order to spot differences between what is really taking place and what was originally planned. Unless we are willing to measure, very little control is possible. And as the module subtitle indicates, willingness to measure has its rewards. What gets measured tends to happen.

When IBM appointed Linda Sanford head of its sales force, she came with an admirable performance record earned during a 22-year career with the company. Notably, Sanford grew up on a family farm, where she developed an appreciation for measuring results. "At the end of the day, you saw what you did, knew how many rows of strawberries you picked." This experience carried over into her work at IBM. She earned a reputation for walking around the factory just to see "at the end of the day how many machines were going out of the back dock."[7]

Linda Sanford is known for her emphasis on control as a senior vice president at IBM.

• Control compares results with objectives and standards.

The third step in the control process is to compare actual results with objectives and standards. You might remember its implications by this **control equation**:

$$\text{Need for action} = \text{Desired performance} - \text{Actual performance.}$$

As with any other problem solving, don't forget that the need for action can point you in two possible directions. It can point toward the need to deal with a performance threat or deficiency (when actual is less than desired) or to explore a performance opportunity (when actual is more than desired).

The question of what constitutes desired performance plays an important role in the control equation and its implications. Ideally this is clarified when the original objectives and standards are set, such as in the earlier example of ethics at GE. But there are other approaches available. Some organizations use *engineering comparisons*. An example is UPS. The firm carefully measures the routes and routines of its drivers to establish the times expected for each delivery. When a delivery manifest is scanned as completed, the driver's time is registered in an electronic performance log that is closely monitored by supervisors.

Organizations, just as we, make use of *historical comparisons* as well. These use past experience as a basis for evaluating current performance. Similarly, *relative comparisons* are also common. These benchmark our performance against that being achieved by other people, work units, or organizations.

• Control takes corrective action as needed.

The final step in the control process occurs when action is taken to address gaps between desired and actual performance. You might hear the term **management by exception** used in this regard. It is the practice of giving attention to high-priority situations that show the greatest need for action.

Management by exception basically adds discipline to our use of the control equation by focusing attention not just on needs for action but also on the highest priority needs for action. In this way it can save valuable time, energy, and other resources that might be spent correcting things of lesser importance while those of greater importance get missed or delayed. Of course, managers should stay alert to two types of action priorities. The first is a problem situation that must be understood right away so corrective action can restore performance to the desired level. The second is an opportunity situation that must be understood right away so that an already high level of performance can be continued or further increased in the future.

Trendsetters

Patricia Karter Shows Brands with Values Are Really Sweet.

A sweet treat is what one gets when digging into one of Dancing Deer Baking's Cherry Almond Ginger Chew cookies. The company, founded by Patricia Karter, sells about $8 million worth of them and other confectionary concoctions every year. Each product is made with all natural ingredients, packaged in recycled materials, and produced in inner city Boston.

Dancing Deer began in 1994 with a $20,000 investment and two ovens in a former pizza shop. It may not have been the original plan, but growth came quickly as the bakery prospered. Customer demand led to expansion; an acquisition led to further expansion; being recognized on national TV as having the "best cake in the nation" fueled growth further.

It isn't easy to stay on course and in control while changing structures, adding people, and building brands for competitive advantage. But for Karter the anchor point has always been clear: let core values be the guide. Dancing Deer's employees get stock options and free lunches; 35% of profits from the firm's Sweet Home cakes are donated to help the homeless find accommodations and jobs. When offered a chance to make a large cookie sale to Williams-Sonoma, Karter declined because the contract would have required use of preservatives. Williams-Sonoma was so impressed that it contracted to sell her bakery mixes. Instead of lost opportunity, the firm gained more sales.

"There's more to life than selling cookies," says the Dancing Deer's Web site, "but it's not a bad way to make a living." And Karter hopes growth will soon make Dancing Deer "big enough to make an impact, to be a social economic force." The firm's Web site sums up the story to date this way: "It has been an interesting journey. Our successes are due to luck, a tremendous amount of dedication and hard work, and a commitment to having fun while being true to our principles. We have had failures as well—and survived them with a sense of humor."

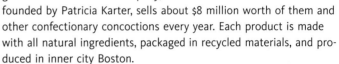

Management by exception focuses attention on differences between actual and desired performance.

Study Guide

6.1
What Is Important to Know about the Control Process?

Rapid review

- Controlling is the process of measuring performance and taking corrective action as needed.
- The control process begins when performance objectives and standards are set; both input standards for work efforts and output standards for work results can be used.
- The second step in control is to measure actual performance; the third step compares these results with objectives and standards to determine the need for corrective action.
- The final step in the control process involves taking action to resolve problems and improve things in the future.
- The control equation states: Need for Action = Desired Performance − Actual Performance.
- Management by exception focuses attention on the greatest need for action.

Terms to define

After-action review
Controlling
Input standards
Management by exception
Output standards

Be sure you can

- explain the role of controlling in the management process
- list the steps in the control process
- explain how planning and controlling should work together in management
- differentiate output standards and input standards
- state the control equation
- explain management by exception

Questions for discussion

1. What performance standards should guide a hospital emergency room or fire department?
2. Can one control performance equally well with input standards and output standards?
3. What are the possible downsides to management by exception?

6.2 How Do Managers Exercise Control?

• Managers use feedforward, concurrent, and feedback controls.

You should recall discussions in earlier modules of how organizations operate as open systems that interact with their environments in an input-throughput-output cycle. **Figure 6.3** now shows how three types of managerial controls—feedforward, concurrent, and feedback—apply to each phase.[8]

FIGURE 6.3

What Are the Differences Between Feedforward, Concurrent, and Feedback Controls?

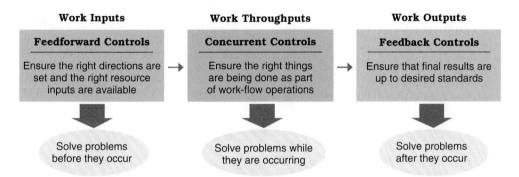

Organizations are input-throughput-output systems, and each point in the cycle offers its own opportunities for control over performance. Feedforward controls try to solve problems before they occur, by making sure the production systems have high-quality inputs. Concurrent controls try to solve problems as they occur, by monitoring and correcting problems during the work process. Feedback controls try to correct problems after they have occurred and inform the system so that similar mistakes can be avoided in the future.

Feedforward controls, also called *preliminary controls*, take place before work begins. Their goal is to prevent problems before they occur. This is a forward-thinking and proactive approach to control, one that we should all try to follow whenever we can. A good example is the area of quality control, where the saying might be: quality in, quality out.

At McDonald's, preliminary control of food ingredients plays an important role in the firm's quality program. The company requires that suppliers of its hamburger buns produce them to exact specifications, covering everything from texture to uniformity of color. Even in overseas markets, the firm works hard to develop local suppliers that can supply it with ingredients of dependable quality.[9]

Concurrent controls focus on what happens during the work process; they take place while people are doing their jobs. The goal is to solve problems as they occur. Sometimes called *steering controls*, they make sure that things are always going according to plan. The ever-present shift leaders at McDonald's restaurants are a good example of how this happens through direct supervision. They constantly observe what is taking place, even while helping out with the work. They also intervene immediately to correct things on the spot. The question continually being asked is: "What can we do to improve things right now?"

By the way, how often do you hear this question in your courses? Most student course evaluations are examples of **feedback controls** done not during

Feedforward control ensures clear directions and needed resources before the work begins.

Concurrent control focuses on what happens during the work process.

Feedback control takes place after completing an action.

Close control over all aspects of the work process is characteristic of McDonald's operations.

News Feed 🔊

"Elsewhere Class" Struggles to Balance Work and Leisure.

Welcome to elsewhere! If you think that college is complicated in terms of conflicting demands, wait until you hit the real world of work. Young professionals are finding that they never seem to be in the right place at the right time. Blending the demands of work and the opportunities of leisure just don't often balance out.

"Elsewhere" is the place you are thinking about even though physically you are somewhere different. You may be at home or out shopping or at a sports event. Yet, you're thinking it's time to check my messages on the cell phone, laptop, or iPhone. In a time of high technology and dual-career couples, young professionals are more and more living in what sociologist Dan Conley describes as "a blended world of work and leisure, home and office." He calls this new generation of workers the "Elsewhere Class" and says: "we feel like we are in the right place at the right time only when in transit, moving from point A to B. Constant motion is a balm to an anxious culture where we are haunted by the feeling that we are frauds, expendable in the workplace because so much of our service work is intangible."

Characteristics of the Elsewhere Class are a bit startling. Some 27% of "high income" earners say their work weeks top 50 hours. American workers put in more hours at work than those in other industrialized nations; they outwork Germans by seven hours per week and outwork the French by six weeks a year. Among women, two-thirds of mothers with young children hold paying jobs; and although the home is increasingly gender neutral, women still spend more hours on household duties.

The recession and financial crises have certainly added lots of pressure to everyday living. But for the Elsewhere Generation, already struggling with work-life balance in their fast-paced lives, the stress can be extreme. One has to wonder: How well will the Elsewheres cope and what does tomorrow have in store for them?

Reflect and React:

Do you know members of the Elsewhere Class? Do you see in them signs that support this report? What are the implications for society of these pressures to continually think about and deal with work responsibilities, even when home or at leisure? Are we losing control of our lives?

but at the end of a course. All such *post-action controls* take place after a job or project is completed. Most course evaluation systems ask you "Was this a good learning experience?" only when the class is almost over; servers ask us "Was everything okay?" after we finish our meals; probably the last question a computer maker asks before your machine is shipped from the factory floor is: "Does it work?"

Although these are all good questions, they show how feedback controls focus mainly on the quality of finished products. This type of control may prevent you from receiving a defective computer, but it may not help you much in the restaurant or at school. However, if carried a step further into the organizational learning phase, feedback controls can help make sure that identified problems won't happen again in the future.

• Managers use both internal and external controls.

We all exercise self-control in our daily lives; we do in respect to managing our money, our relationships, our eating and drinking, and more. Managers can take advantage of this human capacity by unlocking and setting up conditions that support **internal control** in the workplace. This happens when motivated individuals and groups are allowed to exercise self-discipline in fulfilling job expectations.

According to Douglas McGregor's Theory Y perspective, introduced in an earlier module, people are ready and willing to exercise self-control in their work.[10] But he also points out that they are most likely to do this when they participate in setting performance objectives and standards. Furthermore, the potential for self-control is increased when capable people have a clear sense of organizational mission, know their goals, and have the resources necessary to do their jobs well.

Internal control occurs through self-discipline and self-control.

External control occurs through direct supervision or administrative systems.

Bureaucratic control influences behavior through authority, policies, procedures, job descriptions, budgets, and day-to-day supervision.

In addition to encouraging and allowing internal control, managers also set up and use various forms of **external control** to structure situations and make sure things happen as planned.[11] The alternatives here include bureaucratic or administrative control, clan control, and market control.

The logic of **bureaucratic control** traces to the influence of authority, policies, procedures, job descriptions, budgets, and day-to-day supervision to make sure that people behave in ways consistent with organizational interests. In many ways you can think of this as administrative control that flows through the organization's hierarchy of authority. As discussed in the last module of planning, for example, organizations typically have policies and procedures regarding sexual harassment, with the goal being to make sure that members behave toward one another respectfully and in ways that offer no suggestion of sexual pressures or improprieties.

Whereas bureaucratic control emphasizes hierarchy and authority, **clan control** influences behavior through norms and expectations set by the organizational culture. This represents the power of collective identity, where persons who share values and identify strongly with one another and the organization tend to behave in ways that are consistent with one another's expectations. If you want to see the power of clan control in operation, just look around the typical college classroom and campus. You'll see it reflected in the dress, the language, and the behavior as students tend to behave consistent with the expectations of those peers and groups that they identify with. The same holds true in organizations, where employees and members of strong culture organizations display common behavior patterns.

Market control is essentially the influence of market competition on the behavior of organizations and their members. Business firms show the influence of market control in the way that they adjust products, pricing, promotions, and other practices in response to customer feedback as reflected in sales and profitability. A good example in this regard is the growing emphasis on "green" products and practices. When a firm such as Wal-Mart starts to get good publicity from its expressed commitment to eventually power all of its stores with renewable energy, for example, the effect is felt by its competitors.[12] They have to adjust practices in return in order to avoid giving up this public relations advantage to Wal-Mart. In this sense the time-worn phrase "keeping up with the competition" is really another way of expressing the dynamics of market controls in operation.

• Managing by objectives integrates planning and controlling.

A useful technique for integrating planning and controlling is **managing by objectives**. It is a structured process of regular communication in which a supervisor or team leader and a subordinate or team member both jointly set performance objectives and review accomplished results.[13] As **Figure 6.4** shows, the process creates an agreement between the two parties regarding performance objectives for a given time period, plans for accomplishing them, standards for measuring them,

Self-Assessment
This is a good point to complete the self-assessment "*Internal/External Control*" found on page 133.

Clan control influences behavior through norms and expectations set by the organizational culture.

Market control is essentially the influence of market competition on the behavior of organizations and their members.

Managing by objectives is a process of joint objective setting between a superior and a subordinate.

FIGURE 6.4
How Does Managing by Objectives Integrate Planning and Controlling?

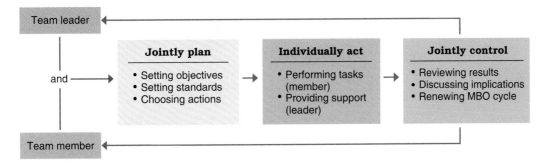

Managing by objectives is a structured process of communication between a supervisor and a subordinate, or team leader and team members. Planning is accomplished when both parties communicate to identify the subordinate's performance objectives. This is a form of participatory planning, and the goal is agreement. Informed by the objectives, the supervisor provides support for the subordinate as work progresses. Controlling is accomplished when the two parties meet at scheduled times to jointly discuss progress and results, and make new plans setting future performance objectives.

Tips to Remember 🅱

How to Write a Good Performance Objective

- *Clarify the target*—be specific; clearly describe the key result to be accomplished.
- *Make it measurable*—state how the key result will be measured and documented.
- *Define the timetable*—identify a date by which the key result will be accomplished.
- *Avoid the impossible*—be realistic; don't promise what cannot be accomplished.
- *Add challenge*—be optimistic; build in "stretch" to make the accomplishment significant.

Improvement objectives
document intentions to improve performance in a specific way.

Personal development objectives
document intentions to accomplish personal growth, such as expanded job knowledge or skills.

and procedures for reviewing them. After reaching an agreement on these matters, both parties are supposed to work closely together to fulfill its terms.

Two types of objectives are most important. **Improvement objectives** document intentions for improving performance in a specific way. An example is "to reduce quality rejects by 10%." **Personal development objectives** focus on personal growth activities, often those resulting in expanded job knowledge or skills. An example is "to learn the latest version of a computer spreadsheet package."

Good objectives are specific, time defined, challenging, and measurable. In the latter respect, it is important to state objectives specifically and as quantitatively as possible. Ideally, this involves agreement on a *measurable end product*, for example, "to reduce housekeeping supply costs by 5% by the end of the fiscal year." But this can be hard to do for some jobs. For example, how could you measure the performance objective "to improve communications with my team members"? Rather than abandon objectives in such cases, performance objectives can often be stated as *verifiable work activities*. In this example, the team leader can commit to holding weekly team meetings as a means for achieving better communications.

You might already be wondering if managing by objectives can become too complicated a process.[14] Critics note that problems can arise when objectives are linked too closely with pay, focused too much on easy accomplishments, involve excessive paperwork, and end up being dictated by supervisors.

But the advantages of making objectives a clear part of the ongoing conversation between managers and those reporting to them are also clear. It can focus workers on the most important tasks and priorities, while focusing supervisors on the best ways to help them meet agreed-upon objectives. Because the process involves direct face-to-face communication, furthermore, it can lead to better interpersonal relationships. And by increasing employees' participation in decisions that affect their work, it also encourages self-management.[15] Would you be surprised to learn that research shows participating in goal setting helps increase a person's motivation to perform as expected?[16]

Study Guide

6.2
How Do Managers Exercise Control?

Rapid review

- Feedforward controls try to make sure things are set up right before work begins; concurrent controls make sure that things are being done correctly; feedback controls assess results after an action is completed.
- Internal control is self-control that occurs as people take personal responsibility for their work.
- External control is accomplished by use of bureaucratic, clan, and market control systems.
- Management by objectives is a process through which team leaders work with team members to "jointly" set performance objectives and review performance results.

Terms to define

Bureaucratic control

Clan control

Concurrent control

External control

Feedback control

Feedforward control

Improvement objectives

Internal control

Management by objectives

Market control

Personal development objectives

Be sure you can

- illustrate the use of feedforward, concurrent, and feedback controls
- explain the nature of internal or self control
- differentiate among bureaucratic, clan, and market controls
- list the steps in the MBO process as it might operate between a team leader and a team member

Questions for discussion

1. How does bureaucratic control differ from clan control?
2. What is Douglas McGregor's main point regarding internal control?
3. Can MBO work when there are problems in the relationship between a team leader and a team member?

6.3 What Are Some Useful Organizational Control Systems and Techniques?

Most organizations use a variety of comprehensive and system-wide controls. On the human resources side you are likely to encounter management by objectives and employee discipline. On the operations side you should be familiar with quality control, purchasing and inventory controls, and the use of breakeven analysis.

• Quality control is a foundation of modern management.

If managing for high performance is a theme of the day, *quality control* is one of its most important watchwords. In fact, businesses that want to compete as world-class companies are now expected to have **ISO certification** by the International Standards Organization in Geneva, Switzerland. Any organization that is ISO certified has undergone a rigorous assessment by outside auditors to verify that it meets international quality standards.

You will also often hear the term **total quality management (TQM)**, used to describe operations that make quality an everyday performance objective and strive to always do things right the first time.[17] A foundation of TQM is the quest for **continuous improvement**, meaning that one is always looking for new ways to improve on current performance.[18] The notion is that you can never be satisfied, that something always can and should be improved upon.[19]

The quality theme permeates modern management, and the work of W. Edwards Deming is a cornerstone of the quality movement. His approach to quality emphasizes constant innovation, use of statistical methods, and commitment to training in the fundamentals of quality assurance. His principles are quite straightforward. If you want quality you have to tally defects, analyze and trace them to the sources, make corrections, and keep records of what happens afterwards.[20] A basic tool, for example, is the **control chart** such as that shown in **Figure 6.5**.

ISO certification verifies an organization meets international quality standards.

Total quality management (TQM) commits to quality objectives, continuous improvement, and doing things right the first time.

Continuous improvement involves always searching for new ways to improve work quality and performance.

Control charts are graphical ways of displaying trends so that exceptions to quality standards can be identified

FIGURE 6.5

A Sample Control Chart Showing Upper and Lower Control Limits.

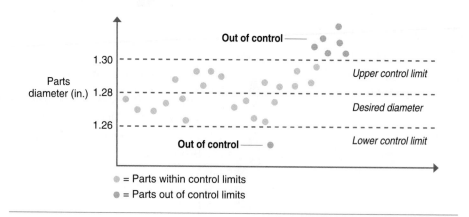

- ○ = Parts within control limits
- ● = Parts out of control limits

Control charts are graphical ways of displaying trends so that exceptions to quality standards can be identified for special attention. In the figure, for example, an upper control limit and a lower control limit specify the allowable tolerances for measurements of a machine part. As long as the manufacturing process produces parts that fall within these limits, things are "in control."

However, as soon as parts start to fall outside the limits, it is clear that something is going wrong that is affecting quality. The process can then be investigated, even shut down, to identify the source of the errors and correct them.

The power of statistics allows sampling to be efficiently used as the basis for decision making and quality management. Many manufacturers now use a **Six Sigma** program, meaning that statistically the firm's quality performance will tolerate no more than 3.4 defects per million units of goods produced or services completed. This translates to a perfection rate of 99.9997%. As tough as it sounds, Six Sigma is a common quality standard for many, if not most, major competitors in our demanding global marketplace.

Six Sigma is a quality standard of 3.4 defects or less per million products or service deliveries.

• Gantt charts and CPM/PERT are used in project management and control.

It might be something personal such as planning an anniversary party for one's parents, preparing for a renovation to your home, or watching the completion of a new student activities building on a campus. What these examples and others like them share in common is that they are relatively complicated tasks with multiple components that have to happen in a certain sequence, and that must be completed by a specified date. In management we call them **projects**, one-time events that are often complex and with unique components and an objective that must be met within a defined time period.

Project management is responsibility for the overall planning, supervision, and control of projects. Basically, a project manager's job is to ensure that a project is well planned and then completed according to plan—on time, within budget, and consistent with objectives. In practice this is often assisted by two techniques known as Gantt charts and CPM/PERT.

A **Gantt chart**, previously introduced in Module 2.3 and depicted in **Figure 2.4**, graphically displays the scheduling of tasks that go into completing a project. This approach was developed in the early twentieth century by Henry Gantt, an industrial engineer, and it has become a mainstay of project management ever since. Because the Gantt chart provides a visual overview of what needs to be done on a project it allows for progress checks to be made at different time intervals. It also assists with event or activity sequencing, making sure that things get accomplished in time for later work to build upon them. One of the biggest problems with projects, for example, is when delays in early activities create problems for later ones.

A companion to the Gantt chart is **CPM/PERT**, a combination of the critical path method and the program evaluation and review technique. Both CPM and PERT are network modeling approaches that originated separately and have now converged. Project planning based on CPM/PERT uses a network chart like the one shown in **Figure 6.6**. Such charts are developed by breaking a service or production project into a series of small sub-activities that each have clear beginning and end points. These points become "nodes" in the charts and the arrows between nodes indicate precedence relationships that show in what order things must be completed. The full diagram shows all the interrelationships that must be coordinated for the entire project to be successfully completed.

Use of CPM/PERT techniques helps project managers track activities, making sure activities happen in the right sequence and on time. If you look at the network in Figure 6.6 you should notice that the time required for each activity can

Projects are one-time activities with many component tasks that must be completed in proper order and according to budget.

Project management makes sure that activities required to complete a project are planned well and accomplished on time.

A **Gantt chart** graphically displays the scheduling of tasks required to complete a project.

CPM/PERT is a combination of the critical path method and the program evaluation and review technique.

FIGURE 6.6

Sample CPM/PERT Network Diagram.

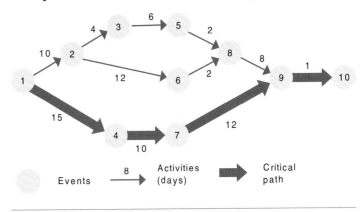

be easily computed and tracked. The pathway from start to conclusion that involves paths with the longest completion times is called the **critical path**. It represents the shortest possible time in which the entire project can be finished, assuming everything goes according to schedule and plans. In the example, the critical path is 37 days.

The **critical path** is the pathway from project start to conclusion that involves activities with the longest completion times.

• Inventory controls help save costs.

Cost control ranks right up there with quality control as an important performance concern. And a very good place to start is with inventory. The goal of **inventory control** is to make sure that any inventory is only big enough to meet one's immediate performance needs. The **economic order quantity** form of inventory control, shown in **Figure 6.7**, automatically orders a fixed number of items every time an inventory level falls to a predetermined point. The order sizes are mathematically calculated to minimize costs of inventory. The best example is your local supermarket. It routinely makes hundreds of daily orders on an economic order quantity basis.

Inventory control ensures that inventory is only big enough to meet immediate needs.

The **economic order quantity** method places new orders when inventory levels fall to predetermined points.

FIGURE 6.7

Inventory Control by Economic Order Quantity, or EOQ.

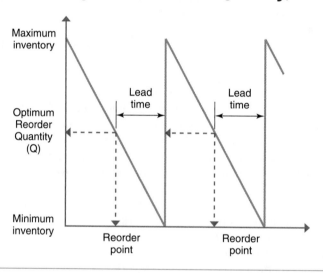

Another and very popular approach to inventory control is **just-in-time scheduling (JIT)**. First made popular by the Japanese, these systems reduce costs and improve workflow by scheduling materials to arrive at a workstation or facility just in time for use. Because JIT nearly eliminates the carrying costs of inventories, it is an important business productivity tool. When a major hurricane was predicted to hit Florida, Wal-Mart's computer database anticipated high demand for, of all things, strawberry Pop-Tarts. Its JIT system delivered them to the stores just in time for the storm.[21]

Just-in-time scheduling (JIT) routes materials to workstations just in time for use.

• Breakeven analysis shows where revenues will equal costs.

When business executives are deliberating new products or projects, a frequent control question is: "What is the **breakeven point**?" A breakeven point is computed using this formula:

$$\text{Breakeven Point} = \text{Fixed Costs} \div (\text{Price} - \text{Variable Costs})$$

Figure 6.8 shows that breakeven occurs at the point where revenues just equal costs. You can also think of it as the point where losses end and profit begins.

Managers rely on **breakeven analysis** to perform "what-if" calculations under different projected cost and revenue conditions. See, for example, if you can calculate some breakeven points. These are the types of cost control analyses that business executives perform every day.

Suppose the proposed target price for a new product is $8 per unit, fixed costs are $10,000, and variable costs are $4 per unit. What sales volume is required to break even? (*Answer:* Breakeven at 2500 units). What happens if you are good at cost control and can keep variable costs to $3 per unit? (*Answer:* Breakeven at 2000 units). Now, suppose you can only produce 1000 units in the beginning and at the original costs. At what price must you sell them to break even? (*Answer:* $14).

• Financial ratios and balanced scorecards strengthen organizational controls.

The pressure is ever present for all organizations to use their financial resources well and to achieve high performance. In business the analysis of a firm's financial performance is an important aspect of managerial control.

At a minimum, managers should be able to understand the following financial performance measures: (1) *liquidity*—ability to generate cash to pay bills; (2) *leverage*—ability to earn more in returns than the cost of debt; (3) *asset management*—ability to use resources efficiently and operate at minimum cost; and (4) *profitability*—ability to earn revenues greater than costs. All of these indicators can be assessed using a variety of financial ratios, including those listed in **Table 6.1**—*Major Financial Ratios for Organizational Control*. Notice in the table that up and down arrows show the preferred directions that a manager would like the ratios to move.

Such financial ratios provide an information framework for historical comparisons within the firm and for external benchmarking relative to industry performance. They can also be used to set financial targets or goals to be shared with employees and tracked to indicate success or failure in their accomplishment. At Civco Medical Instruments, for example, a financial scorecard is distributed monthly to all employees. They always know factually how well the firm is doing. This helps them focus on what they can do differently and better, and strengthens personal commitments to future improvements in the firm's "bottom line."[22]

Speaking of scorecards, "what gets measured happens" the old adage says. And it is true. If an instructor takes class attendance and assigns grades based on it, students tend to come to class; if an employer tracks the number of customers each employee serves per day, employees tend to serve more customers. Do the same principles hold for organizations?

FIGURE 6.8
Breakeven Analysis Helps Managers Make What-If Decisions.

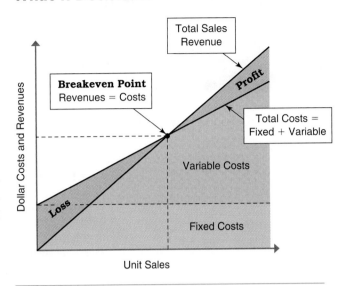

[**TABLE** 6.1]

Major Financial Ratios for Organizational Control

Liquidity—measures ability to meet short-term obligations.

- *Current Ratio* = Current Assets/Current Liabilities
- *Quick Ratio* = Current Assets-Inventory/Current Liabilities
- ↑ Higher is better: You want more assets and fewer liabilities.

Leverage—measures use of debt.

- *Debt Ratio* = Total Debts/Total Assets
- ↓ Lower is better: You want fewer debts and more assets.

Asset Management—measures asset and inventory efficiency.
- *Asset Turnover* = Sales/Total Assets
- *Inventory Turnover* = Sales/Average Inventory
- ↑ Higher is better: You want more sales and fewer assets or lower inventory.

Profitability
- *Net Margin* = Net Profit after Taxes/Sales
- *Return on Assets* (RAO) = Net Profit after Taxes/Total Assets
- *Return on Equity* (ROE) = Net Income/Owner's Equity
- ↑ Higher is better: You want as much profit as possible for sales, assets, and equity.

Like sports teams, organizations perform better when all members know how to keep score.

A **balanced scorecard** measures performance on financial, customer service, internal process, and innovation and learning goals.

Strategic management consultants Robert S. Kaplan and David P. Norton think so. They advocate using what is called the **balanced scorecard** in respect to management control.[23] It gives top managers, as they say, "a fast but comprehensive view of the business." The basic principle is that to do well and to win, you have to keep score.

Developing a balanced scorecard for any organization begins with a clarification of the organization's mission and vision—what it wants to be, and how it wants to be perceived by its key stakeholders. Next, the following questions are used to develop balanced scorecard goals and performance measures.

- *Financial Performance*—To improve financially, how should we appear to our shareholders? Sample goals: survive, succeed, prosper. Sample measures: cash flow, sales growth and operating income, increased market share, and return on equity.
- *Customer Satisfaction*—To achieve our vision, how should we appear to our customers? Sample goals: new products, responsive supply. Sample measures: percentage sales from new products, percentage on-time deliveries.
- *Internal Process Improvement*—To satisfy our customers and shareholders, at what internal business processes should we excel? Sample goals: manufacturing excellence, design productivity, new product introduction. Sample measures: cycle times, engineering efficiency, new product time.
- *Innovation and Learning*—To achieve our vision, how will we sustain our ability to change and improve? Sample goals: technology leadership, time to market. Sample measures: time to develop new technologies, new product introduction time versus competition.

When balanced scorecard measures are taken and routinely recorded for critical managerial review, Kaplan and Norton expect organizations to perform better in those areas. Again, what gets measured happens. Think about the possibilities here. How can the balanced scorecard approach be used by the following organizations: an elementary school, a hospital, a community library, a mayor's office, a fast food restaurant? How do the performance dimensions and indicators vary among these different types of organizations? And if balanced scorecards make sense, why is it that more organizations don't use them?

Study Guide

6.3
What Are Some Useful Organizational Control Systems and Techniques?

Rapid review

- Economic order quantities and just-in-time deliveries are common approaches to inventory cost control.
- The breakeven equation is: Breakeven Point = Fixed Costs ÷ (Price − Variable Costs).
- Breakeven analysis identifies the points where revenues will equal costs under different pricing and cost conditions.
- Financial control of business performance is facilitated by analysis of economic value added, market value added, and a variety of financial ratios, such as those dealing with liquidity, leverage, assets, and profitability.
- The balanced scorecard measures overall organizational performance in respect to four areas: financial, customers, internal processes, innovation.

Terms to define

Balanced scorecard
Breakeven analysis
Breakeven point
Control chart
CPM/PERT
Discipline
Economic order quantity
Gantt chart
Inventory control
ISO certification
Just-in-time scheduling
Six Sigma
Total quality management

Be sure you can

- explain how supply chain management helps organizations control purchasing costs
- explain two common approaches to inventory cost control
- explain the role of continuous improvement in TQM
- state the equation used to calculate a breakeven point
- explain breakeven analysis
- name the common financial ratios used in organizational control
- identify the balanced scorecard components and control questions

Questions for Discussion

1. Can a firm such as Wal-Mart ever go too far in controlling its inventory costs?
2. Is the concept of total quality management out of date?
3. What are the main components in the "balanced scorecard"?

Multiple choice

1. After objectives and standards are set, what step comes next in the control process?

   (a) Measure results.
   (b) Take corrective action.
   (c) Compare results with objectives.
   (d) Modify standards to fit circumstances.

2. When a soccer coach tells her players at the end of a losing game, "You really played well and stayed with the game plan," she is using a/an _____ as a measure of performance.

   (a) input standard
   (b) output standard
   (c) historical comparison
   (d) relative comparison

3. When an automobile manufacturer is careful to purchase only the highest-quality components for use in production, this is an example of an attempt to ensure high performance through _____ control.

   (a) concurrent
   (b) statistical
   (c) inventory
   (d) feedforward

4. Management by exception means _____.

   (a) managing only when necessary
   (b) focusing attention where the need for action is greatest
   (c) the same thing as concurrent control
   (d) the same thing as just-in-time delivery

5. A total quality management program is most likely to be associated with _____.

   (a) EOQ
   (b) continuous improvement
   (c) RFID
   (d) breakeven analysis

6. The _____ chart graphically displays the scheduling of tasks required to complete a project.

   (a) exception   (b) Taylor
   (c) Gantt   (d) after-action

7. When MBO is done right, who does the review of a team member's performance accomplishments?

   (a) the team member
   (b) the team leader
   (c) both the team member and team leader
   (d) the team leader, the team member, and a lawyer

8. A good performance objective is written in such a way that it _____.

   (a) has a flexible timetable
   (b) is general and not too specific
   (c) is impossible to accomplish
   (d) can be easily measured

9. A manager is not living up to the concept of MBO if he or she _____.

   (a) sets performance objectives for subordinates
   (b) stays in touch and tries to support subordinates in their work
   (c) jointly reviews performance results with subordinates
   (d) keeps a written record of subordinates' performance objectives

10. If an organization's top management establishes a target of increasing new hires of minority and female candidates by 15% in the next six months, this is an example of a/an _____ standard for control purposes.

    (a) input
    (b) output
    (c) management by exception
    (d) concurrent

11. When a supervisor working alongside of an employee corrects him or her when a mistake is made, this is an example of _____ control.

    (a) feedforward   (b) external
    (c) concurrent   (d) preliminary

12. In CPM/PERT, "CPM" stands for _____.

    (a) critical path method
    (b) control planning management
    (c) control plan map
    (d) current planning method

13. In a CPM/PERT analysis, the focus is on _____ and the event _____ that link them together with the finished project.

    (a) costs, budgets   (b) activities, sequences
    (c) timetables, budgets   (d) goals, costs

14. When one team member advises another team member that "your behavior is crossing the line in terms of our expectations for workplace civility," she is exercising a form of _____ control over the other's inappropriate behaviors.

    (a) clan   (b) market
    (c) internal   (d) preliminary

15. Among the financial ratios often used for control purposes, Current Assets/Current Liabilities is known as the _____.

(a) debt ratio
(b) net margin
(c) current ratio
(d) inventory turnover ratio

16. In respect to Return on Assets (ROA) and the Debt Ratio, the preferred directions when analyzing them from a control standpoint are _____.

(a) decrease ROA, increase Debt
(b) increase ROA, increase Debt
(c) increase ROA, decrease Debt
(d) decrease ROA, decrease Debt

Short response

17. What type of control is being exercised in the U.S. Army's after-action review?

18. How do quality circles contribute to a TQM program?

19. How can a just-in-time system reduce inventory costs?

20. What four questions could help develop a balanced scorecard for a small business?

Integration & application

21. Put yourself in the position of a management consultant who specializes in MBO. The local Small Business Enterprise Association has asked you to be the speaker for its luncheon next week. The president of the association says that the group would like to learn more about the topic: "How to Use Management by Objectives for Better Planning and Control."

Questions: Your speech will last 15 to 20 minutes. What is the outline for your speech? How will you explain the potential benefits of MBO to this group of small business owners?

Self-Assessment

Internal/External Control

Instructions

Circle either "a" or "b" to indicate the item you most agree with in each pair of the following statements.

1. (a) Promotions are earned through hard work and persistence.
   (b) Making a lot of money is largely a matter of breaks.

2. (a) Many times the reactions of teachers seem haphazard to me.
   (b) In my experience I have noticed that there is usually a direct connection between how hard I study and the grades I get.

3. (a) The number of divorces indicates that more and more people are not trying to make their marriages work.
   (b) Marriage is largely a gamble.

4. (a) It is silly to think that one can really change another person's basic attitudes.
   (b) When I am right I can convince others.

5. (a) Getting promoted is really a matter of being a little luckier than the next guy.
   (b) In our society an individual's future earning power is dependent on his or her ability.

6. (a) If one knows how to deal with people, they are really quite easily led.
   (b) I have little influence over the way other people behave.

7. (a) In my case the grades I make are the results of my own efforts; luck has little or nothing to do with it.
   (b) Sometimes I feel that I have little to do with the grades I get.

8. (a) People such as I can change the course of world affairs if we make ourselves heard.
   (b) It is only wishful thinking to believe that one can really influence what happens in society at large.

9. (a) Much of what happens to me is probably a matter of chance.
   (b) I am the master of my fate.

10. (a) Getting along with people is a skill that must be practiced.
    (b) It is almost impossible to figure out how to please some people.

Scoring

Give yourself 1 point for 1b, 2a, 3a, 4b, 5b, 6a, 7a, 8a, 9b, 10a. Check your total against this rubric: 8–10 =

high *internal* locus of control, 6–7 = moderate *internal* locus of control, 5 = *mixed* locus of control, 3–4 = moderate *external* locus of control, 0–2 = high *external* locus of control.

Interpretation

This instrument offers an impression of your tendency toward an *internal locus of control or external locus of control*. Persons with a high internal locus of control tend to believe they have control over their own destinies. They may be most responsive to opportunities for greater self-control in the workplace. Persons with a high external locus of control tend to believe that what happens to them is largely in the hands of external people or forces. They may be less comfortable with self-control and more responsive to external controls in the workplace.

 For further exploration go to WileyPlus

Case Snapshot

Electronic Arts—Inside Fantasy Sports

Electronic Arts is one of the largest and most profitable third-party video game makers. But despite its dominance in the market, EA's position is beginning to waver. The company's management tried to acquire Take2Interactive, a tough competitor, but failed. Can EA maintain the pole position in a crowded and contentious sports gaming market?

Online Interactive Learning Resources

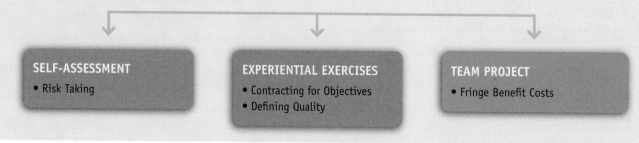

SELF-ASSESSMENT	EXPERIENTIAL EXERCISES	TEAM PROJECT
• Risk Taking	• Contracting for Objectives • Defining Quality	• Fringe Benefit Costs

7 Strategy and Strategic Management

Insight and Hard Work Deliver Results

Passion, Values, and Commitment Make for Strategic Success. Can you name this firm? Its headquarters is in Ventura, California. It sells outdoor clothing and gear, and its products are top quality and high priced. It is known for a commitment to sustainability and respect for the natural environment. Its larger competitors include North Face and Columbia Sportswear. Its earnings are consistently above the industry average. Its workforce is loyal and inspired. And you are as likely to find its founder Yvon Chouinard climbing a mountain in Yosemite or the Himalayas as working in the office. It is also what most analysts would call a strategic success story.

Well, the firm we are talking about is Patagonia, and its mission is clear: "Build the best product, cause no unnecessary harm, use business to inspire and implement solutions to the environmental crisis." Chouinard says: "Most people want to do good things but don't. At Patagonia it's an essential part of your

Trendsetters
Roger W. Ferguson Jr. ready for strategic leadership at TIAA-CREF

News Feed
Clean energy strategy hurt by financial crisis.

Case Snapshot
Dunkin' Donuts—Betting dollars on donuts

life." He leads Patagonia with a personal commitment to sustainability and expects the firm to live up to its responsibilities as a steward of the natural environment. In his words: "So we work steadily to reduce those harms. We use recycled polyester in many of our clothes and only organic, rather than pesticide-intensive, cotton." If you browse online for jobs at Patagonia, you'll find that the company's Web site states: "We're especially interested in people who share our love of the outdoors, our passion for quality and our desire to make a difference."

In strategic management it is important that operating objectives align with and drive the organization toward its mission. Chouinard says he wants to run Patagonia "so that it's here 100 years from now and always makes the best-quality stuff." The objective is growth, but modest, not extreme or uncontrolled, growth. Presently this means growing about 5% per year. He also believes in talent and self-control. "I have an M.B.A. theory of management: Management by Absence. I take off for weeks at a time and never call in. We hire the best people we can and then leave them to do their jobs."

7.1 What Types of Strategies Are Used by Organizations?

Recent changes in the automobile industry have been fast, dramatic, and, hopefully, strategically well done. There was a time when the automakers were quite literally in the driver's seat. Henry Ford once said of his Model T's: "The customer can have any color he wants as long as it's black."[3] Not so anymore in our era of high gasoline prices, tight credit, and lots full of unsold cars. We're part of a shift in the way businesses make plans and appeal to customers. Stephen Haeckel, director of strategic studies at IBM's Advanced Business Institute, has described the shift as "a difference between a bus, which follows a set route, and a taxi, which goes where customers tell it to go."[1]

The bus-taxi analogy should be insightful for managers today, and it can also be applied to your career strategy. Will you be acting like the bus following the set route, or the taxi following opportunities? Don't be afraid to move back and forth between the worlds of business strategy and personal strategy as our discussions in this module develop. The applications go both ways. And just like you and your career progress, success in the business world requires leaders with the abilities to move their organizations forward strategically. "If you want to make a difference as a leader," says *Fast Company* magazine, "you've got to make time for strategy."[2]

• Strategy is a comprehensive plan for achieving competitive advantage.

A **strategy** is a comprehensive action plan that identifies long-term direction for an organization and guides resource utilization to accomplish its goals. Strategy focuses leadership attention on the competitive environment. It represents a "best guess" about what to do to be successful in the face of rivalry and changing conditions.

A good strategy also provides leaders with a plan for allocating and using resources with consistent **strategic intent**. Think of this as having all organizational energies directed toward a unifying and compelling target or goal.[3] Coca-Cola, for example, describes its strategic intent as "To put a Coke within 'arm's reach' of every consumer in the world."

Ultimately, a good strategy helps an organization achieve **competitive advantage**. This means that it is able to outperform rivals. In fact, the best strategies provide *sustainable* competitive advantage. This means that they operate in successful ways that are hard for competitors to imitate. Wal-Mart, for example, is well-known for its abilities to save costs through highly efficient supply chain management. This is made possible by a competitive advantage in information technology utilization; some say its computer system rivals the Department of Defense's in size.[4] This is a tough act for other retailers, even Target, to follow. It's one of the things that helps keep Wal-Mart almost always a step ahead of its competitors.

• Organizations use strategy at the corporate, business, and functional levels.

You can identify strategies at three levels in most organizations. At the top level, **corporate strategy** provides direction and guides resource allocations for the organization as a whole. The *strategic question* at the corporate strategy level is: In what industries and markets should we compete? In large, complex organizations, such as PepsiCo, IBM, and General Electric, decisions on corporate

A **strategy** is a comprehensive plan guiding resource allocation to achieve long-term organization goals.

Strategic intent focuses organizational energies on achieving a compelling goal.

A **competitive advantage** means operating in successful ways that are difficult to imitate.

A **corporate strategy** sets long-term direction for the total enterprise.

strategy identify how the firm intends to compete across multiple industries, businesses, and markets.

Business strategy focuses on the strategic intent for a single business unit or product line. The *strategic question* at the business strategy level is: How are we going to compete for customers within this industry and in this market? Typical business strategy decisions include choices about product and service mix, facilities locations, new technologies, and the like. For smaller, single-business enterprises, business strategy is the corporate strategy.

Functional strategy guides activities to implement higher-level business and corporate strategies. This level of strategy unfolds within a specific functional area such as marketing, manufacturing, finance, and human resources. The *strategic question* for functional strategies is: How can we best utilize resources within the function to support implementation of the business strategy? Answers to this question involve a wide variety of practices and initiatives to improve things such as operating efficiency, product quality, customer service, or innovativeness.

• Growth and diversification strategies focus on expansion.

At the levels of corporate and business strategy you will often read and hear about organizations trying to get bigger.[5] They are pursuing **growth strategies** to increase the size and scope of current operations. In some industries, such as fast food, companies view growth as necessary for long-run profitability. You should probably question this assumption and probe deeper right from the start. Is growth always the best path? And if the choice is to grow, how should it be accomplished?

A strategy of growth through **concentration** seeks expansion within an existing business area, one in which the firm has experience and presumably expertise. You don't see McDonald's trying to grow by getting involved in bookstores or gasoline stations; it keeps opening more restaurants at home and abroad. You don't see Wal-Mart trying to grow by buying a high-end department store chain or even opening Wal-Mart convenience stores; it keeps opening new stores at the rate of 500+ per year. These are classic growth by concentration strategies.

A distinctly different strategy is growth through **diversification**. In this case, expansion occurs by entering new business areas. As you might expect, there is more risk to diversification because the firm may be moving outside its existing areas of competency. One way to moderate the risk is to grow through *related diversification*, expanding into similar or complementary new businesses areas. PepsiCo did this when it purchased Tropicana. Although Tropicana's fruit juices were new to Pepsi, the business is related to its expertise in the beverages industry.

Trendsetters 👤

Roger W. Ferguson Jr. Ready for Strategic Leadership at TIAA-CREF

Leading a huge financial institution with over $70 billion under its management is a big challenge. Doing so when the economy is in recession and the entire financial services industry is in crisis is something else. But Roger W. Ferguson Jr. is well prepared and ready for the job. In 2009, *Black Enterprise* magazine listed him as one of the "100 most powerful African Americans in corporate America."

Ferguson has taken over an organization whose bureaucracy and systems are often criticized by financial advisors. But his experience and capabilities seem well up to the task. With a PhD in economics, his prior experience includes vice chairman of the Board of Governors of the Federal Reserve System and chairman of Swiss Re America Holding Corp. And when U.S. President Barack Obama set up a new Economic Advisory Board and charged its members "to meet regularly so that I can hear different ideas and sharpen my own, and seek counsel that is candid and informed by the wider world," Roger W. Ferguson Jr. was chosen as a member.

Ferguson leads a firm that proudly proclaims "Diversify isn't just smart financial advice. It's a sound hiring policy as well." The firm includes "promoting diversity" in its mission, and states the belief that "all benefit from a work environment that fosters respect, integrity and opportunity for people from a wide variety of backgrounds."

It will be up to Ferguson to further build on that tradition. In 1997, with the appointment of Herbert M. Allison Jr., TIAA-CREF became the first of America's 100 largest companies to hire an African American as CEO. Twelve years later it still stands out from the pack. Ferguson joins only six other African American executives serving as CEOs of Fortune 500 companies.

A **business strategy** identifies how a division or strategic business unit will compete in its product or service domain.

A **functional strategy** guides activities within one specific area of operations.

A **growth strategy** involves expansion of the organization's current operations.

Growth through **concentration** means expansion within an existing business area.

In **diversification**, expansion occurs by entering new business areas.

Some firms get involved in *unrelated diversification* that pursues growth in entirely new business areas. Did you know, for example, that Exxon once owned Izod? Does that make sense? Can you see why growth through unrelated diversification might cause problems? In fact, research is quite clear that business performance may decline with too much unrelated diversification.[6]

Diversification can also take the form of **vertical integration**. This is where a business acquires its suppliers *(backward vertical integration)* or its distributors *(forward vertical integration)*. Backward vertical integration has been a historical pattern in the automobile industry as firms purchased parts suppliers, although you'll find that recent trends are to reverse this. In beverages, both Coca-Cola and PepsiCo have pursued forward vertical integration by purchasing some of their major bottlers.

> Growth through **vertical integration** is by acquiring suppliers or distributors.

• Restructuring and divestiture strategies focus on consolidation.

When organizations run into performance difficulties, perhaps brought about by too much growth and diversification, these problems have to be solved. A **retrenchment strategy** seeks to correct weaknesses by making radical changes to current ways of operating.

The most extreme form of retrenchment is **liquidation**, where a business closes down and sells its assets to pay creditors. A less extreme and more common form of retrenchment is **restructuring**. This involves making major changes to cut costs, gain short-term efficiencies, and buy time for new strategies to improve future success.

When a firm is in desperate financial condition and unable to pay its bills, a situation faced by Chrysler and General Motors during the financial crisis, restructuring by **Chapter 11 bankruptcy** is an option under U.S. law. The intent is to protect the firm from creditors while its management reorganizes things in an attempt to restore solvency. The goal is for the firm to emerge from bankruptcy and resume operations as a stronger and profitable business.

One of the restructuring approaches often in the news lately is **downsizing**, cutting down the size of operations and reducing the workforce.[7] When you learn of organizations reducing budgets or staffs by across-the-board cuts, however, you might be a bit skeptical. Research has shown that downsizing is more successful when cutbacks are done selectively, in ways that focus on key performance objectives.[8]

Finally, restructuring by **divestiture** involves selling parts of the organization to refocus on core competencies, cut costs, and improve operating efficiency. This type of retrenchment often occurs when organizations have become overdiversified. An example is eBay's purchase for $3.1 billion of the Internet telephone service Skype. The expected synergies between Skype and eBay's online auction business never developed, and by the time a divestment decision was made, Skype's estimated sale value was just over $1 billion.[9]

> A **retrenchment strategy** changes operations to correct weaknesses.

> **Liquidation** is where a business closes and sells its assets to pay creditors.

> **Restructuring** reduces the scale or mix of operations.

> **Chapter 11 bankruptcy** protects an insolvent firm from creditors during a period of reorganization to restore profitability.

> **Downsizing** decreases the size of operations.

> **Divestiture** sells off parts of the organization to refocus attention on core business areas.

• Global strategies focus on international business initiatives.

International business offers a variety of growth opportunities, but they can be engaged in quite different ways.[10] A firm pursuing a **globalization strategy** tends to view the world as one large market. With that in mind, it tries to advertise and sell standard products for use everywhere. For example, Gillette sells and advertises its latest razors around the world.

Firms pursuing a *multidomestic strategy* try to customize products and advertising to fit local cultures and needs. Bristol Myers, Procter & Gamble, and

> A **globalization strategy** adopts standardized products and advertising for use worldwide.

Unilever, for example, all vary their products according to consumer preferences in different countries and cultures. And, eBay links its auction business with local needs and cultures by buying into e-commerce firms operating in different countries, such as Korea's Gmarket, Inc.[11]

A third approach is the *transnational strategy*, which seeks a balance between efficiencies in global operations and responsiveness to local markets. You should recall that a transnational firm tries to operate without a strong national identity, hoping to blend instead with the global economy. Firms using a transnational strategy try to fully utilize business resources and tap customer markets worldwide. Ford, for example, draws upon design, manufacturing, and distribution expertise all over the world to build car platforms. These are then modified within regions to build cars that meet local tastes.

• Cooperative strategies find opportunities in alliances and partnerships.

One of the trends today is toward more cooperation among organizations, such as the joint ventures that are a common form of international business. They are one among many forms of **strategic alliances** in which two or more organizations join together in partnership to pursue an area of mutual interest. One way to cooperate strategically is through outsourcing alliances, contracting to purchase important services from another organization. Many organizations today, for example, are outsourcing their IT function to firms such as EDS, Infosys, and IBM in the belief that these services are better provided by a firm that specializes and maintains its expertise in this area.

Cooperation in the supply chain also takes the form of supplier alliances, in which preferred supplier relationships guarantee a smooth and timely flow of quality supplies among alliance partners. Another common approach today is cooperation in distribution alliances, in which firms join together to accomplish product or services sales and distribution.

The term often used to describe cooperation strategies that involve strategic alliances with competitors is **co-opetition**. It applies to situations in which competitors work cooperatively with rivals on projects that can benefit both parties. The notion of co-opetition reflects what scholars M. Brandenburger and Barry J. Nalebuff call a "revolution mindset" in which the executive recognizes that business can be conducted on a playing field of both competitors and potential cooperating partners.[12] This shifts strategic decision making away from a win–lose game with a fixed pie of possible returns to a new one of collaboration to

News Feed

Clean Energy Strategy Hurt by Financial Crisis

There is a lot of buzz these days about going "green" in the many ways that we use and produce power. Wind power, solar power, tidal power, and more are in the news, and when it comes to automobiles, electric cars are certainly part of the buzz. Indeed, you would think that new start-ups would be popping up all over to get into the market and ride the momentum of sustainability and alternative energy.

For awhile the Norwegian firm Think Global AS was a top player in the electric car industry. With venture capital and 350 state-of-the-art plug-in cars to show the firm's potential, it was on track to produce 10,000 vehicles in its first full production year. But then the financial crisis hit. Just as Think Global was trying to expand, economies worldwide went into fast and furious contraction. And as economies turned down, venture capital disappeared, including the $60–100,000 million of new funds Think Global founders were counting on to get through that first manufacturing cycle. CEO Richard Canny said: "We were so close to break-even and being cash-flow positive." Instead they ended up declaring bankruptcy. Canny lamented: "It doesn't seem right that the traditional auto companies are getting massive public money to stave off their decline, while newcomers in the electric-car space are being starved of capital."

At the same time that Think Global was going out of business, other electric car start-ups were still hanging on, including REVA Electric Car Company in the cheap mini-car market and Fisker Automotive in the luxury high-end price range. Yet the start-ups were all hurt as the financial crisis, government pressure, and government monies helped the established auto firms reinvigorate their electric car options. And green cars weren't the only casualties of the crisis. Alternative energy start-ups involving such things as wind farms and solar panel parks suffered as well.

Reflect and React

Is it fair that the large automakers get government support while start-up firms such as Think Global, offering truly new and green car alternatives, are left to suffer in stressed venture capital markets? Was Think trying to move too fast? Was its problem only bad timing? Is bankruptcy a strategy that might actually help the firm get back on track for future success?

In a **strategic alliance**, organizations join together in partnership to pursue an area of mutual interest.

Co-opetition is the strategy of working with rivals on projects of mutual benefit.

An **e-business strategy** strategically uses the Internet to gain competitive advantage.

A **B2B business strategy** uses IT and Web portals to link organizations vertically in supply chains.

A **B2C business strategy** uses IT and Web portals to link businesses with customers.

find ways of making the pie bigger for everyone. For example, Red Hat sells Linux software and so does IBM, but the two firms cooperate on aspects of Linux development. The idea is that better software creates a larger market for Linux that will benefit both firms.[13]

• E-business strategies focus on using the Internet for business success.

Without a doubt, one of the most frequently asked questions these days for the business executive is: "What is your **e-business strategy**?" This is the strategic use of the Internet to gain competitive advantage.[14] And, in fact, there are several different ways that businesses can try to make money through the Internet. **Table 7.1**—*Web-Based Business Models*, lists some common options along with examples of each.[15]

Among the terms you will hear used in this regard are B2B (business-to-business) and B2C (business-to-customer) applications. **B2B business strategies** use IT and Web portals to vertically link organizations with members of their supply chains. For example, Dell Computer sets up special Web site services that allow its major corporate customers to manage their accounts online. Wal-Mart links its suppliers to the firm's information systems so they can manage inventories for their own products electronically.

As individuals, we often do business with firms using **B2C business strategies**, using IT and Web portals to link with customers. Whenever you buy a music download from Apple's iTunes Store, order a book from Amazon.com, or shop online for a new Dell notebook PC, you are the "C" in a B2C strategy. And if you are looking for benchmarking standards for excellence, these firms are good starting points.

[**TABLE** 7.1]

Web-Based Business Models

Advertising Model
Providing free information or services and then generating revenues from paid advertising to viewers (e.g., Yahoo!, Google)

Brokerage Model
Bringing buyers and sellers together for online business transactions and taking a percentage from the sales (e.g., CarsDirect, eBay, Priceline)

Infomediary Model
Providing free service in exchange for collecting information on users and selling it to other businesses (e.g., Epinions, Yelp)

Merchant Model
E-tailing or selling products direct to customers through the Web (e.g., Amazon, Netflix)

Referral Model
Providing free listings and getting referral fees from online merchants for directing potential customers to them (e.g., Shopzilla, PriceGrabber)

Subscription Model
Selling access to high-value content through a subscription Web site (e.g., The Wall Street Journal Interactive, Consumer Reports Online)

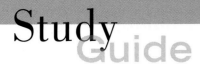
Study Guide

7.1
What Types of Strategies Are Used by Organizations?

Rapid review

- A strategy is a comprehensive plan that sets long-term direction for an organization and guides resource allocations to achieve sustainable competitive advantage, being able to operate in ways that outperform the competition.
- Corporate strategy sets the direction for an entire organization; business strategy sets the direction for a large business unit or product division; functional strategy sets the direction within business functions.
- Organizations follow growth strategies that expand existing business areas through concentration, or pursue new ones by related or unrelated diversification.
- Organizations follow retrenchment strategies that allow periods of consolidation where operations are streamlined for better performance through restructuring and divestiture.
- Global strategies pursue international business opportunities by multidomestic and transnational approaches.
- E-business strategies use information technology and the Internet to pursue competitive advantage, with popular forms being B2B and B2C.

Terms to define

B2B business strategy
B2C business strategy
Business strategy
Chapter 11 bankruptcy
Competitive advantage
Concentration
Co-opetition
Corporate strategy
Diversification
Divestiture
Downsizing
E-business strategy
Functional strategy
Globalization strategy
Growth strategy
Liquidation
Restructuring
Retrenchment strategy
Strategic intent
Strategy
Strategic alliance
Vertical integration

Be sure you can

- differentiate strategy, strategic intent, and competitive advantage
- differentiate corporate, business, and functional levels of strategy
- list and explain major types of growth and diversification strategies
- list and explain restructuring and divestiture strategies
- explain alernative global strategies
- differentiate B2B and B2C as e-business strategies

Questions for discussion

1. With things changing so fast today, is it really possible for a business to achieve "sustainable" competitive advantage?
2. Why is growth such a popular business strategy?
3. Is it good news or bad news for investors when a business announces that it is restructuring?

7.2 How Are Strategies Formulated and Implemented?

The late and great management guru Peter Drucker once said: "The future will not just happen if one wishes hard enough. It requires decision—now. It imposes risk—now. It requires action—now. It demands allocation of resources, and above all, of human resources—now. It requires work—now."[16] Drucker's views fit squarely with the module subtitle: Insights and hard work deliver results. Now let's talk a bit more about the hard work of strategic management.

• The strategic management process formulates and implements strategies.

Strategic management is the process of formulating and implementing strategies.

Strategy formulation is the process of creating strategies.

Strategy implementation is the process of putting strategies into action.

Figure 7.1 shows **strategic management** as the process of formulating and implementing strategies to accomplish long-term goals and sustain competitive advantage. **Strategy formulation** is the process of crafting strategy. It involves assessing the organization and environment to plan new strategies to deliver future competitive advantage. **Strategy implementation** is the process of putting strategies into action. It involves leading and activating the entire organization to put strategies to work.

FIGURE 7.1
What Are the Steps in the Strategic Management Process?

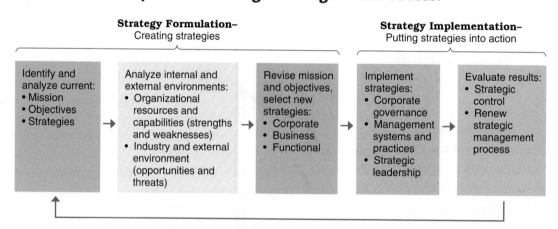

The strategic management process involves responsibilities for both formulating and implementing organizational strategies. The process begins by analyzing mission and objectives to set a baseline for strategy formulation. Then organizational resources and capabilities are analyzed, and strategies are crafted at corporate, business, and functional levels. Finally, the strategies must be put into action. This requires strategic leadership to ensure that all organizational resources and systems fully support strategy implementation.

Can you see that both activities are necessary, that success is only possible when strategies are both well formulated and well implemented? Competitive advantage in business or success in a career doesn't just happen; it is created when great strategies are implemented to full advantage.

• Strategy formulation begins with the organization's mission and objectives.

The **mission** is the organization's reason for existence in society.

Strategy formulation begins with review and clarification of organizational mission and objectives.[17] You should remember that the **mission** describes the purpose of an organization, its reason for existence in society.[18] The best organizations have clear missions that communicate a sense of direction and motivate members to work hard in their behalf.[19] They also link these missions with well-chosen **operating objectives** that serve as short-term guides to performance.[20]

A sampling of typical business operating objectives includes: profitability, cost efficiency, market share, product quality, innovation, and social responsibility. When mission and objectives are clear, a strategic planning baseline is established. From here, the next step in strategy formulation is to understand how well the organization is currently positioned to fulfill its mission and objectives.

Operating objectives are specific results that organizations try to accomplish.

• SWOT analysis identifies strengths, weaknesses, opportunities, and threats.

A **SWOT analysis** involves a detailed examination of organizational *strengths* and *weaknesses*, and environmental *opportunities* and *threats*. As **Figure 7.2** shows, the results of this examination can be portrayed in a straightforward and very useful planning matrix.

Tips to Remember
How to Assess Key Operating Objectives of Organizations

When executives meet to discuss how well an organization is doing, these operating objectives are often under scrutiny.

- *Profits*—operating with revenues greater than costs
- *Cost efficiency*—operating with low costs; finding ways to lower costs
- *Market share*—having a solid and sustainable pool of customers
- *Product quality*—producing goods and services that satisfy customers
- *Talented workforce*—attracting and retaining high quality employees
- *Innovation*—using new ideas to improve operations and products
- *Social responsibility*—earning the respect of multiple stakeholders

FIGURE 7.2
What Does a SWOT Analysis Try to Discover?

A **SWOT analysis** examines organizational strengths and weaknesses, and environmental opportunities and threats.

Internal Assessment of the Organization

What are our strengths?
- Manufacturing efficiency?
- Skilled workforce?
- Good market share?
- Strong financing?
- Superior reputation?

What are our weaknesses?
- Outdated facilities?
- Inadequate R & D?
- Obsolete technologies?
- Weak management?
- Past planning failures?

SWOT Analysis

What are our opportunities?
- Possible new markets?
- Strong economy?
- Weak market rivals?
- Emerging technologies?
- Growth of existing market?

What are our threats?
- New competitors?
- Shortage of resources?
- Changing market tastes?
- New regulations?
- Substitute products?

External Assessment of the Environment

The SWOT analysis is a way of identifying organizational strengths and weaknesses, and environmental opportunities and threats. It is a structured process that forces strategists to discover key facts and conditions with potential consequences for performance. It also organizes this information in a structured manner that is useful for making strategy decisions. Managers using a SWOT analysis should be looking for organizational strengths that can be leveraged as core competencies to make future gains, as well as environmental opportunities that can be exploited.

A **core competency** is a special strength that gives an organization a competitive advantage.

When looking at the organization's strengths, one goal is to find among them **core competencies**. These are special strengths that the organization has or does exceptionally well in comparison with its competitors. When an organization's core competencies are unique and costly for others to imitate, they become potential sources of competitive advantage.[21]

Organizational weaknesses, of course, are the flip side of the picture. Although it might take some extra discipline to do it, they must also be investigated and understood to develop a realistic perspective on the organization's capabilities. The same discipline holds when examining conditions in the environment. It's not only the opportunities that count—such as new markets, a strong economy, weak competitors, and emerging technologies. The threats must be considered also—perhaps the emergence of new competitors, resource scarcities, changing customer tastes, and new government regulations.

And again, don't forget the career planning implications. If you were to analyze your strategic readiness for career advancement right now, what would your personal SWOT look like?

• Porter's five forces model examines industry attractiveness.

Harvard scholar and consultant Michael Porter says, "A company without a strategy is willing to try anything."[22] With a good strategy in place, by contrast, the organization can focus its entire resources on its overall goal. Porter goes on to suggest that managers must craft strategy with a good understanding of the industry within which they are competing. He offers the "five forces" model in **Figure 7.3**, with a focus on what he calls industry attractiveness.

> Force 1: *Competitors*—intensity of rivalry among firms in the industry.
> Force 2: *New entrants*—threats of new competitors entering the market.
> Force 3: *Suppliers*—the bargaining power of suppliers.
> Force 4: *Customers*—the bargaining power of buyers.
> Force 5: *Substitutes*—threats of substitute products or services.[23]

FIGURE 7.3

Porter's Five Forces Model of Industry Attractiveness.

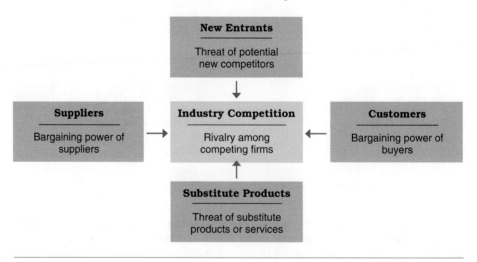

Can you recognize how Porter's five forces influence industry attractiveness? An unattractive industry will have intense competitive rivalries, substantial threats in the form of possible new entrants and substitute products, and powerful suppliers and buyers who dominate any bargaining with the firm. As you might expect, this is a very challenging environment for strategy formulation.

A very attractive industry will have little existing competition, few threats from new entrants or substitutes, and low bargaining power among suppliers and buyers. Obviously, strategy formulation under these conditions should be less of a problem.

• Porter's competitive strategies model examines business or product strategies.

Once industry forces are understood, Porter's attention shifts to how a business or its products can be strategically positioned relative to competitors. He believes that competitive strategies can be built around differentiation, cost leadership, and focus.

A **differentiation strategy** seeks competitive advantage through uniqueness. Organizations try to develop goods and services that are clearly different from those of the competition. The strategic objective is to attract customers who stay loyal to the firm's products and lose interest in its competitors.

Success with a differentiation strategy depends on customer perceptions of product quality and uniqueness. This requires organizational strengths in marketing, research and development, and creativity. An example is Polo Ralph Lauren, retailer of upscale classic fashions and accessories. In Ralph Lauren's words, "Polo redefined how American style and quality is perceived. Polo has always been about selling quality products by creating worlds and inviting our customers to be part of our dream."[24] If you've seen any Polo ads in magazines or television, you'll know that the company aggressively markets this perception.

A **cost leadership strategy** seeks competitive advantage by operating with lower costs than competitors. This allows organizations to make profits while selling products or services at low prices their competitors can't match. The objective is to continuously improve the operating efficiencies of production, distribution, and other organizational systems.

Success with the cost leadership strategy requires tight cost and managerial controls, as well as products or services that are easy to create and distribute. This is what might be called the "Wal-Mart" strategy: do everything you can to keep costs so low that you can offer customers the lowest prices and still make a reasonable profit. You can see this strategy in many places. In financial services, for example, the Vanguard Group keeps costs low and offers mutual funds to customers with minimum fees. Its Web site proudly proclaims that Vanguard's low average expense ratios allow investors to "keep more of what you earn."[25] In personal computers Dell and HP face increasingly strong competition from Acer, whose strategy *Business Week* describes as using a "bare-boned cost structure to get extremely aggressive on price."[26]

Porter's generic *focus strategy* concentrates attention on a special market segment, with the objective of serving its needs better than anyone else. It can be pursued in two forms. In the **focused differentiation strategy**, the organization concentrates on one special market segment and tries to offer customers in that segment a unique product. In the **focused cost leadership strategy**, the organization concentrates on one special market segment and tries in that segment to be the provider with lowest costs. Low-fare airlines, for example, offer heavily discounted fares and "no frills" service for customers who want to travel point-to-point for the lowest prices.

Can you apply these four competitive strategies to an actual situation, say, alternative sodas in the soft-drink industry? Porter would begin by asking and answering two questions for each soda: What is the market scope—is the target market for the drink broad or narrow? What is the potential source of competitive advantage—is it in a lower price or in product uniqueness?

A **differentiation strategy** offers products that are unique and different from the competition.

A **cost leadership strategy** seeks to operate with lower costs than competitors.

Porter's competitive strategies

- *Differentiation*—make products that are unique and different.
- *Cost leadership*—produce at lower cost and sell at lower price.
- *Focused differentiation*—use differentiation and target needs of a special market.
- *Focused cost leadership*—use cost leadership and target needs of a special market.

A **focused differentiation strategy** offers a unique product to a special market segment.

A **focused cost leadership strategy** seeks the lowest costs of operations within a special market segment.

FIGURE 7.4

What Are the Strategic Options in Porter's Competitive Strategies Model?

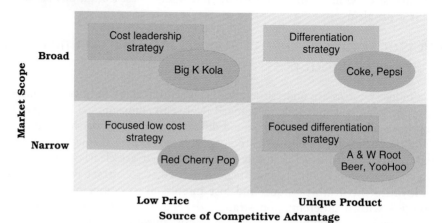

Porter's competitive strategies model asks two basic questions to identify alternative business and product strategies. First, what is the market scope—broad or narrow? Second, what is the expected source of competitive advantage—lower price or product uniqueness? The four possible combinations of answers result in differentiation, cost leadership, focused differentiation, and focused cost leadership strategies. The figure uses examples from the soft drink industry to show how these strategies can be used for different products.

Figure 7.4 shows how answers to these questions might strategically position some soft drinks with which you might be familiar. The makers of Coke and Pepsi follow a differentiation strategy. They spend billions on advertising to convince consumers that their products are high quality and uniquely desirable. Big K Kola, a Kroger product, sells as a cheaper alternative. In order to make a profit at the lower selling price, Kroger must follow a cost leadership strategy.

What about a can of A & W Root Beer or a can of Vanilla Coke? In Porter's model they represent a strategy of focused differentiation—products with unique tastes for customers wanting quality brands. This is quite different from the strategy behind your local convenience store's version of "Red Cherry Pop." This is a classic case of focused cost leadership—a product with a unique taste for customers who want a low price.

• Portfolio planning examines strategies across multiple businesses or products.

As you might expect, strategic management gets quite complicated for companies that operate multiple businesses selling many different products and services. A good example is the global conglomerate General Electric. The firm owns a portfolio of diverse businesses ranging from jet engines, to capital services, to medical systems, to power systems, and even cable television. CEO Jeffrey Immelt faces a difficult strategic question all the time: How should GE's resources be allocated across this mix, or portfolio, of businesses?[27]

If you think about it, Immelt's strategic management problem at GE is similar to what we face with managing our personal assets. How, for example, do you manage a mix of cash, stocks, bonds, and real estate investments? What do you increase, what do you sell, and what do you hold? These are the same questions that Immelt and other executives ask; they are *portfolio-planning* questions, and they have major strategic implications. Shouldn't they be made systematically, rather than haphazardly?[28]

The Boston Consulting Group has proposed a strategic planning approach shown in **Figure 7.5** and known as the **BCG Matrix**. This portfolio-planning framework asks managers to analyze business and product strategies based on the industry or market growth rate and the market share held by the firm.[29]

The **BCG Matrix** analyzes business opportunities according to market growth rate and market share.

FIGURE 7.5

In What Ways Is the BCG Matrix Useful in Strategic Planning?

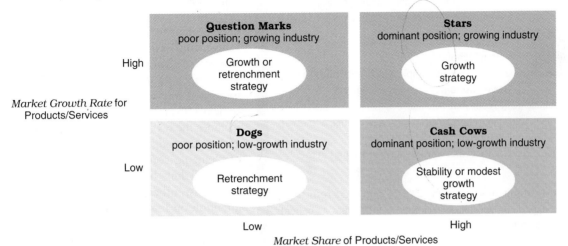

The BCG Matrix is useful in situations where managers must make strategic decisions that allocate scarce organizational resources among multiple and competing uses. This is a typical situation for organizations that have a range of businesses or products. The BCG Matrix sorts businesses or products into four strategic types (Dogs, Stars, Question Marks, and Cash Cows), based on market shares held and market growth rates. Specific master strategies are recommended for each strategic type.

Stars in the BCG Matrix have high-market shares in high-growth markets. They produce large profits through substantial penetration of expanding markets. The preferred strategy for stars is growth; the BCG Matrix recommends making further resource investments in them. Stars are not only high performers in the present, they offer future potential to do the same or even more so.

Cash cows have high-market shares in low-growth markets. They produce large profits and a strong cash flow, but with little upside potential. Because the markets offer little growth opportunity, the preferred strategy for cash cows is stability or modest growth. Like real dairy cows, the BCG Matrix advises firms to "milk" these businesses to generate cash for investing in other more promising areas.

Question marks have low-market shares in high-growth markets. Although they may not generate much profit at the moment, the upside potential is there because of the growing markets. Question marks make for difficult strategic decision making. The BCG Matrix recommends targeting only the most promising question marks for growth, while retrenching those that are less promising.

Dogs have low-market shares in low-growth markets. They produce little if any profit, and they have low potential for future improvement. The preferred strategy for dogs is straightforward: retrenchment by divestiture.

• Strategic leadership ensures strategy implementation and control.

A discussion of the corporate history on Patagonia Inc.'s Web site includes this statement: "During the past thirty years, we've made many mistakes but we've never lost our way for very long."[30] Not only is the firm being honest in its public information, it is also communicating an important point about the strategic

Stay Tuned ⓔ

Cost-Cutting Abounds When Times Get Tough.

How do companies try to deal with recession? A survey of 245 large U.S. firms indicates that the alternatives executives are pursuing in face of an economic crisis involve more than employee layoffs.

- 13% expect to cut the size of their workforces within 12 months.
- 24% plan to raise employee contributions to health insurance.
- 12% plan to reduce 401(K) contributions.
- 18% will cut back tuition reimbursement, subsidized dining, and other perks.
- 50% expect to increase cost-cutting with any further declines in the economy.

Along with the cost-cutting, however, some 29% of employers resorting to layoffs are also expanding severance packages in such areas as benefits coverage and job-search help.

Your Thoughts?

Layoffs and other forms of cost-cutting make the news everyday during recessions and financial crises, but do we read and hear as much about executive pay cuts? How broadly is the "pain" of cost-cutting shared in the organizational pyramid? Are there ways to cut costs and still be considered a good employer?

Strategic leadership inspires people to implement organizational strategies.

Strategic control makes sure strategies are well implemented and that poor strategies are scrapped or changed.

Self-Assessment

This is a good point to complete the self-assessment *"Facts and Inferences"* found on page 153.

management process; mistakes will be made. No matter how thorough or well intended the analysis, the chance exists that one's strategic choices might be wrong.

In our dynamic and often-uncertain environment, in fact, the premium is on **strategic leadership**—the capability to inspire people to successfully engage in a process of continuous change, performance enhancement, as well as implementation and control of organizational strategies.[31] In order to excel at strategic management, a leader must have the ability to not only make strategic choices, but to learn from any mistakes made. This includes the willingness to exercise control and make modifications to meet the needs of changing conditions. At times the lessons will link back to poor selection of strategies; other times they will focus attention on implementation failures.

In this respect, one of the big lessons learned in studying how business firms fared in the recent economic crisis is that a strategic leader has to maintain **strategic control**. This means that the CEO and other top managers should be always in touch with the strategy, how well it is being implemented, whether the strategy is generating performance success or failure, and the need for the strategy to be tweaked or changed.

Michael Porter, whose five forces and competitive strategy models for strategic management were discussed earlier, places a great emphasis on the role of CEO as chief strategist. He describes the task in the following ways.[32]

- *A strategic leader has to be the guardian of trade-offs.* It is the leader's job to make sure that the organization's resources are allocated in ways consistent with the strategy. This requires the discipline to sort through many competing ideas and alternatives to stay on course and not get sidetracked.
- *A strategic leader also needs to create a sense of urgency.* The leader must not allow the organization and its members to grow slow and complacent. Even when doing well, the leader keeps the focus on getting better and being alert to conditions that require adjustments to the strategy.
- A strategic leader needs to make sure that everyone understands the strategy. Unless strategies are understood, the daily tasks and contributions of people lose context and purpose. Everyone might work very hard, but without alignment to strategy, the impact is dispersed and fails to advance common goals.
- *A strategic leader must be a teacher.* It is the leader's job to teach the strategy and make it a "cause," says Porter. In order for strategy to work, it must become an ever-present commitment throughout the organization. This means that a strategic leader must be a great communicator. Everyone must understand the strategy and how it makes the organization different from others.

Study Guide

7.2
How Are Strategies Formulated and Implemented?

Rapid review

- Strategic management is the process of formulating and implementing strategies to achieve sustainable competitive environment.
- A SWOT analysis sets a foundation for strategy formulation by systematically assessing organizational strengths and weaknesses, and environmental opportunities and threats.
- Porter's five forces model analyzes industry attractiveness in terms of competitors, new entrants, substitute products, and the bargaining powers of suppliers and buyers.
- Porter's competitive strategies model examines how business and product strategies are created around differentiation (distinguishing one's products from the competition), cost leadership (minimizing costs relative to the competition), and focus (concentrating on a special market segment).
- The BCG Matrix is a portfolio-planning approach that classifies businesses or product lines as stars, cash cows, question marks, or dogs, and associates each with a suggested master strategy.
- Strategic leadership is the responsibility for activating people and all organizational resources and systems to continually pursue and fully accomplish strategy implementation.

Terms to define

BCG Matrix
Core competencies
Cost leadership strategy
Differentiation strategy
Focused cost leadership strategy
Focused differentiation strategy
Mission
Operating objectives
Strategic control
Strategic management
Strategic leadership
Strategy formulation
Strategy implementation
SWOT analysis

Be sure you can

- describe the strategic management process
- explain Porter's five forces model
- explain Porter's competitive strategies model
- describe the purpose and use of the BCG Matrix
- explain the responsibilities of strategic leadership

Questions for discussion

1. Can an organization have a good strategy but a poor sense of mission?
2. Would a monopoly receive a perfect score for industry attractiveness in Porter's five forces model?
3. Does the BCG Matrix oversimplify a complex strategic management problem?

[Test Prep]

1. Which is the best first question to ask when starting the strategic management process?

    (a) "What is our mission?"
    (b) "How well are we currently doing?"
    (c) "How can we get where we want to be?"
    (d) "Why aren't we doing better?"

2. The ability of a firm to consistently outperform its rivals is called _____.

    (a) vertical integration
    (b) competitive advantage
    (c) strategic intent
    (d) core competency

3. General Electric is a complex conglomerate that owns both NBC Universal and GE Healthcare, firms operating in very different industries. The strategies pursued for each of these units within GE would best be called _____-level strategies.

    (a) corporate   (b) business
    (c) functional   (d) transnational

4. An organization that is downsizing by cutting staff to reduce costs can be described as pursuing a _____ strategy.

    (a) liquidation   (b) divestiture
    (c) retrenchment   (d) stability

5. When you buy music downloads online, the firm selling them to you is engaging in which type of e-business strategy?

    (a) B2C   (b) B2B
    (c) HTTP   (d) WWW

6. A _____ in the BCG Matrix would have a high-market share in a low-growth market.

    (a) dog   (b) cash cow
    (c) question mark   (d) star

7. In Porter's five forces model, which of the following conditions is most favorable from the standpoint of industry attractiveness?

    (a) many competitive rivals
    (b) many substitute products
    (c) low bargaining power of suppliers
    (d) few barriers to entry

8. If Google's top management were to announce that the firm was going to buy Federal Express, this would indicate a strategy of _____.

    (a) diversification
    (b) concentration

    (c) horizontal integration
    (d) vertical integration

9. The alliances that link together firms in supply chain management relationships are examples of how businesses try to use _____ strategies.

    (a) B2C   (b) growth
    (c) cooperation   (d) concentration

10. Among the global strategies that international businesses might pursue, the _____ strategy is the one that most tries to tailor products to fit local needs and cultures in different countries.

    (a) concentration   (b) globalization
    (c) e-business   (d) multidomestic

11. When Coke and Pepsi spend millions on ads trying to convince customers that their products are unique, they are pursuing a _____ strategy.

    (a) transnational
    (b) concentration
    (c) diversification
    (d) differentiation

12. When using Porter's model of competitive strategies, a firm that wants to compete with its rivals in a broad market by selling a very low-priced product would need to successfully implement a _____ strategy.

    (a) retrenchment
    (b) differentiation
    (c) cost leadership
    (d) diversification

13. Restructuring by downsizing operations and reducing staff is a form of _____ strategy.

    (a) retrenchment   (b) growth
    (c) concentration   (d) incremental

14. According to Porter's five forces model, _____ is a good indicator that an industry is unattractive from a competitive standpoint.

    (a) many suppliers
    (b) few customers
    (c) few substitute products
    (d) difficult entry

15. Which is as example of a cooperative strategy?

    (a) retrenchment
    (b) strategic alliance
    (c) bankruptcy
    (d) vertical integration

16. What is the difference between corporate strategy and functional strategy?

17. Why is a cost leadership strategy so important when one wants to sell products at lower prices than competitors?

18. What strategy should be pursued for a "question mark" in the BCG Matrix, and why?

19. What is "strategic leadership"?

Integration & application

20. Kim Harris owns and operates a small retail store, selling the outdoor clothing of an American manufacturer to a predominantly college-student market. Lately, a large department store outside of town has started selling similar but lower-priced clothing manufactured in China, Thailand, and Bangladesh. Kim is starting to lose business to this store. She has asked your instructor to have a student team analyze the situation and propose some strategic alternatives to best deal with this threat. You are on the team.

Questions: Why would a SWOT analysis be helpful in addressing Kim's strategic management problem? How could Porter's competitive strategies model be helpful as well?

Facts and Inferences

Instructions

Read the following report. Then, indicate whether you think the observations are true, false, or doubtful. Write T if the observation is definitely true, F if the observation is definitely false, and ? if the observation may be either true or false. Judge each observation in order. Do not reread the observations after you have indicated your judgment, and do not change any of your answers.[33]

A well-liked college instructor had just completed making up the final examinations and had turned off the lights in the office. Just then a tall, broad figure with dark glasses appeared and demanded the examination. The professor opened the drawer. Everything in the drawer was picked up, and the individual ran down the corridor. The president was notified immediately.

1. The thief was tall, broad, and wore dark glasses.
2. The professor turned off the lights.
3. A tall figure demanded the examination.
4. The examination was picked up by someone.
5. The examination was picked up by the professor.
6. A tall, broad figure appeared after the professor turned off the lights in the office.
7. The man who opened the drawer was the professor.
8. The professor ran down the corridor.
9. The drawer was never actually opened.
10. Three persons are referred to in this report.

Scoring

The correct answers in reverse order (starting with 10) are: ?, F, ?, ?, T, ?, ?, T, T, ?. Your instructor may have additional information on these correct answers.

Interpretation

To begin, ask yourself if there was a difference between your answers and those of the group for each item. If so, why? Why do you think people, individually or in groups, may answer these questions incorrectly? Good planning depends on good decision making by the people doing the planning. Being able to distinguish "facts" and understand one's "inferences" are important steps toward improving the planning process. Involving others to help do the same can frequently assist in this process.

For further exploration go to WileyPlus

Case Snapshot

Dunkin' Donuts: Betting Dollars on Donuts

Dunkin' Donuts has long been a staple on the East Coast. But the brand is now on an aggressive campaign to move into previously uncharted territory, attempting to capture market share and dominance in new regions. It has taken a risk by adding many nontraditional menu items. Will customers bite big, sending a competitive message to Starbucks? Or is Dunkin' Donuts in danger of diluting its brand?

Online Interactive Learning Resources

SELF-ASSESSMENT
• Critical Thinking

EXPERIENTIAL EXERCISES
• Strategic Scenarios
• Personal Career Planning

TEAM PROJECT
• Saving Legacy Companies

8 Organization Structure and Design

Learning Outline

8.1 What Is Organizing as a Managerial Responsibility?

- Organizing is one of the management functions
- Organization charts describe the formal structures of organizations
- Organizations also operate with informal structures
- Informal structures have good points and bad points

8.2 What Are the Most Common Types of Organization Structures?

- Functional structures group together people using similar skills
- Divisional structures group together people by products, customers, or locations
- Matrix structures combine the functional and divisional structures
- Team structures use many permanent and temporary teams
- Network structures extensively use strategic alliances and outsourcing

8.3 What Are the Trends in Organizational Design?

- Organizations are becoming flatter, with fewer levels of management
- Organizations are increasing decentralization
- Organizations are increasing delegation and empowerment
- Organizations are becoming more horizontal and adaptive
- Organizations are offering more alternative work schedules

Build-A-Bear excels at personalizing the production process. If you think the kids are having fun in the store, check out Build-A-Bear's Web site (www.buildabear.com); it's something else. Started by Maxine Clark after she left her job at Payless ShoeSource in 1996, Build-A-Bear Workshop Inc. grew rapidly, attracted venture capital, and now operates 150+ stores in up-scale shopping malls in the United States and Canada. The concept is simple; pick out a bear or bunny or turtle that you like, add stuffing, and then create your own pet with clothing, shoes, and accessories. Each pet is unique—cheerleader, girl scout . . . you name it—personalized to the user's tastes and interests. Kids and accompanying adults love it, and now you can build your bear on the Web storefront as well.

Each Build-A-Bear store is carefully organized. Guest Bear Builders move along the Bear Pathway from the Choose Me work station on to Stuff Me and finally to Name Me as their personal creation takes shape. Sounds a lot like organizations, doesn't it? Until you get to the "making it personal" part. That's where organizations often struggle—how to bring together hundreds, thousands,

Trendsetters
Alan Mulally makes mark
by restructuring Ford.

News Feed
Job fears the talk of the
informal structure

Case Snapshot
Nike—Spreading out to
stay together.

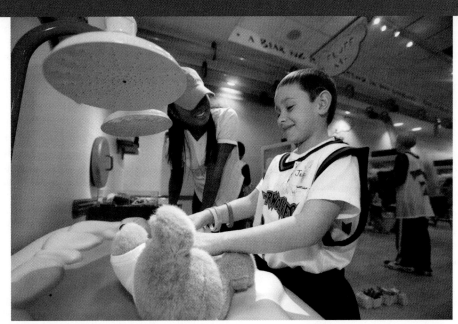

even hundreds of thousands of people in arrangements that make sense and allow personal talents to shine through.

Maxine Clark obviously had the talent, creativity, and ambition to build a successful business. Some consider the Build-A-Bear concept to be brilliant. And even a quick stop into one of the stores or a look at the fascinating options available on the Web storefront would confirm that. Clark's career began with May Company and children's marketing. By the time she resigned to start Build-A-Bear, she was president of the May subsidiary, Payless ShoeSource. While there she moved the company to distinction as a leading seller of children's shoes and was even named "one of the 30 Most Powerful People In Discount Store Retailing."

Children can now find Build-A-Bear stores internationally in places like Ireland and Japan, and expansion continues to be in the cards. Clark's current challenge is to manage the growth by continually adapting and redesigning her company to best meet its new global opportunities. When you think about, it's a lot like her young customers who love to build their own bears.

8.1 What Is Organizing as a Managerial Responsibility?

Like most things, it is much easier to talk about high-performing organizations than to actually create them. We might say in the context of the opening example that it's a lot harder to build an organization than build a bear! In true contingency fashion, there is no one best way to do things; no one organizational form meets the needs of all circumstances. Furthermore, what works well at one moment in time can quickly become outdated, even dysfunctional, in another. This is why you often read and hear about organizations making changes and reorganizing in an attempt to improve their performance.

In most organizations, most of the time nothing is constant, at least not for long. This is a major reason why management scholar Henry Mintzberg points out that people often have problems.[1] Whenever job assignments and reporting relationships change, whenever the organization grows or shrinks, whenever old ways of doing things are reconfigured, people naturally struggle to understand the new ways of working. And perhaps even more importantly, they will worry about the implications for their jobs and careers.

• Organizing is one of the management functions.

Most of us like to be organized—at home, at work, when playing games. We tend to get uncomfortable and anxious when things are disorganized. It shouldn't surprise you, therefore, that people in organizations need answers to such questions as: "Where do I fit in?" "How does my work relate to that of others?" "Who runs things?" "How do I get problems answered?"[2] People need these answers to such questions when they first join an organization, when they take new jobs, and whenever things are substantially changed.

Organizing arranges people and resources to work toward a goal.

This is where and why **organizing** comes into play as one of the four functions of management shown in **Figure 8.1**. It is the process of arranging people and resources to work together to accomplish the goals. Planning sets the goals; through organizing managers begin to carry them out.[3]

FIGURE 8.1

The Importance of Organizing in the Management Process.

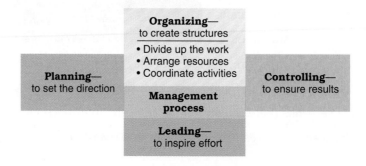

• Organization charts describe the formal structures of organizations.

When managers organize things, they arrange people and jobs into meaningful working relationships. They clarify who is to do what, who is in charge of whom, and how different people and work units are supposed to cooperate with one another. This creates what we call the **organization structure**, a formal arrangement that links the various parts of an organization to one another.

You probably know the concept of structure best in terms of an **organization chart**. This is a diagram, like the one in **Figure 8.2**, of positions and reporting relationships within an organization.[4] A typical organization chart identifies major job titles and shows the hierarchy of authority and communication that links them together. It should give the viewer a sense of the organization's **division of labor**—people and groups performing different jobs, ideally ones for which they are well skilled. It should also indicate how the various parts are linked together so that everyone's work contributes to a common purpose.

Check out **Table 8.1**—*What You Can Learn from an Organization Chart*. And indeed you can learn quite a bit from an organization chart, but only in respect to the **formal structure**. This is the "official" structure, or the way things are supposed to operate. It is supposed to align positions, people, and responsibilities in ways that best accomplish an organization's strategy and goals. But as things change over time, managers often find themselves constantly tinkering with the formal structure in the attempt to get the alignment right. And sometimes, frankly, the current structure doesn't make sense. When Carol Bartz asked to see Yahoo's organization chart before taking over as CEO, for example, she said: "It was like a Dilbert cartoon. It was very odd." Her response was: "You need management here."[5]

Problems with the organization structure were evident in recent controversies over performance failures in large companies such as General Motors, AIG, and Citibank. Some blame the failures on structures that allowed the same person to be both Chairman of the Board and CEO. What happens to corporate governance when the CEO essentially reports to himself or herself as Board Chair? How does this structure provide for critical oversight of top management by the board of directors? As you might expect, many firms are now changing their organization charts to separate the job of Board Chairman from that of CEO; in other words, strengthening governance by not allowing the same person to fill both positions.[6]

Getting to know the formal structure is just a starting point for organizational understanding. It's useful but not fully informative. Things may well have changed since the organization chart was last updated. And the realities of any organization are usually much more complicated than what any such chart can describe anyway.

• Organizations also operate with informal structures.

Behind every formal structure also lies an **informal structure**. You might think of this as a "shadow" organization made up of unofficial, but often critical, working relationships between organizational members. Like any shadow, the shape of the informal structure will be blurry and possibly shifting. You may have to work hard to understand its full complexities.

Figure 8.3 shows how unofficial groupings create the informal structure of an organization. If you could draw the informal structure for your organization, and this would be an interesting exercise, you would find relationships cutting across levels and moving from side to side. Some would be work-related, reflecting how people have

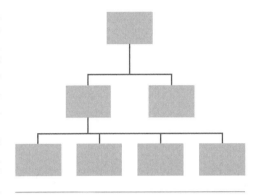

FIGURE 8.2
Organization Charts Show the Formal Structure.

Organization structure is a system of tasks, reporting relationships, and communication linkages.

An **organization chart** describes the arrangement of work positions within an organization.

The **division of labor** is people and groups performing different jobs.

Formal structure is the official structure of the organization.

Informal structure is the set of unofficial relationships among an organization's members.

[**TABLE** 8.1]

What You Can Learn from an Organization Chart

Division of work—Positions and titles show work responsibilities.
Supervisory relationships—Lines between positions show who reports to whom in the chain of command.
Span of control—The number of persons reporting to a supervisor.
Communication channels—Lines between positions show routes for formal communication flows.
Major subunits—How jobs are grouped together in work units, departments, or divisions.
Staff positions—Staff specialists that support other positions and parts of the organization.
Levels of management—The number of management layers from top to bottom.

FIGURE 8.3
The Informal Structure Consists of Unofficial Groups that Create a "Shadow" Organization.

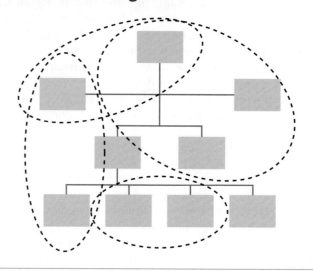

found it best to get their jobs done. Many others would be personal, reflecting who meets for coffee, stops in for office chats, meets together in exercise groups, and spends time together as friends, not just co-workers.[7]

A tool known as **social network analysis** is one way of identifying the informal structures and their embedded social relationships that are active in an organization. Such an analysis typically asks people to identify others whom they turn to for help most often, whom they communicate with regularly, and who energizes and de-energizes them.[8]

The results of a social network analysis are often described as a map showing lines running from person to person according to frequency of communication and type of relationship maintained. The map shows who is linked with whom and how a lot of work really gets done in organizations, in contrast to the formal arrangements shown on the organization chart. This information is useful for redesigning the formal structure for better performance, identifying who the key people are in terms of performance and mentoring others, and also legitimizing the informal networks people use in their daily work.[9]

• Informal structures have good points and bad points.

Let's start with the good points of informal structures and social networks. They can be very helpful in getting work accomplished. Indeed, they may be essential in many ways to organizational success.

Through the emergent and spontaneous relationships of informal structures, people can easily find help getting things done when necessary. One of the first things you probably learned in college was that knowing secretaries and departmental assistants is a very good way to get into classes that are "closed" or find out about new courses that will be offered. Think about all the different ways you use informal structures to get things done; most people in most organizations do the same.

The relationships available in the informal structure can play important roles in helping people learn their jobs and solve problems while doing them. This occurs

Social network analysis identifies the informal structures and their embedded social relationships that are active in an organization.

as people assist one another not because the structure requires it, but because they know and like one another. The relationships also provide a lot of social and emotional support. Informal structures give people access to friendships, conversations, and advice that can help make the normal workday pleasant and a bad workday less troublesome.

Informal structures can be especially helpful during times of change when out-of-date formal structures may fail to provide the support people need to deal with new or unusual situations. Because it takes time to change or modify formal structures, the informal structure helps fill the void. For these reasons and possibly more, it can be argued that informal structures are essential for any organization to succeed. They fill gaps missing in the formal structure and help compensate for its inadequacies, both task-related and people-related.

Yet, let's not forget the potential bad points to informal structures. Because they exist outside the formal system, things that happen in them may work against the best interests of the organization as a whole. Informal structures can be susceptible to rumor, carry inaccurate information, breed resistance to change, and even distract members from their work efforts. And if you happen to end up as an "outsider" rather than an "insider," you may feel less a part of things. Some American managers in Japanese firms, for example, have complained about being excluded from what they call the "shadow cabinet." This is an informal group of Japanese executives who hold the real power and sometimes act to the exclusion of others.[10]

News Feed

Job Fears the Talk of the Informal Structure

Scene: Worker sitting in office cubicle overhears a conversation taking place in the next cubicle. Words such as "project being terminated" and "job cuts will be necessary" draw him over to the wall to hear more. At lunch he shares the conversation with two friends and the word quickly spreads that their employer is going to announce layoffs.

Well there's nothing new about eavesdropping and rumor; they're both facts of life in general and of organizational life in particular. But the job losses of a down economy have heightened the informal buzz surrounding the "What's going to happen next here?" concerns. Rumors, some accurate and others not, are flying around the informal networks of organizations.

The Society for Human Resource Management reported that after the economy suffered a round of massive layoffs, human resource (HR) professionals observed in their firms a 23% increase in workplace eavesdropping and a 54% increase in "gossip and rumors about downsizings and layoffs." Cafeterias are hotspots, and one HR director says she even notices people trying to hang out in hallways and sit as close as possible to executives in cafeterias in attempts to overhear conversations. On the other hand, one manager says he does his own eavesdropping to try to learn what he can from employee conversations; he calls it "alert listening."

Reflect and React:

Is the informal organization operating in a functional or dysfunctional way in these examples? What are the lessons here in terms of managing the informal structure and social networks of organizations? Why does the informal structure become even more significant as a source of rumor in times of crisis?

Study Guide

8.1
What Is Organizing as a Managerial Responsibility?

Rapid review

- Organizing is the process of arranging people and resources to work toward a common goal.
- Structure is the system of tasks, reporting relationships, and communication that links people and positions within an organization.
- Organization charts describe the formal structure, and how an organization should ideally work.
- The informal structure of an organization consists of the unofficial relationships that develop among its members.
- Informal structures create relationships for social support and task assistance, but can be susceptible to rumors.

Terms to define

Division of labor
Formal structure
Informal structure
Organization chart
Organization structure
Organizing
Social network analysis

Be sure you can

- explain the importance of organizing as a management function
- differentiate formal and informal structures
- discuss potential good and bad points about informal structures

Questions for discussion

1. Why is organizing such an important management function?
2. If organization charts are imperfect, why bother with them?
3. Could an organization consistently perform well without the help of its informal structure?

8.2 What Are the Most Common Types of Organization Structures?

A traditional principle of organizing is that performance improves with a good division of labor whose parts are well coordinated. The process of trying to arrange this is called **departmentalization**, and it can take different forms.[11] The most basic ones are the functional, divisional, matrix, team, and network structures. As you read about each, don't forget, organizations rarely use only one type of structure. Most often they will use a mixture, with different parts and levels having different structures because of their unique needs.

Departmentalization is the process of grouping together people and jobs into work units.

• Functional structures group together people using similar skills.

Take a look at **Figure 8.4**. What organizing logic do you see? In these **functional structures** people with similar skills and performing similar tasks are grouped together into formal work units. In business, for example, typical functions include marketing, finance, accounting, production, management information systems, and human resources. The assumption is that if the functions are well chosen and each does its work properly, the business should operate successfully.

A **functional structure** groups together people with similar skills who perform similar tasks.

FIGURE 8.4

What Does a Typical Functional Structure Look Like?

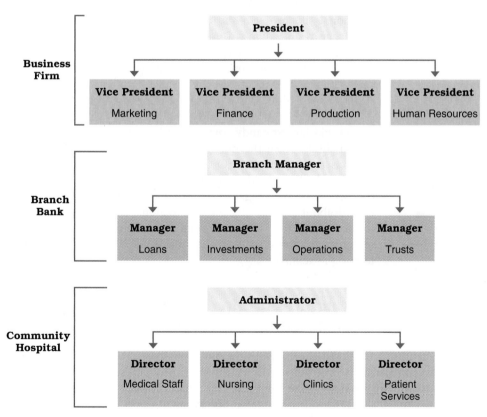

Functional structures are common in organizations of all types and sizes. In a typical business you might have vice presidents or senior managers heading the traditional functions of accounting, human resources, finance, manufacturing, marketing, and sales. In a bank, they may head such functions as loans, investments, and trusts. In a hospital, managers or administrators are usually in charge of functions such as nursing, clinics, and patient services.

Potential advantages of functional structures

- Economies of scale make efficient use of human resources.
- Functional experts are good at solving technical problems.
- Training within functions promotes skill development.
- Career paths are available within each function.

Functional structures are not limited to businesses, and the figure also shows how other types of organizations such as banks and hospitals may use them.

Functional structures work well for small organizations that produce only one or a few products or services. They also tend to work best for organizations, or parts of organizations, dealing with relatively stable environments where the problems are predictable and demands for change are limited. And they offer benefits to individuals. Within a given function, say, marketing, people share technical expertise, interests, and responsibilities. They also can advance in responsibilities and pursue career paths within the function. Perhaps you work or plan to work someday in this type of setup.

Although functional structures have a clear logic, there are some potential downsides as well. When an organization is divided up into functions, it is sometimes hard to pinpoint responsibilities for things such as cost containment, product or service quality, and innovation.

With everyone focused on meeting functional goals, the sense of overall performance accountability may get lost. This tendency may be reinforced when employee training emphasizes functional needs and neglects broader organizational issues, values, and objectives. And people may find that they get trapped in functional career niches that are hard to break out of to gain experiences in other areas.

Another significant concern is something that you might hear called the **functional chimneys** or **functional siloes problem**. Shown in **Figure 8.5**, this is when performance suffers due to a lack of communication, coordination, and problem solving across functions. Instead of cooperating with one another, members of functions sometimes end up either competing or selfishly focusing on functional goals rather than broader organizational objectives. CEO Carol Bartz described a functional silo problem she discovered at Yahoo this way: "The homepage people didn't want to drive traffic to the finance page because they wanted to keep them on the home page."[12] Such problems of poor cooperation and even just plain lack of helpfulness across functions can be very persistent. It often takes alert and strong managers such as Bartz to get things resolved.

Have you had a Mars candy bar recently? Well, Mars Inc. is the world's largest candy company and, like most firms of its size, it also suffers from the functional chimneys problem. When Paul Michels took over as CEO he realized that "the top team was siloed and replete with unspoken agendas. Members did not see the benefit of working together as a team; they were only concerned about success in their own region." Michels' solution was to move Mars toward a horizontal structure that broke the habits of functional thinking by realigning people and mindsets around teams and teamwork.[13]

The **functional chimneys** or **functional siloes problem** is a lack of communication and coordination across functions.

FIGURE 8.5
The Functional Chimneys Problem.

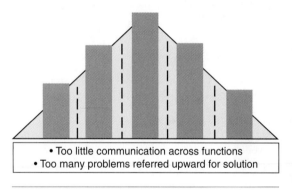

- Too little communication across functions
- Too many problems referred upward for solution

• Divisional structures group together people by products, customers, or locations.

A **divisional structure** groups together people working on the same product, in the same area, or with similar customers.

A second organizational alternative is the **divisional structure** shown in **Figure 8.6**. It groups together people who work on the same product, serve similar customers, and/or are located in the same area or geographical region.[14] The idea is to use the divisional focus to overcome disadvantages of a functional structure, such as the functional chimneys problem. For example, Toyota shifted to a divisional structure in its North American operations during the economic crisis. Engineering, manufacturing, and sales were brought together under a common boss, instead of each function reporting to its own top executive. One analyst said: "The problem is every silo reported back to someone different, but now they need someone in charge of the whole choir."[15]

FIGURE 8.6
What Are Some Ways Organizations Use Divisional Structures?

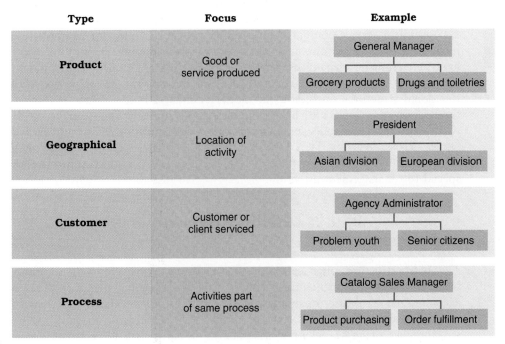

Type	Focus	Example
Product	Good or service produced	General Manager — Grocery products, Drugs and toiletries
Geographical	Location of activity	President — Asian division, European division
Customer	Customer or client serviced	Agency Administrator — Problem youth, Senior citizens
Process	Activities part of same process	Catalog Sales Manager — Product purchasing, Order fulfillment

In product structures, divisions are based on the product or service provided, such as consumer products and industrial products. In geographic structures, divisions are based on geography or territories, such as an Asia–Pacific division and a North American division. In customer structures, divisions are based on customers or clients served, such as graduate students and undergraduate students in a university.

Product structures group together jobs and activities devoted to a single product or service. They identify a common point of managerial responsibility for costs, profits, problems, and successes in a defined market area. An expected benefit is that the product division will be able to respond quickly and effectively to changing market demands and customer tastes. When Fiat took over Chrysler after it emerged from bankruptcy, CEO Sergio Marchionne said he wanted a new structure to "speed decision making and improve communication flow." His choice was to use product divisions; each of the firm's three brands—Chrysler, Jeep, and Dodge, was given its own chief executive and assigned responsibility for its own profits and losses.[16] The "new" General Motors took the same approach and organized around four product divisions—Buick, Cadillac, Chevrolet, and GMC, when it also emerged from bankruptcy protection. CEO Fritz Henderson said: "100 percent of our product, technology and marketing spend will now be focused behind the four core brands . . ."[17]

Geographical structures, or *area structures*, group together jobs and activities conducted in the same location or geographical region. Companies typically use geographical divisions when they need to focus attention on the unique product tastes or operating requirements of particular regions. As UPS operations expanded worldwide, for example, the company announced a change from a product to a geographical organizational structure. The company created two geographical divisions—the Americas and Europe/Asia, with each area responsible for its own logistics, sales, and other business functions.

Customer structures group together jobs and activities that serve the same customers or clients. The major appeal of customer divisions is the ability to

Potential advantages of divisional structures
- Expertise focused on special products, customers, regions
- Better coordination across functions within divisions
- Better accountability for product or service delivery
- Easier to grow or shrink in size as conditions change

A **product structure** groups together people and jobs working on a single product or service.

A **geographical structure** brings together people and jobs performed in the same location.

A **customer structure** groups together people and jobs that serve the same customers or clients.

The Cleveland Clinic created a top-rated cardiac program by organizing around teams of physicians and nonphysicians focused on treating heart patients.

best serve the special needs of the different customer groups. This is a common structure for complex businesses in the consumer products industries. 3M Corporation, for example, structures itself to focus on such diverse markets as consumer and office, specialty materials, industrial, health care, electronics and communications, transportation, graphics, and safety. Customer structures are also useful in service companies and social agencies. Banks, for example, use them to give separate attention to consumer and commercial customers for loans; government agencies use them to focus on different client populations.

Divisional structures are supposed to avoid some of the major problems of functional structures, including functional chimneys. But, as with any structural alternative, they, too, have potential disadvantages. They can be costly when economies of scale get lost through the duplication of resources and efforts across divisions. They can also create unhealthy rivalries between divisions that end up competing with one another for scarce resources, prestige, or special top management attention.

• Matrix structures combine the functional and divisional structures.

A **matrix structure** combines functional and divisional approaches to emphasize project or program teams.

The **matrix structure**, often called the *matrix organization*, combines the functional and divisional structures to try to gain the advantages of each. This is accomplished by setting up permanent teams that operate across functions to support specific products, projects, or programs.[18] Workers in a typical matrix structure, like **Figure 8.7**, belong to at least two formal groups at the same time—a

FIGURE 8.7

How Does a Matrix Structure Combine Functional and Divisional Structures?

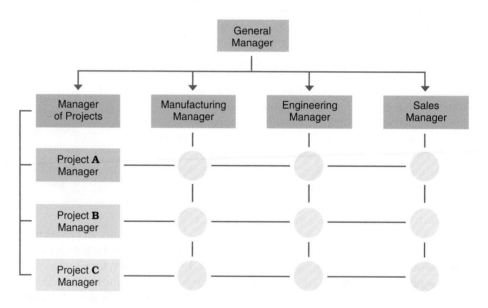

Functional personnel assigned to both projects and functional departments

A matrix structure is designed to combine the best of the functional and divisional forms. In a typical matrix the normal functions create a traditional vertical structure, with heads of marketing and manufacturing, and so on. Then, a new horizontal structure is added to create cross-functional integration. This is done using teams that are staffed by members from the functions. Team members report to two bosses—their functional bosses and their cross-functional team bosses.

functional group, and a product, program, or project team. They also report to two bosses—one within the function and the other within the team.

The matrix structure has gained a strong foothold in the workplace, with applications in such diverse settings as manufacturing (e.g., aerospace, electronics, pharmaceuticals), service industries (e.g., banking, brokerage, retailing), professional fields (e.g., accounting, advertising, law), and the nonprofit sector (e.g., government agencies, hospitals, universities).

The use of permanent **cross-functional teams** in matrix structures creates several potential advantages. These are teams whose members come together from different functional departments to work on a common task. Everyone, regardless of his or her departmental affiliation, is required to work closely with others on the cross-functional team—no functional chimneys tendencies allowed. They share expertise and information to solve problems at the team level and make sure that their programs or projects get accomplished in the best ways possible.

Still, matrix structures aren't perfect; they can't overcome all disadvantages of their functional and divisional parents. The two-boss system of the matrix can lead to power struggles if functional supervisors and team leaders make confusing or conflicting demands on team members. Matrix structures can be costly because they require a whole new set of managers, the leaders who run the cross-functional teams.[19] And as you might guess, team meetings in the matrix can be time consuming.

Potential advantages of matrix structures

- Performance accountability rests with program, product, or project managers.
- Better communication across functions
- Teams solve problems at their levels.
- Top managers spend more time on strategy.

A **cross-functional team** brings together members from different functional departments.

• Team structures use many permanent and temporary teams.

Some organizations are adopting **team structures** that extensively use permanent and temporary teams to solve problems, complete special projects, and accomplish day-to-day tasks.[20] As **Figure 8.8** shows, these teams are often formed across functions and staffed with members whose talents match team tasks.[21]

A **team structure** uses permanent and temporary cross-functional teams to improve lateral relations.

FIGURE 8.8

How Do Team Structures Capture the Benefits of Cross-Functional Teams?

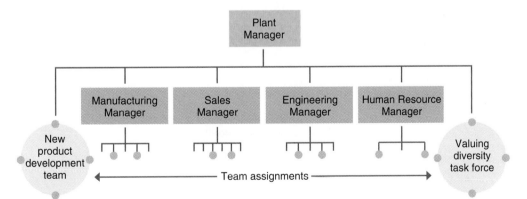

Team structures make extensive use of teams to improve organizations through better communication and problem solving across functions. Some teams are temporary, such as a project team that convenes to create a new product and then disbands when finished. Other teams are more permanent. They bring together members from different functions to work together on standing issues and common problems, such as quality control, diversity management, labor-management relations, or health care benefits.

Potential advantages of team structures

- Team assignments improve communication, cooperation, and decision making.
- Team members get to know each other as persons, not just job titles.
- Team memberships boost morale and increase enthusiasm and task involvement.

The goals are to reduce the functional chimneys problem, tap the full benefits of group decision making, and gain as much creativity in problem solving as possible.

At Polaroid Corporation a research team developed a new medical imaging system in three years, when most had predicted it would take six. As one Polaroid executive noted, "Our researchers are not any smarter, but by working together they get the value of each other's intelligence almost instantaneously."[22]

Things don't always work this well in team structures, however, since the complexities of teams and teamwork can create other problems. As with the matrix, team members sometimes have to deal with conflicting loyalties between their team and functional assignments. Teamwork always takes time. And like any team situation, the quality of results often depends on how well the team is managed and how well team members gel as a group. This is why you'll most likely find organizations with team structures, such as Polaroid, investing heavily in team building and team training.

• Network structures extensively use strategic alliances and outsourcing.

A **network structure** uses IT to link with networks of outside suppliers and service contractors.

Another development in organizational structures dramatically reduces the need for full-time staff by making extensive use of strategic alliances and outsourcing. Shown by example in **Figure 8.9**, a **network structure** links a central core of full-time employees with a surrounding set of "networks" composed of relationships

FIGURE 8.9

How Do Network Structures Take Advantage of Strategic Alliances and Outsourcing?

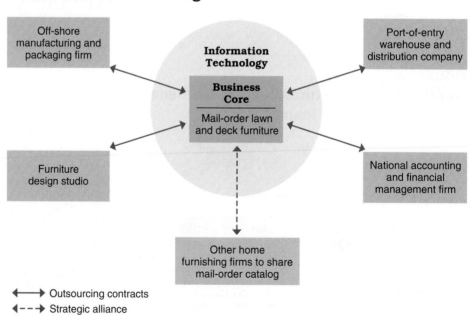

Organizations using network structures replace some full-time positions and functions with services provided by alliance partners and outsourcing contractors. In these structures, "core" employees performing essential operations at the center of a "network" that links them with a shifting mix of outside partners and contractors. The example in this figure shows that a small group of people can run a mail-order business in this manner. A lot of network activities are made easy and cost efficient by using the latest information technologies.

to outside contractors and partners that supply essential services. Because the central core is relatively small and the surrounding networks can be expanded or shrunk as needed, the potential advantages are lower costs, more speed, and greater flexibility in dealing with changing environments.[23]

Instead of doing everything for itself with full-time employees, the network organization employs a minimum staff and contracts out as much work as possible. It makes use of **strategic alliances** by cooperating with other firms to pursue business activities of mutual interest. Some are *outsourcing alliances* in which they contract to purchase important services from another organization. Others may be *supplier alliances* that link businesses in preferred supplier-customer relationships that guarantee a smooth and timely flow of quality supplies among the partners.

In a **strategic alliance**, organizations join together in partnership to pursue an area of mutual interest.

The example in the figure shows a network structure for a company that sells lawn and deck furniture over the Internet and by mail order. The firm employs only a few full-time "core" employees. Other business requirements are met through a network of alliances and outsourcing relationships. A consultant creates product designs; suppliers produce them at low-cost sites around the world. A supply chain management firms gets products shipped to and distributed from a rented warehouse. A quarterly catalog is mailed as part of a strategic alliance with two other firms that sell different home furnishings. Accounting services are outsourced. Even the company Web site that supports customer and network relationships is maintained by an outside contractor.

This may sound a bit radical, but it isn't. It is an increasingly common arrangement that might even raise some entrepreneurial opportunities for you. Could the growing popularity of network organization concepts make it easier for you to start your own business someday?

If network structures are highly streamlined, efficient, and adaptable, don't you wonder why even more organizations aren't adopting them? Part of the answer may lie in inertia, simply being caught up in old ways and finding it very hard to change. Another reason is the management complication of having to deal with a vast and sometimes shifting network of contracts and alliances. If one part of the network breaks down or fails to deliver, the entire system may suffer the consequences. Also, outsourcing might have hidden costs. Not too long ago, for example, Delta Air announced that it was shutting down its call-center operations in India because too many customers were complaining about communication difficulties with service providers.[24]

As information technology continues to evolve, a variation of the network structure is appearing. Called the **virtual organization**, it uses information technologies to operate a constantly shifting network of alliances.[25] The goal is to use virtual networks to eliminate boundaries that traditionally separate a firm from its suppliers and customers, and its internal departments and divisions from one another. The intense use of IT allows virtual relationships to be called into action as needed; when the work is done, they are disbanded or left idle until next needed.

A **virtual organization** uses information technologies to operate as a shifting network of alliances.

If you really think about it, each of us is probably already a part of virtual organizations. Do you see similarities, for example, with the MySpace, Facebook, or LinkedIn communities? Isn't the virtual organization concept similar to how we manage our relationships online—signing on, signing off, getting things done as needed with different people and groups, and all taking place instantaneously, temporarily, and without the need for face-to-face contacts?

Study Guide

8.2
What Are the Most Common Types of Organization Structures?

Rapid review

- Functional structures group together people using similar skills to perform similar activities.
- Divisional structures group together people who work on a similar product, work in the same geographical region, or serve the same customers.
- A matrix structure uses permanent cross-functional teams to try to gain the advantages of both the functional and divisional approaches.
- Team structures make extensive use of permanent and temporary teams, often cross functional, to improve communication, cooperation, and problem solving.
- Network structures maintain a staff of core full-time employees and use contracted services and strategic alliances to accomplish many business needs.

Terms to define

Customer structure

Departmentalization

Divisional structure

Functional chimneys problem

Functional siloes problem

Functional structure

Geographical structure

Matrix structure

Product structure

Cross-functional teams

Network structure

Strategic alliance

Team structure

Virtual organization

Be sure you can

- compare the functional, divisional, and matrix structures
- draw charts to show how each structure might be used in a business
- list advantages and disadvantages of each structure
- explain the functional chimneys problem
- describe how cross-functional and project teams operate in team structures
- illustrate how an organization familiar to you might operate as a network structure
- list advantages and disadvantages of the network approach to organizing

Questions for discussion

1. Why use functional structures if they are prone to functional chimneys problems?
2. Could a matrix structure improve performance for an organization familiar to you?
3. How can the disadvantages of group decision making hurt team structures?

8.3 What Are the Trends in Organizational Design?

Just as organizations vary in size and type, so too do the variety of problems and opportunities they face.[26] This is why they use different ways of organizing—from the functional, divisional, and matrix structures, to the team and network structures reviewed in the previous module. Now it is time to probe further, recognizing that there is still more to the story of how managers try to align their organizations with the unique situations that they face.

This process of alignment is called **organizational design**. It deals with the choices managers make to configure their organizations to best meet the problems and opportunities posed by their environments.[27] And because every organization faces its own set of unique challenges, there is no "one fits all" best design. It's best to think of organizational design as a problem-solving activity where managers strive to always have the best possible configuration to meet current demands. Among today's developments, some recognizable design trends are evident.

• Organizations are becoming flatter, with fewer levels of management.

When organizations grow in size, they tend to get taller by adding more and more levels of management. This raises costs. It also increases the distance between top management and lower levels, making it harder for the levels to communicate with one another. This increases the risks of decision-making delays and poorly informed decisions.

For these and other reasons, taller organizations are generally viewed as less efficient, less flexible, and less customer-sensitive.[28] You shouldn't be surprised that the trend is for organizations to get flatter. One of the first announcements by Procter & Gamble's new CEO Robert McDonald was that he would be taking steps to "create a simpler, flatter and more agile organization . . . because simplification reduces cost, improves productivity and enhances employee satisfaction." His plan involved cutting the number of levels of management in the firm from nine to seven.[29]

When organizations do get flatter, as in the case of Procter & Gamble, one of the things often affected is **span of control**—the number of persons directly reporting to a manager. When span of control is narrow, a manager supervises only a few people; a manager with a wide span of control supervises many people. Flatter organizations tend to have wider spans of control that require fewer levels of management; taller organizations tend to have narrow spans of control and many levels of management.

Trendsetter

Alan Mulally Makes Mark by Restructuring Ford.

Why is it that a CEO brought in from outside the industry fared the best as the big three automakers went into crisis mode during the economic downturn? That's a question that Ford Motor Company's chairman, William Clay Ford Jr., is happy to answer. And the person he's talking about is Alan Mulally, a former Boeing executive hired by Ford to retool the firm and put it back on a competitive track.

Many wondered at the time if an "airplane guy" could run an auto company. It isn't easy to come in from outside an industry and successfully lead a huge firm. But Mulally's management experience and insights are proving well up to the task. One consultant remarked: "The speed with which Mulally has transformed Ford into a more nimble and healthy operation has been one of the more impressive jobs I've seen." He went on to say that without Mulally's impact, Ford might well have gone out of business.

In addition to many changes to modernize plants and streamline operations, Mulally has tackled the bureaucratic problems common to many extremely large organizations—particularly those dealing with functional chimneys and a lack of open communication. William Ford says that the firm had a culture that "loved to meet" and in which managers got together to discuss the message they wanted to communicate to the top executives. Mulally changed all that with a focus on transparency and data-based decision making, cooperation between Ford's divisions, and a more centralized approach to global operations that build vehicles to sell in many markets. When some of the senior executives balked and tried to go directly to Ford with their complaints, he refused: "I didn't permit it," he says, thus reinforcing Mulally's authority to run the firm his way.

As for Mulally's success, only time will tell how the firm does in extremely difficult circumstances. For now, however, Ford is outperforming GM and Chrysler, and Mulally has gained lots of respect for his executive prowess. One of his senior managers says: "I'm going into my fourth year on the job. I've never had such consistency of purpose before."

Organizational design is the process of configuring organizations to meet environmental challenges.

Span of control is the number of persons directly reporting to a manager.

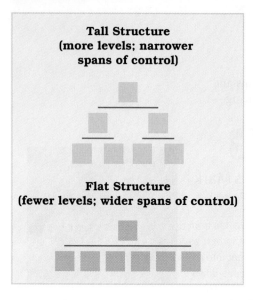

Tall Structure
(more levels; narrower spans of control)

Flat Structure
(fewer levels; wider spans of control)

With **centralization** top management keeps the power to make most decisions.

With **decentralization** top management allows lower levels to help make many decisions.

• Organizations are increasing decentralization.

While we are talking about levels of management, the next question becomes: Should top management make the decisions and the lower levels just carry them out? The answer increasingly heard is "No," at least not for all decisions. When top management keeps the power to make most decisions, the setup is called **centralization**. When top management allows employees at lower levels to make decisions in their areas of responsibility and on those matters where they are best prepared or informed, the setup is called **decentralization**.

If you had to choose right now, wouldn't you go for decentralization? Well, you wouldn't be wrong, since it is a characteristic of the more progressive organizations.[30] But you would not be exactly right, either. Do you really want lower levels making major decisions and changing things whenever they see fit?

The reality is that there is no need for a trade-off between these two alternatives; an organization can have both. One of the unique opportunities of today's high-tech world is that top management can decentralize and still maintain centralized control. Computer networks and advanced information systems allow top managers to easily stay informed about day-to-day performance results at all levels throughout an organization. Because they have this information readily available, it is easier for them to operate in more decentralized ways.[31]

• Organizations are increasing delegation and empowerment.

Delegation is the process of entrusting work to others.

Decentralization brings with it another trend that is good for organizations and their members: increased delegation and empowerment. **Delegation** is the process of entrusting work to others by giving them the right to make decisions and take action. It is the foundation for decentralization.

Every manager really needs to know how and when to delegate. Even if you are already good at it, there are probably ways to get even better. On those days when you complain that "I just can't get everything done," for example, the real problem may be that you are trying to do everything yourself. Delegation involves deciding what work you should do yourself and what you should allow others to accomplish. It sounds easy, but there is skill to doing delegation right.[32]

A classical management principle states: Authority should equal responsibility when a supervisor delegates work to a subordinate. This principle warns managers not to delegate without giving the subordinate sufficient authority to perform. Can you think of a time when you were asked to get something done but didn't have the authority to do it? This was probably frustrating and perhaps it even caused you to lose respect for the manager who failed to understand the basic steps in delegation.

Three steps in delegation

1. *Assign responsibility*—explain tasks and expectations to others.
2. *Grant authority*—allow others to act as needed to complete task.
3. *Create accountability*—require others to report back, complete task.

Unfortunately, some managers go even one step further; they fail to delegate at all. Whether because they are unwilling or unable to trust others or are too inflexible in how they want things done, the failure to delegate is more common than you might think. And it creates problems. A failure to delegate not only makes it hard for people to do their jobs, it overloads the manager with work that really should be done by others.

Empowerment gives people freedom to do their jobs as they think best.

But let's remember that the trend is in the direction of more, not less, delegation. And when delegation is done well it leads to **empowerment**. This is the process of giving people the freedom to contribute ideas, make decisions, show initiative, and do their jobs in the best possible ways. Empowerment is the engine that powers decentralization; it is the foundation from which organizations become faster, more flexible, and adaptable in today's dynamic environments.

• Organizations are becoming more horizontal and adaptive.

You should remember the concept of **bureaucracy** from earlier discussion in this book. Its distinguishing features are clear-cut division of labor, strict hierarchy of authority, formal rules and procedures, and promotion based on competency. According to Max Weber, bureaucracies should be orderly, fair, and highly efficient.[33] Yet, the chances are your image of a bureaucracy is an organization bogged down with "red tape," which acts cumbersome and impersonal and is sometimes overcome to the point of inadequacy by rules and procedures.

Where, you might ask, is the decentralization, delegation, and empowerment that we have just been talking about? Well, researchers have looked into the question and arrived at some interesting answers. When Tom Burns and George Stalker investigated 20 manufacturing firms in England, they found that two quite different organizational forms could be successful.[34] The key was "fit" with challenges in the firm's external environment.

A more bureaucratic form of organization, which Burns and Stalker called the **mechanistic design**, thrived in stable environments. It was good at doing routine things in predictable situations. But in rapidly changing and uncertain situations, a much less bureaucratic form, called the **organic design**, performed best. It was adaptable and better suited to handle change and less predictable situations.

Figure 8.10 portrays these two approaches as opposite extremes on a continuum of organizational design alternatives. The figure points out that organizations with mechanistic designs typically operate as "tight" structures of the traditional vertical and bureaucratic form.[35] They are good for production efficiency. A ready example

A **bureaucracy** emphasizes formal authority, rules, order, fairness, and efficiency.

Self-Assessment
This is a good point to complete the self-assessment "*Organizational Design Preference*" found on page 178.

Mechanistic designs are bureaucratic, using a centralized and vertical structure.

Organic designs are adaptive, using a decentralized and horizontal structure.

FIGURE 8.10

What Are the Major Differences Between Mechanistic and Organic Organizational Designs?

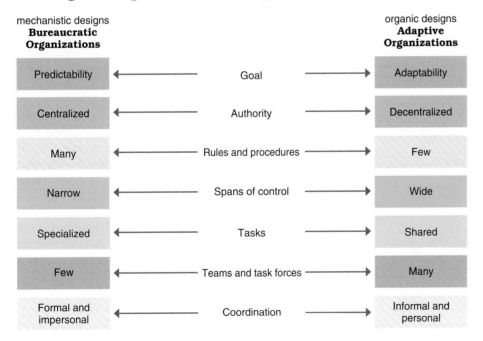

mechanistic designs **Bureaucratic Organizations**		organic designs **Adaptive Organizations**
Predictability	Goal	Adaptability
Centralized	Authority	Decentralized
Many	Rules and procedures	Few
Narrow	Spans of control	Wide
Specialized	Tasks	Shared
Few	Teams and task forces	Many
Formal and impersonal	Coordination	Informal and personal

Some indicators of a more organic design are decentralization, few rules and procedures, wider spans of control, sharing of tasks, use of teams and task forces, and informal or personal approaches to coordination. This organic design is most associated with success in dynamic and changing environments. The more mechanistic design has mainly bureaucratic features and is more likely to have difficulty in change environments but to be successful in more stable ones.

is your local fast-food restaurant. On your next visit, why not look things over? Think about it also the next time you turn on your PC and "Microsoft" pops up. *Business Week* claims that the software giant suffers from "bureaucratic red tape" and endless meetings that bog employees down and limit their abilities to be creative and on top of market demands.[36] *The Wall Street Journal* takes the case even further, suggesting that Microsoft should be broken into three smaller pieces to free the firm from "bureaucracy that's stifling entrepreneurial spirits."[37] The idea is to create new and smaller components with more organic designs—decentralization, flatter, wider spans of control, and fewer rules and procedures.

The organic organizational design is more horizontal and less vertical than its mechanistic counterpart. It operates with more emphasis on empowerment and teamwork, and gets a lot of work done through informal structures and interpersonal networks maintained by its members.[38] The result is an organization that is adaptive and flexible, and whose employees are allowed to be more spontaneous in dealing with changing markets and environments.[39] This type of design is good for creativity and innovation. Doesn't this sound like just the type of organization most likely to succeed today?[40]

• Organizations are using more alternative work schedules.

A **compressed workweek** allows a worker to complete a full-time job in less than five days.

With the massive job losses that accompanied the recent economic decline, the potential for readjusting work schedules to keep more people working gained prominence in the news. We read and heard more and more about such things as unpaid days off once a week or every two weeks, reduced hours in the work week, extended schedules for unpaid vacations, and more.

In fact, management scholars have been pointing out for quite some time how organizations and their members can benefit from alternative ways of scheduling work. The fact is—just because it's been normal to work 40 hours each week in the past doesn't make this the only or best way to schedule work time.[41]

A **compressed workweek** allows a worker to complete a full-time job in less than the standard five days of 8-hour shifts.[42] Its most common form is the "4–40," that is, accomplishing 40 hours of work in four 10-hour days. This is found at USAA, a diversified financial services company that has ranked among the 100 best companies to work for in America. A large part of the firm's San Antonio workforce is on a four-day schedule, with some working Monday through Thursday, and others working Tuesday through Friday.[43]

Although compressed workweeks can cause scheduling problems, possible customer complaints, and even union objections, the benefits are there as well. USAA reports improved morale, as well as lower overtime costs, less absenteeism, and decreased use of sick leave.

Stay Tuned

What Recession Means in Job Losses

The hard realities of recession are reflected in the anguish of those losing jobs. The recent economic crisis was dramatic in causing job losses, as the following data from the Center for Economic Progress show.

Monthly Job Losses

Your Thoughts?

The job losses in the chart are staggering. What does this mean in terms of personal career management and even academic program selection? When employers are faced with such realities, what options do they have? Can more jobs be protected through alternative forms of cost-cutting?

The term **flexible working hours**, also called *flextime*, describes any work schedule that gives employees some choice in daily work hours. A typical flextime schedule offers choices of starting and ending times, while still putting in a full workday. Some people may start earlier and leave earlier, while others do the opposite. The flexibility provides opportunities to attend to personal affairs such as medical appointments, home emergencies, and children's school schedules.

All top 100 companies in *Working Mother* magazine's list of best employers for working moms offer flexible scheduling. Reports indicate that flexibility in dealing with nonwork obligations reduces stress and unwanted job turnover. The women's sports apparel company Athleta, for example, attributes its low turnover rate compared with the industry average to flexible scheduling.[44]

Another work scheduling alternative is **job sharing**, where two or more persons split one full-time job. This often involves each person working one-half day, but it can also be done on weekly or monthly sharing arrangements. Both the employees and the organizations benefit when talented people who cannot devote a full day to work are kept or brought back into the workforce.

Then there is remote work, virtual offices, or work at home.[45] Whatever you call it, many people do some form of **telecommuting**. They spend at least a portion of scheduled work hours outside the office linked with co-workers, customers, and bosses by a variety of advanced information technologies. And it's popular. Estimates are that 27% of American workers spent at least one day a month working at home.[46]

When asked what they like, telecommuters report increased productivity, fewer distractions, the freedom to be their own boss, and the benefit of having more time for themselves. But there are potential negatives as well. Some telecommuters report working too much, having less time to themselves, difficulty separating work and personal life, and having less time for family.[47] One says: "You have to have self-discipline and pride in what you do, but you also have to have a boss that trusts you enough to get out of the way."[48] Tips to Remember offers several guidelines for how to make telecommuting work for you.[49]

Tips to Remember
How to Make Telecommuting Work for You

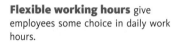

- Treat telecommuting like any workday; keep regular hours.
- Limit nonwork distractions; set up private space dedicated to work.
- Establish positive routines and work habits; be disciplined.
- Report regularly to your boss and main office; don't lose touch.
- Seek out human contact; don't become isolated.
- Use technology: instant messaging, intranet links, Net meetings.
- Keep your freedoms and responsibilities in balance.
- Reward yourself with time off; let flexibility be an advantage.

Flexible working hours give employees some choice in daily work hours.

Job sharing splits one job between two people.

Telecommuting involves using IT to work at home or outside the office.

Study Guide

8.3
What Are the Trends in Organizational Design?

Rapid review

- Organizations are becoming flatter, with fewer management levels, operating with fewer staff appointments, using decentralization with centralization, and using more delegation and empowerment.
- Mechanistic organizational designs are vertical and bureaucratic; they perform best in stable environments with mostly routine and predictable tasks.
- Organic organizational designs are horizontal and adaptive; they perform best in change environments requiring adaptation and flexibility.
- Organizations are using alternative work schedules such as the compressed work week, flexible working hours, and job sharing.

Terms to define

Bureaucracy
Centralization
Compressed work week
Decentralization
Delegation
Differentiation
Empowerment
Flexible working hours
Job sharing
Mechanistic design
Organic design
Organizational design
Span of control

Be sure you can

- illustrate the link between tall or flat organizations and spans of control
- explain the reasons for more decentralization and smaller staffs
- list the steps in delegation
- differentiate mechanistic and organic organizational designs
- explain the organizational design implications of the Burns and Stalker study
- explain subsystems design implications of the Lawrence and Lorsch study
- differentiate compressed work week, flexible working hours, and job sharing

Questions for discussion

1. Which, if any, of the organizational trends are unlikely to persist in today's ever-changing economy?
2. Knowing your personality, will you fit in better with an organization that has a mechanistic or an organic design?
3. How can alternative work schedules work to the benefit of both organizations and their members?

[Test Prep]

Multiple choice

1. The main purpose of organizing as a management function is to _____.
   (a) make sure that results match plans
   (b) arrange people and resources to accomplish work
   (c) create enthusiasm for the needed work
   (d) link strategies with operational plans

2. An organization chart is most useful for _____.
   (a) mapping informal structures
   (b) eliminating functional chimneys
   (c) showing designated supervisory relationships
   (d) describing the shadow organization

3. Rumors and resistance to change are potential disadvantages often associated with _____.
   (a) virtual organizations
   (b) informal structures
   (c) functional chimneys
   (d) cross-functional teams

4. When an organization chart shows vice presidents of marketing, finance, manufacturing, and purchasing all reporting to the president, top management is using a _____ structure.
   (a) functional
   (b) matrix
   (c) network
   (d) product

5. The "two-boss" system of reporting relationships is both a potential source of problems and one of the key aspects of _____ structures.
   (a) functional   (b) matrix
   (c) network   (d) product

6. A manufacturing business with a functional structure has recently acquired two other businesses with very different product lines. The president of the combined company might consider using a _____ structure to allow a better focus on the unique needs of each product area.
   (a) virtual   (b) team
   (c) divisional   (d) network

7. An organization using a _____ structure should expect more problems to be solved at lower levels and that top managers will have more time free to engage in strategic thinking.
   (a) virtual   (b) matrix
   (c) functional   (d) product

8. The functional chimneys problem occurs when people in different functions _____.
   (a) fail to communicate with one another
   (b) try to help each other work with customers
   (c) spend too much time coordinating decisions
   (d) focus on products rather than functions

9. An organization that employs just a few "core" or essential full-time employees and outsources a lot of the remaining work shows signs of using a _____ structure.
   (a) functional   (b) divisional
   (c) network   (d) team

10. Which organization structure is likely to have better managerial accountability for product or service delivery?
    (a) virtual   (b) functional
    (c) area division   (d) matrix

11. A "tall" organization will likely have _____ spans of control than a "flat" organization with the same number of members.
    (a) wider   (b) narrower
    (c) more ambiguous (d) less centralized

12. If a student in one of your course groups volunteers to gather information for a case analysis project and the other members agree while telling him to choose the information sources he believes are most important, the group is giving this student _____ to fulfill the agreed-upon task.
    (a) responsibility   (b) accountability
    (c) authority   (d) values

13. The current trend in the use of staff personnel in organizations is to _____.
    (a) give them more authority
    (b) reduce their numbers
    (c) distribute them among all levels of management
    (d) increase their efficiency with better use of IT

14. The bureaucratic organization described by Max Weber is similar to the _____ organization described by Burns and Stalker.
    (a) adaptive   (b) mechanistic
    (c) organic   (d) horizontal

15. Which organization would likely be a good fit for a dynamic and changing external environment?
    (a) vertical   (b) centralized
    (c) organic   (d) mechanistic

16. Why should an organization chart be trusted "only so far"?

17. In what ways can informal structures be good for organizations?

18. How does a matrix structure combine functional and divisional forms?

19. Why is an organic design likely to be quicker and more flexible in adapting to changes than a mechanistic design?

Integration & application

20. Be a consultant to your university or college president. The assignment is: Make this organization more efficient without sacrificing our educational goals. Although the president doesn't realize it, you are a specialist in network structures. You are going to suggest building a network organization, and your ideas are going to be radical and provocative.

Questions: What would be the core of the network—is it the faculty members that teach the various courses, or is it the administration that provides the infrastructure that students and faculty use in the learning experience? What might be outsourced—grounds and facilities maintenance, food services, security, recreation programs, even registration? What types of alliances might prove beneficial—student recruiting, faculty, even facilities?

[Self-Assessment]

Organizational Design Preference

Instructions

In the margin near each item, write the number from the following scale that shows the extent to which the statement accurately describes your views.[50]

> 5 = *strongly agree*
> 4 = *agree somewhat*
> 3 = *undecided*
> 2 = *disagree somewhat*
> 1 = *strongly disagree*

I prefer to work in an organization where:

1. Goals are defined by those in higher levels.

2. Work methods and procedures are specified.

3. Top management makes important decisions.

4. My loyalty counts as much as my ability to do the job.

5. Clear lines of authority and responsibility are established.

6. Top management is decisive and firm.

7. My career is pretty well planned out for me.

8. I can specialize.

9. My length of service is almost as important as my level of performance.

10. Management is able to provide the information I need to do my job well.

11. A chain of command is well established.

12. Rules and procedures are adhered to equally by everyone.

13. People accept the authority of a leader's position.

14. People are loyal to their boss.

15. People do as they have been instructed.

16. People clear things with their boss before going over his or her head.

Scoring and Interpretation

Total your scores for all questions. Enter the score here [_____]. This assessment measures your preference for working in an organization designed along "organic" or "mechanistic" lines. The higher your score (above 64), the more comfortable you are with a mechanistic design; the lower your score (below 48), the more comfortable you are with an organic design. Scores between 48 and 64 can go either way.

Case Snapshot

Nike—Spreading Out to Stay Together

Nike is indisputably a giant in the athletics industry. But the Portland, Oregon, company has grown large precisely because it knows how to stay small. By focusing on its core competencies—and outsourcing all others—Nike has managed to become a sharply focused industry leader. But how does its approach stack up with the realities of a changing economy? And is it the right approach for keeping Nike ahead of its competition?

Online Interactive Learning Resources

SELF-ASSESSMENT
• Networking

EXPERIENTIAL EXERCISES
• Network "U"
• Contingency Workforce

TEAM PROJECT
• Downsizing or Rightsizing?

9
Organizational Culture, Innovation, and Change

Adaptability and Values Set the Tone

Learning Outline

9.1 What Is the Nature of Organizational Culture?

- Organizational culture is the personality of the organization
- Great organizational cultures are customer-driven and performance-oriented
- The observable culture is what you as employee or customer see and hear
- The core culture is found in the underlying values of the organization
- Value-based management supports a strong organizational culture

9.2 How Do Organizations Support and Achieve Innovation?

- Organizations pursue process, product, and business model innovations
- Green innovations support the environment and pursue sustainability
- Social business innovations seek solutions to important societal problems
- Commercializing innovation puts new ideas into use
- Innovative organizations share many common characteristics

9.3 How Do Managers Lead the Processes of Organizational Change?

- Organizations pursue both transformational and incremental changes
- Three phases of planned change are unfreezing, changing, and refreezing
- Managers use force-coercion, rational persuasion, and shared power change strategies
- Change leaders identify and deal positively with resistance to change

Businesses tap design firms for innovation booster. Design has long been the province of the toymakers, apparel manufacturers, and even computer firms. But now more businesses of all types are turning to the expertise of IDEO Inc. and other design firms for innovative ideas that can add value to the bottom line.

At New York's Sloan-Kettering Cancer Center the administrators were concerned about patient experiences with chemotherapy. When IDEO consultants were called in, the first thing they did was spend time observing patients in all stages of therapy. Clinic staffers thought waiting times would be the big issue. But what the consultants found was that stress relating to tests, patient information, and even travel to the clinic was the big issue. And these findings led to innovative solutions—patient phone calls when leaving home so that the clinic could start mixing drugs, new information packets, and special transportation services. Wendy Perchick, head of strategic planning and innovation for the center, says the design firm was hired "to look at problems differently" and the result was "the first time for us to see chemotherapy through the patients' eyes."

Trendsetters
Tom Szaky takes idea from
dorm room to Wal-Mart.

News Feed
Google, P&G fuel innovation
by swapping workers.

Case Snapshot
Apple Inc.—People and
design create the future.

Switch over to toys and you find IDEO working with Mattel Inc. to help improve collaboration among product designers. When executives at the Mexican cement firm Productos Cementeros Mexicanos asked for insights, IDEO consultants saw a need to get in better touch with markets; they took executives for rides in the cement trucks to visit customers and discover new business opportunities.

Educators are recognizing the great potential of blending design with other areas of study. One is Stanford University. It now runs an Institute of Design that executives can attend to learn "design thinking." Another is Case Western Reserve University which is integrating a "design attitude and skills" into its MBA program. And without doubt, organizations of all types are finding that the ideas and approaches of design experts can be a great boost to management thinking on everything from products to processes to business models. Tim Brown, CEO of IDEO, says: "Design thinking is an approach that uses the designer's sensibility and methods for problem solving to meet people's needs in a technologically feasible and commercially viable way. In other words, design thinking is human-centered innovation."

9.1 What Is the Nature of Organizational Culture?

You probably hear the word "culture" a lot these days. In today's global economy, how can we fail to appreciate the cultural differences between people or nations? However, you may not hear about another type of culture that can be just as important: the cultures of organizations. Just as nations, ethnic groups, and families have cultures, organizations also have cultures that help to distinguish them from one another and bind members together with some sense of collective identity.

• Organizational culture is the personality of the organization.

Organizational culture is a system of shared beliefs and values guiding behavior.

Think of the stores that you shop in; the restaurants that you patronize; the place where you work. What is the "atmosphere" like? Do you notice, for example, how major retailers like Anthropologie, Hollister, and Abercrombie & Fitch have Web sites and store climates that seem to fit their brands and customer identities?[1] Such aspects of the internal environments of organizations are important in management and the term used to describe them is **organizational culture**, the system of shared beliefs and values that develops within an organization and guides the behavior of its members.[2]

Whenever someone speaks of "the way we do things here," he or she is talking about the organization's culture. You can think of this as the personality of the organization, something in the background that creates the atmosphere within which people work. Sometimes called the *corporate culture*, it is a key aspect of any organization and work setting. And importantly, the nature of the culture can have a strong impact on an organization's performance and the quality of work experiences of its members. At Zappos.com, the popular e-tailer of shoes and more, CEO Tony Hsieh says: "If we get the culture right, most of the other stuff, like brand and the customer service, will just happen.[3]

• Great organizational cultures are customer-driven and performance-oriented.

Strong cultures are clear, well defined, and widely shared among members.

Although culture is not the sole determinant of what happens in organizations, it does influence what they accomplish, and how. The internal culture has the potential to shape attitudes, reinforce beliefs, direct behavior, and establish performance expectations and the motivation to fulfill them. It helps set the organization's performance tone. Meg Whitman, former eBay CEO, says that organization culture "means the set of values and principles by which you run a company." She believes it creates the "character of the company" and becomes the "moral center" that helps every member understand what is right and what is wrong in terms of personal behavior.[4]

A widely discussed study of successful businesses concluded that organizational culture had a positive impact on long-term performance.[5] The cultures in these organizations provided for a clear vision that allowed people to rally around the goals and work hard to accomplish them.[6] The cultures discouraged dysfunctional work behaviors and encouraged positive ones, helping commit members to doing things for and with one another that are good for the organization. And they were also **strong cultures**—clear, well defined, and widely shared among members.[7] Honda is a good example. Its culture is tightly focused around "The Honda Way"—principles emphasizing ambition, respect for ideas, open communication, work enjoyment, harmony, and hard work.

When IBM's Research Director, John E. Kelly III, says—"If we don't fail a third of the time, we're not stretching enough," he's not just making a point; he's describing essential dimensions of IBM's corporate culture.[8] From his comments

The atmosphere in each Anthropologie store clearly communicates the firm's organizational culture.

you should be picturing an organization that encourages risk taking and seeks extraordinarily high performance. Tips to Remember suggests how you can learn to read and understand an organization's culture, whether as a job applicant, employee, or customer. Acquiring this important skill can guide you toward working for, and with, the organizations that best fit your career goals and personal preferences.

Have you visited Disneyland or Disney World? If so, you have experienced firsthand an organization with a "strong" organizational culture. Think about how the employees acted, how the park ran, and how consistently and positively all visitors were treated. Strong organizational cultures such as Disney's are clear, well defined, and widely shared among members.[9] They encourage positive work behaviors and discourage dysfunctional ones. They also commit members to doing things for and with one another that are in the best interests of the organization.

Strong and positive cultures like the one found at Disney don't happen by chance. They are created through **socialization**. This is the process of helping new members learn the culture and values of the organization, as well as the behaviors and attitudes that are shared among its members.[10] Such socialization often begins in an anticipatory sense with one's education, such as the importance of professional appearance and interpersonal skills for business students. It then continues with an employer's orientation and training programs which, when well done, can be strongly influential on the new member. And, as you well realize, some organizations give much more attention to such training than others.

Disney is one of those employers that invests heavily in socialization and training of its members. Each new Disney employee attends a program called "traditions." It educates them on the company history, its language and lore, as well as the founding story. All is done in the context of the global reach of the Disney brand. This commitment to socialization and a strong culture began with the founder, Walt Disney, who is quoted as saying: "You can dream, create, design and build the most wonderful place in the world, but it requires people to make the dream a reality."[11]

Tips to Remember 🅑

SCORES—How to Read an Organization's Culture

S—How tight or loose is the *structure*?
C—Are decisions *change* oriented or driven by the status quo?
O—What *outcomes* or results are most highly valued?
R—What is the climate for *risk taking*, innovation?
E—How widespread is *empowerment*, worker involvement?
S—What is the competitive *style*, internal and external?

Socialization is the process through which new members learn the culture of an organization.

• The observable culture is what you see and hear as an employee or customer.

One way that you can try to understand organizational culture is shown in **Figure 9.1**, depicting two levels—the outermost or "observable" culture and the inner or "core" culture.[12] You might think of this in the sense of an iceberg. What lies below the surface and is harder to see is the core culture. That which stands out above the surface and is more visible to the discerning eye is the observable culture. Both need to be understood.

The **observable culture** is what you see in people's behaviors and hear in their conversations. It includes how people dress at work, arrange their offices, speak to and behave toward one another, and talk about and treat their customers. You'll notice it not only as an employee, but also when being served as a customer or client. Test this out the next time you go in a store, restaurant, or service establishment. How do people look, act, and behave? How do they treat one another? How do they treat customers? What's in their conversations? Are they enjoying themselves? When you answer these questions you are starting to describe the observable culture of the organization.

The **observable culture** is what you see and hear when walking around an organization.

The Disney commitment to socialization around a strong organizational culture is legendary.

FIGURE 9.1
What Are the Main Components of Organizational Culture?

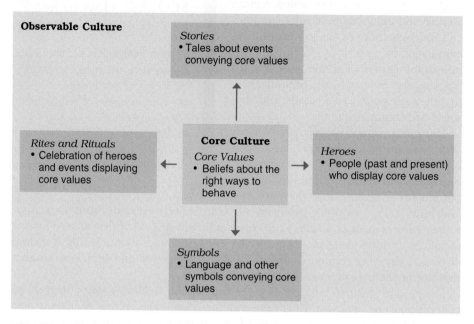

With a bit of effort one can easily identify the organizational culture. The most visible part is the observable culture. It is shown in the stories, rituals, heroes, and symbols that are part of the everyday life of the organization. The deeper, below-the-surface part is the core culture. It consists of the values that influence the beliefs, attitudes, and work practices among organizational members.

The observable culture is also found in the stories, heroes, rituals, and symbols that are part of daily organizational life. In the university it includes the pageantry of graduation and honors ceremonies; in sports teams it's the pregame rally, sidelines pep talk, and all the "thumping and bumping" that takes place after a good play. In workplaces such as Apple, Hewlett-Packard, Zappos, and Amazon, it's in the stories told about the founders and the firm's history, as well as spontaneous celebrations of a work accomplishment or personal milestone such as a co-worker's birthday or wedding.

The presence or absence of such things, and the ways they are practiced, can say a lot about an organization's culture. They represent, communicate, and carry the culture over time, keeping it visible and clear in all members' eyes. New members learn the organization's culture through them; all members keep the culture alive by sharing and joining in them. And you have to admit, in some organizations this observable culture is far richer and more positive than in others.

• The core culture is found in the underlying values of the organization.

Core culture is found in the underlying values of the organization.

Core values are beliefs and values shared by organization members.

A second and deeper level of organizational culture is called the **core culture**. It consists of the **core values** or underlying assumptions and beliefs that shape and guide people's behaviors. Values in some of the best companies, for example, have been found to emphasize performance excellence, innovation, social responsibility, integrity, worker involvement, customer service, and teamwork.[13] And successful organizations that operate with such values are often described as having "strong" cultures.

Statements of an organization's values are typically found on Web sites, in mission statements, and in executive speeches. Examples are: "Service above all else"—Nordstrom; "Science-based innovation"—Merck; "Fanatical attention to consistency and detail"—Disney. Another example is Herman Miller, the innovative and award-winning manufacturer of designer furniture that calls itself "a high-performance, values-driven community of people tied together by a common purpose." The firm's Web site further states: "For 50 years participation has been central to Herman Miller. It still is. We believe in participation because we value and benefit from the richness of ideas and opinions of thousands of people. Participation enables employee-owners to contribute their unique gifts and abilities to the corporate community."[14]

When trying to read or understand an organization's culture, however, don't be fooled by values statements alone. It's easy to write a set of values, post them on the Web, and talk about them. It's a lot harder to live up to them. If an organization's stated values are to have any positive effects, everyone in the organization from top to bottom must reflect the values in day-to-day actions. That is characteristic of successful strong culture organizations. And in this sense, managers have a special responsibility to "walk the values talk" and make the expressed values real. After all, how might you react if you found out senior executives in your organization talked up values such as honesty and ethical behavior, but then acted quite differently, such as by spending company funds on lavish private parties and vacations?

> **Core values support a strong culture at Herman Miller**
> - Making a meaningful contribution to our customers
> - Cultivating community, participation, and people development
> - Creating economic value for shareholders and employee-owners
> - Responding to change through design and innovation
> - Living with integrity and respecting the environment and career development

• Value-based management supports a strong organizational culture.

When managers do practice the core values, model them for others, and communicate and reinforce them in all that they do, this is called **value-based management**. It is managing with a commitment to actively help develop, communicate, and represent shared values within an organization. A good test of the value-based management of any organization or team can be done by assessing how things work on criteria such as these.

Value-based management actively develops, communicates, and enacts shared values.

- *Relevance*—Core values support key performance objectives.
- *Integrity*—Core values provide clear, consistent ethical anchors.
- *Pervasiveness*—Core values are understood by all members.
- *Strength*—Core values are accepted by all members.

An incident at Tom's of Maine provides an example of value-based management.[15] After a big investment in a new deodorant, founder Tom Chappell was dismayed when he learned that customers were very dissatisfied with it. But having founded the company on values that include fairness and honesty in all matters, he decided to reimburse customers and pull the product from the market. Even though it cost the company more than $400,000, Tom did what he believed was the right thing. He was living up to the full spirit of the company's values and also setting a very positive example for others in the firm to follow. This is what value-based management is all about.

It is now popular to discuss something called **workplace spirituality** along with value-based management. Although the first tendency might be to associate the term "spirituality" with religion, it is used in management to reflect practices that try to nourish people's inner lives by bringing meaning to work and engaging each other with a sense of shared community.[16]

The core values in a culture of workplace spirituality will have strong ethics foundations, recognize the value of individuals and respect their diversity, and

Workplace spirituality involves practices that create meaning and shared community among organizational members.

focus on creating meaningful work tasks and jobs. These factors contribute to an organizational purpose that offers identifiable value to society. When someone works in a culture of workplace spirituality, in other words, the person should derive personal pleasure from knowing that what is being accomplished is personally meaningful, created through community, and valued by others.

Tom Chappell is a good example of value-based management in action, and he led Tom's of Maine with a strong commitment to workplace spirituality. He also proved in his handling of the new deodorant problem to be a good **symbolic leader**, someone who uses symbols well to communicate values and maintain a desired organizational culture. Symbolic managers and leaders both act and talk the "language" of the organization. They are always careful to behave in ways that live up to the espoused core values; they are ever-present role models for others to emulate and follow.

A **symbolic leader** uses symbols to establish and maintain a desired organizational culture.

One thing you'll notice is that symbolic leaders are careful to use spoken and written words to describe people, events, and even the competition in ways that reinforce and communicate core values. Language metaphors—the use of positive examples from another context—are very powerful in this regard. For example, newly hired workers at Disney are counseled to always think of themselves not as employees but as key "members of the cast" that work "on stage." After all, they are told, Disney isn't just any business; it is an "entertainment" business.

Tom Chappell built a firm on strong values and the belief that you can do good while doing business.

Successful symbolic leaders continually highlight and even dramatize core values and the observable culture. They tell key stories over and over again, and they encourage others to tell them. They may refer to the "founding story" about the entrepreneur whose personal values set a key tone for the enterprise. They remind everyone about organizational heroes, past and present, whose performances exemplify core values. They often use rites and rituals to glorify the performance of the organization and its members. At Mary Kay Cosmetics, gala events at which top sales performers share their tales of success are legendary. So, too, are the lavish incentive awards presented at these ceremonies, especially the pink luxury cars given to the most successful salespeople.[17]

Study Guide

9.1
What is the Nature of Organizational Culture?

Rapid review

- Organizational culture is a system of shared values and beliefs that guides the behavior of members; it is an internal climate that creates the personality of the organization and also sets its performance tone.
- High-performing organizations tend to have strong cultures that are positive influences on employee behaviors, teamwork, and attitudes.
- The observable culture is found in the everyday rites, rituals, stories, heroes, and symbols of the organization.
- The core culture consists of the core values and fundamental beliefs on which the organization is based.
- Value-based management communicates, models, and reinforces core values throughout the organization.
- Symbolic leadership uses words and symbols to communicate the organizational culture.

Terms to define

Core culture

Core values

Observable culture

Organizational culture

Strong cultures

Symbolic leader

Value-based management

Workplace spirituality

Be sure you can

- explain organizational culture as the personality of an organization
- describe how strong cultures influence organizations
- define and explain the process of socialization
- distinguish between the observable and the core cultures
- explain value-based management
- explain symbolic leadership

Questions for discussion

1. Can an organization achieve success with a good organizational design but a weak organizational culture?
2. When you are in your local bank or any other retail establishment as a customer, what do you see and hear around you that identifies its observable culture?
3. What core values would you choose if you were creating a new organization and wanted to establish a strong performance-oriented culture?

9.2 How Do Organizations Support and Achieve Innovation?

When a car drove out of Tokyo one day, the event hardly seemed remarkable at the time. But when it arrived some 900 kilometers later on the northern island of Hokkaido, Mitsubishi's president considered it a notable feat. The car, powered by a new engine technology, had made the trip without refueling! In fact, the gas tank still had fuel to spare. Company engineers had long studied the challenge without successfully solving it. Finally, through a lot of hard work, information sharing, and learning, they achieved a breakthrough.[18]

It also may have seemed unremarkable, at first, when a group of Motorola engineers, designers, and marketers met in a Chicago office. But it wasn't just any office; it became the Motorola's innovation lab known as Moto City—a special place located away from corporate headquarters and free of its bureaucracy. This team's task was simple but challenging: Come up with a better cell phone. What they created together was the Motorola Razr. It was a smashing success, with 12.5 million selling its first year on the market.[19]

What we are discussing in these examples is **innovation**, the process of developing new ideas and putting them into practice.[20] The late management consultant Peter Drucker called innovation "an effort to create purposeful, focused change in an enterprise's economic or social potential."[21] Said a bit differently, it is the act of converting new ideas into usable applications with positive economic or social consequences. And if you stop and think about it, your office, home, car, and backpack are probably full of examples of innovations that enrich your life.

> **Innovation** is the process of taking a new idea and putting it into practice.

• Organizations pursue process, product, and business model innovations.

Innovation in and by organizations has traditionally been discussed in these three forms. First, **process innovations** result in better ways of doing things. Second, **product innovations** result in the creation of new or improved goods and services. Third, **business model innovations** result in new ways of making money for the firm.[22] Consider these examples of each type as found in firms listed in *Business Week* as among "The World's Most Innovative Companies."[23]

> **Process innovations** result in better ways of doing things.
>
> **Product innovations** result in new or improved goods or services.
>
> **Business model innovations** result in ways for firms to make money.

- *Process Innovation*—Southwest Airlines continues to improve operations underpinning its low-cost business strategy; IKEA transformed retail shopping for furniture and fixtures; Amazon.com keeps improving the online shopping experience; Nike allows online shoppers at NikeID to design their own sneakers; Proctor & Gamble reorganized to bring design executives into the top management circle; Facebook opened its software platform to third-party developers, with Yahoo! and Google following.
- *Product Innovation*—The Blackberry from Research in Motion ushered in a new era of hand-held mobile devices; Apple introduced us to the iPod and iPhone worlds, and made the "app" a must-have for smart phones; Amazon brought us the Kindle e-book reader; Toyota has been the market mover in new hybrid vehicles; Pure Digital technologies came out with the low-cost Flip Video camcorder; Tata Group of India has introduced a $2500 car, the Nano, for low income earners.
- *Business Model Innovation*—Virgin Group Ltd. uses "hip lifestyle" branding to infuse its many businesses, including Virgin Galactic, a new space tourism initiative; Starbucks continues to turn its coffee machine into a global branding business; eBay created the world's largest online marketplace; Google thrives on advertising revenues driven by ever-expanding

and great Web technology; Apple created iTunes for inexpensive and legal music downloads; Amazon.com sells its proprietary Web services to other firms.

• Green innovations pursue and support the goals of sustainability.

Today we can add **green innovation** to the prior list. Green innovations support sustainability and reduce the carbon footprint of an organization or its products. The possibilities abound.[24] Sometimes it's the small things that count, such as replacement of air travel with videoconferencing. Vodafone estimates that in one year it eliminated 13,500 flights employees would otherwise take to attend meetings. This cut some 5000 tons of carbon emissions. In other ways, green innovation gets more expansive. Sierra Nevada Brewing Company fuels its generators with a blend of purchased natural gas and biogas from a water treatment plant. Adding in solar energy, the firm generates 80% of its own power, cutting electricity costs while also reducing air pollution.

Take a look around and you find many more examples of green innovation. Patagonia buys used garments, breaks them down, and reweaves the fibers for clothing sold in its Common Threads line. The savings in energy costs and carbon emissions are over 70%.[25] And factories in Kenya are producing the "Kyoto Box Oven" developed by local resident John Bohmer. It harnesses the sun's energy and costs about $5 to make from cardboard and other easily-found materials. The goal is to free poor people from dependence on wood-fired cooking ovens, and thus reduce deforestation and global warming. Bohmer says: "A lot of scientists are working on ways to send people to Mars. I was looking for something a little more grassroots, a little simpler."[26]

Green innovation is the process of turning ideas into innovations that reduce the carbon footprint of an organization or its products.

• Social business innovations seek solutions to important societal problems.

It can be said that innovation is the act of converting new ideas into usable applications with positive economic or social value. And although the tendency is to view business innovation in a purely economic context, it's important to remember that it applies equally well when we talk about the world's social problems—poverty, famine, literacy, diseases, and the general conditions for economic and social development.

Social business innovation stems from creativity that manifests itself as **social entrepreneurship**.[27] It is a unique form of entrepreneurship that seeks novel ways to solve pressing social problems. You can think of it as creativity and innovation for social good, such as the Kyoto Box Oven just discussed.

What do you do, for example, about chronic hunger that is the leading cause of death among African children? Sympathy wasn't enough for Andrew Youn. He's a social entrepreneur whose efforts have made a world of difference for many African families.[28] After returning from a Northwestern University internship in South Africa, Youn attacked the problem of chronic child hunger with an innovative program—the One Acre Fund. It provides small loans to Kenya's poor families, enabling them to work their land with high quality seed, fertilizer, equipment, and training. The goal is to help farmers "grow their way out of poverty" by finding ways to increase crop yields and avoid the devastating effects of Kenya's three-month "hunger season." The One Acre Fund won the SC Johnson Award for

Social entrepreneurship pursues creative and innovative ways to solve pressing social problems.

Social entrepreneurship finds innovative ways to solve pressing social problems.

Socially Responsible Entrepreneurship, and has expanded into Rwanda. Says Youn: "The mothers are absolutely inspiring. The things they do out of necessity are heroic."

• Commercializing innovation puts new ideas into use.

The management of innovation requires encouragement and support for both *invention*—the act of discovery, and *application*—the act of use. This means that managers need to invest in and build work environments that stimulate creativity and an ongoing stream of new ideas. They must also make sure that good ideas for new or modified processes and products are actually implemented.

Commercializing innovation turns ideas into economic value added.

In business it is the process of **commercializing innovation** that turns new ideas into actual products, services, or processes that can increase profits through greater sales or reduced costs.[29] For example, 3M Corporation owes its success to the imagination of employees such as Art Fry. He's the person whose creativity turned an adhesive that "wasn't sticky enough" into the blockbuster product known worldwide today as Post-It Notes®. It's tempting to believe that commercializing an innovation such as the Post-It Note is easy; you might even consider it a "no brainer." But it isn't necessarily so. Art Fry and his colleagues had to actively "sell" the Post-It idea to 3M's marketing group and then to senior management before getting the financial support they needed to turn the invention into a salable product. **Figure 9.2** shows how new product ideas such as Post-It might move through the typical steps of commercializing innovation.

FIGURE 9.2

Steps in the Process of Commercializing Innovation.

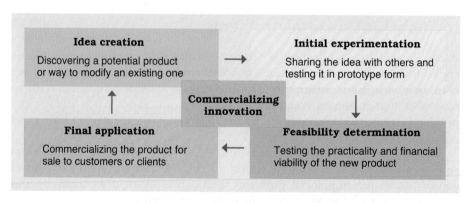

Idea creation
Discovering a potential product or way to modify an existing one

Initial experimentation
Sharing the idea with others and testing it in prototype form

Commercializing innovation

Final application
Commercializing the product for sale to customers or clients

Feasibility determination
Testing the practicality and financial viability of the new product

When reading the earlier example of Patagonia's innovative Common Threads project that collects old garments and breaks them down to create reusable fibers, you might have said—"common sense." But the idea was almost four years in process. Like 3M's Post-It Notes® there was a lot involved in turning a good idea into a for-sale product. One way to describe the full set of responsibilities for commercializing innovation is in what consultant Gary Hamel calls the wheel of innovation.[30]

1. *Imagining*—thinking about new possibilities; making discoveries by ingenuity or communicating with others; extending existing ways

2. *Designing*—testing ideas in concept; discussing them with peers, customers, clients, or technical experts; building initial models, prototypes, or samples

Japanese firms show that hard work and persistence often generate innovations.

3. *Experimenting*—examining practicality and financial value through experiments and feasibility studies

4. *Assessing*—identifying strengths and weaknesses, potential costs and benefits, and potential markets or applications; and making constructive changes

5. *Scaling*—gearing up and implementing new processes; putting to work what has been learned; commercializing new products or services

The ultimate test of successful innovation is whether the entire process meets the real needs of the organization and its marketplace. In talking about Procter & Gamble's approach to innovation, for example, former CEO A. G. Lafley says: "We have figured out how to keep the consumer at the center of all our decisions, as a result we don't go wrong."[31] He is pointing out that new ideas alone do not guarantee success; they must be relevant, and they must be well implemented. "You need creativity and invention," Lafley says, "but until you can connect that creativity to the customer in the form of a product or service that meaningfully changes their lives, I would argue you don't yet have innovation."[32]

• Innovative organizations share many common characteristics.

How do you view Microsoft? Do you see a firm whose strategy and culture drive an innovation powerhouse? Or do see what *PC World* describes as "a stodgy old corporation churning out boring software"? There are quite a few critics that believe Microsoft meets the latter description, not the former. Craig Mundie, Microsoft's chief research and strategy officer, claims his firm hasn't lost its innovative edge and pledges to do better at "communicating about the tremendous things this company does."[33] But claiming innovation and demonstrating innovation are two different things. The proof for Mundie and Microsoft will be in what the firm delivers in the future and how its products are received in the marketplace.

Truly innovative organizations such as 3M, Google, and Apple have built enduring organizational capacities to innovate. And most innovative organizations like this share common features like those in **Figure 9.3**.[34]

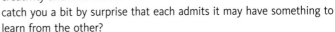

News Feed

Google and Procter & Gamble Swap Workers to Fuel Innovation

They are two solid business names—Google and Procter & Gamble. They are also two firms well regarded for creativity and innovation. Does it catch you a bit by surprise that each admits it may have something to learn from the other?

To begin, the organizational cultures are quite different. P&G employees sometimes call themselves "Proctoids" when joking about the rigid culture; "Googlers" work in a fashion-forward culture full of flexibility, funkiness, and fun. So it may have been with some apprehension that teams from each firm recently traded cultures to spend time with the other. As it turns out, they learned quite a bit.

Procter & Gamble is a marketing innovator and leads the corporate world in advertising spending. Yet its online ad budget is very low at just the time when a growing number of its customers spend more time browsing the Internet than watching TV. Time spent at Google, the world's Web master, was a chance to get closer in touch with that medium and come up with new ideas to guide its online ad strategy. "One of the best learning of my first week at Google," said one Proctoid, was that online searches for coupons had skyrocketed by 50% in 12 months.

Tech-savvy Googlers learned ideas for refined online advertising, but were shocked at the lack of blogging at P&G. "Where are the bloggers?" one asked after learning about a new Pampers ad featuring Salma Hayek. How could such a large promotion be launched without "motherhood" bloggers, persons running Web sites devoted to child rearing, being invited to the news conference? In response, P&G invited the mommy-bloggers for a special visit to the baby division headquarters. They reported an increase into the millions of visitors to their Web sites during this campaign.

Reflect and React:

Job swapping isn't new within an organization, so why has it taken so long for it to gain popularity between organizations? Does it surprise you that firms such as Google and Procter & Gamble are taking this approach? What other organizations including those in your community might make good job-swapping partners for these firms?

FIGURE 9.3

Common Characteristics of Highly Innovative Organizations.

Highly Innovative Organizations				
Strategy includes innovation	Culture values innovation	Responsive structures and systems	Top management support	Staffing for creativity and innovation

Core values at IDEO encourage innovation and allow new ideas to continually flourish.

In highly innovative organizations the *corporate strategy and culture support innovation.* The strategies of the organization include and highlight innovation; the culture of the organization, as reflected in the visions and values of senior management and the framework of policies and expectations, emphasizes an innovation spirit. If you think back to the opening example of the design firm IDEO, for example, we are talking about a firm whose Web site says: "Our values are part mad scientist (curious, experimental), bear-tamer (gutsy, agile), *reiki* master (hands-on, empathetic), and midnight tax accountant (optimistic, savvy). These qualities are reflected in the smallest details to the biggest endeavors, composing the medium in which great ideas are born and flourish."[35]

Organization cultures that encourage innovation are tolerant of differences, not risk adverse, and value creativity more than conformity. That type of culture is precisely the goal communicated by Sony CEO Howard Stringer when he addressed a meeting of the firm's top global executives. Concerned that Sony was falling behind its rivals and was not as innovative as it could be, Stringer placed a large part of the blame on Sony's corporate culture. He told the executives: "I'm asking you to get mad" and pointedly said he wanted their businesses run in more "energetic," "bold," and "imaginative" ways.[36] Innovation is already part of the culture at Google where engineers are allowed one day per week to work on ideas not driven by their jobs. Managers also attend "innovation reviews" where they present new ideas from their areas to the firm's senior executives.[37]

In highly innovative organizations, *organization structures support innovation.* Bureaucracy is an enemy of innovation. More and more organizations are trying to break its confines by taking advantage of horizontal designs team structures that break up functional chimneys and silos. *Business Week* describes the goal this way: "Instead of assembly line, think swarming beehive. Teams of people from different disciplines gather to focus on a problem. They brainstorm, tinker and toy with different approaches."[38]

The term **skunkworks** is often used to describe special units set free from the normal structure and given separate locations, special resources, and their own managers, all with the purpose of achieving innovation. Yahoo, for example, has created the "Brickhouse." It's basically an idea incubator set up in a separate facility where Yahoo staffers, some in bean bag chairs and playing with Nerf balls, work on ideas submitted from all over the company. "The goal," says Salim Ismail who heads Brickhouse, "is to take the idea, develop it, and make sure it's seen by senior management quickly."[39] In other words, Brickhouse exists so that good ideas don't get lost in Yahoo's bureaucracy.

Skunkworks are special creative units set free from the normal structure for the purpose of innovation.

In highly innovative organizations, *staffing supports innovation*. Step one in meeting this goal is to make creativity an important criterion when hiring and moving people into positions of responsibility. Step two is allowing their creative talents to fully operate by following through on the practices just discussed—strategy, culture, structure, and leadership. Step three involves putting people in key roles that are focused on meeting the needs of the innovation process itself. These critical innovation roles include:

- *Idea generators*—people who create new insights from internal discovery or external awareness or both.
- *Information gatekeepers*—people who serve as links between people and groups within the organization and with external sources.
- *Product and process champions*—people who advocate and push for change and innovation, and for the adoption of specific product or process ideas.
- *Project managers*—people who perform technical functions needed to keep an innovative project on track with necessary resource support.
- *Innovation leaders*—people who encourage, sponsor, and coach others to keep the innovation values, goals, and energies in place.

Amazon's long-term thinking and willingness to fail help support creativity and innovation at the firm.

In highly innovative organizations, *top management supports innovation*. Google's CEO Eric Schmidt is a good example. Considered a master at fueling innovation, he allows the firm's engineers to spend 20% of their time on projects of their own choosing.[40] The best top managers tolerate criticisms and differences of opinion. They know that success doesn't always come in a straight line and admit that mistakes are often part of the innovation process.

When it comes to top management support for innovation, Johnson & Johnson's former CEO James Burke believes that managers should eliminate risk-averse climates and replace them with organizational cultures in which innovation is a norm. He once said: "I try to give people the feeling that it's okay to fail, that it's important to fail."[41] And at Amazon, CEO Jeff Bezos said this when talking about the firm's innovative electronic reader, the Kindle: "Our willingness to be misunderstood, our long-term orientation and our willingness to repeatedly fail are the three parts of our culture that make doing this kind of thing possible."[42]

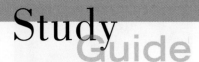
Study Guide

9.2
How Do Organizations Support and Achieve Innovation?

Rapid review

- Innovation is a process that turns creative ideas into products or processes that benefit organizations and their customers.
- Organizations pursue process, product, and business model innovations.
- Organizations pursue green innovations that support sustainability.
- Organizations pursue social business innovations to tackle important societal problems.
- The process of commercializing innovation turns new ideas into useful applications.
- Highly innovative organizations tend to have supportive cultures, strategies, structures, staffing, and top management.

Terms to define

Business model innovation
Commercializing innovation
Creativity
Green innovation
Innovation
Process innovations
Product innovations
Skunkworks
Social business innovation

Be sure you can

- discuss differences between process, product, and business model innovations
- explain green innovation and social business innovation
- list five steps in the process of commercializing innovation
- list and explain four characteristics of innovative organizations
- identify the critical innovation roles in organizations

Questions for discussion

1. Are there any potential downsides to making organizational commitments to green innovation?
2. What are the biggest trouble points in a large organization that might prevent a great idea from becoming a commercialized innovation?
3. What difference does a leader make in terms of how innovative an organization becomes?

9.3 How Do Managers Lead the Processes of Organizational Change?

Innovation is only one part of the story when it comes to organizations keeping up with the times. Look at the changes now taking place in industry world-wide. Firms are struggling and it's not always because they don't have the right ideas, it's because they have difficulty rallying the entire organization and all of its resources around goals. In other words, they have difficulty creating organizational change.

Like many other new CEOs, when Angel Martinez became head of Rockport Company he wanted to change traditional ways of doing things and increase the company's future competitiveness. But instead of embracing the changes he sponsored, employees resisted. Martinez said they "gave lip service to my ideas and hoped I'd go away."[43] He was trying, if not succeeding, to be a **change leader**. These are managers who act as *change agents*, who take leadership responsibility for changing the existing pattern of behavior of another person or social system.[44]

A **change leader** tries to change the behavior of another person or social system.

In theory, every manager should act as a change leader. But the reality described in **Figure 9.4** is that people in organizations show major tendencies toward the status quo—accepting things as they are and not wanting to change. And it's the status quo that creates lots of difficulties as organizations strive to innovate and managers try to lead the processes of change.

FIGURE 9.4
Change Leaders versus Status Quo Managers

Change leaders	Status quo managers
• Confident of ability • Willing to take risks • Seize opportunity • Expect surprise • Make things happen	• Threatened by change • Bothered by uncertainty • Prefer predictability • Support the status quo • Wait for things to happen

• Organizations pursue both transformational and incremental changes.

Many, if not most, people are arguing that only major, frame-breaking, radical change can save the large legacy companies hammered by the global financial crisis, and firms such as General Motors and Chrysler are at the top of the lists. They are talking about **transformational change** resulting in a major and comprehensive redirection of the organization—new vision, new strategy, new culture, new structure, and even new people.[45]

Transformational change results in a major and comprehensive redirection of the organization.

As you might expect, transformation change is intense, highly stressful, and very complex to achieve. Reports are that as many as 70% or more of large-scale change efforts actually fail.[46] And a main reason for failure is bad implementation, especially the failure of top management to build commitments within the workforce so that almost everyone actively supports and follows through with change goals.[47] The advice offered to would-be leaders of such large-scale changes includes these guidelines.[48]

- Establish a sense of urgency for change.
- Form a powerful coalition to lead the change.
- Create and communicate a change vision.
- Empower others to move change forward.
- Celebrate short-term wins and recognize those who help.
- Build on success; align people and systems with new ways.
- Stay with it; keep the message consistent; champion the vision.

Incremental change bends and adjusts existing ways to improve performance.

But let's not forget another more modest, frame-*bending* side to organizational change. This is **incremental change**, that which tweaks and nudges existing systems and practices to better align them with emerging problems and opportunities. The intent isn't to break and remake the system, but to move it forward through continuous improvements.

Leadership of incremental change focuses on building on existing ways of doing things with the goal of doing them better in the future. Common incremental changes in organizations involve new products, new processes, new technologies, and new work systems. You might think of this in the context of a good total quality management program, one where the search is always on for better ways and higher performance.

One shouldn't get the idea, by the way, that incremental change is somehow inferior to transformational change. Rather, most would argue that both are important; incremental changes keep things tuned up (like the engine on a car) in between transformations (when the old car is replaced with a new one). Putting the two together probably offers organizations the best of both worlds. When GE's former CEO Jack Welch first took the top job, for example, he was concerned about the firm's performance. So he began an aggressive top-down restructuring that led to major workforce cuts and a trimmer organization structure. Once underway, however, he created a structure for bottom-up change driven by employee involvement. He called the program Work-Out.[49]

In GE's Work-Out sessions managers are supposed to respond right away to change suggestions from their subordinates.

In GE's Work-Out sessions, employees confronted their managers in a "town meeting" format. The manager sat or stood in front listening to suggestions from subordinates about removing performance obstacles and improving operations. Welch expected the managers to respond immediately to the suggestions, and to try to implement as many of them as possible. From the top, Welch initiated the Work-Out program to drive organizational change from the bottom up.

• Three phases of planned change are unfreezing, changing, and refreezing.

Managers seeking to lead change in organizations can benefit from a simple but helpful model developed by the psychologist Kurt Lewin. He describes how change situations can be analyzed and addressed in three phases: *unfreezing*— preparing a system for change; *changing*—making actual changes in the system; and *refreezing*—stabilizing the system after change.[50]

Unfreezing is the phase during which a situation is prepared for change.

Unfreezing is the stage in which managers help others to develop, experience, and feel a real need for change. The goal here is to get people to view change as a way of solving a problem or taking advantage of an opportunity. Some might call this the "burning bridge" phase, arguing that in order to get people to jump off a bridge, you might just have to set it on fire. Managers can simulate the burning bridge by engaging people with facts and information that communicate the need for change—environmental pressures, declining performance, and examples of alternative approaches. And as you have probably experienced, conflict can help people to break old habits and recognize new ways of thinking about or doing things.

The **changing** phase is where actual change takes place. Ideally these changes are planned in ways that give them the best opportunities for success, having maximum appeal and posing minimum difficulties for those being asked to make them.[51] Although this phase should follow unfreezing in Lewin's model, he believes it is often started too early. When change takes place before people and systems are ready for it, the likelihood of resistance and change failure is much greater. In this sense Lewin might liken the change process to building a house; you need to put a good foundation in place before you begin the framing.

As shown in **Figure 9.5**, the final stage in the planned change process is **refreezing**. Here, the focus is on stabilizing the change to make it as long lasting as needed. Linking change with rewards, positive reinforcement, and resource support all help with refreezing. Of course, in today's dynamic environments

Changing is the phase where a planned change actually takes place.

Refreezing is the phase at which change is stabilized.

FIGURE 9.5

What Are the Change Leader's Responsibilities in Lewin's Three Phases of Planned Organizational Change?

Phase 1 Unfreezing

Change leader's task:

create a felt need for change

This is done by:

- Establishing a good relationship with the people involved.
- Helping others realize that present behaviors are not effective.
- Minimizing expressed resistance to change.

Phase 2 Changing

Change leader's task:

implement change

This is done by:

- Identifying new, more effective ways of behaving.
- Choosing changes in tasks, people, culture, technology, structures.
- Taking action to put these changes into place.

Phase 3 Refreezing

Change leader's task:

stabilize change

This is done by:

- Creating acceptance and continuity for the new behaviors.
- Providing any necessary resource support.
- Using performance-contingent rewards and positive reinforcement.

Kurt Lewin identified three phases of the planned change process. The first is unfreezing, the phase where people open up and become receptive to the possibility of change. The second is changing, where the actual change happens and the new ways of doing things are put into place. Third is refreezing, the phase where changes are stabilized to become part of ongoing routines. Lewin believed that change agents often neglect unfreezing and move too quickly into the changing phase, thus setting the stage for change failures. They may also neglect refreezing with the result that any achieved change has only temporary effects.

there may not be a lot of time for refreezing before things are ready to change again. You may well find that refreezing in Lewin's sense probably gives way quite often to a phase of evaluating and reassessing. We begin preparing for or undertaking more change even while trying to take full advantage of the present one.

• Managers use force-coercion, rational persuasion, and shared power change strategies.

When it comes to a manager actually being able to move people and systems toward change, the issue boils down to change strategy. **Figure 9.6** summarizes three common change strategies—force-coercion, rational persuasion, and shared power. Each should be understood and most likely used by all change leaders.[52]

FIGURE 9.6

What Happens When a Change Leader Uses Alternative Change Strategies?

Change Strategy	Power Bases	Managerial Behavior	Likely Results
Force–Coercion Using position power to create change by decree and formal authority	Legitimacy Rewards Punishments	*Direct forcing* and unilateral action *Political maneuvering* and indirect action	Faster, but low commitment and only temporary compliance
Rational Persuasion Creating change through rational persuasion and empirical argument	Expertise	*Informational efforts* using credible knowledge, demonstrated facts, and logical argument	
Shared power Developing support for change through personal values and commitments	Reference	*Participative efforts* to share power and involve others in planning and implementing change	Slower, but high commitment and longer term internalization

Force-coercion strategies use authority, offers of rewards, and threats of punishments to push change forward. The likely results are, at best, temporary compliance. Rational persuasion strategies use information, facts, and logic to present a persuasive case in support of change. The likely outcomes are compliance with reasonable commitment. Shared power strategies engage others and allow them to participate in the change process, from initial planning through implementation. The high involvement tends to build more internalization and greater commitments to change.

A **force-coercion strategy** pursues change through formal authority and/or the use of rewards or punishments.

A **force-coercion strategy** uses the power bases of legitimacy, rewards, and punishments as the primary inducements to change.[53] It comes in at least two types. In a *direct forcing* strategy, the change agent takes direct and unilateral action to command that change take place. This involves the exercise of formal authority or legitimate power, offering special rewards and/or threatening punishment. In *political maneuvering*, the change agent works indirectly to gain special advantage over other persons to force the change. This involves bargaining, obtaining control of important resources, forming alliances, or granting favors.

One thing to remember is that most people will probably respond to force-coercion in a limited way, and most likely out of fear of punishment or hope for a reward. The result is usually temporary compliance with the change agent's desires; the new behavior continues only so long as the opportunity for rewards and punishments exists. This is why force-coercion may be most useful as an unfreezing strategy. It can help to break people from old habits and create some impetus to try new ones. An example is General Electric's Work-Out program as discussed earlier.[54] Jack Welch started Work-Out to create a forum for active employee empowerment. But he made participation mandatory from the start; he used his authority to force employees to participate. And he was confident in doing so because he believed that, once started, the program would prove valuable enough to survive and prosper on its own. It did.

An alternative to force-coercion is the **rational persuasion strategy**, attempting to bring about change through persuasion backed by special knowledge, information, facts, and rational argument. The likely outcome of rational persuasion is compliance with reasonable commitment. This is actually the strategy that you learn and practice so much in school, when writing reports and making formal presentations on group projects. And you'll do a lot of it in the real world as well. But, as you fully realize, the strategy is dependent on very good facts and information, as well as the change agent's ability to communicate them persuasively.

The persuasive power in this strategy works best when the change agent has credibility as an expert. But the credibility can also be gained from external consultants or experts, or by case examples, demonstration projects, or benchmarks. Ford, for example, has sent managers to Disney World to learn about customer loyalty, hoping to stimulate them to lead customer-service initiatives of their own.[55] A Ford vice president says, "Disney's track record is one of the best in the country as far as dealing with customers." In this sense the power of rational persuasion is straightforward: If it works for Disney, why can't it work for Ford?

A **shared power strategy** engages people in a collaborative process of identifying values, assumptions, and goals from which support for change will naturally emerge. Although slow, the process is likely to yield high commitment. Sometimes called a *normative re-educative strategy*, this approach relies on empowerment and participation. The change leader works together with others as a team to develop the consensus needed to support change. This requires being comfortable and confident in allowing others to influence decisions that affect the planned change and its implementation. And because it entails a high level of involvement, this strategy is often quite time consuming. But shared power can deliver major benefits in terms of longer-lasting and internalized change.

The great power of the shared power strategy lies with unlocking the creativity and experience of people within the system. Unfortunately, many managers hesitate to use it for fear of losing control or of having to compromise on

Trendsetters

Tom Szaky Takes Idea from Dorm Room to Wal-Mart

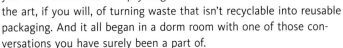

Talk about "sustainability," "green," and "recycling." If you buy Tom Szaky's book *Revolution in a Bottle,* you enter the world of "upcycling"— the art, if you will, of turning waste that isn't recyclable into reusable packaging. And it all began in a dorm room with one of those conversations you have surely been a part of.

Szaky is what many call an "eco-capitalist," someone who brings environmentalism into the world of business and consumers. While a freshman at Princeton University he ordered a million red worms with the goal of learning how to use them to recycle campus garbage and reduce landfill usage. One thing led to another, including conversations with classmate Jon Beyer, and before long the original idea of eco-friendly waste management became one of creating and selling liquid fertilizer made from worm excrement. While making the liquid fertilizer proved pretty easy, being able to afford the expensive plastic bottles to package it in was a lot more difficult. That's when more conversations, this time with entrepreneur Robin Tator, led to the idea of collecting and reusing bottles sent for recycling.

The idea worked so well that a new firm called TerraCycle quickly took shape with a mission to "find a meaningful use for waste materials." The original liquid fertilizer became TerraCycle Plant Food. Now the firm *upcycles* a variety of waste products such as cookie wrappers, drink containers, and discarded juice packs into usable products ranging from tote bags to containers of various sorts to pencil cases. And "yes," lots of them are found on Wal-Mart's shelves.

Szaky says about the innovation process: "Unlike most companies, which spend years in product development and testing, TerraCycle moves through these stages very quickly. First we identify a waste stream, then we figure out what we can make from that material. This is our strength—creatively solving the 'what the hell do we make from it' issue. If a retailer bites, we are in full production in a matter of weeks."

A **rational persuasion strategy** pursues change through empirical data and rational argument.

A **shared power strategy** pursues change by participation in assessing change needs, values, and goals.

important organizational goals. However, Harvard scholar Teresa M. Amabile points out that managers and change leaders can share power regarding choice of means and processes, even if they can't debate the goals. "People will be more creative," she says, "if you give them freedom to decide how to climb particular mountains. You needn't let them choose which mountains to climb."[56]

• Change leaders identify and deal positively with resistance to change.

S A
Self-Assessment
This is a good point to complete the self-assessment *"Tolerance for Ambiguity"* found on page 203.

You may have heard the adage that "change can be your best friend." At this point, however, we should probably add: "but only if you deal with resistance in the right ways." When people resist change, they are most often defending something important to them that now appears threatened. A change leader can learn a lot by listening to resistance and then using it to gain ideas for improving the change and change process.[57]

The list in **Table 9.1**—*Why People May Resist Change* probably contains some familiar items. Surely you've seen some or all of these forms of change resistance in your own experience. And honestly now, haven't you also been a resistor at times? When you were, how did the change leader or manager respond? How do you think they should have responded?

It is tempting to view resistance to change as something that must be overcome or defeated. But this mindset can easily cause problems. Perhaps a better way is to view resistance as feedback, as a source of information about how people view the change and its impact on them. Armed with this feedback, a good change leader should be able to achieve a better fit among the change, the situation, and the people involved.

[TABLE 9.1]

Why People May Resist Change

Fear of the unknown—not understanding what is happening or what comes next
Disrupted habits—feeling upset to see the end of the old ways of doing things
Loss of confidence—feeling incapable of performing well under the new ways of doing things
Loss of control—feeling that things are being done "to" you rather than "by" or "with" you
Poor timing—feeling overwhelmed by the situation or that things are moving too fast
Work overload—not having the physical or psychic energy to commit to the change
Loss of face—feeling inadequate or humiliated because it appears that the old ways weren't good ways
Lack of purpose—not seeing a reason for the change and/ or not understanding its benefits

Researchers have found that once resistance appears in organizations, managers try to deal with it in various ways, and some of their choices are better than others.[58] *Education and communication* uses discussions, presentations, and demonstrations to educate people about a change before it happens. *Participation and involvement* allows others to contribute ideas and help design and implement the change. *Facilitation and support* provides encouragement and training, channels for communicating problems and complaints, and ways of helping to overcome performance pressures. *Negotiation and agreement* offers incentives to those who are actively resisting or ready to resist, trying to make trade-offs in exchange for cooperation.

Although very different, each of the prior strategies for dealing with resistance to change has a role to play in organizations. Two other approaches, also found in management practice, are considerably more risky and prone to negative side effects. Change leaders who use *manipulation and cooptation* try to covertly influence resistors by providing information selectively and structuring events in favor of the desired change. When they use *explicit and implicit coercion*, they try to force resistors to accept change by threatening them with a variety of undesirable consequences if they do not go along as asked. Would you agree that most people don't like to be on the receiving end of these strategies?

Study Guide

9.3
How Do Managers Lead the Processes of Organizational Change?

Rapid review

- Transformational change makes radical changes in organizational directions; incremental change makes continuing adjustments to existing ways and practices.
- Change leaders are change agents who take responsibility for helping to change the behavior of people and organizational systems.
- Lewin's three phases of planned change are unfreezing (preparing a system for change), changing (making a change), and refreezing (stabilizing the system with a new change in place).
- Successful change agents understand the force-coercion, rational persuasion, and shared power change strategies, and the different outcomes likely to follow the use of each.
- People resist change for a variety of reasons, including fear of the unknown and force of habit; this resistance can be a source of feedback that can help improve the change process.
- Effective change agents deal with resistance positively and in a variety of ways, including education, participation, facilitation, manipulation, and coercion.

Terms to define

Change leader
Changing
Force-coercion strategy
Incremental change
Organization development
Planned change
Rational persuasion strategy
Refreezing
Shared power strategy
Transformational change
Unfreezing

Be sure you can

- differentiate transformational and incremental change
- discuss a change leader's responsibilities for each phase of the change process
- explain the force-coercion, rational persuasion, and shared power change strategies
- discuss the pros and cons of each change strategy
- list reasons why people resist change
- identify strategies for dealing with resistance to change

Questions for discussion

1. When is it better to pursue incremental rather than transformational change?
2. Can the refreezing phase of planned change ever be completed in today's dynamic environment?
3. Should managers avoid the force-coercion change strategy altogether?

Test Prep

1. Stories about past accomplishments and heroes such as company founders are all part of an organization's _____ culture.

   (a) observable   (b) underground
   (c) functional   (d) core

2. Planned and spontaneous ceremonies and celebrations of work achievements illustrate how _____ help build strong corporate cultures.

   (a) rewards   (b) heroes
   (c) rites and rituals   (d) core values

3. When managers at Disney World use language metaphors, telling workers they are "on stage" as "members of the cast," they are engaging in _____ leadership.

   (a) symbolic   (b) competitive
   (c) multicultural   (d) stakeholder

4. An organization with a strong culture is most likely to have _____.

   (a) tight, bureaucratic structure
   (b) loose, flexible design
   (c) small staff size
   (d) clearly communicated mission

5. Innovation, social responsibility, and customer service are examples of _____ which can be foundations for an organization's core culture.

   (a) rites and rituals
   (b) values
   (c) subsystems
   (d) integrating devices

6. What does the "O" stand for in the SCORES model for reading an organization's culture?

   (a) opportunity   (b) optimum
   (c) options   (d) outcomes

7. Product innovations create new goods or services for customers, while _____ innovations create new ways of doing things in the organization.

   (a) content   (b) process
   (c) quality   (d) task

8. The first step in Hamel's wheel of innovation is _____.

   (a) imagining   (b) assessing
   (c) experimenting   (d) scaling

9. The innovation process isn't really successful in an organization until a new idea is _____.

   (a) tested as a prototype
   (b) proven to be financially feasible
   (c) put into practice
   (d) discovered or invented

10. The basic idea of a "skunkworks" is to _____.

    (a) find ways to reduce costs and increase efficiency
    (b) establish special free space in which people work together to achieve innovations
    (c) make sure that any innovation occurs according to pre-set plans
    (d) give people free time in their jobs to be personally creative

11. Green innovation is most associated with the concept of _____.

    (a) observable culture   (b) core culture
    (c) sustainability   (d) skunkworks

12. A manager using a force-coercion strategy is most likely relying on _____ power to bring about the planned change.

    (a) expertise   (b) reference
    (c) position   (d) information

13. The most participative of the planned change strategies is _____.

    (a) negotiation and agreement
    (b) rational persuasion
    (c) shared power
    (d) education and communication

14. When one deals with resistance by trying to covertly influence others, offering only selective information and/or structuring events in favor of the desired change, this is an example of _____.

    (a) rational persuasion
    (b) manipulation and cooptation
    (c) negotiation
    (d) facilitation

15. The responses most likely to be associated with use of a force-coercion change strategy are best described as _____.

    (a) internalized behaviors   (b) compliance behaviors
    (c) cooptation behaviors   (d) cooperative behaviors

16. What core values might be found in high-performance organizational cultures?

17. What is the difference between process, product, and business model innovation?

18. How do a manager's responsibilities for change leadership vary among Lewin's three phases of planned change?

19. What are the possible differences in outcomes for managers using force-coercion and shared power change strategies?

Integration & application

20. One of the common experiences new college graduates have in their first jobs is that they often "spot things that need to be changed." They are full of new ideas, and they are ready and quick to challenge existing ways of doing things. They are enthusiastic and well-intentioned. But more often than most probably expect, their new bosses turn out to be skeptical, not too interested, or even irritated; co-workers who have been in place for some time may feel and act the same.

Questions: What is the new employee to do? One option is to just forget it and take an "I'll just do my job" approach. Let's reject that. So then, how can you in your next new job be an effective change leader? How can you use change strategies and deal with resistance from your boss and co-workers in a manner that builds your reputation as someone with good ideas for positive change?

Tolerance for Ambiguity

Instructions

To determine your tolerance for ambiguity, rate each of the following items on this seven-point scale.[59]

1	2	3	4	5
strongly disagree	moderately disagree	slightly disagree		slightly agree

6	7
moderately agree	strongly agree

_____ **1.** An expert who doesn't come up with a definite answer probably doesn't know too much.

_____ **2.** There is really no such thing as a problem that can't be solved.

_____ **3.** I would like to live in a foreign country for a while.

_____ **4.** People who fit their lives to a schedule probably miss the joy of living.

_____ **5.** A good job is one where what is to be done and how it is to be done are always clear.

_____ **6.** In the long run it is possible to get more done by tackling small, simple problems rather than large, complicated ones.

_____ **7.** It is more fun to tackle a complicated problem than it is to solve a simple one.

_____ **8.** Often the most interesting and stimulating people are those who don't mind being different and original.

_____ **9.** What we are used to is always preferable to what is unfamiliar.

_____ **10.** A person who leads an even, regular life in which few surprises or unexpected happenings arise really has a lot to be grateful for.

_____ **11.** People who insist upon a yes or no answer just don't know how complicated things really are.

_____ **12.** Many of our most important decisions are based on insufficient information.

_____ **13.** I like parties where I know most of the people more than ones where most of the people are complete strangers.

_____ **14.** The sooner we all acquire ideals, the better.

_____ **15.** Teachers or supervisors who hand out vague assignments give a chance for one to show initiative and originality.

_____ **16.** A good teacher is one who makes you wonder about your way of looking at things.

_____ Total

Scoring

To obtain a score, first *reverse* your scores for items, 3, 4, 7, 8, 11, 12, 15, and 16 (i.e., a rating of 1 = 7, 2 = 6, 3 = 5, etc.), then add up your scores for all 16 items. The higher your total the higher your indicated tolerance for ambiguity.

Source: Based on Budner, S. Intolerance of Ambiguity as a Personality Variable, *Journal of Personality*, Vol. 30, No. 1, (1962), pp. 29–50.

 For further exploration go to WileyPlus

Case Snapshot

Apple Inc.—People and Design Create the Future

For more than 30 years Apple Computer has generated some of America's greatest business successes . . . and experienced major failures. The firm ignited the personal computer industry in the 1970s when its Macintosh staggered "big blue"—IBM, and established Apple as a leader in both technology and design. But the firm stagnated while a series of CEOs squandered opportunities, and then rebounded when cofounder and former CEO Steve Jobs returned to the helm. Since then the world has reveled in iPods, iPhones, and iMacs. What is next for a firm that faces a tough economy and stiff competition as it continually tries to reinvent itself?

Online Interactive Learning Resources

SELF-ASSESSMENT
• Empowering Others

EXPERIENTIAL EXERCISES
• Which Organizational Culture Fits You?
• Force-Field Analysis

TEAM PROJECTS
• Organizational Culture Survey
• Innovation Audit

Human Resource Management

Nurturing Turns Potential into

Great employers respect diversity and value people. *Working Mother* magazine's annual listing of the "100 Best Companies for Working Mothers" has become an important management benchmark—both for employers who want to be able to be among the best and for potential employees who only want to work for the best. The magazine has achieved prominence as a major supporter of mothers with work careers.

A recent list of best employers for multicultural women includes Allstate, American Express, Deloitte, Ernst & Young, IBM, and General Mills. In terms of making the selections, *Working Mother* says: "All of our winning companies not only require manager training on diversity issues but also rate manager performance partly on diversity results, such as how many multicultural women advance."

Monthly topics in *Working Mother* cover the full gamut from kids to health to personal motivation and more. Self-described as helping women "integrate their professional lives, their family lives and their inner lives,"

Trendsetters
Susan Arnold follows trailblazing career path.

News Feed
Age bias complaints are on the increase.

Case Snapshot
Netflix—Making movie magic

Performance

Working Mother mainstreams coverage of work-life balance issues and needs for women. The magazine is part of Working Mother Media, a conglomerate headed by CEO Carol Evans. It has a monthly readership of over 3 million and is well worth a look.

In one issue an article reported on moms who "pushed for more family-friendly benefits and got them." The writer described how Kristina Marsh worked to get lactation support for nursing mothers as a formal benefit at Dow Corning, and how Beth Schiavo started a Working Moms Network in Ernst & Young's Atlanta offices and then got it approved as a nationwide corporate program. As soon as a woman announces that she is pregnant, a network forms to support and assist her. About the program in support of working moms, Schiavo said: "The goal is to make sure these women understand that, yes, it can be an intimidating time, but all the aspects of a career at Ernst & Young are still there for you."

WORKING MOTHER

GOLD RUSH
Shine from head to toe with these fashion finds

Recession-Proof Your Family
Smart (super easy) money moves

Benefits Under Fire
Meet the employers fighting to protect your hard-won work/life perks

Make Room for Daddy
The stigma that keeps men from taking parental leave

Talk Your Way Out of Anything
Clever comebacks for life's sticky situations

+ THE ULTIMATE 3-MINUTE WORKOUT
Hint: We don't mean your abs

100 BEST COMPANIES
ALL YOU NEED TO KNOW ABOUT THE BEST JOBS FOR MOMS

OCTOBER 2008 $3.50 workingmother.com

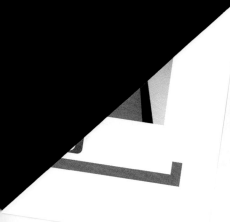

10.1 What Are the Purpose and Legal Context of Human Resource Management?

The key to managing people in ways that lead to profit, productivity, innovation, and real organizational learning ultimately lies in how you think about your organization and its people. . . . When you look at your people, do you see costs to be reduced? . . . Or, when you look at your people do you see intelligent, motivated, trustworthy individuals—the most critical and valuable strategic assets your organization can have?

These comments are from Jeffrey Pfeffer's book, *The Human Equation: Building Profits by Putting People First.*[1] What is your experience? Do you find employers treating people as costs or as assets? And what difference does this seem to make? Pfeffer and his colleague, John F. Veiga, believe it does make a performance difference, a potentially big one. After reviewing the evidence they conclude: "There is a substantial and rapidly expanding body of evidence . . . that speaks to the strong connection between how firms manage their people and the economic results achieved."[2]

The core argument being advanced here is that organizations will perform better when they treat their members better.[3] And when it comes to how people are treated at work, we enter the territory of "human resource management."

• Human resource management attracts, develops, and maintains a talented workforce.

Human resource management (HRM) is the process of attracting, developing, and maintaining a high-quality workforce.

The process of **human resource management (HRM)** attracts, develops, and maintains a talented and energetic workforce. Its purpose is to ensure that an organization is always staffed with the best people available so that it gets important jobs done in the best possible ways. You might state the *goal of HRM* this way: to build organizational performance capacity through people. This means making sure that highly capable and enthusiastic people are always in the right positions and working with the support they need to be successful. The three major responsibilities of human resource management are typically described as:

1. *Attracting a quality workforce*—human resource planning, employee recruitment, and employee selection.
2. *Developing a quality workforce*—employee orientation, training and development, and performance management.
3. *Maintaining a quality workforce*—career development, work-life balance, compensation and benefits, retention and turnover, and labor-management relations.

Human Resource Management	→	Attracting talented employees	→	Developing talented employees	→	Keeping talented employees

• Strategic human resource management aligns human capital with organizational strategies.

Human capital is the economic value of people with job-relevant abilities, knowledge, ideas, energies, and commitments.

High-performing organizations thrive on strong foundations of **human capital**, the economic value of a workforce with job-relevant abilities, knowledge, experience, ideas, energies, and commitments. And when Sheryl Sandberg left her senior management post with Google to become Facebook's Chief Operating Officer, she made human capital her top priority. She strengthened the firm's human resource management systems with updated approaches for employee performance reviews, innovative recruiting methods, and new management training.[4] These initiatives are consistent with the concept of **strategic human resource management**—mobilizing human capital through the HRM process to best implement organizational strategies.[5]

One indicator that the HRM process is truly strategic to an organization is when it is headed by a senior executive reporting directly to the chief executive officer. When former Home Depot executive Denis Donovan became the firm's first vice president for human resources, he said: "CEOs and boards of directors are learning that human resources can be one of your biggest game-changers in terms of competitive advantage."[6] The strategic importance of HRM has also been linked to the spate of corporate ethics scandals. "It was a failure of people and that isn't lost on those in the executive suite," says Susan Meisinger, past president of the Society for Human Resource Development.[7]

There are many career opportunities in the human resource management profession. HRM departments are common in most organizations. And HRM specialists are increasingly important in an environment complicated by legal issues, labor shortages, economic turmoil, changing corporate strategies, changing personal values, and more. As outsourcing of professional services becomes more popular, a growing number of firms provide specialized HRM services such as recruiting, compensation, outplacement, and the like. The Society for Human Resource Management, or SHRM, is a professional organization dedicated to keeping its membership up to date in all aspects of HRM and its complex legal environment.

• Government legislation protects workers against employment discrimination.

The opening example of *Working Mother* magazine highlights the importance of valuing diversity in human resources and being fully inclusive of all people with the talent and desire to do good work. Job-relevant talent is not restricted because of anyone's race, gender, religion, marital or parental status, sexual orientation, ethnicity, or other diversity characteristics. And any time these characteristics interfere with finding, hiring, and utilizing the best employees, the loss in human capital will be someone else's gain.[8]

If valuing people is at the heart of human resource management, **job discrimination** should be its enemy. It occurs when an organization denies someone employment or a job assignment or an advancement opportunity for reasons that are not performance relevant.

As **Table 10.1** indicates, there are a number of U.S. laws designed to protect workers from job discrimination. An important cornerstone of this legal protection is *Title VII of the Civil Rights Act of 1964*, amended by the *Equal Employment Opportunity Act of 1972* and the *Civil Rights Act (EEOA) of 1991*. These acts provide for **equal employment opportunity (EEO)**, giving everyone the right to employment without regard to sex, race, color, national origin, or religion. It is illegal under Title VII to use any of these as criteria when making decisions about hiring, promoting, compensating, terminating, or otherwise changing someone's terms of employment.

Strategic human resource management mobilizes human capital to implement organizational strategies.

Discrimination occurs when someone is denied a job or job assignment for non-job-relevant reasons.

Equal employment opportunity (EEO) is the right to employment and advancement without regard to race, sex, religion, color, or national origin.

[TABLE 10.1]

A Sample of U.S. Laws Against Employment Discrimination

Equal Pay Act of 1963	Requires equal pay for men and women performing equal work in an organization.
Title VII of the Civil Rights Act of 1964 (as amended)	Prohibits discrimination in employment based on race, color, religion, sex, or national origin.
Age Discrimination in Employment Act of 1967	Prohibits discrimination against persons over 40; restricts mandatory retirement.
Occupational Health and Safety Act of 1970	Establishes mandatory health and safety standards in workplaces.
Pregnancy Discrimination Act of 1978	Prohibits employment discrimination against pregnant workers.
Americans with Disabilities Act of 1990	Prohibits discrimination against a qualified individual on the basis of disability.
Civil Rights Act of 1991	Reaffirms Title VII of the 1964 Civil Rights Act; reinstates burden of proof by employer, and allows for punitive and compensatory damages.
Family and Medical Leave Act of 1993	Allows employees up to 12 weeks of unpaid leave with job guarantees for childbirth, adoption, or family illness.

The intent of equal employment opportunity is to ensure everyone the right to gain and keep employment based only on their ability and job performance. The Equal Employment Opportunity Commission (EEOC) enforces the legislation through its federal power to file civil lawsuits against organizations that do not provide timely resolution of any discrimination charges lodged against them. These laws generally apply to all public and private organizations that employ 15 or more people.

Title VII also requires organizations to show **affirmative action** in their efforts to ensure equal employment opportunity for members of *protected groups*, those historically underrepresented in the workforce. Employers are expected to analyze existing workforce demographics, compare them with those in the relevant labor markets, and set goals for correcting any underrepresentation that might exist. These goals are supported by *affirmative action plans* that are designed to ensure that an organization's workforce represents women and minorities in proportion to their labor market availability.[9]

> **Affirmative action** is an effort to give preference in employment to women and minority group members.

> **Bona fide occupational qualifications** are employment criteria justified by capacity to perform a job.

You are likely to hear debates over the pros and cons of affirmative action. Criticisms tend to focus on the use of group membership, or female or minority status, as a criterion in employment decisions.[10] The issues raised include claims of *reverse discrimination* by members of majority populations. White males, for example, may claim that preferential treatment given to minorities in a particular situation interferes with their individual rights.

As a general rule, the legal protections of EEO do not restrict an employer's right to establish **bona fide occupational qualifications**. These are criteria for employment that an organization can clearly justify as relating to a person's capacity to perform a job. However, the EEO bars the use of employment qualifications based on race and color under any circumstances; those based on sex, religion, and age are very difficult to support.[11]

As you can see, legal protection against employment discrimination is quite extensive. Listed below are four examples of possible areas of discrimination and laws that govern them.

- *Disabilities*—The *Americans with Disabilities Act of 1990 as amended in 2008* prevents discrimination against people with disabilities. The law requires employers to focus their employment decisions on a person's abilities and what he or she can do.
- *Age*—The *Age Discrimination in Employment Act of 1967 as amended in 1978 and 1986* protects workers against mandatory retirement ages. Age discrimination occurs when a qualified individual is adversely affected by a job action that replaces him or her with a younger worker.

News Feed

Age Bias Complaints Are on the Increase

The Equal Employment Opportunity Commission is reporting an increased number of age bias complaints. Some 24,600 complaints were filed in 2008, up from 19,103 in the prior year. Expectations are that there will be even more as older employees find themselves included in the job losses suffered in a recessionary economy.

Federal age discrimination laws protect employees aged 40 and up, and the proportion of workers in this age group is increasing with what some call the "graying" of the American workforce. When an older worker is laid off or loses his or her job, the possibility of age discrimination exists. However, attorneys say that it's hard to prove, especially when workers of all ages are getting the axe as companies cut payrolls in crisis times. "There's always the fine line between what discrimination is and what is a legitimate business decision," says one.

About 20% of age discrimination suits result in some financial settlement in favor of the person filing the claim, but this doesn't always include getting the job back. And there is no doubt that older workers face tough job searches. AARP cites data that unemployment for workers over 50 lasts 27 more weeks than for younger ones.

Age bias filings aren't alone among increased discrimination cases lodged with the EEOC. Also on the list are more complaints about retaliation, sexual harassment, race bias, and disability bias.

Reflect and React:

What is the "fine line," as the attorney said in this report, between job discrimination and legitimate business decisions? If a company has to lay off 10% of its workforce and decides to let go the more senior workers first in hopes of keeping the long-term loyalties of younger workers, is there anything wrong with that? Do tough economic times make it easier for employers to discriminate and get away with it?

- *Pregnancy*—The *Pregnancy Discrimination Act of 1978* protects female workers from discrimination because of pregnancy. A pregnant employee is protected against termination or adverse job action because of the pregnancy and is entitled to reasonable time off work.
- *Family matters*—The *Family and Medical Leave Act of 1993* protects workers who take unpaid leaves for family matters from losing their jobs or employment status. Workers are allowed up to 12 weeks leave for childbirth, adoption, personal illness, or illness of a family member.

Even though these and other legal protections are extensive, we should be realistic. Laws can help, but they can't guarantee that you will never be affected by employment discrimination. Just read the papers and listen to the news. You'll often find reports on people taking employers to court with claims that they have been discriminated against based on gender, race, age, or other personal characteristics.[12] Not too long ago a woman wrote to the *Wall Street Journal*, for example, with this question: "I was interviewing for a sales job and the manager asked me what child care arrangements I had made . . . Was his question legal?" The answer, according to an employment attorney, is that the manager's question is "a perfect example of what not to ask a job applicant" and "could be considered direct evidence of gender bias against women based on negative stereotypes."[13]

• Employee rights and concerns influence the legal environment of work.

When Lilly Ledbetter was about to retire from Goodyear, she realized that male co-workers were being paid more. She sued. At issue is the *Equal Pay Act of 1963*, which provides for men and women to be equally paid for doing equal work in terms of skills, responsibilities, and working conditions. She initially lost the case because the Supreme Court said she had delayed too long in filing the claim. But she was smiling when the Lilly Ledbetter Fair Pay Act became the very first bill signed by President Barack Obama. It expanded worker's rights to sue employers on equal-pay issues, starting a six-month clock with each paycheck received. Obama said he signed it not only in honor of Lilly but also of his own grandmother "who worked in a bank all her life, and even after she hit that glass ceiling, kept getting up again."[14]

Comparable worth holds that persons performing jobs of similar importance should receive comparable pay.

It's important to stay up to date on the legal context of HRM as it changes and grows more complex almost every day. Although we can't be exhaustive, here is a sampling of employee rights and other concerns that you will find often have legal implications.

Have you heard about **comparable worth**? This is the notion that persons performing jobs of similar importance should be paid comparable salaries. Take an example. Should a long-distance truck driver receive higher pay than an elementary school teacher? They often do, and one has to wonder: "Why?" Is it because driving trucks is a traditionally male occupation and teaching elementary-age children a traditionally female occupation? Advocates of comparable worth argue that pay differences like these are sometimes due to a gender bias that is embedded in historical pay disparities for various occupations. What do you think?

When he signed the Lilly Ledbetter Fair Pay Act, President Barack Obama said "making our economy work means making sure it works for everybody."

Pregnancy discrimination penalizes a woman in a job or as a job applicant for being pregnant.

Pregnancy discrimination is against the law, but pregnancy bias complaints filed with the U.S. Equal Employment Opportunity Commission still increased 14% from 2006 through 2007. A spokesperson for the National Partnership of Women & Families said that problems of pregnancy discrimination are "escalating" and require "national attention."[15] And recent research paints a bleak picture as well. Actors played roles of visibly pregnant and nonpregnant applicants for jobs as corporate attorneys and college professors. Results showed that interviewers were more negative toward the "pregnant" females, making comments such as "she'll try to get out of doing work" and "she would be too moody."[16]

Workplace privacy is the right to privacy while at work.

Another issue that is increasingly important in our high-tech world of work is **workplace privacy**—the right of individuals to privacy on the job.[17] Employers, of course, should be able to monitor and assess the work performance and behavior of their employees. But monitoring can become invasive, sometimes crossing legal and ethical lines.

Are you prepared to deal with privacy issues at work? Most employers can monitor e-mails and Internet searches to track your use of the computer while on the job. Technology allows employers to identify who is called by telephone and how long conversations last; work performance in many jobs can be electronically documented moment to moment. All of this information and more can be stored in vast databases that may be used and even passed on to others without your permission. Until the legal status of high-tech surveillance is cleared up, one consultant says the best assumption to make is that we have "no privacy at work."[18]

The outsourcing, restructurings, and search for greater cost efficiencies that are taking place in business today have created another legal issue—the status of part-time and temporary workers. Don't be surprised if you are asked some day to work only "as needed," as a "free lancer," or to work as an **independent contractor**. This would mean that you are expected to work for an agreed-upon period or for an agreed-upon task and without becoming part of the permanent workforce.

Independent contractors are hired on temporary contracts and are not part of the organization's permanent workforce.

Although offering both employment and perhaps attractive flexibility, these jobs can have their downsides. Many people find themselves caught up in a status known as *permatemp*; they are regularly employed but denied access to standard health care, pension, and other fringe benefits. This is a murky area under the law and it is attracting more public attention, including that of labor unions.

Study Guide

10.1
What Are the Purpose and Legal Context of Human Resource Management?

Rapid review

- The human resource management process involves attracting, developing, and maintaining a quality workforce.
- Job discrimination occurs when someone is denied an employment opportunity for reasons that are not job relevant.
- Equal employment opportunity legislation guarantees people the right to employment and advancement without discrimination.
- Current legal issues in the work environment deal with comparable worth, workplace privacy, and rights of independent contractors, among other matters.
- Labor relations and collective bargaining are closely governed by law, and can be cooperative or adversarial in nature.

Terms to define

Affirmative action

Bona fide occupational qualifications

Comparable worth

Equal employment opportunity (EEO)

Human resource management (HRM)

Independent contractors

Job discrimination

Pregnancy discrimination

Workplace privacy

Be sure you can

- explain the purpose of human resource management
- differentiate job discrimination, equal employment opportunity, and affirmative action
- identify the major laws protecting against employment discrimination
- explain the issues of comparable worth, workplace privacy, and independent contractors

Questions for discussion

1. How might the forces of globalization affect human resource management in the future?
2. Are current laws protecting American workers against discrimination in employment sufficient, or do we need additional ones?
3. What employee-rights issues and concerns would you add to those discussed here?

10.2 What Are the Essential Human Resource Management Practices?

To attract and retain the right people to its workforce, an organization must first know exactly what it is looking for. It must have a clear understanding of the purpose and requirements of the jobs, and the talents that people need to do them well. And then, it must have the systems in place to fill the jobs with enthusiastic and high-performing workers.

• Human resource planning matches staffing with organizational needs.

A marketing manager at IDEO, the Palo Alto-based design firm, once said: "If you hire the right people . . . if you've got the right fit . . . then everything will take care of itself."[19] It really isn't quite that simple, but getting the right people on board is certainly a great starting point for success.

Human resource planning is the process of analyzing an organization's staffing needs and determining how to best fill them. The process begins with a review of organizational mission, objectives, and strategies to establish a baseline for forecasting human resource requirements. Once this is done, managers can assess the existing workforce and make recruiting, training, and career development plans to best meet future needs. At Procter & Gamble, for example, a replacement planning approach called "Build from Within" keeps at least three potential candidates identified as replacements for any of the firm's 50 top manager positions. "We can fill a spot in an hour," says former CEO A. G. Lafley. "That's the beauty of our system."[20]

Human resource planning analyzes staffing needs and identifies actions to fill those needs.

Recruitment is a set of activities designed to attract a qualified pool of job applicants.

Selection is choosing whom to hire from a pool of qualified job applicants.

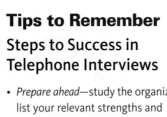

Tips to Remember

Steps to Success in Telephone Interviews

- *Prepare ahead*—study the organization; list your relevant strengths and capabilities.
- *Practice answers to common questions*— What do you know about our organization? Why do you want this job? What are your strengths? What are your career goals?
- *Minimize Distractions*—be in a quiet room, with privacy, without interruptions; set aside enough time to talk as long as the interviewer wants.
- *Dress professionally*—this increases confidence, sets your interview tone.
- *Practice your verbal skills*—what you say and how you sound affects your first impression; use correct telephone etiquette—e.g., no answering other calls.
- *Have materials handy*—have all supporting documents within easy reach.
- *Have your questions ready*—show insight and interest; don't hesitate to ask questions during the interview.
- *Ask what happens next*—ask how to follow up, what information you can provide.

• Recruitment and selection attract and hire qualified job applicants.

Recruitment is what organizations do to attract a qualified pool of applicants to an organization. **Selection** involves choosing to hire from this pool the persons who offer the greatest performance potential. You should already be familiar with both from the job applicant side, perhaps in collegiate recruiting for internships or full-time jobs.

The basic elements in the recruitment and selection processes are most typically:

- advertising job vacancies
- preliminary contacts with job candidates
- initial screening interview
- formal application, in-depth interviews
- employment testing
- reference checks.

Check out the Tips to Remember for ideas on how to succeed in telephone interviews.[21] Are you ready? They are an increasingly common recruiting practice. The typical telephone interview can last an hour or more and get into lots of specifics that traditionally have been covered in face-to-face conversation. After being asked to describe her major past accomplishments, one job candidate said "I was taken aback by how specific the interviewer was getting."[22]

One thing to look and press for in an interview is a **realistic job preview**, one that gives you both the good points and the bad points of the job and organization.[23] You might be easily misled when the interviewer adopts a more traditional "tell and sell" approach, perhaps trying to hide or gloss over the potential negatives. It's far better to get a realistic and full picture of the situation before you decide to accept any offer, not after.

Instead of "selling" only positive features, this approach tries to be open and balanced in describing the job and organization. Both favorable and unfavorable aspects are covered. How can you tell if you are getting a realistic job preview? The interviewer in a realistic job preview might use phrases such as "Of course, there are some downsides. . . ." "Things don't always go the way we hope. . . ." "Something that you will want to be prepared for is. . . ." "We have found that some new hires had difficulty with. . . ." And if you don't hear these phrases, ask the tough questions yourself. This type of conversation helps the candidate establish realistic job expectations and better prepare for the inevitable "ups and downs" of a new job. Higher levels of early job satisfaction and less inclination to quit prematurely are among the expected benefits.

It's quite common that job candidates are asked to take employment tests. Some test job-specific knowledge and skills; others focus more on intelligence, aptitudes, personality, or general interests. Regardless of the intent, however, any employment test should be both reliable and valid. **Reliability** means that the test provides a consistent measurement, returning the same results time after time. **Validity** means that the test score is a good predictor of future job performance, with a high score associated with high job performance and vice versa.

One of the popular developments in testing is the use of **assessment centers**. This approach evaluates a person's job potential by observing his or her performance in experiential activities designed to simulate daily work. A related approach is **work sampling**, which asks you to work on actual job tasks while observers grade your performance. Google uses a form of this with its "Code Jams." These are essentially contests that the firm runs to find the most brilliant software coders. Google awards winners with financial prizes and job offers. Code Jams are held worldwide. A company spokesperson says: "Wherever the best talent is, Google wants them."[24]

Realistic job previews help candidates understand the potential positives and negatives of a new job.

Realistic job previews provide job candidates with all pertinent information about a job and organization.

Reliability means a selection device gives consistent results over repeated measures.

Validity means scores on a selection device have demonstrated links with future job performance.

An **assessment center** examines how job candidates handle simulated work situations.

Work sampling evaluates applicants as they perform actual work tasks.

• Socialization and orientation integrate new employees into the organization.

Once hired, a new member of any organization has to "learn the ropes" and become familiar with "the way things are done." **Socialization** is the process of influencing the expectations, behavior, and attitudes of a new employee in a desirable way. It begins with the human resource management practice of **orientation**—a set of activities designed to familiarize new employees with their jobs, co-workers, and key values, policies, and other aspects of the organization as a whole.

Socialization systematically influences the expectations, behavior, and attitudes of new employees.

Orientation familiarizes new employees with jobs, co-workers, and organizational policies and services.

For years, Disney has been considered a master at this. During orientation at its Disney World Resort in Buena Vista, Florida, new employees learn the corporate culture. They also learn that the company places a premium on personality and expects all employees—from entertainers to ticket sellers to groundskeepers—"to make the customer happy." A Disney HRM specialist notes: "We can train for skills. We want people who are enthusiastic, who have pride in their work, who can take charge of a situation without supervision."[25] Obviously, a good orientation program such as Disney's can go a long way toward setting the stage for high performance, job satisfaction, and work enthusism among new employees. Is this your experience?

• Training continually develops employee skills and capabilities.

At this point you should probably be keeping a list of things to look for in your next employer. Here's another one: a willingness to invest in training so that you are continuously learning and updating your job skills. Training is so important at Procter & Gamble that managers are rated on how well they train and develop those reporting to them; those that develop reputations as great trainers usually get the promotions.[26]

Mentoring and coaching relationships can be important sources of training and development for early career employees.

Coaching occurs as an experienced person offers performance advice to a less-experienced person.

Mentoring assigns early career employees as protégés to more senior ones.

In **reverse mentoring** younger and newly-hired employees mentor senior executives, often on latest developments with digital technologies.

We all need training, especially today when new knowledge and technologies quickly make so many of our existing skills obsolete. A great employer won't let this happen. Instead of trying to save costs, it willingly spends on training and views it as an investment in human resources.[27] In fact, you should probably ask questions about training opportunities in any job interview. And if the interviewer struggles for answers or evades the questions, you're getting a pretty good indication that the organization isn't likely to pass the "great employer" test.

A convenient and powerful training approach that you should be inquiring about is **coaching**. This is where an experienced person provides performance advice to someone else. Ideally, a new employee is assigned a coach who can model desired work behaviors and otherwise help him or her to learn and make progress. Sometimes the best coach is the manager. Other times it may be a co-worker. Always, the key is for the coach to be willing and able to show a newcomer by example how things should be done.

You should also be interested in **mentoring**. This is where a new or early-career employee is assigned as a protégé to someone senior in his or her area of expertise, perhaps a high-level manager. Good mentoring programs can be a great boost to a newcomer's career. Mentors are supposed to take an interest in the junior person, provide guidance and advice on skills and career progress, and otherwise inform him or her about how one gets ahead career wise in the organization.

Cisco systems provides mentoring to young employees by linking its "Legacy Leaders Network"—made up of pre-retirement baby boomers, with the "New Hire Network"—consisting of Gen Ys just starting out with the firm. Executives at the firm believe this approach to mentoring has helped in recruiting a new generation of employees. And in an approach called **reverse mentoring**, some enlightened employers are using younger and newly-hired to mentor senior executives. This often involves technology-savvy Gen-Yers tutoring their seniors on how to use social media such as Facebook and Twitter, as well as updating them with the latest in digital technologies. Reverse mentoring programs are not only informative for senior managers, they also provide the Gen Yers with an important sense of buy-in and contribution. One human resource management consultant says: "It's exactly the kind of thing that's needed today because Gen-Yers really want to be involved."[28]

• Performance management appraises and rewards accomplishments.

Once a person is hired and on the job, one of the important functions of HRM is performance management. This involves using various techniques of **performance appraisal** to formally assess and give feedback on someone's work accomplishments.[29] The purposes of performance appraisal are twofold: first, to evaluate and document performance for the record; second, to initiate a process of development that can improve performance in the future.[30]

In order for an appraisal method to have credibility it must satisfy reliability and validity criteria, just as with employment tests.[31] Any manager who hires, fires, or promotes based on performance appraisals, for example, may need to defend such actions in discrimination-based lawsuits. It is hard to make a defense if the performance appraisal method is faulted because of reliability or validity problems.

One of the most basic performance appraisal methods is a **graphic rating scale**. It is a checklist or scorecard for rating an employee on preselected personal traits or performance characteristics such as work quality, attendance, and punctuality. Although simple, quick, and commonly used, graphic rating scales have questionable reliability and validity. At best they should probably be used only with additional appraisal tools.

A more advanced approach to performance appraisal uses a **behaviorally anchored rating scale (BARS)**. This describes actual behaviors that exemplify various levels of performance achievement in a job. The example in **Figure 10.1** shows a BARS for a customer service representative. "Extremely poor" performance is described with the behavioral anchor "rude or disrespectful treatment of a customer." Because the BARS relates performance assessments to specific descriptions of work behavior, it is more reliable and valid than the graphic rating scale. The behavioral anchors are also useful as benchmarks for training in job skills and objectives.

Performance appraisal is the process of formally evaluating performance and providing feedback to a job holder.

Self-Assessment
This is a good point to complete the self-assessment *"Performance Appraisal Assumptions"* found on page 234.

A **graphic rating scale** uses a checklist of traits or characteristics to evaluate performance.

A **behaviorally anchored rating (BARS)** uses specific descriptions of actual behaviors to rate various levels of performance.

FIGURE 10.1
What Does a Behaviorally Anchored Rating Scale Look Like?

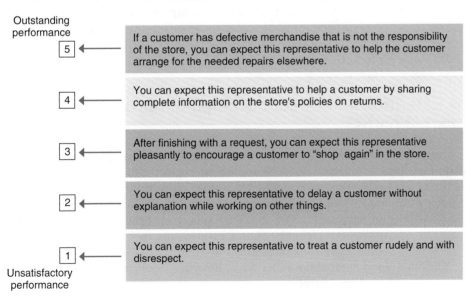

A *behaviorally anchored rating scale (BARS)* uses actual descriptions of positive and negative job behaviors to anchor rating points. In this example of how a customer service representative handles a merchandise return, various alternative behaviors are clearly identified. Consistent and documented rude or disrespectful behavior toward customers by a salesperson would earn a rating of "extremely poor." This specificity makes the BARS more reliable and valid.

Many performance appraisals today use the 360°
approach to gather feedback and evaluations.

The **critical-incident technique**
keeps a log of someone's effective
and ineffective job behaviors.

360° feedback includes in the
appraisal process superiors, subordinates,
peers, and even customers.

A **multi-person comparison**
compares one person's performance
with that of others.

The **critical-incident technique** keeps an actual log of a person's effective and ineffective job behaviors. Using the case of the customer service representative again, a critical-incidents log might include this *positive example*: "Took extraordinary care of a customer who had purchased a defective item from a company store in another city." Or it might include this *negative example*: "Acted rudely in dismissing the complaint of a customer who felt that we mistakenly advertised a sale item."

Not all performance appraisals are completed only by one's immediate boss. It is increasingly popular to include more of a job's stakeholders in the appraisal process. The new workplace often involves use of peer appraisal that includes in the process others who work regularly and directly with a job holder, and upward appraisal that includes subordinates reporting to the job holder. An even broader stakeholder approach is known as **360° feedback**, where superiors, subordinates, peers, and even internal and external customers are involved in the appraisal of a job holder's performance.[32] The approach normally includes a self-appraisal as well.

One of the latest developments with 360° feedback taps the power of social networking to provide quick and on-demand feedback through the likes of Facebook and Twitter.[33] Accenture uses a computer program called Performance Multiplier that allows users to post projects, goals, and status updates for review by others. And a Toronto-based start-up company offers a program called Rypple. Users post questions in 140 characters or less; for example: "What did you think of my presentation?" or "How could I have run that meeting better?" Anonymous responses are compiled by the program and the 360°-type feedback is then sent to the person posting the query.

Finally, some performance management systems use **multi-person comparisons** to avoid the problem of everyone being rated "about the same." Instead, they make managers rate and rank people relative to one another. Those multi-person comparisons can be done by *rank-ordering* people from top to bottom in order of performance achievement, with no ties allowed. They can be done by *paired comparisons* that first evaluate each person against every other, and then create a summary ranking based on the number of superior scores. Or they can be done by a *forced distribution* that places each person into a frequency distribution with fixed performance classifications—such as top 10%, next 40%, next 40%, and bottom 10%.

• Retention and career development provide career paths.

After all the investments in recruitment, selection, orientation, training, and appraisal, an employer would be foolish to neglect efforts to retain the best employees for as long as possible. Of course, there are many issues in retention, with compensation and benefits certainly of obvious importance. If one isn't willing to pay at or above market levels, with benefits to match, it goes without saying that the organization's investments in human resources may be lost as people leave for better jobs elsewhere.

Career development manages how a person grows and progresses in a career.

Given a good compensation package, however, another significant retention issue becomes **career development**—the process of managing how a person grows and progresses in responsibility from one point in a career to the next. After initial entry, our career paths within organizations become subject to many considerations. Lots of choices will have to be made dealing with promotions, transfers, overseas assignments, mentors, higher degrees, even alternative employers and retirement.

Ideally, the employer and the individual work closely together in making career development choices. Using Procter & Gamble as an example again, the head of human resources Moheet Nagrath says that career tracks are built to match individual goals and company needs. For someone who wants to become a top manager someday, for example, they will plot moves through various brands as well as domestic and international locations. "If you train people to work in different countries and businesses," he says, "you develop a deep bench."[34]

With people changing jobs frequently today, career development is becoming more and more a personal responsibility. This means that we each have to be diligent in **career planning**, the process of systematically matching career goals and individual capabilities with opportunities for their fulfillment. It involves answering such questions as "Who am I?" "Where do I want to go?" and "How do I get there?"

Some suggest that we should view a career as something that should be rationally planned and pursued in a logical step-by-step fashion. Others argue for much greater flexibility, allowing our career to progress in a somewhat random fashion as we respond to unexpected opportunities as they arise. A well-managed career will probably include elements of each. And a carefully thought-out career plan can point you in a general direction; an eye for opportunity helps fill in the details as you proceed along the way. Are you ready?

Career planning is the process of matching career goals and individual capabilities with opportunities for their fulfillment.

Trendsetters

Susan Arnold Follows Trailblazing Career Path

With an MBA in hand, Susan Arnold joined Procter & Gamble in 1980 as a brand assistant for Dawn and Ivory Snow detergents. After a 29-year career she was called a "trailblazer" by the *Wall Street Journal*, rising to be the first female head of P&G's global beauty business with responsibility for some 300 brands. She tripled the size of global business to $20 billion, and went on to become president and vice chairwoman of global business units for the firm.

Before stepping down from her position at P&G, Arnold turned down many offers from executive recruiters trying to lure her to other top management positions. Now, after fulfilling her announced intention to retire at 55, the question is: Who's going to land Arnold as their new No. 1?

One observer said that in the past "she always got yanked back by P&G" when the job offers came in from firms such as Walgreen Co. This time, however, she has put herself into play, and speculation abounds. Executive recruiter Patricia Cook expects Arnold to accept the top job only at a company that is "really big and really global." That would put her in the ranks of the few women who now head Fortune 500 companies. And it would make her the only openly gay CEO of a large American business.

Arnold's reputation is one of a "hard charging executive unafraid to take on a fight." She is credited with making the Olay brand a major billion-dollar winner for P&G. *Fortune* magazine ranked her #7 on its listing of the 50 most powerful businesswomen in America, while *Forbes* ranked her as the 47th most powerful woman in the world—ahead of Queen Elizabeth II of Great Britain.

Study Guide

10.2
What Are the Essential Human Resource Management Practices?

Rapid review

- Human resource planning is the process of analyzing staffing needs and identifying actions that should be taken to satisfy them over time.
- Recruitment is the process of attracting qualified job candidates to fill vacant positions; realistic job previews try to provide candidates with accurate information on the job and organization.
- Assessment centers and work sampling are increasing common selection techniques; employment tests should meet the criteria of reliability and validity.
- Orientation is the process of formally introducing new employees to their jobs and socializing them with performance expectations.
- Training keeps workers' skills up to date and job relevant; important training approaches include coaching and mentoring.
- Performance appraisal methods include graphic rating scales, behaviorally anchored rating scales, critical incidents, 360° feedback, and multi-person comparisons; any appraisal method should meet the criteria of reliability and validity.
- Employee retention programs try to keep skilled workers in jobs and on career paths that are satisfying to them as well as making performance contributions for the employer.

Terms to define

Behaviorally anchored rating
Career planning
Coaching
Critical incident technique
Forced distribution
Graphic rating scale
Human resource planning
Mentoring
Performance appraisal
Recruitment
Reliability
Reverse mentoring
Selection
Socialization
360° feedback
Validity
Work sampling

Be sure you can

- list steps in the recruitment process
- explain realistic job previews
- illustrate reliability and validity in employment testing
- illustrate how an assessment center might work
- explain the importance of socialization and orientation
- describe coaching and mentoring as training approaches
- discuss strengths and weaknesses of alternative performance appraisal methods

Questions for discussion

1. Is it realistic to expect that you can get a "realistic job preview" during the interview process?
2. Suppose a new employer doesn't formally assign someone to be your coach or mentor; what should you do?
3. What are some of the possible downsides to receiving 360° feedback?

10.3 What Are Some of the Current Issues in Human Resource Management?

"Hiring good people is tough," starts an article in the *Harvard Business Review*. The sentence finishes with "keeping them can be even tougher."[35] The point is that it isn't enough to hire and train workers to meet an organization's immediate needs; they must also be successfully nurtured, supported, and retained. When the Society for Human Resource Management surveyed employers, it learned that popular tools for maintaining a quality workforce included flexible work schedules and personal time off, competitive salaries, and good benefits—especially health insurance.[36]

• Today's lifestyles increase demands for flexibility and work-life balance.

Today's fast-paced and complicated lifestyles have contributed to increased concerns for **work-life balance**, how people balance the demands of careers with their personal and family needs.[37] Not surprisingly, the "family-friendliness" of an employer is now frequently used as a screening criterion by job candidates. It is also used in "best employer" rankings by magazines such as *Business Week*, *Working Mother*, and *Fortune*.[38] If you have any doubts at all regarding the importance of work-life issues, consider these facts:[39]

Work-life balance involves balancing career demands with personal and family needs.

- 78% of American couples are dual wage earners
- 63% believe they don't have enough time for spouses and partners
- 74% believe they don't have enough time for their children
- 35% are spending time caring for elderly relatives
- both baby boomers (87%) and Gen Ys (89%) rate flexible work as important
- both baby boomers (63%) and Gen Ys (69%) want opportunities to work remotely at least part of the time

Work-life balance is enhanced when workers have flexibility in scheduling work hours, work locations, and even such things as vacations and personal time off. Flexibility allows people to more easily manage their personal affairs and work responsibilities, and it has been shown that workers who have flexibility, at least with start and stop times, are less likely to leave their jobs.[40] Job designs that include flexible work hours and other alternative work schedules are an increasingly popular starting point.[41] One example is Motorola, where all employees in its Chicago technology-acceleration group work flexible schedules at the office or from home. Another is Abbott Labs in Columbus, Ohio, where Wednesday is the only day employees have to be in the office; other days are open to flexible scheduling.[42]

Many employers also create flexibility by directly helping workers handle family matters through such things as on-site day-care and elder-care, and concierge services for miscellaneous needs such as dry cleaning and gift purchasing. Some have moved into innovative programs that include work sabbaticals—Schwab offers four weeks after five years employment; unlimited vacation days—a Dublin, Ohio, advertising agency lets workers take as many vacation days as they want; purchased vacation time—Xerox allows workers to buy vacation days using payroll deductions; and on-call doctors—Microsoft sends doctors to employees' homes to keep them out of emergency rooms.[43] The accounting

Flexibility and work-life balance are big issues when it comes to attracting and retaining talented workers.

firm KPMG even keeps a "wellness scorecard" on employees to identify if they are missing vacations or working too hard; they are contacted by supervisors to discuss work patterns and ways to slow down.[44]

• Compensation plans influence employee recruitment and retention.

Pay! It may be that no other work issue receives as much attention.

Base compensation in the form of a market competitive salary or hourly wage helps in hiring the right people. The way pay increases are subsequently handled can have a big impact on employees' job attitudes, motivation, and performance, and also influence their tendencies to "look around" for better jobs elsewhere.

The trend in compensation today is largely toward "pay-for-performance."[45] If you are part of a **merit pay** system, your pay increases will be based on some assessment of how well you perform. The notion is that a good merit raise is a positive signal to high performers and a negative signal to low performers, thus encouraging both to work hard in the future. Although this logic makes sense, merit systems are not problem-free. A survey reported by the *Wall Street Journal* found that only 23% of employees believed they understood their companies' reward systems.[46] Typical questions are: Who assesses performance? Suppose the employee doesn't agree with the assessment? Is the system fair and equitable to everyone involved? Is there enough money available to make the merit increases meaningful for those who receive them?

A good merit pay system that is based on a solid foundation of agreed-upon and well-defined performance measures can handle these questions and more. For example, at the restaurant chain Applebee's International Inc., managers know that part of their merit pay will be determined by what percentage of their best workers are retained. In an industry known for high turnover, Applebee's wants to retain its best workers and the company makes this a high-priority goal for managers. It also makes their pay increases contingent on how well they do.[47] But this system can still break down if Applebee's managers don't perceive that it is administered in a fair, consistent, and credible fashion.

There's a bit more to the Applebee's story. If you are one of the employees that managers want to retain, you might be on the receiving end of "Applebucks"—small cash bonuses that are given to reward performance and raise loyalty to the firm.[48] This is a modest example; the "bonus" can also take larger proportions. How would you like to someday receive a letter like this one, once sent to two top executives by Amazon.com's chairman Jeff Bezos? "In recognition and appreciation of your contributions," his letter read, "Amazon.com will pay you a special bonus in the amount of $1,000,000."[49]

Bonus pay plans provide one-time or lump-sum payments to employees based on the accomplishment of specific performance targets or some other extraordinary contribution, such as an idea for a work improvement. Bonuses have been most common at the executive level, but many companies now use them more extensively across levels.[50] Whereas some bonus systems award bonuses to individuals, such as the Applebee's and Amazon examples, others award them to everyone in the group or division responsible for high performance. For example, steelmaker Nucor paid out $40 million to give workers bonuses from $1,000–$2,000 after the firm had a record performance.[51]

In contrast to straight bonuses, **profit sharing** plans distribute to employees a proportion of net profits earned by the organization in a performance period. **Gain sharing** plans extend the profit sharing concept by allowing groups of employees to share in any savings or "gains" realized when their efforts result in measurable cost reductions or productivity increases.

Merit pay awards pay increases in proportion to performance contributions.

Bonus pay plans provide one-time payments based on performance accomplishments.

Profit sharing distributes to employees a proportion of net profits earned by the organization.

Gain sharing plans allow employees to share in cost savings or productivity gains realized by their efforts.

Applebee's bases part of managers' merit pay on how well they do in retaining the best workers.

Another approach is to grant employees **stock options** linked to their performance or as part of their hiring packages.[52] Stock options give the owner the right to buy shares of stock at a future date at a fixed price. They gain financially the more the stock price rises above the original option price; they lose if the stock price ends up lower. Some companies "restrict" the stock options so that they come due only after designated periods of employment. This practice is meant to tie high performers to the employer and is often called the "golden handcuff." The Hay Group reports that the most admired U.S. companies are also ones that offer stock options to a greater proportion of their workforces.[53]

Stock options give the right to purchase shares at a fixed price in the future.

• Fringe benefits are an important part of employee compensation packages.

Benefits! They rank right up there in importance with pay as a way of helping to attract and retain workers. How many times does a graduating college student hear—"be sure to get a job with benefits!"?[54]

Any mention of **fringe benefits** can be a hot button in conversations about work today. They include nonmonetary forms of compensation such as health insurance and retirement plans. They can add as much as 20% or more to a typical worker's earnings and, at times, the cost of benefits increases faster than the cost of wages and salaries.[55]

Fringe benefits are nonmonetary forms of compensation such as health insurance and retirement plans.

Fringe benefit costs, especially medical insurance and retirement, are a major worry for employers. Many are attempting to gain control over health care expenses by shifting more of the insurance costs to the employee and by restricting options in choosing health care providers. Many are also encouraging healthy lifestyles as a way of decreasing health insurance claims.

The growing significance of work-life balance in the new social contract is reflected in a trend toward more **family-friendly benefits** that help employees to better balance work and nonwork responsibilities. These include child care, elder care, flexible schedules, parental leave, and part-time employment options, among others. **Flexible benefits** programs that let the employee choose a personalized set of benefits within a certain dollar amount are increasingly common as are **employee assistance programs** that help employees deal with troublesome personal problems. Called EAP programs, they may include assistance in dealing with stress, counseling on alcohol and substance abuse problems, referrals for domestic violence and sexual abuse, family and marital counseling, and advice on community resources.

Family-friendly benefits help employees achieve better work-life balance.

Flexible benefits programs allow choice to personalize benefits within a set dollar allowance.

Employee assistance programs help employees cope with personal stresses and problems.

You'll probably hear a lot about fringe benefits in conversations with family and friends. A quick check of online discussions, for example, uncovered this question: "If I don't get the raise I was hoping for, What are some of the possible fringe benefits other than medical insurance that I might ask for to make up the difference?" Here's a list of the suggestions the questioner received: 401(k) or 403(b) options, life & disability insurance, lower premiums on health insurance, vision insurance, free fitness center membership, extra vacation time, more flexible hours, okay to work from home or the car, longer lunch periods, use of a company car, and new office furniture. If you're looking for a new job or getting ready to negotiate for a pay raise, what might be on your list of desired fringe benefits?

• Labor relations and collective bargaining are closely governed by law.

Labor unions are organizations to which workers belong and that deal with employers on the workers' behalf.[56] They act as a collective "voice" for their members, bringing them a power in dealing with their employers that wouldn't

A **labor union** is an organization that deals with employers on the workers' collective behalf.

Stay Tuned 🅱

Union Membership Declines Among U.S. Workers Overall.

The percentage of wage and salary workers in the United States who belong to unions has been on the decline. The latest figures show 12.4% of workers overall and 19% of white-collar workers belonging to unions. The highest unionization, 38.7%, is among education, training, and library workers. Some 67% of respondents to a Harris survey said that unions are too involved in politics.

Labor union membership trends

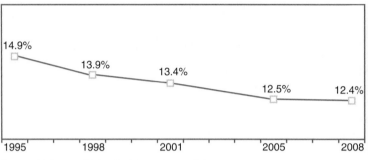

Source: U.S. Bureau of Labor Statistics and www.afl-cio.org.

Your Thoughts?

Does the decline in union membership mean that workers have pretty much decided they don't need union representation any more? Or do other factors explain these trends? In times of economic recession and huge job losses experienced by American workers do you expect union membership will start increasing?

A **labor contract** is a formal agreement between a union and an employer about the terms of work for union members.

Collective bargaining is the process of negotiating, administering, and interpreting a labor contract.

Two-tier wage systems pay new hires less than workers already doing the same jobs with more seniority.

otherwise be available to them as individuals. Historically, this voice of the unions has played an important role in American society. And even though unions are often associated with wage and benefit concerns, it seems that what often causes workers to join unions are things such as poor relationships with supervisors, favoritism or lack of respect by supervisor, little or no influence with employer, and failure of employer to provide a mechanism for grievance and dispute resolution.[57]

As bargaining agents, unions negotiate legal contracts affecting many aspects of the employment relationship for their members. These **labor contracts** typically specify the rights and obligations of employees and management with respect to wages, work hours, work rules, seniority, hiring, grievances, and other conditions of work.

The front line in the legal context of the labor-management relationship is **collective bargaining**, the process that brings management and union representatives together in negotiating, administering, and interpreting labor contracts. During a collective bargaining session, these parties exchange a variety of demands, proposals, and counterproposals. Several rounds of bargaining may take place before a contract is reached or a dispute resolved. Sometimes the process breaks down, and one or both parties walk away. The impasse can be short or lengthy, in some cases leading to labor actions that can last months and even years before agreements are reached.

One of the areas where unions and employers are increasingly finding themselves on different sides of the bargaining issue relates to so-called **two-tier wage systems.** These are systems that pay new hires less than workers already doing the same jobs with more seniority. At a Goodyear factory in Alabama where a two-tiered system is in place, one of the high-seniority workers says: "If I was doing the same job, working just as hard and earning what they make, I'd be resentful."[58] Agreeing in collective bargaining to a two-tier system isn't likely to be the preference of union negotiators. But the management side offers at least one strong argument it its favor; getting a two-tier agreement in the labor contract can help keep the firm profitable and retain jobs in America than would otherwise be lost foreign outsourcing.

When labor-management relations take on the adversarial character shown in **Figure 10.2**, the conflict can be prolonged and costly for both sides. That's not good for anyone, and there is quite a bit of pressure these days for more cooperative union-management relationships. Wouldn't it be nice if unions and management would work together in partnership, trying to address the concerns of both parties in ways that best meet the great challenges and competitive pressures of a global economy?

The trend seems to be in the direction of more labor-management cooperation. When Southwest Airlines and the Transport Workers Union reached agreement

FIGURE 10.2

What Happens When Labor-Management Relations Become Adversarial?

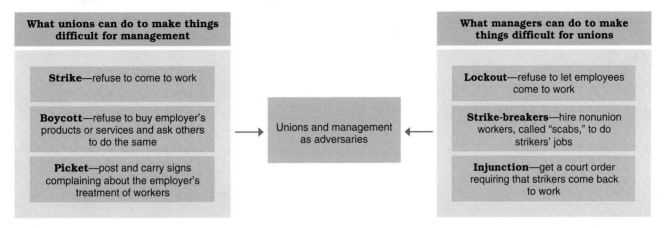

When union and management representatives meet in collective bargaining, it would be nice if things were always cooperative. Unfortunately, they sometimes turn adversarial, and each side has weapons at its disposal to make things hard for the other. Unions can resort to strikes, boycotts, and picketing. Management can use lockouts, strike-breakers, and court injunctions to force strikers back to work. Although each side can find justifications in defense of using such tactics, they can also come with high price tags in terms of lost worker earnings and company profits.

on contract terms for 9,800 flight attendants, the process had taken about eight months and covered pay raises, retirement contributions, leaves, and job security. But the Local 556 union president said it had all been handled "with a spirit of cooperation and partnership."[59]

What is happening in the U.S. auto industry is another example. The companies are in crisis due to foreign competition; their workers are in crisis as job losses threaten careers and lifestyles; their communities are in crisis as plant shutdowns create economic hardships. These problems are not easily solved, and any solutions are likely to be long term and to require substantial compromises and changes on both sides. The United Automobile Workers Union covers 42,000 of Ford's workers. In negotiations during the crisis, the union made concessions on benefits cuts, made work rule changes, and cancelled pay increases to help Ford stay competitive with the cost structures of foreign automakers such as Toyota.[60] You'll most probably note ups and downs, complaints, and controversies, as the automakers and unions bargain back and forth. But it's also likely that you'll see each side bending a bit, over time, as they try to work things out in the best ways possible.

Study Guide

10.3
What Are Some Current Issues in Human Resource Management?

Rapid review

- Complex demands of job and family responsibilities have made work-life balance programs increasingly important in human resource management.
- Compensation and benefits packages must be attractive so that an organization stays competitive in labor markets.
- Labor unions are organizations to which workers belong and that deal with employers in the employees' behalf.
- The collective bargaining process and labor-management relations are carefully governed by law.

Terms to define

Bonus pay

Gain sharing

Merit pay

Profit sharing

Collective bargaining

Employee assistance program

Flexible benefits

Family-friendly benefits

Labor contract

Labor union

Stock options

Two-tier wage system

Work-life balance

Be sure you can

- define work-life balance and discuss its significance for the human resource management process
- explain why compensation and benefits are important in human resource management
- differentiate bonuses and profit sharing as forms of performance-based pay
- define the terms labor union, labor contract, and collective bargaining
- explain the role of labor unions and the process of collective bargaining
- compare the adversarial and cooperative approaches to labor-management relations

Questions for discussion

1. Are we giving too much attention these days to issues of work-life balance?
2. Can a good argument be made that merit pay just doesn't work?
3. Given current economic trends, is it likely that unions will gain in popularity?

[Test Prep]

1. Human resource management is the process of _____, developing, and maintaining a high-quality workforce.

   (a) attracting   (b) compensating
   (c) appraising   (d) selecting

2. A _____ is a criterion that organizations can legally justify for use in screening candidates for employment.

   (a) job description
   (b) bona fide occupational qualification
   (c) realistic job preview
   (d) BARS

3. _____ programs are designed to ensure equal employment opportunities for groups historically underrepresented in the workforce.

   (a) Realistic recruiting   (b) Mentoring
   (c) Affirmative action   (d) Coaching

4. An organization should replace an employment test that yields different results over time when taken by the same person because it lacks _____.

   (a) validity   (b) reliability
   (c) realism   (d) behavioral anchors

5. The assessment center approach to employee selection relies heavily on _____ to evaluate a candidate's job skills.

   (a) intelligence tests
   (b) simulations and experiential exercises
   (c) 360° feedback
   (d) formal one-on-one interviews

6. If a woman in a traditionally female occupation complains that a man in a traditionally male occupation is unfairly earning more pay even though the skill requirements for both jobs are equal, she is raising an issue known as _____.

   (a) equal employment opportunity
   (b) comparable worth
   (c) bona fide occupational qualification
   (d) reverse discrimination

7. Socialization of newcomers occurs during the _____ step of the staffing process.

   (a) orientation
   (b) recruiting
   (c) selecting
   (d) training existing workforce
   (e) review organizational mission, objectives, and strategies

8. Which phrase is most consistent with a recruiter offering a job candidate a realistic job preview?

   (a) "There are just no downsides to this job."
   (b) "No organization can be as good an employer as this one."
   (c) "Don't ask me about negatives because there just aren't any."
   (d) "Let me tell you what you might not like once you start work."

9. The _____ purpose of performance appraisal is being addressed when a manager describes training options that might help an employee improve future performance.

   (a) development   (b) evaluation
   (c) judgmental   (d) legal

10. When a team leader must rate 10% of team members as "superior," 80% as "good," and 10% as "unacceptable" for their performance on a project, this is an example of the _____ approach to performance appraisal.

    (a) graphic
    (b) critical-incidents
    (c) behaviorally anchored rating scale
    (d) forced distribution

11. The first step in strategic human resource planning is to _____.

    (a) forecast human resource needs
    (b) forecast labor supplies
    (c) assess the existing workforce
    (d) review organizational mission, objectives, and strategies

12. Whereas bonus plans pay employees for special accomplishments, profit sharing plans reward them for _____.

    (a) helping to increase profits
    (b) regular attendance
    (c) positive work attitudes
    (d) suggestions that lead to cost reductions

13. An employee with family problems that are starting to interfere with work would be pleased to learn that his employer had a(n) _____ plan to help on such matters.

    (a) employee assistance
    (b) cafeteria benefits
    (c) comparable worth
    (d) collective bargaining

14. In the United States, the _____ Act of 1947 protects employers from unfair labor practices by unions.

    (a) Wagner   (b) Taft-Hartley
    (c) Labor Union   (d) Hawley-Smoot

15. A manager who _____ is displaying a commitment to valuing human capital.

    (a) believes payroll costs should be reduced wherever possible

    (b) is always looking for new ways to replace people with machines

    (c) protects workers from stress by withholding information from them about the organization's performance

    (d) views people as assets to be nurtured and developed over time

Short response

16. Why is orientation important in the HRM process?

17. How does mentoring work as an on-the-job training approach?

18. When is an employment test or a performance appraisal method reliable?

19. How do the graphic rating scale and the BARS differ as performance appraisal methods?

Integration & application

20. Sy Smith is not doing well in his job. The problems began to appear shortly after Sy's job changed from a manual to a computer-based operation. He has tried hard, but is just not doing well in learning how to use the computer to meet performance expectations. He is 45 years old, with 18 years with the company. He has been a great worker in the past and is both popular and influential among his peers. Along with his performance problems, you have also noticed that Sy is starting to sometimes "badmouth" the firm.

Questions: As Sy's manager, what options would you consider in terms of dealing with the issue of his retention in the job and in the company? What would you do and why?

Performance Appraisal Assumptions

Instructions

In each of the following pairs of statements, check the one that best reflects your assumptions about performance evaluation.[61]

1. (a) a formal process that is done annually
   (b) an informal process done continuously

2. (a) a process that is planned for subordinates
   (b) a process that is planned with subordinates

3. (a) a required organizational procedure
   (b) a process done regardless of requirements

4. (a) a time to evaluate subordinates' performance
   (b) a time for subordinates to evaluate their manager

5. (a) a time to clarify standards
   (b) a time to clarify the subordinate's career needs

6. (a) a time to confront poor performance
   (b) a time to express appreciation

7. (a) an opportunity to clarify issues and provide direction and control
   (b) an opportunity to increase enthusiasm and commitment

8. (a) only as good as the organization's forms
   (b) only as good as the manager's coaching skills

Interpretation

In general, the "a" responses show more emphasis on the *evaluation* function of performance appraisal. This largely

puts th...
ordinate's ...
purposes. Th...
on the *counsel*...
supervisor is conce...
do better and with l...
what he or she needs t...

 For further exploration go to WileyPlus

Case Snapshot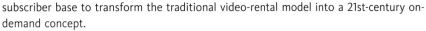

Netflix—Making Movie Magic

How can the most successful video-delivery company beat its already unbelievable one-day turnaround time? By making a growing portion of its immense catalog available for instant download. Netflix leverages emerging technologies, superior customer service, and an ever-growing subscriber base to transform the traditional video-rental model into a 21st-century on-demand concept.

Online Interactive Learning Resources

SELF-ASSESSMENT
• Work-Life Balance

EXPERIENTIAL EXERCISES
• You Be the Judge
• Upward Appraisal

TEAM PROJECT
• Fringe Benefit Costs

supervisor in the role of documenting a sub-
performance for control and administrative
e "b" responses show a stronger emphasis
g or *development* function. Here, the
ned with helping the subordinate
arning from the subordinate
be able to do better.

Each of Us

Learning Outline

11.1 What Are the Foundations for Effective Leadership?

- Leadership is one of the four functions of management
- Leaders use position power to achieve influence
- Leaders use personal power to achieve influence
- Leaders bring vision to leadership situations
- Leaders display different traits in the quest for leadership effectiveness
- Leaders display different styles in the quest for leadership effectiveness

11.2 What Are the Contingency Leadership Theories?

- Fiedler's contingency model matches leadership styles with situational differences
- The Hersey-Blanchard situational leadership model matches leadership styles with the maturity of followers
- House's path-goal theory matches leadership styles with task and follower characteristics
- Leader–member exchange theory describes how leaders treat in-group and out-group followers
- The Vroom-Jago model describes a leader's choice of alternative decision-making methods

11.3 What Are Current Issues and Directions in Leadership Development?

- Transformational leadership inspires enthusiasm and extraordinary performance
- Emotionally intelligent leadership handles emotions and relationships well
- Interactive leadership emphasizes communication, listening, and participation
- Moral leadership builds trust from a foundation of personal integrity
- Servant leadership is follower centered and empowering

Employees are a firm's most important customers. When most people think of Southwest Airlines, they think of reasonable prices and a service spirit. How does the firm do it? The answer traces back to one word: leadership.

And when it comes to leadership, Southwest's well-known founder Herb Kelleher is often considered a role model. You can learn more about Kelleher, his business model, and his leadership style in the case for this chapter. When he retired as CEO, his successor Colleen Barrett had "big shoes to fill." But she picked up nicely where he left off and added some leadership touches of her own.

In an interview with *Bi$_z$Ed* magazine, Barrett links the airline's success with its high-priority commitment to all employees, something set into the culture by Kelleher. She also points to three types of customers: employees, passengers, and shareholders. Whereas many would consider it unusual to define employees as an organization's most important customers, Barrett says it has a purpose: "If senior leaders regularly communicate with employees;

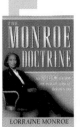

Trendsetters
Lorraine Monroe's leadership turns vision into inspiration.

News Feed
Why Peter Drucker's leadership advice still matters

Case Snapshot
Southwest Airlines—How Herb Kelleher led the way

if we're truthful and factual, if we show them that we care, and if we do our best to respond to their needs, they'll feel good about their work environment and they'll be better at serving the passenger."

There's no human resources department on Southwest's organization chart. Instead, there's a People and Leadership Development Department. This is consistent with Kelleher's vision. "Competitors have tried and failed to copy us," he says, "because they can't copy our people." This is what we've come to expect from a company whose listing symbol on the New York Stock Exchange is LUV. After Barrett retired, Southwest's veteran Gary Kelly became president and CEO. True to form, one of his first leadership statements was: "We all pledge to continue to keep the LUV alive and the Warrior Spirit strong that Herb and Colleen inspired in all 34,000 Southwest employees."

11.1 What Are the Foundations for Effective Leadership?

Leadership is the process of inspiring others to work hard to accomplish important tasks.

A glance at the shelves in your local bookstore will quickly confirm that **leadership**, the process of inspiring others to work hard to accomplish important tasks, is one of the most popular management topics.[1] Consultant and author Tom Peters says that the leader is "rarely—possibly never—the best performer."[2] They don't have to be; leaders thrive through and by the successes of others. But not all managers live up to these expectations. Warren Bennis, a respected scholar and consultant, claims that too many U.S. corporations are "over-managed and under-led." The late Grace Hopper, the first female admiral in the U.S. Navy, advised that "You manage things; you lead people."[3] The bottom line is that leaders become great by bringing out the best in people.

• Leadership is one of the four functions of management.

Leadership is one of the four functions that make up the management process shown in **Figure 11.1**. *Planning* sets the direction and objectives; *organizing* brings together the resources to turn plans into action; *leading* builds the commitments and enthusiasm for people to apply their talents to help accomplish plans; and *controlling* makes sure things turn out right.

FIGURE 11.1

The Importance of Leading in the Management Process.

Where do you stand on leadership skills and capabilities?[4] If, as the module subtitle suggests, "A leader lives in each of us," what leader resides in you?

Of course, managers face sometimes daunting challenges in their quest to succeed as leaders. The time frames for getting things accomplished are becoming shorter. Leaders are expected to get things right the first time, with second chances sometimes few and far between. The problems to be resolved through leadership are complex, ambiguous, and multidimensional. Leaders are expected to stay focused on long-term goals even while dealing with problems and pressures in the short term.[5] Anyone aspiring to career success in leadership must rise to these challenges, and more, becoming good at all the interpersonal skills discussed in this part of *Exploring Management 2/e*—communication, motivation, teamwork, conflict, and negotiation.

• Leaders use position power to achieve influence.

Are you surprised that our discussion of leadership and leadership development starts with "power"? Harvard professor Rossabeth Moss Kanter once called it "America's last great dirty word."[5] She was concerned that too many people, managers among them, are not only uncomfortable with the concept, but also they don't realize how indispensable it is to leadership.

Power is the ability to get someone else to do something you want done, the ability to make things happen the way you want them to. Isn't that a large part of management, being able to influence other people? So, where and how do managers get power?

As shown in **Figure 11.2**, there are basically two sources of managerial power.[6] First is the power of the position, being "the manager." This power includes rewards, coercion, and legitimacy. Second is the power of the person, who you are and what your presence means in a situation. This power includes expertise and reference. Of course, some of us do far better than others at mobilizing and using power from these multiple sources.[7]

Power is the ability to get someone else to do something you want done.

FIGURE 11.2

Sources of Position Power and Personal Power as Used by Leaders.

Sources of power...

Power of the POSITION: Based on things managers can offer to others	Power of the PERSON: Based on how managers are viewed by others
Rewards: "If you do what I ask, I'll give you a reward."	**Expertise**—as a source of special knowledge and information
Coercion: "If you don't do what I ask, I'll punish you."	**Reference**—as a person with whom others like to identify
Legitimacy: "Because I am the boss, you *must* do as I ask."	

When it comes to position power, **reward power** is the capability to offer something of value as a means of influencing the behavior of other people. To use reward power, a manager says, in effect: "If you do what I ask, I'll give you a reward."

Very often the available rewards are things such as pay raises, bonuses, promotions, special assignments, and verbal or written compliments. As you might expect, reward power can work well as long as people want the reward and the manager or leader makes it continuously available. But take the value of the reward or the reward itself away, and the power is quickly lost.

Coercive power is the capability to punish or withhold positive outcomes as a way of influencing the behavior of other people. To mobilize coercive power, a manager is really saying: "If you don't do what I want, I'll punish you."

Managers have access to lots of possible punishments, including threatened or actual reprimands, pay penalties, bad job assignments, and even termination. How do you or would you feel when threatened in these ways? If you're like me, you'll most likely resent both the threat and the person making it. Sure, you might act as requested, or at least go through the motions, but you're unlikely to continue doing so once the threat no longer exists.

Legitimate power is the capacity to influence through authority. It is the right by virtue of one's status as the manager, or person in charge, to exercise control over persons in subordinate positions. To mobilize legitimate power, a manager is basically saying: "I am the boss; therefore you are supposed to do as I ask."

Reward power achieves influence by offering something of value.

Coercive power achieves influence by punishment.

Legitimate power achieves influence by formal authority.

Just like many of the athletes and celebrities we see in television ads, referent power allows leaders to influence others through positive identification.

Expert power achieves influence by special knowledge.

Referent power achieves influence by personal identification.

You might consider legitimate power in the context of your management course. When the instructor assigns homework, exams, and group projects, don't you most often do what is requested? Why? You do it because the requests seem legitimate in the context of the course. But if the instructor moves outside of the course boundaries, such as requiring you to attend a campus sports event, the legitimacy is lost and your compliance is much less likely.

• Leaders use personal power to achieve influence.

After all is said and done, we need to admit that position power alone isn't going to be sufficient for any manager. In fact, how much personal power you can mobilize through expertise and reference may well make the difference someday between success and failure in a leadership situation, and even a career.

Expert power is the ability to influence the behavior of others because of special knowledge and skills. When a manager uses expert power, the implied message is, "You should do what I want because of my special expertise or information."

A leader's expertise may come from technical understanding or access to information relevant to the issue at hand. It can be acquired through formal education and evidenced by degrees and credentials. It is also acquired on the job, through experience, and by gaining a reputation as someone who is a high performer and really understands the work. Building expertise in these ways, in fact, may be one of your biggest early career challenges.

There's still more to personal power. Think of all the television commercials that show high-visibility athletes and personalities advertising consumer products. What's really going on here? The intent is to attract customers to the products through identification with the athletes and personalities. The same holds true in leadership. **Referent power** is the ability to influence the behavior of others because they admire and want to identify positively with you. When a manager uses referent power, the implied message is: "You should do what I want in order to maintain a positive self-defined relationship with me."

If referent power is so valuable, do you know how to get it? It is probably derived in large part from and maintained by good interpersonal relationships, ones that create admiration and respect for us in the eyes of others. My wife sums this up very simply, saying: "It's a lot easier to get people to do what you want when they like you, than when they dislike you." Doesn't this make sense? Isn't this good advice for how to approach your work and the people with whom you work every day?

Trendsetters

Lorraine Monroe's Leadership Turns Vision into Inspiration.

Dr. Lorraine Monroe's career in the New York City Schools began as a teacher. She went on to serve as assistant principal, principal, and Vice-Chancellor for Curriculum and Instruction. But her career really took off when she founded the Frederick Douglass Academy, a public school in Harlem, where she grew up. Under her leadership as principal, the school became highly respected for educational excellence. The academy's namesake was an escaped slave who later became a prominent abolitionist and civil rights leader.

Through her experiences Monroe formed a set of beliefs centered on a leader being vision driven and follower centered. She believes leaders must always start at the "heart of the matter" and that "the job of a good leader is to articulate a vision that others are inspired to follow." She believes in making sure all workers know they are valued and that their advice is welcome, and that workers and managers should always try to help and support one another. "I have never undertaken any project," she says, "without first imagining on paper what it would ultimately look like. . . . all the doers who would be responsible for carrying out my imaginings have to be informed and let in on the dream."

About her commitment to public leadership, Monroe states: "We can reform society only if every place we live—every school, workplace, church, and family—becomes a site of reform." She now serves as a leadership consultant and runs the Lorraine Monroe Leadership Institute. Its goal is to train educational leaders in visionary leadership and help them go forth to build high-performing schools that transform children's lives.

Lorraine Monroe's many leadership ideas are summarized in what is called the "Monroe Doctrine." It begins with this advice: "The job of the leader is to uplift her people—not just as members of and contributors to the organization, but as individuals of infinite worth in their own right."

• Leaders bring vision to leadership situations.

"Great leaders," it is said, "get extraordinary things done in organizations by inspiring and motivating others toward a common purpose."[8] In other words, they use their power exceptionally well. And frequently today, successful leadership is associated with **vision**—a future that one hopes to create or achieve in order to improve upon the present state of affairs. According to John Wooden, former stand-out men's basketball coach at UCLA: "Effective leadership means having a lot of people working toward a common goal. And when you have that with no one caring who gets the credit, you're going to accomplish a lot."[9]

The term **visionary leadership** describes a leader who brings to the situation a clear and compelling sense of the future, as well as an understanding of the actions needed to get there successfully.[10] But simply having the vision of a desirable future is not enough. Truly great leaders are extraordinarily good at turning their visions into accomplishments. This means being good at communicating the vision and getting people motivated and inspired to pursue the vision in their daily work. You can think of it this way: visionary leadership brings meaning to people's work, making what they do seem worthy and valuable.

A **vision** is a clear sense of the future.

Visionary leadership brings to the situation a clear sense of the future and an understanding of how to get there.

• Leaders display different traits in the quest for leadership effectiveness.

For centuries, people have recognized that some persons use power and perform very well as leaders, whereas others do not. You've certainly seen this yourself. How can such differences in leadership effectiveness be explained?

An early direction in leadership research tried to answer this question by identifying traits and personal characteristics shared by effective leaders.[11] Not surprisingly, results showed that physical characteristics such as height, weight, and physique make no difference. But a study of over 3400 managers found that followers rather consistently admired leaders who were honest, competent, forward-looking, inspiring, and credible.[12] Another comprehensive review is summarized in **Table 11.1**—*Traits Often Shared by Effective Leaders*.[13] You might use this list as a quick check of your leadership potential.

In addition to leadership traits, researchers have also studied how successful and unsuccessful leaders behaved when working with followers. Most of this research focused on two sets of behaviors: task-oriented behaviors and people-oriented behaviors. A leader high in concern for task generally plans and defines work goals, assigns task responsibilities, sets clear work standards, urges task completion, and monitors performance results. A leader high in concern for people acts warm and supportive toward followers, maintains good social relations with them, respects their feelings, shows sensitivity to their needs, and displays trust in them.

[TABLE 11.1]

Traits Often Shared by Effective Leaders

Drive—successful leaders have high energy, display initiative, and are tenacious.

Self-confidence—successful leaders trust themselves and have confidence in their abilities.

Creativity—successful leaders are creative and original in their thinking.

Cognitive ability—successful leaders have the intelligence to integrate and interpret information.

Business knowledge—successful leaders know their industry and its technical foundations.

Motivation—successful leaders enjoy influencing others to achieve shared goals.

Flexibility—successful leaders adapt to fit the needs of followers and the demands of situations.

Honesty and integrity—successful leaders are trustworthy; they are honest, predictable, and dependable.

• Leaders display different styles in the quest for leadership effectiveness.

Leaders who show different combinations of task and people behaviors are often described as having unique **leadership styles**, such as you have probably observed in your own experiences. A popular approach to leadership

Leadership style is the recurring pattern of behaviors exhibited by a leader.

styles is shown in **Figure 11.3.** Someone who emphasizes task over people is often described as "autocratic."[14] An **autocratic leader** holds on to authority, delegates little, keeps information to himself or herself, and tends to act in a unilateral command-and-control fashion. Have you ever worked for someone fitting this description? How would you score his or her leadership effectiveness?

A leader with an **autocratic style** acts in unilateral command-and-control fashion.

FIGURE 11.3

Managerial Styles in Blake and Mouton's Leadership Grid.

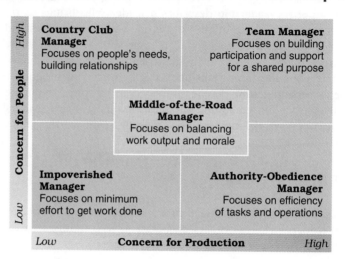

It is common to describe leaders in terms of how their day-to-day styles show concern for people and concern for task. In the "Leadership Grid" shown here, the leader low in concerns for both people and task is described as "laissez-faire" and very ineffective. The leader high in concern for task but low in concern for people is "autocratic" and focused on performance. The leader high in concern for people and low in concern for task is has a "human relations" style that focuses mainly on people and relationships. The "democratic" leader is high in concerns for both people and task. This person is often highly successful as a true team manager who is able to engage people to accomplish common goals.

A leader with a **human relations** style emphasizes people over tasks.

A leader who emphasizes people over task is often referred to as a **human relations leader.** This leader is interpersonally engaging, caring about others, and sensitive to feelings and emotions, and tends to act in ways that emphasize harmony and good working relationships.

Interestingly, researchers at first believed that the human relations style was the most effective for a leader. However, after pressing further, the conclusion emerged that the most effective leaders were strong in concerns for both people and task.[15] Sometimes called a **democratic leader,** a person with this style shares decisions with subordinates, encourages participation, and supports the team-work needed for high levels of task accomplishment.

A leader with a **democratic style** encourages participation with an emphasis on task and people.

One of the results of the early research on leader behaviors was the emergence of training programs designed to help people learn how to be good at both task-oriented and people-oriented behaviors needed for leadership success. How about you? Where do you fit on the leadership grid? What leadership training would be best for you? Hopefully you're not starting out with a **laissez-faire style,** low on both task and people concerns.

A leader with a **laissez-faire style** is disengaged, showing low task and people concerns.

Study Guide

11.1
What Are the Foundations for Effective Leadership?

Rapid review

- Leadership, as one of the management functions, is the process of inspiring others to work hard to accomplish important tasks.
- Leaders use power, from two primary sources: position power that includes rewards, coercion, and legitimacy, and personal power that includes expertise and reference.
- The ability to communicate a vision or clear sense of the future is considered essential to effective leadership.
- Personal characteristics that have been associated with leadership success include drive, integrity, and self-confidence.
- Research on leader behaviors focused attention on concerns for task and concerns for people, with the leader high on both and using a democratic style considered most effective.

Terms to define

Autocratic leader

Coercive power

Democratic leader

Expert power

Human relations leader

Laissez-faire leader

Leadership

Leadership style

Legitimate power

Power

Referent power

Reward power

Vision

Visionary leadership

Be sure you can

- illustrate how managers use position and personal power
- define vision and give an example of visionary leadership
- list five traits of successful leaders
- describe alternative leadership styles based on concern for task and concern for people

Reflect/React

1. When, if ever, is a leader justified in using coercive power?
2. How can a young college graduate gain personal power when moving into a new job as team leader?
3. In what ways can a human relations leader have difficulty getting things done in an organization?

11.2 What Are the Contingency Leadership Theories?

Even as you consider your leadership style and tendencies, you should know that researchers eventually concluded that no one style always works best. Not even the democratic or "high-high" leader is successful all of the time. This finding led scholars to explore a **contingency leadership perspective**, that is, what is effective as a leadership style varies according to the nature of the situation and people involved.

The **contingency leadership perspective** suggests that what is successful as a leadership style varies by the situation and the people involved.

• Fiedler's contingency model matches leadership styles with situational differences.

One of the first contingency models of leadership was put forth by Fred Fiedler. He proposed that leadership success depends on achieving a proper match between your leadership style and situational demands.[16] And he believed that each of us has a predominant leadership style that is strongly rooted in our personalities. This is important because it suggests that a person's leadership style, yours or mine, is going to be quite enduring and difficult to change.

Fiedler uses an instrument called the *least-preferred co-worker scale (LPC)* to classify our leadership styles as either task motivated or relationship motivated. By the way, the LPC scale is available on this book's student Web site. Why not complete it and see how Fiedler would describe your style?

Leadership situations are analyzed in Fiedler's model for leader–member relations, task structure, and position power. **Figure 11.4** shows the three contingency variables can exist in eight different combinations, with each representing a different leadership challenge. The most favorable situation provides high control for the leader (good leader–member relations, high task structure, strong position power); the least favorable situation provides low control for the leader (poor leader–member relations, low task structure, weak position power).

S A
Self-Assessment
This is a good point to complete the self-assessment *"LPC Scale"* found on page 250.

FIGURE 11.4

What Are the Best Matches of Leadership Style and Situation According to Fiedler's Contingency Model?

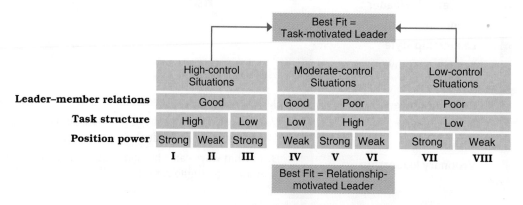

Fiedler believes that leadership success requires the right style-situation match. He classifies leadership styles as either task motivated or relationship motivated, and views them as strongly rooted in our individual personalities. He describes situations according to the leader's position power, quality of leader–member relations, and amount of task structure. In situations that are most favorable and unfavorable for leaders, his research shows the task-motivated style as a best fit. In more intermediate situations, the relationship-motivated style provides the best fit.

Fiedler's research revealed an interesting pattern when he studied the effectiveness of different styles in these leadership situations. As shown in the figure, a task-oriented leader is most successful in either very favorable (high-control) or very unfavorable (low-control) situations. In contrast, a relationship-oriented leader is more successful in situations of moderate control.

Don't let the apparent complexity of the figure fool you; Fiedler's logic is quite straightforward and, if on track, has some interesting career implications. It suggests that you should know yourself well enough to recognize your predominant leadership style. And you should seek out or create leadership situations for which this style is a good match, while avoiding those for which it is a bad match.

Let's do some quick examples. First, assume that you are the leader of a team of bank tellers. The tellers seem highly supportive of you, and their job is clearly defined. You have the authority to evaluate their performance and to make pay and promotion recommendations. This is a high-control situation consisting of good leader–member relations, high task structure, and high position power. By checking Figure 11.4 you can see that a task-motivated leader is recommended.

Now suppose you are chairperson of a committee asked to improve labor-management relations in a manufacturing plant. Although the goal is clear, no one knows exactly how to accomplish it—task structure is low. Further, not everyone believes that a committee is even the right way to approach the situation—poor leader–member relations are likely. Finally, committee members are free to quit any time they want—you have little position power. The figure shows that in this low-control situation a task-motivated leader should be most effective.

Finally, assume that you are the new head of a clothing section in a large department store. Because you won the job over one of the popular sales clerks you now supervise, leader–member relations are poor. Task structure is high since the clerk's job is well defined. But your position power is low because clerks work under a seniority system, with a fixed wage schedule. The figure shows that this moderate-control situation requires a relationship-motivated leader.

• The Hersey-Blanchard situational leadership model matches leadership styles with the maturity of followers.

In contrast to Fiedler's notion that leadership style is hard to change, the Hersey-Blanchard situational leadership model suggests that successful leaders do adjust their styles. They do so contingently and based on the maturity of followers, as indicated by their readiness to perform in a given situation.[17] "Readiness," in this sense, is based on how able and willing or confident followers are to perform required tasks. As shown in **Figure 11.5**, the possible combinations of task-oriented and relationship-oriented behaviors result in four leadership styles.

- *Delegating*—allowing the group to take responsibility for task decisions; a low-task, low-relationship style
- *Participating*—emphasizing shared ideas and participative decisions on task directions; a low-task, high-relationship style
- *Selling*—explaining task directions in a supportive and persuasive way; a high-task, high-relationship style
- *Telling*—giving specific task directions and closely supervising work; a high-task, low-relationship style

FIGURE 11.5

Leadership Implications of the Hersey-Blanchard Situational Leadership Model.

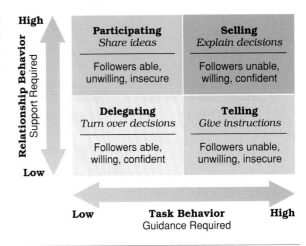

The delegating style works best in high-readiness situations with able and willing or confident followers. The telling style works best at the other extreme of low readiness, where followers are unable and unwilling or insecure. The participating style is recommended for low-to-moderate readiness (followers able but unwilling or insecure); the selling style for moderate-to-high readiness (followers unable but willing or confident).

Hersey and Blanchard further believe that leadership styles should be adjusted as followers change over time. The model also implies that if the correct styles are used in lower-readiness situations, followers will "mature" and grow in ability, willingness, and confidence. This allows the leader to become less directive as followers mature. Although this situational leadership model is intuitively appealing, limited research has been accomplished on it to date.[18]

• House's path-goal theory matches leadership styles with task and follower characteristics.

Another contingency leadership approach is the path-goal theory advanced by Robert House.[19] This theory suggests that leaders are effective when they help followers move along paths through which they can achieve both work and personal goals. The best leaders create positive "path-goal" linkages, raising motivation by removing barriers and rewarding progress.

Like Fiedler's approach, House's path-goal theory seeks the right fit between leadership and situation. But unlike Fiedler, House believes that a leader can use four leadership styles: directive, supportive, achievement-oriented, and participative.

When choosing among the different styles, House suggests that the leader's job is to "add value" to a situation. This means acting in ways that contribute things that are missing, and not doing things that can otherwise take care of themselves. For example, if you are the leader of a team whose members are expert and competent at their tasks, why would you need to be directive? They have the know-how to provide their own direction. More likely, the value you can add to this situation would be found in a participative leadership style that helps unlock the expertise of team members and apply it fully to the tasks at hand.

> **Four leadership styles in House's path-goal theory**
>
> 1. *Directive leader*—lets others know what is expected; gives directions, maintains standards.
> 2. *Supportive leader*—makes work more pleasant; treats others as equals, acts friendly, shows concern.
> 3. *Achievement-oriented leader*—sets challenging goals; expects high performance, shows confidence.
> 4. *Participative leader*—involves others in decision making; asks for and uses suggestions.

The details of path-goal theory provide a variety of research-based guidance of this sort to help leaders contingently match their styles with situational characteristics.[20] When job assignments are unclear, *directive leadership* helps to clarify task objectives and expected rewards. When worker self-confidence is low, *supportive leadership* can increase confidence by emphasizing individual abilities and offering needed assistance. When task challenge is insufficient in a job, *achievement-oriented leadership* helps to set goals and raise performance aspirations. When performance incentives are poor, *participative leadership* might clarify individual needs and identify appropriate rewards.

Path-goal theory has contributed to the recognition of what are called **substitutes for leadership**.[21] These are aspects of the work setting and the people involved that can reduce the need for a leader's personal involvement. In effect, they make leadership from the "outside" unnecessary because leadership is already provided from within the situation.

Substitutes for leadership are factors in the work setting that direct work efforts without the involvement of a leader.

Possible substitutes for leadership include subordinate characteristics such as ability, experience, and independence; task characteristics such as how routine it is and the availability of feedback; and organizational characteristics such as clarity of plans and formalization of rules and procedures. When these substitutes are present, managers are advised to avoid duplicating them. Instead, they should concentrate on doing other and more important things.

• Leader–member exchange theory describes how leaders treat in-group and out-group followers.

One of the things you may have noticed in your work and study groups is the tendency of leaders to develop "special" relationships with some team members. This notion is central to leader–member exchange theory, or LMX theory as it is often called.[22] This contingency theory is described in **Figure 11.6** and recognizes that in most, or at least many, leadership situations, not everyone is treated the same by the leader.

People fall into "in-groups" and "out-groups," and the group you are in can have quite a significant influence on your experience with the leader. Those in the "in-group" are often considered the best performers. They enjoy special and trusted high-exchange relationships with the leaders that can translate into special assignments, privileges, and access to information. Those in the "out-group" are often excluded from these attributions and benefits; they have a low-exchange relationship with the leader.

The premise underlying leader–member exchange theory is that as a leader and follower interact over time, their exchanges end up defining the follower's role.[23] Look around, and you're likely to see examples of this in classroom situations between instructors and certain students, and in work situations between bosses and certain subordinates.

For the follower in a high-LMX relationship, being part of the leader's inner circle or in-group can have positive implications. It's often motivating and satisfying to be on the inside of things in terms of getting rewards, access to information, and other favorable treatments. Being in the out-group because of a low-LMX relationship, however, can mean fewer rewards, less information, and little or no special attention. And as to the leader, it is nice to be able to call on and depend upon the loyal support of those in the in-group. But the leader may also be missing out on opportunities that would come from working more closely with out-group members.

Research on leader–member exchange theory places most value on its usefulness in describing leader–member relationships. The notions of high-LMX and low-LMX relationships seem to make sense and correspond to working realities experienced by many people. Also, research finds that members of leaders' in-groups seem to get more positive performance evaluations, report higher levels of job satisfaction, and be less prone to turnover than are members of out-groups.[24]

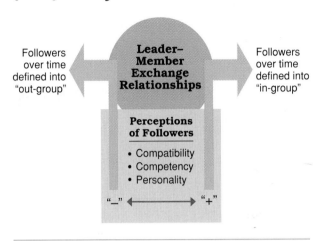

FIGURE 11.6
Elements of Leader–Member Exchange (LMX) Theory.

• The Vroom–Jago model describes a leader's choice of alternative decision-making methods.

Yet another contingency leadership theory focuses on how managers lead through their use of decision-making methods. The Vroom–Jago leader-participation model views a manager as having three decision options, and in true contingency fashion, no one option is always superior to the others.[25] When facing a problem situation, the leader's choices are:

1. **Authority decision**—The manager makes an individual decision how to solve the problem and then communicates the decision to the group.

2. **Consultative decision**—The manager makes the decision after sharing the problem with and getting suggestions from individual group members or the group as a whole.

3. **Group decision**—The manager convenes the group, shares the problem, and then either facilitates a group decision or delegates the decision to the group.

An **authority decision** is made by the leader and then communicated to the group.

A **consultative decision** is made by a leader after receiving information, advice, or opinions from group members.

A **group decision** is made by group members themselves.

FIGURE 11.7

Leadership Implications of Vroom–Jago Leader-Participation Model.

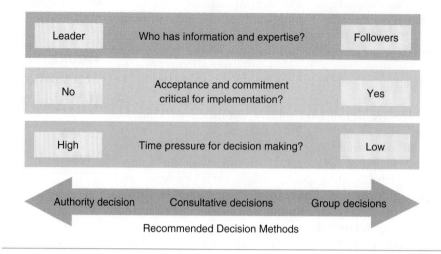

Leader	Who has information and expertise?	Followers
No	Acceptance and commitment critical for implementation?	Yes
High	Time pressure for decision making?	Low

Authority decision   Consultative decisions   Group decisions

Recommended Decision Methods

Leadership success results when the leader's choice of decision-making method best matches the nature of the problem to be solved.[26] As shown in **Figure 11.7**, the rules for making the choice involve three criteria: (1) *decision quality*—based on who has the information needed for problem solving; (2) *decision acceptance*—based on the importance of follower acceptance of the decision to its eventual implementation; and (3) *decision time*—based on the time available to make and implement the decision.

In true contingency fashion, each of the decision methods is appropriate in certain situations, and each has its advantages and disadvantages.[27] Authority decisions work best when leaders personally have the expertise needed to solve the problem, they are confident and capable of acting alone, others are likely to accept and implement the decision they make, and little or no time is available for discussion. By contrast, consultative and group decisions are recommended when:

- the leader lacks sufficient expertise and information to solve this problem alone.
- the problem is unclear and help is needed to clarify the situation.
- acceptance of the decision and commitment by others are necessary for implementation.
- adequate time is available to allow for true participation.

Using consultative and group decisions offers important leadership benefits.[28] Participation helps improve decision quality by bringing more information to bear on the problem. It helps improve decision acceptance as participants gain understanding and become committed to the process. It also contributes to leadership development by allowing others to gain experience in the problem-solving process. However, a potential cost of participation is lost efficiency. Participation often adds to the time required for decision making, and leaders don't always have extra time available. When problems must be resolved immediately, the authority decision may be the only option.[29]

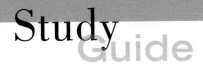
Study Guide

11.2
What Are the Contingency Leadership Theories?

Rapid review

- Fiedler's contingency model describes how situational differences in task structure, position power, and leader–member relations may influence the success of task-motivated and relationship-motivated leaders.
- The Hersey-Blanchard situational model recommends using task-oriented and people-oriented behaviors, depending on the "maturity" levels of followers.
- House's path-goal theory describes how leaders add value to situations by using supportive, directive, achievement-oriented, and/or participative styles as needed.
- Leader–member exchange theory recognizes that leaders respond differently to followers in "in-groups" and "out-groups"
- The Vroom–Jago leader-participation theory advises leaders to choose decision-making methods—authority, consultative, group—that best fit the problems to be solved.

Terms to define

Authority decision

Consultative decision

Contingency leadership perspective

Group decision

Substitutes for leadership

Be sure you can

- explain Fiedler's contingency model for matching leadership style and situation
- identify the three variables used to assess situational favorableness in Fiedler's model
- identify the four leadership styles in the Hersey-Blanchard situational leadership model
- explain the importance of follower "maturity" in the Hersey-Blanchard model
- describe the best use of directive, supportive, achievement-oriented, and participative leadership styles in House's path-goal theory
- explain how leader–member exchange theory deals with "in-groups" and "out-groups" among a leader's followers

Questions for discussion

1. What are the potential career development implications of Fiedler's contingency leadership model?
2. What are the implications of follower "maturity" for leaders trying to follow the Hersey-Blanchard situational leadership model?
3. Is it wrong for a team leader to allow the formation of "in-groups" and "out-groups" in his or her relationships with team members?

A charismatic leader has the capacity to communicate a vision that arouses and inspires followers.

A **charismatic leader** develops special leader-follower relationships and inspires followers in extraordinary ways.

Transactional leadership directs the efforts of others through tasks, rewards, and structures.

Transformational leadership is inspirational and arouses extraordinary effort and performance.

11.3 What Are Current Issues and Directions in Leadership Development?

By now you should be thinking seriously about your leadership qualities, tendencies, styles, and effectiveness. You should also be thinking about your personal development as a leader. And, in fact, if you look at what people say about leaders in their workplaces, you should be admitting that most of us have considerable room to grow in this regard.[30]

• Transformational leadership inspires enthusiasm and extraordinary performance.

For a while now it has been popular to talk about "super leaders," persons whose visions and strong personalities have an extraordinary impact on others.[31] Martin Luther King and his famous "I have a dream" speech delivered August 1963 on the Washington Mall serves as a good example. Some call people like King **charismatic leaders** because of their ability to inspire others in exceptional ways. We used to think charisma was limited to only a few lucky persons who were born with it. Today, it is linked with a broader set of personal qualities that most of us should be able to develop with foresight and practice.

Leadership scholars James MacGregor Burns and Bernard Bass have pursued this theme. They begin by describing the traditional leadership approaches we have discussed so far as **transactional leadership**.[32] You might picture the transactional leader engaging followers in a somewhat mechanical fashion, "transacting" with them by using power, employing behaviors and styles that seem to be the best choices at the moment for getting things done.

What is missing in the transactional approach, say Burns and Bass, is attention to things typically associated with charismatic super leaders—"enthusiasm" and "inspiration," for example. These are among the qualities that they associate with something called **transformational leadership**.[33] Transformational leaders (see Tips to Remember) use their personalities to inspire followers and get them so highly excited about their jobs and organizational goals that they strive for truly extraordinary performance accomplishments.[34] Indeed, the easiest way to spot a truly transformational leader is through his or her followers. They are likely to be enthusiastic about the leader and loyal and devoted to his or her ideas, and to work exceptionally hard together to support them.

Tips to Remember B

Six Essentials of Transformational Leadership

Vision—has ideas and a clear sense of direction; communicates them to others; develops excitement about accomplishing shared "dreams"

Charisma—uses power of personal reference and emotion to arouse others' enthusiasm, faith, loyalty, pride, and trust in themselves

Symbolism—identifies "heroes" and holds spontaneous and planned ceremonies to celebrate excellence and high achievement

Empowerment—helps others grow and develop by removing performance obstacles, sharing responsibilities, and delegating truly challenging work

Intellectual stimulation—gains the involvement of others by creating awareness of problems and stirring their imaginations

Integrity—is honest and credible; acts consistently and out of personal conviction; follows through on commitments

• Emotionally intelligent leadership handles emotions and relationships well.

The role of personality in transformational leadership raises another popular area of inquiry in leadership development—**emotional intelligence**. Popularized by the work of Daniel Goleman, emotional intelligence, or EI for short, is an ability to understand emotions in yourself and others, and use this understanding to handle one's social relationships effectively.[35] "Great leaders move us," say Goleman and his colleagues. "Great leadership works through emotions."[36] Think about it; is this the leader in you?

Emotional intelligence (EI) is the ability to manage our emotions in social relationships.

According to Goleman's research, emotional intelligence is an important influence on leadership success, especially in more senior management positions. In his words: "the higher the rank of the person considered to be a star performer, the more emotional intelligence capabilities showed up as the reason for his or her effectiveness."[37] This is a pretty strong endorsement for considering whether EI is one of your leadership assets. Important, too, is Goleman's belief that we can all learn basic emotional intelligence skills.[38]

To put Goleman's ideas into perspective, consider four primary emotional intelligence competencies as shown in the small figure. *Self-awareness* is the ability to understand our own moods and emotions, and to understand their impact on our work and on others. *Social awareness* is the ability to empathize, to understand the emotions of others, and to use this understanding to better deal with them. *Self-management*, or self-regulation, is the ability to think before acting and to be in control of otherwise disruptive impulses. *Relationship management* is the ability to establish rapport with others in ways that build good relationships and influence their emotions in positive ways.

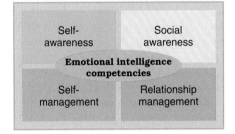

• Interactive leadership emphasizes communication, listening, and participation.

Sara Levinson, President of NFL Properties Inc., of New York, once asked the all-male members of her management team: "Is my leadership style different from a man's?"[39] Would you be surprised to learn that they answered "Yes," telling her that just by asking the question she was providing evidence of the difference; they described her as a leader who emphasized communication, always gathering ideas and opinions from others. And when Levinson probed further by asking "Is this a distinctly 'female' trait?" they said it was.

This example poses an interesting question: Are there gender differences in leadership? Before you jump in with your own answer, let's be clear on three things. First, research largely supports the **gender similarities hypothesis** that males and females are very similar to one another in terms of psychological properties.[40] Second, research leaves no doubt that both women and men can be effective leaders.[41] Third, what research on gender in leadership does show is that men and women are sometimes perceived as using somewhat different styles, perhaps arriving at leadership success from different angles.[42] And, the perceived differences are quite interesting.

The **gender similarities hypothesis** holds that males and females have similar psychological make-ups.

Some studies report male leaders being viewed as directive and assertive, using position power to get things done in traditional command-and-control ways.[43] A recent study employing 360° assessments found women were rated more highly than men in all but one area of leadership—visioning.[44] One possible explanation is that women just aren't perceived as visionaries because they act less directive as leaders. And indeed, other studies report female leaders acting more participative than men. They are also rated by peers, subordinates, and supervisors as strong on motivating others, emotional intelligence, persuading, fostering communication, listening to others, mentoring, and supporting high-quality work.[45]

This pattern of behaviors associated with female leaders has been called an **interactive leadership style**.[46] Interactive leaders are democratic, participative, and inclusive, often approaching problems and decisions through teamwork.[47] They focus on building consensus and good interpersonal relations through

Interactive leadership is strong on motivating, communicating, listening, and relating positively to others.

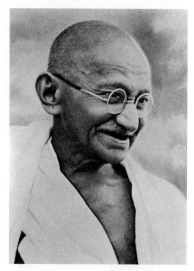

As a moral leader Mahatma Gandhi rallied nonviolent civil disobedience to support India's independence from Great Britain.

emotional intelligence, communication, and involvement. They tend to get things done with personal power, seeking influence over others through support and interpersonal relationships.

Rosabeth Moss Kanter says, "Women get high ratings on exactly those skills required to succeed in the Global Information Age, where teamwork and partnering are so important."[48] Her observations are backed up by data from Catalyst and McKinsey & Co. that show firms having more female directors and executives outperform others.[49] But let's be careful. One of the risks in any discussion of gender and leadership is placing individual men and women into boxes in which they don't necessarily belong.[50] Perhaps we should focus instead on the notion of interactive leadership. The likelihood is that this style is a very good fit with the needs of today's organizations and workers.[51] And, furthermore, there is every reason to believe that both men and women can do interactive leadership equally well. What do you think?

• Moral leadership builds trust from a foundation of personal integrity.

Would you be surprised that a Harris Poll found only 37% of U.S. adults in a survey willing to describe their top managers as acting with "integrity and morality"?[52] Based on that result, it may not surprise you that a *Business Week* survey found that just 13% of top executives at large U.S. firms rated "having strong ethical values" as a top leadership characteristic.[53] Don't you have to wonder: Where is the moral leadership that we so often hear talked about?

In contrast to the findings described in these surveys, there can be little doubt that society today is demanding more **ethical leadership** in our organizations. We want, even if we don't always have, leaders to act ethically and maintain an ethical organizational culture, and both help and require others to behave ethically in their work.[54] We hope, that this theme has been well communicated throughout this book. We hope too, that you will agree that long-term success in work, and in life, can be built only on a foundation of solid ethical behavior.[55]

But where do we start when facing up to the challenge of building capacities for ethical leadership? Peter Drucker's answer would be: **integrity**![56] You must start with honest, credible, and consistent behavior that puts your values into action. When a leader has integrity, he or she earns the trust of followers. And when followers believe that their leaders are trustworthy, they are more willing to try and live up to the leader's expectations. Southwest Airlines CEO Gary Kelly seems to have gotten the message. He says: "Being a leader is about character . . . being straightforward and honest, having integrity, and treating people right." And there's a payoff; one of his co-workers says this about Kelly's leadership impact: "People are willing to run through walls for him."[57]

Ethical leadership has integrity and appears to others as "good" or "right" by moral standards.

Integrity in leadership is honesty, credibility, and consistency in putting values into action.

Stay Tuned 🅱

U.S. Workers Report Their Concerns about Leaders.

Harris Interactive periodically conducts surveys of workers' attitudes toward their jobs and employers. The results for "leaders" and "top managers" reveal lots of shortcomings.

- 37% believe their top managers display integrity and morality.
- 39% believe leaders most often act in best interest of organization.
- 22% see leaders as ready to admit mistakes.
- 46% believe their organizations give them freedom to do their jobs.
- 25% of women and 16% of men believe their organizations pick the best people for leadership.
- <33% of managers are perceived by followers as "strong leaders."

What Are Your Thoughts?

How do the leaders you have experienced stack up—"strong," "weak," or just plain average? What makes the most difference in the ways leaders are viewed in the eyes of followers?

• Servant leadership is follower centered and empowering.

Peter Drucker points out that great leaders view leadership as a responsibility and not a rank. This view is consistent with the concept of **servant leadership**. It is based on a commitment to serving others, and to helping people use their talents to full potential while working together in organizations that benefit society.[58]

You might think of servant leadership with this question in mind: Who is most important in leadership, the leader or the followers? For those who believe in servant leadership, there is no doubt about the correct answer: the followers. Servant leadership is "other centered" and not "self-centered." And once one shifts the focus away from the self and toward others, what does that generate in terms of leadership opportunities? **Empowerment** for one thing. This is the process of giving people job freedom and helping them gain power to achieve influence within the organization.[59]

Max DePree, former CEO of Herman Miller and a noted leadership author, praises leaders who "permit others to share ownership of problems—to take possession of the situation."[60] Lorraine Monroe of the School Leadership Academy says: "The real leader is a servant of the people she leads . . . a really great boss is not afraid to hire smart people. You want people who are smart about things you are not smart about."[61] Robert Greenleaf, who is credited with coining the term servant leadership, says: "Institutions function better when the idea, the dream, is to the fore, and the person, the leader, is seen as servant to the dream."[62]

Reach back and take a good look. Is the leader in you capable of being a servant?

Servant leadership means serving others, and helping them use their talents to help organizations best serve society.

Empowerment gives people job freedom and power to influence affairs in the organization.

News Feed

Why Peter Drucker's Leadership Advice Still Matters

When Peter Drucker died at the age of 95 in the year 2005, the former CEO of GE, Jack Welch, said: "The world knows he was the greatest management thinker of the last century." That could be an understatement. Drucker was renowned worldwide for his many books, consultancies, newspaper columns, and sage advice on matters of management, organizations, business and society, and executive leadership. Here's a sampler of his enduring advice on leaders and leadership.

- Good leaders have integrity; they mean what they say.
- Good leaders earn and keep the trust of followers.
- Good leaders define and establish a sense of mission.
- Good leaders set clear goals, priorities, and standards.
- Good leaders accept leadership as responsibility, not rank.
- Good leaders understand and accept that every decision is risky.
- Good leaders surround themselves with talented people.

Reflect and React

What does Drucker's advice mean to you? Can you translate each of his points into a "leadership lesson" of personal value? Is there anything you would add to this list based on your experience?

Study Guide

11.3
What Are Current Issues and Directions in Leadership Development?

[**Rapid review**

- Transformational leaders use charisma and emotion to inspire others toward extraordinary efforts in support of change and performance excellence.
- Emotional intelligence, the ability to manage our emotions and relationships effectively, is an important leadership capability.
- The interactive leadership style, sometimes associated with women, emphasizes communication, involvement, and interpersonal respect.
- Moral or ethical leadership is built from a foundation of personal integrity, creating a basis for trust and respect between leaders and followers.
- A servant leader operates with a commitment to serving followers by empowering them and unlocking their personal talents in the quest for goals and accomplishments that help organizations best serve society.

[**Terms to define**

Charismatic leader

Emotional intelligence

Empowerment

Ethical leadership

Integrity

Interactive leadership style

Servant leadership

Transactional leadership

Transformational leadership

[**Be sure you can**

- differentiate transformational and transactional leadership
- list personal qualities of transformational leaders
- explain how emotional intelligence contributes to leadership success
- discuss research findings on interactive leadership
- list Drucker's three essentials of good old-fashioned leadership
- explain the role of integrity as a foundation for moral leadership
- explain the concept of servant leadership

[**Questions for discussion**

1. Should all managers be expected to excel at transformational leadership?
2. How do women lead differently than men?
3. Is servant leadership inevitably moral leadership?

Test Prep

1. When managers use offers of rewards and threats of punishments to try and get others to do what they want them to do, they are using which type of power?
   (a) formal authority (b) position
   (c) referent (d) personal

2. When a manager says, "Because I am the boss, you must do what I ask," what power base is being put into play?
   (a) reward (b) legitimate
   (c) moral (d) referent

3. The personal traits that are now considered important for managerial success include _____.
   (a) self-confidence (b) gender
   (c) age (d) personality

4. In the research on leader behaviors, which style of leadership describes the preferred "high-high" combination?
   (a) transformational (b) transactional
   (c) laissez-faire (d) democratic

5. In Fiedler's contingency model, both highly favorable and highly unfavorable leadership situations are best dealt with by a _____ leadership style.
   (a) task-oriented
   (b) laissez-faire
   (c) participative
   (d) relationship-oriented

6. Which leadership theorist argues that one's leadership style is strongly anchored in personality and therefore very difficult to change?
   (a) Daniel Goleman (b) Peter Drucker
   (c) Fred Fiedler (d) Robert House

7. Vision, charisma, integrity, and symbolism are all attributes typically associated with _____ leaders.
   (a) people-oriented (b) democratic
   (c) transformational (d) transactional

8. In terms of leadership behaviors, someone who focuses on doing a very good job of planning work, setting standards, and monitoring results would be described as _____.
   (a) task oriented
   (b) servant oriented
   (c) achievement oriented
   (d) transformational

9. In the discussion of gender and leadership it was pointed out that some perceive women as having tendencies toward _____, a style that seems a good fit with developments in the new workplace.
   (a) interactive leadership
   (b) use of position power
   (c) command-and-control
   (d) transactional leadership

10. In House's path-goal theory, a leader who sets challenging goals for others would be described as using the _____ leadership style.
    (a) autocratic
    (b) achievement-oriented
    (c) transformational
    (d) directive

11. Someone with a clear sense of the future and the actions needed to get there is considered a _____ leader.
    (a) task-oriented (b) people-oriented
    (c) transactional (d) visionary

12. Leader power = _____ power × _____ power.
    (a) reward, punishment
    (b) reward, expert
    (c) legitimate, position
    (d) position, personal

13. The interactive leadership style, sometimes associated with women, is characterized by _____.
    (a) inclusion and information sharing
    (b) use of rewards and punishments
    (c) command and control
    (d) emphasis on position power

14. A leader whose actions indicate an attitude of "do as you want and don't bother me" would be described as having a(n) _____ leadership style.
    (a) autocratic (b) country club
    (c) democratic (d) laissez-faire

15. The critical contingency variable in the Hersey-Blanchard situational model of leadership is _____.
    (a) follower maturity
    (b) LPC
    (c) task structure
    (d) emotional intelligence

16. Why are both position power and personal power essential in management?

17. Use Fiedler's terms to list the characteristics of situations that would be extremely favorable and extremely unfavorable to a leader.

18. Describe the situations in which path-goal theory would expect a participative leadership style and a directive leadership style to work best.

19. How do you sum up in two or three sentences the notion of servant leadership?

Integration & application

20. When Marcel Henry took over as leader of a new product development team, he was both excited and apprehensive. "I wonder," he said to himself on the first day in his new assignment, "if I can meet the challenges of leadership." Later that day, Marcel shares this concern with you during a coffee break.

Questions: Based on the insights of this module, how would you describe to him the personal implications in this team setting of current thinking on transformational and moral leadership?

Least Preferred Co-Worker Scale

Instructions

Think of all the different people with whom you have ever worked—in jobs, in social clubs, in student projects, or whatever. Next, think of the one person with whom you could work least well—that is, the person with whom you had the most difficulty getting a job done. This is the one person—a peer, boss, or subordinate—with whom you would least want to work. Describe this person by circling numbers at the appropriate points on each of the following pairs of bipolar adjectives. Work rapidly. There is no right or wrong answer.

Pleasant	8 7 6 5 4 3 2 1	Unpleasant
Friendly	8 7 6 5 4 3 2 1	Unfriendly
Rejecting	1 2 3 4 5 6 7 8	Accepting
Tense	1 2 3 4 5 6 7 8	Relaxed
Distant	1 2 3 4 5 6 7 8	Close
Cold	1 2 3 4 5 6 7 8	Warm
Supportive	8 7 6 5 4 3 2 1	Hostile

Boring	1 2 3 4 5 6 7 8	Interesting
Quarrelsome	1 2 3 4 5 6 7 8	Harmonious
Gloomy	1 2 3 4 5 6 7 8	Cheerful
Open	8 7 6 5 4 3 2 1	Guarded
Backbiting	1 2 3 4 5 6 7 8	Loyal
Untrustworthy	1 2 3 4 5 6 7 8	Trustworthy
Considerate	8 7 6 5 4 3 2 1	Inconsiderate
Nasty	1 2 3 4 5 6 7 8	Nice
Agreeable	8 7 6 5 4 3 2 1	Disagreeable
Insincere	1 2 3 4 5 6 7 8	Sincere
Kind	8 7 6 5 4 3 2 1	Unkind

Scoring

This is called the "least-preferred co-worker scale" (LPC). Compute your LPC score by totaling all the numbers you circled; enter that score here [LPC = ___].

Interpretation

The LPC scale is used by Fred Fiedler to identify a person's dominant leadership style. Fiedler believes that this style is a relatively fixed part of one's personality and is therefore difficult to change. This leads Fiedler to his contingency views, which suggest that the key to leadership success is finding (or creating) good "matches" between style and situation.

If your score is 73 or above on the LPC scale, Fiedler considers you a "relationship-motivated" leader; if it is 64 or below on the scale, he considers you a "task-motivated" leader. If your score is between 65 and 72, Fiedler leaves it up to you to determine which leadership style is most accurate.

 For further exploration go to WileyPlus

Case Snapshot
Southwest Airlines—How Herb Kelleher Led the Way.

To say that the airline industry has had problems is an understatement. The largest carriers—including American, United, Delta, and USAir—have lost billions of dollars. But Southwest Airlines has remained profitable. How did a little airline get so big and do so well? Its success springs from its core values, developed by Herb Kelleher, cofounder and former CEO, and embraced daily by the company's 34,000 employees: humor, altruism, and "LUV" (the company's stock ticker symbol).

Online Interactive Learning Resources

MORE SELF-ASSESSMENTS
- "T-P" Leadership
- "T-T" Leadership

EXPERIENTIAL EXERCISES
- Sources of Power
- Leading by Participation

TEAM PROJECT
- Gender and Leadership

12

Communication

Listening Is the Key to Understanding

Learning Outline

12.1 What Is Communication and When Is It Effective?

- Communication is a process of sending and receiving messages with meanings attached
- Communication is effective when the receiver understands the sender's messages
- Communication is efficient when it is delivered at low cost to the sender
- Communication is persuasive when the receiver acts as the sender intends

12.2 What Are the Major Barriers to Effective Communication?

- Poor use of communication channels makes it hard to communicate effectively
- Poor written or oral expression makes it hard to communicate effectively
- Failure to spot nonverbal signals makes it hard to communicate effectively
- Physical distractions make it hard to communicate effectively
- Status differences make it hard to communicate effectively

12.3 How Can We Improve Communication with People at Work?

- Active listening helps people say what they really mean
- Constructive feedback is specific, timely, and relevant
- Open communication channels build trust and improve upward communication
- Office spaces can be designed to encourage interaction and communication
- Appropriate use of technology can facilitate more and better communication
- Sensitivity and etiquette can improve cross-cultural communication

Communication deserves a top spot on your list of basic career skills. How well we communicate and collaborate with others has a big impact on how we are perceived and received as friends, co-workers, and leaders. But not everyone gets it right all the time; most of us probably get it right some of the time, while also making our fair share of mistakes. All of us could probably benefit from experiences such as the ones Richard S. Herlich, Robert Siddall, and Lisa DiTrullio had at the Center for Creative Leadership, headquartered in Greensboro, North Carolina. The center, or CCL, is internationally regarded for its excellent training programs and executive coaching in the communication and interpersonal skills essential to leadership.

Richard Herlich went to the CCL after being promoted to be the director of marketing for his firm. "I thought I had the perfect style," he said. But in

Trendsetters
Evan Williams and Biz
Stone have us all a-Twitter.

News Feed
Millennials may need
special handling.

Case Snapshot
Facebook—Communicating
the Web2.0 way

feedback sessions following role-playing exercises he learned that wasn't how others saw him. Instead, he was perceived as aloof and a poor communicator. Robert Siddall learned through feedback that he was too structured and domineering. He worked with instructors on a more "coaching" style of management. After returning to his job, Siddall's performance ratings went up as his relationships with coworkers improved. He reported: "If I start screaming and yelling, they say—'Old Bob, old Bob.'"

Lisa DiTrullio used her time at the CCL to gain confidence and launch a new career. She says: "The feedback reassures and reenergizes you around what you're doing well and helps you identify areas for development." She says the CCL experience gave her "momentum and energy" to take her to the "next level" of accomplishment.

12.1 What Is Communication and When Is It Effective?

Communication is at the heart of the management process.[1] You might think of it as the glue that binds together the four functions of planning, organizing, leading, and controlling. Henry Mintzberg described managers as information nerve centers, continually gathering information, processing it, using it for problem solving, and sharing it with others.[2] John Kotter described effective general managers as entwined in complex webs of interpersonal networks through which they implement work priorities and agendas.[3] And from the firing line itself, Pam Alexander, as CEO of Ogilvy Public Relations Worldwide, says: "Relationships are the most powerful form of media. Ideas will only get you so far these days. Count on personal relationships to carry you further."[4]

Having read all this, would it surprise you that when the American Management Association asked members to rate the communication skills of their managers, only 22.1% rated them "high"?[5] The respondents also rated their bosses only slightly above average on transforming ideas into words, credibility, listening and asking questions, and written and oral presentations.[6] And even though communication skills regularly top the lists of characteristics looked for by corporate recruiters, why is it that 81% of college professors in one survey rated high school graduates as "fair" or "poor" in writing clearly?

Strong communication skills such as those shown in **Figure 12.1** can and should differentiate you from others wanting the same job or internship. But how do you stack up on the capabilities identified in this figure? Can you convince a recruiter that you have the communication skills necessary for success in your career field?

FIGURE 12.1

Quick Check of Your Basic Communication Skills.

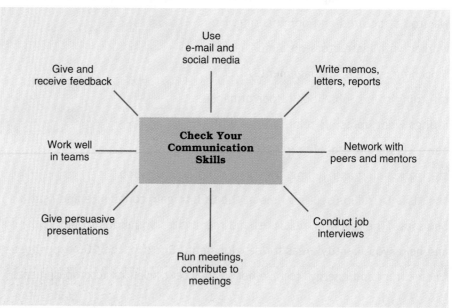

• Communication is a process of sending and receiving messages with meanings attached.

Communication is the process of sending and receiving symbols with meanings attached.

As you ponder the prior questions, think also about this definition: **communication** is an interpersonal process of sending and receiving symbols with messages attached to them. Although the definition sounds simple and commonsense enough, there is a lot of room for error when we actually implement the process in communicating with others. There are many places where things can be done well or poorly, and our communications fare better or worse as a consequence.

Figure 12.2 summarizes the key elements in the communication process this way. In communication a *sender* encodes an intended message into meaningful symbols, both verbal and nonverbal. He or she sends the *message* through a *communication channel* to a *receiver*, who then decodes or interprets its meaning. This *interpretation* may or may not match the sender's original intentions. When present, *feedback* reverses the process and conveys the receiver's response back to the sender.

FIGURE 12.2
What Are the Major Elements in the Process of Interpersonal Communication?

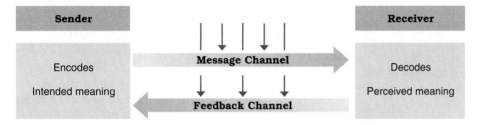

The communication process begins when a sender encodes an intended meaning into a message. This message is then transmitted through a channel to a receiver. The receiver next decodes the message into perceived meaning. Finally, the receiver may transmit feedback back to the sender. The communication process is effective when the perceived meaning of the receiver is the same as the intended meaning of the sender.

A useful way to describe the communication process shown in the figure is as a series of questions. Ask: "Who?" (sender) "says what?" (message) "in what way?" (channel) "to whom?" (receiver) "with what result?" (interpreted meaning). A useful way to test out the process in actual practice is to ask yet another important question: Do receiver and sender understand things the same ways?

• Communication is effective when the receiver understands the sender's messages.

The ability to communicate well both orally and in writing is a critical managerial skill and the foundation of effective leadership. Through communication, people exchange and share information with one another, and influence one another's attitudes, behaviors, and understandings. Communication allows managers to establish and maintain interpersonal relationships, listen to others, deal with conflicts, negotiate, and otherwise gain the information needed to create high performance workplace. But all this assumes that the communication goes as intended, and that raises the important issue of "effectiveness."

Effective communication occurs when the receiver fully understands the sender's intended message; the intended meaning matches the received meaning. As you well know, this outcome can't be taken for granted; it just doesn't always happen.

In **effective communication** the receiver fully understands the intended meaning.

Trendsetters 👤

Evan Williams and Biz Stone Have Us All a-Twitter.

"**M**y Siamese #cat Skimbleshanks is up a tree . . . At Wilco concert—Jeff Tweedy is so cool . . . Home alone ☹ with Willie Nelson ☺ . . . Flying to Ireland, wish me luck driving . . . Just saw Todd with Stephanie!"

So who cares? Well, it turns out that almost everyone cares, just as Evan Williams and Biz Stone, cofounders of Twitter, the microblog Web site, had anticipated. They're the guys who moved texting into the upper limits. And the quick, easy, and ever-present social networking offered through Twitter isn't just for friends and family—companies are using it, radio and television shows are using it, and, of course, celebrities are using it.

Sending 140 character or less "tweets" by mobile text, instant messaging, or Web quickly hit the mark with traffic rising to over 6 million users in a year's time and now over 40 million. Williams and Stone are thinking millions, too—dollars, that is. Expectations are that the firm will be sold and that the bidding will be high. "I guess we have a lot of things we think we can prove," Stone says, "to provide the infrastructure for a new kind of communication, and then support the creativity that emerges." For his part, Williams points out "we're totally focused on making the best user experience possible and building a defensible communications network."

Both Stone and Williams have been part of the Internet business community through many past ventures, including Blogger, which was purchased by Google. Williams is even credited with coining the word "blog" and Stone has published two books on blogging. No wonder that Williams, self-described as "An American entrepreneur, originally a farm boy from Nebraska, who's been very lucky in business and life," has this to say: "We really believe Twitter is potentially massive in terms of its impact on millions and millions of people." How else can you so easily find out where people are and what they are doing right now?

From what Stone calls "the side project that took," the Twitter revolution has grown into something of transformative proportions. But problems are popping up for the firm and its founders. Williams and Stone are dealing with rapid growth in both users and employees, lack of business expertise on the staff, and the need to find ways to turn the Twitter user experience into a source of revenue generation. Williams says: "If it weren't growing nearly as fast, we would be building a lot more things."

How often have you wondered what an instructor is really asking for in an assignment, or struggled to understand the instructor's point during a class lecture? Or how often have you been angry when a friend or loved one just "didn't seem to get" your message and, unfortunately, didn't respond in the desired way? And, of course, how often have you sent a letter, SMS, or e-mail, or left a voice message, only to receive back an "angry" or "distressed" reply that wasn't at all appropriate to your intended message? These are all examples of well-intentioned communications that went awry; they were not effective. And we can't afford too many of them in our personal relationships or in our work responsibilities.

• Communication is efficient when it is delivered at low cost to the sender.

One reason why communication is not always effective, and the prior examples are good cases-in-point, is a trade-off between effectiveness and efficiency. **Efficient communication** occurs at minimum cost in terms of resources expended. And of these costs, time and convenience, in particular, often become very influential in how we choose to communicate.

Picture your instructor speaking individually, face-to-face, with each student about this module. This could be very effective, but it would certainly be inefficient in terms of the cost of his or her time. This is why we often send text messages, leave voice-mail messages, and use e-mail, rather than speak directly with other people. These alternatives are more efficient than one-on-one and face-to-face communications. Although quick and easy, are they always effective? The next time you have something important to communicate, you might pause and consider the trade-offs between effectiveness and efficiency. A low-cost approach such as an e-mail note to a distribution list may save time, but it may not result in everyone getting the same mean-

Efficient communication occurs at minimum cost to the sender.

ing from the message. Without opportunities to ask questions and clarify the message, erroneous interpretations are possible.

By the same token, an effective communication may not always be efficient. If a team leader visits each team member individually to explain a new change in procedures, this may guarantee that everyone truly understands the change. But it may also take a lot of the leader's time. A team meeting would be more efficient. In these and other ways, potential trade-offs between effectiveness and efficiency must be recognized in communication.

• Communication is persuasive when the receiver acts as the sender intends.

In life and in management we often want not just to be heard, but to be followed. That is, we want our communication to "persuade" the other party to believe or behave in a specific way that we intend. **Persuasive communication** is that which gets someone else to accept, support, and act consistent with the sender's message.[7]

If you agree that managers get most things done through other people, you should also agree that managers must be very good at persuasive communication. Yet, scholar and consultant Jay Conger believes that many managers "confuse persuasion with bold stands and aggressive arguing." This sounds a lot like the so-called "debates" that we watch on television as advocates of different political viewpoints face off against one another. A lot is said, some of it quite aggressively, but little in the way of influence on the other speaker or the listening audience really takes place. Conger believes that the approach can also raise questions about one's credibility.[8] Conger defines **credible communication** as that which earns trust, respect, and integrity in the eyes of others. And without it, he claims there is little chance for successful persuasion.

The late Sam Walton, Wal-Mart's founder, was considered a master of persuasive communication. Conger says this is a learned skill, one based on personal power of expertise and reference. Consider an example—classic Walton in action. Stopping once to visit a Memphis store, he called everyone to the front, saying: "Northeast Memphis, you're the largest store in Memphis, and you must have the best floor-cleaning crew in America. This floor is so clean, let's sit down on it." Picture this. Walton is kneeling casually while wearing his Wal-Mart baseball cap. He congratulated the employees on their fine work. "I thank you. The company is so proud of you we can hardly stand it," he said. "But," he added, "you know that confounded Kmart is getting better, and so is Target. So what's our challenge?" Walton asked. "Customer service," he replied in answer to his own question. And everyone present took his message to heart.[9]

Master communicators like Wal-Mart's founder the late Sam Walton are good at connecting with people in credible and persuasive ways.

Persuasive communication presents a message in a manner that causes others to accept and support it.

Credible communication earns trust, respect, and integrity in the eyes of others.

Study Guide

12.1
What Is Communication and When Is It Effective?

Rapid review

- Communication is the interpersonal process of sending and receiving symbols with messages attached to them.
- Effective communication occurs when the sender and the receiver of a message both interpret it in the same way.
- Efficient communication occurs when the sender conveys the message at low cost.
- Noise is anything that interferes with the effectiveness of communication.
- Persuasive communication results in the recipient acting as the sender intends.
- Credibility earned by expertise and good relationships is essential to persuasive communication.

Terms to define

Communication
Communication channel
Credible communication
Effective communication
Efficient communication
Persuasive communication

Be sure you can

- describe the communication process and identify its key components
- define and give an example of effective communication
- define and give an example of efficient communication
- explain why an effective communication is not always efficient
- explain the role of credibility in persuasive communication

Questions for discussion

1. In what situations can you accept less communication effectiveness in order to gain communication efficiency?
2. Can persuasive communication occur without the sender having credibility?
3. What can a manager do to gain the credibility needed for truly persuasive communication?

12.2 What Are the Major Barriers to Effective Communication?

Look now at **Figure 12.3** which updates the earlier description of the communication process. This time the figure includes the presence of **noise**, which is anything that interferes with the effectiveness of the communication process. In international business, for example, one should be prepared to deal with language differences in communication. When Yoshihiro Wada was president of Mazda Corporation, he had to use interpreters when meeting with representatives of the firm's U.S. joint venture partner, Ford. He estimated that he lost 20% of his intended meaning in the exchange between himself and the interpreter, and another 20% between the interpreter and the Americans.[10]

Noise is anything that interferes with the communication process.

FIGURE 12.3
Noise Is Anything That Interferes with the Communication Process.

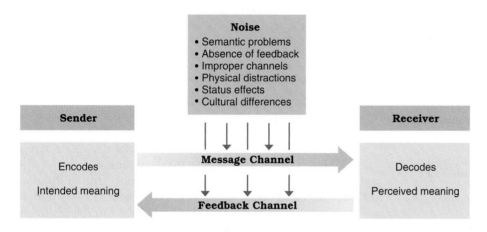

Yoshihiro's problem is pretty easy to recognize. It's not easy to communicate in a second language, and messages do get lost in translation. We expect that in the world of international business and travel. But do you recognize how noise can play a role in everyday text messaging, such as the boxed exchange between a high-tech millennial and a low-tech baby boomer manager? Common sources of noise that often create communication barriers include poor choice of channels, poor written or oral expression, failures to recognize nonverbal signals, physical distractions, and status differences.

• Poor use of communication channels makes it hard to communicate effectively.

Problems can arise from a poor choice of **communication channel**, the medium used to carry the message.[11] Written channels such as memos, e-mails, and text messages work well for conveying simple messages or questions that require extensive dissemination quickly. Spoken channels are more personal and can create a supportive, even inspirational, relationship between sender and receiver. They work especially well face-to-face, when we need to convey complex or difficult messages and when we need immediate feedback.

People communicate with one another using a variety of channels. Choice of channels is important, since they vary in **channel richness**, the capacity to carry

A **communication channel** is the medium used to carry a message.

Channel richness is the capacity of a communication channel to effectively carry information.

information in an effective manner.[12] **Figure 12.4** shows that face-to-face communication is very high in richness, enabling two-way interaction and real-time feedback. Things such as written reports, memos, and e-mail messages are very low in richness because of impersonal, one-way interaction with limited opportunity for feedback. Managers need to understand the limits of the possible channels and choose wisely when using them for communication.

FIGURE 12.4
Channel Richness and the Use of Communication Media.

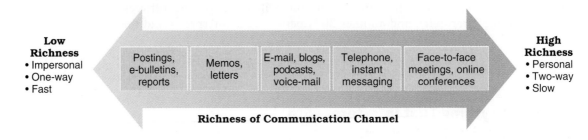

[**TABLE** 12.1]

Essential Ingredients of Successful Presentations

Be Prepared
Know what you want to say; know how you want to say it; rehearse saying it.

Set the Right Tone
Focus on your audience; make eye contact and act pleasantly and confidently.

Sequence Your Points
State your purpose, make important points, follow with details, and then summarize.

Support Your Points
Give specific reasons for your points; state them in understandable terms.

Accent the Presentation
Use good visual aids; provide supporting handouts when possible.

Add the Right Amount of Polish
Attend to details; have room, materials, and arrangements ready to go.

Check the Technology
Check everything ahead of time; make sure it works and know how to use it.

Don't Bet on the Internet
Beware of plans to make real time Internet visits; save sites on a disk and use a browser to open the file.

Be Professional
Be on time; wear appropriate attire; act organized, confident, and enthusiastic.

• Poor written or oral expression makes it hard to communicate effectively.

We all know that it isn't easy to write a concise letter or report, or deliver a great oral presentation. In fact, it takes a lot of practice. There's no getting around it; good writing and good speaking (see **Table 12.1**—*Essential Ingredients of Successful Presentations*) are the products of plain old hard work.[13] But it's well worth the investment. Are you willing to make it? Take the test: How many drafts do you write for memos, letters, and reports? How often do you practice for an oral presentation?

A survey of 120 companies by the National Commission on Writing found that over one-third of their employees were considered deficient in writing skills, and that employers were spending over $3 billion each year on remedial training.[14] Consider the following "bafflegab" found among some executive communications.

A business report said: "Consumer elements are continuing to stress the fundamental necessity of a stabilization of the price structure at a lower level than exists at the present time." *Why couldn't the report say*: "Consumers keep saying that prices must go down and stay down."?

A manager said: "Substantial economies were affected in this division by increasing the time interval between distributions of data-eliciting forms to business entities." *Why couldn't the manager say*: "The division saved money by sending out fewer questionnaires."?

• Failure to spot nonverbal signals makes it hard to communicate effectively.

The ways we use **nonverbal communication** can also work for or against our communication effectiveness. It takes place through hand movements, facial expressions, body posture, eye contact, and the use of interpersonal space.[15] And it can be a powerful means of transmitting messages. Research shows that up to 55% of a message's impact comes through nonverbal communication.[16] A good listener, for example, knows how to read the "body language" of a speaker while listening to the words being spoken. In fact, a potential side effect of the growing use of electronic mail, computer networking, and other communication technologies is that the added communication of nonverbal signals, such as gestures, voice intonation, or eye movements, are lost.

Think of how nonverbal signals play out in your own communications. A simple hand gesture, for example, can show whether someone is speaking positive or negative, excited or bored, or even engaged or disengaged with you.[17] Also, we can't forget that sometimes our body may be "talking" for us even as we otherwise maintain silence. And when we do speak, our body may sometimes "say" different things than our words convey. This is called a **mixed message**, when a person's words communicate one thing while his or her nonverbal actions communicate something else.

Nonverbal communication takes place through gestures, expressions, posture, and even use of interpersonal space.

A **mixed message** results when words communicate one message while actions, body language, or appearance communicate something else.

• Physical distractions make it hard to communicate effectively.

Also, don't neglect the role of *physical distractions* in disrupting communication. Have you ever tried to talk with someone about an important matter, only to have that conversation interrupted by phone calls? Any number of distractions, from drop-in visitors to instant messages to ringing cell phones, can interfere with the effectiveness of a communication attempt. Some of these distractions are evident in the following conversation between an employee, George, and his manager.[18]

> Okay, George, let's hear your problem [phone rings, boss picks it up, promises to deliver a report "just as soon as I can get it done"]. Uh, now, where were we—oh, you're having a problem with your technician. She's [manager's secretary brings in some papers that need his immediate signature; secretary leaves]—you say she's overstressed lately, wants to leave. I tell you what, George, why don't you [phone rings again, lunch partner drops by], uh, take a stab at handling it yourself. I've got to go now.

Besides what may have been poor intentions in the first place, the manager in this example did not do a good job of communicating with George. This problem could be easily corrected. Many communication distractions can be avoided or at least minimized through proper planning. If George has something important to say, the manager should set aside adequate time for the meeting. Additional interruptions such as telephone calls and drop-in visitors could be eliminated by issuing appropriate instructions to the secretary. One basic lesson from this incident is: plan ahead. If you have something important to say or hear, set aside adequate time, choose the right location, and take steps to avoid interruptions—including turning the cell phone off.

Filtering is the intentional distortion of information to make it more favorable to the recipient.

• **Status differences make it hard to communicate effectively.**

The risk of ineffective communication may be highest when people are communicating upward in organizations, and with their immediate boss in particular. Haven't you heard people say things like this? "Criticize my boss? I'd get fired." "It's her company, not mine." "I can't tell him that; he'll just get mad at me."

We have to be realistic; the hierarchy of authority is a potential barrier to effective communication between lower and higher levels in organizations. This problem arises because of **filtering**—the intentional distortion of information to make it appear favorable to the recipient. You know this as "telling the boss or instructor what he or she wants to hear." And it's more common than many people think. Consultant Tom Peters calls it "Management Enemy Number 1."[19]

Whether caused by fear of retribution for bringing bad news, an unwillingness to identify personal mistakes, or just a general desire to please, the end result of filtering is the same. Lower levels "cleanse" the information sent to higher levels; the higher levels, although well intentioned, make poor decisions because their information is inaccurate or incomplete. And the consequences can be significant. Consider a "corporate cover-up" once discovered at an electronics company. Workers were predating product shipments and falsifying paperwork to artificially show that they were meeting unrealistic sales targets set by the president. At least 20 persons cooperated in the deception, and it was months before top management found out.

News Feed

Millennials May Need Special Handling.

Perhaps you've noticed it too. The "Millennials," born between 1980 and 1995, and also called "Gen Ys," "Echo Boomers," or the "Net Generation," have a unique way about them. They grew up special, they are challenging as students, and they have unique expectations of their bosses and employers.

A CBS *60 Minutes* report had this to say about Millennials—" . . . raised by doting parents who told them they were special, played in little leagues with no winners or losers, or all winners . . . laden with trophies for just participating, and they think your business-as-usual ethics are for the birds." *The Wall Street Journal* says that this generation wants "a good workplace environment . . . meaningful responsibility, continuous feedback from managers and peers, an active say in what goes on and a good work-life-balance."

Is it any surprise, then, that employers like IBM are offering suggestions such as these to managers of Millennials? Keep expectations clear, set milestones, and avoid surprises; stay in touch with regular feedback. Spend a lot of time listening and keep the communication channels open. Respect preferences for informality and flexibility. Welcome instant messages and give lots of personal access. Provide mentors.

Above all, remember the need for feedback. As an Aetna manager says: "Other generations have not felt they were so empowered to ask or sometimes demand feedback." In an Ernst & Young survey, 85% of Gen Ys claimed to want "frequent and candid performance feedback," compared with only half of Baby Boomers. Brittany Rotondo, 26 years old and working for Accenture, is a good example. "I'm definitely a feedback kind of person," she says. "It's always incredibly important for me to know how my work is perceived and the impact it's having."

Reflect and React:

Can you recognize these traits in yourself and others? Where do you agree and disagree with these descriptions? Is the advice given here for managing Millennials sound? And, by the way, are you sure Millennials are really so different from prior generations in what they want from work?

Study Guide

12.2
What Are the Major Barriers to Effective Communication?

Rapid review

- Noise interferes with the effectiveness of communication.
- Poor choice of channels can reduce communication effectiveness.
- Poor written or oral expression can reduce communication effectiveness.
- Failure to accurately read nonverbal signals can reduce communication effectiveness.
- Filtering caused by status differences can reduce communication effectiveness.

Terms to define

Communication channel
Filtering
Mixed message
Noise
Nonverbal communication

Be sure you can

- list common sources of noise that can interfere with effective communication
- discuss how the choice of channels influences communication effectiveness
- give examples of poor language choices in written and oral expression
- clarify the notion of mixed messages and how they affect communication
- explain how filtering operates in upward communication

Questions for discussion

1. When might it not be appropriate to use SMS texting to convey a message in a work situation?
2. Suppose someone just isn't a good writer or speaker; what can he or she do to improve communication skills?
3. How can a manager avoid the problem of status differences where her direct reports filter information that is passed upward?

12.3 How Can We Improve Communication with People at Work?

With all the possible noise in the communication process, don't you wonder how we ever communicate effectively? Fortunately, there are a number of things we can do to overcome or minimize the effects of communication barriers as well as improve our communication behaviors. They include active listening, constructive use of feedback, opening upward communication channels, understanding the use of space, utilizing technology, and valuing diversity.

• Active listening helps people say what they really mean.

When people talk, they are trying to communicate something. That "something" may or may not be what they are saying. Managers must be very good at listening. Legendary UCLA men's basketball coach from 1964 through 1975, John Wooden, winner of ten NCAA championships and named by ESPN as "coach of the century," says: "Many leaders don't listen . . . We'd all be a lot wiser if we listened more—not just hearing the words, but listening and not thinking about what you are going to say."[21]

Active listening helps the source of a message say what he or she really means.

Active listening is the process of taking action to help someone say what he or she really means.[20] It requires being sincere while listening to someone, and trying to find the full meaning of a message. It also involves being disciplined, controlling one's emotions, and withholding premature evaluations or interpretations that can turn off rather than turn on the other party's willingness to communicate.

Different responses to the following two questions contrast how a "passive" listener and an "active" listener might act in real workplace conversations.

Question 1: "Don't you think employees should be promoted on the basis of seniority?"

Passive listener's response: "No, I don't!"

Active listener's response: "It seems to you that they should, I take it?"

Question 2: "What does the supervisor expect us to do about these out-of-date computers?"

Passive listener's response: "Do the best you can, I guess."

Active listener's response: "You're pretty disgusted with those machines, aren't you?"

The prior examples help show how active listening can facilitate communication in difficult circumstances, rather than discourage it. As you think further about active listening, keep these rules in mind.[22]

1. *Listen for message content:* Try to hear exactly what content is being conveyed in the message.

2. *Listen for feelings:* Try to identify how the source feels about the content in the message.

3. *Respond to feelings:* Let the source know that her or his feelings are being recognized.

4. *Note all cues:* Be sensitive to nonverbal and verbal messages; be alert for mixed messages.

5. *Paraphrase and restate:* State back to the source what you think you are hearing.

It is often said that the most important rule in communicating is to stop talking and start listening.

• Constructive feedback is specific, timely, and relevant.

When Lydia Whitfield, a marketing vice president at Avaya, asked one of her managers for feedback, she was surprised. He said: "You're angry a lot." Whitfield learned from the experience, saying: "What he and other employees saw as my anger, I saw as my passion."[23] **Feedback** is the process of telling other people how you feel about something they did or said, or about the situation in general.

The art of giving feedback is an indispensable skill for managers. When poorly given, critical feedback can easily come off as threatening and create more resentment than positive action. When the feedback is *constructive*, however, the receiver is more likely to listen and carefully consider the message, and even make some personal commitment to using it to best advantage.[24]

Take a look at Tips to Remember for suggestions for giving constructive feedback. Are there things you can learn to do better? Would you agree that constructive feedback is essential if performance appraisals are to be helpful for developmental purposes?

Tips to Remember 🅱

How to Give Constructive Feedback

- *Choose the right time*—Give feedback at a time when the receiver seems most willing or able to accept it.
- *Be genuine*—Give feedback directly and with real feeling, based on trust between you and the receiver.
- *Be specific*—Make sure that feedback is specific rather than general; use good, clear, and preferably recent examples to make your points.
- *Stick to the essentials*—Make sure the feedback is valid; limit it to things the receiver can be expected to do something about.
- *Keep it manageable*—Give feedback in small doses; never give more than the receiver can handle at any particular time.

Feedback is the process of telling someone else how you feel about something that person did or said.

• Open communication channels build trust and improve upward communication.

Managers really can't afford to be on the receiving end of the filtering problem caused by the status differences we discussed earlier. They need good information from the people who work for them if they are to make good decisions. But good information can be hard to get, particularly when things like status barriers interfere with the upward communication process.

One way of keeping communication channels open is **management by wandering around (MBWA)**. As the name implies, MBWA takes place when managers get out of their offices and simply spend time walking around and talking face-to-face with people. It is a way of breaking down status barriers and building relationships; it encourages people to share with their managers more and better information about themselves and their work.

Open communication has been one of the hallmarks of how Nucor CEO Daniel R. DiMicco handled the impact of recession on his firm and its employees. Instead of staying behind closed doors talking about the crisis with other executives, DiMicco doubled the time he spent out in the firm's plants talking with employees. He and his managers try to keep everyone informed about the status of orders for the firm's products. And the open communication is well appreciated. One employee sent a card to top management saying "Thank you for caring about me and my family."[25]

An even more extreme effort to open communication channels was made by CEO Stephen Martin, the boss who "went underground" at a firm in England for two weeks. He posed with an assumed name as an office worker and kept his ears and eyes open wide while going about his daily work. After the experience, Martin said: "They (workers) said things to me that they never would have told their manager". . . "Our key messages were just not getting through to people". . . "We were asking the impossible of some of them." But

Managers using **MBWA** spend time out of their offices, meeting and talking with workers at all levels.

when he shared these concerns with the firm's managers, the response was: "They never told us that!"[26]

Besides MBWA, there are many ways for managers to break status barriers to keep the communication channels open. Like college professors, they can get a lot of benefits from holding *open office hours*, setting aside time in their busy calendars to welcome walk-in visits. Today this approach can be easily expanded by using everything from e-mail to instant messaging to social networking groups to Twitter, and more. The technology is available; all we have to do is open the channels and use it well.

Holding regular *employee group meetings* is another helpful technique. Here, a rotating schedule of "shirtsleeve" meetings brings top managers into face-to-face contact with mixed employee groups throughout an organization. Some organizations even use *employee advisory councils* whose members are elected by their fellow employees. Such councils meet with management on a regular schedule to discuss and react to new policies and programs that will affect employees.

And again, any and all such ideas for openinig communication channels with employees can be easily implemented in electronic space. Traditional face-to-face group meetings can be replaced with *computer conferencing* and *videoconferencing* to overcome time and distance limitations. *Social networking* using public programs such as Facebook or dedicated in-house ones gives managers further opportunities to maintain open communication on a continuous basis. At Nokia, employee bloggers use assumed names to log-in to the company-supported Blog-Hub to complain about everyday workplace affairs and to offer ideas. And management listens. One Blogger wondered why the styluses for touchscreen handsets were always grey; now the firm offers a choice of colors. "I don't think you can mandate innovation," says executive vice-president Mary T. McDowell, "our role is to keep the skids greased."[27]

• Office spaces can be designed to encourage interaction and communication.

Look at **Figure 12.5** and think about your office and those of persons with whom you often visit. What messages do they send to visitors, just by the layouts and furnishings? And it's not only individual offices that count in this respect. Architects and consultants are helping executives build entire office spaces that are conducive to the intense, multilevel, and cross-functional communications desired today.

FIGURE 12.5

Furniture Placement and Nonverbal Communication in the Office.

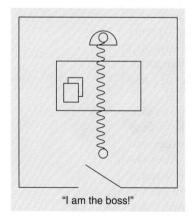
"I am the boss!"

"I am the boss, but let's talk"

"Forget I'm the boss, let's talk"

The way we use space, **proxemics**, is an important but sometimes neglected influence on communication.[28] We know that physical distance between people conveys varying intentions in terms of intimacy, openness, and status as they communicate with one another. But we might not be as sensitive to how the physical layout of an office can do the same things. When former Google executive Tim Armstrong became CEO of AOL, for example, one of his first decisions was to remove the glass doors separating the executive offices from other workers. The only way to open them previously had been with a company key card.[29]

Sun Microsystems invested in space design for its new facility in San Jose, California. Public spaces were designed to encourage communication among persons from different departments. The project relied on extensive suggestions from the employees. And the results seemed to justify the effort. One employee called it "the most productive workspace I have ever been in."[30] At Google headquarters, or Googleplex, telecommuters work in specially designed office "tents." These are made of acrylics to allow both the sense of private personal space and transparency.[31] And at b&a advertising in Dublin, Ohio, "open space" supports the small ad agency's emphasis on creativity; after all, its Web address is www.babrain.com. Face-to-face communication is the rule at b&a, to the point where internal e-mail among employees is banned. There are no offices or cubicles, and all office equipment is portable. Desks have wheels so that informal meetings can happen by people repositioning themselves for spontaneous collaboration. Even the formal meetings are held "standing up" in the company kitchen.[32]

• Appropriate use of technology can facilitate more and better communication.

Knowing how and when to use e-mail, text messaging, and social networking is now a top issue in workplace communications. "Thnx for the IView! I Wud Luv to Work 4 U!!;)" may be quite understandable "textspeak" for some people, but it isn't the follow-up message that most employers like to receive from job candidates.[33]

When Tory Johnson, President of Women for Hire Inc., received a thank-you note by e-mail from an intern candidate, it included "hiya," "thanx," three exclamation points—"!!!," and two emoticons ☹ ☺. She says: "That e-mail just ruined it for me." The risk of everyday shorthand in e-mails and texting is that we become too casual overall in its use, forgetting that how a message is received is in large part determined by the receiver. Even though textspeak and emoticons are the norm in social networks, for example, staffing executives at KPMG, which hires hundreds of new college grads and interns each year, consider them "not professional."

Communication technology has created another force to be reckoned with— the **electronic grapevine**. Electronic messages fly with speed and intensity around organizations and the Internet at large, assisted by blogs, chat rooms, tweets, and more. And, the results can be functional when the information is accurate and useful. General Electric, for example, started a "Tweet Squad" to advise the rest of the organization how social networking could be used to improve internal collaboration; the insurer MetLife has its own social network, connect.MetLife, which facilitates collaboration through a Facebook-like setting.[34]

But let's not forget, the electronic grapevine can be dysfunctional when the information it broadcasts is false, distorted, malicious, or rumor based. Not too long ago a YouTube video appeared showing two Domino's Pizza employees doing all sorts of nasty things to sandwiches they were making for delivery. It was soon viewed over a million times and Domino's faced a crisis of customer confidence. Although the video was pulled by one of its authors—

Proxemics is the study of the way we use space.

Self-Assessment
This is a good point to complete the self-assessment "*Feedback and Assertiveness*" found on page 272.

Millennial text to baby boomer
Omg sorry abt mtg nbd 4 now b rdy nxt time g2g ttl

Baby boomer text to millennial
Missed you at meeting. It was important. Don't forget next one. Stop by office.

The **electronic grapevine** uses computer technologies to transmit information around informal networks inside and outside of organizations.

Stay Tuned

Employees Have Cause to Worry about Electronic Monitoring.

An American Management Association survey of 304 U.S. companies found the following:

- 66% monitor Internet connections.
- 65% block Web sites: pornography (96%), games (61%), social networking (61%), shopping/auction (27%), and sports (21%).
- 45% track key strokes and keyboard time.
- 43% store and review computer files.
- 43% monitor e-mail.
- 45% monitor telephone time and numbers dialed.
- >25% have fired employees for misuse of e-mail.
- >30% have fired employees for misuse of the Internet.

Another survey of large firms and advertising agencies by the Creative Group found that 57% of bosses thought it was "okay" to Web surf while at work, but they suggested that time should be no more than about one-half hour per day.

What Are Your Thoughts?

Is this type of employer "snooping" justified? What boundaries should be set on employer invasion of employee privacy? Is there anything special about the fact that in the advertising industry the majority of executives thought personal Web surfing was alright?

who apologized for "faking" how they worked, both employees were fired. But negative chat spread around the Internet and the Domino's brand was damaged. The firm's management finally created a Twitter account to present its own view of the situation and posted a YouTube video message from the CEO.[35]

Purpose and privacy are also important issues in the electronic workplace. Employers express concerns that too much work time gets spent handling personal e-mail, and in social networking and Web browsing. Employees can also be too casual and inappropriate in what they put out on the Web. Here's a real tweet that became an Internet sensation: "Cisco just offered me a job! Now I have to weigh the utility of a fatty paycheck against the daily commute to San Jose and hating the work."[36] What would you do if you were the Cisco recruiter who had just made this person a job offer?

When it comes to e-mail and various types of Web use, the best advice comes down to this: Find out the employer's policy and follow it. And, don't assume that you ever have electronic privacy.[37] Enterprise Rent-A-Car, for example, uses Google alerts to learn when an employee has used the company name or a co-worker's name in an online post.[38]

• Sensitivity and etiquette can improve cross-cultural communication.

After taking over as the first American to be CEO of the Dutch publisher Wolters Kluwer, Nancy McKinstry initiated major changes in strategy and operations—cutting staff, restructuring divisions, and investing in new business areas. She first described the new strategy as "aggressive" in speaking with her management team. But after learning the word wasn't well received by Europeans, she switched to "decisive." She says: "I was coming across as too harsh, too much of a results-driven American to the people I needed to get on board," says McKinstry, offering us a nice lesson in cross-cultural communication.[39]

There is no doubt that cultural differences are a ready source of potential problems in communication. And keep in mind that you don't have be doing international business or taking a foreign vacation for this to be relevant. Just going to work and out to shop is a cross-cultural journey for most of us today. Furthermore, you should recall that **ethnocentrism** is a major source of intercultural difficulties. It is the tendency to consider one's culture superior to any and all others.

Tendencies toward ethnocentrism can hurt cross-cultural communication in at least three ways. First, they may cause someone to not listen well to what others have to say. Second, they may cause someone to address or speak with others in ways that alienate them. And third, they may involve use of inappropriate stereotypes.

Ethnocentrism is the tendency to consider one's culture superior to any and all others.

Just recognizing tendencies toward ethnocentrism is a starting point for improving cross-cultural communication. You can spot it in conversations as arrogance in one's tone, manners, gestures, and words. But success in cross-cultural communication also takes sensitivity and a willingness to learn about how different people see, do, and interpret things. This involves a basic awareness of **cultural etiquette**, the use of appropriate manners, language, and behaviors when communicating with people from other cultures. Cutural etiquette begins with recognition that the ways and customs of our culture, things we might naturally be inclined to use, do, or say, won't necessarily work in the same ways or mean the same things in another. Knowing the etiquette helps avoid basic cross-cultural mistakes.

An obvious and common problem of cultural etiquette involves language differences. Messages can easily get lost in translation, as advertising miscues often demonstrate. A Pepsi ad in Taiwan intended to say "The Pepsi Generation" came out as "Pepsi will bring your ancestors back from the dead." A KFC ad in China intended to convey "finger lickin' good" came out as "eat your fingers off."[40] Other etiquette problems may trace to cultural differences in nonverbal communication, everything from the use of gestures to interpersonal space.[41] The American "thumbs-up" sign is an insult in Ghana and Australia; signaling "OK" with thumb and forefinger circled together is not okay in parts of Europe; whereas we wave "hello" with an open palm, in West Africa it's an insult, suggesting the other person has five fathers.[42]

Cultural etiquette is use of appropriate manners and behaviors in cross-cultural situations.

Sample cultural variations in nonverbal communications

- *Eye movements (oculesics)*—Chinese and Japanese may only show anger in their eyes; a point often missed by westerners.

- *Touching (haptics)*—Asian cultures typically dislike touching behaviors; Latin cultures tend to use them in communicating.

- *Body motions (kinesics)*—gestures, shrugs, and blushes can mean different things; "thumbs up" means "A-OK" in America, but is vulgar in the Middle East.

Study Guide

12.3
How Can We Improve Communication with People at Work?

Rapid review

- Active listening, through reflecting back and paraphrasing, can help overcome barriers and improve communication.
- Interactive management through MBWA and use of structured meetings, suggestion systems, and advisory councils can improve upward communication.
- Organizations can design and use office architecture and physical space to improve communication.
- Information technology, such as e-mail, instant messaging, and intranets, can improve communication in organizations, but it must be well used.
- Ethnocentrism, and feelings of cultural superiority, can interfere with the effectiveness of cross-cultural communication; with sensitivity and cultural etiquette, such communication can be improved.

Terms to define

Active listening

Cultural etiquette

Electronic grapevine

Ethnocentrism

Feedback

Management by wandering around (MBWA)

Proxemics

Be sure you can

- illustrate the practice of active listening
- list the rules for giving constructive feedback
- explain how MBWA can improve upward communication
- explain how space design influences communication
- identify ways technology utilization influences communication
- explain the concept of cultural etiquette

Questions for discussion

1. Which rules for active listening do you think most people break?
2. Is MBWA a sure winner, or could a manager have problems with it?
3. How could you redesign your office space to make it more communication friendly?

[Test Prep]

Multiple choice

1. Who is responsible for encoding a message in the communication process?

   (a) sender   (b) receiver
   (c) observer   (d) consultant

2. Issues of "respect" and "integrity" are associated with _____ in communication?

   (a) noise
   (b) filtering
   (c) credibility
   (d) ethnocentrism

3. Which of the following is the best example of a supervisor making feedback evaluative rather than descriptive in communicating with one of her direct reports?

   (a) You are a slacker.
   (b) You are not responsible.
   (c) You cause me lots of problems.
   (d) You have been late to work three days this month.

4. A manager who uses paraphrasing and reflecting back of what someone else is saying in order to encourage them to say what they really mean is using a communication technique known as _____.

   (a) mixed messaging
   (b) active listening
   (c) constructive feedback
   (d) filtering

5. When the intended meaning of the sender and the interpreted meaning of the receiver are the same, communication is _____.

   (a) effective   (b) persuasive
   (c) passive   (d) efficient

6. One of the rules for giving constructive feedback is to make sure that it is always _____.

   (a) general rather than specific
   (b) indirect rather than direct
   (c) given in small doses
   (d) delivered at a time convenient for the sender

7. When a worker receives an e-mail memo from the boss with information about changes to his job assignment and ends up confused because he doesn't understand it, the boss has erred by making a bad choice of _____ for communicating the message.

   (a) words   (b) channels
   (c) nonverbals   (d) filters

8. _____ is a form of interactive management that helps improve upward communication.

   (a) Attribution   (b) Mediation
   (c) MBWA   (d) Proxemics

9. A _____ communication channel is higher in richness than a _____ channel.

   (a) written memo, e-mail
   (b) text message, video conference
   (c) instant message, e-mail
   (d) voice mail, telephone conversation

10. If a visitor to a foreign culture makes gestures commonly used at home even after learning that they are offensive to locals, the visitor can be described as _____.

    (a) a passive listener
    (b) ethnocentric
    (c) more efficient than effective
    (d) an active listener

11. In order to be truly and consistently persuasive when communicating in the workplace, a manager should build credibility by making sure _____.

    (a) rewards for compliance with requests are clear
    (b) penalties for noncompliance with requests are clear
    (c) everyone knows who is the boss
    (d) to have good relationships established with others

12. A manager who understands the influence of proxemics in communication is likely to _____.

    (a) avoid sending mixed messages
    (b) arrange work spaces so as to encourage interaction
    (c) be very careful choosing written and spoken words
    (d) send frequent e-mail messages to team members

13. When a person's words say one thing but his or her body language suggests something quite different, the person is said to be communicating _____.

    (a) a mixed message
    (b) noise
    (c) through the wrong channel
    (d) destructive feedback

14. The advice for managers to spend time out of the office every day, talking with and listening to people doing their jobs, is part of a communication approach known as _____.

    (a) active listening
    (b) cultural etiquette
    (c) MBWA
    (d) credibility

15. A manager skilled at active listening would most likely try to _____ when interacting with an angry co-worker who is complaining about a work problem?

   (a) suggest that the conversation be held at a better time.
   (b) point out that the conversation would be better held at another location.
   (c) express displeasure in agreement with the co-workers complaint
   (d) rephrase the co-worker's complaint to encourage him to say more

Short response

16. What is the goal of active listening?

17. Why is it that well-intentioned managers sometimes make bad decisions based on information received from their subordinates?

18. What are four errors managers might make when trying to give constructive feedback to others?

19. How does ethnocentrism influence cross-cultural communication?

Integration & application

20. Glenn Pool was recently promoted to be the manager of a new store being opened by a large department store chain. Glenn wants to start out right, making sure that communications are always good between him, the six department heads, and the 50 full-time and part-time sales associates. He knows that he'll be making a lot of decisions in the new job and he wants to be sure that he is always well informed about store operations, and that everyone is always "on the same page" about important priorities. Put yourself in Glenn's shoes.

Questions: What steps should Glenn take right from the beginning to ensure that he and the department managers communicate well with one another? What can he do to open up and maintain good channels of communication with the sales associates?

Feedback and Assertiveness

Instructions

For each statement below, decide which of the following answers best fits you.[43]
1 = Never true; 2 = Sometimes true; 3 = Often true; 4 = Always true

_____ 1. I respond with more modesty than I really feel when my work is complimented.

_____ 2. If people are rude, I will be rude right back.

_____ 3. Other people find me interesting.

_____ 4. I find it difficult to speak up in a group of strangers.

_____ 5. I don't mind using sarcasm if it helps me make a point.

_____ 6. I ask for a raise when I feel I really deserve it.

_____ 7. If others interrupt me when I am talking, I suffer in silence.

_____ 8. If people criticize my work, I find a way to make them back down.

_____ 9. I can express pride in my accomplishments without being boastful.

_____ 10. People take advantage of me.

_____ 11. I tell people what they want to hear if it helps me get what I want.

_____ 12. I find it easy to ask for help.

_____ 13. I lend things to others even when I don't really want to.

_____ 14. I win arguments by dominating the discussion.

_____ 15. I can express my true feelings to someone I really care for.

_____ 16. When I feel angry with other people, I bottle it up rather than express it.

_____ 17. When I criticize someone else's work, they get mad.

_____ 18. I feel confident in my ability to stand up for my rights.

Scoring and Interpretation

Obtain your scores as follows:

Aggressiveness tendency score—Add items 2, 5, 8, 11, 14, and 17.

Passiveness tendency score—Add items 1, 4, 7, 10, 13, and 16.

Assertiveness tendency score—Add items 3, 6, 9, 12, 15, and 18.

The maximum score in any single area is 24. The minimum score is 6. Try to find someone who knows you well. Have this person complete the instrument also as it relates to you. Compare his or her impression of you with your own score. What is this telling you about your behavior tendencies in social situations?

 For further exploration go to WileyPlus

Case Snapshot

Facebook— Communicating the Web2.0 Way

Social networking Web sites are a dime a dozen these days, so how does Facebook stay at the top? By expanding its user base and working with developers and advertisers to create fresh content that keeps users at the site for hours on end. But can Facebook handle the challenges of international expansion and stereotypes about its youthful leadership?

Online Interactive Learning Resources

SELF-ASSESSMENT
• Listening

EXPERIENTIAL EXERCISES
• Upward Appraisal
• How to Give and Take Criticism

TEAM PROJECT
• How Words Count

13 Individual Behavior

There's Beauty in Individual Differences

Learning Outline

13.1 How Do Perceptions Influence Individual Behavior?

- Perceptual distortions can obscure individual differences
- Perception can cause attribution errors as we explain events and problems
- Impression management is a way of influencing how others perceive us

13.2 How Do Personalities Influence Individual Behavior?

- The Big Five personality traits describe work-related individual differences
- The Myers-Briggs Type Indicator is a popular approach to personality assessment
- Many personality traits influence work behavior
- People with Type A personalities tend to stress themselves
- Stress has consequences for work performance and personal health

13.3 How Do Attitudes, Emotions, and Moods Influence Individual Behavior?

- Attitudes predispose people to act in certain ways
- Job satisfaction is a positive attitude toward one's job and work experiences
- Job satisfaction influences work behavior
- Job satisfaction has a complex relationship with job performance
- Emotions and moods are positive and negative states of mind that influence behavior

Don't forget the real people behind those successful organizations. The headline reads: "Spanx queen leads from the bottom line." The story goes: woman unhappy with the way she looks in white pants cuts feet off panty hose, puts them on, and attends party. The result is: Sara Blakely founds a $250+ million business called Spanx.

"I knew this could open up so many women's wardrobes," Blakely says, "All women have that clothing in the back of the closet that they don't wear because they don't like the way it looks." With this notion, $5,500 of her own money, and the idea for "body shaping" underwear, she set out to start a business. Her unique blend of skills and personality made it all work.

When her first attempts to convince manufacturers to make product samples met with resistance—with one

274

Trendsetters
Richard Branson leads
with personality and
flamboyance.

News Feed
Racial bias embedded in
the perceptions of many

Case Snapshot
Panera Bread—Positive
attitude is a recipe for
success.

calling it "a stupid idea," Blakely persisted until one agreed. She aspired to place Spanx in "high end" department stores. But again, department stores kept turning her down. Still Blakely kept at it and finally persuaded a buyer at Neiman Marcus to give Spanx its first big chance.

Blakely sent Oprah Winfrey samples and sales really took off; Oprah voted Spanx "one of her favorite things." And it was about this time that Blakely realized additional skills were needed to handle the firm's fast-paced growth. She recognized her limits and "was eager to delegate my weaknesses." So, she turned day-to-day operations over to a chief executive officer, leaving herself free to pursue creativity, new products, and brand development. Her drive to succeed extends beyond product and business goals alone. She has since started the Sara Blakely Foundation with the express purpose of "supporting and empowering women around the world."

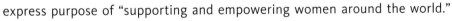

13.1 How Do Perceptions Influence Individual Behavior?

When people communicate with one another, everything passes through two silent but influential shields: the "perceptions" of the sender and the receiver. **Perception** is the process through which people receive and interpret information from the environment. It is the way we form impressions about ourselves, other people, and daily life experiences.

As suggested in **Figure 13.1**, you might think of perception as a bubble that surrounds us and influences significantly the way we receive, interpret, and process information received from our environments.[1] And because our individual idiosyncrasies, backgrounds, values, and experiences influence our perceptions, this means that people can and do view the same things quite differently. These differences in perceptions influence how we communicate and behave in relationship to one another.

> **Perception** is the process through which people receive and interpret information from the environment.

FIGURE 13.1

How Does Perception Influence Communication?

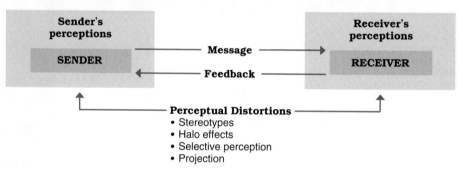

- Stereotypes
- Halo effects
- Selective perception
- Projection

Perception is the process of receiving and interpreting information from our environment. It acts as a screen or filter through which we interpret messages in the communication process. And perceptions influence how we behave in response to information received. Because people often perceive the same things quite differently, perception is an important issue in respect to individual behavior at work. Perceptual distortions in the form of stereotypes, halo effects, projection, and selective perception can lead to inaccurate assumptions regarding other people and events.

• Perceptual distortions can obscure individual differences.

Given the complexity of the stimuli constantly flowing toward us from our environments, human beings use various means of simplifying and organizing their perceptions. One of the most common of these tendencies is the use of **stereotypes**. This occurs when you identify someone with a group or category, and then use the attributes associated with the group or category to describe the individual. Although this makes things easier by reducing the need to deal with unique individual characteristics, it is an oversimplification. By using the stereotype we end up missing the real individual.

Some of the most common stereotypes in the workplace, and in life in general, relate to such factors as gender, age, race, and physical ability. Consider how managers might use gender stereotyping to misconstrue work behavior. If they see men in a discussion, they might think they are discussing a new deal; if it's a group of women, they might perceive what they are doing as gossiping. And then there's the question of opportunity. Why are so few top executives in

> A **stereotype** assigns attributes commonly associated with a group to an individual.

industry African Americans or Hispanics or women? Only a small proportion of U.S. managers sent on international assignments by their employers are women. Do you wonder why? A Catalyst study of women in global business blames gender stereotypes that place women at a disadvantage to men for international jobs. The perception seems to be that women lack the abilities or willingness for working abroad.[2]

A **halo effect** occurs when we use one characteristic of a person or situation to form an overall impression. You probably do this quite often, as do I. For example, when meeting someone new, receiving a positive smile might create a halo effect that results in a positive overall impression. By contrast, the halo effect of an unfamiliar hairstyle or manner of dressing may create a negative impression.

Halo effects cause the same problems as do stereotypes; they obscure individual differences. The person who smiles might have a very negative work attitude; the person with the unique hair style might be a top performer. Halo effects are especially significant in performance evaluations where one factor, such as a person's punctuality or lack of it, may become the halo that inaccurately determines the overall performance rating.

Selective perception is the tendency to single out for attention those aspects of a situation or person that reinforce or appear consistent with one's existing beliefs, values, or needs.[3] And what do we often do with information that conflicts with this perception? We simply screen it out. This happens in organizations when people from different departments or functions—such as marketing and manufacturing—tend to see things only from their own point of view. Like the other perceptual distortions, selective perception can bias our views of situations and individuals. One of the great benefits of teamwork and consultative decision making is the pooling of ideas and perceptions of many people, thus making it harder for selective perception to create problems.

Projection occurs when we assign our personal attributes to other individuals. Some call this the "similar-to-me" error. A classic projection error is to assume that other persons share our needs, desires, and values. Suppose, for example, that you enjoy a lot of responsibility and challenge in your work as a team leader. You might move quickly to increase responsibilities and challenges for team members, wanting them to experience the same satisfactions as you. But this involves projection. Instead of designing jobs to best fit their needs, you have designed their jobs to fit yours. In fact, an individual team member may be quite satisfied and productive doing his or her current job, one that seems routine to you. We can control projection errors through self-awareness and a willingness to communicate and empathize with other persons, that is, to try to see things through their eyes.

News Feed 🔊

Racial Bias Embedded in the Perceptions of Many

Although leaders are going to great lengths to increase diversity in their organizations' workforces, the presence of diversity alone may not be enough to change the racial perceptions of many workers. At least that's the conclusion of a study completed by researchers Ashleigh Shelby Rosette of Duke University, Geoffrey Leonardelli of the University of Toronto, and Katherine Phillips of Northwestern University.

In a paper entitled "The White Standard: Racial Bias in Leader Categorization," they report studies in which undergraduate and graduate students were asked to evaluate descriptions of fictitious CEOs and managers. When no racial information was provided in the descriptions, the students tended to describe business leaders as White more often than nonleaders. Even when the leader's race was disclosed as African American, Hispanic, Asian, or White, students associated successful leadership more with Whites and viewed Whites as having greater leadership potential. The results held even when information provided in the descriptions showed no differences among leaders in their performance accomplishments.

The reported findings held regardless of the race of the evaluators, causing the researchers to conclude that racial bias couldn't be explained on the basis "that people who are white give preferential treatment to other people who are white. . . . Americans of all races associate successful leadership with being white . . ."

Reflect and React:

Do racial stereotypes help to explain the findings of this study? Can you detect similar patterns in everyday conversations as friends and acquaintances talk about the performance of leaders in business, civic organizations, universities, and student associations? What are the implications of this study for you and your career?

A **halo effect** uses one attribute to develop an overall impression of a person or situation.

Selective perception is the tendency to define problems from one's own point of view.

Projection assigns personal attributes to other individuals.

• Perception can cause attribution errors as we explain events and problems.

Attribution is the process of creating explanations for events.

One of the ways in which perception exerts its influence on behavior is through **attribution**. This is the process of developing explanations or assigning perceived causes for events. It is natural for people to try to explain what they observe and the things that happen to them. And one of the most significant places for this is the workplace. What happens when you perceive that someone else in a job or student group isn't performing up to expectations? How do you explain this? And, depending on the explanation, what do you do to try and correct things?

Fundamental attribution error overestimates internal factors and underestimates external factors as influences on someone's behavior.

When someone else is the poor performer, the likelihood is for us to commit something called **fundamental attribution error**. This is a tendency to blame other people when things go wrong, whether or not this is really true. If I perceive that a student is doing poorly in my course, for example, this error pops up as a tendency to "blame" the student—perhaps perceiving a lack of ability or an unwillingness to study hard enough. But that perception may not be accurate, as you may well agree. Perhaps there's something about the course design, its delivery, or my actions as an instructor that are contributing to the problem—a deficiency in the learning environment, not the individual.

Consider another case. This time it's you having a performance problem—at school, at work, wherever. How do you explain it? Again, the likelihood of error is high, this time due to **self-serving bias**. This is the tendency for people to blame their personal failures or problems on external causes, and underestimate the role of personal responsibility. This is the "It's not my fault!" error. Of course, the flip side is to claim personal responsibility for any successes—"It was me; I did it!" This is also self-serving bias.

Self-serving bias underestimates internal factors and overestimates external factors as influences on someone's behavior.

So what's the significance of these error tendencies? Actually, it is quite substantial. When we perceive things incorrectly we are likely to take the wrong actions, and miss solving a lot of problems in the process. When other people's performance is too quickly blamed on them, we may never realize that the real cause of the problem rested in the environment. While we are trying to correct things through training, motivation, or even replacement, the real opportunity for improving performance may be missed—clarifying goals, making more resources available, extending deadlines, for example. And when we too quickly blame the environment for our problems, we never, or rarely, face up to the personal responsibilities for making positive changes in our behavior.

Think about self-serving bias the next time you hear someone blaming your instructor for a poor course grade. And think about fundamental attribution error the next time you jump on a group member who didn't perform according to your standards. Our perceptions aren't always wrong, but they should always be double-checked and tested for accuracy. There are no safe assumptions when it comes to the power of attributions.

• Impression management is a way of influencing how others perceive us.

Richard Branson, CEO of the Virgin Group, may be one of the richest and most famous executives in the world. One of his early business accomplishments was the successful start-up of Virgin Airlines, now a major competitor of British Airways (BA). In a memoir, the former head of BA, Lord King, said: "If Richard Branson had worn a shirt and tie instead of a goatee and jumper, I would not have underestimated him."[4] This is an example of how much our impressions count—both positive and negative. Knowing this, scholars today emphasize the importance of **impression management**, the systematic attempt to influence how others perceive us.[5]

Impression management tries to create desired perceptions in the eyes of others.

You might notice that we often do bits and pieces of impression management as a matter of routine in everyday life. This is especially evident when we enter new situations—perhaps a college classroom or new work team, and as we prepare to meet people for the first time such as going out with a new friend for a social occasion or heading off to a job interview. In these and other situations we tend to dress, talk, act, and surround ourselves with things that reinforce a desirable self-image and help to convey that same image to other persons. When well done, impression management can help us to advance in jobs and careers, form relationships with people we admire, and even create pathways to desired social memberships.

Some basic tactics of impression management are worth remembering: dressing in ways that convey positive appeal in certain circumstances—for example, knowing when to dress up and when to dress down; using words to flatter other people in ways that generate positive feelings toward you; making eye contact and smiling when engaged in conversations to create a personal bond; and displaying a high level of energy suggestive of work commitment and initiative.[6]

Trendsetters

Richard Branson Leads with Personality and Flamboyance.

Could you imagine starting an airline? Richard Branson decided he would and called it Virgin Atlantic. His career began in his native England with a student literary magazine and small mail-order record business. Since then he's built "Virgin" into one of the world's most recognized brand names.

Virgin Group is a business conglomerate employing some 25,000 people around the globe. It holds over 200 companies, including Virgin Mobile, Virgin Records, and even a space venture—Virgin Galactic. It's all very creative and ambitious—but that's Branson. "I love to learn things I know little about," he says.

But if you bump into Branson on the street you might be surprised. He's casual, he's smiling, and he's fun; he's also brilliant when it comes to business and leadership. Branson has been listed among the 25 most influential business leaders. His goal is to build Virgin into "the most respected brand in the world." And as the man behind the brand he's described as "flamboyant," something that he doesn't deny and also considers a major business advantage that keeps him and his ventures in the public eye.

About leadership Branson says: "Having a personality of caring about people is important. . . . You can't be a good leader unless you generally like people. That is how you bring out the best in them." His own style, he claims, was shaped by his family and childhood. At age 10 his mother put him on a 300-mile bike ride to build character and endurance. At 16 he started a student magazine. By the age of 22 he was launching Virgin record stores. And by the time he was 30 Virgin Group was running at high speed.

As for himself Branson says he'll probably never retire. Now known as Sir Richard after being knighted in 1999, he enjoys Virgin today "as a way of life" that he greatly enjoys. But he also says, "In the next stage of my life I want to use our business skills to tackle social issues around the world . . . Malaria in Africa kills four million people a year. AIDS kills even more . . . I don't want to waste this fabulous situation in which I've found myself."

Study Guide

13.1
How Do Perceptions Influence Individual Behavior?

Rapid review

- Perception acts as a filter through which all communication passes as it travels from one person to the next.
- Different people may interpret the same message differently.
- Fundamental attribution error occurs when we blame others for performance problems while excluding possible external causes.
- Self-serving bias occurs when, in judging our own performance, we take personal credit for successes and blame failures on external factors.
- Stereotypes, projections, halo effects, and selective perception can distort perceptions and reduce communication effectiveness.
- Through impression management we influence the way that others perceive us.

Terms to define

Attribution

Fundamental attribution error

Halo effect

Impression management

Perception

Projection

Selective perception

Self-serving bias

Stereotype

Be sure you can

- describe how perception influences behavior
- explain how stereotypes, halo effects, selective perceptions, and projection operate in the workplace
- explain the concepts of attribution error and self-serving bias
- illustrate how someone might use impression management during a job interview

Questions for discussion

1. Are there times when a self-serving bias is actually helpful?
2. How do advertising firms use stereotypes in a positive way?
3. Does the notion of impression management contradict the idea of personal integrity?

13.2 How Do Personalities Influence Individual Behavior?

Think of how many times you've complained about someone's "bad personality" or told a friend how much you like someone else because they had such a "nice personality." Well, the same holds true at work. Perhaps you have been part of or the object of conversations like these: "I can't give him that job. He's a bad fit; with a personality like that, there's no way he can work with customers." Or "Put Erika on the project; her personality is perfect for the intensity that we expect from the team."

In management we use the term **personality** to describe the combination or overall profile of enduring characteristics that makes each of us unique. And as the prior examples suggest, this uniqueness can have consequences for how we behave and how that behavior is regarded by others.

Personality is the profile of characteristics making a person unique from others.

• The Big Five personality traits describe work-related individual differences.

We all know that variations among personalities are both real and consequential in our relationships with everyone from family to friends to co-workers. Although there are many personality traits, scholars have identified a short list of five that are especially significant in the workplace. Known as the Big Five, these personality traits are extraversion, agreeableness, conscientiousness, emotional stability, and openness to experience.[7]

Take a look at the descriptions in **Table 13.1**—*How to Identify the Big Five Personality Traits*. You can probably spot them pretty easily in people with whom you work, study, and socialize, as well as in yourself. And while you're at it, why not use the table as a quick check of your personality? Then ask: What are the implications for my interpersonal and working relationships?

A considerable body of research links the Big Five personality traits with work and career outcomes. The expectation is that people with more extroverted, agreeable, conscientious, emotionally stable, and open personalities will have more positive relationships and experiences in organizations.[8] Conscientious persons tend to be highly motivated and high performing in their work, while emotionally stable persons tend to handle change situations well. It's also likely that Big Five traits are implicit criteria used by managers when making judgments about people at work, handing out job assignments, building teams, and more. Psychologists even use the Big Five to steer people in the direction of career choices that may provide the best personality-job fits. Extraversion, for example, is a good predictor of success in management and sales positions.

• The Myers-Briggs Type Indicator is a popular approach to personality assessment.

Another popular approach to personality assessment is the Myers-Briggs Type Indicator, a sophisticated questionnaire that probes into how people act or feel in various situations. Called the MBTI for short, it was developed by Katherine

[**TABLE** 13.1]

How to Identify the Big Five Personality Traits

Extroversion

An extravert is talkative, comfortable, and confident in interpersonal relationships; an introvert is more private, withdrawn, and reserved.

Agreeableness

An agreeable person is trusting, courteous, and helpful, getting along well with others; a disagreeable person is self-serving, skeptical, and tough, creating discomfort for others.

Conscientiousness

A conscientious person is dependable, organized, and focused on getting things done; a person who lacks conscientiousness is careless, impulsive, and not achievement oriented.

Emotional stability

A person who is emotionally stable is secure, calm, steady, and self-confident; a person lacking emotional stability is excitable, anxious, nervous, and tense.

Openness to Experience

A person open to experience is broad-minded, imaginative, and open to new ideas; a person who lacks openness is narrow-minded, has few interests, and resists change.

Sample Myers-Briggs types

- ESTJ (extraverted, sensing, thinking, judging)—practical, decisive, logical, and quick to dig in; common among managers.
- ENTJ (extraverted, intuitive, thinking, judging)—analytical, strategic, forceful, quick to take charge; common for leaders.
- ISFJ (introverted, sensing, feeling, judging)—conscientious, considerate, and helpful; common among team players.
- INTJ (introverted, intuitive, thinking, judging)—insightful, free thinking, determined; common for visionaries.

Briggs and her daughter Isabel Briggs-Myers from foundations set forth in the work of psychologist Carl Jung.[9]

Jung's model of personality differences included three main distinctions. First, extraversion and introversion, as just discussed, were used to describe personality differences in ways people relate with others. Second, Jung described how people vary in the way they gather information—by sensation (emphasizing details, facts, and routine), or by intuition (looking for the "big picture" and being willing to deal with various possibilities). Third, he described how they vary in ways of evaluating information—by thinking (using reason and analysis) or by feeling (responding to the feelings and desires of others).

To the personality distinctions in Jung's original model, Briggs and Briggs-Myers added a fourth dimension. It describes how people vary in the ways they relate to the outside world—judging or perceiving. This results in the four dimensions of the Myers-Briggs Type Indicator that can be briefly described as follows.[10]

- *Extraversion vs. introversion (E or I)*—whether a person tends toward being outgoing and sociable or shy and quiet.
- *Sensing vs. intuitive (S or N)*—whether a person tends to focus on details or on the big picture in dealing with problems.
- *Thinking vs. feeling (T or F)*—whether a person tends to rely on logic or emotions in dealing with problems.
- *Judging vs. perceiving (J or P)*—whether a person prefers order and control or acts with flexibility and spontaneity.

Based on MBTI scores, an individual is classified into one of the 16 possible personality types that result from combinations of these four dimensions. A sample is shown in the small box. The neat and understandable nature of the classification has made the MBTI very popular in management training and development, although it receives mixed reviews from researchers.[11] Employers and trainers tend to like it because once a person is "typed" on the Myers-Briggs, for example as an ESTJ or ISFJ, they can be trained to both understand their own styles and to learn how to better work with people having different styles.

Locus of control is the extent to which one believes that what happens is within one's control.

Authoritarianism is the degree to which a person defers to authority and accepts status differences.

FIGURE 13.2

Beyond the "Big Five," What Other Personality Traits and Tendencies Influence Human Behavior at Work?

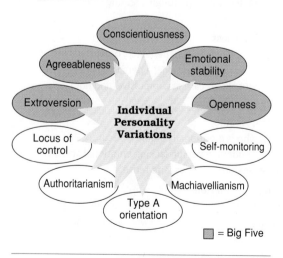

= Big Five

• Many personality traits influence work behavior.

In addition to the Big Five dimensions and the Myers-Briggs Type Indicator, there are other personality traits that can influence how people behave and work together.[12] Those shown in **Figure 13.2** include locus of control, authoritarianism, Machiavellianism, self-monitoring, and Type A orientation.

Scholars have a strong interest in **locus of control**, noting that some people believe they control their destinies while others believe what happens is beyond their control.[13] "Internals" are more self-confident and accept responsibility for their own actions; "externals" are prone to blaming others and outside forces when bad things happen. Interestingly, research suggests that internals tend to be more satisfied and less alienated from their work.

Authoritarianism is the degree to which a person defers to authority and accepts status differences.[14] Someone with an authoritarian personality might act rigid and control-oriented as a leader. Yet this same person is often subservient in a follower capacity. People with an authoritarian personality tend to obey orders. Of course, this can create problems when their supervisors ask them to do unethical or even illegal things.

In his sixteenth-century book *The Prince*, Niccolo Machiavelli gained lasting fame for his advice on how to use power to achieve personal goals.[15] Today we use the term **Machiavellianism** to describe someone who is emotionally detached in using power or acts manipulatively. We usually view a "high-Mach" personality as exploitative and unconcerned about others, seemingly guided only by the rule that the end justifies the means. Those with "low-Mach" personality, by contrast, allow others to exert power over them.

Finally, **self-monitoring** reflects the degree to which someone is able to adjust and modify behavior in new situations.[16] Persons high in self-monitoring tend to be learners, comfortable with feedback, and both willing and able to change. Because they are flexible, however, others may perceive them as constantly shifting gears and hard to read. A person low in self-monitoring is predictable and tends to act consistently. But this consistency may not fit differing circumstances.

People who are strong in self-monitoring are open to feedback and flexible in responding to new situations.

• People with Type A personalities tend to stress themselves.

Stress is a state of tension experienced by individuals facing extraordinary demands, constraints, or opportunities.[17] As you consider stress in your life and in your work, you might think about how your personality deals with it. Researchers describe the **Type A personality**, also shown among the personality traits in **Figure 13.2**, as someone who is high in achievement orientation, impatience, and perfectionism. Type A's are likely to bring stress on themselves, even in circumstances that others find relatively stress-free.[18] Do the suggestions for how to spot Type A personalities in the Tips to Remember describe you?

The work environment has enough potential *stressors*, or sources of stress, without this added burden of a stress-prone personality. Some 34% of workers in one survey actually said that their jobs were so stressful that they were thinking of quitting.[19] The stress they were talking about comes from long hours of work, excessive e-mails, unrealistic work deadlines, difficult bosses or co-workers, unwelcome or unfamiliar work, and unrelenting change.[20]

As if this isn't enough for Type A's to deal with, for them and the rest of us there's the added kicker of stress in our personal lives. Things such as family events (e.g., the birth of a new child), economics (e.g., a sudden loss of extra income), and personal issues (e.g., a preoccupation with a bad relationship) are all sources of potential emotional strain. Depending on how we deal with them, personal stressors can spill over to negatively affect our behavior at work. Of course, the effects also hold in reverse; work stressors can have spillover impact on our personal lives.

Machiavellianism is the degree to which someone uses power manipulatively.

Self-monitoring is the degree to which someone is able to adjust behavior in response to external factors.

Stress is a state of tension experienced by individuals facing extraordinary demands, constraints, or opportunities.

A **Type A personality** is oriented toward extreme achievement, impatience, and perfectionism.

Self-Assessment

This is a good point to complete the self-assessment "*Stress Test*" found on page 292.

• Stress has consequences for work performance and personal health.

How does all of this add up as an influence on your work and life? It's tempting to view stress all in the negative. But don't forget that stress can have its positive side as well.[21] Consider the analogy of a violin.[22] When a violin string is too loose, the sound produced by even the most skilled player is weak and raspy. When the string is too tight, the sound gets shrill and the string might even snap. But when the tension on the string

Tips to Remember

How to Spot Type A Personalities

1. Always moving, walking, and eating rapidly
2. Impatient, disliking waiting
3. Doing or trying to do several things at once
4. Feeling guilty when relaxing
5. Trying to schedule more in less time
6. Using nervous gestures such as clenched fists
7. Hurrying or interrupting the speech of others

Like the beautiful sound from a properly tuned violin string, moderate stress, not too little or too much, can be a source of creative tension that boosts performance.

Constructive stress is a positive influence on effort, creativity, and diligence in work.

Destructive stress is a negative influence on one's performance.

Job burnout is physical and mental exhaustion from work stress.

Workplace rage is aggressive behavior toward co-workers or the work setting.

Personal wellness is the pursuit of a personal health-promotion program.

is just right, it creates a most beautiful sound. Just enough stress, in other words, may optimize performance.

Constructive stress is energizing and performance enhancing.[23] You've probably felt this as a student. Don't you sometimes do better work "when the pressure is on," as we like to say? Moderate but not overwhelming stress can help us by encouraging effort, stimulating creativity, and enhancing diligence.

Just like tuning a violin string, however, achieving the right balance of stress for each person and situation is difficult. **Destructive stress** is dysfunctional because it is or seems to be so intense or long-lasting that it overloads and breaks down a person's physical and mental systems. One of its outcomes is **job burnout**. This is a sense of physical and mental exhaustion that can be incapacitating both personally and professionally. Another is **workplace rage**—overly aggressive behavior toward co-workers, bosses, or customers.[24] An extreme example is the "bossnapping" which made the news in France where workers at a Caterpillar plant took their plant manager hostage and held him for 24 hours in protest of layoffs. A local sociologist said: "Kidnapping your boss is not legal. But it's a way workers have found to make their voices heard."[25]

Medical research also indicates that too much stress can reduce resistance to disease and increase the likelihood of physical and/or mental illness. It may contribute to health problems such as hypertension, ulcers, substance abuse, overeating, depression, and muscle aches.[26]

So what can we do about stress; how can it be managed? The best strategy is to prevent it from reaching excessive levels in the first place. If we can identify our stressors, whether work-related or personal, we can often take action to avoid or minimize their negative consequences. And as managers, we can take steps to help others who are showing stress symptoms. Things like temporary changes in work schedules, reduced performance expectations, long deadlines, and even reminders to take time off can all help. And when it comes to taking time off, the latest advice is that you can work better by working less. A Society for Human Resource Management Survey reports that some 70% of people suffer from self-imposed pressures and often work late or on weekends. But a study by the Boston Consulting Group also reports that actually requiring people to take time off from their work can be beneficial in terms of more job satisfaction and better work-life balance. The professional services firm KPMG follows this advice. Its managers now use "wellness scorecards" to help monitor whether or not employees are skipping vacations or working too much overtime.[27]

Finally, there is really no substitute for **personal wellness**. In management we use this term to describe the pursuit of a personal health-promotion program.[28] This begins by taking personal responsibility for your physical and mental health. It means getting rest, exercise, and proper nutrition. It means dealing with things like smoking and alcohol or drug abuse. It means committing to a healthy lifestyle, one that helps you deal with stress and the demands of life and work.

Study Guide

13.2
How Do Personalities Influence Individual Behavior?

Rapid review

- The Big Five personality factors are extroversion, agreeableness, conscientiousness, emotional stability, and openness.
- Additional personality dimensions of work significance are locus of control, authoritarianism, Machiavellianism, problem-solving style, and self-monitoring.
- The Myers-Briggs Type Indicator identifies personality types based on extraversion-introversion, sensing-intuitive, thinking-feeling, and judging-perceiving.
- Stress is a state of tension that accompanies extraordinary demands, constraints, or opportunities.
- For some people, having a Type A personality creates stress as a result of continual feelings of impatience and pressure.
- Stress can be destructive or constructive; a moderate level of stress typically has a positive impact on performance.

Terms to define

Agreeableness

Authoritarianism

Conscientiousness

Constructive stress

Destructive stress

Emotional stability

Extraversion

Job burnout

Locus of control

Machiavellianism

Openness

Personal wellness

Personality

Self-monitoring

Stress

Type A personality

Workplace rage

Be sure you can

- list the Big Five personality traits and give work-related examples of each
- list five more personality traits and give work-related examples for each
- list and explain the four dimensions used to create personality types in the MBTI
- identify common stressors in work and personal life
- describe the Type A personality
- differentiate constructive and destructive stress
- explain personal wellness as a stress management strategy

Questions for discussion

1. Which personality trait would you add to the Big Five to make it six?
2. What are the advantages of having people of different MBTI types working on the same team?
3. Can you be an effective manager and not have a Type A personality?

13.3 How Do Attitudes, Emotions, and Moods Influence Individual Behavior?

At one time, Challis M. Lowe was one of only two African American women among the five highest-paid executives in over 400 U.S. corporations.[29] She attained this success after a 25-year career that included several changes of employers and lots of stressors—working-mother guilt, a failed marriage, gender bias on the job, and an MBA degree earned part-time. Through it all she says: "I've never let being scared stop me from doing something. Just because you haven't done it before doesn't mean you shouldn't try." Would you agree that Lowe has what we often call a "can-do" attitude?

• Attitudes predispose people to act in certain ways.

An **attitude** is a predisposition to act in a certain way.

An **attitude** is a predisposition to act in a certain way toward people and environmental factors.[30] Challis Lowe seemed disposed to take risks and embrace challenges. This positive attitude influenced her behavior when dealing with the inevitable problems, choices, and opportunities of work and career.

To fully understand attitudes, positive or negative, you must recognize their three components shown in **Figure 13.3**. First is the *cognitive component*, which reflects a belief or value. You might believe, for example, that your management course is very interesting. Second is the *affective or emotional component*, which reflects a specific feeling. For example, you might feel very good about being a management major. Third is the *behavioral component*, which reflects an intention to behave consistently with the belief and feeling. Using the same example again, you might say to yourself: "I am going to work hard and try to get A's in all my management courses."

FIGURE 13.3
Three Components of Individual Attitudes.

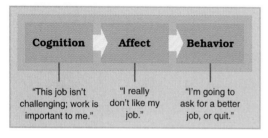

Have you noticed, however, that attitudes aren't always good predictors of behavior? Despite pledging to work hard as a student, you may not; despite wanting a more challenging job, you might stay with the current one because of family or other nonwork reasons. In these types of cases we fail to live up to our own expectations. Usually that's not a good feeling.

Cognitive dissonance is discomfort felt when attitude and behavior are inconsistent.

The psychological concept of **cognitive dissonance** describes the discomfort we feel in situations where our attitude is inconsistent with our behavior.[31] Most of us manage this dissonance by rethinking our attitude to make it seem to fit the behavior ("Oh well, work isn't really that important, anyway"), changing future behavior to fit the attitude (not putting extra time in at work; focusing more attention on leisure and personal hobbies), or rationalizing in ways that make the attitude and behavior seem compatible ("I'm in no hurry; there will be a lot of opportunities for new jobs in the future").

• Job satisfaction is a positive attitude toward one's job and work experiences.

Job satisfaction is the degree to which an individual feels positive about a job and work experience.

People hold attitudes about many things in the workplace—bosses, each other, tasks, organizational policies, performance goals, paychecks, and more. A comprehensive or catch-all work attitude is **job satisfaction**, the degree to which an individual feels positive or negative about various aspects of his or her job and work experiences.[32]

When researchers study and people talk about job satisfaction, several things are usually at issue. Job satisfaction typically reflects attitudes toward the *job itself* (responsibility, interest, challenge), *quality of supervision* (task help, social support), *co-workers* (harmony, respect, friendliness), *opportunities* (promotion, learning, growth), *pay* (actual and perceived), *work conditions* (comfort, safety, support), and *security* (job and employment).

If you watch or read the news, you'll regularly find reports on job satisfaction. You'll also find lots of job satisfaction studies in the academic literature. Interestingly, the majority of people tend to report being somewhat or completely satisfied with their jobs.[33] And in respect to things that create job satisfaction, a global study finds pay, contrary to what you might expect, is less important than things like opportunities to do interesting work, recognition for performance, work-life balance, chances for advancement, and job security.[34]

Job satisfaction influences work behavior.

At the beginning of this book we identified two primary goals or concerns of an effective manager—to help others both achieve high performance and experience job satisfaction. Surely you can agree that job satisfaction is important on quality-of-work-life grounds alone. Don't people deserve to have satisfying work experiences? Of course they do. But, an important question remains: Is job satisfaction important in other than a "feel good" sense?

Researchers tell us that there is a strong relationship between job satisfaction and **withdrawal behaviors** in the forms of *absenteeism* and turnover. In respect to absenteeism, workers who are more satisfied with their jobs are absent less often than those who are dissatisfied. In respect to turnover, satisfied workers are more likely to stay, and dissatisfied workers are more likely to quit their jobs. The consequences of these withdrawal behaviors can be significant; absenteeism and excessive turnover are expensive for employers. In fact, one study found that changing retention rates up or down results in magnified changes to corporate earnings. It also warns about the negative impact on corporate performance of declining employee loyalty and high turnover.[35]

Researchers also identify a relationship between job satisfaction and **organizational citizenship behaviors**.[36] This is a set of behaviors that basically represent a willingness to "go beyond the call of duty" or "go the extra mile" in one's work.[37] A person who is a good organizational citizen does things that, although not required, help advance the performance of the organization. You might observe this as a service worker who goes to extraordinary lengths to take care of a customer, a team member who is always willing to take on extra tasks, or a friend who is always working extra hours at no pay just to make sure things are done right for his employer.

On a related dimension, a survey of 55,000 American workers by the Gallup Organization suggests that higher profits[38] for employers arise when workers have a high sense of **employee engagement**. This is a positive work attitude resulting in a strong sense of belonging or connection with one's job and employer. It shows up both in high involvement—being willing to help others and always trying to do something extra to improve performance, and in high commitment—feeling and speaking positively about the organization. Things that

Stay Tuned

Job Satisfaction Trends

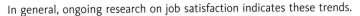

When reporters from *Fortune* asked a sample of American workers about their job satisfaction, they received the following feedback:

- 37% completely satisfied
- 47% somewhat satisfied
- 10% somewhat dissatisfied
- 4% completely dissatisfied
- 2% not sure

In general, ongoing research on job satisfaction indicates these trends.

- Job satisfaction has been declining since 1995.
- Job satisfaction tends to run higher in smaller firms than in large ones.
- Job satisfaction tends to run together with overall life satisfaction.

What Are Your Thoughts?

Do these data seem consistent with your work experiences and those of your friends and family? How do you think the many job layoffs of the recent economic crisis have affected job satisfaction? Are people with jobs going to be "satisfied" just for having them, or will the uncertainty over keeping their jobs make people "less satisfied" in general?

Withdrawal behaviors include absenteeism—not showing up for work, and turnover—quitting one's job.

Organizational citizenship behaviors are the extras people do to go the additional mile in their work.

Employee engagement is a strong sense of belonging and connection with one's work and employer.

counted most toward employee engagement in the Gallup research were believing one has the opportunity to do one's best every day, believing one's opinions count, believing fellow workers are committed to quality, and believing there is a direct connection between one's work and the company's mission.

• Job satisfaction has a complex relationship with job performance.

The data on the job satisfaction and performance relationship, as you might expect, are somewhat complicated.[39] When you think of this, remember a sign that once hung in a tavern near a Ford plant in Michigan: "I spend 40 hours a week here, am I supposed to work too?"

There are three different arguments on the satisfaction and performance relationship as depicted in **Figure 13.4**. One is that job satisfaction causes performance; "a happy worker is a productive worker." The second is that performance causes job satisfaction. The third is that job satisfaction and performance are intertwined, influencing one another, and mutually linked with other factors such as the availability of rewards. Can you make a case for each argument based on your personal experiences?

Although it was in doubt for quite some time, recent conclusions are that there is probably a modest link between job satisfaction and performance.[40] But keep the stress on the word "modest" in the last sentence. We need to be careful before rushing to conclude that making people happy is a sure-fire way to improve their job performance. The reality is that some people will like their jobs, be very satisfied, and still not perform very well. That's just part of the complexity regarding individual differences.

The link between performance and satisfaction holds pretty much to the same pattern. High-performing workers are likely to feel satisfied. But again, a realistic position is probably best; not everyone is likely to fit the model. Some people may get their work done and even meet high performance expectations while still not feeling high job satisfaction. Can you think of a time where this was the case for you?

Finally, it is quite likely that job satisfaction and job performance influence one another. But the relationship is also most likely to hold under certain "conditions." Those conditions are the subject of a lot of research, particularly on the role of rewards. One of the more popular positions is that job performance followed by rewards that are valued and perceived as fair will create job satisfaction; this in turn will likely increase motivation to work hard to achieve high performance in the future.

• Emotions and moods are positive and negative states of mind that influence behavior.

We have already discussed **emotional intelligence** as an important human skill for managers and an important leadership capability. Daniel Goleman defines "EI" as an ability to understand emotions in ourselves and in others and to use this understanding to manage relationships effectively.[41] But what is an emotion and how does it influence our behavior—positively and negatively?

An **emotion** is a strong feeling directed toward someone or something. For example, you might feel positive emotion or elation when an instructor congratulates you on a fine class presentation; you might feel negative emotion or anger when an instructor criticizes you in front of the class. In both cases the object of your emotion is the instructor, but in each case the impact of the instructor's behavior on your feelings is quite different. And your behavior in

---

FIGURE 13.4

Three Possible Arguments in the Job Satisfaction and Performance Relationship.

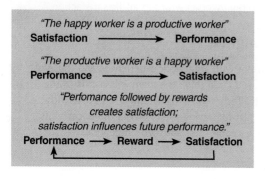

Emotional intelligence is an ability to understand emotions and manage relationships effectively.

Emotions are strong feelings directed toward someone or something.

response to the aroused emotions is likely to differ as well—perhaps breaking into a wide smile with the compliment, or making a nasty comment in response to the criticism.

Goleman's point on emotional intelligence is that we perform better in such situations when we are good at recognizing and dealing with emotions in ourselves and others. In other words, EI allows us to avoid having our emotions "get the better of us."

Whereas emotions tend to be short-term and clearly targeted, **moods** are different but equally significant. They are more generalized positive and negative feelings or states of mind that may persist for some time. Everyone seems to have occasional moods, and we each know the full range of possibilities they represent. How often do you wake up in the morning and feel excited, refreshed, and just happy, or feel low, depressed, and generally unhappy? And what are the consequences of these different moods for your behavior with friends and family, and at work or school? How do moods affect a person's "likability," and how does this affect how they perform at work or school?

Moods are generalized positive and negative feelings or states of mind.

Researchers are increasingly interested in **mood contagion**, the spillover effects of one's mood onto others.[42] Findings indicate that positive emotions of leaders can be "contagious," causing followers to display more positive moods and both be more attracted to the leaders and willing to rate the leaders more highly. As you might expect, mood contagion can also have inflationary and deflationary effects on the moods of co-workers and teammates, as well as family and friends.[43]

Mood contagion is the spillover of one's positive or negative moods onto others.

When it comes to moods and the workplace, a *Business Week* article claims that it pays to be likable; "harsh is out, caring is in." Some CEOs are even hiring executive coaches to help them manage emotions and moods to come across as more personable and friendly in relationships with others. There's a bit of impression management to consider here. If a CEO, for example, goes to a meeting in a good mood and gets described as "cheerful," "charming," "humorous," "friendly," and "candid," she or he may be viewed as on the upswing. But if the CEO is in a bad mood and comes away perceived as "prickly," "impatient," "remote," "tough," "acrimonious," or even "ruthless," she or he may be seen as on the downhill slope.

Study Guide

13.3
How Do Attitudes Emotions, and Moods Influence Individual Behavior?

Rapid review

- An attitude is a predisposition to respond in a certain way to people and things.
- Cognitive dissonance occurs when a person's attitude and behavior are inconsistent.
- Job satisfaction is an important work attitude, reflecting a person's evaluation of the job, co-workers, and other aspects of the work setting.
- Job satisfaction influences such behaviors as absenteeism, turnover, and organizational citizenship.
- Job satisfaction has a complex and reciprocal relationship with job performance.
- Emotions are strong feelings that are directed at someone or something; they influence behavior, often with intensity and for short periods of time.
- Moods are generalized positive or negative states of mind that can be persistent influences on one's behavior.

Terms to define

Attitude

Cognitive dissonance

Emotion

Employee engagement

Job satisfaction

Mood

Mood contagion

Organizational citizenship behaviors

Withdrawal behaviors

Be sure you can

- identify the three components of an attitude
- explain cognitive dissonance
- describe possible measures of job satisfaction
- explain the potential consequences of job satisfaction for absenteeism and turnover
- explain the link between job satisfaction, organizational citizenship, and employee engagement
- list and describe three alternative explanations in the job satisfaction–performance relationship
- explain how emotions and moods influence work behavior

Questions for discussion

1. Is cognitive dissonance a good or bad influence on us?
2. How can a manager deal with someone who has high job satisfaction but is a low performer?
3. What are the lessons of mood contagion for how a new team leader should behave?

[Test Prep]

1. Among the Big Five personality traits, _____ indicates someone who tends to be responsible, dependable, and careful in respect to tasks.

   (a) authoritarian   (b) agreeable
   (c) conscientious   (d) emotionally stable

2. A person with a/an _____ personality would most likely act unemotional and manipulative when trying to influence others to achieve personal goals.

   (a) extroverted   (b) sensation-thinking
   (c) self-monitoring   (d) Machiavellian

3. When a person tends to believe that he or she has little influence over things that happen in life, this indicates a/an _____ personality.

   (a) low emotional stability
   (b) external locus of control
   (c) high self-monitoring
   (d) intuitive-thinker

4. A person with a/an _____ problem-solving style is most likely to be comfortable with abstraction and unstructured situations, and to avoid getting involved in details.

   (a) sensation-thinker   (b) intuitive-thinker
   (c) sensation-feeler   (d) intuitive-feeler

5. If a new team leader changes job designs for persons on her work team mainly "because I would prefer to work the new way rather than the old," the chances are that she is committing a perceptual error known as _____.

   (a) halo effect   (b) stereotyping
   (c) extroversion   (d) projection

6. If a manager allows one characteristic of a person, say, a pleasant personality, to bias performance ratings of that individual overall, the manager is falling prey to a perceptual distortion known as _____.

   (a) halo effect   (b) impression management
   (c) extroversion   (d) projection

7. Use of special dress, manners, gestures, and vocabulary words when meeting a prospective employer in a job interview are all examples of how people use _____ in daily life.

   (a) halo effect
   (b) impression management
   (c) introversion
   (d) mood contagion

8. _____ is a form of attribution error that involves blaming the environment for problems that we may have caused ourselves.

   (a) Self-serving bias
   (b) Fundamental attribution error
   (c) Projection
   (d) Self-monitoring

9. _____ is a form of attribution error that involves blaming yourself for problems caused by others _____.

   (a) Self-serving bias
   (b) Fundamental attribution error
   (c) Projection
   (d) Self-monitoring

10. The _____ component of an attitude is what indicates a person's belief about something, while the _____ component indicates a specific positive or negative feeling about it.

    (a) cognitive/affective
    (b) emotional/affective
    (c) cognitive/attributional
    (d) behavioral/attributional

11. The term used to describe the discomfort someone feels when his or her behavior turns out to be inconsistent with a previously expressed attitude is _____.

    (a) alienation
    (b) cognitive dissonance
    (c) job dissatisfaction
    (d) job burnout

12. Job satisfaction is known from research to be a very good predictor of _____.

    (a) job performance
    (b) job burnout
    (c) conscientiousness
    (d) absenteeism

13. A person who is always willing to volunteer for extra work or to help someone else with his or her work or to contribute personal time to support an organizational social event can be said to be high in _____.

    (a) job performance
    (b) self-serving bias
    (c) emotional intelligence
    (d) organizational commitment

14. A/an _____ represents a rather intense but short-lived feeling about a person or a situation, whereas a/an _____ describes a more generalized positive or negative state of mind.

(a) stressor, role ambiguity
(b) external locus of control, internal locus of control
(c) self-serving bias, halo effect
(d) emotion, mood

15. Which statement about the job satisfaction–job performance relationship is most true based on research?

(a) A happy worker will be a productive worker.
(b) A productive worker will be a happy worker.
(c) A productive worker well rewarded for performance will be a happy worker.
(d) There is no relationship between being happy and being productive in a job.

Short response

16. What is the most positive profile of Big Five personality traits in terms of positive impact on work behavior?

17. What is the relationship between stress and performance?

18. How does the halo effect differ from selective perception?

19. If you were going to develop a job satisfaction survey, exactly what would you try to measure?

Integration & application

20. When Scott Tweedy picked up a magazine article on "How to manage health-care workers," he was pleased to find some apparent advice. Scott was concerned about poor or mediocre performance by several of the respiratory therapists in his clinic. The author of the article said that the "best way to improve performance is to make your workers happy." Well, Scott was happy upon reading this and made a pledge to himself to start doing a much better job of "making the therapists happy."

Questions: Should Scott charge ahead, or should he be concerned about this advice? What do we know about the relationship between job satisfaction and performance, and how can this apply to Scott's performance problems?

Self-Assessment

Stress Test

Instructions

Complete the following questionnaire. Circle the number that best represents your tendency to behave on each bipolar dimension.[44]

Am casual about appointments	1 2 3 4 5 6 7 8	Am never late
Am not competitive	1 2 3 4 5 6 7 8	Am very competitive
Never feel rushed	1 2 3 4 5 6 7 8	Always feel rushed
Take things one at a time	1 2 3 4 5 6 7 8	Try to do many things at once
Do things slowly	1 2 3 4 5 6 7 8	Do things fast
Express feelings	1 2 3 4 5 6 7 8	"Sit on" feelings
Have many interests	1 2 3 4 5 6 7 8	Have few interests but work

Scoring

Total the numbers circled for all items, and multiply this by 3; enter the result here [_____].

Points	Personality Type
120+	A+
106–119	A
100–105	A–
90–99	B+
below 90	B

Case Snapshot

Panera Bread—Positive Attitude Is a Recipe for Success.

Panera Bread is in the business of satisfying customers. With fresh-baked breads, gourmet soups, and efficient service, the relatively new franchise has surpassed all expectations for success. But how did a start-up food company get so big, so fast? Credit founder Ron Schaich's passion and intensity, as well as his uncanny ability to spot and respond to timely market trends.

Online Interactive Learning Resources

MORE SELF-ASSESSMENTS
- Internal/External Control
- Emotional Intelligence

EXPERIENTIAL EXERCISE
- Job Satisfaction Preferences

TEAM PROJECT
- Difficult Personalities

14 Motivation

Learning Outline

Loyal employer shares wealth with employees. At the age of 83, Charlie Butcher finally sold his family firm to the S.C. Johnson Company. And it was a good deal for Charlie and family—$18 million! But there's quite a bit more to this story than personal gain. You see, after selling the firm, Charlie shared the $18 million with the firm's employees!

He handed out checks the day after the sale, written to an average of $55,000 per person. How did everyone react? The president, Paul P. McClaughlin, said the employees "just filled up with tears. They would just throw their arms around Charlie and give him a hug." Butcher's administrative assistant Lynne Ouellette summed it up this way: "Charlie really wanted to take care of the hourly folks and people who put in a lot of years."

If you knew Charlie, they say, this wouldn't be a surprise. He always believed in people. This was just another chance to confirm the theory that he'd been practicing for years. If you treat talented people well, they'll create business success. Charlie tied job satisfaction and performance, saying: "When people are happy in their jobs, they are at least twice as productive."

Trendsetters
Pat Christen fights disease with video game therapy.

News Feed
Volunteers find they do well by doing good.

Case Snapshot
Pixar Animation Studios—Home of the creative geniuses

This was Charlie's answer to a perplexing question in social science: Why do some people work enthusiastically, while others hold back? More answers are possible, and most begin with respect for people in all of their talents and diversity. Either you respect people, or you don't, and this makes a big difference in how they respond to you. The best managers already know this. Like Charlie Butcher, they lead with full awareness that "productivity through people" is the foundation for long-term success.

In an interview, Charlie once reminded his audience that he believed the employees are what made his business successful. "I meant it," he said, "and when the opportunity came to put my money where my mouth was, that's exactly what I did." When he published the book *How to Succeed in Business by Giving Away Millions*, it wasn't, as you might expect, a best seller. But Charlie lived his message. Charlie's gone now, but his obituary called him a businessman "known for his generosity and passion for knowledge and justice."

14.1 How Do Human Needs and Job Designs Influence Motivation to Work?

Did you know that J. K. Rowling's first *Harry Potter* book was rejected by 12 publishers?[1] Thank goodness she didn't give up. In management we use the term **motivation** to describe forces within the individual that account for the level, direction, and persistence of effort expended at work. Simply put, a highly motivated person works hard at a job; an unmotivated person does not. A manager who leads through motivation creates conditions that consistently inspire other people to work hard.

A highly motivated workforce is obviously indispensable. So how do we get there? Why do some people work enthusiastically, persevering in the face of difficulty and often doing more than required to turn out an extraordinary performance? Why do others hold back, quit at the first negative feedback, and do the minimum needed to avoid reprimand or termination?

• Maslow described a hierarchy of needs topped by self-actualization.

One of the best starting points in exploring the issue of motivation is theories from psychology that deal with differences in individual **needs**—unfulfilled desires that stimulate people to behave in ways that will satisfy them. And as you might expect, there are different theories about human needs and how they may affect people at work.

Abraham Maslow's theory of human needs is an important foundation in the history of management thought. He described a hierarchy built on a foundation of **lower-order needs** (physiological, safety, and social concerns) and moving up to **higher-order needs** (esteem and self-actualization).[2] Whereas lower-order needs focus on physical well-being and companionship, the higher-order needs reflect psychological development and growth.

A key part of Maslow's thinking about how needs affect human behavior relies on two principles. The *deficit principle* states that a satisfied need is not a motivator of behavior. People act in ways that satisfy deprived needs, ones for which a "deficit" exists. For example, we eat because we are hungry; we call a friend when we are lonely; we seek approval from others when we are feeling insecure.

The *progression principle* states that people try to satisfy lower-level needs first and then move step-by-step up the hierarchy. This happens up until the level of self-actualization; the more these needs are satisfied, the stronger they will grow. According to Maslow, opportunities for self-fulfillment should continue to motivate a person as long as the other needs remain satisfied.

Maslow's theory is a good starting point for examining human needs and their potential influence on motivation. It seems to make sense, for example, that managers should try to understand the needs of people working with and for them. And isn't it a manager's job to help others find ways of satisfying their needs through work? **Figure 14.1** gives some suggestions along these lines.

• Alderfer's ERG theory deals with existence, relatedness, and growth needs.

A well-regarded alternative to Maslow's work is the ERG theory proposed by Clayton Alderfer.[3] His theory collapses Maslow's five needs categories into three.

Abraham Maslow described a hierarchy of lower-order and higher-order needs that influence motivation.

Motivation accounts for the level, direction, and persistence of effort expended at work.

A **need** is an unfulfilled physiological or psychological desire.

Lower-order needs are physiological, safety, and social needs in Maslow's hierarchy.

Higher-order needs are esteem and self-actualization needs in Maslow's hierarchy.

FIGURE 14.1

What Are the Opportunities for Need Satisfaction in Maslow's Hierarchy?

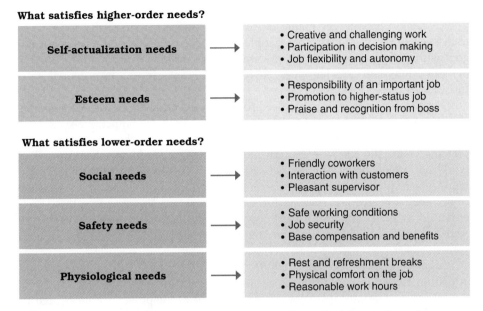

What satisfies higher-order needs?

| Self-actualization needs | → | • Creative and challenging work
• Participation in decision making
• Job flexibility and autonomy |
| Esteem needs | → | • Responsibility of an important job
• Promotion to higher-status job
• Praise and recognition from boss |

What satisfies lower-order needs?

Social needs	→	• Friendly coworkers • Interaction with customers • Pleasant supervisor
Safety needs	→	• Safe working conditions • Job security • Base compensation and benefits
Physiological needs	→	• Rest and refreshment breaks • Physical comfort on the job • Reasonable work hours

For higher-order need satisfaction, people realize self-actualization by doing creative and challenging work and participating in important decisions; they boost self-esteem through promotions and praise, and by having responsibility for an important job. For lower-order need satisfaction, people meet social needs through positive relationships with co-workers, supervisors, and customers; they achieve safety needs in healthy working conditions and a secure job with good pay and benefits; and they realize physiological needs by having reasonable work hours and comfortable work spaces.

Existence needs are desires for physiological and material well-being. **Relatedness needs** are desires for satisfying interpersonal relationships. **Growth needs** are desires for continued psychological growth and development.

ERG theory also rejects Maslow's deficit and progression principles. Instead, Alderfer suggests that any or all of the needs can influence individual behavior at any given time. His theory also suggests that a satisfied need doesn't lose its motivational impact. Instead, Alderfer describes a *frustration-regression principle* through which an already-satisfied lower-level need can become reactivated when a higher-level need cannot be satisfied. Perhaps this is why unionized workers frustrated by assembly line jobs (low growth need satisfaction) give so much attention in labor negotiations to things such as job security and wage levels (existence need satisfaction).

Don't be quick to reject either Maslow or Alderfer in favor of the other. Although questions can be raised about both theories, each adds value to our understanding of how individual needs can influence motivation.[4]

• McClelland identified acquired needs for achievement, power, and affiliation.

In the late 1940s, David McClelland and his colleagues began experimenting with the Thematic Apperception Test (TAT) of human psychology.[5] The TAT asks people to view pictures and write stories about what they see. Researchers then analyzed the stories' contents, looking for themes that display individual needs.

Existence needs are desires for physiological and material well-being.

Relatedness needs are desires for satisfying interpersonal relationships.

Growth needs are desires for continued psychological growth and development.

Need for achievement is the desire to do something better, to solve problems, or to master complex tasks.

Need for power is the desire to control, influence, or be responsible for other people.

Need for affiliation is the desire to establish and maintain good relations with people.

From this research McClelland identified *three acquired needs* that he considers central to understanding human motivation. The **need for achievement** is the desire to do something better or more efficiently, to solve problems, or to master complex tasks. The **need for power** is the desire to control other people, to influence their behavior, or to be responsible for them. The **need for affiliation** is the desire to establish and maintain friendly and warm relations with other people.

McClelland encourages managers to learn how to recognize the strength of each need in them and in other people. And because each need can be associated with a distinct set of work preferences, his insights offer helpful ideas for designing jobs and creating work environments that are rich in potential need satisfactions.

Consider someone high in the need for achievement. Do you, for example, like to put your competencies to work, take moderate risks in competitive situations, and often prefer to work alone? Need achievers are like this, and their work preferences usually follow a pattern. Persons high in need for achievement like work that offers challenging but achievable goals, feedback on performance, and individual responsibility. If you take one or more of these away, they are likely to become frustrated and their performance may suffer. As a manager, these preferences offer pretty straightforward insights for dealing with a high need achiever. And if you are that person, these are the things you should be talking about with your manager.

Insights are there for the other needs as well. People high in the need for affiliation prefer jobs offering companionship, social approval, and satisfying interpersonal relationships. People high in the need for power are motivated to behave in ways that have a clear impact on other people and events; they enjoy being in positions of control.

David McClelland identified needs for achievement, affiliation, and power as sources of motivation.

Importantly, McClelland distinguishes between two forms of the power need.[6] The need for *personal power* is exploitative and involves manipulation for the pure sake of personal gratification. As you might imagine, this type of power need is not respected in management. By contrast, the *need for social power* is the positive face of power. It involves the use of power in a socially responsible way, one that is directed toward group or organizational objectives rather than personal ones. This need for social power is essential to managerial leadership.

One interesting extension of McClelland's research found that successful senior executives tended to have high needs for social power that, in turn, were higher than otherwise-strong needs for affiliation. Can you explain these results? It may be that managers high in the need for affiliation alone may let their desires for social approval interfere with business decisions. But with a higher need for power, they may be more willing to sometimes act in ways that other persons may disagree with. In other words, they'll do what is best for the organization even if it makes some people unhappy. Does this make sense?

• Herzberg's two-factor theory focuses on higher-order need satisfaction.

Frederick Herzberg's work on needs took a slightly different route. He began with extensive interviews of people at work, and then content analyzed their answers. The result is known as the two-factor theory.[7]

When questioned about what "turned them on," Herzberg found that his interview respondents mainly talked about the nature of the job itself. They were telling him about what they did. Herzberg called these **satisfier factors**, or *motivator factors*, and described them as part of *job content*. They include such things as a sense of achievement, feelings of recognition, a sense of responsibility, the opportunity for advancement, and feelings of personal growth. They are most consistent with the higher-order needs of Maslow and the existence needs of Alderfer.

A **satisfier factor** is found in job content, such as a sense of achievement, recognition, responsibility, advancement, or personal growth.

When questioned about what "turned them off," Herzberg found that his respondents talked about quite different things. They were mostly telling him about where they worked, not about what they did. Herzberg called these **hygiene factors** and described them as part of *job context*. They include such things as working conditions, interpersonal relations, organizational policies and administration, technical quality of supervision, and base wage or salary. These seem more associated with Maslow's lower-order needs and Alderfer's existence and relatedness needs.

A **hygiene factor** is found in the job context, such as working conditions, interpersonal relations, organizational policies, and salary.

The two-factor theory is shown in **Figure 14.2**. It views hygiene factors as influencing high or low job *dis*satisfaction. By contrast, satisfier factors influence high or low job satisfaction. The distinction is important. Herzberg is saying that you can't increase job satisfaction by improving the hygiene factors. You will only get less dissatisfaction. And although you might agree that minimizing dissatisfaction is an important goal, you need to understand that Herzberg believes it won't deliver much by way of increased motivation. At least that's his theory.

FIGURE 14.2

Core Elements in Herzberg's Two-Factor Theory of Motivation.

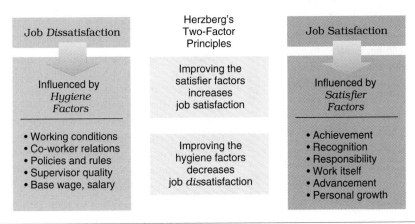

The satisfier factors found in job content are the real keys to job satisfaction according to Herzberg. He believes that it's only by improving on them that we can expect more motivation and higher performance. And to create these high-content jobs he suggests the technique of *job enrichment*. Essentially, it involves building into a job more opportunities for people to manage themselves and exercise self-control over their work. We'll discuss this job design approach in more detail in the next module.

Although scholars have criticized Herzberg's theory as being method-bound and difficult to replicate, it makes us think about both job content and job context.[8] It cautions managers not to expect too much by way of motivational improvements from investments in things such as special office fixtures and even high base salaries. And it focuses attention on how the job itself can be designed to provide for responsibility, growth, and other sources of higher-order need satisfactions.

SA
Self-Assessment
This is a good point to complete the self-assessment "*Two-Factor Profile*" found on page 313.

• The core characteristics model integrates motivation and job design.

One of the ways that an understanding of individual needs can be directly applied in the workplace is through **job design**, the allocation of specific work

Job design is the allocation of specific work tasks to individuals and groups.

News Feed

Volunteers Find They Do Well by Doing Good.

"When times are tough," the old adage goes, "the tough get going." Many times it's the volunteers who make that extra bit of difference to our local communities and society as a whole. And for some who suffered layoffs in a down economy, volunteering opened new doors for both social contribution and self-fulfillment.

At the very time that nonprofits are suffering from declining endowments and shrinking contributions, a new pool of volunteers is appearing to help. Laine Seator lost her management job and started volunteering. She puts in 35-hour weeks working for five different organizations. She's finding that her time is well spent; she's helping others and also gaining new skills in grant writing and strategic planning that should help with future job hunting. "In a regular job," she says, "you'd need to be a director or management staff to be able to do these types of things, but on a volunteer basis they welcome the help."

A United Way director in Boise, Idaho, claims that today's volunteers are highly skilled in ways "that we could never afford to hire." One of those volunteers is Rick Overton who lost his copywriting job. After volunteering with United Way he says: "It's hard to describe how much better it feels to get to the end of the day and, even if you haven't made any money, feel like you did some good for the world."

If you're interested in volunteering, don't hesitate to go online for help. Virtual matchmaking services can be found at sites such as usaservice.org, volunteermatch.org, idealist.org, and 1-800-volunteer.org.

Reflect and React:

Do you know the opportunities available for volunteer work in your community? To what extent do you participate in them? Is it possible that you might seek a career with a nonprofit, perhaps trading off some income potential from a private-sector career for the satisfaction of working for a nonprofit with a strong social mission?

tasks to individuals and groups. If you really think about it, you should see that for a job to be highly motivational it should provide a good fit between the needs and talents of the individual, and the task to be performed. And as you might expect, just what constitutes a good fit is going to vary from one individual and situation to the next.

Herzberg, known for the two-factor theory just discussed, poses the challenge this way: "If you want people to do a good job," he says, "give them a good job to do."[9] He goes on to argue that this is best done through **job enrichment**, the practice of designing jobs rich in content that offers opportunities for higher-order need satisfaction. For him, an enriched job allows the individual to perform planning and controlling duties normally done by supervisors. In other words, job enrichment allows for a lot of self-management.

Modern management theory values job enrichment and its motivating potential. However, in true contingency fashion, it recognizes that not everyone may have needs consistent with enriched jobs. This perspective is reflected in the core characteristics model developed by J. Richard Hackman and his associates. It offers a way for managers to design jobs that best fit the needs of both the people doing them and the organization.[10]

Figure 14.3 shows that the core characteristics model approaches job design with a focus on five "core" job characteristics: skill variety, task identity, task significance, autonomy, and job feedback. Can you think of any specific jobs that might score high or low on these characteristics?

Job enrichment increases job content by adding work planning and evaluating duties normally performed by the supervisor.

1. *Skill variety*—the degree to which a job requires a variety of different activities to carry out the work, and involves the use of a number of different skills and talents of the individual.

2. *Task identity*—the degree to which the job requires completion of a "whole" and identifiable piece of work, one that involves doing a job from beginning to end with a visible outcome.

3. *Task significance*—the degree to which the job has a substantial impact on the lives or work of other people elsewhere in the organization, or in the external environment.

4. *Autonomy*—the degree to which the job gives the individual freedom, independence, and discretion in scheduling work and in choosing procedures for carrying it out.

5. *Feedback from the job itself*—the degree to which work activities required by the job result in the individual obtaining direct and clear information on his or her performance.

FIGURE 14.3
The Core Characteristics Model of Job Design.

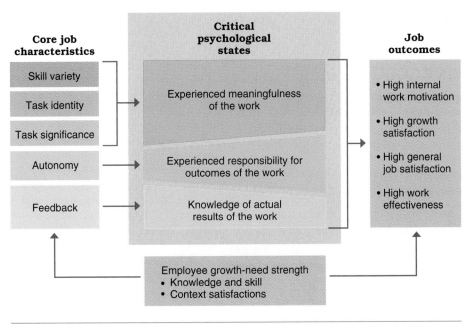

The higher a job scores on these core characteristics, the more enriched it is. But as you consider this model, don't forget that it is a contingency approach that recognizes that not everyone will be a good fit for a highly enriched job. Those who are expected to respond most favorably to job enrichment are likely to have strong growth needs, appropriate job knowledge and skills, and be otherwise satisfied with the job context. When these conditions are weak or absent, the results from job enrichment may turn out less favorable than expected.

Study Guide

14.1
How Do Human Needs and Job Designs Influence Motivation to Work?

Rapid review

- Motivation involves the level, direction, and persistence of effort expended at work; a highly motivated person can be expected to work hard.
- Maslow's hierarchy of human needs suggests a progression from lower-order physiological, safety, and social needs, up to higher-order ego and self-actualization needs.
- Alderfer's ERG theory identifies existence, relatedness, and growth needs.
- Herzberg's two-factor theory identifies satisfier factors in job content as influences on job satisfaction; hygiene factors in job context are viewed as influences on job dissatisfaction.
- McClelland's acquired needs theory identifies the needs for achievement, affiliation, and power, all of which may influence what a person desires from work.
- The core characteristics model of job design focuses on skill variety, task identity, task significance, autonomy, and feedback.

Terms to define

Growth needs

Higher-order needs

Hygiene factors

Job design

Job enrichment

Lower-order needs

Motivation

Need

Need for achievement

Need for affiliation

Need for power

Satisfier factors

Be sure you can

- describe work practices that can satisfy higher-order and lower-order needs in Maslow's hierarchy
- contrast Maslow's hierarchy with ERG theory
- describe hygiene factors and satisfier factors in Herzberg's theory
- explain needs for achievement, affiliation, and power in McClelland's theory
- differentiate the needs for personal and social power
- describe work preferences for a person with a high need for achievement
- explain how a person's growth needs and skills can affect his or her responses to job enrichment

Questions for discussion

1. Was Maslow right in suggesting we each have tendencies toward self-actualization?
2. Is high need for achievement always good for managers?
3. Why can't job enrichment work for everyone?

14.2 How Do Thought Processes and Decisions Affect Motivation to Work?

Have you ever received an exam or project grade and felt good about it, only to get discouraged when you hear about someone who didn't work as hard getting the same or better grade? Or have you ever suffered a loss of motivation when the goal set by your boss or instructor seems so high that you don't see any chance at all for succeeding?

My guess is that most of us have had these types of experiences, and perhaps fairly often.[11] They raise another question that those who study work motivation are very interested in answering: What influences people's decisions whether to work hard in various situations? The equity, expectancy, and goal-setting theories all offer possible answers.

• Equity theory explains how social comparisons can motivate individual behavior.

The *equity theory of motivation* is best known in management through the work of J. Stacy Adams.[12] Based on the logic of social comparisons, it pictures us continually checking our situations against those of others. Any perceived inequities in these comparisons will motivate us to engage in behaviors that correct them. Adams's equity theory of motivation is summarized in **Figure 14.4**.

FIGURE 14.4

Equity Theory and the Role of Social Comparison in Motivation.

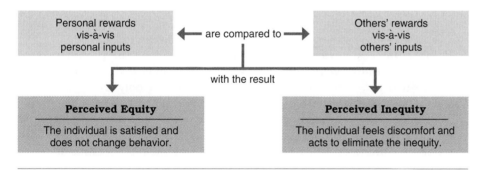

How have you reacted when your grade seems unfair compared with others? Did you reduce your efforts in the future? Drop the course? Rationalize that you really didn't work that hard either? Complain to the instructor and request a higher grade? All of these are ways to reduce the perceived grading inequity. And they are the same types of behaviors that perceived inequity can motivate people to pursue at work. Only instead of grades, the sources of inequity are more likely to be pay raises, job assignments, work schedules, office "perks," and the like. Pay, of course, is the really big one!

Research on equity theory has largely occurred in the laboratory. It is most conclusive with respect to the *perceived negative inequity* that we have just been discussing. People who feel underpaid, for example, experience a sense of anger. This causes them to try and restore perceived equity to the situation, such as by reducing current work efforts to compensate for the missing rewards, asking for more rewards or better treatment, or even by quitting the job.[13]

Interestingly, there is also some evidence for an equity dynamic among people who feel overpaid. This *perceived positive inequity* is associated with a sense of guilt. The individual becomes motivated to restore perceived equity by increasing the quantity or quality of work, taking on more difficult assignments, or working overtime.

Stay Tuned 🅑

Women Still Behind in Pay and Top Jobs

A report by the nonprofit research firm Catalyst and consulting firm McKinsey & Co. found that firms outperform when they have a larger proportion of female executives. So, what are the equity and motivational implications of these data also reported by Catalyst?

- Women constitute 46% of the U.S. workforce and the percentage is growing.
- Women receive 6 out of every 10 college degrees.
- Female CEOs earn 85% of what male CEOs earn.
- Thirteen women are among CEOs of America's Fortune 500 (F500) firms.
- Women hold 15% of director positions on F500 corporate boards.
- Women of color hold 3% of director positions on F500 corporate boards.
- Women hold 6% of top earner positions in F500 firms.

What Are Your Thoughts?

How do you explain the disparity between college degrees earned by women and the number of women represented among top CEOs and on corporate boards? For young women graduating from college today, are these data motivating or de-motivating in respect to the potential for a satisfying career in management?

Think about this finding for a minute. If valid, it suggests that managers, or instructors, might over-reward individuals today in order to motivate them to work harder in the future. Do you think this really works? What if one of your instructors decides to inflate the grades of students on early assignments, thinking that perceived positive inequities will motivate them to study harder for the rest of the course. Would you work harder? Or would you perhaps work less?

Although there are no clear answers available in equity theory, there are some very good insights. The theory is a reminder that rewards perceived as equitable should positively affect satisfaction and performance; those perceived as inequitable may create dissatisfaction and cause performance problems. In the current economic environment, for example, executive pay and benefits have caused equity complaints from rank and file workers as well as the public at large. When John Thain became CEO of Merrill Lynch, the firm had just lost $8 billion and he began cutting staff to save costs. But he took a $15 million signing bonus and spent $1.2 million to renovate his new office. After public outcries, he later agreed to pay back the office expenses saying they were "a mistake in the light of the world we live in today."[14]

Probably the best advice from equity theory is to anticipate potential equity problems whenever rewards of any type are being allocated. We should also recognize that people may compare their situations not only with co-workers, but with workers elsewhere in the organization and senior executives, and even persons employed by other organizations. And we should always understand that people behave according to their perceptions. If someone perceives inequity, it is likely to affect his or her behavior whether the manager sees the situation the same way or not.

• Expectancy theory considers motivation = expectancy × instrumentality × valence.

Victor Vroom offers another approach to motivation. His *expectancy theory* asks: What determines the willingness of an individual to work hard at tasks important to the organization?[15] Vroom answers this question with an equation: Motivation = Expectancy × Instrumentality × Valence. You can remember it as M = E × I × V.

The core elements of this theory are shown in **Figure 14.5**. **Expectancy** is a person's belief that working hard will result in achieving a desired level of task performance (sometimes called *effort-performance expectancy*). **Instrumentality** is a person's belief that successful performance will lead to rewards and other potential outcomes (sometimes called *performance-outcome expectancy*). **Valence** is the value a person assigns to the possible rewards and other work-related outcomes.

The use of multiplication signs in the expectancy equation (M = E × I × V) have important implications. Mathematically speaking, a zero at any location on the right side of the equation will result in zero motivation. This means that we cannot neglect any of these factors—expectancy, instrumentality, or valence; each has an influence on motivation.

Expectancy is a person's belief that working hard will result in high task performance.

Instrumentality is a person's belief that various outcomes will occur as a result of task performance.

Valence is the value a person assigns to work-related outcomes.

FIGURE 14.5
Core Elements in the Expectancy Theory of Motivation.

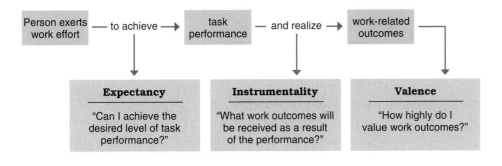

Are you ready to test this theory? Most of us assume that people will work hard to get promoted. But is this necessarily true? Expectancy theory predicts that motivation to work hard for a promotion will be low if any one or more of three conditions apply. If *expectancy is low*, motivation suffers. The person feels that he or she cannot achieve the performance level necessary to get promoted. So why try? If *instrumentality is low*, motivation suffers. The person lacks confidence that high performance will actually result in being promoted. So why try? If *valence is low*, motivation suffers. The person doesn't want a promotion, preferring less responsibility in the present job. So, if it isn't a valued outcome, why work hard to get it?

Figure 14.6 summarizes the management implications of expectancy theory. It is a reminder that different people are likely to come up with different answers to the question: "Why should I work hard today?" Knowing this, Vroom's advice

FIGURE 14.6
How Can Managers Apply the Insights of Expectancy Theory?

To Maximize Expectancy

| Make the person feel competent and capable of achieving the desired performance level | → | • Select workers with ability
• Train workers to use ability
• Support work efforts
• Clarify performance goals |

To Maximize Instrumentality

| Make the person confident in understanding which rewards and outcomes will follow performance accomplishments | → | • Clarify psychological contracts
• Communicate performance–outcome possibilities
• Demonstrate what rewards are contingent on performance |

To Maximize Valence

| Make the person understand the value of various possible rewards and work outcomes | → | • Identify individual needs
• Adjust rewards to match these needs |

Managers should act in ways that maximize expectancies, instrumentalities, and valences for others. To maximize expectancy, hire capable workers, train and develop them continuously, and communicate goals and confidence in their skills. To maximize instrumentality, clarify and stand by performance-reward linkages. Finally, to maximize valence, understand individual needs and try to tie work outcomes to important sources of need satisfaction.

As CEO of Bob Evans Farms, Steven Davis knows that setting goals can go a long way in building motivation for high performance accomplishments.

is to always try and build high expectancies that make people believe that if they try hard, they can perform. Managers should also build a sense of instrumentality that allows people to see what results from high performance. And they should make sure that valence is always high for these likely work outcomes.

• Goal-setting theory shows that well-chosen and well-set goals can be motivating.

The *goal-setting theory* described by Edwin Locke recognizes the motivational influence of task goals.[16] His basic premise is that task goals can be highly motivating, but only *if* they are the right goals and *if* they are set in the right ways.[17]

When Steven A. Davis was a child he got a lot of encouragement from his parents: "They never said that because you are an African American you can only go this far or do only this or that," he says, "they just said 'go for it.'" Davis also says that when he graduated from college he set goals—to be corporate vice president in 10 years and a president in 20. He made it; Davis rose through a variety of management jobs to become president of Long John Silver's, part of Yum Brands. He is now CEO of Bob Evans Farms in Columbus, Ohio.[18] Victor Vroom would point out that Davis's parents increased his motivation by creating high positive expectancy during his school years. Edwin Locke would add that Davis found lots of motivation through the goals he set as a college graduate.

Goals give direction to people in their work. Goals clarify the performance expectations between leaders and followers, among co-workers, and even across subunits in an organization. Goals establish a frame of reference for task feedback, and they provide a foundation for control and self-management.[19] In these and related ways, Locke believes goal setting is a very practical and powerful motivational tool.

But what is a motivational goal? Research by Locke and his associates indicates that managers and team leaders should focus on how specific and difficult goals are, and how likely it is that others will accept and commit to them.[20] As you might suspect, this is a tall order. It is no easy task for managers to work with others to set the right goals in the right ways. And as Tips to Remember recommends, an important key to the goal-setting process is participation. Goals are most motivating when the individual has participated in setting them.

The concept of management by objectives, described in Module 6.2 as an integrative approach to planning and controlling, can be a good example. When done well, MBO brings together team leaders and team members in a participative process of goal setting and performance review. Consistent with goal-setting theory, the positive impact of MBO is most likely when specific and difficult goals are set in ways that create mutual understanding and increase acceptance and commitment.

Although all this sounds ideal and good, we have to be realistic. We can't always choose our own goals; there are many times in work when goals come to us from above and we are expected to help accomplish them. Does this mean that the motivational properties of goal setting are lost? Not necessarily; even though the goals are set, there may be opportunities to participate in how to best pursue them. Locke's research also suggests that workers will respond positively to externally imposed goals if they trust the supervisors assigning them and they believe the supervisors will adequately support them.

Goals

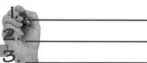

Tips to Remember ℮

How to Make Goal Setting Work for You

- *Set specific goals*—avoid more generally stated ones, such as "Do your best."
- *Set challenging goals*—when realistic and attainable, they motivate better than easy ones.
- *Build commitment*—people work harder for goals they accept and believe in.
- *Clarify priorities*—expectations should be clear on which goals to pursue first.
- *Provide feedback*—people need to know how well they are doing.
- *Reward results*—don't let accomplishments pass unnoticed.

Study Guide

14.2
How Do Thought Processes and Decisions Affect Motivation to Work?

Rapid review

- Adams's equity theory recognizes that social comparisons take place when rewards are distributed in the workplace.
- In equity theory, any sense of inequity is considered a motivating state that causes a person to behave in ways that can reduce the perceived inequity.
- Vroom's expectancy theory states that motivation = expectancy $\times$ instrumentality $\times$ valence.
- Managers using expectancy theory are advised to make sure rewards are achievable (maximizing expectancies), predictable (maximizing instrumentalities), and individually valued (maximizing valence).
- Locke's goal-setting theory emphasizes the motivational power of goals that are specific and challenging, as well as set through participatory means.
- The joint goal-setting process in management by objectives provides a framework for managers to apply goal-setting theory in practice.

Terms to define

Expectancy

Instrumentality

Valence

Be sure you can

- explain the role of social comparison in Adams's equity theory
- apply the equity theory to explain how people with felt negative inequity behave
- differentiate the terms expectancy, instrumentality, and valence
- explain the implications of Vroom's expectancy equation, $M = E \times I \times V$
- explain Locke's goal-setting theory
- describe the fit between goal-setting theory and MBO

Questions for discussion

1. Is it against human nature to work harder in response to perceived positive inequity?
2. Can a person with low expectancy ever be motivated to work hard at a task?
3. Will goal-setting theory work if the goals are fixed and only the means are open for discussion?

14.3 What Role Does Reinforcement Play in Motivation?

The theories discussed so far focus on people satisfying needs, resolving felt inequities, and/or pursuing positive expectancies and task goals. Instead of looking within the individual to explain motivation in these ways, *reinforcement theory* takes a different approach. It views human behavior as determined by its environmental consequences.

• Operant conditioning influences behavior by controlling its consequences.

The premises of reinforcement theory rely on what E. L. Thorndike called the **law of effect**: People generally repeat behavior that results in a pleasant outcome, and avoid behavior that results in an unpleasant outcome.[21] Psychologist B. F. Skinner used this notion to popularize the concept of **operant conditioning**. This is the process of applying the law of effect to influence behavior by manipulating its consequences.[22] You may think of operant conditioning as learning by reinforcement, and **Figure 14.7** shows how managers might apply four reinforcement strategies in the work setting.

> The **law of effect** states that behavior followed by pleasant consequences is likely to be repeated; behavior followed by unpleasant consequences is not.
>
> **Operant conditioning** is the control of behavior by manipulating its consequences.

FIGURE 14.7

How Do Managers Apply Reinforcement Strategies to Influence Work Behavior?

To strengthen quality work, a supervisor might use positive reinforcement by praising the individual, or negative reinforcement by no longer complaining to him about poor quality work. To discourage poor quality work, a supervisor might use extinction (withholding things that are positively reinforcing such outcomes) or punishment (associating the poor-quality work with unpleasant results for the individual).

> **Positive reinforcement** strengthens a behavior by making a desirable consequence contingent on its occurrence.
>
> **Negative reinforcement** strengthens a behavior by making the avoidance of an undesirable consequence contingent on its occurrence.

Positive reinforcement strengthens or increases the frequency of desirable behavior by making a pleasant consequence contingent on its occurrence. *Example:* A manager nods to express approval to someone who makes a useful comment during a staff meeting. **Negative reinforcement** increases the frequency of or strengthens desirable behavior by making the avoidance of an unpleasant consequence contingent on its occurrence. *Example:* A manager who has nagged a worker every day about tardiness does not nag when the worker comes to work on time.

Punishment decreases the frequency of or eliminates an undesirable behavior by making an unpleasant consequence contingent on its occurrence. *Example:* A manager issues a written reprimand to an employee whose careless work creates quality problems. **Extinction** decreases the frequency of or eliminates an undesirable behavior by making the removal of a pleasant consequence contingent on its occurrence. *Example:* After observing that co-workers are providing social approval to a disruptive employee, a manager counsels co-workers to stop giving this approval.

Looking again at the case described in Figure 14.7, the supervisor's goal is to improve work quality as part of a total quality management program. Notice that both positive and negative reinforcement strategies strengthen desirable behavior when it occurs. Punishment and extinction strategies weaken or eliminate undesirable behaviors.

• Positive reinforcement connects desirable behavior with pleasant consequences.

Among the reinforcement strategies, positive reinforcement deserves special attention. It should be part of any manager's motivational strategy. In fact, it should be part of our personal life strategies as well—as parents working with children, for example.

Sir Richard Branson, well-known founder of Virgin Group, is a believer in positive reinforcement. "For the people who work for you or with you, you must lavish praise on them at all times," he says. "If a flower is watered, it flourishes. If not, it shrivels up and dies." And besides, he goes on to add: "It's much more fun looking for the best in people."[23] David Novak, CEO of Yum Brands Inc., is another believer in the power of positive reinforcement. He claims that one of his most important tasks as CEO is "to get people fired up." He adds: "You can never underestimate the power of telling someone he's doing a good job."[24]

Whether we are talking about a pink Cadillac, pay raise, verbal praise, or any other forms of positive reinforcement, two laws govern the process. The *law of contingent reinforcement* states: For a reward to have maximum reinforcing value, it must be delivered only if the desired behavior is exhibited. The *law of immediate reinforcement* states: The more immediate the delivery of a reward after the occurrence of a desirable behavior, the greater the reinforcing value of the reward. **Table 14.1**—*Guidelines for Positive Reinforcement and Punishment* presents several useful guidelines for using these laws.

One of the ways to mobilize the power of positive reinforcement is through **shaping**. This is the creation of a new behavior by the positive reinforcement of successive approximations to it. The timing of positive reinforcement can also

Trendsetters

Pat Christen Fights Disease with Video Game Therapy.

While many teens play video games just for fun, teens with cancer can now play a video game that can help them beat the disease. Picture a teenager with cancer but not too good keeping up with his medication schedules. Now picture him playing the video game Re-Mission and maneuvering a nanobot by the name of Roxxi through the body of a cancer patient to destroy cancer cells. And finally, think about the article in the medical journal *Pediatrics* that reports that patients who play the game at least one hour a week do a better job of holding to their medication schedules.

What's going on here is the brainchild of HopeLab, a nonprofit led by president and CEO Pat Christen with the mission of combining "rigorous research with innovative solutions to improve the health and quality of life of young people with chronic illness." The nonprofit was founded by Pam Omidyar who as an immunology researcher and gaming enthusiast saw the possible link between games and fighting disease.

Christen came to HopeLab after 20 years of nonprofit management experience, and focuses on strategic management and business development. The goal is always to find innovative ways to improve the lives of young people fighting illnesses. Her previous positions included president and executive director of the San Francisco AIDS Foundation and president of the Pangaea Global AIDS Foundation. In the latter capacity she helped found a state-of-the-art AIDS clinic and research center in Uganda. Her career began in Kenya, East Africa, where she served as a Peace Corps volunteer after graduating from Stanford University.

Re-Mission is one positive step in the war against childhood cancer. With the founding vision of Pam Omidyar and the strategic leadership of Pam Christen, HopeLab received the Social Enterprise Award of the Year from *Fast Company* magazine. One of its current priorities is to unleash the power of video gaming to help in the fight against childhood obesity.

Punishment discourages a behavior by making an unpleasant consequence contingent on its occurrence.

Extinction discourages a behavior by making the removal of a desirable consequence contingent on its occurrence.

Shaping is positive reinforcement of successive approximations to the desired behavior.

[TABLE 14.1]

Guidelines for Positive Reinforcement and Punishment

Positive Reinforcement:
- Clearly identify desired work behaviors.
- Maintain a diverse inventory of rewards.
- Inform everyone what must be done to get rewards.
- Recognize individual differences when allocating rewards.
- Follow the laws of immediate and contingent reinforcement.

Punishment:
- Tell the person what is being done wrong.
- Tell the person what is being done right.
- Make sure the punishment matches the behavior.
- Administer the punishment in private.
- Follow the laws of immediate and contingent reinforcement.

make a difference in its impact. A *continuous reinforcement schedule* administers a reward each time a desired behavior occurs. An *intermittent reinforcement schedule* rewards behavior only periodically. In general, continuous reinforcement will likely elicit a desired behavior more quickly than will intermittent reinforcement. Also, behavior acquired under an intermittent schedule will be more permanent than will behavior acquired under a continuous schedule.

• Punishment connects undesirable behavior with unpleasant consequences.

As a reinforcement strategy, punishment attempts to eliminate undesirable behavior by making an unpleasant consequence contingent with its occurrence. To punish an employee, for example, a manager may deny a valued reward, such as verbal praise or merit pay, or administer an unpleasant outcome, such as a verbal reprimand or pay reduction. Like positive reinforcement, punishment can be done poorly or it can be done well. All too often, it is done both too frequently and poorly. If you look again at **Table 14.1** you'll find advice on how to best handle punishment when it is necessary as a reinforcement strategy.

Perhaps this discussion of punishment raises other questions in your mind. The use of reinforcement techniques in work settings has produced many success stories of improved safety, decreased absenteeism and tardiness, and increased productivity.[25] But there are still debates over both the results and the ethics of controlling human behavior.

Some people worry that use of operant conditioning principles ignores the individuality of people, restricts their freedom of choice, and fails to recognize that people can be motivated by things other than extrinsic rewards. Others agree that reinforcement involves the control of behavior, but argue that control is part of every manager's job. The ethical issue, they say, isn't whether to use reinforcement principles, but is whether or not we use them well in the performance context of the organization.[26]

Study Guide

14.3
What Role Does Reinforcement Play in Motivation?

Rapid review

- Reinforcement theory views human behavior as determined by its environmental consequences.
- The law of effect states that behavior followed by a pleasant consequence is likely to be repeated; behavior followed by an unpleasant consequence is unlikely to be repeated.
- Managers use strategies of positive reinforcement and negative reinforcement to strengthen desirable behaviors.
- Managers use strategies of punishment and extinction to weaken undesirable work behaviors.
- Positive reinforcement and punishment both work best when applied according to the laws of contingent and immediate reinforcement.

Terms to define

Extinction

Law of effect

Negative reinforcement

Operant conditioning

Positive reinforcement

Punishment

Shaping

Be sure you can

- explain the law of effect and operant conditioning
- illustrate how positive reinforcement, negative reinforcement, punishment, and extinction can influence work behavior
- explain the reinforcement technique of shaping
- describe how managers can use the laws of immediate and contingent reinforcement when allocating rewards

Questions for discussion

1. Is operant conditioning a manipulative way to influence human behavior?
2. When is punishment justifiable as a reinforcement strategy?
3. Is it possible for a manager, or parent, to only use positive reinforcement?

Test Prep

1. Maslow's progression principle stops working at the level of _____ needs.
   (a) growth
   (b) self-actualization
   (c) achievement
   (d) self-esteem

2. Lower-order needs in Maslow's hierarchy correspond to _____ needs in ERG theory.
   (a) growth
   (b) affiliation
   (c) existence
   (d) achievement

3. A worker high in need for _____ power in McClelland's theory tries to use power for the good of the organization.
   (a) position
   (b) expert
   (c) personal
   (d) social

4. In the _____ theory of motivation, an individual who feels under-rewarded relative to a co-worker might be expected to reduce his or her work efforts in the future.
   (a) ERG
   (b) acquired needs
   (c) two-factor
   (d) equity

5. Which of the following is a correct match?
   (a) McClelland–ERG theory
   (b) Skinner–reinforcement theory
   (c) Vroom–equity theory
   (d) Locke–expectancy theory

6. In Herzberg's two-factor theory, base pay is considered a/an _____ factor.
   (a) hygiene
   (b) satisfier
   (c) equity
   (d) higher-order

7. The expectancy theory of motivation says that: motivation = expectancy × _____ × _____.
   (a) rewards/valence
   (b) instrumentality/valence
   (c) equity/instrumentality
   (d) rewards/valence

8. When a team member shows strong ego needs in Maslow's hierarchy, the team leader should find ways to link this person's work on the team task with _____.
   (a) compensation tied to group performance
   (b) individual praise and recognition for work well done
   (c) lots of social interaction with other team members
   (d) challenging individual performance goals

9. When someone has a high and positive "expectancy" in expectancy theory of motivation, this means that the person _____.
   (a) believes he or she can meet performance expectations
   (b) highly values the rewards being offered
   (c) sees a relationship between high performance and the available rewards
   (d) believes that rewards are equitable

10. The law of _____ states that behavior followed by a positive consequence is likely to be repeated, whereas behavior followed by an undesirable consequence is not likely to be repeated.
    (a) reinforcement
    (b) contingency
    (c) goal setting
    (d) effect

11. When a job allows a person to do a complete unit of work, for example, process an insurance claim from point of receipt from the customer to point of final resolution for the customer, it would be considered high on which core characteristic?
    (a) Task identity
    (b) Task significance
    (c) Task autonomy
    (d) Feedback

12. _____ is a positive reinforcement strategy that rewards successive approximations to a desirable behavior.
    (a) Extinction
    (b) Negative reinforcement
    (c) Shaping
    (d) Merit pay

13. The purpose of negative reinforcement as an operant conditioning technique is to _____.
    (a) punish bad behavior
    (b) discourage bad behavior
    (c) encourage desirable behavior
    (d) offset the effects of shaping

14. The underlying premise of reinforcement theory is that _____.

(a) behavior is a function of environment
(b) motivation comes from positive expectancy
(c) higher order needs stimulate hard work
(d) rewards considered unfair are de-motivators

15. Both Barry and Marissa are highly motivated college students. Knowing this I can expect them to be _____ in my class.

(a) hard working   (b) high performing
(c) highly satisfied   (d) highly dissatisfied

Short response

16. What preferences does a person high in the need for achievement bring to the workplace?

17. Why is MBO a way to apply goal-setting theory?

18. What are three ways a worker could reduce the discomforts of perceived negative inequity over a pay raise?

19. How can shaping be used to encourage desirable work behaviors?

Integration & application

20. I overheard a conversation between two Executive MBA students. One was telling the other: "My firm just contracted with Musak to have mood music piped into the offices at various times of the workday." The other replied: "That's a waste of money; there should be better things to do if the firm is really interested in increasing motivation and performance."

Questions: Is the second student right or wrong, and why?

[SA Self-Assessment]

Two-Factor Profile

Instructions

On each of the following dimensions, distribute a total of 10 points between the two options. For example:

Summer weather	(7)	(3)	*Winter weather*

1. Very responsible job   (___) (___) Job security

2. Recognition for work accomplishments   (___) (___) Good relations with co-workers

3. Advancement opportunities at work   (___) (___) A boss who knows his/her job well

4. Opportunities to grow and learn on the job   (___) (___) Good working conditions

5. A job that I can do well   (___) (___) Supportive rules, policies of employer

6. A prestigious or high-status job   (___) (___) A high base wage or salary

Scoring

MF = _____

Summarize your total score for all items in the *left-hand column* and write it here.

HF = _____

Summarize your total score for all items in the *right-hand column* and write it here.

Interpretation

The "MF" score indicates the relative importance that you place on the motivating, or satisfier, factors in Herzberg's two-factor theory. This shows how important job content is to you. The "HF" score indicates the relative importance that you place on hygiene, or dissatisfier, factors in Herzberg's two-factor theory. This shows how important job context is to you.

 For further exploration go to WileyPlus

Case Snapshot

Pixar Animation Studios—Home of the Creative Geniuses

Pixar has delivered a series of wildly successful animated movies featuring plucky characters and intensely lifelike animation. Yet some of the most memorable ones—*Toy Story*, *Finding Nemo*, and *The Incredibles*—were almost never made. Find out how Apple guru Steve Jobs, whose company struggled to stay alive during its early years, took these upstarts of animation to success.

Online Interactive Learning Resources

SELF-ASSESSMENT
- Student Engagement Survey

EXPERIENTIAL EXERCISES
- Why Do We Work?
- Compensation and Benefits Debate

TEAM PROJECT
- CEO Pay

15 Teams and Teamwork

Two Heads Really Can Be Better

The beauty is in the teamwork. What distinguishes a group of people from a high-performance team? For one, it's the way members work with one another to achieve common goals. A vivid example is a NASCAR pit crew. When a driver pulls in for a pit stop, the team must jump in to perform multiple tasks flawlessly and in perfect order and unison. A second gained or lost can be crucial to a NASCAR driver's performance. Team members must be well trained and rehearsed to efficiently perform on race day.

When Ryan Newman won the Daytona 500 by a mere .092 seconds over runner-up Kurt Busch, it was time that could have been easily lost—not just on the track, but in the pits. "You can't win a race with a 12-second stop, but you can lose it with an 18-second stop," says Trent Cherry, the coach of Newman's pit crew.

Pit crew members are often former college and professional athletes. They are all conditioned and

Trendsetters
Amazon's Jeff Bezos believes in two-pizza teams.

News Feed
Reality TV rubs off on "reality" team building.

Case Snapshot
NASCAR—Fast cars, passion, and teamwork create wins.

Than One

trained to execute intricate maneuvers while taking care of tire changes, car adjustments, fueling, and related matters on a crowded pit lane. Each crew member is an expert at one task. But each is also fully aware of how that job fits into every other *task* that must be performed in a few-second pit stop interval. The duties are carefully scripted for each individual's performance and equally choreographed to fit together seamlessly at the team level. Every task is highly specialized and interdependent; if the jacker is late, for example, the wheel changer can't pull the wheel.

Pit crews plan and practice over and over again, getting ready for the big test of race day performance. The crew chief makes sure that everyone is in shape, well trained, and ready to contribute to the team. "I don't want seven all-stars," Trent Cherry says, "I want seven guys who work as a team."

15.1 Why Is It Important to Understand Teams and Teamwork?

We can't all be race car drivers or members of pit crews as in the opening example, but we're part of teams every day. And it's time to recognize a basic fact: teams are hard work, but they are worth it. The beauty of teams is accomplishing something far greater than what's possible for an individual alone. Indeed, two heads can be better than one. But the key word is *can*. While we all know that teams can be great, they're often not. How frequently have you heard someone declare "Too many cooks spoil the broth." or "A camel is an elephant put together by a committee."?

So let's start this discussion realistically. On one level there seems little to debate; groups and teams have a lot to offer organizations. But at another level, you have to sometimes wonder if the extra effort is really worth it. Teams can be more pain than gain. There's a lot to learn about them and about their roles in organizations if we are to participate in and help lead teams for real performance gains.[1]

• Teams offer synergy and other benefits to organizations and their members.

A **team** is a collection of people who regularly interact to pursue common goals.

Teamwork is the process of people actively working together to accomplish common goals.

Synergy is the creation of a whole greater than the sum of its individual parts.

A **team** is a small group of people with complementary skills who work together to accomplish shared goals while holding each other mutually accountable for performance results.[2] Teams are essential to organizations of all types and sizes. Many tasks are well beyond the capabilities of individuals alone.[3] And in this sense, **teamwork**, people actually working together to accomplish a shared goal, is a major high-performance asset.[4]

The term **synergy** means the creation of a whole that exceeds the sum of its parts. When teams perform well, it's because of synergy that pools many diverse talents and efforts to create extraordinary results. This is the force behind the great NASCAR pit crews described in the opening feature. It is also a key force in most, if not all, performance contexts.

Check research on success in the NBA. Scholars find that both good and bad basketball teams win more the longer the players have been together. Why? A "teamwork effect" creates wins because players know each other's moves and playing tendencies. Shift to the hospital operating room. Scholars notice an interesting pattern: the same heart surgeons had lower death rates for similar procedures performed in hospitals where the surgeons did more operations. Why? The researchers claim it's because the doctors had more time working together with the surgery teams—anesthesiologists, nurses, and other surgical technicians. They say it's not only the surgeon's skills that count; the skills of the team and the time spent working together count, too.[5]

Is there any doubt that teams can have a performance edge?[6] And don't forget—teams are good not only for organizations, but also for their members. Just as in life overall, being part of a work team or informal group can strongly influence our attitudes and behaviors. The personal relationships can help people do their jobs better—making contacts, sharing ideas, responding to favors, and bypassing roadblocks. And being part of a team often helps satisfy important needs that may be difficult to meet in the regular work setting or life overall. In teams one can find social relationships, a sense of security and belonging, and emotional support.

Why teams are good for organizations

- More resources for problem solving
- Improved creativity and innovation
- Improved quality of decision making
- Greater commitments to tasks
- Increased motivation of members
- Better control and work discipline
- More individual need satisfaction

• Teams often suffer from common performance problems.

Notwithstanding all this positive talk, however, we all know that working in groups isn't always easy or productive. Problems with teams not only happen; they are quite common.[7] One of the most troublesome is **social loafing**—the presence of one or more "free-riders" who slack off and allow other team members to do most of the work.[8] For whatever reason, perhaps in the absence of spotlight on personal performance, individuals sometimes work less hard, not harder, when they are part of a group.

What can you, as a team leader, do when someone is free-riding? You might take actions to make individual contributions more visible, reward individuals for their contributions, make task assignments more interesting, and keep group size small so that free-riders are more visible. This makes them more susceptible to pressures from peers and to critical leader evaluations. And if you've ever considered free-riding, think again. You may get away with it in the short term, but your reputation will suffer much longer.

Other common problems of teams include personality conflicts and differences in work styles that antagonize others and disrupt relationships and accomplishments. Sometimes group members withdraw from active participation due to uncertainty over tasks or battles about goals or competing visions. Ambiguous agendas or ill-defined problems can also cause fatigue and loss of motivation when teams work too long on the wrong things, having little to show for it.

Finally, not everyone is always ready to do group work. This might be due to lack of motivation, but it may also stem from conflicts with other work deadlines and priorities. Low enthusiasm for group work may also result from perceptions of poor team organization or progress, as well as by meetings that seem to lack purpose. These and other difficulties can easily turn the great potential of teams into frustration and failure.

Social loafing occurs in teams when some members slack off and allow others to do most of the work.

Social loafing is the tendency of some people to avoid responsibility by free-riding in groups.

• Organizations are networks of formal teams and informal groups.

A **formal team** is one that is officially designated for a specific organizational purpose. You'll find such teams described on organization charts and going by different labels—examples are *departments* (e.g., market research department), *work units* (e.g., audit unit), *teams* (e.g., customer service team), or *divisions* (e.g., office products division).

A **formal team** is officially recognized and supported by the organization.

Formal teams are headed by supervisors, managers, department heads, team leaders, and the like. Some people, in fact, describe organizations as interlocking networks of teams in which managers and leaders play "linking pin" roles.[9] This means that they serve both as head of one work team and as a subordinate member in the next-higher-level one. It's important to recognize, as shown in **Figure 15.1**, that managers play more than one role in groups and teams. Although

FIGURE 15.1
Some of the Roles Managers Play in Teams.

Supervisor

Network facilitator

Helpful participant

External coach

often serving as the supervisor or team leader, they also act as network facilitators, helpful participants, and external coaches.

The informal structure of an organization also consists of **informal groups**. They emerge from natural or spontaneous relationships among people. Some are *interest groups* whose members pursue a common cause, such as a women's career network. Some are *friendship groups* that develop for a wide variety of personal reasons, including shared hobbies and other nonwork interests. Others are *support groups* where members basically help one another do his or her job.

An **informal group** is unofficial and emerges from relationships and shared interests among members.

• Organizations use committees, task forces, and cross-functional teams.

You will find many types of formal teams and groups in organizations.[10] A **committee** brings together people outside of their daily job assignments to work in a small team for a specific purpose. The task agenda is specific and ongoing. For example, an organization may have standing committees for diversity and compensation.[11] A designated head or chairperson typically leads the committee and is held accountable for its performance.

A **committee** is designated to work on a special task on a continuing basis.

Project teams or **task forces** bring together people from various parts of an organization to work on common problems, but on a temporary rather than continuing basis. Project teams, for example, might be formed to develop a new product or service, redesign an office layout, or provide specialized consulting for a client.[12] A task force might be formed to address employee retention problems or come up with ideas for redesigning office space.[13]

The **cross-functional team** whose members come from different functional units is indispensable to organizations that emphasize adaptation and horizontal integration.[14] Members of cross-functional teams are supposed to work together on specific problems or tasks, sharing information and exploring new ideas. They are expected to help knock down the "walls" that otherwise separate departments and people in the organization. At Tom's of Maine, for example, the company uses "Acorn Groups"—symbolizing the fruits of the stately oak tree—to help launch new products. These groups bring together members of all departments to work on new ideas from concept to finished product. The goal is to minimize problems and maximize efficiency through cross-departmental cooperation.[15]

Another development is use of **employee involvement teams**. These groups of workers meet on a regular basis, with the goal of applying their expertise and attention to continuous improvement. A popular form of employee involvement team is the **quality circle**, a group of workers that meets regularly to discuss and plan specific ways to improve work quality.[16] After receiving special training in problem solving, team processes, and quality issues, members of the quality circle try to suggest ways to raise productivity through quality improvements.

A **project team** or **task force** is convened for a specific purpose and disbands after completing its task.

A **cross-functional team** operates with members who come from different functional units of an organization.

An **employee involvement team** meets on a regular basis to help achieve continuous improvement.

A **quality circle** is a team of employees who meet periodically to discuss ways of improving work quality.

Stay Tuned 🅱

Unproductive Meetings Are Major Time Wasters.

A Microsoft survey of some 38,000 workers around the world raises concerns about teamwork and productivity. The chief culprits are bad meetings, poor communication, and unclear goals.

- The average worker spends 5.6 hours per week in meetings.
- 69% of meetings attended are considered ineffective.
- 32% of workers complained about poor team communication and unclear objectives.
- 31% complained about unclear priorities.
- 29% complained about procrastination.

What Are Your Thoughts?

Do these data match with your experiences with team meetings? Given the common complaints about meetings, what can a team leader do to improve them? Think about the recent meetings you have attended; in what ways were the best meetings different from the worst ones?

• Virtual teams are increasingly common in organizations.

A vice president for human resources at Marriott once called electronic meetings "the quietest, least stressful, most productive meetings you've ever had."[17] She was talking about a type of group that is increasingly common in today's organizations: the **virtual team**.[18] This is a group of people who work together and solve problems through computer-mediated rather than face-to-face interactions. And, the constant emergence of new technologies is making virtual collaboration both easier and more common. At home it may be MySpace or Facebook; at the office it's likely to be Intranet discussion groups, editable Web sites called "wikis," and other online meeting resources.[19]

In terms of potential advantages, the virtual environment allows teamwork by people who may be located at great distances from one another. It offers cost and time efficiencies. And it can help reduce interpersonal problems that might otherwise occur when a team is dealing with controversial issues.[20] As you probably realize already from working in college study teams, virtual teamwork is also useful because it allows for online discussions to be archived along with any information shared among team members. This creates an easily accessible historical record of team activity and also provides a useful data bank that any team member can use when needed.

Virtual teams cut across physical distance as computers allow people to work together without being face-to-face.

Are there any downsides to virtual groups? For sure there can be problems, and often they occur for the same reasons as in other groups.[21] Members of virtual teams can have difficulties establishing good working relationships. The lack of face-to-face interaction limits the role of emotions and nonverbal cues in the communication process, perhaps depersonalizing relations among team members.[22] Yet as more people have experience in online forums, and with effort and sound management, teams working in virtual space rather than face-to-face are proving their performance potential.[23]

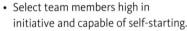

Tips to Remember
Steps to Successful Virtual Teams

- Select team members high in initiative and capable of self-starting.
- Select members who will join and engage the team with positive attitudes.
- Select members known for working hard to meet team goals.
- Begin with social messaging that allows members to exchange information about each other to personalize the process.
- Assign clear goals and roles so that members can focus while working alone and also know what others are doing.
- Gather regular feedback from members about how they think the team is doing and how it might do better.
- Provide regular feedback to team members about team accomplishments.

• Self-managing teams are a form of job enrichment for groups.

In a growing number of organizations, traditional work units consisting of first-level supervisors and their immediate subordinates are being replaced with **self-managing teams**. Sometimes called autonomous work groups, these are teams of workers whose jobs have been redesigned to create a high degree of task interdependence, and that have been given group authority to make many decisions about how they work.[24]

Self-managing teams operate with participative decision making, shared tasks, and responsibility for many of the managerial tasks performed by supervisors in more traditional settings. The "self-management" responsibilities include planning and scheduling work, training members in various tasks, distributing tasks, meeting performance goals, ensuring high quality, and solving day-to-day operating problems. In some settings the team's authority may even extend to "hiring" and "firing" its members when necessary. A key feature is multitasking, in which team members each have the skills to perform several different jobs.

Members of a **virtual team** work together and solve problems through computer-based interactions.

Members of a **self-managing team** have the authority to make decisions about how they share and complete their work.

FIGURE 15.2
What Are the Management Implications of Self-Managing Teams?

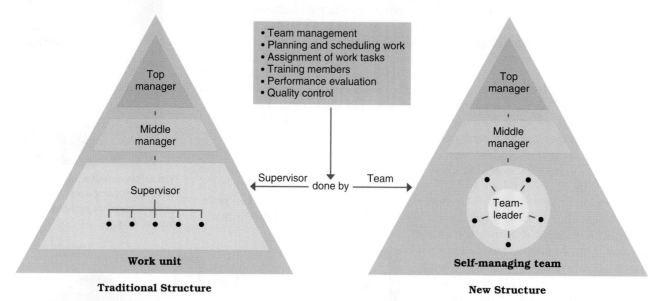

Members of self-managing teams make decisions together on team membership, task plans and job assignments, training and performance evaluations, and quality control. Because they essentially manage themselves in these ways, they no longer need a traditional supervisor or department head. Instead, the team leader performs this role with the support of team members. The team leader and team as a whole report to the next higher level of management and are held collectively accountable for performance results.

As shown in **Figure 15.2**, typical characteristics of self-managing teams are as follows:

- Members are held collectively accountable for performance results.
- Members have discretion in distributing tasks within the team.
- Members have discretion in scheduling work within the team.
- Members are able to perform more than one job on the team.
- Members train one another to develop multiple job skills.
- Members evaluate one another's performance contributions.
- Members are responsible for the total quality of team products.

Within a self-managing team the emphasis is always on participation. The leader and members are expected to jointly decide how the work gets done. A true self-managing team emphasizes team decision making, shared tasks, high involvement, and collective responsibility for accomplished results. The expected advantages include better performance, decreased costs, and higher morale. Of course, these results are not guaranteed. Managing the transition to self-managing teams from more traditional setups isn't always easy. The process requires leadership committed to both empowerment and a lot of support for those learning to work in new ways.

Study Guide

15.1
Why Is It Important to Understand Teams and Teamwork?

Rapid review

- A team consists of people with complimentary skills working together for shared goals and holding each other accountable for performance.
- Teams benefit organizations by providing for synergy that allows the accomplishment of tasks that are beyond individual capabilities alone.
- Social loafing and other problems can limit the performance of teams.
- Teams can suffer from social loafing when a member slacks off and lets others do the work.
- Organizations use a variety of committees, task forces, project teams, cross-functional teams, and virtual teams, all of which are increasingly common.
- Self-managing teams allow team members to perform many tasks previously done by supervisors, while virtual teams use computers to link members across time and space.

Terms to define

Committee

Cross-functional team

Employee involvement team

Formal team

Informal group

Project team

Quality circle

Self-managing team

Social loafing

Synergy

Task force

Team

Teamwork

Virtual team

Be sure you can

- define team and teamwork
- describe the roles managers play in teams
- explain the potential advantages and disadvantages of virtual teams
- explain synergy and the benefits of teams
- discuss social loafing and other potential problems of teams
- differentiate formal and informal groups
- explain how committees, task forces, and cross-functional teams operate
- describe potential problems faced by virtual teams
- list the characteristics of self-managing teams

Questions for discussion

1. Do committees and task forces do better work when they are given short deadlines?
2. Are there some things that should be done only by face-to-face teams, not virtual ones?
3. Why do people in groups often tolerate social loafers?

15.2 What Are the Building Blocks of Successful Teamwork?

So far we've really been talking about the types of teams in organizations. Now it's time to talk in more detail about the teamwork that can make them successful. Look at **Figure 15.3**. It diagrams a team as an open system that, like the organization itself, transforms a variety of inputs through teamwork into outputs.[25] It also shows that an **effective team** should be accomplishing three output goals—task performance, member satisfaction, and team viability.[26]

An **effective team** achieves high levels of task performance, membership satisfaction, and future viability.

FIGURE 15.3

What Are the Foundations of Team Effectiveness?

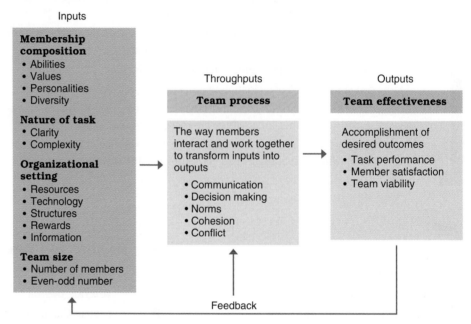

An effective team achieves high levels of task performance and member satisfaction, and remains viable for the future. The foundations of effectiveness begin with inputs—things such as membership composition, nature of the task, resources and support in the organizational setting, and team size. The foundations of effectiveness further rest with team process—how well the members utilize their talents and other inputs to create the desired outputs. Key process factors include stages of development, norms and cohesion, task and maintenance activities, communication, and decision making.

The first outcome of an effective team is a high *task performance*. When you are on a team, ask: Did we accomplish our tasks and meet expectations? The second outcome of an effective team is *member satisfaction*. Ask: Are we individually and collectively pleased with our participation in the process? The third outcome of an effective team is *viability for future action*. Ask: Can this team be successful again in the future?[27]

Procter & Gamble's former CEO A. G. Lafley says that team effectiveness comes together when you have "the right players in the right seats on the same bus, headed in the same direction."[28] The open systems model in Figure 14.3 shows that a team's effectiveness is influenced by inputs—"right players in the right seats," and by process—"on the same bus, headed in the same direction." You can remember the implications by this *Team Effectiveness Equation*.

Team effectiveness = Quality of inputs + (Process gains − Process losses)

• Teams need the right members and inputs to be effective.

The foundations for team effectiveness are set when a team is formed. The better the inputs, we can argue, the more likely that the team will achieve success. One of the most important inputs of any group is the nature of the membership. You can think of a team's **membership composition** as the mix of abilities, skills, backgrounds, and experiences. And for anyone creating a team, this raises one of the most important decisions to be made: Just who should be on the team?

In the ideal world, managers carefully form teams by choosing members whose talents and interests fit well with the job to be done. If you were in charge of a new team, wouldn't you want to select members this way? It's a good starting point, but some interesting research raises other issues in team membership as well. For example, it turns out that the most creative teams include a mix of experienced people and those who haven't worked together before.[29] The experienced members, or incumbents, have the connections; the newcomers add fresh thinking. Researchers also warn about risks when team members are too similar in background, training, and experience. Such teams tend to under-perform even though the members may feel very comfortable with one another.[30]

What are your experiences on this issue? Do you seem to get along better in teams whose members are pretty much all alike? Have you encountered problems on teams whose members are diverse and different from one another?

Another input that influences team effectiveness is the *nature of the task* itself. Clearly defined tasks make it easier for team members to combine their work efforts. Complex tasks require more information exchange and intense interaction than do simpler tasks. Think task complexity the next time you fly. And check out the ground crews. You should notice some similarities between them and teams handling pit stops for NASCAR racers. In fact, if you fly United Airlines there's a good chance the members of the ramp crews have been through "Pit Crew U." United is among many organizations that are sending employees to Pit Instruction & Training in Mooresville, North Carolina. At this facility, where real racing crews train, United's ramp workers learn to work intensely and under pressure while meeting the goals of teamwork, safety, and job preparedness. The goal is better teamwork to reduce aircraft delays and service inadequacies.[31]

Predictably, the *organizational setting* makes a difference. A key issue here is support—how well the organization supports

> **Membership composition** is the mix of abilities, skills, backgrounds, and experiences among team members.

Trendsetters

Amazon's Jeff Bezos Believes in Two-Pizza Teams.

Amazon.com's founder and CEO Jeff Bezos is a great fan of teams. But he also has a simple rule when it comes to sizing the firm's product development teams: "If two pizzas aren't enough to feed a team, it's too big."

Bezos wrote the business plan for Amazon while driving cross-country. He started the firm in his garage, and even when his Amazon stock grew to $500 million he was still driving a Honda and living in a small apartment in downtown Seattle. Clearly, he's a unique personality and also one with a great business mind. His goal with Amazon was to "create the world's most customer-centric company, the place where you can find and buy anything you want online."

If you go to Amazon.com and click on the "Gold Box" at the top, you'll be tuning in to his vision. It's a place for special deals, lasting only an hour and offering everything from a power tool to a new pair of shoes. Such online innovations don't just come out of the blue. They're part and parcel of the management philosophy Bezos has instilled at the firm.

The Gold Box and many of Amazon's successful innovations are products of "two-pizza teams." Described as "small," "fast-moving," and "innovation engines," these teams typically have 5–8 members and thrive on turning new ideas into business potential. These are teams that two pizzas can nicely feed.

Bezos views Amazon's two-pizza teams as a way of fighting bureaucracy and decentralizing, even as a company grows large and very complex. He is also a fan of what he calls fact-based decisions. He says they help to "overrule the hierarchy. The most junior person in the company can win an argument with the most senior person with fact-based decisions."

Don't expect to spot a stereotyped corporate CEO in Jeff Bezos. His standard office attire is still blue jeans and blue collared shirt. And, yes, he does live in an expensive house and probably drives more than one car. But a family friend describes him and his wife as "very playful people." Perhaps "playful" is another word for the two-pizza team, as long as its members also keep their eyes on keeping the business successful.

the team in terms of information, material resources, technology, organization structures, available rewards, and even physical space. Having support, as we have all probably experienced, can make a big difference in how well we perform in groups and individually.

Team size also makes a difference. Size affects how members work together, handle disagreements, and reach agreements. The number of potential interactions increases geometrically as teams increase in size, which congests communications. So how big should a team be? In general, teams larger than six or seven members can be difficult to manage for the purpose of creative problem solving. When voting is required, you should also remember that teams with odd numbers of members help to prevent ties. Amazon.com's founder and CEO Jeff Bezos is a great fan of teams. But he also has a simple rule when it comes to sizing the firm's product development teams: No team should be larger than two pizzas can feed.[32]

• Teams need the right processes to be effective.

Team process is the way team members work together to accomplish tasks.

Although having the right inputs available to a team is important, it does not guarantee effectiveness. **Team process** counts, too. This is the heart of teamwork—the way the members of any team actually work together as they transform inputs into outputs. Also called *group dynamics*, the process aspects of any group or team include how members get to know each other, develop expectations and loyalty, communicate, handle conflicts, and make decisions.

Again, don't forget the equation: Team effectiveness = Quality of inputs × (Process gains − Process losses). A positive process takes full advantage of group inputs and creates gains that raise team effectiveness. But any problems with group process can quickly drain energies and create losses that reduce effectiveness. This is what occurs, for example, when team members have difficulty managing diversity. When the internal dynamics fail in any way, team effectiveness can quickly suffer. Haven't you been on teams where people seemed to spend more time dealing with personality conflicts than with the task?

• Teams move through different stages of development.

A synthesis of research suggests that five distinct phases occur in the life cycle of any team.[33] Known as the stages of team development, they are:

1. *Forming*—a stage of initial orientation and interpersonal testing.
2. *Storming*—a stage of conflict over tasks and working as a team.
3. *Norming*—a stage of consolidation around task and operating agendas.
4. *Performing*—a stage of teamwork and focused task performance.
5. *Adjourning*—a stage of task completion and disengagement.

An effective team meets and masters key process challenges each step of the way as it moves through the five stages of development. One of these challenges is membership diversity. As shown in **Figure 15.4**, diverse teams often experience complications that can hurt effectiveness. But if they are well handled, membership diversity offers special opportunities that can improve long-term performance. Diverse teams expand the variety of talents, ideas, perspectives, and experiences available for problem solving.[34]

FIGURE 15.4
How Diversity Influences Performance During the Stages of Team Development.

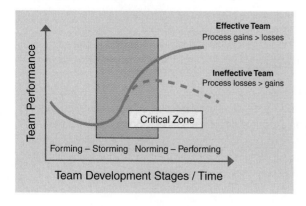

The *forming stage of team development* is one of initial task orientation and interpersonal testing. For example, new members likely ask: "What can or does the team offer me?" "What will they ask me to contribute?" "Can my efforts serve the task needs of the team while also meeting my needs?" In this stage, people begin to identify with other members and with the team itself. They focus on getting acquainted, establishing interpersonal relationships, discovering what is considered acceptable behavior, and learning how others perceive the team's task. Difficulties in the forming stage tend to be greater in more culturally and demographically diverse teams.

The *storming stage of team development* is a period of high emotionality. Tension often emerges between members over tasks and interpersonal concerns. There may be periods of conflict, outright hostility, and even infighting as individuals try to impose their preferences on others. But, with progress, this is also the stage where members clarify task agendas and begin to understand one another's interpersonal styles. Attention begins to shift toward obstacles that may impede task accomplishment; team members start looking for ways to meet team goals while also satisfying individual needs. The storming stage is part of a "critical zone" in team development where process failures cause lasting problems but process successes set the foundations for future effectiveness.

Cooperation is an important issue for teams in the *norming stage of team development*. At this point, members of the team begin to coordinate their efforts as a working unit and tend to operate with shared rules of conduct. The team feels a sense of leadership, with each member starting to play useful roles. Most interpersonal hostilities give way to a precarious balancing of forces as norming builds initial integration. Norming is also part of the critical zone. When this stage is well managed, team members are likely to develop initial feelings of closeness, a division of labor, and a sense of shared expectations. This helps protect the team from disintegration, while members continue their efforts to work well together.

Teams in the *performing stage of team development* are more mature, organized, and well functioning. This is a stage of total integration in which team members often creatively deal with both complex tasks and any interpersonal conflicts. The team operates with a clear and stable structure, members are motivated by team goals, and the team scores high on the criteria of team maturity shown in **Figure 15.5**.[35]

The storming stage of team development is a period of tension and high emotionality among members.

Self-Assessment

This is a good point to complete the self-assessment "*Team Leader Skills*" found on page 337.

FIGURE 15.5

Criteria for Assessing the Process Maturity of a Team.

	Very poor			Very good	
1. Trust among members	1	2	3	4	5
2. Feedback mechanisms	1	2	3	4	5
3. Open communications	1	2	3	4	5
4. Approach to decisions	1	2	3	4	5
5. Leadership sharing	1	2	3	4	5
6. Acceptance of goals	1	2	3	4	5
7. Valuing diversity	1	2	3	4	5
8. Member cohesiveness	1	2	3	4	5
9. Support for each other	1	2	3	4	5
10. Performance norms	1	2	3	4	5

The *adjourning stage of team development* is the final stage for temporary committees, task forces, and project teams. Here, team members prepare to achieve closure and disband, ideally with a sense that they have accomplished important goals. As you may have experienced yourself, after working intensely with others for a period of time, breaking up the close relationships actually can be quite emotional.

• Team performance is affected by norms and cohesiveness.

Have you ever felt pressure, subtle or not, from other group members when you do something wrong—come late to a meeting, fail to complete an assigned task, or act out of character? What you are experiencing is related to group **norms**, or behaviors expected of team members.[36] A norm is a rule or standard that guides behavior. When violated, team members are usually pressured to conform; in the extreme, violating a norm can result in expulsion from the group or social ostracism.

Any number of norms can be operating in a group at any given time. During the forming and storming stages of development, for example, norms often focus on expected attendance and levels of commitment. By the time the team reaches the performing stage, norms have formed around adaptability, change, and desired levels of achievement. And without doubt one of the most important norms for any team is the *performance norm*. It defines the level of work effort and performance that team members are expected to contribute.

Not surprisingly, teams with positive performance norms are likely to be more successful in accomplishing their tasks than those with negative performance norms. But how do you build teams with the right norms? Actually, there are a number of things leaders can and should do.[37]

- Act as a positive role model.
- Reinforce the desired behaviors with rewards.
- Control results by performance reviews and regular feedback.
- Train and orient new members to adopt desired behaviors.
- Recruit and select new members who exhibit the desired behaviors.
- Hold regular meetings to discuss progress and ways of improving.
- Use team decision-making methods to reach agreement.

Whether the team members will accept and conform to norms is largely determined by **cohesiveness**, the degree to which members are attracted to and motivated to remain part of a team.[38] Members of a highly cohesive team value their membership. They try to conform to norms and behave in ways that meet the expectations of other members, and they get satisfaction from doing so. In this way, at least, a highly cohesive team is good for its members. But does the same hold true for team performance?

Figure 15.6 shows that teams perform best when the performance norm is positive and cohesiveness is high. In this best-case scenario, cohesion results in conformity to the positive norm which ultimately benefits team performance. When the performance norm is negative in a cohesive team, however, high conformity to the norm creates a worst-case scenario. In this situation, members join together in restricting their efforts to perform.

What are the implications of this relationship between norms and cohesiveness? Basically it boils down to this: Each of us should be aware of what can be done to build both positive norms and high cohesiveness in our teams. In respect to cohesiveness, this means such things as keeping team size as small as possible, working to gain agreements on team goals, increasing interaction among members, rewarding team outcomes rather than individual performance, introducing competition with other teams, and putting together team members who are very similar to one another.

A **norm** is a behavior, rule, or standard expected to be followed by team members.

Cohesiveness is the degree to which members are attracted to and motivated to remain part of a team.

FIGURE 15.6
How Do Norms and Cohesiveness Influence Team Performance?

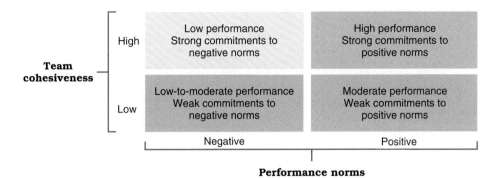

Group norms are expected behaviors for team members; cohesiveness is the strength of attraction members feel toward the team. When cohesiveness is high, conformity to norms is high. Positive performance norms in a highly cohesive group create a desirable situation, with high-performance outcomes likely. However, negative performance norms in a highly cohesive group can be troublesome; conformity by members to the negative norms creates low-performance outcomes.

• Team performance is affected by task and maintenance roles.

Research on the group process identifies two types of activities that are essential if team members are to work well together over time.[39] **Task activities** contribute directly to the team's performance purpose; **maintenance activities** support the emotional life of the team as an ongoing social system. Although you might expect that these are things that team leaders or managers should be doing, this is only partially correct. In fact, all team members should share the responsibilities for task and maintenance leadership.

The concept of **distributed leadership** in teams makes every member continually responsible for both recognizing when task or maintenance activities are needed and taking actions to provide them. Leading through task activities involves making an effort to define and solve problems and advance work toward performance results. Without the relevant task activities such as initiating agendas and sharing information, teams have difficulty accomplishing their objectives. Leading through maintenance activities, such as encouraging others and reducing tensions, helps strengthen and perpetuate the team as a social system.

Both task and maintenance activities stand in distinct contrast to the dysfunctional or **disruptive behaviors** that team leaders and effective members should avoid. These include obvious self-serving behaviors that you often see and perhaps even engage in yourself—things such as aggressiveness, excessive joking, and nonparticipation. Think about this the next time one of your groups is drifting in the direction of ineffectiveness.

A **task activity** is an action taken by a team member that directly contributes to the group's performance purpose.

A **maintenance activity** is an action taken by a team member that supports the emotional life of the group.

Distributed leadership is when any and all members contribute helpful task and maintenance activities to the team.

Disruptive behaviors are self-serving and cause problems for team effectiveness.

• Team performance is affected by use of communication networks.

Teams can use the different communication networks shown in **Figure 15.7** as they work and interact together.[40] In a **decentralized communication network**, all members communicate directly with one another. Sometimes called the *all-channel* or *star* structure, this arrangement works well for tasks that require lots of creativity, information processing, and problem solving. Use of a decentralized communication network creates an interacting team in which all members

A **decentralized communication network** allows all members to communicate directly with one another.

FIGURE 15.7
What Communication Networks Are Used in Teams?

Pattern	Diagram	Characteristics
Interacting Group Decentralized communication network		High interdependency around a common task Best at complex tasks
Coaching Group Centralized communication network		Independent individual efforts on behalf of common task Best at simple tasks
Counteracting Group Restricted communication network		Subgroups in disagreement with one another Slow task accomplishment

Members of teams communicate and interact together in different ways. A decentralized structure is where all members communicate with one another. It works best when tasks are complex and the need for information sharing is high. When tasks are simple and easily broken down into small parts, a centralized structure works well. It coordinates members' communications through one central point. A restricted communication network sometimes forms when subgroups break off to do separate work or due to member alienation. Any lack of communication between the subgroups can create performance problems.

actively work and share information with each other. The result is that member satisfaction on successful interacting teams is usually high.

When tasks are less demanding team members can often divide up the work and then simply coordinate the final results using a **centralized communication network**, sometimes called the *wheel* or *chain* structure. Its basic characteristic is the existence of a central "hub" through which one member, often the team leader, collects and distributes information among the other members. Most members of such coaching teams work independently and pass completed tasks to the hub member who pools them to create the finished product. The hub member often experiences the most satisfaction on successful coaching teams.

When teams break into subgroups, either on purpose or because members are experiencing issue-specific disagreements, the resulting interaction pattern may create a **restricted communication network**. Left unmanaged, this counteracting team environment can deteriorate to the point where subgroups fail to adequately communicate with one another and even engage in outwardly antagonistic relations. Although the poor communication characteristic of such situations often creates problems, there are times when counteracting teams might be intentionally set up to encourage conflict and help test out specific decisions or chosen courses of action.

In a **centralized communication network**, communication flows only between individual members and a hub or center point.

Subgroups in a **restricted communication network** contest each others' positions and restrict interactions with one another.

15.2
What Are the Building Blocks of Successful Teamwork?

Rapid review

- An effective team achieves high levels of task performance, member satisfaction, and team viability.
- Important team input factors include the membership characteristics, nature of the task, organizational setting, and group size.
- A team matures through various stages of development, including forming, storming, norming, performing, and adjourning.
- Norms are the standards or rules of conduct that influence the behavior of team members; cohesion is the attractiveness of the team to its members.
- In highly cohesive teams, members tend to conform to norms; the best situation for a manager or leader is a team with positive performance norms and high cohesiveness.
- Distributed leadership occurs when team members step in to provide helpful task and maintenance activities and discourage disruptive activities.
- Effective teams make use of alternative communication networks and decision-making methods to best complete tasks.

Terms to define

Centralized communication network

Cohesiveness

Disruptive behaviors

Distributed leadership

Effective team

Maintenance activity

Membership composition

Norm

Restricted communication network

Task activity

Team process

Be sure you can

- list the outputs of an effective team
- identify inputs that influence team effectiveness
- discuss how diversity influences team effectiveness
- list five stages of group development
- explain how norms and cohesion influence team performance
- list ways to build positive norms and to change cohesiveness
- illustrate task, maintenance, and disruptive activities in teams
- describe how groups use decentralized and centralized communication networks

Questions for discussion

1. What happens if a team can't get past the storming stage?
2. Why would a manager ever want to reduce the cohesion of a work group?
3. What can a manager do to increase the cohesiveness of a work team?

Characteristics of high-performance teams

- clear and elevating goals
- task-driven, results-oriented structure
- competent, hard-working members
- collaborative culture
- high standards of excellence
- external support and recognition
- strong, principled leadership

15.3 How Can Managers Create and Lead High-Performance Teams?

Whichever type of group or team we are talking about, and wherever in an organization it may be located, high-performance results can't be left to chance. Although we know that high-performance teams generally share the characteristics noted in the box, not all teams reach this level of excellence.[41] Just as in the world of sports, there are many things that can go wrong and cause problems for work teams.

• Team building helps team members learn to better work together.

One of the ways to build capacity for long-term team effectiveness is a practice known as **team building**. This is a set of planned activities used to analyze the functioning of a team, and then make constructive changes to increase its operating effectiveness.[42] Most systematic approaches to team building begin with awareness that a problem may exist or may develop within the team. Once aware of problems, members then work together to gather data and fully understand the problem. Action plans are made together and then are collectively implemented. Results are evaluated by team members working together. As difficulties or new problems are discovered, the team-building process recycles.

There are many ways to gather data on team functioning, including structured and unstructured interviews, questionnaires, and team meetings. Regardless of the method used, the basic principle of team building remains the same. The process requires a careful and collaborative assessment of the team's inputs, processes, and results. All members should participate in data gathering, assist in data analysis, and collectively decide on actions to be taken.

Sometimes teamwork can be improved when people share the challenges of unusual and even physically demanding experiences. On one fall day, for example, a team of employees from American Electric Power (AEP) went to an outdoor camp for a day of team-building activities. They worked on problems such as how to get six members through a spider-web maze of bungee cords strung two feet above the ground. When her colleagues lifted Judy Gallo into their hands to pass her over the obstacle, she was nervous. But a trainer told the team this was just like solving a problem together at the office. The spider web was just another performance constraint, like the difficult policy issues or

News Feed

Reality TV Rubs Off on "Reality Team Building"

Chances are that while you have probably tuned in to one of the many TV reality shows, you couldn't imagine actually being on one. But get ready, your next corporate training stop may be reality based. It seems some organizations are finding the "reality" notion is a great way to accomplish team building and drive innovation.

Best Buy gave employees a chance to prove their own business ideas, sending small teams to live together for 10 weeks in Los Angeles apartments. The purpose was to prove out new ideas and lay the groundwork for new lines of business as well as potential independent businesses. One of the ideas was for Best Buy Studio, a new venture serving small businesses with web design services and consulting. Jeremy Sevush came up with the idea, and with support from his team was able to implement it shortly after moving out of the apartment. He says: "Living together and knowing we only had 10 weeks sped up our team-building process."

John Wolpert runs the program for Best Buy from his consulting firm UpStart™. He claims: "There's something magical about taking smart people out of their safety zones and making them spend night and day together."

Some call the reality team building experiences "extreme brainstorming," and it seems to fit today's generation of workers. In a program called Real Whirled, small teams from Whirlpool live together for seven weeks while using the company's appliances. IBM has a program called Extreme Blue to incubate new business ideas.

Reflect and React:

Are Best Buy, Whirlpool, and IBM on to something with the notion of reality team building? Using their ideas, can you design a "mini" reality team-building experience that might add value to the operation of a local store or business? How could team building be used in the academic setting to make the typical college course something really innovative?

financial limits they might face at work. After "high-fives" for making it through the web, Judy's team jumped tree stumps together, passed hula hoops while holding hands, and more. Says one team trainer, "We throw clients into situations to try and bring out the traits of a good team."[43]

Team building is a set of collaborative activities to gather and analyze data on a team and make changes to increase its effectiveness.

• Team performance is affected by use of decision-making methods.

The best teams don't limit themselves to just one **decision-making** method. In true contingency-management fashion, they choose and use methods that best fit the problems at hand.[44] Edgar Schein, a respected scholar and consultant, describes how teams can make decisions by at least six different methods.[45]

In *decision by lack of response*, one idea after another is suggested without any discussion taking place. When the team finally accepts an idea, all alternatives have been bypassed and discarded by simple lack of response rather than by critical evaluation. In *decision by authority rule*, the leader, manager, committee head, or some other authority figure makes a decision for the team. Although time efficient, the quality of the decision depends on whether the authority figure has the necessary information; its implementation depends on how well other team members accept the top-down approach. In *decision by minority rule*, two or three people dominate or "railroad" the team into making a mutually agreeable decision. How often have you heard: "Does anyone object? Okay, let's go ahead with it."

One of the most common ways teams make decisions, especially when early signs of disagreement arise, is *decision by majority rule*. This method is consistent with a democratic political system, but is often used without awareness of its potential problems. The very process of voting can create coalitions; that is, some people will be "winners" and others will be "losers." In all likelihood, you've been on the losing side at times. How did it feel? If you're like me, it may have made you feel left out, unenthusiastic about supporting the majority decision, and even hoping for a future chance to win.

Teams are often encouraged to try for *decision by* **consensus**. This is where full discussion leads to most members favoring one alternative, with the other members agreeing to support it. After reaching a consensus, even those who may have opposed the decision know that the other team members listened to their concerns. Consensus doesn't require unanimity, but it does require that team members are able to argue, engage in reasonable conflict, and still get along with and respect one another.[46]

A *decision by unanimity* may be the ideal state of affairs. Here, all team members agree on the course of action to take. This is a logically perfect method for decision making in teams, but it is also extremely difficult to attain in actual practice. One of the reasons that teams sometimes turn to authority decisions, majority voting, or even minority decisions is the difficulty of managing the team process to achieve consensus or unanimity.

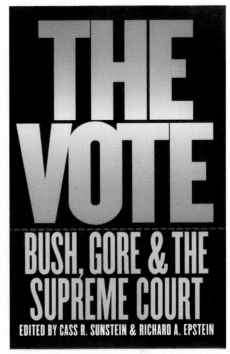

Decision by majority rule can create groups of "winners" and "losers" that have trouble working well together.

Decision making is the process of making choices among alternative courses of action.

Consensus is reached when all parties believe they have had their say and been listened to, and agree to support the group's final decision.

• Team performance suffers when groupthink leads to bad decisions.

How often have you held back stating your views in a meeting, agreed to someone else's position when it really seemed wrong, or went along with a boss's suggestions even though you disagreed?[47] If and when you do these things, you are likely involved in **groupthink**, the tendency for members of highly cohesive groups to lose their critical evaluative capabilities.[48] It tends to occur when teams strive for consensus or unanimity, seeking agreements and trying to avoid disagreements.[49]

Psychologist Irving Janis ties a variety of well-known historical blunders to groupthink, including the lack of preparedness of U.S. naval forces for the Japanese

Groupthink is a tendency for highly cohesive teams to lose their evaluative capabilities.

TABLE 15.1

Symptoms of Groupthink

Illusions of invulnerability—Members assume that the team is too good for criticism or beyond attack.

Rationalizing unpleasant and disconfirming data—Members refuse to accept contradictory data or to thoroughly consider alternatives.

Belief in inherent group morality—Members act as though the group is inherently right and above reproach.

Stereotyping competitors as weak, evil, and stupid—Members refuse to look realistically at other groups.

Applying direct pressure to deviants to conform to group wishes—Members refuse to tolerate anyone who suggests the team may be wrong.

Self-censorship by members—Members refuse to communicate personal concerns to the whole team.

Illusions of unanimity—Members accept consensus prematurely, without testing its completeness.

Mind guarding—Members protect the team from hearing disturbing ideas or outside viewpoints.

attack on Pearl Harbor, the Bay of Pigs invasion under President Kennedy, and the many roads that led to U.S. involvement in Vietnam. In all likelihood, it is present all too often, in any team, at any level, in all sorts of organizations.

Teams experiencing groupthink often display the behaviors such as those shown in **Table 15.1**—*Symptoms of Groupthink*. They act this way because they want to avoid doing anything that might detract from feelings of goodwill—including raising critical questions about a suggested course of action. But when everyone publicly agrees with a suggestion while privately having serious doubts about it, groupthink occurs. The result is often a bad decision.

When and if you encounter groupthink or believe your group is headed in that direction, Janis suggests a number of things leaders might do to avoid or minimize the groupthink effects. These include assigning one member to act as a critical evaluator or "devil's advocate" during each meeting; creating subteams to work on the same issues and then share their findings; bringing in outsiders to offer viewpoints on group processes and decisions; holding a "second chance" meeting after an initial decision is made; and being purposely absent from some meetings to let the group deliberate on its own.

• Special techniques can increase creativity in team decision making.

Among the potential benefits that teams can bring to organizations is increased creativity. Two techniques that are particularly helpful for tapping creativity in group decision making are brainstorming and the nominal group technique.[50] Both can now be pursued in computer-mediated or virtual team discussions, as well as in face-to-face formats.

In **brainstorming**, teams of 5 to 10 members meet to generate ideas. Brainstorming teams typically operate within these guidelines: All criticism is ruled out—judgment or evaluation of ideas must be withheld until the idea-generation process has been completed. "Freewheeling" is welcomed—the wilder or more radical the idea, the better. Quantity is important—the greater the number of ideas, the greater the likelihood of obtaining a superior idea. Building on one another's ideas is encouraged—participants should suggest how ideas of others can be turned into better ideas, or how two or more ideas can be joined into still another hybrid idea.

Brainstorming engages group members in an open, spontaneous discussion of problems and ideas.

By prohibiting criticism, the brainstorming method reduces fears of ridicule or failure on the part of individuals. Ideally, this results in more enthusiasm, involvement, and a freer flow of ideas among members. But there are times when team members have very different opinions and goals. The differences may be so extreme that a brainstorming meeting might deteriorate into antagonistic arguments and harmful conflicts.

The **nominal group technique** structures interaction among team members discussing problems and ideas.

When brainstorming doesn't work, a **nominal group technique** could help. This approach uses a highly structured meeting agenda to allow everyone to contribute ideas without the interference of evaluative comments by others. Participants are first asked to work alone and respond in writing with possible solutions to a stated problem. Ideas are then shared in round-robin fashion without any criticism or discussion; all ideas are recorded as they are presented. Ideas are next discussed and clarified in round-robin sequence, with no evaluative comments allowed. Next, members individually and silently follow a written voting procedure that allows for all alternatives to be rated or ranked in priority order. Finally, the last two steps are repeated as needed to further clarify the process.

Study Guide

15.3
How Can Managers Create and Lead High-Performance Teams?

Rapid review

- Team building is a collaborative approach to improving group process and performance.
- Teams can make decisions by lack of response, authority rule, minority rule, majority rule, consensus, and unanimity.
- Although group decisions often make more information available for problem solving and generating more understanding and commitment, the potential liabilities of group decision making include social pressures to conform and greater time requirements.
- Groupthink is a tendency of members of highly cohesive teams to lose their critical evaluative capabilities and make poor decisions.
- Techniques for improving creativity in teams include brainstorming and the nominal group technique.

Terms to define

Brainstorming

Consensus

Decision making

Groupthink

Nominal group technique

Team building

Be sure you can

- describe the typical steps in the team-building process
- list and discuss the different ways groups make decisions
- define the term groupthink and identify its symptoms
- list at least four symptoms of groupthink
- explain how brainstorming and the nominal group techniques can improve creativity

Questions for discussion

1. Is team building for everyone?
2. How does consensus differ from unanimity in group decision making?
3. Is groupthink found only in highly cohesive teams, or could it exist in pre-cohesive ones?

Multiple choice

1. When a group of people is able to achieve more than what its members could by working individually, this is called _____.
   (a) distributed leadership
   (b) consensus
   (c) team viability
   (d) synergy

2. A "quality circle" is an example of how organizations try to use _____ groups for performance advantage.
   (a) virtual
   (b) informal
   (c) employee involvement
   (d) self-managing

3. An effective team is defined as one that achieves high levels of task performance, member satisfaction, and _____.
   (a) resource efficiency
   (b) team viability
   (c) group consensus
   (d) creativity

4. In the open-systems model of teams, the _____ is an important input factor.
   (a) communication network
   (b) decision-making method
   (c) performance norm
   (d) diversity of membership

5. A basic rule of team dynamics might be stated this way: The greater the _____ in a team, the greater the conformity to norms.
   (a) membership diversity
   (b) cohesiveness
   (c) task clarity
   (d) competition among members

6. Groupthink is most likely to occur in teams that are _____.
   (a) large in size
   (b) diverse in membership
   (c) high performing
   (d) highly cohesive

7. A team performing very creative and unstructured tasks is most likely to succeed using _____.
   (a) a decentralized communication network
   (b) decisions by majority rule
   (c) decisions by minority rule
   (d) more task than maintenance activities

8. Members of a team tend to become more motivated and better able to deal with conflict during the _____ stage of team development.
   (a) forming
   (b) norming
   (c) performing
   (d) adjourning

9. A _____ decision is one in which all members agree on the course of action to be taken.
   (a) consensus
   (b) unanimous
   (c) majority
   (d) synergy

10. The best way to try and increase the cohesiveness of a team would be to _____.
    (a) start competition with other groups
    (b) add more members
    (c) reduce isolation from other groups
    (d) increase the heterogeneity of members

11. Members of a team tend to start to get coordinated and comfortable with one another in the _____ stage of team development.
    (a) forming   (b) norming
    (c) performing   (d) adjourning

12. One way for a manager to build positive norms within a team is to _____.
    (a) act as a positive role model
    (b) increase group size
    (c) introduce groupthink
    (d) isolate the team

13. The team effectiveness equation states the following: team effectiveness = quality of inputs + (_____ − process losses).
    (a) process gains
    (b) leadership impact
    (c) membership ability
    (d) problem complexity

14. A team member who does a good job at summarizing discussion, offering new ideas, and clarifying points made by others is providing leadership by contributing _____ activities to the group process.
    (a) required
    (b) task
    (c) disruptive
    (d) maintenance

15. When a group member engages in social loafing, one of the recommended strategies for dealing with this situation is to _____.

    (a) redefine tasks to make individual contributions more visible

    (b) ask another member to force this person to work harder

    (c) give the person extra rewards and hope he or she will feel guilty

    (d) forget about it

Short response

16. What are the major differences among a task force, employee involvement group, and a self-managing team?

17. How can a manager influence team performance by modifying group inputs?

18. How do cohesiveness and performance norms together influence team performance?

19. What are two symptoms, and two possible remedies, of groupthink?

Integration & application

20. Mariel Espinoza has just been appointed manager of a production team operating the 11 PM to 7 AM shift in a large manufacturing firm. An experienced manager, Mariel is pleased that the team members seem to really like and get along well with one another, but she notices that they also appear to be restricting their task outputs to the minimum acceptable levels.

    Questions: How might Mariel improve this situation?

Self-Assessment

Team Leader Skills

Instructions

Consider your experiences in groups and work teams. Ask: "What skills do I bring to team leadership situations?" Then, complete the following inventory by rating yourself on each item using this scale.[51]

1 = Almost never, 2 = Seldom, 3 = Sometimes,
4 = Usually, 5 = Almost always

_____ 1. I facilitate communications with and among team members between team meetings.

_____ 2. I provide feedback/coaching to individual team members on their performance.

_____ 3. I encourage creative and out-of-the-box thinking.

_____ 4. I continue to clarify stakeholder needs/expectations.

_____ 5. I keep team members' responsibilities and activities focused within the team's objectives and goals.

_____ 6. I organize and run effective and productive team meetings.

_____ 7. I demonstrate integrity and personal commitment.

_____ 8. I have excellent persuasive and influence skills.

_____ 9. I respect and leverage the team's cross-functional diversity.

_____ 10. I recognize and reward individual contributions to team performance.

_____ 11. I use the appropriate decision-making style for specific issues.

_____ 12. I facilitate and encourage border management with the team's key stakeholders.

_____ 13. I ensure that the team meets its team commitments.

_____ 14. I bring team issues and problems to the team's attention and focus on constructive problem solving.

_____ 15. I provide a clear vision and direction for the team.

Scoring and Interpretation

Add your scores for the items listed next to each dimension below to get an indication of your potential strengths and weaknesses on seven dimensions of team leadership. The higher the score, the more confident you are on the particular skill and leadership capability. When considering the score, ask yourself if others would rate you the same way.

1,9	Building the Team
2,10	Developing People
3,11	Team Problem Solving/Decision Making
4,12	Stakeholder Relations
5,13	Team Performance
6,14	Team Process
7,8,15	Providing Personal Leadership

 For further exploration go to WileyPlus

Case Snapshot

NASCAR—Fast Cars, Passion, and Teamwork Create Wins.

By only his second full year of NASCAR Winston Cup Series racing, the young Ryan Newman was rapidly becoming a racing phenomenon. He has since had spectacular consecutive racing seasons, including winning the Daytona 500. What accounts for the success of a top NASCAR driver?

Online Interactive Learning Resources

SELF-ASSESSMENT
• Team Contributions

EXPERIENTIAL EXERCISES
• After Meeting Project Review
• Work Team Dynamics

TEAM PROJECT
• Superstars on the Team

16
Conflict and Negotiation

Working Together Isn't Always Easy

Not even the folks at National Public Radio are immune to conflict. Yes, that's right, even at NPR, what *Fast Company* magazine calls "the country's brainiest, brawniest news-gathering giant," there can be a fair amount of conflict behind the scenes as NPR central and its member stations try to work together. And that's precisely what new CEO Vivian Schiller knows she has to master.

Money, of course, is the crux of the matter. NPR itself doesn't broadcast anything; it produces several shows such as *Morning Edition* and *All Things Considered*. These are sent to local stations that combine them with local programming for their audiences. The nonprofit member stations survive through donations, while paying dues and fees to NPR for rights of affiliation and use of the national shows.

The problem is that just about anyone can access NPR content over the Internet; there's even an NPR app for iPhones. In one month alone NPR had 14 million Podcast downloads. And if you can get programs through NPR's Web site, you don't need to listen to and support the local channel. Right?

Trendsetters
UN Secretary General Ban Ki-Moon pursues world peace.

News Feed
Bloggers' rights a growing point of conflict

Case Snapshot
AFL-CIO: Managing dissent while supporting labor

One of NPR's own commentators, Paul Farhi describes the problem this way: "If I'm running a station in Chapel Hill or Bloomington, I pay dues to NPR to get marquee programming that brings people to my station . . . I don't care about your digital initiative. . . . You're siphoning my dues to build your national brand. That's the essence of the conflict."

With experience at five other major media organizations, most recently the NYTimes.com and previously Discovery Channel, CNN, and TBS, Schiller is confident as CEO. She talks not about conflict and NPR being viewed as a "competitor" to the local stations, but about "opportunity" and says her job is to "figure out a way to work together so that people in every community who go to their local NPR–member station sites can get the benefit of NPR's international, national, and local coverage in a seamless experience." But her task is going to be challenging; there's a lot to be worked out in the NPR–member station relationships. At KCRW in Los Angeles, general manager Ruth Seymour says: "There is hope on NPR's part that somehow we can work collaboratively online. I am truly dubious about it. In online, everybody is competitive with everybody else."

16.1 What Should We Know about Dealing with Conflict?

Conflict is a disagreement over issues of substance and/or an emotional antagonism.

Substantive conflict involves disagreements over goals, resources, rewards, policies, procedures, and job assignments.

Emotional conflict results from feelings of anger, distrust, dislike, fear, and resentment as well as from personality clashes.

The opening vignette of National Public Radio and Vivian Schiller's challenges as its new CEO is just another example of a common fact of organizational life—conflict. Among your interpersonal, team, and leadership skills, the ability to deal with conflicts is critical. Managers spend a lot of time dealing with it, just as we do in everyday life. But *conflict* is one of those words like *communication* or *power*. We use it a lot, but rarely think it through to the specifics.

In management, the term **conflict** refers to disagreements among people. And in our experiences, it can emerge or form around two quite different types of issues—substantive and emotional.[1]

News Feed

Bloggers' Rights a Growing Point of Conflict

It is easy and tempting to set up your own blog, write about your experiences and impressions, and then share your thoughts with others online. So, why not do it? Catherine Sanderson, a British citizen living and working in Paris, might have asked this question before launching her blog, Le Petite Anglaise. At one point it was so "successful" that she had 3,000 readers. But the Internet diary included reports on her experiences at work—and her employer, the accounting firm Dixon Wilson, wasn't at all happy when it became public knowledge.

Even though Sanderson was blogging anonymously, her photo was on the site, and the connection was eventually discovered. Noticed, too, was her running commentary about bosses, colleagues, and life at the office. One boss, she wrote, "calls secretaries 'typists.'" A Christmas party was described in detail, including an executive's "unforgivable faux pas." Under the heading "Titillation," she told how she displayed cleavage during a video conference at the office.

It's all out now. News reports said that one of the firm's partners was "incandescent with rage" after learning what Sanderson had written about him. Now Sanderson is upset. She says that she was "dooced"—a term used to describe being fired for what one writes in a blog. She wants financial damages and confirmation of her rights, on principle, to have a private blog.

Reflect and React:

What are bloggers' rights? Suppose in your spare time you write an anonymous blog about life "inside" your organization. Would you expect anything less than termination upon discovery? Who has what rights when it comes to communicating in public about one's work experiences and impressions?

• Conflicts can occur over substantive or emotional issues.

When Paul Michaels became CEO of Mars Inc., the large candy maker, he decided to tackle the problem of a lack of teamwork among the top managers. His approach was to remind them of the company value—efficiency, and then put them into a two-day team building retreat. Reports are that there were "heated discussions about what they needed to accomplish, who was responsible for what and who had the authority to make what decisions."[2] This is an example of **substantive conflict**. They often involve disagreements over such things as goals and tasks; the allocation of resources; the distribution of rewards, policies, and procedures; and job assignments. You are in a substantive conflict with someone when, for example, each of you wants to solve a problem by following a different strategy.

Those managers attending the Mars team building retreat had more than pure substance issues on their minds. With one another they brought up "unacceptable interpersonal behavior," "riding roughshod over others," and "backbiting and subterfuge." These clashes entered into the realm of **emotional conflict**. These conflicts result from feelings of anger, distrust, dislike, fear, and resentment, as well as relationship problems. You know this form of conflict as a clash of personalities or emotions, when you don't want to agree with another person just because you don't like or are angry with him.

What do you think will happen at NPR as CEO Schiller works to blend the multiple interests and agendas of the national organization with those of its member stations? My guess is that the conflict will be both substantive and emotional. And when the two get intertwined, it gets very complicated and difficult to resolve the conflicts.

Most people encounter substantive and emotional conflicts almost every day. Many are minor and pass quickly; others are more major, perhaps very upsetting and even consuming enormous amounts of our time and energies. But we shouldn't fear these conflicts. Rather, we really need to understand and learn how to best deal with them.

In fact, not all conflict is bad, and the absence of conflict isn't always good. As the saying goes, a smooth ride isn't always the best ride; the absence of conflict can sometimes be a signal that something is wrong. Can you imagine yourself in a managerial situation where you need to create conflict, not reduce it?

• Conflicts can be both functional and dysfunctional.

Take a look at **Figure 16.1**. It shows the inverted U curve of the conflict intensity and performance relationship. Notice that although conflict at the extremes is harmful, conflict in the middle region is beneficial.

FIGURE 16.1

What Is the Relationship Between Conflict Intensity and Performance?

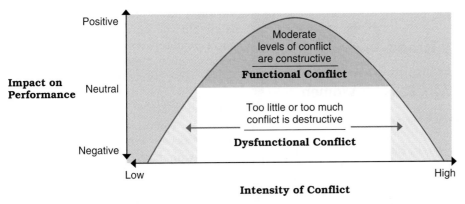

This U curve indicates that there are two sides to the conflict-performance relationship—a positive side and a negative one. When conflict occurs at moderate levels, creating tension but not overwhelming us, it can often lead to increased performance. By contrast, too little conflict (no tension) or too much conflict (extraordinary tension) can lead to lower performance.

Conflict of moderate intensity can be constructive, offering the potential to actually improve performance. This **functional conflict** stimulates us toward greater work efforts, more creativity in problem solving, and even to cooperate more with others. It helps keep things in check, and to make sure that alternatives are carefully considered in decision making, and often provides the creative edge that makes the difference between "okay" and "really great" performance.

We know the destructive side of conflict as well. You probably recognize **dysfunctional conflict** best when it overloads you physically or mentally, making it hard to concentrate or make real progress on goals. Perhaps you've been in groups where a few people get into emotional conflicts that seem never ending. Their intensity spills over to affect everyone, making it harder to work together and even creating tendencies for the group to just do the bare minimum to get by.

Functional conflict is constructive and helps boost task performance.

Dysfunctional conflict is destructive and hurts task performance.

TABLE 16.1

Causes of Conflicts in Organizations

Role ambiguities—when people aren't sure what they are supposed to do, conflict with others is likely; task uncertainties increase odds of working at cross-purposes at least some of the time.

Resource scarcities—When people have to share resources with one another and/or when they have to compete with one another for resources, the conditions are ripe for conflict.

Task interdependencies—When people must depend on others doing things first before they can do their own jobs, conflicts often occur; dependency on others creates anxieties and other pressures.

Competing objectives—When people work on objectives that are competing, conflict is a natural byproduct; win-lose conditions pit people against one another.

Structural differentiation—When people work in parts of the organization where structures, goals, time horizons, and even staff compositions are very different, conflict is likely with other units.

Unresolved prior conflicts—When conflicts go unresolved, they remain latent and often reemerge in the future as the basis for conflicts over the same or related matters.

Stay Tuned 🅱

Work-Family Conflict Rises for Men, Falls for Women.

The Families and Work Institute published a report on a long-term study of 3,500 workers. Ellen Galinsky, the institute's president, says the findings show a "revolutionary change in attitudes and behaviors among both women and men." One implication is the need for more flexible work arrangements and support for work-life conflicts. Some study findings are:

- 45% of men report work-family conflict vs. 39% of women; in 1977 the figure was 34% for both.
- 31% of women say their husbands do ≥50% of child care vs. 21% in 1992.
- 2/3 of men under the age of 29 say they want more job responsibility.
- 69% of working mothers under the age of 29 want to move up the career ladder vs. 66% of women without children; in 2002 the figures were 48% for young working mothers and 61% for those without children.
- 44% of income in dual-career families is provided by women vs. 39% in 1997.

What Are Your Thoughts?

Knowing yourself, your friends, and your classmates, are these data representative of what you would expect? Projecting this study ahead another 10 years, what major changes in the data would you expect? What are the implications of these trends and issues for your career and personal life?

But remember, again, that too little conflict also can be dysfunctional. Perhaps this has happened to you in teams where nobody wanted to disagree with a suggestion that, if you admitted it, just wasn't very good. This lack of substantive conflict can cause groupthink, promote complacency, and result in the loss of a creative, high-performance edge.

• Organizations have many sources of potential conflict.

As **Table 16.1**—*Causes of Conflicts in Organizations* shows, the workplace is a natural home for conflict. Its sources rest with role ambiguities, resource scarcities, task interdependencies, and more. Even unresolved prior conflicts are breeding grounds for more conflict in the future. And the types of conflicts that can involve us are also many and varied. Some of the conflicts are internal ones where we own all or part of the conflict experience. Others are due in large part to our group memberships, or roles in the organization structure.

Do you recognize when you are experiencing *intrapersonal conflicts?* These are conflicts caused by incompatible goals or expectations, and they commonly appear in three forms. *Approach–approach conflict* occurs when a person must choose between two positive and equally attractive alternatives—perhaps a job transfer to another city versus having a network of close friends and family in the current location. *Avoidance–avoidance conflict* occurs when a person must choose between equally unattractive alternatives. For example, you might one day face either losing your job or accepting a job transfer to a faraway town. *Approach–avoidance conflict* occurs when a person faces a choice with both positive and negative aspects, such as taking a higher-paying job that will require excessive work that is bound to interfere with family time.

Of course you're familiar with the dynamics and anxieties caused by *interpersonal conflict* between individuals. Sometimes these are substantive, such as disagreements between supervisors and subordinates over a performance evaluation. Other times they are purely emotional, resting with personality differences.

The same possibilities evidence themselves as *intergroup conflict* that occurs between representatives of different groups. For example, can you imagine the conflict between members of the marketing department, who want to quickly satisfy a customer's order, and those in manufacturing, who decide to delay the order because of other priorities? How would you, as a manager, work to resolve this issue? It might be addressed by creating cross-functional teams and task forces for interdepartmental coordination, or seeking greater integration through a team or matrix organization structure.

Finally, if we look at the organization as a whole, we can often spot *inter-organizational conflict* that takes place between organizations. These are the conflicts senior executives have to deal with as they manage the boundary relationships between their organizations and the external environment. For example, conflict may develop between business firms and outside regulators or consumer advocacy groups, between labor unions and the employers of their members, and even between nations.

• People use different interpersonal conflict management styles.

With all this potential for conflict in and around organizations, how do people deal with it? Interpersonally, people respond to conflict through different combinations of cooperative and assertive behaviors.[3]

Think about how you tend to behave when in conflict with someone else. In terms of *cooperativeness*, do you often try to satisfy the other person's needs and concerns? Or are you uncooperative? In terms of *assertiveness*, do you act assertively to satisfy your own needs and concerns? Or are you nonassertive when facing conflict? **Figure 16.2** shows that different combinations of cooperative and assertive behaviors result in five conflict management styles—avoidance, accommodation, competition, compromise, and collaboration.[4]

In **avoidance**, everyone withdraws and pretends that conflict doesn't really exist, hoping that it will simply go away. You might think of this as two roommates angry over a large late fee for a video rental and each unwilling to mention it to the other. **Accommodation** plays down differences and highlights

Avoidance pretends that a conflict doesn't really exist.

Accommodation or smoothing plays down differences and highlights similarities to reduce conflict.

FIGURE 16.2
What Are the Five Common Styles of Interpersonal Conflict Management?

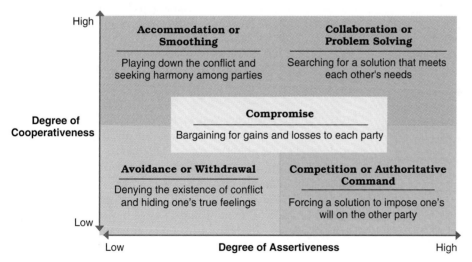

In interpersonal conflict situations, a combination of cooperative and aggressive behaviors results in five possible conflict management styles. Competition occurs when aggression dominates our behavior and accommodation occurs when cooperation dominates. Avoidance occurs with both low aggression and cooperation, whereas compromise occurs with moderate amounts of both. When both cooperation and aggression are high, true collaboration and problem solving are more likely to occur.

similarities and areas of agreement. Peaceful coexistence through recognition of common interests is the goal even though the real cause for the conflict doesn't get addressed. In our example, the roommates might agree to split the late fee but still not determine who was at fault and why, so that the problem can be avoided in the future. Both avoidance and accommodation are forms of **lose-lose conflict** in the sense that no one achieves her or his true desires, and the underlying conflict remains unresolved, often to recur in the future.

In **competition**, one party wins through superior skill or outright domination. Although the first example that may come to mind is sports and second most likely some form of physical contest, competition is common in management. It occurs here as authoritative command, where a higher-level supervisor simply dictates to subordinates what will happen in a conflict situation. **Compromise** occurs through trade-offs, where each party to the conflict gives up and gains something of value. An example here is a union-management negotiation where each party to a conflict over wages gives in bit by bit until a point is reached that both can agree upon. Competition and compromise are forms of **win-lose conflict** where each party strives to gain at the other's expense. But whenever one party loses something, it tends not to go away; the antecedents are put into place for future conflicts.

Unlike the prior methods, **collaboration** tries to find and address the problem and reconcile the real differences underlying a conflict. As you would expect, it is often time-consuming and stressful. But, it's also the most effective conflict management style in terms of real conflict resolution. Collaboration turns a difficult situation into a **win-win conflict**, where things are resolved to everyone's mutual benefit—no avoiding, no smoothing, no domination, and no compromising; a real agreement is reached. From experience you should recognize that this approach to conflict depends on the willingness of all parties to dig in, confront the issues, and openly and honestly discuss them. When it works, such collaboration eliminates the underlying causes of a conflict and creates real win-win outcomes.

The small box is a reminder that each of the five conflict management styles can be useful.[5] Most of us probably use each at least some of the time. But we should make good choices, being sure to fit our style to the requirements of each unique conflict situation. It's also worth remembering that unresolved or suppressed conflicts often sow the seeds for future conflicts. Only true **conflict resolution**, characteristic of the collaborative style, eliminates the underlying causes of a conflict in ways that should prevent similar conflicts in the future.

• Structural approaches can help deal with conflicts in organizations.

Most managers will tell you that not all conflict management in groups and organizations can be resolved at the interpersonal level. Think about it. Aren't there likely to be times when personalities and emotions prove irreconcilable? In such cases a structural approach to conflict management can often help.

Take the case of conflict that really traces to a resource issue—someone or some group doesn't have enough, or two parties have to share from a common pool. The structural solution is to *make more resources available* to everyone. Although costly and not always possible, this is a straightforward way to resolve resource-driven conflicts.

When people are stuck in conflict and just can't seem to appreciate one another's points of view, *appealing to higher-level goals* can sometimes focus their attention on one mutually desirable outcome. In a course team where members are

---

In lose-lose conflict no one achieves his or her true desires and the underlying reasons for conflict remain unaffected.

Competition or authoritative command uses force, superior skill, or domination to win a conflict.

Compromise occurs when each party to the conflict gives up something of value to the other.

In win-lose conflict one party achieves its desires and the other party does not.

Collaboration or problem solving involves working through conflict differences and solving problems so everyone wins.

In win-win conflict the conflict is resolved to everyone's benefit.

Conflict resolution is the removal of the substantial and/or emotional reasons for a conflict.

When to use alternative conflict management strategies

- *Collaboration or problem solving*—is the preferred way to gain true conflict resolution when time and cost permit.

- *Avoidance or withdrawal*—may be used when an issue is trivial, when more important issues are pressing, or when people need to cool down temporarily and regain perspective.

- *Competition or authoritative command*—may be used when quick and decisive action is vital or when unpopular actions must be taken.

- *Accommodation or smoothing*—may be used when issues are more important to others than to yourself or when you want to build "credits" for use in later disagreements.

- *Compromise*—may be used to arrive at temporary settlements of complex issues or to arrive at expedient solutions when time is limited.

arguing over content choices for a Power Point presentation, for example, it might help to remind everyone that the goal is to impress the instructor and get an "A" for the presentation. An appeal to higher goals offers a common frame of reference that can be very helpful for analyzing differences and reconciling disagreements.

When appeals to higher goals don't work, it may be that *changing the people* is necessary. That is, a manager may need to replace or transfer one or more of the conflicting parties to eliminate the conflict. And when the people can't be changed, they may have to be separated by *altering the physical environment*. Sometimes it is possible to rearrange facilities, workspace, or workflows to physically separate conflicting parties and decrease opportunities for contact with one another.

Organizations also use a variety of *integrating devices* to help in managing conflicts between groups. These approaches include assigning people to formal liaison roles, convening special task forces, setting up cross-functional teams, and even switching to the matrix form of organization. Providing by *training in interpersonal skills* can also help prepare people to communicate and work more effectively in situations where conflict is likely. In fact, such "soft" or "people" skills are often right at the top when corporate recruiters list criteria for recruiting new college graduates. You can't succeed in today's horizontal and team-oriented organizational structures if you can't work well with other people, even when disagreements are inevitable.

Finally, it's useful to know that by *changing reward systems* it is sometimes possible to reduce conflicts that arise when people feel they have to compete with one another for attention, pay, and other rewards. An example is shifting pay bonuses or even team project grades to the group level so that individuals benefit in direct proportion to how well the team performs as a whole. This is a way of reinforcing teamwork and reducing tendencies of team members to compete with one another.

Self-Assessment

This is a good point to complete the self-assessment "*Conflict Management Strategies*" found on page 356.

Study Guide

16.1
What Should We Know about Dealing with Conflict?

Rapid review

- Interpersonal conflict occurs as disagreements between people over substantive or emotional issues.
- Moderate levels of conflict can be functional for performance, stimulating effort and creativity.
- Too little conflict is dysfunctional when it leads to complacency.
- Too much conflict is dysfunctional when it overwhelms us.
- Conflict in and around organizations occurs at the intrapersonal, interpersonal, intergroup, and interorganizational levels.
- Tendencies toward cooperativeness and assertiveness create the interpersonal conflict management styles of avoidance, accommodation, compromise, competition, and collaboration.
- Conflict in organizations can also be managed through structural approaches that involve changing people, goals, resources, or work arrangements.

Terms to define

Accommodation

Avoidance

Collaboration

Competition

Compromise

Conflict

Conflict resolution

Dysfunctional conflict

Emotional conflict

Functional conflict

Lose-lose conflict

Substantive conflict

Win-lose conflict

Win-win conflict

Be sure you can

- differentiate substantive and emotional conflict
- differentiate functional and dysfunctional conflict
- list and give examples of four levels of conflict in and around organizations
- explain the common causes of conflict in organizations
- explain the conflict management styles of avoidance, accommodation, competition, compromise, and collaboration
- discuss the structural approaches to conflict management

Questions for discussion

1. Is substantive or emotional conflict more difficult for people to handle?
2. Is the absence of conflict always a problem?
3. When is it better to avoid conflict rather than directly engage in it?

16.2 How Can We Negotiate Successfully?

Situation: Your employer offers you a promotion, but the pay raise being offered is disappointing.

Situation: You have enough money to order one new computer for your department, but two members of your team really need one.

Situation: Your team members are having a "cook out" on Saturday afternoon and want you to attend; your husband wants you to go with him to a neighboring town to visit his mother in the hospital.

Situation: Someone on your sales team has to fly to Texas to visit an important client; you've made the last two trips out of town and don't want to go. Another member of the team hasn't traveled in a long time and "owes" you a favor.

• Negotiation is a process of reaching agreement.

These are but a few examples of the many work situations that lead to **negotiation**—the process of making joint decisions when the parties involved have alternative preferences, perhaps to the point of outright conflict. Stated a bit differently, negotiation is a way of reaching agreement.[6]

People negotiate over salary, merit raises, performance evaluations, job assignments, work schedules, work locations, and many other considerations. Nothing could serve you better than learning some basic negotiating skills to deal with these and similar situations in the future. The learning begins by recognizing two goals in the negotiation process—substance goals and relationship goals.

Substance goals in negotiation focus on outcomes. They relate to what is being negotiated—the pay raise or who gets the computer, for example. **Relationship goals** in negotiation focus on the people issues and processes. They are tied to the way people work together while negotiating and how they will be able to work together again in the future.

It's a mistake to rank either substance or relationship goals over the other; both are important. It's rare that we can be satisfied to get what we want while damaging relationships in the process. But by the same token, how often do you want to sacrifice what you want just to preserve a relationship?

A negotiation can be considered an **effective negotiation** when issues of substance are resolved, and working relationships among the negotiating parties are maintained or even improved in the process.[7] One test for an effective negotiation is the question: "Now that it's over, am I and is the other party willing to implement the decision and follow through as agreed?"[8] Also, an effective

Negotiation is the process of making joint decisions when the parties involved have different preferences.

Substance goals in negotiation focus on outcomes.

Relationship goals in negotiation focus on people's relationships and interpersonal processes.

Effective negotiation resolves issues of substance while maintaining a positive process.

Tips to Remember

"Ins" and "Outs" of Negotiating Salaries

Have you ever wished that you had asked for more when negotiating a starting salary or a pay raise? And, even if you had asked, would it have made a difference? Here's what the experts recommend.

- *Prepare, prepare, prepare*—do the research and find out what others make for a similar position inside and outside the organization, including everything from salary to benefits, bonuses, incentives, and job perks.
- *Document and communicate*—identify and communicate your performance value; put forth a set of accomplishments that show how you have saved or made money and created value in your present job or for a past employer.
- *Identify critical skills and attributes*—make a list of your strengths and link each of them with potential contributions to the new employer; show how "you" offer talents and personal attributes of immediate value to the work team.
- *Advocate and ask*—be your own best advocate; the rule in salary negotiation is "Don't ask, don't get." But don't ask too soon; your boss or interviewer should be the first to bring up salary.
- *Stay focused on the goal*—your goal is to achieve as much as you can in the negotiation; this means not only doing well at the moment but also getting better positioned for future gains.
- *View things from the other side*—test your requests against the employer's point of view; ask if you are being reasonable, convincing, and fair; ask how the boss could explain to higher levels and to your peers a decision to grant your request.
- *Don't overreact to bad news*—never "quit on the spot" if you don't get what you want; be willing to search for and consider alternative job offers.

negotiation usually scores well on these three criteria: (1) *quality*—negotiating a "wise" agreement that is truly satisfactory to all sides; (2) *cost*—negotiating efficiently, using up minimum resources and time; and (3) *harmony*—negotiating in a way that fosters, rather than inhibits, interpersonal relationships.[9]

• Negotiation can be approached in distributive or integrative ways.

The way each party approaches a negotiation can have a significant impact on its effectiveness.[10] In the book *Getting to Yes*, Roger Fisher and William Ury describe differences in "distributive negotiation" (which they don't like) and "integrative negotiation" (which they advocate).

Distributive negotiation is a process in which each party focuses mainly on staking out claims for certain preferred outcomes. In *hard distributive negotiation* things become highly competitive as each party focuses on narrow self-interests, trying to gain from losses by the other. As you might expect, these win-lose conditions often damage working relationships. In *soft distributive negotiation* one party basically backs off and accepts a loss, perhaps just "to get things over with." But when one party acts accommodative, it may be done with underlying resentment and little personal conviction.

Fisher and Ury see the pitfalls and recognize the limitations of distributive negotiation. They much prefer the alternative of **integrative negotiation**, often called *principled negotiation*. This approach takes more of a win-win orientation that considers the interests of all parties. The goal is an outcome that is based on the merits of individual claims, and that serves each party's desires as much as possible. Ideally, no one should lose in an integrative negotiation, and relationships shouldn't be harmed.

When asked by an interviewer to illustrate how the integrative approach to negotiation differs from a distributive one, William Ury gave this example.[11] A union worker presents a manager with a list of requests. The manager says: "That's your solution, now what's the problem?" The union worker responds with a list of problems. The manager says: "Well, I can't give you *that* solution, but I think we can solve your problem this way." Can you see the manager's attempt to be "integrative" here?

• Integrative agreements require commitment, trust, and information.

It isn't easy to gain integrative agreements; Fisher and Ury don't deny that fact. Rather, they offer the four rules in the accompanying box as starting points for moving in an integrative rather than distributive direction.[12] Commitment to the process, proper attitudes, and good information are all necessary foundations for integrative agreements. Each negotiating party must be willing to trust, share information with, and ask reasonable questions of the other.

Integrative agreements are more likely when each party knows both what it really wants and what the other wants. Consider the case of labor–management negotiations over wage terms in a new contract.[13] A union negotiator has told her management counterpart that the union wants a new wage of $15.00 per hour. This expressed preference is the union's initial offer. However, she also has in mind a minimum reservation point of $13.25 per hour. This is the lowest wage rate that she will accept for the union. Now take the seat of the management negotiator. He has a different perspective. His

Distributive negotiation focuses on win-lose claims made by each party for certain preferred outcomes.

Integrative negotiation uses a win-win orientation to reach solutions acceptable to each party.

Fisher and Ury's four rules for integrative negotiation

1. Separate the people from the problem.
2. Focus on interests, not on positions.
3. Generate many alternatives before deciding what to do.
4. Insist that results be based on some objective standard.

FIGURE 16.3

How Does the Bargaining Zone Operate in Classic Two-Party Negotiation?

	Bargaining Zone		
$12.75/hour	$13.25/hour	$13.75/hour	$15.00/hour
Mi	Ur	Mr	Ui

Mi = Management's initial offer   Mr = Management's maximum reservation point
Ur = Union's minimum reservation point   Ui = Union's initial offer

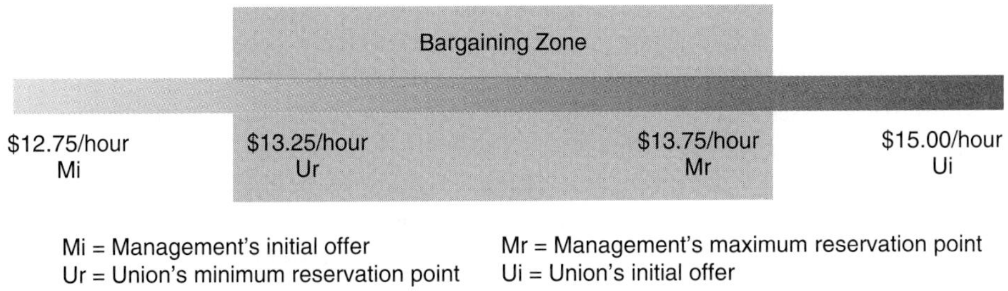

The bargaining zone in a negotiation is set by the difference in the minimum and maximum reservation points of the negotiating parties. In this example of a salary negotiation, and even though each would like a better deal, the union representatives know that they would accept a wage offer as low as $13.25 an hour (their minimum reservation point) and the management representatives know they would pay as much as $13.75 an hour (their maximum reservation point). Within these two extremes lies the bargaining zone—each party would settle on a wage between $13.25 and $13.75. Outside of this zone, each party is prepared to walk away without an agreement.

initial offer is $12.75 per hour, with $13.75 per hour representing his maximum reservation point.

Classic two-party negotiation defines the **bargaining zone** as the distance between one party's minimum reservation point and the other party's maximum reservation point. In this example, and as described in **Figure 16.3**, the bargaining zone of $13.25 per hour to $13.75 per hour is a "positive" one, since the reservation points of the two parties overlap. There is room for true negotiation. If, however, the union's minimum reservation point exceeded the management's maximum reservation point, no room would exist for bargaining.

A key task for any negotiator is to discover each party's reservation points. That's the only way to really know if a positive bargaining zone exists. If it does, negotiations can proceed effectively. Otherwise, negotiations will stall until either one party or the other, or both, are willing to modify the original stance.

By the way, one of the most important negotiations we ever have with our employers is over our starting salary. In your next salary negotiation will you be well prepared and able to find the bargaining zone?

A **bargaining zone** is the area between one party's minimum reservation point and the other party's maximum reservation point.

• Successful negotiation should meet high ethical standards.

In the midst of negotiations like the one just described, it may be easy for participants to drift off into manipulative, deceitful, and even dishonest behaviors. This is the *trap of ethical misconduct*. Sometimes the motivation to behave unethically arises from an undue emphasis on personal gain or self-satisfaction. This may be experienced as a desire to "get just a bit more" or to "get as much as you can" from a negotiation. The motivation to behave unethically may also result from a sense of competition. This may be experienced as a desire to "win" a negotiation just for the sake of winning it and the misguided belief that someone else must "lose" in order for you to win. And, as we are all well aware, the motivation to behave unethically can be driven by all-consuming greed and the quest for profits in negotiation situations where money is at issue.

Even in the toughest of negotiations it's important to maintain integrity and avoid the trap of ethical misconduct.

Think about the roles that honor and personal integrity play in negotiation. Are they worth sacrificing? As has been said so many times in this book, there is no substitute for ethical behavior. Keep this in mind and watch for tendencies in yourself and in others to do unethical things when negotiating, and then try to explain them away with inappropriate rationalizing: "It was really unavoidable," "Oh, it's harmless," "The results justify the means," or "It's really quite fair and appropriate."[14] These excuses for questionable behavior are, and will always be, morally and organizationally unacceptable.

Long-run losses may follow ill-gotten short-run gains for negotiators using unethical tactics. They often get tagged with bad reputations and incur lasting legacies of distrust, disrespect, and dislike in the eyes of others. Someone who acts unethically in a negotiation may get what he or she wants, but end up paying the price when targeted for "revenge" in later negotiations.

Trendsetters

UN Secretary General Ban Ki-Moon Pursues World Peace

Talk about conflict and negotiation! Whose job could be more intense in this regard than that of Ban Ki-Moon, the 37th Secretary General of the United Nations? On any given day he could be getting off the plane in some far part of the world to meet with heads of state, or dealing with problems in Somalia, or marshalling aid for relief in some natural disaster, or handling delicate disagreements with and among the UN's member nations.

But Mr. Ban is well prepared, having come to his post with 37 years of experience in public and government service. Prior to becoming Secretary General he served as the Republic of Korea's Minister of Foreign Affairs and Trade, and was well traveled and highly respected in global leadership circles. Mr. Ban speaks Korean, English, and French, and his principles to world peace and prosperity are reflected in his priorities as found on the United Nations Web site. They include

Peace and security—"By enhancing our capacity for preventive diplomacy and supporting sustainable peace processes, we will build long-term solutions and respond more effectively to conflict."

Climate change—"If we care about our legacy for succeeding generations, this is the time for decisive global action. The UN is the natural forum for building consensus and negotiating future global action—all nations can take firm steps towards being carbon-neutral."

Development—"While threats to peace must be addressed, my concern lies equally with those men, women and children of the world struggling to make ends meet—it is intolerable that almost 1 billion people still live on less than $1 a day . . . I will mobilize political will and hold leaders to their commitment to allocate adequate resources and development aid . . ."

UN Reform—"Global problems demand global solutions—and going it alone is not a viable option . . . I do have faith in human decency, diligence and incremental progress. Above all, I believe in results, not rhetoric. The fundamental purposes and principles of this Organization are inspiring and enduring—we need to renew our pledge to live up to them."

• Negotiators should guard against common negotiation pitfalls.

At this point I think you'll agree that the negotiation process can be very complex. Even the best-intentioned negotiators can fail. Sometimes we get trapped and do the wrong things not because of ethical lapses, but because we don't recognize and act to avoid common negotiating errors or pitfalls.

The first negotiation pitfall is the *myth of the "fixed pie."* This assumes that in order for you to gain, the other person must give something up. Negotiating under this belief fails to recognize that we can sometimes either expand or better utilize the pie to everyone's advantage. A second negotiation error is *nonrational escalation of conflict.* The negotiator in this case becomes committed to previously stated demands and allows personal needs for enhancing ego and saving face to exaggerate the perceived importance of satisfying them.

The third common negotiating error or pitfall is *overconfidence and ignoring the other's needs.* The negotiator becomes overconfident, believes that his or her position is the only correct one, and fails to see the needs of the other party and the merits in its position. The fourth error is *too much telling and too little hearing.* When committing the "telling" problem, parties to a negotiation don't really make themselves understood to each other. When committing the "hearing" problem, they fail to listen sufficiently in order to understand what each is saying.[15]

Another potential negotiation pitfall, and one increasingly important in our age of globalization, is *premature cultural comfort.* This occurs when a negotiator is too quick to assume that he or she understands the intentions, positions, and meanings being communicated by a negotiator from a different culture. Scholar Jeanne Brett says, for example, that negotiators from low-context cultures can run into difficulties when dealing with ones from high-context cultures. The low-context negotiator is used to getting information through direct questions and answers; the high-context negotiator is likely to communicate indirectly using nondeclarative language and nonverbal signals and without explicitly stated positions.[16]

The next time you're involved in a negotiation that is not going well, stop to consider if you, or the other party, is getting caught up in ethical misconduct or one of the other negotiation pitfalls. They're not ideas; they're real. They're also likely to trap you someday if your guard isn't up.

We are sometimes too quick to assume we understand intentions and positions of negotiators from different cultures.

• Mediation and arbitration are forms of third-party negotiations.

For any of the reasons just discussed, and more, it may not always be possible to achieve integrative agreements. And when disputes reach the point of impasse, third-party approaches are often the next best choice for resolving things.

Mediation involves a neutral third party who tries to improve communication between negotiating parties and keep them focused on relevant issues. The mediator generally does not issue a ruling or make a decision, but often takes an active role in discussions. This may include making suggestions in an attempt to move the parties toward agreement.

In **mediation** a neutral party tries to help conflicting parties improve communication to resolve their dispute.

Arbitration, such as salary arbitration in professional sports, is a stronger form of dispute resolution. It involves a neutral third party, the arbitrator, who acts as a "judge" and issues a binding decision. This usually includes a formal hearing in which the arbitrator listens to both sides and reviews all facets of the case before making a ruling.

In **arbitration** a neutral third party issues a binding decision to resolve a dispute.

Some organizations formally provide for a process called *alternative dispute resolution*. This approach utilizes mediation and arbitration, but only after direct attempts to negotiate agreements between the conflicting parties has failed. Often an ombudsperson, or designated neutral third party who listens to complaints and disputes, plays a key role in the process.

Study Guide

16.2
How Can We Negotiate Successfully?

Rapid review

- Negotiation is the process of making decisions and reaching agreement in situations in which the participants have different preferences.
- Effective negotiation occurs when both substance goals (dealing with outcomes) and relationship goals (dealing with processes) are achieved.
- The distributive approach to negotiation emphasizes win-lose outcomes; the integrative approach, or principled negotiation approach, emphasizes win-win outcomes.
- Ethical problems in negotiation can arise when people become manipulative and dishonest in trying to satisfy their self-interests at any cost.
- Participants in negotiations sometimes fall prey to pitfalls such as the myth of the fixed pie, irrational escalation, overconfidence, and too much telling with too little hearing.
- When negotiations are at an impasse, third-party approaches such as mediation and arbitration offer alternative and structured ways for dispute resolution.

Terms to define

Arbitration
Bargaining zone
Distributive negotiation
Integrative negotiation
Mediation
Negotiation
Relationship goals
Substance goals

Be sure you can

- differentiate substance and relationship goals in negotiation
- explain distributive and integrative negotiation
- explain the role of the bargaining zone in negotiation
- discuss the ethical challenges of negotiation
- list potential negotiation pitfalls
- differentiate between mediation and arbitration in dispute resolution

Questions for discussion

1. If you have a good relationship with someone, are you likely to give in too easily when negotiating?
2. Is it possible to completely avoid distributive negotiation?
3. What can you do when the person you are negotiating with seems trapped by the myth of the fixed pie?

Multiple choice

1. A conflict is most likely to be functional and have a positive impact on group performance when it is _____.

   (a) based on emotions
   (b) resolved by arbitration
   (c) caused by resource scarcities
   (d) of moderate intensity

2. When a manager points out that two persons in conflict should agree on higher-level goals and then work backward from there to resolve the conflict, this is an example of a/an _____ approach to conflict management.

   (a) avoidance   (b) structural
   (c) accommodation   (d) distributive

3. The interpersonal conflict management style with the greatest potential for true conflict resolution is _____.

   (a) compromise   (b) competition
   (c) smoothing   (d) collaboration

4. When people are highly cooperative but not very assertive in a conflict situation, the likelihood is that they will be using which conflict management style?

   (a) avoidance   (b) authoritative
   (c) smoothing   (d) collaboration

5. If you are in a situation where you must choose between an attractive job transfer to another city and having a great network of friends and family in your current location, you might experience _____ conflict.

   (a) lose-lose
   (b) approach–avoidance
   (c) approach–approach
   (d) interorganizational

6. If you are an observer in a labor–management negotiation and notice that each side is taking a competitive stance, staking out its claims for desired outcomes, the likelihood is that this negotiation is _____ in nature.

   (a) intrapersonal   (b) principled
   (c) approach–avoidance   (d) distributive

7. The criteria of an effective negotiation include high quality, low cost, and _____.

   (a) harmony   (b) timeliness
   (c) efficiency   (d) personal gain

8. The distance between one party's minimum reservation point and the other party's maximum reservation point in a negotiation over salary is called the _____.

   (a) bargaining zone
   (b) zone of indifference
   (c) fixed pie effect
   (d) escalation point

9. When a negotiator becomes committed to previously stated demands and becomes concerned about saving face by not compromising on them, a negotiation error known as _____ is occurring.

   (a) overconfidence
   (b) poor ethics
   (c) irrational exuberance
   (d) non-rational escalation

10. When a professional baseball player reaches an impasse negotiating for a contract renewal with his present club, the matter is often referred to _____ where an outside person acts as a judge and makes the decision for them.

    (a) arbitration
    (b) alternative dispute resolution
    (c) mediation
    (d) principled negotiation

11. Gaining the highest possible salary offer from a potential employer is an example of a/an _____ goal in negotiation.

    (a) emotional   (b) process
    (c) principled   (d) substance

12. Which conflict management strategy is most likely to take on a win-win character?

    (a) authoritative command
    (b) collaboration
    (c) competition
    (d) compromise

13. When a team leader appeals to members in conflict to remember the goals set for the team as a whole as they debate the issues, she is taking a/an _____ approach to conflict management.

    (a) avoidance
    (b) structural
    (c) dysfunctional
    (d) self-serving

14. When people are highly cooperative and very assertive in a conflict situation, the likelihood is that they will be using which conflict management style?
    (a) avoidance
    (b) authoritative
    (c) smoothing
    (d) problem solving

15. The first rule of thumb for gaining integrative agreements in negotiations is to _____.
    (a) separate the people from the problems
    (b) focus on positions
    (c) deal with a minimum number of alternatives
    (d) avoid setting standards for measuring outcomes

Short response

16. What interpersonal styles create lose-lose and win-lose outcomes in conflict management?

17. Why is conflict of moderate intensity considered functional?

18. What is the difference between substance and relationship goals in negotiation?

19. How does arbitration differ from mediation?

Integration & application

20. When Professor Kraham received her teaching assignments for spring semester from the department head, she was surprised. Instead of teaching her normal load of one management course and one organizational behavior course, she was given two strategic management courses. She will have to do a lot of extra work preparing for the strategic management classes and this is going to leave less time available for the research she needs to complete to stay on track for promotion and tenure. She is determined to raise the issue with the department head and try to negotiate a better teaching schedule.

Questions: What type of conflict is Professor Kraham experiencing in this situation? What suggestions would you give her for how to negotiate with the department head in a way that will result in an integrative agreement?

Conflict Management Strategies

Instructions

Think of how you behave in conflict situations in which your wishes differ from those of others. In the space to the left, rate each of the following statements on a scale of "1" = 5 "not at all" to "5" = 5 "very much."[17] *When I have a conflict at work, school, or in my personal life, I do the following:*

_____ 1. I give in to the wishes of the other party.

_____ 2. I try to realize a middle-of-the-road solution.

_____ 3. I push my own point of view.

_____ 4. I examine issues until I find a solution that really satisfies me and the other party.

_____ 5. I avoid a confrontation about our differences.

_____ 6. I concur with the other party.

_____ 7. I emphasize that we have to find a compromise solution.

_____ 8. I search for gains.

_____ 9. I stand for my own and the other's goals.

_____ 10. I avoid differences of opinion as much as possible.

_____ 11. I try to accommodate the other party.

_____ 12. I insist we both give in a little.

_____ 13. I fight for a good outcome for myself.

_____ 14. I examine ideas from both sides to find a mutually optimal solution.

_____ 15. I try to make differences seem less severe.

_____ 16. I adapt to the other party's goals and interests.

_____ 17. I strive whenever possible toward a fifty-fifty compromise.

_____ 18. I do everything to win.

_____ 19. I work out a solution that serves my own as well as the other's interests as much as possible.

_____ 20. I try to avoid a confrontation with the other person.

Scoring

Total your scores for items as follows.

Yielding tendency: 1 + 6 + 11 + 16 = _____.

Compromising tendency: 2 + 7 + 12 + 17 = _____.

Forcing tendency: 3 + 8 + 13 + 18 = _____.

Problem-solving tendency: 4 + 9 + 14 + 19 = _____.

Avoiding tendency: 5 + 10 + 15 + 20 = _____.

Interpretation

Each of the scores above approximates one of the conflict management styles discussed in the chapter. Look back to Figure 15.4 and make the match ups. Although each style is part of management, only collaboration or problem solving leads to true conflict resolution. You should consider any patterns that may be evident in your scores and think about how to best handle the conflict situations in which you become involved.

 For further exploration go to WileyPlus

Case Snapshot

AFL-CIO: Managing Dissent While Supporting Labor

The AFL-CIO, once America's preeminent labor organization, has been fragmented in recent years by dissent within its ranks. But this is nothing new to organized labor. Learn how differing opinions within the labor movement aided the formation of both the AFL and CIO and caused their eventual merger.

Online Interactive Learning Resources

SELF-ASSESSMENT	EXPERIENTIAL EXERCISES	TEAM PROJECT
• Feedback and Assertiveness	• Conflict Dialogues • The Ugli Orange	• Negotiating Salaries

17

Diversity and Global Cultures

There Are New Faces in the Neighborhood

Tiny car from India may teach Detroit a lesson.
Is the next automobile revolution starting in India? It could well be. Tata Motors Ltd. had to use a computerized lottery to select buyers for the first 100,000 "Nano's" that came off its assembly lines. Conceived by founder Ratan Tata, the Nano is known as the "$2,000 people's car" and has caught lots of attention around the world.

Tata's vision came straight from the busy streets of India, where a common sight is to see an entire family packed together on a motorcycle and fighting for their way against buses, trucks, and cars in intense hair-raising traffic. He wanted his firm to build and sell a car that millions of low-income Indians could afford, one that would allow them to move up from the two-wheel transportation market to the safer four-wheel market. Enter the Nano; designed to be small—10.2 feet long, fuel efficient, low emission, and cheap enough to be a viable purchase for India's low-income workers.

Conceived in India, in response to needs of Indian customers, the Nano is now poised to challenge the legacy automakers. It was six years in the making, with suppliers brought into the design process right from the

358

Trendsetters
David Segura, Hispanic Business Entrepreneur of the Year

News Feed
Internet censorship fuels global debate.

Case Snapshot
Toyota—Looking far into the future

start. The goal was design features that help cut costs—a single windshield wiper, use of glue rather than welds on some parts, simplified door levers, and no power steering.

Not only is the Nano manufactured in typical large plants such as Pune in Maharashtra state, plans are to ship it in components that can then be assembled almost anywhere by local mechanics in small shops. He says: "A bunch of entrepreneurs could establish an assembly operation and Tata Motors would train their people, would oversee their quality assurance, and they would become satellite assembly operations for us. So we would create entrepreneurs across the country that would produce the car. We would produce the mass items and ship them as kits. That is my idea of dispersing wealth."

The first proud Nano owner, Ashok Vichare, said: "This is the smallest and cheapest car in India—That's why I bought it." And Vikas Sehgal, an analyst with Booz & Co., says: "The Nano shows that a new world order is possible in the auto industry. It shows a glimpse of what is to come." Isn't it interesting that this "glimpse" into the future is coming not from Detroit or Stuttgart or Nagoya, but from India?

17.1 What Should We Know about Diversity in the Workplace?

In Module 1.3 we first discussed diversity in respect to age, race, ethnicity, gender, physical ability, and sexual orientation. A broad definition of workplace **diversity** would also include differences in such areas as religious beliefs, education, experience, family status, national cultures, and perhaps more.[1] In his book *Beyond Race and Gender,* diversity consultant R. Roosevelt Thomas Jr. goes so far as to say that "diversity includes everyone . . . white males are as diverse as their colleagues."[2]

Trendsetters

David Segura, Hispanic Business Entrepreneur of the Year

David Segura grew up in a family of executives; his grandparents were Mexican immigrants, finding work in the automotive industry, and his father worked at Ford Motor Company. And after graduating from the University of Michigan-Dearborn with a degree in computer science he, too, joined Ford. But Segura wanted more—a business of his own.

It all started when he met the president of Hacienda Mexican Foods while both were volunteering at a Wayne State University tutoring program for inner-city kids in Detroit. Segura later went on to do some IT consulting for her firm. But when it came time to be paid she said he had so much potential she would only write a check to his company, not to him personally. The next day he founded VisionIT Inc., with $100 and Hacienda as his first client.

Today VisionIT is a $100+ million company serving many Fortune 500 clients. It provides IT staffing, managed services, and consulting services based on what Segura calls the FAST approach—focused on clients, agile, streamlined, and rich with talented people. Segura is the CEO and his sister Christine Rice is president. She says: "It's been a tremendous journey. Being an entrepreneur takes tremendous effort. Nothing is easy." About being successful in the technology industry where Hispanics are not well represented, Segura says: "VisionIT is a firm of much diversity and we are showing that a company is at its best when it fully utilizes the talents of all backgrounds and ethnicities."

Hispanic Business magazine in 2008 named Segura its Hispanic Entrepreneur of the Year, based on the success of his firm and his commitment to the community. When accepting the award he said it was a "truly humbling experience" and thanked the VisionIT team "whose shared vision and commitment made this day possible." Also in 2008, Segura received the Ernst & Young Entrepreneur of the Year award.

When Segura became an entrepreneur he saw it as a way to have a positive impact on society. He continues to pursue that impact not only by running a successful large business, but also by helping young people enter the world of IT through college scholarships and company internships.

• There is a business case for diversity.

One of Thomas's main points is that diversity is good for organizations, that it is a potential source of competitive advantage. Picture an organization whose diverse employees reflect a mixture of talents and perspectives, and are representative of the firm's customers and clients. Wouldn't this be good for business?

Lou Gerstner, former CEO of IBM, thinks so. He once said that at IBM: "We made diversity a market-based issue . . . it's about understanding our markets which are diverse and multicultural."[3] IBM attributes the growth in its sales to minority-owned and women-owned smaller businesses to the increased presence of women and minorities in its management ranks.[4] Also, the New York research group Catalyst reports that companies with a greater percentage of women on their boards outperform those whose boards have the lowest female representation.[5] Research reported in the *Gallup Management Journal* shows that establishing a racially and ethnically inclusive workplace is good for morale. In a study of 2,014 American workers, those who felt included were more likely to stay with their employers and recommend them to others. Survey questions asked such things as "Do you always trust your company to be fair to all employees?" "At work, are all employees always treated with respect?" "Does your supervisor always make the best use of employees' skills?"[6]

Studies and evidence like that just cited points toward what some call a strong "business case for diversity."[7] But just having a diverse workforce doesn't guarantee success. If all members of this workforce are not fully respected by management and one another, and if they are not actively engaged in day-to-day affairs, it is highly unlikely that any diversity benefits will be realized. In fact, Thomas Kochan and his colleagues at MIT found in their research that it is only when managers make diversity a priority through training and supportive human resource practices that they gain the hoped-for advantages.[8] They advise:

> *To be successful in working with and gaining value from diversity requires a sustained, systemic approach and long-term commitment. Success is facilitated by a perspective that considers diversity to be an opportunity for everyone in an organization to learn from each other how better to accomplish their work and an occasion that requires a supportive and cooperative organizational culture as well as group leadership and process skills that can facilitate effective group functioning.*

Diversity describes race, gender, age, and other individual differences.

• Inclusive organizational cultures value and support diversity.

Just how do managers go about leveraging diversity in the workplace? Many organizations seem to be good or relatively good at attracting new employees of diverse backgrounds to join, but they aren't always successful in keeping them for the long term. This problem of high employee turnover among minorities and women has been called the "revolving door" syndrome.[9] It can reflect a lack of **inclusivity** in the employing organizations—that is, the degree to which they are open to anyone who can perform a job, regardless of race, sexual preference, gender, or other diversity attribute.[10]

Inclusivity is how open the organization is to anyone who can perform a job.

Look around; think about how people are treating those who differ from themselves. What about your experiences at school and at work? Are you always treated with respect and inclusion? Or do you sense at times disrespect and exclusion from certain people or groups you interact with on campus or at work?

When an organization is truly inclusive, its internal climate or organizational culture is rich in beliefs, values, and expectations that respect and empower the full potential of a diverse workforce. The model for inclusivity is the **multicultural organization** that displays commitments to diversity like those in **Table 17.1**—*Characteristics of Multicultural Organizations*.[11] One such organization is Xerox, the first Fortune 500 firm to have an African American woman as CEO—Ursula Burns, and also the first to have one woman succeed another as CEO. When praising Burns's appointment, Ilene Lang, head of the nonprofit Catalyst which supports women in business, said: "Most companies have one woman who might be a possibility to become CEO, Xerox has a range of them." The firm has an Executive Diversity Council, runs diversity leadership programs, and evaluates managers on how well they recruit and develop employees from underrepresented groups. Harvard professor David Thomas says Xerox has "a culture where having women and people of color as candidates for powerful jobs has been going on for two decades."[12]

A **multicultural organization** is based on pluralism and operates with inclusivity and respect for diversity.

[**TABLE** 17.1]

Characteristics of Multicultural Organizations

Pluralism—Members of minority and majority cultures influence key values and policies.

Structural integration—Minority-culture members are well represented at all levels and in all responsibilities.

Informal network integration—Mentoring and support groups assist career development of minority-culture members.

Absence of prejudice and discrimination—Training and task force activities support the goal of eliminating culture-group biases.

Minimum intergroup conflict—Members of minority and majority cultures avoid destructive conflicts.

• Organizational subcultures can create diversity challenges.

We have to be realistic in facing up to the challenges in creating truly multicultural organizations; it isn't always easy to get the members of a workforce to really respect and work well with one another. One of the reasons is the

Organizational subcultures are groupings of people based on shared demographic and job identities.

Ethnocentrism is the belief that one's membership group or subculture is superior to all others.

existence of **organizational subcultures**. These are informal groupings of persons with shared identities.

Organizational subcultures can form around such things as gender, age, race and ethnicity, and even job functions. And they can create diversity challenges. People can get so caught up in their subcultures that they often identify and interact mostly with others who are like themselves. They may develop tendencies toward **ethnocentrism**, acting in ways that suggest that their ways are superior to all others. All of this generally makes it harder for people from different organizational subcultures to work well together.

Consider, for example, the *occupational subcultures* that form as people form shared identities around the work that they do. Some employees may consider themselves "systems people" who are very different from "those marketing people" and even more different still from "those finance people." Even at school, in course project groups, have you noticed how students tend to identify themselves by their majors? Don't some students look down on others who they consider as pursuing "easy" majors, or seem to view their own majors as the most superior ones?

Differences in *ethnic or national subcultures* exist as people from various countries and regions of the world meet and work together in the global economy. And as we all know, it can sometimes be hard to work well with persons whose backgrounds are very different from our own. The best understanding is most likely gained through direct contact and from being open-minded. The same advice holds true with respect to *racial subcultures*. Although one may speak in everyday conversations about "African American" or "Latino" or "Anglo" cultures, one has to wonder, are these subcultures truly understood?[13] If improved cross-cultural understandings can help people work better across national boundaries, how can we create the same understandings to help people from different racial subcultures work better together?

Issues of relationships and discrimination based on *gender subcultures* also continue to complicate the workplace. Some research shows that when men work together, a group culture forms around a competitive atmosphere. Sports metaphors are common, and games and stories often deal with winning and losing.[14] When women work together, a rather different culture may form, with more emphasis on personal relationships and collaboration.[15]

We shouldn't forget age as a potential challenge in a diverse organization. It is the basis for *generational subcultures*. The *Harvard Business Review* reports that today's teenagers, the "Millennial" generation, are highly ambitious and prefer job mobility;[16] Harris and Conference Board polls report younger workers tend to be more dissatisfied than older workers.[17] They are also described as more short-term oriented, giving higher priority to work-life balance, and expecting to hold at least five jobs during their careers.[18] Imagine the conflicts that can occur when a member of the Millennial generation leaves college and goes to work for a manager from the Baby Boomer generation who started working in the late 1960s or early 1970s. As suggested in Tips to Remember, each may have to take special steps to work well with the other.[19]

Tips to Remember

How Millennials and Baby Boomers Can Work Together

Millennials Working with Baby Boomers:

- Show respect—let them know you're willing to learn from them.
- Use face-to-face conversations to be more personal.
- Give full attention when trying to communicate.
- Be diplomatic; workplace politics are a fact of life.
- Show respect for the past; find out what's happened before.

Baby Boomers Working with Millennials:

- Challenge them—give meaningful work.
- Reward them with responsibility and recognition for accomplishments.
- Ask their opinions; avoid command-and-control approaches.
- Link them with an older mentor.
- Give timely feedback; they're used to instantaneous gratification.

• Minorities and women suffer diversity bias in many situations.

The term "diversity" basically means the presence of differences, and that's both important and potentially challenging in its own right. But diversity issues in organizations are further complicated because such differences are often distributed unequally in the power structure. Let's be honest. Most senior executives in large businesses are still older, white, and male; there is more diversity among lower and middle levels of most organizations than at the top. And for some women and minority workers, the **glass ceiling** depicted in **Figure 17.1** is a real barrier to career advancement.[20]

The **glass ceiling** is a hidden barrier to the advancement of women and minorities.

FIGURE 17.1
How Do Glass Ceilings Constrain Career Advancement for Women and Minorities?

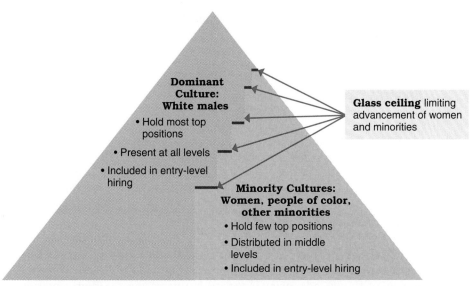

Organizations consist of a majority culture (often white males) and minority cultures (including women, people of color, and other minorities). It is likely that members of the majority culture will dominate higher management levels. One of the potential consequences is a "glass ceiling" effect that, although not publicized, acts as a barrier that sometimes makes it hard for women and minorities to advance and gain entry into higher management ranks.

Jesse Spaulding experienced the glass ceiling while working as a regional manager for a restaurant chain owned by Shoney's. He says that the firm used to operate on the "buddy system," which "left people of color by the wayside" when it came to promotions. Fortunately, things changed when new leadership took over. Their commitments to diversity provided Spaulding with new opportunity. And *Fortune* magazine went on to include Shoney's in its list of America's 50 Best Companies for Minorities.[21]

Minorities and women can face work challenges that range from misunderstandings, to lack of sensitivity, to glass ceiling limitations, to outright job discrimination and various types of harassment. Data from the U.S. Equal Employment Opportunity Commission (EEOC), for example, report an increasing number of bias suits filed by workers, with sex discrimination being a factor in some 30% of them. Sexual harassment in the form of unwanted sexual advances, requests for sexual favors, and sexually laced communications is another problem employees, interns, and volunteers may face in organizations. Indeed, one survey reports some 45 percent of minority respondents had encountered abuse as targets of offensive jokes and conversations in the workplace. The EEOC also reports an increase in filings of pregnancy discrimination complaints. And, of course, pay discrimination is a prominent issue. One senior executive reports her surprise upon finding out that the top performer in her work group, an African American male, was paid 25 percent less than anyone else. This wasn't because his pay had been cut to that level; it was because his pay increases had always trailed those given to white co-workers. The differences added up significantly over time, but no one noticed or stepped forward to make the appropriate adjustment.[22]

People respond to bad treatment at work in different ways. Some may challenge the system by filing complaints, pursuing harassment and discrimination charges, or taking legal action. Some may quit to look for better positions elsewhere, or to pursue self-employment opportunities. Some may try to "fit in," to adapt through **biculturalism** by displaying majority culture characteristics that seem necessary to succeed in the work environment. For example, gays and lesbians might hide their sexual orientation; an African American or Hispanic manager might avoid using words or phrases at work that white colleagues would consider subculture slang; a woman might use football or baseball metaphors in conversations to gain acceptance into male-dominated networks.

> **Biculturalism** is when minority members adopt characteristics of majority cultures in order to succeed.

• Managing diversity should be top leadership priority.

What can leaders and managers do so that people are treated inclusively and don't need to fall back on these types of adaptive behaviors? The process begins with a willingness to recognize that, regardless of their backgrounds, most workers want the same things. They want respect for their talents; they want to be fairly treated; they want to be able to work to the best of their abilities; they want to achieve their full potential. Meeting these expectations requires the best in diversity leadership.

Figure 17.2 describes what R. Roosevelt Thomas calls a continuum of leadership approaches to diversity.[23] At one end is *affirmative action*. Here, leadership commits the organization to hiring and advancing minorities and women. You might think of this as advancing diversity by increasing the representation of diverse members in the organization's workforce. But this is only a partial solution, and the revolving door syndrome may even negate some of its positive impact. Thomas says that the "assumption is that once you get representation, people will assimilate. But we're actually seeing that people are less willing to assimilate than ever before."[24]

FIGURE 17.2

Leadership Approaches to Diversity—from Affirmative Action to Managing Diversity.

Affirmative Action
Create upward mobility for minorities and women

Valuing Differences
Build quality relationships with respect for diversity

Managing Diversity
Achieve full utilization of diverse human resources

Source: Developed from R. Roosevelt Thomas Jr., *Beyond Race and Gender* (New York: AMACOM, 1991), p. 28.

A step beyond affirmative action is what Thomas calls *valuing diversity*. Here, a leader commits the organization to education and training programs designed to help people better understand and respect individual differences. The goal is to teach people of diverse backgrounds more about one another, and how to work well together. Thomas says this training should help us deal with "similarities, differences and tensions." And it should help us answer a fundamental question: "Can I work with people who are qualified that are not like me."[25]

The final step in Thomas's continuum is **managing diversity**. A leader who actively manages diversity is always seeking ways to make an organization truly multicultural and inclusive, and keep it that way. Eastman Kodak might be a good example. The firm is praised by *Business Ethics* magazine for "leading-edge anti-discrimination policies toward gay, bisexual, and transgender employees." It has also received a perfect score from the Human Rights Campaign for its efforts to end sexual discrimination.[26]

Thomas argues quite forcibly that leaders have a performance incentive to embrace managing diversity.[27] A diverse workforce offers a rich pool of talents, ideas, and viewpoints that can help solve complex problems; a diverse workforce aligns well with needs and expectations of diverse customers and stakeholders.[28] Michael R. Losey, president of the Society for Human Resource Management (SHRM), agrees. He says: "Companies must realize that the talent pool includes people of all types, including older workers; persons with disabilities; persons of various religious, cultural, and national backgrounds; persons who are not heterosexual; minorities; and women."[29]

As suggested here and earlier, the arguments are quite compelling in favor of what many call the business case for diversity. When you are next in a conversation about this issue or pause to think about it due to prompting by something you read or encounter, remember these points regarding how a diverse membership can help organizations of all types, from businesses to nonprofits to schools to governments and more.

- Cultural diversity builds strength for dealing with global markets.
- Workforce diversity builds strength for dealing with diverse customers.
- Diverse work teams are high in creativity and innovation.
- Diverse workforces attract new highly talented members.

Managing diversity is building an inclusive work environment that allows everyone to reach his or her potential.

Self-Assessment

This is a good point to complete the self-assessment "*Diversity Awareness*" found on page 376.

Study Guide

17.1
What Should We Know about Diversity in the Workplace?

Rapid review

- Workforce diversity can improve business performance by expanding the talent pool of the organization and establishing better understandings of customers and stakeholders.

- Inclusivity is a characteristic of multicultural organizations that values and respects diversity of their members.

- Organizational subcultures, including those based on occupational, functional, ethnic, racial, age, and gender differences, can create diversity challenges.

- Minorities and women can suffer diversity bias in such forms as job and pay discrimination, sexual harassment, and the glass ceiling effect.

- A top leadership priority should be managing diversity to develop an inclusive work environment within which everyone is able to reach their full potential.

Terms to define

Biculturalism

Diversity

Ethnocentrism

Glass ceiling

Inclusivity

Managing diversity

Multicultural organization

Organizational subcultures

Be sure you can

- identify major diversity trends in American society
- explain the business case for diversity
- explain the concept of inclusivity
- list characteristics of multicultural organizations
- identify subcultures common to organizations
- discuss the types of employment problems faced by minorities and women
- explain Thomas's concept of managing diversity

Questions for discussion

1. Why don't current demographic trends and conditions make it easy to create truly multicultural organizations?

2. What are some of the things organizations and leaders can do to reduce diversity bias faced by minorities and women in the workplace?

3. What does the existence of an affirmative action policy say about an organization's commitment to diversity?

17.2 What Should We Know about Diversity among Global Cultures?

A trip to the grocery store, a day spent at work, a visit to our children's schools—all are possible opportunities for us to have cross-cultural experiences. And you have to admit, there's a lot of new faces in the neighborhood. At my university even a walk across campus can be a trip around the world, but we have to be willing to take it. How about you? Do you greet, speak with, and actively engage people of other cultures? Or are you shy, hesitant, and even inclined to avoid them?[30]

• Culture shock comes from discomfort in cross-cultural situations.

Maybe it is a bit awkward to introduce yourself to an international student or foreign visitor to your community. Maybe the appearance of a Muslim woman in a head scarf or of a Nigerian man in a long over blouse is unusual to the point of being intimidating. Maybe, too, when we do meet or work with someone from another culture we experience something well known to international travelers as **culture shock**. This is feelings of confusion and discomfort when in or dealing with an unfamiliar culture.

International businesses are concerned about culture shock because they need their employees to be successful as they travel and work around the world. Listed below are stages that are often encountered as someone adjusts to the unfamiliar setting of a new culture. The assumption is that knowing about the stages can help the international businessperson, and someone traveling for business or pleasure.[31] Perhaps this understanding might also be applied to our everyday cross-cultural experiences right here at home. The stages of adjustment to a new culture are

- *Confusion*—First contacts with the new culture leave you anxious, uncomfortable, and in need of information and advice.
- *Small victories*—Continued interactions bring some "successes," and your confidence grows in handling daily affairs.
- *Honeymoon*—A time of wonderment, cultural immersion, and even infatuation, with local ways viewed positively.
- *Irritation and anger*—A time when the "negatives" overwhelm the "positives" and the new culture becomes a target of your criticism.
- *Reality*—A time of rebalancing; you are able to enjoy the new culture while accommodating its less desirable elements.

> **Culture shock** is the confusion and discomfort that a person experiences when in an unfamiliar culture.

Stay Tuned

Employee Morale Varies Around the World.

A worldwide study shows that what workers want varies from one country to the next. FDS International of the United Kingdom surveyed 13,832 workers in 23 countries. Here is how selected countries ranked on the overall morale of employees as based on job satisfaction, quality of employer-employee relations, and work-life balance.

Top-Ranked	Some Others
1. The Netherlands	10. United States
2. Ireland and Thailand	11. Canada
3. Switzerland	12. Poland
4. Denmark	13. Korea
5. United Kingdom	14. Australia
	15. Japan

What Are Your Thoughts?

Why do you think employee morale in the United States and Canada trails that of other countries such as The Netherlands, Ireland, and Switzerland? Why might one Asian country such as Thailand score very high in employee morale and another such as Korea score much lower? Are there cultural factors that might make a difference in how employees respond to a survey about their workplace morale?

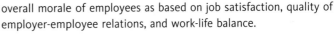

Failure to respect cultural practices can have a negative impact on international business and travel.

• Cultural intelligence is the capacity to adapt to foreign cultures.

A U.S. businessman once went to meet a Saudi Arabian official. He sat in the office with crossed legs and the sole of his shoe exposed, which, unknown to him at the time, is a sign of disrespect in the local culture. He passed documents to the host using his left hand, which Muslims consider unclean. He declined when coffee was offered, suggesting criticism of the Saudi's hospitality. What was the price for these cultural miscues? A $10 million contract was lost to a Korean executive better versed in Arabic ways.[32]

Some might say that this American's behavior was ethnocentric, and he was so self-centered that he ignored and showed no concern for the culture of his Arab host. Others might excuse him as suffering culture shock. Maybe he was so uncomfortable upon arrival in Saudi Arabia that all he could think about was offering his contract and leaving as quickly as possible. Still others might give him the benefit of the doubt. It could have been that he was well intentioned, but didn't have time to learn about Saudi culture before making the trip.

Regardless of the possible reasons for the cultural miscues, however, they still worked to his disadvantage. And there is little doubt that he failed to show **cultural intelligence**—the ability to adapt and adjust to new cultures.[33] People with cultural intelligence have high cultural self-awareness and are flexible in dealing with cultural differences. In cross-cultural situations they are willing to learn from what is unfamiliar; they modify their behaviors to act with sensitivity to another culture's ways. In other words, someone high in cultural intelligence views cultural differences not as threats but as learning opportunities.

Executives at China's Haier Group showed cultural intelligence in the way they responded to problems that popped after the firm opened a new factory in South Carolina.[34] As part of Haier's commitment to quality, workers that make mistakes in its Chinese factories are made to stand on special footprints and publicly criticize themselves by pointing out what they did wrong and what lessons they have learned. When this practice was implemented at the U.S. factory, American workers protested—they thought it was humiliating to stand in the footprints and criticize themselves. But Haier executives didn't respond by forcing the Americans to accept this practice, they changed their approach. The footprints and quality commitment still exist, but American workers now stand in the footprints as a form of public recognition when they do exceptional work. It seems that the Chinese managers in this case listened and learned from their American experiences. And they ended up with a local practice that fits both corporate values and the local culture.

Cultural intelligence is probably a good indicator of someone's capacity for success in international assignments, and in relationships with persons of different cultures. How would you rate yourself? Could cultural intelligence be one of your important personal assets?

Cultural intelligence is the ability to adapt to new cultures.

• The "silent" languages of cultures include context, time, and space.

Nike once featured NBA star LeBron James in a TV ad where he played the role of kung-fu master and battled dragons and Chinese symbols. The ad had to be pulled when Chinese critics claimed it wounded their "national dignity." Another time, McDonalds aired an ad that showed a Chinese man asking for a discount. It was pulled after they received feedback that the ad was "humiliating."[35]

It is easy to recognize differences in the spoken and written languages used by people around the world. And foreign language skills

The silent languages of culture are found in the communication context approach to time and use of space.

can open many doors to cultural understanding. But anthropologist Edward T. Hall points out that there are other "silent" languages of culture that are very significant, too.[36] They are found in the culture's approach to communication context, time, and space.

If we look and listen carefully, Hall believes we should recognize how cultures differ in the ways their members use language in communication.[37] In **low-context cultures** most communication takes place via the written or spoken word. This is common in the United States, Canada, and Germany, for example. As the saying goes: "We say (or write) what we mean, and we mean what we say."

In **high-context cultures** things are different. What is actually said or written may convey only part, and sometimes a very small part, of the real message. The rest must be interpreted from nonverbal signals and the situation as a whole; things such as body language, physical setting, and even past relationships among the people involved. Dinner parties and social gatherings in high-context cultures allow potential business partners to get to know one another. Only after the relationships are established and a context for communication exists is it possible to make business deals.

Hall also notes that the way people approach and deal with time varies across cultures. He describes a **monochronic culture** as one in which people tend to do one thing at a time. This is typical of the United States, where most businesspeople schedule a meeting for one person or group to focus on one issue for an allotted time.[38] And if someone is late for one of those meetings, or brings an uninvited guest, we tend not to like it.

Members of a **polychronic culture** are more flexible toward time and who uses it. They often try to work on many different things at once, perhaps not in any particular order. An American visitor (monochronic culture) to an Egyptian client (polychronic culture) may be frustrated, for example, by continued interruptions as the client greets and deals with people continually flowing in and out of his office.

Finally, Hall points out that most Americans like and value their own space, perhaps as much space as they can get. We like big offices, big homes, big yards; we get uncomfortable in tight spaces and when others stand too close to us in lines. When someone "talks right in our face," we don't like it; the behavior may even be interpreted as an expression of anger.

Members of other cultures can view all of these things quite differently. Hall describes these cultural tendencies in terms of **proxemics**, or how people use interpersonal space to communicate. If you visit Japan, for example, you would notice the difference in proxemics very quickly. Space is precious in Japan; it is respected and its use is carefully planned. Small, tidy homes, offices, and shops are the norm; gardens are tiny but immaculate; public spaces are carefully organized for most efficient use.

Low-context cultures emphasize communication via spoken or written words.

High-context cultures rely on nonverbal and situational cues as well as spoken or written words in communication.

In **monochronic cultures** people tend to do one thing at a time.

In **polychronic cultures** people accomplish many different things at once.

Proxemics is the study of how people use interpersonal space.

Beautiful gardens display how precious space is and how carefully it is used in Japanese culture.

• Hofstede identifies five value differences among national cultures.

As companies expand operations around the world, they need managers with global viewpoints, open to new experiences, and strong on cultural appreciation. Understanding the silent languages just discussed is a good place to start, but cultures are still more complex. Geert Hofstede, a Dutch scholar and international management consultant, explores this complexity in respect to value differences among national cultures.

After studying employees of a United States-based corporation operating in 40 countries, Hofstede identified the four cultural dimensions of power distance, uncertainty avoidance, individualism–collectivism, and masculinity–femininity.[39] Later studies resulted in the addition of a fifth dimension, time orientation.[40]

FIGURE 17.3

How Do Countries Compare on Hofstede's Five Dimensions of National Cultures?

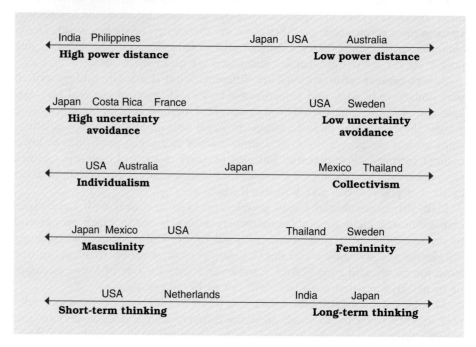

Countries vary on Hofstede's five dimensions of value differences in national cultures. For example, Japan scores somewhat comparatively higher on power distance, and substantially higher on uncertainty avoidance and masculinity; the United States is much more individualistic and short-term oriented. The implications of such cultural differences can be significant. Imagine what they might mean when international business executives try to make deals around the world, or when representatives of national governments try to work out problems.

Figure 17.3 uses the examples of Japan, the United States, and other countries to show how national cultures varied in his research. Can you see why these cultural dimensions can be significant in business and management?

Power distance is the degree to which a society accepts or rejects the unequal distribution of power among people in organizations and the institutions of society. In high power distance cultures such as Japan we would expect to find great respect for age, status, and titles. Could this create problems for an American visitor used to the informalities of a more moderate power distance culture, and perhaps accustomed to first names and casual dress in the office?

Uncertainty avoidance is the degree to which a society tolerates or is uncomfortable with risk, change, and situational uncertainty. In high uncertainty avoidance cultures, such as France, one would expect to find a preference for structure, order, and predictability. Could this be one of the reasons why the French seem to favor employment practices that provide job security? Could this explain why Hong Kong Chinese, from a low uncertainty avoidance culture, are considered very entrepreneurial in business affairs?

Individualism-collectivism is the degree to which a society emphasizes individual accomplishments and self-interests, or collective accomplishments and the interests of groups. In Hofstede's data the United States had the highest individualism score of any country. Think about it; don't you find the "I" and "me" words used a lot in our conversations and meetings? I'm always surprised, for example, how often they occur when students are making team presentations in class. This may reflect our cultural tendency toward individualism. But what

Power distance is the degree to which a society accepts unequal distribution of power.

Uncertainty avoidance is the degree to which a society tolerates risk and uncertainty.

Individualism-collectivism is the degree to which a society emphasizes individuals and their self-interests.

are the implications when we try to work with people from more collectivist national cultures? How, for example, are individualistic Americans perceived in Mexico or Thailand?

Masculinity-femininity is the degree to which a society values assertiveness and materialism, versus feelings, relationships, and quality of life.[41] You might think of it as a tendency to emphasize stereotypical masculine or feminine traits. It also reflects attitudes toward gender roles. Visitors to Japan, with the highest masculinity score in Hofstede's research, may be surprised at how restricted career opportunities can be for women.[42] *The Wall Street Journal* comments: "In Japan, professional women face a set of socially complex issues—from overt sexism to deep-seated attitudes about the division of labor." One female Japanese manager says: "Men tend to have very fixed ideas about what women are like."[43]

Time orientation is the degree to which a society emphasizes short-term or long-term goals and gratifications.[44] Americans are notorious for impatience and desires for quick, even instantaneous, gratifications. Even our companies are expected to achieve short-term results; those failing to meet quarterly financial targets often suffer immediate stock price declines. Many Asian cultures are quite the opposite, valuing persistence and thrift, being patient and willing to work for long-term success. Maybe this helps explain why Japan's auto executives were willing to invest in hybrid technologies and stick with them even though market demand was very low at first.

Although Hofstede's ideas are insightful, his five value dimensions offer only a ballpark look at national cultures, a starting point at best. And Hofstede himself warns that we must avoid the **ecological fallacy**.[45] This is acting with the mistaken assumption that a generalized cultural value, such as individualism in American culture or masculinity in Japanese culture, applies always and equally to all members of the culture.

News Feed

Internet Censorship Fuels Global Debate.

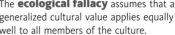

Freedom of expression is a valued human right, at least in America and many other countries. But when working in China, it's best to be careful. A series of incidents raises testy issues of Internet censorship.

The Centre for Democracy and Technology said that "China's actions fail to live up to international norms" and it "is at odds with the rule of law and the right to freedom of expression." What was the problem? China had just blocked access to YouTube, which is owned by Google. This action came after the site had earlier posted footage of unrest in Tibet. Google was highly criticized for allowing the Chinese government to deny access to YouTube sites. "We have a delicate balancing act between being a platform for free expression and also obeying local laws around the world," says YouTube spokesman Ricardo Reyes.

China claims it is acting according to law. But such censorship is a hot issue. After Chinese journalist Shi Tao received a 10-year jail sentence, based in part on information turned over by Yahoo's Hong Kong subsidiary, then CEO Jerry Yang was highly criticized by human-rights and free-speech advocates, and by members of the U.S. Congress.

Also in China, TOM Online, a joint venture of Skype/eBay, was accused of allowing government sources to monitor text chats, track participants in voice calls, and review stored messages about political topics. A spokesperson for TOM says "as a Chinese company we adhere to rules and regulations in China," while Skype spokeswoman Jennifer Caukin says that the parent firm was not aware of the local practice, "deeply apologized," and was "urgently addressing this situation." But *The Wall Street Journal* concludes that "many companies seeking growth in China's dynamic Internet sector have come under criticism that they have been too helpful in enabling censorship in a foreign country."

Reflect and React:

Does culture play a role in this debate on Internet censorship? If you were to profile the United States and China on Hofstede's five dimensions of national cultures, how would they differ? And to what extent might these differences explain alternative views on Internet censorship?

Masculinity-femininity is the degree to which a society values assertiveness and materialism.

Time orientation is the degree to which a society emphasizes short-term or long-term goals.

The **ecological fallacy** assumes that a generalized cultural value applies equally well to all members of the culture.

• Project GLOBE identifies ten country clusters displaying cultural differences.

In project GLOBE, short for Global Leadership and Organizational Behavior Effectiveness, a team of international researchers led by Robert House convened to study leadership, organizational practices, and diversity among world cultures.[46] So far they have collected data from 170,000 managers in 62 countries.

They also discovered that these countries fall into ten culture clusters. Countries within a cluster tend to share societal culture practices with one another, while also differing significantly in many ways from cultural practices of countries in other clusters. The *ten culture clusters* and sample member countries are:

- *Latin America*—Brazil, Ecuador, Mexico
- *Anglo*—Australia, England, U.S.A.
- *Latin Europe*—France, Italy, Spain
- *Nordic Europe*—Denmark, Finland, Sweden
- *Germanic Europe*—Germany, Netherlands, Switzerland
- *Eastern Europe*—Greece, Hungary, Russia
- *Confucian Asia*—China, Japan, Singapore
- *Southern Asia*—India, Malaysia, Philippines
- *Sub-Saharan Africa*—Nigeria, South Africa, Zambia
- *Middle East*—Egypt, Kuwait, Turkey

GLOBE researchers use the nine dimensions shown in **Figure 17.4** to explore and describe cultures among the country clusters.[47] Two of the dimensions are rather direct fits with Hofstede: *power distance*—higher in Confucian Asia and lower in Nordic Europe, and *uncertainty avoidance*—high in Germanic Europe and low in the Middle East.

Three other dimensions are quite similar to Hofstede's. *Gender Egalitarianism* is the degree to which a culture minimizes gender inequalities, similar to Hofstede's masculinity–femininity. It is high in the cultures of Eastern and Nordic Europe and low in those of the Middle East. *Future Orientation* is the degree to

FIGURE 17.4

How Does Project GLOBE Classify Societal Cultures?

	Low-score clusters	Mid-score clusters	High-score clusters
Power distance	Nordic Europe	Sub-Saharan Africa	—
Uncertainty avoidance	Latin America	Southern Asia	Germanic Europe
Gender egalitarianism	Middle East	Anglo	Eastern Europe
Future orientation	Eastern Europe	Latin Europe	Nordic Europe
Institutional collectivism	Latin America	Anglo	Confucian Asia
In-group collectivism	Anglo	Latin Europe	Middle East
Assertiveness	Nordic Europe	Confucian Asia	Germanic Europe
Performance orientation	Eastern Europe	Southern Asia	Confucian Asia
Humane orientation	Germanic Europe	Middle East	Sub-Saharan Africa

A large team of international researchers collaborated in Project GLOBE to examine societal cultures using the nine cultural dimensions shown in the figure. When results from extensive empirical studies were analyzed for 62 countries, they were found to fall into 10 culture clusters. Countries within a cluster share many societal cultural practices; countries tend to differ significantly across clusters in their cultural practices.

which members of a culture are willing to look ahead, delay gratifications, and make investments in the expectation of longer-term payoffs, similar to Hofstede's time orientation. Germanic and Nordic Europe are high on future orientation; Latin America and the Middle East are low. *Institutional Collectivism* is the extent to which the organizations of a society emphasize and reward group action and accomplishments versus individual ones, similar to Hofstede's individualism–collectivism. Confucian Asia and Nordic Europe score high in institutional collectivism, while Germanic and Latin Europe score low.

The remaining four of GLOBE's dimensions offer additional cultural insights. *In-Group Collectivism* is the extent to which people take pride in their families and organizational memberships, acting loyal and cohesive regarding them. This form of collectivism runs high in Latin America and the Middle East, and tends to be low in Anglo and Germanic Europe cultures. *Assertiveness* is described as the extent to which a culture emphasizes competition and assertiveness in social relationships, valuing behavior that is tough and confrontational as opposed to showing modesty and tenderness. Cultures in Eastern and Germanic Europe score high in assertiveness; those in Nordic Europe and Latin America score low.

Performance Orientation is the degree of emphasis on performance excellence and improvements. Anglo and Confucian Asia cultures tend to be high in performance orientation. Countries in these clusters can be expected to reward performance accomplishments and invest in training to encourage future performance gains. *Humane Orientation* reflects tendencies in a society for people to emphasize fairness, altruism, generosity, and caring as they deal with one another. It tends to be high in Southern Asia and Sub-Saharan Africa, and to be low in Latin and Germanic Europe.

The GLOBE research offers a timely, systematic, and empirical look at culture across a large sample of countries. Its results are also being analyzed extensively for their management and leadership implications. Yet, as with other cross-cultural research, the GLOBE project is insightful but not definitive. When combined with the ideas and findings of Hall, Hofstede, and other cross-cultural researchers, however, it too can be useful as we try to better understand the rich diversity of global cultures.[48]

Study Guide

17.2
What Should We Know about Diversity among Global Cultures?

Rapid review

- People can experience culture shock due to the discomfort experienced in cross-cultural situations.
- Cultural intelligence is an individual capacity to understand, respect, and adapt to cultural differences.
- Hall's "silent" languages of culture include the role of context in communication, time orientation, and use of interpersonal space.
- Hofstede's five dimensions of value differences in national cultures are power distance, uncertainty avoidance, individualism–collectivism, masculinity–femininity, and time orientation.
- Project GLOBE groups countries into ten clusters, with cultures similar within clusters and different across them on nine cultural dimensions.

Terms to define

Cultural intelligence

Culture

Culture shock

Ecological fallacy

High-context culture

Individualism-collectivism

Low-context culture

Masculinity-femininity

Monochronic culture

Polychronic culture

Power distance

Proxemics

Time orientation

Uncertainty avoidance

Be sure you can

- explain culture shock and how people may respond to it
- differentiate low-context and high-context cultures, monochronic and polychronic cultures
- list Hofstede's five dimensions of value differences among national cultures
- contrast American culture with that of other countries on each dimension
- explain the insights of project GLOBE for cross-cultural understanding

Questions for discussion

1. Should religion be included on Hall's list of the silent languages of culture?
2. Which of Hofstede's, or project GLOBE's, cultural dimensions might pose the greatest challenges to U.S. managers working in Asia, the Middle East, or Latin America?
3. Even though cultural differences are readily apparent around the world, is the trend today for cultures to converge and become more like one another?

Test Prep

Multiple choice

1. Which of these statements is most consistent with arguments set forth in the business case for diversity?
   (a) Diversity in organizations is inevitable.
   (b) Diversity is valued by all people.
   (c) Diverse workforces are good at dealing with diverse customers.
   (d) Diverse workforces discourage talented new members.

2. When members of minority cultures feel that they have to behave similar to the ways of the majority culture, this tendency is called _____.
   (a) biculturalism
   (b) particularism
   (c) the glass ceiling effect
   (d) multiculturalism

3. The beliefs that older workers are not creative and mostly desire routine, low-stress jobs are examples of stereotypes that might create bad feelings among members of different _____ subcultures in organizations.
   (a) gender
   (b) generational
   (c) functional
   (d) ethnic

4. Among the three leadership approaches to diversity identified by Thomas, which one is primarily directed at making sure that minorities and women are hired by the organization?
   (a) equal employment opportunity
   (b) affirmative action
   (c) valuing diversity
   (d) managing diversity

5. Pluralism and the absence of discrimination and prejudice in policies and practices are two important hallmarks of _____.
   (a) the glass ceiling effect
   (b) a multicultural organization
   (c) quality circles
   (d) affirmative action

6. _____ means that an organization fully integrates members of minority cultures and majority cultures.
   (a) Equal employment opportunity
   (b) Affirmative action
   (c) Symbolic leadership
   (d) Pluralism

7. When members of the marketing department stick close to one another, as well as share jokes and even a slang language, the likelihood is that a/an _____ subculture is forming.
   (a) occupational
   (b) generational
   (c) gender
   (d) functional

8. In _____ cultures, members tend to do one thing at a time; in _____ cultures, members tend to do many things at once.
   (a) monochronic/polychronic
   (b) universal/particular
   (c) collectivist/individualist
   (d) neutral/affective

9. Hofstede's study of national cultures found that the United States is the most highly _____ culture of any countries in his sample.
   (a) individualistic
   (b) collectivist
   (c) feminine
   (d) long-term oriented

10. When a foreign visitor to India attends a dinner, and criticizes as "primitive" a local custom of eating with one's fingers, he or she can be described as acting _____.
    (a) diffuse
    (b) sequentially
    (c) monochronic
    (d) ethnocentric

11. In a high-context culture such as that in Egypt, we would expect to find _____.
    (a) low uncertainty avoidance
    (b) belief in achievement
    (c) an inner-directed orientation toward nature
    (d) emphasis on nonverbal as well as verbal communication

12. It is common in Malaysian culture for people to value teamwork and to display great respect for authority. Hofstede would describe this culture as high in both _____.
    (a) uncertainty avoidance and feminism
    (b) universalism and particularism
    (c) collectivism and power distance
    (d) long-term orientation and masculinity

13. On which dimension of national culture did the United States score highest and Japan score highest in Hofstede's original survey research?

    (a) masculinity, femininity
    (b) long-term, short-term
    (c) individualism, masculinity
    (d) high uncertainty avoidance, collectivism

14. In the Project GLOBE framework, someone from a culture high in _____ would be expected to take a lot of pride in their families and act loyal in their group memberships.

    (a) in-group collectivism
    (b) humane orientation
    (c) institutional collectivism
    (d) future orientation

Short response

15. What is the difference between valuing diversity and managing diversity?

16. How can subculture differences create diversity challenges in organizations?

17. In what ways can the power-distance dimension of national culture become an important issue in management?

18. Why would a global corporation be interested in training its managers to understand cultural differences in what project GLOBE calls "assertiveness"?

Integration & application

19. A friend of mine in West Virginia owns a small manufacturing firm employing about 50 workers. His son spent a semester in Japan as an exchange student. Upon return he said to his Dad: "Boy, the Japanese really do things right; everything is organized in teams; decisions are made by consensus, with everyone participating; no one seems to disagree with anything the bosses say. I think we should immediately start more teamwork and consensus decision making in our factory."

Questions: My friend has asked you for advice. Using insights from Hofstede's framework, what would you say to him? What differences in the Japanese and American cultures should be considered in this situation, and why?

Self-Assessment

Diversity Awareness

Instructions

Indicate "O" for often, "S" for sometimes, and "N" for never in response to each of the following questions as they pertain to where you work or go to school.[49]

1. How often have you heard jokes or remarks about other people that you consider offensive?

2. How often do you hear men "talk down" to women in an attempt to keep them in an inferior status?

3. How often have you felt personal discomfort as the object of sexual harassment?

4. How often do you work or study with persons of different ethnic or national cultures?

5. How often have you felt disadvantaged because members of ethnic groups other than yours were given special treatment?

6. How often have you seen a woman put in an uncomfortable situation because of unwelcome advances by a man?

7. How often does it seem that African Americans, Hispanics, Caucasians, women, men, and members of other minority demographic groups seem to

"stick together" during work breaks or other leisure situations?

8. How often do you feel uncomfortable about something you did and/or said to someone of the opposite sex or a member of an ethnic or racial group other than yours?

9. How often do you feel efforts are made in this setting to raise the level of cross-cultural understanding among people who work and/or study together?

10. How often do you step in to communicate concerns to others when you feel actions and/or words are used to the disadvantage of minorities?

Interpretation

There are no correct answers for the Diversity Awareness Checklist. The key issue is the extent to which you are sensitive to diversity issues in the workplace or university. Are you comfortable with your responses? How do you think others in your class responded? Why not share your responses with others and examine different viewpoints on this important issue?

 For further exploration go to WileyPlus

Case Snapshot

Toyota: Looking Far into the Future

By borrowing the best ideas from American brands and by constant innovation Toyota has become a paragon of auto manufacturing efficiency. Its vehicles are widely known for their quality and longevity—and Toyota's sales numbers are the envy of the American Big Three. Here is how Toyota became so efficient at producing high-quality automobiles. And don't you wonder, what role has national culture played in the firm's global success?

Online Interactive Learning Resources

SELF-ASSESSMENT
• Time Orientation

EXPERIENTIAL EXERCISE
• American Football

TEAM PROJECT
• Diversity Lessons

18 Globalization and International Business

Going Global Isn't Just for Travelers

Globalization gets a workout as businesses travel the world. This is a shopping test: What do Victoria's Secret, Pink, C.O. Bigelow, La Senza, Bath & Body Works, The White Barn Candle Co., and Henri Bendel all have in common?

Answer: Their roots all trace to 1963 and a small woman's clothing store in Columbus, Ohio. That single store has grown into a company with one of the best fashion names in the world—Limited Brands Inc., headed by founder, chairman, and CEO Leslie Wexner. In the retail industry, Wexner has been called a "pioneer of specialty brands" and someone with unique retailing "vision and focus." A member of the CEO's retail all-star team, he also knows international business.

This is a global economy test: Where does the Limited shop to stock its 3,000+ specialty stores? Answer: It shops around the world—anywhere and everywhere it can get quality products at the best prices. But the company also has to be careful. Although it finds high-quality materials at good prices from many reliable

Trendsetters
Victor Fung warns against drift toward protectionism.

News Feed
More global firms employ sweatshop hunters.

Case Snapshot
Harley-Davidson—Style and strategy have global reach.

foreign partners, it also risks getting entangled with some suppliers whose lack of ethics and bad behavior could reflect poorly on its brands.

To protect its image as an international business, The Limited uses its "What We Stand For" policy to guide its relationships with suppliers and subcontractors. The policy states: "We will not do business with individuals or suppliers that do not meet our standards. We expect our suppliers to promote an environment of dignity, respect and opportunity; provide safe and healthy working conditions; offer fair compensation through wages and other benefits; hire workers of legal age, who accept employment on a voluntary basis; and maintain reasonable working hours".

How does Limited Brands do as it travels the world seeking textile business partners and products? Very well, actually. For its role in helping to expand the apparel manufacturing industry in Sub-Saharan Africa to over $1 billion in sales, Limited Brands was given the Special Recognition Award for Business Enterprise in Africa from the Africa-America Institute. In respect to business success, Wexner says: "Better brands. Best brands. I don't believe bigger is better. I believe better is better. Period."

18.1 How Does Globalization Affect International Business?

There is no doubt that our global community is rich with information, opportunities, controversies, and complications. The Internet and television bring on-the-spot news from around the world into our homes; most of the world's newspapers can be read online. It is possible to board a plane in New York and fly nonstop to Bangkok, Thailand, or Mumbai, India, or Cape Town, South Africa. Colleges and universities offer a growing variety of study-abroad programs. And in the business world an international MBA is an increasingly desirable credential.

Speaking of the business side of things, the opening example of Limited Brands was a good place to start thinking about the international sides of business and management. Here are some other conversation starters. IBM employs over 40,000 software developers in India. Mercedes builds M-class vehicles in Alabama; India's Tata Group owns Jaguar and Land Rover; Ford sells its Fiesta model around the world; Japan's Honda, Nissan, and Toyota get 80 to 90% of their profits from sales in America. The front fuselage of Boeing's new 787 Dreamliner is made by a Japanese company; 60% of the plane's components are made by foreign firms. Nike earns the vast majority of its sales outside of the U.S., with its complex worldwide web of contractors including over 120 factories in China alone. And Anheuser-Busch is now owned by the Belgian firm InBev.[1]

Similar trends and patterns are evident in other industries, and the growing power of global businesses affects all of us in our roles as citizens, consumers, and career-seekers. If at all in doubt, take a look at what you are wearing. You might be surprised how hard it is to find a garment or a shoe that is really "Made in America."

• Globalization involves the growing interdependence of the world's economies.

In the **global economy,** resources, markets, and competition are worldwide in scope.

Globalization is the process of growing interdependence among elements of the global economy.

Insourcing is the creation of domestic jobs by foreign employers.

This is the age of the **global economy** in which resource supplies, product markets, and business competition are worldwide rather than purely local or national in scope.[2] It is also a time heavily influenced by the forces of **globalization**, defined in earlier chapters as the process of growing interdependence among the components in the global economy.[3] Harvard scholar and consultant Rosabeth Moss Kanter describes globalization as "one of the most powerful and pervasive influences on nations, businesses, workplaces, communities, and lives."[4]

Globalization means a lot of things, many of them well reflected in the turmoil caused by the recent recession and financial crisis. What about your work and career plans? Do you have a good idea of how much globalization affects your life? If you come to Ohio, where I live, you'll find almost 1 out of every 20 persons employed in the private sector working for foreign firms.[5] These are jobs created by **insourcing**, ones provided domestically by foreign employers. At last count there were more than 5 million such jobs in the U.S. economy.

Perhaps you are or will someday be holding one, working in America for a foreign employer just like Allen Kinzer. He was the first U.S. manager hired by Honda to work in its Marysville, Ohio, plant. Now retired, he says: "It wasn't easy blending the cultures; anyone who knew anything about the industry at the time would have to say it was a bold move." Bold move, indeed! Honda now employs over 13,000 people in its multiple U.S. plants, which produce over 500,000 cars per year. It is only one

Through direct investments in the United States, foreign firms provide many jobs for domestic workers.

among hundreds of foreign firms offering employment opportunities to U.S. workers.[6]

Outsourcing is the other side of the job story. It involves shifting jobs to foreign locations to save costs by taking advantage of lower-wage skilled labor in other countries. John Chambers, CEO of Cisco Systems Inc., pretty much lays it on the line for all of us when he says: "I will put my jobs anywhere in the world where the right infrastructure is, with the right educated workforce, with the right supportive government."[7]

Outsourcing shifts local jobs to foreign locations to take advantage of lower-wage labor in other countries.

• Globalization creates a variety of international business opportunities.

Sony, Limited Brands, IKEA, and other firms like them are large **international businesses**. They do business by conducting for-profit transactions of goods and services across national boundaries. Such businesses, from small exporters and importers to the huge multinational corporations (MNCs), form the foundations of world trade, helping to move raw materials, finished products, and specialized services from one country to another in the global economy. And they all "go global" for good reasons.

An **international business** conducts commercial transactions across national boundaries.

Nike is one of those brands that may come to mind as an exemplar of international businesses; its swoosh is one of the world's most globally recognized brands. But did you know that Nike does no domestic manufacturing? All of its products come from sources abroad. Consider also New Balance. This Boston firm has been in business for more than 100 years and it sells in some 120 countries. New Balance still produces at factories in the United States, even while manufacturing in China and elsewhere, making extensive use of global suppliers and licensing some of its products internationally.[8]

While competing in the same industry, Nike and New Balance are pursuing somewhat different strategies as they deal with the opportunities and threats of a global economy. Both stories are good examples of how businesses naturally grow and go international for reasons such as these.[9]

Global firms seek profits, customers, suppliers, capital, and labor as they do business in many countries.

- *Profits*—Global operations offer greater profit potential through expanded operations
- *Customers*—Global operations offer new markets to gain customers and sell products and services
- *Suppliers*—Global operations offer access to products, services, and raw materials
- *Capital*—Global operations offer access to alternative providers of financial resources
- *Labor*—Global operations offer access to labor markets with low-cost, talented workers
- *Risk*—Global operations offer risk management by spreading assets among multiple countries

Today you can also add to this list *economic development*—where a global firm does business in foreign countries with direct intent to advance local economic development. An example is coffee giants Green Mountain Coffee Roasters, Peet's Coffee & Tea, and Starbucks working in Rwanda with the nonprofit TechnoServe. Funded by the Bill & Melinda Gates Foundation, TechnoServe's goal is to help raise the incomes for African coffee farmers by improving their production and marketing methods. Partner firms send advisors to help teach the coffee growers how to meet their standards so that the local products can be sourced for sale worldwide. It's a win-win for all; the global firm gets a quality product at a good price, the growers gain skills and market opportunities, and the local economy improves. Peet's director of coffee purchasing, Shirin Moayyad, says: "If they produce a high-quality produce we'll pay more for it."[10]

• International business is done by global sourcing, import/export, licensing, and franchising.

Not only is there more than one reason for getting into international business, there are several ways of doing it. And getting started with the forms of international business shown in **Figure 18.1** can be relatively easy.

FIGURE 18.1

Common Forms of International Business—from Market Entry to Direct Investment Strategies.

Market entry strategies			Direct investment strategies	
Global sourcing	Exporting and importing	Licensing and franchising	Joint ventures	Foreign subsidiaries

Increasing involvement in ownership and control of foreign operations

In **global sourcing,** firms purchase materials or services around the world for local use.

A common first step in international business is **global sourcing** such as that described in the opening example of Limited Brands. Through global sourcing, a business purchases materials, manufacturing components, or services from around the world. This is basically taking advantage of international wage gaps by contracting for goods and services in low-cost foreign locations.

In automobile manufacturing, for example, global sourcing may mean designs from Italy, windshields and instrument panels from Mexico, antilock braking systems from Germany, and electronics from Malaysia. In services, it may mean setting up customer-support call centers in the Philippines, contracting for computer software engineers in Russia, or having medical x-rays read by physicians in India.

China is a major global sourcing destination and has become the world's manufacturer for many essential items.

Firms selling toys, shoes, electronics, furniture, and clothing are among those that make extensive use of global sourcing. The goal is to take advantage of international wage gaps and by sourcing products in countries that can produce them at the lowest costs. China, as suggested by the box, is a major outsourcing destination and in many areas of manufacturing it has become the factory for the world. It manufactures, believe it or not, 70% of the world's umbrellas, 72% of U.S. shoes, 50% of U.S. appliances, and 80% of U.S. toys.[11] And if you follow the news you'll find many more examples; the global sourcing trend shows little signs of slowing down.

In **exporting,** local products are sold abroad.

Importing is the process of acquiring products abroad and selling them in domestic markets.

In **licensing,** one firm pays a fee for rights to make or sell another company's products.

A second form of international business involves **exporting**—selling locally made products in foreign markets, and **importing**—buying foreign-made products and selling them in domestic markets. Because the growth of export industries creates local jobs, governments often support these business initiatives. Franklin Jacobs is the founder of a commercial furniture company, St. Louis-based Falcon Products Inc. While on a tour through Europe, he says, "I discovered that my products were a lot better and a lot cheaper." With the help of the U.S. government, he rented exposition space in London, showcased his furniture, and landed over $200,000 in orders. He then built an export program that added jobs at his St. Louis firm.[12]

Another form of international business is the **licensing** agreement, where foreign firms pay a fee for rights to make or sell another company's products in a specified region. The license typically grants access to a unique manufacturing technology, special patent, or trademark. In effect the foreign firm provides the local firm with the technology and knowledge to offer its products or services for local sales. One of the business risks of the company granting a license is the appearance of counterfeit brands.[13] New Balance, for example, licensed a Chinese supplier to produce one of its brands. Even after New Balance revoked the license, the supplier continued to produce and distribute the shoes around Asia. New Balance ended up facing costly and complex litigation in China's courts.[14]

In **franchising**, a foreign firm buys the rights to use another's name and operating methods in its home country. When companies such as McDonald's or Starbucks franchise internationally, they sell facility designs, equipment, product ingredients, recipes, and management systems to foreign investors. They also typically retain certain product and operating controls to protect their brand's image.

China Manufactures
for the World

• **70% of world's umbrellas**
• **60% of world's buttons**
• **72% of U.S. shoes**
• **50% of U.S. appliances**
• **80% of U.S. toys**

In **franchising,** a firm pays a fee for rights to use another company's name and operating methods.

• International business is done by joint ventures and wholly owned subsidiaries.

Sooner or later, some firms that are active in international business decide to make costly direct investments in operations in foreign countries. One common way to do this is through a **joint venture**. This is a co-ownership arrangement in which the foreign and local partners agree to pool resources, share risks, and jointly operate the new business. Sometimes the joint venture is formed when a foreign partner buys part ownership in an existing local firm; in other cases it is formed as an entirely new operation that the foreign and local partners start up together.

International joint ventures are types of **global strategic alliances** in which foreign and domestic firms act as partners by sharing resources and knowledge for mutual benefit. Basically, each partner hopes to gain through cooperation things they couldn't do or would have a hard time doing alone. For the local partner an alliance may bring access to technology and opportunities to learn new skills. For the outside partner an alliance may bring access to new markets and the expert assistance of locals that understand them.[15]

A **joint venture** operates in a foreign country through co-ownership with local partners.

In a **global strategic alliance** each partner hopes to achieve through cooperation things they couldn't do alone.

Joint ventures were the business forms of choice for the world's large automakers when they decided to pursue major operations in China. Recognizing the local complexities, they decided it was better to cooperate with local partners than try to enter the Chinese markets on their own. Of course, any such business deals pose potential risks as well. Not long ago, GM executives noticed that a new car from a fast-growing local competitor, partially owned by GM's Chinese joint venture partner, looked very similar to one of its models. GM claims its design was copied. The competitor denied it, and even pursued plans to export the cars, called "Cherys," for sale in the United States.[16]

Tips to Remember
Checklist for Choosing a Good Joint Venture Partner

• Familiar with your firm's major business
• Employs a strong local workforce
• Values its customers
• Has potential for future expansion
• Has strong local market for its own products
• Has good profit potential
• Has sound financial standing
• Has reputation for ethical decision making
• Has reputation for socially responsible practices

In contrast to the international joint venture, which is a cross-border partnership, a **foreign subsidiary** is a local operation completely owned and controlled by a foreign firm. It might be a local firm that was purchased in its entirety; it might be a brand new operation built up as a start-up, or **greenfield venture**. Quite often, the decision to set up a foreign subsidiary is made only after the foreign firm has gained experience in the local environment through earlier joint ventures.

A **foreign subsidiary** is a local operation completely owned by a foreign firm.

A **greenfield venture** establishes a foreign subsidiary by building an entirely new operation in a foreign country.

• International business is complicated by different legal and political systems.

When it comes to risk in international business, including the licensing and joint venture problems just discussed, some of the biggest complications come from differences in legal and political systems. When firms conduct business abroad they are expected to abide by local laws, some of which may be unfamiliar. In the United States, for example, executives of foreign-owned companies must comply with antitrust issues that prevent competitors from regularly talking to one another, something that they may not be used to at home. They also must deal with a variety of laws regarding occupational health and safety, equal employment opportunity, sexual harassment, and other matters. All of these laws, and more, may be different from the legal environments they are used to at home.

Trendsetters

Victor Fung Warns Against Drift Toward Protectionism

Li & Fung. You've probably never heard the name but *Fast Company* magazine includes it among the 10 most innovative companies in China and says the "middle-man consumer-products business has its prints on just about anything with a 'Made in China' label." Founded in 1906 in Guangzhou, China, by Fung Pak-liu and Li To-ming, Li & Fung is now a close to $20 billion conglomerate headquartered in Hong Kong and with core businesses in export trading, distribution, and retailing. The export sourcing firm, Li & Fung Limited, is one of the world's largest supply chain management companies, handling production for firms like Limited Brands, Timberland, and Liz Claiborne.

Dr. Victor Fung is currently the Chairman of the Li & Fung group of companies. He is Fung Pak-liu's grandson, and holds a doctorate in business administration and bachelor's and master's degrees from MIT. In addition to running his conglomerate and its world-wide reach, Fung is serving as chairman of the International Chamber of Commerce. It is in that role that he has been speaking out with a "please deliver" message to global business leaders.

Fung publicly warned the Group of 20 industrialized nations not to drift into protectionism during the global financial and economic crisis. He expressed worry about President Nicolas Sarkozy's call to keep auto jobs in France and the chorus of voices supporting "Buy America" in the United States.

"If we take away what we've nurtured all these years in the multi-lateral trading systems, then we do so at our peril," he said. Pointing to the Great Depression, he observes that the protectionism it spawned actually caused a loss of jobs around the world and made the crisis worse. According to Fung, "Protectionism actually serves to destroy jobs in the economy."

Noting also that the Chinese word for "crisis" is a combination of "danger" and "opportunity," he also urged business leaders to take steps now to gain advantage when the economic rebound comes.

As you might imagine, the more home-country and host-country laws differ, the more difficult and complex it is for international businesses to adapt to local ways. Intel, for example, was fined $1.45 billion by the European Union for breaking its antitrust laws. Neelie Kroes, the EU's antitrust regulator, said: "Intel has harmed millions of European consumers by deliberately acting to keep competitors out of the market for computer chips for many years."[17]

Common legal problems faced by international businesses involve incorporation practices and business ownership; negotiating and implementing contracts with foreign parties; handling foreign exchange; and intellectual property—patents, trademarks, and copyrights.

The issue of intellectual property is particularly sensitive these days. You might know this best in terms of concerns about movie and music downloads, photocopying of books and journals, and sale of fake designer fashions. Many Western businesses know it as lost profits due to their products or designs being copied and sold as imitations by foreign firms.

After a lengthy and complex legal battle, Starbucks won a major intellectual property case it had taken to the Chinese courts. A local firm was using Starbucks' Chinese name, "Xingbake" (*Xing* means "star" and *bake* is pronounced "bah kuh"), and was also copying its café designs.[18] Hewlett Packard has also had some success chasing Chinese counterfeiters. In one instance and working with local police, the firm's investigators tracked illicit ink cartridges to 14 warehouses in China, seized $88 million of equipment and materials, and obtained jail sentences for two local manufacturers.[19]

When international businesses believe they are being mistreated in foreign countries, or when local companies believe foreign competitors are disadvantaging them, their respective governments might take the cases to the **World Trade Organization (WTO)**. This global institution was established to promote free trade and open markets around the world. A quick look at the WTO website, for example, finds this justification for its work: "liberal trade policies—that allow the unrestricted flow of goods and services—sharpen competition, motivate innovation and breed success. They multiply the rewards that result from producing the best products, with the best design, at the best price."

The 140 members of the WTO give one another **most favored nation status—** the most favorable treatment for imports and exports. Members also agree to work together within its framework to try and resolve some international business problems. But controversies are still inevitable. For example, in one claim filed with the WTO against China, the United States complained that China's "legal structure for protecting and enforcing copyright and trademark protections" was "deficient" and not in compliance with WTO rules. China's official response was that the suit was out of line with WTO rules and that "We strongly oppose the U.S. attempt to impose on developing members through this case."[20]

Even though WTO members are supposed to give one another most favored nation status in treatments of imports and exports, trade barriers are still common among countries. **Tariffs** are one type of trade barrier. They are basically taxes that governments impose on imports in order to limit them. Another form of trade barrier and one of the big issues of the day is **protectionism**. This is where governments try to protect local firms from foreign competition and save jobs for local workers. You will see such issues reflected in many political campaigns and debates. And the issues aren't easy. Government leaders, including the president of the United States, face internal political dilemmas involving the often-conflicting goals of seeking freer international trade while still protecting domestic industries. Such dilemmas make it sometimes difficult to reach international agreements on trade matters and create controversies for the WTO in its role as a global arbiter of trade issues.

The **World Trade Organization (WTO)** is a global institution established to promote free trade and open markets around the world.

Most favored nation status gives a trading partner the most favorable treatment for imports and exports.

Tariffs are taxes governments levy on imports from abroad.

Protectionism is a call for tariffs and favorable treatments to protect domestic firms from foreign competition.

Study Guide

18.1
How Does Globalization Affect International Business?

Rapid review

- The forces of globalization create international business opportunities to pursue profits, customers, capital, and low-cost suppliers and labor in different countries.
- The least costly ways of doing business internationally are to use global sourcing, exporting and importing, and licensing and franchising.
- Direct investment strategies to establish joint ventures or wholly owned subsidiaries in foreign countries represent substantial commitments to international operations.
- Environmental differences, particularly in legal and political systems, can complicate international business activities.
- The World Trade Organization (WTO) is a global institution established to promote free trade and open markets around the world.

Terms to define

Exporting

Foreign subsidiary

Franchising

Global economy

Global sourcing

Global strategic alliance

Globalization

Importing

Insourcing

International business

Joint venture

Licensing agreement

Outsourcing

Tariffs

World Trade Organization (WTO)

Be sure you can

- explain how globalization impacts our lives
- list five reasons that companies pursue international business opportunities
- describe and give examples of how firms do international business by global sourcing, exporting/importing, franchising/licensing, joint ventures, and foreign subsidiaries
- discuss how differences in legal environments can affect businesses operating internationally
- explain the purpose of the World Trade Organization

Questions for discussion

1. Why would a government want to prohibit a foreign firm from owning more than 49% of a local joint venture?
2. Are joint ventures worth the risk of being taken advantage of by foreign partners, as with GM's "Chery" case in China?
3. What aspects of the U.S. legal environment might prove complicated for a Russian firm starting new operations in the United States?

18.2 What Are Global Corporations and How Do They Work?

If you travel abroad these days, many of your favorite brands and products will travel with you. You can have a McDonald's sandwich in 119 countries, follow it with a Haagen-Dazs ice cream in some 50 countries, and then brush up with Procter & Gamble's Crest in 80 countries. Economists even use the "Big Mac" index to track purchasing power parity among the world's currencies. The index compares the price in a currency such as the U.S. dollar of the McDonald's sandwich around the world.[21]

Although many international businesses exist, they don't all pursue world-wide missions and strategies or earn huge revenues abroad. There is quite a difference between Nike and McDonald's, which earn the majority of their profits outside of the United States, for example, and the small St. Louis furniture maker Falcon Products mentioned earlier as exporting to foreign customers when the opportunity arises.

Big Mac Index (2009 Data)	
United States	$3.54
Australia	$2.19
Brazil	$3.45
China	$1.83
Euro area	$4.38
Mexico	$2.30
Russia	$1.73
Sweden	$4.58
Turkey	$3.13

• Global corporations or MNCs do substantial business in many countries.

A **global corporation** or **multinational corporation (MNC)** has extensive international operations in many foreign countries, and derives a substantial portion of its sales and profits from international sources.[22]

The world's largest MNCs are identified in annual listings such as *Fortune* magazine's Global 500 and the *Financial Times*' FT Global 500. They include names very familiar to consumers, such as Wal-Mart, BP, Toyota, Nestlé, BMW, Hitachi, Caterpillar, Sony, and Samsung. Also on the list are some you might not recognize such as big oil and gas producers like PetroChina (China), Gazprom (Russia), Total (France), and Petrobas (Brazil).[23]

Also important on the world scene are *multinational organizations* whose nonprofit missions and operations span the globe. Examples include the International Federation of Red Cross and Red Crescent Societies, the United Nations, and the World Bank.

Most MNCs retain strong national identifications even while operating around the world. Is there any doubt in your mind that Wal-Mart and Dell are "American" firms whereas Honda and Sony are "Japanese"? Most likely not, but that may not be the way their executives would like the firms viewed. And, by the way, which company is really more American—the Indian giant Tata Group which gets more than 50% of its revenues from North America, or IBM, which gets 65% of its revenues outside of the United States?[24]

Top managers of many multinationals are trying to move their firms toward becoming **transnational corporations**. That is, they would like to operate world-wide and without being identified with one national home.[25] Nestlé is a good example. When you buy the firm's products do you have any idea that it is a registered Swiss company? Executives at Nestlé, for example, view the entire world as their domain for acquiring resources, locating production facilities, marketing goods and services, and establishing brand image. They seek total integration of global operations, try to make major decisions from a global perspective, distribute work among worldwide points of excellence, and employ senior executives from many different countries.

A **global corporation** or **multinational** corporation has extensive international business dealings in many foreign countries.

A **transnational corporation** is an MNC that operates worldwide on a borderless basis.

• The actions of global corporations can be controversial at home and abroad.

The recent U.S. economic downturn and national elections raised important questions that relate, in part at least, to the growth of the "transnational" concept of global business. Does a company's nationality matter to the domestic economy?

Does it matter to an American whether local jobs come from a domestic giant such as AT&T or a foreign one such as Toyota?[26] And how about what some call the "globalization gap" in which large multinationals gain disproportionately from the forces of globalization while smaller firms and many countries do not.[27]

Have you ever thought about how much power multinational corporations wield in the world economy? The United Nations reports that they hold one-third of the world's productive assets and control 70% of world trade. Revenues of Exxon/Mobil, for example, are equivalent to Egypt's GDP; Finland's budget is 20% less than the annual sales of its premier multinational Nokia.[28] Furthermore, more than 90% of these MNCs are based in the Northern Hemisphere. While this economic power is undoubtedly good for the business leaders and investors, it can be threatening to small and less-developed countries and their domestic industries.

Ideally, global corporations and the countries that host their foreign operations should all benefit. But, as **Figure 18.2** shows, things can go both right and wrong in MNC-host country relationships.

FIGURE 18.2

What Can Go Right and Wrong in Relationships Between MNCs and Their Host Countries?

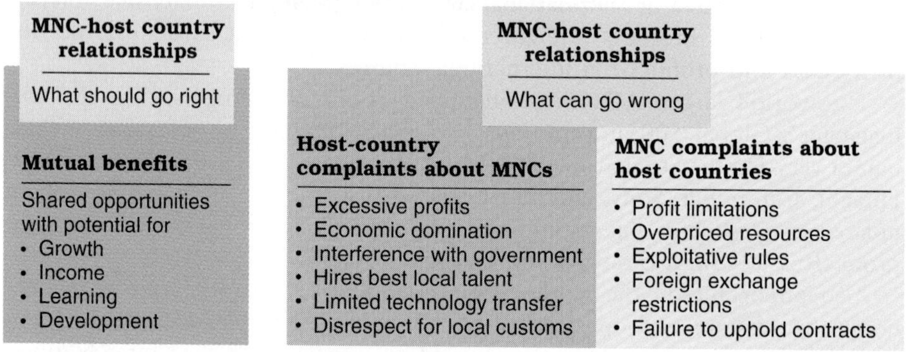

When things go right, both the MNC and its host countries gain. The MNC gets profits or resources, and the host country often sees more jobs and employment opportunities, higher tax revenues, and useful technology transfers. But when things go wrong, each finds ways to blame the other.

MNCs may complain that the host country bars it from taking profits out of country, overprices local resources, and imposes restrictive government rules. Host countries may accuse the MNCs of hiring the best local talent, failing to respect local customs, making too much profit, and failing to transfer really useful technology.[29] Another complaint is that MNCs may use unfair practices, such as below-cost pricing, to drive local competitors out of business. This is one of the arguments in favor of *protectionism*, discussed earlier as the use of laws and practices to protect a country's domestic businesses from foreign competitors.

MNCs can also run into difficulties in their home or headquarters countries. If a multinational cuts local jobs and then moves or outsources the work to another country, local government and community leaders will quickly criticize the firm for its lack of social responsibility. After all, they will say, shouldn't you be creating local jobs and building the local economy? Perhaps you might agree with this view. But can you see why business executives might disagree?

• Managers of global corporations face a variety of ethical challenges.

The ethical aspects of international business are often in the news. In just one day, March 24, 2008, for example, *The Wall Street Journal* contained articles on:

Brazil—where Alcoa is spending over $35 million on health services, a water system, and technical training for local residents in the area of a mine it wants to expand; Indonesia—where locals suffer shortages of coal, natural gas, and palm oil at the same time that export of the same commodities are increasing to China, India, and Japan; and China—where the government's harsh treatment of Tibetan unrest dampened prospects for foreign direct investments in the region.[30]

Take a moment to think where you stand on the underlying issues in these examples, and think also about other areas of ethical challenge that face global corporations. One of the issues and challenges is that the employees of MNCs sometimes get involved in **corruption**. That is, they resort to illegal practices, such as bribes, to further their business interests in foreign countries.

In the United States, the **Foreign Corrupt Practices Act** makes it illegal for U.S. firms and their representatives to engage in corrupt practices overseas. This prevents them from paying or offering bribes or excessive commissions, including non-monetary gifts, to foreign officials or employees of state-run companies in return for business favors.[31] Such a ban makes sense, but critics claim that it fails to recognize the realities of business as practiced in many foreign nations. They believe it puts U.S. companies at a competitive disadvantage because they can't offer the same "deals" as businesses from other nations—deals that the locals may regard as standard business practices. Lucent Technologies, for example, was fined $2.5 million for paying travel expenses for executives of Chinese government-owned telecom companies to visit Disney World and other U.S. tourist spots. The trips were entered into the company's official records as "factory tours."[32]

What do you think? Should U.S. legal standards apply to American companies operating abroad? Or should they be allowed to practice business in whatever way the local setting considers acceptable? A good case in point involves doing business in countries with weak employment laws.

Global businesses may end up working with local firms best described as **sweatshops**, places in which employees work at low wages for long hours and in poor, even unsafe, conditions.[33] They may also work with those using **child labor**, the full-time employment of children for work otherwise done by adults.[34] As you might guess, the owners of such places might be in a good position to offer low prices to foreign companies buying their products. But just because the factory is legal by local standards, does this justify doing business with its owners?

The fact is that even the most well-intentioned of MNCs can end up in troublesome relationships with their global suppliers. Nike Inc., for example, contracts with hundreds of manufacturing sites around the world. When problems with employee treatment at some of them came to light, Nike was threatened with consumer boycotts. The firm now lists on its Web site all countries it does business in and who its suppliers are, as well as results from social audits of its international labor practices.[35]

Corruption involves illegal practices to further one's business interests.

The **Foreign Corrupt Practices Act** makes it illegal for U.S. firms and their representatives to engage in corrupt practices overseas.

Sweatshops employ workers at very low wages, for long hours, and in poor working conditions.

Child labor is the full-time employment of children for work otherwise done by adults.

Stay Tuned

Corruption and Bribes Haunt International Business.

If you want a world free of corruption and bribes, you have a lot in common with the nonprofit activist organization Transparency International. From its headquarters in Berlin, "TI" publishes regular surveys and reports on corruption and bribery around the world. Here are some recent data.

Corruption: Best and worst out of 180 countries in perceived corruption in doing business.
   Best—1. Denmark, 2. New Zealand, 3. Sweden, 4. Singapore, 5. Finland
   Worst—180. Somalia, 179. Myanmar, 178. Iraq, 177. Haiti, 176. Afghanistan
   In Betweens—18. USA, 28. Spain, 57. Greece, 72. Mexico, 80. Brazil

Bribery: Best and worst of 20 countries in likelihood of home-country firms willingness's to pay bribes abroad. [& = ties]
   Best—Belgium & Canada, Netherlands & Switzerland, Germany & Japan & United Kingdom
   Worst—Russia, China, Mexico, India, Italy & Brazil
   In Betweens—Australia, France & United States, Spain, South Korea & Taiwan

What Are Your Thoughts?

What patterns do you detect in these data, if any? Does it surprise you that the United States didn't make the "best" lists? How would you differentiate between the terms "corruption" and "bribery" as they apply in international business?

News Feed 📶

More Global Firms Employ Sweatshop Hunters.

Help Wanted—Sweatshop Hunter One of the world's premier fashion merchandisers seeks an experienced executive to head staff in charge of monitoring international suppliers for ethics and social responsibility practices. The successful candidate will have a strong commitment to ethics and social responsibility in business, strong communication skills and cultural intelligence, confidence in handling conflict situations, and the capacity to work well in relationships spanning shop-floor workers to chief executives.

This ad is fabricated; the job it features is real.

At Hewlett-Packard it's filled by Bonnie Nixon-Gardiner. She has a middle-management appointment, overseeing the work of some 70 auditors, and with major responsibilities for keeping track of over 200 supplier factories. Nixon-Gardiner and her staff travel the world inspecting HP suppliers with the goal of making sure that working conditions are up to HP's standards. She describes her goal this way: "My 10-year vision is for [consumers to know that] when you touch a technology product you are guaranteed it was made in a social and environmentally responsible way."

Picture this—Nixon-Gardiner arrives at Foxconn Electronics in Long Hua, China. Her hosts try to move her into a conference room, but she declines and opts to walk about the factory with its multiple buildings and 200,000 employees. "Look," she tells her hosts when they balk, "this isn't going to work unless you're totally transparent with me."

She found that the noise was too loud for workers on some machines; the firm agreed to purchase ear protectors. On a later visit she called for and got more changes—special enclosures for the machines and purchase of the best ear protection devices available. Her no-nonsense but polite approach has been described by a colleague as "it's like being kissed and slapped at the same time."

Reflect and React:

How would you like a job like this? Should all international businesses have a similar position? What special skills and capabilities does Nixon-Gardiner need to succeed in this job? Were you surprised that she is described as a "middle manager"? With these responsibilities, should she be on the top management team?

Sustainable development meets the needs of the present without hurting future generations.

• Global corporations face growing calls to support sustainable development.

Global warming, industrial pollution, hazardous waste disposal, depletion of natural resources. You should recognize these and related concerns as worldwide issues. Yet we also want the products and economic development that come from manufacturing, transportation, power generation, and consumption of resources—everything from timber, to iron ore and minerals, to oil.

How do we satisfy the needs of the present without sacrificing those of future generations? What are the implications, for example, of growing resource needs of rapidly growing economies such as India and China?

In a book entitled *Collapse*, scholar Jared Diamond argues that "resource exhaustion" is linked with "social catastrophe," and that both are of increasing likelihood on the world stage. He suggests, for example, that if China's 1.3 billion people were to reach the prosperity of Americans, the worldwide demand for resources would double and require "another earth" to provide them.[36]

Concerns for our natural environment and its resources have given rise to the notion of **sustainable development**, a popular guideline advanced by activist groups and one increasingly accepted by global corporations. The term means "development that meets the needs of the present without compromising the ability of future generations to meet their own needs."[37] While some might consider this concept idealistic, would you be willing to consider it a worthwhile guide for international business activities?

For a global firm to fulfill a commitment to sustainable development, its executives must lead in ways that demonstrate stewardship in protecting the natural environment and preserving its resources for future generations. As a step in this direction, several of the world's largest mining firms, including DeBeers, Rio Tinto, Newmont, and Anglo-American, have proposed that the United Nations develop a "badge of excellence" establishing environmental and safety standards in the mining industry.[38] Also, the Davos World Economic Forum now publishes an annual list of the Global 100 Most Sustainable Corporations in the World; among recent honorees are Google, Hewlett-Packard, and Intel.[39]

• Planning and controlling are complicated in global corporations.

Setting goals, making plans, controlling results—all of these standard management functions can become quite complicated in the international arena. Picture a home office somewhere in the United States, say, Chicago. The MNC's foreign operations are scattered in Asia, Africa, South America, and Europe. Somehow, planning and controlling must span all locations, meeting home office needs and those of foreign affiliates.

One of the risks of international business is **currency risk**, or fluctuations in foreign exchange rates. Companies such as Dell and IBM, for example, make a lot of sales abroad. These sales are in foreign currencies; eventually, a good part of the revenues must be converted into dollars. But as exchange rates vary, the dollar value of sales revenues goes up and down over time. Companies have to plan for these risks of exchange rate fluctuations affecting business profits.

When the dollar is weak against the Euro it takes more in dollars to buy one Euro. But this is good for companies making lots of sales in Euros because they get more dollars when trading in the Euros. It is also good for American exporters that sell to Euro-zone customers because their customers' Euros have more purchasing power for products priced in dollars. But suppose the dollar strengthens against the Euro; what happens then to firms with large sales in Euro-zone countries? Consider these examples of alternative currency risk scenarios that a U.S. exporter might face when making sales in France for Euro 100,000.

> *Scenario 1:* Weak dollar
> .75 Euros = 1 $US
> Take home revenue = $133,000
> *Scenario 2:* Strong dollar
> 1.35 Euros = 1 $US
> Take home revenue = $74,000

Global businesses also must deal with **political risk**, the potential loss in value of an investment in or managerial control over a foreign asset because of instability and political changes in the host country. The major threats of political risk today come from terrorism, civil wars, armed conflicts and military disruptions, shifting government systems through elections or forced takeovers, and new laws and economic policies. Although such things can't be prevented, they can be anticipated to some extent by a planning technique called **political-risk analysis**. It tries to forecast the probability of disruptive events that can threaten the security of a foreign investment. Given the world we now live in, can you see the high stakes of such analysis?

• Organizing can be difficult in global corporations.

Even with plans in place, it isn't easy to organize for international operations. When just starting international activities, businesses often appoint a vice president or another senior manager to oversee them. But as global business expands, a more complex arrangement is usually necessary.

One possible choice for organizing an MNC is the *global area structure* shown in **Figure 18.3.** It arranges production and sales functions into separate geographical units and assigns a top manager to oversee them—such as Area Manager Africa or Area Manager Europe. This allows activities in major areas of the world to be run by executives with special local expertise.[40]

Another organizing option is the *global product structure*, also shown in the figure. It gives worldwide responsibilities to product group managers, for example, a global sales and marketing group, who are assisted by area specialists who work as part of the corporate staff. These specialists provide expert guidance on the unique needs of various countries or regions.

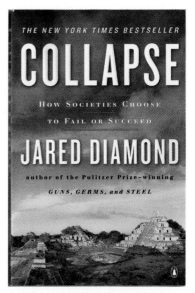

Concerns for sustainable development question how global businesses can satisfy present needs without hurting future generations.

Currency risk is possible loss because of fluctuating exchange rates.

Political risk is the possible loss of investment in or control over a foreign asset because of instability and political changes in the host country.

Political-risk analysis forecasts how political events may impact foreign investments.

FIGURE 18.3
How Can Multinational Corporations Organize for Global Operations?

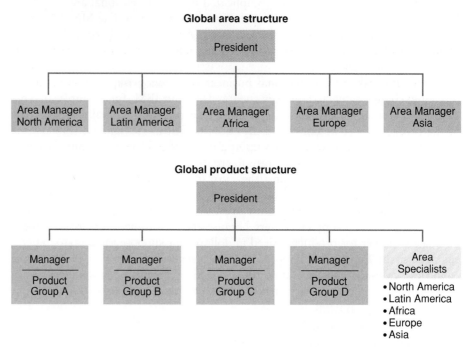

Some firms initially organize for international business by adding a new senior management position, such as head of international operations, to the existing structure. When the international side of the business grows, the structure often gets more sophisticated. One approach is a global area structure that assigns senior managers to oversee all product operations in major parts of the world. Another is the global product structure in which area specialists advise other senior managers on business practices in their parts of the world.

Of course no organizational structure can work without the right people in place. And one of a business leader's most important jobs anywhere is to ensure that the firm is staffed with a talented workforce. When it comes to staffing international operations, an often-heard rule of thumb is: "Hire competent locals, use competent locals, and listen to competent locals." Yet, in addition to hiring locals, most any global firm also employs **expatriate workers**. These are home country employees sent to live and work in foreign countries on short-term or long-term assignments.[41]

An **expatriate** lives and works in a foreign country.

Not only do expatriate assignments offer the individuals challenging work experiences, they also help the firms develop a pool of culturally aware managers with global horizons and interpersonal networks of global contacts. But not everyone performs well in an overseas assignment. The risk of failure can sometimes be reduced when employers provide pre-departure training and cultural orientation, extra support in the foreign environment, special attention to the needs of an expatriate's family members, and extra assistance on the return home.[42] Does expatriate work sound appealing to you? Take a look at this list of *personal attributes for success in an expatriate assignment.*

- High degree of self-awareness
- Cultural sensitivity
- Desire to live and work abroad
- Family flexibility and support
- Technical job competence

• Leading is challenging in global corporations.

As executives in businesses and other types of organizations press forward with global initiatives, the challenges of leading diverse workforces and constituencies across national and cultural borders have to be mastered. Consider two short cases—one a success story and another still considered a "work in progress."[43]

> *Honda* Allen Kinzer, now retired, was the first American manager Honda hired for its Marysville, Ohio, plant. Although people were worried whether or not U.S. workers could adapt to the Japanese firm's production methods, technology, and style, it all worked out, says Kinzer: "It wasn't easy blending the cultures; anyone who knew anything about the industry at the time would have to say it was a bold move." Bold move, indeed! Honda now produces almost 500,000 cars per year in America. It is only one among hundreds of foreign firms offering employment opportunities to U.S. workers.

> *Haier* You may know the brand as popular in dorm-room refrigerators; there's hardly a consumer in China that doesn't know it—the Haier Group is one of the country's best-known appliance makers. With goals to become a major player in the American market Zhang Ruimin, Haier's CEO, built a factory in South Carolina. The idea was to manufacture in America and take a larger share of the refrigerator market. But the plant was expensive by Chinese standards and also started production just at the time when the U.S. economy was heading down. Also Haier's parent organizational culture with a top-down management style clashed with expectations of the American workforce. As it did in China, the factory management required workers to wear caps that showed different ranks and seniority, something that didn't fit well with the Americans. But CEO Zhang says he is open to cultural learning and committed to global expansion for his firm. "First the hard, then smooth," he says, "that's the way to win."

What about you? Is it possible that you will work at home someday for a foreign employer and in a management capacity? Are you interested in a management assignment abroad as an expatriate employee? Are you informed about the world and what is taking place with the advance of globalization?

There is no doubt the forces of globalization and growth of international businesses are creating needs for more **global managers**, ones aware of international developments and competent in working across cultures.[44] In fact, *The Wall Street Journal* calls it a business imperative, saying that global companies need managers who "understand different countries and cultures" and "intuitively understand the markets they are trying to penetrate."[45]

A truly global manager is always inquisitive in staying abreast of international events and trends in our ever changing world, such as those featured throughout this book. A truly global manager is also informed about cultural differences as discussed in Modules 17.1 and 17.2. And a truly global manager is highly skilled in leadership competencies that extend well across cultural boundaries. In terms of these essential global leadership skills, Project GLOBE researchers, mentioned in Module 17.2 for their extensive cross-cultural studies, are quite confident in drawing some evidence-based conclusions.[46] As shown in the small box, such things as being trustworthy, informed, communicative, and inspiring are universally praised as positive leadership characteristics that facilitate success; things like being a loner and acting autocratic are viewed negatively across cultures as things that inhibit leadership success. So we might say that being informal and culturally sensitive are essential steps in the right direction for a global manager. But the ultimate test of greatness will further depend on showing strong leadership skills wherever and with whomever one may be working.

Are you willing to admit that the world isn't just for traveling anymore, and to embrace it as a career opportunity? Is it possible that you might stand out to a potential employer as someone with the leadership skills to excel as a global manager?

Universal *Facilitators* of Leadership Success

- Acting trustworthy, just, honest
- Showing foresight, planning
- Being positive, dynamic, motivating
- Inspiring confidence
- Being informed and communicative
- Being a coordinator and team builder

Universal *Inhibitors* of Leadership Success

- Being a loner
- Acting uncooperative
- Being irritable
- Acting autocratic

A **global manager** is culturally aware and informed on international affairs.

18.2
What Are Global Corporations and How Do They Work?

Rapid review

- A multinational corporation (MNC) is a business with extensive operations in several foreign countries; a transnational corporation attempts to operate without national identity and with a worldwide mission and strategies.

- MNCs can benefit host countries by paying taxes, bringing in new technologies, and creating employment opportunities; MNCs can also hurt host countries by interfering with local government and politics, extracting excessive profits, and dominating the local economy.

- The Foreign Corrupt Practices Act prohibits representatives of U.S. international businesses from engaging in corrupt practices abroad.

- Planning and controlling in MNCs must take into account such things as currency risk and political risk in changing environmental conditions.

- Organizing for multinational operations often involves use of a global product structure or a global area structure.

- Leading in MNCs involves staffing the firm with talented local employees, and with expatriates and global managers who are capable of working in different cultures and countries.

Terms to define

Child labor

Corruption

Currency risk

Expatriate workers

Foreign Corrupt Practices Act

Global manager

Global corporation

Multinational corporation (MNC)

Political risk

Political-risk analysis

Protectionism

Sustainable development

Sweatshop

Transnational corporation

Be sure you can

- differentiate a multinational corporation from a transnational corporation
- list common host-country complaints and three home-country complaints about MNC operations
- explain the challenges of corruption, sweatshops, and child labor for MNCs
- discuss the implications of political risk for MNCs
- differentiate the global area structure and global product structure
- discuss the challenges of expatriate work
- list competencies of a global manager

Questions for discussion

1. Should becoming a transnational corporation be the goal of all MNCs?
2. Is there anything that MNCs and host governments can do to avoid conflicts and bad feelings with one another?
3. Are laws such as the Foreign Corrupt Practices Act unfair to American companies trying to compete around the world?

[Test Prep]

1. In addition to gaining new markets, the reasons why businesses go international include the search for _____.

   (a) political risk
   (b) protectionism
   (c) lower labor costs
   (d) most favored nation status

2. When Rocky Brands decided to increase its international operations by buying 70% ownership of a manufacturing company in the Dominican Republic, Rocky was engaging in which form of international business?

   (a) import/export
   (b) licensing
   (c) foreign subsidiary
   (d) joint venture

3. When Limited Brands buys cotton in Egypt and has pants sewn from it in Sri Lanka according to designs made in Italy for sale in the United States, this is a form of international business known as _____.

   (a) licensing
   (b) importing
   (c) joint venturing
   (d) global sourcing

4. A common form of international business that falls into the category of a direct investment strategy is _____.

   (a) exporting
   (b) joint venturing
   (c) licensing
   (d) global sourcing

5. A joint venture is a form of _____ in which each of the partners expects to gain something of value from working with the other.

   (a) global strategic alliance
   (b) green field venture
   (c) sustainable development
   (d) protectionism

6. When a Hong Kong firm makes an agreement with The Walt Disney Company to legally make jewelry in the shape of Disney cartoon characters, Disney is engaging in a form of international business known as _____.

   (a) exporting
   (b) licensing
   (c) joint venturing
   (d) franchising

7. One major difference between an international business and a transnational corporation is that the transnational tries to operate _____.

   (a) without a strong national identity
   (b) in at least six foreign countries
   (c) with only expatriate managers at the top
   (d) without corruption

8. The Foreign Corrupt Practices Act makes it illegal for _____.

   (a) U.S. businesses to work with subcontractors running foreign sweatshop operations
   (b) foreign businesses to pay bribes to U.S. government officials
   (c) U.S. businesses to make "payoffs" abroad to gain international business contracts
   (d) foreign businesses to steal intellectual property from U.S. firms operating in their countries

9. The World Trade Organization, or WTO, would most likely become involved in disputes between countries over _____.

   (a) exchange rates
   (b) ethnocentrism
   (c) nationalization
   (d) tariffs and protectionism

10. The athletic footwear maker New Balance discovered that exact copies of its running shoe designs were on sale in China under the name "New Barlun." This is an example of a/an _____ problem in international business.

    (a) most favored nation
    (b) global strategic alliance
    (c) joint venture
    (d) intellectual property rights

11. A global corporation whose executives worry that the firm's need for resources today will cause problems of resource shortages for future generations must successfully address the issue of _____.

    (a) sustainable development
    (b) protectionism
    (c) currency risk
    (d) franchising

12. When foreign investment creates new jobs that are filled by local domestic workers, some call the result _____ as opposed to the more controversial notion of outsourcing.

    (a) globalization
    (b) insourcing
    (c) joint venturing
    (d) licensing

13. If a new government comes into power and seizes all foreign assets in the country without any payments to the owners, the loss to foreign firms is considered a _____ risk of international business.

    (a) franchise
    (b) political
    (c) currency
    (d) corruption

14. If an international business firm has separate vice presidents in charge of its Asian, African, and European divisions, it is most likely using a global _____ structure.

(a) product
(b) functional
(c) area
(d) matrix

15. A person who is sent overseas by his or her employer to work for an extended period of time in a foreign subsidiary is called a/an _____.

(a) expatriate employee
(b) global manager
(c) transnational manager
(d) foreign worker

Short response

16. What is the difference between a joint venture and wholly owned subsidiary?

17. List three reasons why host countries sometimes complain about MNCs.

18. What does it mean in an international business sense if a U.S. senator says she favors "protectionism"?

19. What is the difference between currency risk and political risk in international business?

Integration & application

20. Picture yourself sitting in a discussion group at the local bookstore and proudly signing copies of your newly published book, *Business Transitions in the New Global Economy*. A book buyer invites a comment from you by stating: "I am interested in your point regarding the emergence of transnational corporations. But, try as I might, a company like Ford or Procter & Gamble will always be 'as American as Apple pie' for me."

Questions: How would you respond in a way that both (a) clarifies the difference between a multinational and a transnational corporation, and (b) explains reasons why Ford or P&G may wish not to operate as or be viewed as "American" companies?

Self-Assessment

Global Readiness

Instructions

Rate yourself on each of the following items as an indicator of your readiness to participate in the global work environment.[47] *Use this scale: 1 = Very Poor, 2 = Poor, 3 = Acceptable, 4 = Good, 5 = Very Good*

1. I understand my own culture in terms of its expectations, values, and influence on communication and relationships.

2. When someone presents me with a different point of view, I try to understand it rather than attack it.

3. I am comfortable dealing with situations where the available information is incomplete and the outcomes unpredictable.

4. I am open to new situations and am always looking for new information and learning opportunities.

5. I have a good understanding of the attitudes and perceptions toward my culture as they are held by people from other cultures.

6. I am always gathering information about other countries and cultures and trying to learn from them.

7. I am well informed regarding the major differences in government, political, and economic systems around the world.

8. I work hard to increase my understanding of people from other cultures.

9. I am able to adjust my communication style to work effectively with people from different cultures.

10. I can recognize when cultural differences are influencing working relationships and adjust my attitudes and behavior accordingly.

Scoring and Interpretation

The goal is to score as close to a perfect "5" as possible.

Items $(1 + 2 + 3 + 4)/4 = $ _____ Global Mindset Score
Items $(5 + 6 + 7)/3 = $ _____ Global Knowledge Score
Items $(8 + 9 + 10)/3 = $ _____ Global Work Skills Score

A *global mindset* is receptive to and respectful of cultural differences; *global knowledge* includes the continuing quest to know and learn more about other nations and cultures; *global work skills* allow you to work effectively across cultures.

 For further exploration go to WileyPlus

Case Snapshot

Harley-Davidson—Style and Strategy Have Global Reach.

Harley-Davidson celebrated a century in business with a year-long International Road Tour. The party culminated in the company's hometown, Milwaukee. Harley is a true American success story. Once near death in the face of global competition, Harley reestablished itself as the dominant maker of big bikes in the United States. However, success breeds imitation and Harley once again faces a mixture of domestic and foreign competitors encroaching on its market. Can it meet the challenge?

Online Interactive Learning Resources

SELF-ASSESSMENT
• Time Orientation

EXPERIENTIAL EXERCISE
• American Football

TEAM PROJECT
• Globalization Pros and Cons

19

Entrepreneurship and Small Business

Taking Risks Can Make Dreams Come True

Learning Outline

19.1 What Is Entrepreneurship and Who Are Entrepreneurs?

- Entrepreneurs are risk takers who spot and pursue opportunities
- Entrepreneurs often share similar personal characteristics
- Women and minority entrepreneurs are growing in numbers
- Social entrepreneurs seek novel solutions to pressing social problems

19.2 What Should We Know about Small Businesses and How to Start One?

- Small businesses are mainstays of the economy
- Small businesses must master three life-cycle stages
- Family-owned businesses can face unique challenges
- Most small businesses fail within five years
- A small business should start with a sound business plan
- There are different forms of small business ownership
- There are different ways of financing a small business

Qué bueno es; women set the pace in entrepreneurship. When Anita Santiago moved to the United States from Venezuela, she thought: "I'll never be able to land a job." But she did, in the advertising business. Four years later she started her own firm, Anita Santiago Advertising, to focus on Spanish language advertising for the Latin community. Her goal was also to help communicate her culture to large companies. *Que gran idioma tengo* (What a great language I have) reads the front page of her Web site, quoting Chilean poet Pablo Neruda. "I can see culture from both sides," says Santiago. "You can't learn that from a book."

This is a success story—a person with a great idea, taking the risk, starting a business. Could this be you someday? Perhaps, but you also need to be realistic. There's a very high failure rate for start-up small businesses. Each year there are many people with good ideas who can't find the resources to turn them into reality, or don't implement them well because they don't have good business skills.

Trendsetters
Zainab Salbi makes mark as social activist and entrepreneur.

News Feed
Social entrepreneurs turn dreams into progress.

Case Snapshot
Sprinkles—Leading a sweet trend

About 50% of those owning small businesses are women, but they own only 2.6% of small businesses with revenues of $1 million or more. The disparity should make you wonder. Nell Merlino, creator of Take Our Daughters to Work Day, points out that women entrepreneurs face special challenges and "still have far less access to capital than men because of today's process." Along with Iris Burnett, she founded Count-Me-In for Women's Economic Independence as a way of helping female entrepreneurs get started, dream big, and succeed in breaking through the $1 million barrier.

Geneva Francais is one of Count-Me-In's clients. She got a $1,500 loan to support her homemade cooking sauce—"Geneva's Splash." She says: "A bank would not lend a woman money when she is 65 years old. It's as simple as that." Heather McCartney was also an early client. An avid cookie baker, she was inspired by a trip to South Africa to embrace African tribal arts and culture. A $5,000 loan from Count-Me-In helped Ethnic Edibles, her line of African-motif cookies and cookie cutters.

Don't you think more people, women and men, should have this type of chance? Shouldn't everyone be "counted in" for economic independence?

19.1 What Is Entrepreneurship and Who Are Entrepreneurs?

Entrepreneurship is dynamic, risk-taking, creative, growth-oriented behavior.
An **entrepreneur** is willing to pursue opportunities in situations that others view as problems or threats.

Anita Santiago, Heather McCartney, Iris Burnett, Geneva Francais, and Nell Merlino share a personal quality that is much valued in today's challenging economic times: **entrepreneurship**. Each showed original thinking and then acted upon it to create something new for society—an advertising agency, homemade cooking sauce, a cookie company, and a venture capital firm. They are **entrepreneurs**, persons who are willing to take risks to pursue opportunities that others either fail to recognize, or view as problems or threats.

And if the opening examples aren't enough, consider the stories of two "young" entrepreneurs. At the age of 22 Richard Ludlow turned down a full-time job offer and an MBA admission to start New York's Academic Earth. It is an online location for posting and sharing faculty lectures and other educational materials. His goal is to both make a profit and help society by lowering the cost of education. And while in high school Jasmine Lawrence created her own natural cosmetics after having problems with a purchased hair relaxer. Products from her firm, Eden Body Works, can now be found at Wal-Mart and Whole Foods.[1] Is there something in your experience that could be a pathway to similar entrepreneurship?

[**TABLE** 19.1]

Debunking Common Myths about Entrepreneurs

- *Entrepreneurs are born, not made.*
  Not true! Talent gained and enhanced by experience is a foundation for entrepreneurial success.
- *Entrepreneurs are gamblers.*
  Not true! Entrepreneurs are risk takers, but the risks are informed and calculated.
- *Money is the key to entrepreneurial success.*
  Not true! Money is no guarantee of success. There's a lot more to it than that; many entrepreneurs start with very little.
- *You have to be young to be an entrepreneur.*
  Not true! Age is no barrier to entrepreneurship; with age often comes experience, contacts, and other useful resources.
- *You have to have a degree in business to be an entrepreneur.*
  Not true! But it helps to study and understand business fundamentals.

A **first-mover advantage** comes from being first to exploit a niche or enter a market.

• Entrepreneurs are risk takers who spot and pursue opportunities.

H. Wayne Huizenga, former owner of AutoNation, Blockbuster Video, and the Miami Dolphins, and a member of the Entrepreneurs' Hall of Fame, describes being an entrepreneur this way: "An important part of being an entrepreneur is a gut instinct that allows you to believe in your heart that something will work even though everyone else says it will not." You say, "I am going to make sure it works. I am going to go out there and make it happen."[2] In business we talk about this as an entrepreneur's skill at gaining **first-mover advantage**, moving faster than competitors to spot, exploit, and enter a new market or an unrecognized niche in an existing one.

So who are these entrepreneurs and who might become one someday? To begin the discussion take a look at **Table 19.1**—*Debunking Common Myths about Entrepreneurs*.[3] With the myths out of the way, let's meet some real ones, people that built successful long-term businesses from good ideas and hard work.[4] As you read about these creative and confident individuals, think about how you might apply their experiences to your own life and career. After all, it could be very nice to be your own boss someday.

• Anita Roddick

In 1973 Anita Roddick was a 33-year-old housewife looking for a way to support herself and her two children. She spotted a niche for natural-based skin and health care products, and started mixing and selling them from a small shop in Brighton, England. The Body Shop PLC has grown to some 1,500 outlets in 47 countries with 24 languages, selling a product every half-second to one of its 86 million customers. Known for her commitment to human rights, the environment, and economic

development, Roddick believed in business social responsibility, saying: "If you think you're too small to have an impact, try going to bed with a mosquito."

• Earl Graves

With a vision and a $175,000 loan, Earl G. Graves, Sr. started *Black Enterprise* magazine in 1970. That success grew into the diversified business information company Earl G. Graves Ltd.—a multimedia company covering television, radio, and digital media including BlackEnterprise.com. Among his many accomplishments are: named by *Fortune* Magazine as one of the 50 most powerful and influential African Americans in corporate America; recipient of the Lifetime Achievement Award from the National Association of Black Journalists; and selection for the Junior Achievement Wroldwide U.S. Business Hall of Fame. He has written a best-selling book *How to Succeed in Business Without Being White* and is a member of many business and nonprofit boards. Today the business school at his college alma mater, Baltimore's Morgan State University, is named after him. Graves says: "I feel that a large part of my role as publisher of *Black Enterprise* is to be a catalyst for black economic development in this country."

• David Thomas

Have you had your Wendy's today? A lot of people have, and there's quite a story behind it. The first Wendy's restaurant opened in Columbus, Ohio, in November 1969. It's still there, although there are also about 5,000 others now operating around the world. What began as founder David Thomas's dream to own one restaurant grew into a global enterprise. He went on to become one of the world's best-known entrepreneurs: "the world's most famous hamburger cook." But there's more to Wendy's than profits and business performance. The company strives to help its communities, with a special focus on schools and schoolchildren. An adopted child, he founded the Dave Thomas Foundation for Adoption.

• Entrepreneurs often share similar personal characteristics.

Although we might think of all entrepreneurs as founding a new business that achieves large-scale success, many operate on a smaller and less public scale. Entrepreneurs also include those who buy a local Subway Sandwich or Papa John's franchise, open a small retail shop selling used video games or bicycles, or start a self-employed service business such as financial planning or management consulting.[5] Entrepreneurs are found within larger organizations as well. Called **intrapreneurs**, they are people who step forward and take risk to introduce a new product or process, or pursue innovations that can change the organization in significant ways.

Intrapreneurs display entrepreneurial behavior as employees of larger firms.

But what makes entrepreneurs different? Do you see any common patterns in the prior stories? Researchers tell us that most entrepreneurs are very self-confident, determined, self-directing, resilient, adaptable, and driven by excellence.[6] A report in the *Harvard Business Review* suggests that they have strong interests in both "creative production" and "enterprise control." They like to start things. This is creative production; they enjoy working with the unknown and finding unique solutions to problems. They like to run things. This is enterprise control; they enjoy making progress toward a goal.[7]

Research finds that entrepreneurs tend to have unique backgrounds and personal experiences.[8] *Childhood experiences and family environment* seem to make a difference. Evidence links entrepreneurs with parents who were entrepreneurial and self-employed. Similarly, entrepreneurs are often raised in families that encourage responsibility, initiative, and independence. Another issue is *career or work history*. Entrepreneurs who try one venture often go on to others. Prior work experience in the business area or industry is helpful.

Entrepreneurs also tend to emerge during certain *windows of career opportunity*. Most start their business between the ages of 22 and 45, an age spread that seems to allow for risk taking. However, age is no barrier. When Tony DeSio was 50 he founded the Mail Boxes Etc. chain. He sold it for $300 million when he was 67 and suffering heart problems. Within a year he launched PixArts, another franchise chain based on photography and art.[9] Undoubtedly, entrepreneurs seek independence and the sense of mastery that comes with success. That seems to keep driving DeSio. When asked by a reporter what he liked most about entrepreneurship, he replied: "Being able to make decisions without having to go through layers of corporate hierarchy—just being a master of your own destiny."

Test yourself. Look at the personality traits and characteristics here and in **Figure 19.1**.[10] How do you stack up as a potential entrepreneur?[11]

- *Internal locus of control:* Entrepreneurs believe that they are in control of their own destiny; they are self-directing and like autonomy.
- *High energy level:* Entrepreneurs are persistent, hard working, and willing to exert extraordinary efforts to succeed.
- *High need for achievement:* Entrepreneurs are motivated to accomplish challenging goals; they thrive on performance feedback.
- *Tolerance for ambiguity:* Entrepreneurs are risk takers; they tolerate situations with high degrees of uncertainty.
- *Self-confidence:* Entrepreneurs feel competent, believe in themselves, and are willing to make decisions.
- *Passion and action orientation:* Entrepreneurs try to act ahead of problems; they want to get things done and not waste valuable time.

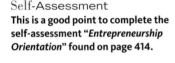

Self-Assessment

This is a good point to complete the self-assessment "*Entrepreneurship Orientation*" found on page 414.

FIGURE 19.1

Personality Traits and Characteristics Common Among Entrepreneurs.

- *Self-reliance and desire for independence:* Entrepreneurs want independence; they are self-reliant; they want to be their own bosses, not work for others.
- *Flexibility:* Entrepreneurs are willing to admit problems and errors, and willing to change a course of action when plans aren't working.

And while talking about the characteristics of entrepreneurs, let's be sure to dispel some of the common myths floating around about them.[12] To begin, it is not true that entrepreneurs are born, not made. Talent gained and enhanced by experience is a foundation for entrepreneurial success. It is not true that entrepreneurs are gamblers. Entrepreneurs are risk takers, but the risks are informed and calculated. It is not true that money is the key to enterpreneurial success. Money is no guarantee of success. There's a lot more to it than that; many entrepreneurs start with very little. It is not true that you have to be young to be an entrepreneur. Age is no barrier to entrepreneurship; with age often comes experience, contacts, and other useful resources. And, it is not true that you have to have a degree in business to be an entrepreneur. Indeed, you may not need a degree at all. Although a business degree is not necessary, it can be helpful to study and understand business fundamentals.

• Women and minority entrepreneurs are growing in numbers.

Sometimes it takes an outside stimulus or a special set of circumstances to awaken one's entrepreneurial tendencies. When economists speak about entrepreneurs, they differentiate between those who are driven by the quest for new opportunities and those who are driven by absolute need.[13] Those in the latter group pursue **necessity-based entrepreneurship.** They start new ventures because they see no other employment options or they find career doors closed, perhaps due to hitting glass ceilings.

The National Foundation for Women Business Owners (NFWBO) reports that women already own over 9 million businesses in the United States and are starting new businesses at twice the rate of the national average. Most indicate being motivated by a new idea or by realizing that they could do for themselves what they were already doing for other employers.

Among women leaving private-sector employment to pursue entrepreneurship, one survey reports 33% believing they were not being taken seriously by their prior employer and 29% having experienced "glass ceiling" issues.[14] In its publication *Women Business Owners of Color: Challenges and Accomplishments,* the NFWBO discusses the motivations of women of color to pursue entrepreneurship because of glass ceiling problems. These include not being recognized or valued by their prior employers, not being taken seriously, and seeing others promoted ahead of them.[15]

Necessity-based entrepreneurship is when people start new ventures because they have few or no other employment options.

Stay Tuned

Minority Entrepreneurs Lead the Way

Career difficulties may help explain why minority entrepreneurship is one of the fastest-growing sectors of our economy. Consider these facts and trends from recent reports.

- Minority-owned businesses are the fastest growing sector of the American economy; there are over 4 million minority-owned firms and annual sales reach almost $700 billion.
- Minority entrepreneurs employ over 4 million U.S. workers, and create almost 5 million jobs—and the trend is up.
- In the last census of small businesses, those owned by African Americans had grown by 45%, by Hispanics 31%, and by Asians 24%.
- During this same time small businesses owned by women also had grown by 24%.

What Are Your Thoughts?

How can we explain the growth of minority-owned businesses? Is minority entrepreneurship a way to fight economic disparities in society? And when it comes to entrepreneurship, do you have any ideas or plans of your own?

News Feed

Social Entrepreneurs Turn Dreams into Progress

Fast Company magazine is always on the lookout for organizations that are run with "innovative thinking that can transform lives and change the world." It recognizes the organizations and those social entrepreneurs who created them with a listing on its prestigious annual Honor Roll of Social Enterprises of the Year. Here are some recent winners.

Chip Ransler and Manoj Sinha tackled the lack of power faced by many of India's poor villagers. As University of Virginia business students, they realized that 350 million of the people without reliable electricity lived in the country's rice-growing regions. And in those regions tons of rice husks were being discarded with every harvest. Ransler and Sinha found a way to create biogas from the husks and use the gas to fuel small power plants. It works and Husk Power Systems is a reality. But with more than 125,000 villages suffering a lack of power, Ransler says "there's a lot of work to be done."

Neal Keny-Guyer, CEO of Mercy Corps, is tackling the crowded field of micro-finance in Indonesia. There are more than 50,000 micro lenders serving 50 million people. But as many as 110 million Indonesians struggle to live on $2 per day. Keny-Guyer's organization bought a local bank that was in trouble and then restructured it to serve as a banker for micro lenders. The goal was to boost the impact of micro-finance in Indonesia by supporting it with top flight financial tools and technology, as well as capital. Keny-Guyer says the goal was "real impact," and that the successful program will be expanded to other countries.

Rose Donna and Joel Selanikio are tackling public health problems in sub-Saharan Africa. Noting that developing nations are often bogged down in the paperwork of public health, they created software to make the process quicker and more efficient, increasing the reliability of the resulting databases. The UN, World Health Organization, and the Vodafone Foundation are now helping their firm DataDyne move the program into 22 other African nations.

Reflect and React

What drives people like those in the examples to pursue entrepreneurship for social gains instead of money? What ideas can you come up with that could turn social entrepreneurship by yourself and others into positive impact on your local community, or on other social problems worldwide?

A **social entrepreneur** takes risks to find new ways to solve pressing social problems.

• Social entrepreneurs seek novel solutions to pressing social problems.

In an early discussion in this book we identified **social entrepreneurs** as persons whose entrepreneurial ventures involve novel ways to help solve pressing social problems.[16] You can think of these problems as the likes of poverty, illiteracy, poor health, and even social oppression. It is the creative and entrepreneurial person indeed, who devotes her or his time and resources in the hope of achieving a positive impact on such difficult problems.

Social entrepreneurs share many characteristics with other entrepreneurs. But there is also one big difference: instead of the profit motive, they are driven by a social mission.[17] Their personal quests are to start and run organizations that help solve social problems, or at least help make lives better for people who are disadvantaged. In many ways the opening example of Nell Merino is an example of a social entrepreneur in action. She saw a problem with women getting the financing they needed to start small businesses to better themselves, their families, and their communities. That sense of need gave rise to Count-Me-In which she started as an online micro credit operation to raise capital that can be used to make loans of $500–$10,000 to women with promising business ideas.[18]

When you think social entrepreneur, think too about what is happening in your community along these lines. Lots of times social entrepreneurship goes without much notice, flying under the radar so to speak; most attention often goes to business entrepreneurs making lots of money, or trying to do so. Yet there are many examples you can find of people who have made the commitment to social entrepreneurship. Deborah Sardone, for example, is the owner of a housekeeping service in Texas; a classic business entrepreneur. But after noticing that her clients with cancer really struggled with everyday household chores, she started Cleaning for a Reason. It's a nonprofit that builds networks of linkages with cleaning firms around the country, each of which offers free home cleaning to cancer patients.[19]

Study Guide

19.1
What Is Entrepreneurship and Who Are Entrepreneurs?

Rapid review

- Entrepreneurship is original thinking that creates value for people, organizations, and society.
- Entrepreneurs take risks to pursue opportunities others may fail to recognize.
- Entrepreneurs such as Mary Kay Ash, Richard Branson, Earl Graves, and Anita Roddick can be a source of learning and inspiration for others.
- Entrepreneurs tend to be creative people who are self-confident, determined, resilient, adaptable, and driven to excel; they like to be masters of their own destinies.
- Women and minorities are well represented among entrepreneurs, with some of this being driven by necessity or the lack of alternative career options.
- Social entrepreneurs apply their energies to create innovations that help to solve important problems in society.

Terms to define

Entrepreneur

Entrepreneurship

First-mover advantage

Intrapreneur

Necessity-based entrepreneurship

Social entrepreneur

Be sure you can

- explain the concept of entrepreneurship
- explain the concept of first-mover advantage
- explain why people such as Mary Kay Ash and Earl Graves are entrepreneurs
- list personal characteristics often associated with entrepreneurs
- explain trends in entrepreneurship by women and minorities
- explain what makes social entrepreneurs unique

Questions for discussion

1. Does an entrepreneur always need to have first-mover advantage in order to succeed?
2. Are there any items on the list of entrepreneurial characteristics that are essential "must haves" for someone to succeed in any career, not just entrepreneurship?
3. Could necessity-driven entrepreneurship be an indicator of some deeper problems in our society?

19.2 What Should We Know about Small Businesses and How to Start One?

A **small business** has fewer than 500 employees, is independently owned and operated, and does not dominate its industry.

The SBA defines a **small business** as one with 500 or fewer employees, with the number varying a bit by industry. The SBA also views a small business as one that is independently owned and operated and that does not dominate its industry.[20] Almost 99% of U.S. businesses meet this definition. Some 87% employ fewer than 20 persons. And interestingly enough, recent data show that business owners rank highest among 10 other occupations in terms of contentment based on things like physical and mental health, job satisfaction, and quality of life overall.[21] As to what it's like to be a small business owner, "I'm still excited to get up and go to work every day," says Roger Peugot who owns a 14-employee plumbing firm. He adds: "Even when things get tough, I'm still in control."[22]

• Small businesses are mainstays of the economy.

Most nations rely on their small business sector. Why? Among other things, small businesses offer major economic advantages. In the United States, for example, small businesses employ some 52% of private workers, provide 51% of private-sector output, receive 35% of federal government contract dollars, and provide as many as 7 out of every 10 new jobs in the economy.[23] Smaller businesses are especially prevalent in the service and retailing sectors of the economy. Higher costs of entry make them less common in other industries such as manufacturing and transportation.

And then there's the Internet. Have you looked at the action on eBay recently? Can you imagine how many people might now be running small trading businesses from their homes? If you're one of them, you're certainly not alone. The SBA believes that some 85% of small firms are already conducting business over the Internet.[24] Even established "bricks-and-mortar" small retailers are finding the Internet ripe with opportunities.

That's what happened to Rod Spencer and his S&S Sports Cards store in Worthington, Ohio. In fact, he closed the store not because business was bad, but because it was really good. When his Internet sales greatly exceeded in-store sales, Spencer decided to follow the world of e-commerce. He now works from home, saving the cost of renting retail space and hiring store employees. "I can do less business overall," Rod says, "and make a higher profit."[25]

• Small businesses must master three life-cycle stages.

Figure 19.2 describes the typical progression in the life cycle of a small business.[26] The new firm begins with the *birth stage*—where the entrepreneur struggles to get the new venture established and survive long enough to really test the marketplace. The firm then passes into the *breakthrough stage*—where the business model begins to work well, growth takes place, and the complexity of the business expands significantly. Next is the *maturity stage*—where the entrepreneur experiences market success and financial stability, but also has to face competitive challenges in a dynamic environment.

Small business owners often face control and management dilemmas as their firms move through life-cycle stages. When their firms experience growth, including possible diversification or global expansion, they can encounter problems making the transition from entrepreneurial leadership to professional strategic leadership. The former brings the venture into being and sees it through the early stages of life; the latter manages and leads the venture into maturity as an

FIGURE 19.2
What Are the Stages in the Life Cycle of an Entrepreneurial Firm?

Birth Stage
- Establishing the firm
- Getting customers
- Finding the money

Fighting for existence and survival

Breakthrough Stage
- Working on finances
- Becoming profitable
- Growing

Coping with growth and takeoff

Maturity Stage
- Refining the strategy
- Continuing growth
- Managing for success

Investing wisely and staying flexible

It is typical for small businesses to move through three life-cycle stages. During the *birth* stage, the entrepreneur focuses on getting things started—bringing a product to market, finding initial customers, and earning enough money to survive. *Breakthrough* is a time of rapid growth when the business model really starts working well. Growth often slows in the *maturity* stage where financial success is realized, but also where the entrepreneur often needs to make adjustments to stay successful in a dynamic marketplace.

ever-evolving and perhaps still-growing corporate enterprise. If the entrepreneur is incapable of meeting or unwilling to meet the firm's leadership needs in later life-cycle stages, continued business survival and success may well depend on the business being sold or management control being passed to professionals.

• Family-owned businesses can face unique challenges.

Among the reasons given for getting started in small businesses, you'll find the owners saying they were motivated to be their own bosses, be in control of their own futures, fulfill dreams, and become part of a family-owned business.[27] Indeed, **family businesses**, those owned and financially controlled by family members, represent the largest percentage of businesses operating worldwide. The Family Firm Institute reports that family businesses account for 78% of new jobs created in the United States, and provide 60% of the nation's employment.[28]

Family businesses must master the same challenges as other small or large businesses, such as devising strategy, achieving competitive advantage, and ensuring operational excellence. When everything goes right, the family firm can be an ideal situation. Everyone works together, sharing values and a common goal: working together to support the family. But things don't always turn out this way or stay this way, especially as a business changes hands over successive generations.

"Okay, Dad, so he's your brother. But does that mean we have to put up with inferior work and an erratic schedule that we would never tolerate from anyone else in the business?"[29] Welcome to the **family business feud**, a problem that can lead to small business failure. The feud can be about jobs and who does what, business strategy, operating approaches, finances, or other matters. It can be between spouses, among siblings, between parents and children. It really doesn't matter. Unless family business feuds are resolved satisfactorily, the firm may not survive.

A survey of small and midsized family businesses indicated that 66% planned on keeping the business within the family.[30] The management question is: Upon leaving, how will the current head of the company distribute assets and determine who will run the business? This introduces the **succession problem**, how to handle

Family businesses are owned and financially controlled by family members.

A **family business feud** can lead to small business failure.

The **succession problem** is the issue of who will run the business when the current head leaves.

Owners of family businesses often face the succession problem of how to transfer leadership to the next generation.

the transfer of leadership from one generation to the next. The data on succession are eye opening. About 30% of family firms survive to the second generation; 12% survive to the third generation; only 3% are expected to survive beyond that.[31]

If you were the owner of a successful family business, what would you do? Wouldn't you want to have a **succession plan** that clearly spells out how leadership transition and related matters, including financial ones, are to be handled when the time for changeover occurs?

A **succession plan** describes how the leadership transition and related financial matters will be handled.

• Most small businesses fail within five years.

Does the prospect of starting your own small business sound good? It should, but a word of caution is called for as well. What Figure 19.2, discussed earlier, didn't show is a very common event in the life cycle of a small business: failure.

Small businesses have a scarily high failure rate. The SBA reports that as many as 60 to 80% of new businesses fail in their first five years of operation.[32] Part of this might be explained as a "counting" issue, since the government counts as a "failure" any business that closes, whether it is due to the death or retirement of an owner, sale to someone else, or the inability to earn a profit. Nevertheless, the fact remains: a lot of small business start-ups don't make it.

The recent economic downturn was especially hard on small firms.[33] Reports are that over 4 million closed in one three-month period, with most facing major sales revenue and credit problems. Beth Wood, a family business expert with MassMutual says: "They've seen reductions in top line revenue that they just can't react fast enough to." And reflecting on problems with his family restaurant, former owner Georgia Roussos said: "You had to discount so heavily to get someone in the door that it just wasn't profitable anymore." When the restaurant finally closed, her family suffered emotionally not just for themselves, but for their former employees as well; 55 people, some serving as long as 35 years, lost their jobs.

Look at **Figure 19.3** and consider the many possible causes of small business failures.[34] Most of the failures result from poor judgment and management mistakes made by entrepreneurs and owners. So if you decide to launch your own venture someday, you'll need to learn from these mistakes. This is just as important as studying success stories.

FIGURE 19.3
Eight Reasons Why Many Small Businesses Fail.

• A small business should start with a sound business plan.

When people start new businesses or even start new units within existing ones, they can greatly benefit from another type of plan—a sound **business plan**. This plan describes the goals of the business and the way it intends to operate, ideally in ways that can help obtain any needed start-up financing.[35]

Banks and other financiers want to see a business plan before they loan money or invest in a new venture. Senior managers want to see a business plan before they allocate scarce organizational resources to support a new entrepreneurial project. You should also want a small business plan. It helps sort out your ideas, map strategies, and pin down your business model; this detailed and disciplined thinking can increase the likelihood of success. Says Ed Federkeil, who founded a small business called California Custom Sport Trucks: "It gives you direction instead of haphazardly sticking your key in the door every day and saying—'What are we going to do?' "[36]

Although there is no single template for a successful business plan, most would agree on the general framework presented in Tips to Remember.[37] Any business plan should include an executive summary, cover certain business fundamentals, be well organized with headings, be easy to read, and be relatively short. In addition to advice available in books and magazines, you should also be able to find many online resources for the development of a business plan.

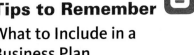

Tips to Remember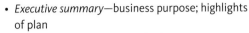
What to Include in a Business Plan

- *Executive summary*—business purpose; highlights of plan
- *Industry analysis*—nature of industry, economic trends, legal or regulatory issues, risks
- *Company description*—mission, owners, legal form
- *Products and services*—major goods or services, uniqueness vis-à-vis competition
- *Market description*—size, competitor strengths and weaknesses, five-year sales goals
- *Marketing strategy*—product characteristics, distribution, promotion, pricing
- *Operations description*—manufacturing or service methods, suppliers, controls
- *Staffing*—management and worker skills needed and available, compensation, human resource systems
- *Financial projection*—cash flow projections 1–5 years, breakeven points
- *Capital needs*—amount needed, amount available, amount being requested
- *Milestones*—timetable for completing key stages of new venture

A **business plan** describes the direction for a new business and the financing needed to operate it.

• There are different forms of small business ownership.

One of the important choices when starting a new venture is the legal form of ownership. There are a number of alternatives, each with respective advantages and disadvantages.

A **sole proprietorship** is simply an individual or a married couple that pursues business for a profit. The business often operates under a personal name, such as "Tiaña Lopez Designs." Because a sole proprietorship is simple to start, run, and terminate, it is the most common form of U.S. small business ownership. If you were to choose this for your small business, however, you have to remember that any owner of a sole proprietorship is personally liable for all business debts and claims.

A **partnership** is formed when two or more people agree to contribute resources to start and operate a business together. Most partnerships are set up with legal and written agreements that document what each party contributes in resources and skills, and how profits and losses are to be shared. You would be ill advised to enter into a serious partnership without such an agreement. But the choice of partnership type is important also.

In a **general partnership**, the simplest and most common form, the owners share management responsibilities. Each is supposed to be directly involved in

A **sole proprietorship** is an individual pursuing business for a profit.

A **partnership** is when two or more people agree to contribute resources to start and operate a business together.

In a **general partnership**, owners share management responsibilities.

A **limited partnership** consists of a general partner who manages the business and one or more limited partners.

A **corporation** is a legal entity that exists separately from its owners.

A **limited liability corporation, LLC**, combines the advantages of the sole proprietorship, partnership, and corporation.

Debt financing involves borrowing money from another person, a bank, or a financial institution.

day-to-day operations. This differs from a **limited partnership** consisting of a general partner and one or more "limited" partners. The general manager runs the business; the limited partners do not participate in its day-to-day management. All partners share in profits, but their losses are limited to the amounts of their investments. This limit to one's liabilities is a major advantage. In fact, you'll notice that many professionals, such as accountants and attorneys, join in *limited liability partnerships* because they limit the liability of one partner in case of negligence by any others.

A **corporation**, commonly identified by the "Inc." designation in a name, is a legal entity that exists separately from its owners. Corporations are legally charted by the states in which they are registered, and they can be for-profit, such as Microsoft Inc., or not-for-profit, such as Count-Me-In Inc. There are two major advantages in choosing to incorporate a small business: (1) it grants the organization certain legal rights (for example, to engage in contracts), and (2) the corporation is responsible for its own liabilities. This gives the firm a life of its own and separates the owners from personal liability. The major disadvantages rest with the legal costs of forming the corporation, and the complexity of documentation required to operate as one.

Recently, the **limited liability corporation**, or "LLC," has gained popularity. It combines the advantages of sole proprietorship, partnership, and corporation. For liability purposes, it functions as a corporation, protecting the assets of owners against claims made against the company. For tax purposes, it functions as a partnership in the case of multiple owners, and as a sole proprietorship in the case of a single owner.

• There are different ways of financing a small business.

Starting a new venture takes money. Unless you possess personal wealth that you are willing to risk, that money has to be raised. The two most common ways to raise it are through debt financing and equity financing.

Debt financing involves borrowing money from another person, a bank, or a financial institution. This loan must be paid back over time with interest. A loan also requires collateral that pledges business assets or personal assets, such as a home, to secure the loan in case of default. This is the same type of financing that you probably use when purchasing a home or a car; you borrow money with a promise to repay both the loan amount and interest.

Equity financing gives ownership shares to outsiders in return for their financial investments. And in important contrast to debt financing, this money does not need

Trendsetters

Zainab Salbi Makes Mark as Social Activist and Entrepreneur.

Called "a recognized force for women's rights and self-sufficiency" and "a lifeline for women in war-torn countries," Zainab Salbi grew up in the tyranny of Saddam Hussein's Iraq. It is a long journey from those days of war and strife to Davos, Switzerland, where she was honored as Young Global Leader by the World Economic Forum.

What has she done to earn the praise? Lots. Salbi founded Women for Women International with the mission of "changing the world one woman at a time." The nonprofit organization's Web site says "Women for Women International provides women survivors of war, civil strife and other conflicts with the tools and resources to move from crisis and poverty to stability and self-sufficiency, thereby promoting viable civil societies." The goal is to provide women with training, financial aid, and rights awareness that can help them move from despair and poverty to independence and economic security.

Salbi says, "Women who survive war are strong, resilient and courageous—they just need some support dealing with the aftermath of conflict." Violette of Rwanda is one such survivor. She joined one of the "women's circles" set up by Women for Women International to link women in need with sponsors from other countries. With the encouragement of her sponsor Liz from Boston, Violette built a business of sorghum-based drinks from her experience in sorghum harvesting. She became a community leader and was able to send her children to school.

Elsewhere Salbi's organization has made $4 million in micro-credit loans to help women in Afghanistan start small businesses, organized 1,600 women in Kosovo to create an "Action Agenda for Women," and ran a Men's Leadership Program in Kenya that helped 550 men learn how they could work in their communities to change the attitudes and behaviors of other men who were contributing to violence against women. In just one year alone the organization touched the lives of almost 70,000 women worldwide.

This quote from Salbi seems to sum up her philosophy quite well: "You need strong women—at the grass-roots level—to build a strong society. Women are the barometers."

to be paid back. Instead, the investor assumes the risk of potential gains and losses based on the performance of the business. But in return for taking that risk, the equity investor gains something—part of your original ownership. The amount of ownership and control given up is represented in the number and proportion of ownership shares transferred to the equity investors.

When businesses need equity financing in fairly large amounts, from the tens of thousands to the millions of dollars, they often turn to **venture capitalists**. These are individuals and companies that make money by pooling capital to invest in new ventures. Their hope is that their equity stakes rise in value and can be sold for a profit when the business becomes successful. Sometimes they can be quite aggressive in wanting active management roles to make sure the business grows in value as soon as possible. Then, this value is tapped by an **initial public offering (IPO)**. This is when shares in the business are sold to the public at large, most likely beginning to trade on a major stock exchange.

When an IPO is successful, the market bids up the share prices, thus increasing the value of the original shares held by the venture capitalist and the entrepreneur. When Google's IPO went public, the stock opened at $85 per share; by the end of the day it was already above $100, and it has risen dramatically since. This has been a great return for the founders and original venture capital investors. Check out the current price for a GOOG share on the NASDAQ today and you'll find it worth considerably more. Wouldn't it have been nice to be in on that original IPO?

Entrepreneurs may try to find an **angel investor** when venture capital isn't available or isn't yet interested. This is a wealthy individual who invests in return for equity in a new venture. Angel investors are especially helpful in the late birth and early breakthrough stages of a new venture. Once they jump in, it can raise the confidence and interests of venture capitalists, thus making it easier to attract even more funding. For example, when Liz Cobb wanted to start her sales compensation firm, Incentive Systems, she contacted 15 to 20 venture capital firms. Only 10 interviewed her, and all of those turned her down. However, after she located $250,000 from two angel investors, the venture capital firms renewed their interest, allowing her to obtain her first $2 million in financing. Her firm grew to employ over 70 workers.[38] This isn't quite a Google story, but it's still a good one.

Equity financing gives ownership shares to outsiders in return for their financial investments.

Venture capitalists make large investments in new ventures in return for an equity stake in the business.

An **initial public offering (IPO)** is an initial selling of shares of stock to the public at large.

An **angel investor** is a wealthy individual willing to invest in return for equity in a new venture.

19.2
What Should We Know about Small Businesses and How to Start One?

Rapid review

- Small businesses constitute the vast majority of businesses in the United States and create 7 out of every 10 new jobs in the economy.
- Small businesses have a high failure rate; as many as 60 to 80% of new businesses fail in their first five years of operation.
- Family businesses that are owned and financially controlled by family members can suffer from the succession problem of transferring leadership from one generation to the next.
- A business plan describes the intended nature of a proposed new business, how it will operate, and how it will obtain financing.
- Proprietorships, partnerships, and corporations are different forms of business ownership, with each offering advantages and disadvantages.
- New ventures can be financed through debt financing in the form of loans, and through equity financing, which exchanges ownership shares in return for outside investment.
- Venture capitalists and angel investors invest in new ventures in return for an equity stake in the business.

Terms to define

Angel investor

Business plan

Corporation

Debt financing

Equity financing

Family business

Family business feud

General partnership

Initial public offering (IPO)

Limited partnership

Limited liability corporation (LLC)

Partnership

Small business

Sole proprietorship

Succession plan

Succession problem

Venture capitalists

Be sure you can

- state the SBA definition of small business
- illustrate opportunities for entrepreneurship on the Internet
- list the life-cycle stages of a small business
- list several reasons why many small businesses fail
- discuss the succession problem in family-owned businesses
- list the major elements in a business plan
- differentiate the common forms of small business ownership
- differentiate debt financing and equity financing
- explain the roles of venture capitalists and angel investors in new venture financing

Questions for discussion

1. Given the high economic importance of small businesses, what could local, state, and federal governments do to make it easier for them to prosper?
2. If you were asked to join a small company, what would you look for in its business plan as potential success indicators?
3. Why should the owner of a small but growing business want to be careful when accepting big investments from venture capitalists?

[Test Prep]

Multiple choice

1. Someone who thrives on uncertainty and risk-taking displays an entrepreneurial characteristic known as a/an _____.

   (a) high tolerance for ambiguity
   (b) internal locus of control
   (c) need for achievement
   (d) action orientation

2. _____ is among the personality characteristics commonly found among entrepreneurs.

   (a) External locus of control
   (b) Inflexibility
   (c) Self-confidence
   (d) Low self-reliance

3. When a new business is quick to capture a market niche before competitors, this is called _____.

   (a) intrapreneurship   (b) an initial public offering
   (c) succession planning   (d) first-mover advantage

4. Almost _____% of U.S. businesses meet the definition of "small business" used by the Small Business Administration.

   (a) 40   (b) 99
   (c) 75   (d) 81

5. A small business owner who is concerned about passing the business on to other family members after retirement or death is advised to prepare a _____ plan that documents his or her wishes.

   (a) retirement   (b) succession
   (c) partnership   (d) liquidation

6. One of the most common reasons that new small business start-ups often fail is because _____.

   (a) the owner lacks experience and business skills
   (b) there is too much government regulation
   (c) the owner tightly controls money and finances
   (d) the business grows too slowly

7. A pressing problem faced by a small business in the birth or start-up stage is _____.

   (a) gaining acceptance in the marketplace
   (b) finding partners for expansion
   (c) preparing the initial public offering
   (d) bringing professional skills into the management team

8. A venture capitalist that receives an ownership share in return for investing in a new business is providing _____ financing.

   (a) debt   (b) equity
   (c) limited   (d) corporate

9. In _____ financing, the business owner borrows money as a loan that must eventually be paid along with agreed-upon interest to the lender.

   (a) debt   (b) equity
   (c) partnership   (d) limited

10. If an entrepreneur wants to start a small business, avoid losing any more than the amount of his or her original investment, and avoid costly legal fees for setting up the company, a _____ form of ownership would be a good choice.

    (a) sole proprietorship
    (b) general partnership
    (c) limited partnership
    (d) corporation

11. The first element in a good business plan is usually _____.

    (a) an industry analysis
    (b) a marketing strategy
    (c) an executive summary
    (d) a set of performance milestones

12. Data on current trends in U.S. small business ownership would most likely show that _____.

    (a) the number of businesses owned by women and minorities are growing
    (b) very few small businesses conduct some business by Internet
    (c) large businesses create more jobs than small businesses
    (d) very few small businesses are family owned

13. Among the forms of small business ownership, a _____ protects the owners from any personal liabilities for business losses.

    (a) sole proprietorship   (b) franchise
    (c) limited partnership   (d) corporation

14. _____ take ownership shares in a new venture in return for providing the entrepreneur with critical startup funds.

    (a) Business incubators   (b) Angel investors
    (c) SBDCS   (d) Intrapreneurs

15. The unique feature distinguishing social entrepreneurship is _____.

    (a) lack of other career options
    (b) focus on international markets
    (c) refusal to finance by loans
    (d) commitment to solving social problems

16. What is the relationship between diversity and entrepreneurship?

17. What major challenges do business owners face at each stage in the life cycle of an entrepreneurial firm?

18. What are the advantages of choosing a limited partnership form of small business ownership?

19. What is the difference, if any, between a venture capitalist and an angel investor?

20. Assume that you have a great idea for a potential Internet-based start-up business. In discussing the idea with a friend, she advises you to clearly link your business idea to potential customers, and then describe it well in a business plan. "After all," she says, "you won't succeed without customers and you'll never get a chance to succeed if you can't attract financial backers through a good business plan."

Questions: This sounds like good advice. What questions will you ask and answer to ensure that you are customer-focused in this business? What are the major areas that you would address in your initial business plan?

Entrepreneurship Orientation

Instructions

Answer each of the following questions.[39]

1. What portion of your college expenses did you earn (or are you earning)?
   (a) 50% or more
   (b) less than 50%
   (c) none

2. In college, your academic performance was/is
   (a) above average.
   (b) average.
   (c) below average.

3. What is your basic reason for considering opening a business?
   (a) I want to make money.
   (b) I want to control my own destiny.
   (c) I hate the frustration of working for someone else.

4. Which phrase best describes your attitude toward work?
   (a) I can keep going as long as I need to; I don't mind working for something I want.
   (b) I can work hard for a while, but when I've had enough, I quit.

   (c) Hard work really doesn't get you anywhere.

5. How would you rate your organizing skills?
   (a) superorganized
   (b) above average
   (c) average
   (d) I do well to find half the things I look for.

6. You are primarily a(n)
   (a) optimist.
   (b) pessimist.
   (c) neither.

7. You are faced with a challenging problem. As you work, you realize you are stuck. You will most likely
   (a) give up.
   (b) ask for help.
   (c) keep plugging; you'll figure it out.

8. You are playing a game with a group of friends. You are most interested in
   (a) winning.
   (b) playing well.
   (c) making sure that everyone has a good time.
   (d) cheating as much as possible.

9. How would you describe your feelings toward failure?

 (a) Fear of failure paralyzes me.
 (b) Failure can be a good learning experience.
 (c) Knowing that I might fail motivates me to work even harder.
 (d) "Damn the torpedoes! Full speed ahead."

10. Which phrase best describes you?

 (a) I need constant encouragement to get anything done.
 (b) If someone gets me started, I can keep going,
 (c) I am energetic and hard-working—a self-starter.

11. Which bet would you most likely accept?

 (a) a wager on a dog race
 (b) a wager on a racquetball game in which you play an opponent
 (c) Neither. I never make wagers.

12. At the Kentucky Derby, you would bet on

 (a) the 100-to-1 long shot.
 (b) the odds-on favorite,
 (c) the 3-to-1 shot.
 (d) none of the above.

Scoring

Give yourself 10 points each for answers 1a, 2a, 3c, 4a, 5a, 6a, 7c, 8a, 9c, 10c, 11b, 12c; total the scores and enter the result here [I = ____]. Give yourself 8 points each for answers 3b, 8b, 9b; enter total here [II = ____]. Give yourself 6 points each for answers 2b, 5b; enter total here [III = ____]. Give yourself 5 points for answer 1b; enter result here [IV = ____]. Give yourself 4 points for answer 5c; enter result here [V = ____]. Give yourself 2 points each for answers 2c, 3a, 4b, 6c, 9d, 10b, 11a, 12b; enter total here [VI = ____]. Any other answers are worth 0 points. Total your summary scores for I + II + III + IV + V + VI and enter the result here [EP = ____].

Interpretation

This assessment offers an impression of your *entrepreneurial profile (EP)*. It compares your characteristics with those of typical entrepreneurs, according to this profile: 100+ = Entrepreneur extraordinaire; 80–99 = Entrepreneur; 60–79 = Potential entrepreneur; 0–59 = Entrepreneur in the rough.

 For further exploration go to WileyPlus

Case Snapshot

Sprinkles—Leading a Sweet Trend

Most people think of cupcakes as either homemade snacks or pre-packaged Hostess treats. But Candace Nelson's cupcake-only bakery, Sprinkles, proved that high-end ingredients in a stylish setting could challenge the low-carb craze and inspire food fans to wait in long lines for a bite-sized taste of heaven.

Online Interactive Learning Resources

SELF-ASSESSMENT
• Self-Confidence

EXPERIENTIAL EXERCISE
• Entrepreneurs Among Us

TEAM PROJECT
• Community Entrepreneurs

Case 1: Trader Joe's: Keeping a Cool Edge

The average Trader Joe's stocks only a small percentage of the products of local supermarkets in a space little larger than a corner store. How did this neighborhood market grow to earnings of $7.2 billion, garner superior ratings, and become a model of management? Take a walk down the aisles of Trader Joe's and learn how sharp attention to the fundamentals of retail management made this chain more than the average Joe.

From Corner Store to Foodie Mecca

In more than 300 stores across the United States, hundreds of thousands of customers are treasure hunting. Driven by gourmet tastes but hungering for deals, they are led by cheerful guides in Hawaiian shirts who point them to culinary discoveries such as ahi jerky, ginger granola, and baked jalapeño cheese crunchies.

It's just an average day at Trader Joe's, the gourmet, specialty, and natural-foods store that offers staples such as milk and eggs along with curious, one-of-a-kind foods at below-average prices in twenty-odd states.[1] Foodies, hipsters, and recessionistas alike are attracted to the

chain's charming blend of low prices, tasty treats, and laid-back but enthusiastic customer service. Shopping at Trader Joe's is less a chore than it is immersion into another culture. In keeping with its whimsical faux-nautical theme, crew members and managers wear loud tropical-print shirts. Chalkboards around every corner unabashedly announce slogans such as, "You don't have to join a club, carry a card, or clip coupons to get a good deal."

"When you look at food retailers," says Richard George, professor of food marketing at St. Joseph's University, "there is the low end, the big middle, and then there is the cool edge—that's Trader Joe's."[2] But how does Trader Joe's compare with other stores with an edge, such as Whole Foods? Both obtain products locally and from all over the world. Each values employees and strives to offer the highest quality. However, there's no mistaking that Trader Joe's is cozy and intimate, whereas Whole Foods' spacious stores offer an abundance of choices. By limiting its stock and selling quality products at low prices, Trader Joe's sells twice as much per square foot than other supermarkets.[3] Most retail mega-markets,

such as Whole Foods, carry between 25,000 and 45,000 products; Trader Joe's stores carry only 1,500 to 2,000.[4] But this scarcity benefits both Trader Joe's and its customers. According to Swarthmore professor Barry Schwartz, author of *The Paradox of Choice: Why Less Is More,* "Giving people too much choice can result in paralysis. . . . [R]esearch shows that the more options you offer, the less likely people are to choose any."[5]

Trader Joe's didn't always stand for brie and baguettes at peanut butter and jelly prices. In 1958, the company began life in Los Angeles as a chain of 7-Eleven–style corner stores. Striving to differentiate his stores from those of his competitors in order to survive in a crowded marketplace, founder "Trader" Joe Coulombe, vacationing in the Caribbean, reasoned that consumers are more likely to try new things while on vacation. He transformed his stores into oases of value by replacing humdrum sundries with exotic, one-of-a-kind foods priced persuasively below those of any reasonable competitor.[6] In 1979, he sold his chain to the Albrecht family, German billionaires and owners of an estimated 7,500 Aldi markets in the United States and Europe.[7]

The Albrechts shared Coulombe's relentless pursuit of value, a trait inseparable from Trader Joe's success. Recent annual sales are estimated at $7.2 billion, landing Trader Joe's in the top third of *Supermarket News's* Top 75 Retailers.[8] Because it's not easy competing with such giants as Whole Foods and Dean & DeLuca, the company applies its pursuit of value to every facet of management. By keeping stores comparatively small—they average about 10,000 square feet—and shying away from prime locations, Trader Joe's keeps real estate costs down.[9] The chain prides itself on its thriftiness and cost-saving measures, proclaiming, "Every penny we save is a penny you save" and "Our CEO doesn't even have a secretary."[10,11]

Trader Giotto, Trader José, Trader Ming, and Trader Darwin

Trader Joe's strongest weapon in the fight to keep costs low may also be its greatest appeal to customers: its stock. The company follows a deliciously simple approach to stocking stores: (1) search out tasty, unusual foods from all around the world; (2) contract directly with manufacturers; (3) label each product under one of several catchy house brands; and (4) maintain a small stock, making each product fight for its place on the shelf. This common-sense, low-overhead approach to retail serves Trader Joe's well, embodying its commitment to aggressive cost-cutting.

Most Trader Joe's products are sold under a variant of their house brand—dried pasta under the "Trader Giotto's" moniker, frozen enchiladas under the "Trader José's" label, vitamins under "Trader Darwin's," and so on. But these store brands don't sacrifice quality—readers of *Consumer Reports* awarded Trader Joe's house brands top marks.[12] The house brand success is no accident. According to Trader Joe's President Doug Rauch, the company pursued the strategy to "put our destiny in our own hands."[13]

But playing a role in this destiny is no easy feat. Ten to fifteen new products debut each week at Trader Joe's—and the company maintains a strict "one in, one out" policy. Items that sell poorly or whose costs rise get the heave-ho in favor of new blood, something the company calls the "gangway factor."[14] If the company hears that customers don't like something about a product, out it goes. In just such a move, Trader Joe's phased out single-ingredient products (such as spinach and garlic) from China. "Our customers have voiced their concerns about products from this region and we have listened," the company said in a statement, noting that items would be replaced with "products from other regions until our customers feel as confident as we do about the quality and safety of Chinese products."[15]

Conversely, discontinued items may be brought back if customers are vocal enough, making Trader Joe's the model of an open system. "We feel really close to our customers," says Audrey Dumper, vice president of marketing for Trader Joe's East. "When we want to know what's on their minds, we don't need to put them in a sterile room with a swinging bulb. We like to think of Trader Joe's as an economic food democracy."[16] In return, customers keep talking, and they recruit new converts. Word-of-mouth advertising has lowered the corporation's advertising budget to approximately 0.2% of sales, a fraction of the 4% spent by supermarkets.[17]

Trader Joe's connects with its customers because of the culture of product knowledge and customer involvement that its management cultivates among store employees. Most shoppers recall instances when helpful crew members took the time to locate or recommend particular items. Despite the lighthearted tone suggested by marketing materials and in-store ads,

What About Whole Foods?

In 1978 John Mackey opened a health-food store in Austin, Texas. He teamed with three other local business owners who were also convinced that the natural foods industry was ready for a supermarket format. The original Whole Foods Market opened in 1980 with a staff of only 19 people. It was an immediate success. From this humble beginning emerged Whole Foods, the leading natural-foods supermarket chain.[24] Its bright spacious stores offer not only an abundance of fresh produce and hormone-free meats, but also gourmet prepared dishes, making it a dining destination as well as a grocery store.[25]

According to Mackey, "the purpose of business is not primarily to maximize shareholder value." Like many new businesses, he started out striving to satisfy customers. As the company grew, the emphasis shifted to employees.[26] Keeping in mind three principles—Whole Food, Whole People, and Whole Planet—Whole Foods offers tasty, natural, and organic food within a decentralized, self-directed team culture to create a respectful workplace where employees are treated fairly and are highly motivated to succeed.[27] It also pays better than most retailers, offers good benefits, and entrusts workers at all levels with sensitive financial data. The idea is that happy, empowered employees lead to happy customers.[28]

There's no denying Whole Foods has its share of loyal, happy customers, but even they are feeling these tough economic times. Mockingly nicknamed "Whole Paycheck" for its premium-priced offerings, the company has thrived even though suffering like many other businesses through the recent recession. It is aggressively fighting the stigma of being a high-priced retailer by offering more discounts and promotions, filling their "Whole Deal" newsletter with money-saving tips, and offering customers budget-focused store tours.[29]

An infusion of $425 million by private equity investor Leonard Green & Partners appears to have reinvigorated Whole Foods and helped them to rein in spending, according to analysts. They're enforcing stricter cost controls and trimming planned store openings.[30, 31]

Will Whole Foods be able to change market perception? Or will shoppers continue to reach for the store brand?

Trader Joe's aggressively courts friendly, customer-oriented employees by writing job descriptions highlighting desired soft skills ("ambitious and adventurous, enjoy smiling and have a strong sense of values") as much as actual retail experience.[18]

Those who work for Trader Joe's earn more than their counterparts at other chain grocers. In California, Trader Joe's employees can earn almost 20% more than counterparts at supermarket giants Albertsons or Safeway.[19] Starting benefits include medical, dental, and vision insurance; company-paid retirement; paid vacation; and a 10% employee discount.[20] Assistant store managers earn a compensation package averaging $94,000 a year, and store managers' packages average $132,000. One analyst estimates that a Wal-Mart store manager earning that much would need to run an outlet grossing six or seven times that of an average Trader Joe's.[21]

Outlet managers are highly compensated, partly because they know the Trader Joe's system inside and out (managers are hired only from within the company). Future leaders enroll in training programs such as Trader Joe's University that foster in them the loyalty necessary to run stores according to both company and customer expectations, teaching managers to imbue their part-timers with the customer-focused attitude shoppers have come to expect.[22]

If Trader Joe's has any puzzling trait, it's that the company is more than a bit media-shy. Executives have granted no interviews since the Aldi Group took over. Company statements and spokespersons have been known to be terse—the company's leases even stipulate that no store opening may be formally announced until a month before the outlet opens![23]

The future looks bright for Trader Joe's. More outlets are planned up and down the East Coast and in the Midwest, and the company continues to break into markets hungry for reasonably priced gourmet goodies. But will Trader Joe's struggle to sustain its international flavor in the face of shrinking discretionary income, or will the allure of cosmopolitan food at provincial prices continue to tempt consumers?

Discussion Questions

1. In what ways does Trader Joe's demonstrate the importance of each responsibility in the management process—planning, organizing, leading, and controlling?

2. This is a German company operating in America and sourcing products from around the world. What are the biggest risks that international owner-ship and global events pose for Trader Joe's performance effectiveness and performance efficiency?

3. In a casual and nontraditional work environment such as the one at Trader Joe's, what are the keys to a team leader or supervisor becoming an ef-fective manager?

4. **FURTHER RESEARCH**—Study news reports to find more information on Trader Joe's management and organi-zation practices. Look for comparisons with its competitors and try to identify whether or not Trader Joe's has the right management approach and busi-ness model for continued success. Are there any internal weaknesses or ex-ternal competitors or industry forces that might cause future problems?

Case 2: Zara International: Fashion at the Speed of Light

Spotted! Letizia Ortiz Rocasolano wearing a chic white pant suit at the announcement of her engagement to Spain's Crown Prince Felipe. Within a few weeks, hundreds of European women sported the same look. Welcome to fast fashion, a trend that sees clothing retailers frequently purchasing small quantities of merchandise to stay on top of emerging trends. In this world of "hot today, gauche tomorrow," no company does fast fashion better than Zara International. Shoppers in over 70 countries are fans of Zara's knack for bringing the latest styles from sketchbook to clothing rack at lightning speed—and reasonable prices.

In Fast Fashion, Moments Matter.

Because style-savvy customers expect shorter and shorter delays from runway to store, Zara International employs a creative team of more than 200 professionals to help it keep up with the latest fashions.[1] It takes just two weeks for the company to update existing garments and get them into its stores; new pieces hit the market twice a week.

Defying the recession with its cheap-and-chic Zara clothing chain, Zara's parent company Inditex posted strong sales gains. Low prices and a rapid response to fashion trends are enabling it to challenge Gap Inc. for top ranking among global clothing vendors. The improved results highlight how Zara's formula continues to work even in the economic downturn. The chain specializes in lightning-quick turnarounds of the latest designer trends at prices tailored to the young—about $27 an item.[2] Louis Vuitton fashion director Daniel Piette described Zara as "possibly the most innovative and devastating retailer in the world."[3]

Inditex Group shortens the time from order to arrival by a complex system of just-in-time production and inventory reporting that keeps Zara ahead. Their distribution centers can have items in European stores within 24 hours of receiving an order, and in American and Asian stores in under 48 hours.[4] "They're a fantastic case study in terms of how they manage to get product to their stores so quick," said Stacey Cartwright, CFO of Burberry Group PLC. "We are mindful of their techniques."[5]

Inditex's history in fabrics manufacturing made it good business sense to internalize as many points in the supply chain as possible. Design, production, distribution, and retail sales are all controlled by Inditex to optimize the flow of goods, without having to share profits with wholesalers or intermediary partners. Customers win by having access to new fashions while they're still fresh off the runway. During a Madonna concert tour in Spain, Zara's quick turnaround let young fans at the last show wear Madonna's outfit from the first one.[6]

Twice a week Zara's finished garments are shipped to logistical centers that all simultaneously distribute product to stores worldwide. These small production batches help the company avoid the risk of oversupply. Because batches always contain new products, Zara's stores perpetually energize their inventories.[7] Most clothing lines are not replenished. Instead they are replaced with new designs to create scarcity value—shoppers cannot be sure that designs in stores one day will be available the next.

Store managers track sales data with handheld computers. They can reorder hot items in less than an hour. This lets Zara know what's selling and what's not; when a look doesn't pan out, designers promptly put together new products. According to Dilip Patel, U.K. commercial director for Inditex, new arrivals are rushed to store sales floors still on the black plastic hangers used in shipping. Shoppers who are in the know recognize these designs as the newest of the new; soon after, any items left over are rotated to Zara's standard wood hangers.[8]

Inside and out, Zara's stores are specially dressed to strengthen the brand. Inditex considers this to be of the greatest importance—because that is where shoppers ultimately decide which fashions make the cut. In a faux shopping street in the basement of the company's headquarters, stylists craft and photograph eye-catching layouts that are e-mailed every two weeks to store managers for replication.[9]

Zara stores sit on some of the world's glitziest shopping streets—including New York's Fifth Avenue, near the flagship stores of leading international fashion brands—

which make its reasonable prices stand out. "Inditex gives people the most up-to-date fashion at accessible prices, so it is a real alternative to high-end fashion lines," said Luca Solca, senior research analyst with Sanford C. Bernstein in London. That is good news for Zara as many shoppers trade down from higher-priced chains.[10]

Catfights on the Catwalk

Zara is not the only player in fast fashion. Competition is fierce, but Zara's overwhelming success (recent sales were almost $10 billion) has the competition scrambling to keep up.[11] San Francisco-based Gap, the largest independent clothing retailer by revenue, recently posted a 23% decline in full-year sales and had plans to open a modest 50 new stores.[12] Only time will tell if super-chic Topshop's entry into the American market causes a wrinkle in Zara's success.

Some fashion analysts are referring to all of this as the democratization of fashion: bringing high(er) fashion to low(er) income shoppers. According to James Hurley, a senior research analyst with New York-based Telsey Advisory Group LLC, big-box discount stores such as Target and WalMart are emulating Zara's ability to study emerging fashions and knock out look-a-likes in a matter of weeks. "In general," Hurley said, "the fashion cycle is becoming sharper and more immediately accessible."[13]

A Single Fashion Culture

With a network of over 1,500 stores around the world, Zara International is Inditex's largest and most profitable brand, bringing home 72% of international sales and nearly 67% of revenues.[14] The first Zara outlet opened shop in 1975 in La Coruña.[15] It remained solely a Spanish chain until opening a store in Oporto, Portugal, in 1988. The brand reached the United States and France in 1989 and 1990 with outlets in New York and Paris, respectively.[16] Zara went into mainland China in 2001, and expanded into India in 2009.[17]

Essential to Zara's growth and success are Inditex's 100-plus textile design, manufacturing, and distribution companies that employ more than 80,000 workers.[18] The Inditex group began in 1963 when Amancio Ortega Gaona, chairman and founder of Inditex, got his start in textile manufacturing.[19] After a period of growth, he assimilated Zara into a new holding company, Industria de Diseño Textil.[20] Inditex has a tried-and-true strategy for entering new markets: start with a handful of stores and gain a critical mass of customers. Generally, Zara is the first Inditex chain to break ground in new countries, paving the way for the group's other brands, including Pull and Bear, Massimo Dutti, and Bershka.[21]

Inditex farms out much of its garment production to specialist companies, located on the Iberian Peninsula, which it often supplies with its own fabrics. Although some pieces and fabrics are purchased in Asia—many undyed or only partly finished—the company manufactures about half of its clothing in its hometown of La Coruña, Spain.[22]

H&M, one of Zara's top competitors, uses a slightly different strategy. Around one quarter of its stock is made up of fast-fashion items that are designed in-house and farmed out to independent factories. As at Zara, these items move quickly through the stores and are replaced often by fresh designs. But H&M also keeps a large inventory of basic, everyday items sourced from cheap Asian factories.[23]

Inditex CEO Pablo Isla believes in cutting expenses wherever and whenever possible. Zara spends just 0.3% of sales on ads, making the 3–4% typically spent by rivals seem excessive in comparison. Isla disdains markdowns and sales, as well.[24]

Few can criticize the results of Isla's frugality. Inditex recently opened 439 stores in a single year and was simultaneously named Retailer of the Year during the World Retailer Congress meeting, after raking in net profits of almost $2 billion.[25,26] Perhaps most important in an industry based on image, Inditex secured bragging rights as Europe's largest fashion retailer by overtaking H&M.[27] According to José Castellano, Inditex's deputy chairman, the group plans to double in size in the coming years while making sales of more than $15 billion. He envisions most of this growth taking place in Europe—especially in trend-savvy Italy.[28]

Fashion of the Moment

Although Inditex's dominance of fast fashion seems virtually complete, it isn't without its challenges. For instance, keeping production so close to home becomes difficult when an increasing number of Zara stores are far-flung across the globe. "The efficiency of the supply chain is coming under more pressure the farther abroad they go," notes Nirmalya Kumar, a professor at London Business School.[29]

Analysts worry that Inditex's rapid expansion may pressure its business. The rising number of overseas stores, they warn, adds cost and complexity and is straining its operations. Inditex may no longer be able to manage everything from Spain. But Inditex isn't worried. By closely managing costs, Inditex says its current logistics system can handle its growth until 2012.[30]

José Luis Nueno of IESE, a business school in Barcelona, agrees that Zara is here to stay. Consumers have become more demanding and more arbitrary, he says—and fast fashion is better suited to these changes.[31] But does Zara International have what it takes to succeed in the hypercompetitive world of fast fashion? Or is the company trying to expand too quickly?

Discussion Questions

1. In what ways are elements of the classical management approaches evident at Zara International?
2. How are insights of the behavioral management approaches being used by Zara's management team?
3. How can systems concepts and the notion of contingency thinking explain the success of some of Zara's distinctive practices?
4. **FURTHER RESEARCH**—Gather the latest information on competitive trends in the apparel industry, and the latest actions and innovations of Zara. Is the firm continuing to do well? Is it adapting in ways needed to stay abreast of both its major competition and the pressures of a changing global economy? Is Inditex still providing worthy management benchmarks for other firms to follow?

Case 3: Tom's of Maine: "Doing Business" Means "Doing Good."

Tom's of Maine was one of the first natural health care companies to distribute outside normal channels. The company holds fast to the values that got owners Tom and Kate Chappell started more than three decades ago, providing insight into how a small firm can grow while staying true to its founding principles in the midst of competition. Now that Tom's has been sold to Colgate, one wonders if those principles can be sustained in a large corporate environment.

Getting Going

Tom and Kate Chappell, dreaming of a line of all-natural, environmentally friendly household products, started Tom's of Maine in 1970. The company's first product, a phosphate-free detergent, was environmentally friendly, Tom Chappell says, but "it didn't clean so well."[1] Consumers were interested in environmentally friendly products—and the toothpaste and soap that followed were more successful. All of Tom's products were made with all-natural ingredients and packaged in recycled materials whenever possible. New personal care products, including shampoo and deodorant, were developed without animal testing.[2]

But the road to success wasn't always direct or fast. Tom's stand against "business as usual" made the company wait seven years longer and spend about ten times the usual sum to get the American Dental Association's seal of approval for its fluoride toothpastes. And mistakes were made. At a time when deodorant made up 25% of the business, Chappell reformulated the product for ecological reasons. Later, he realized that the new formulation "magnified the human bacteria that cause odor" in half its users. After much agonizing, Chappell took the product from his shelves at a cost of $400,000, 30% of the firm's projected profits for the year. Dissatisfied consumers were sent refunds and a letter of apology.

One pivotal event was the introduction of baking soda toothpaste. The gritty product had none of the sweetness of commercial toothpastes, and the marketing manager told Chappell, "In all candor, I don't know how we're going to sell it."[3] Tom insisted that the product be test-marketed. It became a best-seller and was quickly copied by Arm and Hammer and Procter & Gamble.[4]

As the company moved from experience to experience, it gained strength and customers, but Tom was still unhappy, saying he was tired of simply "creating new brands and making money." He felt that something was missing.[5] It seemed to him that sales potential was becoming more important than product quality. "We were working for the numbers, and we got the numbers. But I was confused by success, unhappy with success," said Chappell.[6] He later wrote, "I had made a real go of something I'd started. What more could I do in life except make more money? Where was

the purpose and direction for the rest of my life?"[7] Following this line of thinking, Tom Chappell entered Harvard Divinity School.[8]

Sharpening the Focus

The years that Chappell spent as a part-time divinity student gave him a new understanding of his role. "For the first time in my career, I had the language I needed to debate my bean-counters."[9] He realized that his company was his ministry: "I'm here to succeed . . . according to my principles."[10]

Tom's new mission statement reflected both business aspiration and social responsibility, spelling out guiding values for the company that included natural ingredients and high quality. It talked of respecting employees by providing meaningful work, as well as fair pay. Concern for the community and the world required that Tom's of Maine "be a profitable and successful company, while acting in a socially responsible manner."[11] The company began donating 10% of pretax profits to charities—from arts organizations and environmental groups to curbside recycling programs—and supported the Rainforest Alliance.

Tom's also urged its employees to work with charitable causes and allowed them to donate 5% of their work time to volunteer activities. Employees enthusiastically took advantage of the opportunity—when one employee began teaching art classes for emotionally disturbed children, nearly all of the employees got involved.[12] Others worked in soup kitchens and homeless shelters.

The volunteer program required other employees to cover for absent volunteers for an equivalent of 20 days each month, but Colleen Myers, vice president of community life, called volunteer activities valuable to the company as well as the community. "After spending a few hours at a soup kitchen or a shelter, you're happy to have a job. It's a morale booster, and better morale translates pretty directly into better productivity."[13] Sometimes the company benefited even more directly: "The woman who headed up those art classes—she discovered she's a heck of a project manager. We found that out, too."[14]

Not all employee benefits were strictly psychological. The company offered flexible four-day scheduling and subsidized day care, designing even coffee breaks with employee preference in mind. Individual employees were helped to earn high school equivalency degrees and to develop skills required for new positions.[15]

Even as product distribution expanded nationwide, Tom's marketing efforts remained low-key, according to Katie Shisler, vice president of marketing. "We just tell them our story," she said. "We tell them why we have such a loyal base of consumers who vote with their dollars every day. A number of trade accounts appreciate our social responsibility."[16] Tom Chappell agreed: "We're selling a

lot more than toothpaste; we're selling a point of view—that nature is worth protecting."[17]

He stuck by those notions even in face of increased competition. Tom's prices were similar to those of national competitors for baking soda toothpaste, but 20–40% higher for deodorant and mouthwash. But Tom, unworried, believed that "[t]hat's not the way you're going to get market share—you're going to get it by being who you are."[18] He explained his philosophy: "If we try to act like commodities, act like a toothpaste, we give up our souls. Instead, we have to be peculiarly authentic in everything we do.[19] When you start doing that, customers are very aware of your difference," says Tom. "And they like the difference."[20]

Selling the Company

Despite its humble beginnings, Tom's of Maine has been a pioneer in the green movement. Corporate giants began to

take notice and saw great potential for green products as consumers continue to gravitate to organic and eco-friendly products.

In 2006 Tom's of Maine entered into what Tom and Kate called a "partnership" with a global conglomerate, the Colgate-Palmolive Company. For approximately $100 million dollars—or 84% of outstanding shares—they sold the company and retained a minority interest, with Tom staying on as CEO of Tom's of Maine as a free-standing division of Colgate.[21] The Chappells stated in a letter to employees and stakeholders that "after much soul-searching, and many conversations with our children and trusted advisors, we realized that we cannot meet this growing demand alone. We decided to seek a partner to help us. It's been a quest that we entered with trepidation and excitement because we wanted to find a company that would honor our values, and we were unwavering

The Burt's Bees Story

While hitchhiking in the summer of 1984, Roxanne Quimby was picked up by bee keeper Burt Shavitz. Nicknamed "the bee-man," Burt sold honey in pickle jars from the back of his pickup truck and lived in a small turkey coop. The two hit it off and Roxanne offered to help Burt tend to his beehives. Roxanne quickly fell in love with him and his idyllic life in the wilderness. Together they created Burt's Bees, a niche company famous for its beeswax lip balms, lotions, soaps, and shampoos, as well as for its homespun packaging and feel-good, eco-friendly marketing.[25]

Since its foundation, Burt's Bees has been committed to taking care

of the environment. Ms. Quimby has spent more than $50 million to buy 100,000 acres where she tries to restore the land to its natural state, and the company has partnered with corporations such as the Nature Conservancy and the Arbor Day Foundation for conservation efforts.[26] Burt's believes that in order to *take* from nature, it must protect and provide *for* nature. Its ultimate goal is to be the "greenest personal care company on earth." It has offset its operations to 100% carbon neutral. Burt's has set wide-ranging goals to achieve by 2020. By that time, it wants to be operating on 100% renewable energy and it wants none of its waste to be deposited in landfills.[27]

In 2008, Clorox Company, best known for making bleach, purchased Burt's Bees for $913 million. Afterward, scores of customers called Burt's Bees and accused them of selling out. John Replogle, chief executive, says he personally responded to customers who left their phone numbers. "Don't judge Clorox as much by where they've been as much as where they plan to go," he told them.[28]

The Clorox Company, with revenues of $5.3 billion, markets some of consumers' most trusted and recognized brand names, including its namesake bleach and cleaning products, Green Works(TM) natural cleaners, and Brita® water-filtration systems, to name just a few. With 8,300 employees worldwide, the company manufactures products in more than two dozen countries and markets them in more than 100 countries. Clorox states it is committed to making a positive difference in the communities where its employees work and live.[29]

Mr. Replogle calls his job a "mission" and says he is trying to reinvent business with an idea he calls "the Greater Good," based on the founders' ideals. The premise is that if companies are socially responsible, profit will follow.[30]

Now that Clorox owns Burt's Bees, will it continue to maintain its founders' green philosophies? Or, will consumers just tell the company to buzz off?

in our commitment to stay intact in Maine as Tom's of Maine."[22] Afterward, Chappell compared Colgate to a big Tom's of Maine: "I find that we have more in common than we have differences. They have an organization run by human beings, and they're very capable, savvy, and caring human beings."[23]

Tom's Future: A Different Kind of Company?

Tom's of Maine stresses the "common good" in everything and is passionately concerned about corporate, customer, product, community, environmental, and employee wellness. The firm uses the services of a wellness advisory council, provides wellness education, and practices stewardship by using natural, sustainable, and responsible ingredients, products, and packaging. In "doing well by doing good," Tom's has also been recognized as an exemplar for "common good" capitalism.[24]

Tom's of Maine achieved financial success while following its principles. But will the acquisition by a large, profit-seeking corporation make it hard to hold fast to those principles in the future? Will its reputation for commitment to the environment and ethical behavior be threatened in the large corporate environment, or can a little company teach this corporate giant a thing or two about corporate responsibility?

Discussion Questions

1. Does the Tom's of Maine experience prove that anyone can "do business with principles," or are there business realities that make it hard for others to copy this principled management model?

2. What examples and incidents from this brief history of Tom's of Maine illustrate how the personal ethics and values of founders can positively influence an organization as it deals with the challenges of start-up and growth?

3. What are the biggest threats that Tom's faces in its new life within Colgate's global corporate structure, and especially with respect to maintaining what Tom and Kate call "the character, spirit, and values of our company"?

4. **FURTHER RESEARCH**—Find news items reporting on what has happened at Tom's of Maine since being purchased by Colgate. Has the firm been able to operate with the ethics and independence that Tom and Kate had hoped for? Is the company starting to lose its way now that it's part of a global corporate giant?

Case 4: Amazon: One E-Store to Rule Them All

Amazon.com has soared ahead of other online merchants. What the firm can't carry in its 31 world-wide warehouses, affiliated retailers distribute for it. Not content to rest on past laurels, CEO Jeff Bezos has introduced a number of new services to keep customers glued to the Amazon site. And his latest investment is the Kindle, an e-book reader. But will the investments pay off? Can Amazon hold its own in the face of upstart competitors like Zappos.com?

The Rocket Takes Off

Like a bottle rocket propelled by jet fuel, Internet commerce has shot off the launch pad. No matter what the product is that may set a shopper's heart aflutter, some up-and-coming marketer has likely already set up a specialty e-store selling it. But one online vendor has grander aspirations: why stop at selling one line

of products—or two, or twenty—when customers can instead be offered the equivalent of an online Mall of America?

From its modest beginning in Jeff Bezos's garage in 1995, Amazon.com has quickly sprouted into the most megalithic online retailer. Once Bezos saw that Amazon could outgrow its role as an immense book retailer, he began to sell CDs and DVDs. Even its logo was updated to symbolize that Amazon.com sells almost anything you can think of, from A to Z.

And that only takes into account Amazon's U.S. presence. At latest count, customers in six other countries, including China, Japan, and France, can access Amazon sister sites built especially for them.[1] Amazon's 31 "fulfillment centers" around the world enclose more than 9 million square feet of operating space.[2,3]

So what's next? Growth. Bezos continues to diversify Amazon's product offerings and broaden its brand by partnering with existing retailers to add new product lines. It's a win-win proposition for a multitude of companies—including Target, Toys 'R' Us, and Wine.com. The companies profit from the additional exposure and sales (without undercutting their existing business), and Amazon's brand thrives from the opportunity to keep customers who might otherwise shop elsewhere.

Traditional Content, Layers of Value

Not forgetting its roots, Amazon enhanced its media offerings by several key acquisitions. Its purchase of on-demand book self-publisher BookSurge reinforces Amazon's literary heritage: customers publishing memoirs or first books of poetry may, for a small fee, have

their work made available for sale via Amazon's Web site.[4] Considering how many sets of eyes visit the site in the average week, this is a very compelling offer to a writer who may be considering other on-demand services. Readers appreciate the expanded range of literary offerings, and Amazon wins by having more products to sell—products it is paid to stock.

Beyond simply finding more and more products to sell, Bezos realized that to prevent his brand from becoming stagnant, he would have to innovate, creating new levels of service to complement existing products. "We have to say, 'What kind of innovation can we layer on top of that that will be meaningful for our customers?'" Bezos said.[5]

So far, much of this innovation has come from the depth of the free content available to Amazon customers. Far from being a loss leader, Amazon's free content spurs sales and reinforces customers' perception of Amazon's commitment to customer service.

As David Meerman Scott put it in *eContent*, "Here is the flip side of free in action—a smart content company figuring out how to get people to contribute compelling content for free and then building a for-profit business model around it. Amazon.com has built a huge content site by having all of the content provided to it for no cost. Of course, Amazon.com makes money by selling products based on the contributed content on the site—another example of the flip side of free."[6]

Entering Busy Markets

Time and time again, Amazon has squared off against tech industry giant Apple. First, by launching its Amazon MP3 music downloading service and, in a move of digital one-upmanship, offering all of its tracks from the Big 4 record labels without proprietary digital rights management (DRM) software, allowing the files to be played on any MP3 player.[7] Amazon also bought top-shelf audio book vendor Audible.com for $300 million, adding more than 80,000 audio titles to its arsenal; it bought the on-line merchant Zappos.com for $928 million.[8]

The company introduced the Amazon Unbox, which allows customers to purchase or rent thousands of movies and television shows from most major networks. In another snub to Apple, Unbox files initially could only be played on Windows-compatible devices, putting Apple's computers and TV set-top device out of the action. Amazon touts the content as roughly that of DVD quality, though occupying only half as much space. Using a cable broadband connection, Unbox subscribers can expect to download a two-hour movie in approximately two hours—and can begin to watch it after five minutes or so of downloading.[9]

Although Amazon still sells a considerable number of Apple's iPods, in 2007 it unveiled a new device that existed completely outside Apple's catalog—the Amazon Kindle. Part e-book reader, part wireless computer, the Kindle can download and store e-books, RSS feeds, Microsoft Word documents, and digital pictures in most major formats. Bezos sees this as a natural evolution of technology. "Books are the last bastion of analog," he said to *Newsweek*. "Music and video have been digital for a long time, and short-form reading has been digitized, beginning with the early Web. But long-form reading really hasn't."[10]

Apple played the same game to perfection with the iPhone App Store by unleashing its own e-reader application, Stanza. The company seems to have a knack for balancing the benefits of both open and closed architectures. Any Web page can act as an application for the iPhone.[11] By May 2009, Amazon realized the benefit to allowing readers to read books on a variety of devices and introduced the free application "Kindle for iPhone and iPod touch."[12]

Despite Amazon's success in so many new markets, some critics question whether Amazon.com, let alone the Internet, is the best place to make high-involvement purchases. Once again, Bezos is upbeat. "We sell a lot of high-ticket items," he counters. "We sell diamonds that cost thousands of dollars and $8,000 plasma TVs. There doesn't seem to be any resistance, and, in fact, those high-priced items are growing very rapidly as a percentage of our sales."[13]

How Zappos Did It

The brain child of Tony Hsieh, Zappos.com launched in 1999, selling only shoes.[15] He says: "We view shoes as just our foundation. We believe that as long as we are known for our service, then expanding into almost any category is possible. We want Zappos to be known as a service company that happens to sell shoes, handbags, and anything and everything."[16] By 2001, gross sales had reached $8.6 million. That number nearly quadrupled to $32 million in 2002 and continued to grow before soaring to more than $1 billion in 2008. By that time, Zappos carried more than 1,300 brands and 2 million total products, including shoes, handbags, clothes, housewares, electronics, and jewelry.[17] And it had also caught the eye of Amazon's Jeff Bezos. He liked what he was seeing and spent $928 million to buy the firm for Amazon's business stable in 2009.

Tony Hsieh is widely regarded as one of the most innovative Internet marketers of all time. His ability to use technology to connect with his customers has been likened to the Beatles' ability to excite their teenage fans. The blog search engine Land calls Zappos "the poster child for how to connect with customers online." Online resources such as Facebook and Twitter.com help the company connect with their customers, distributors, employees, and other businesses. Sean Kim, Zappos vice president of business development, says "We don't advertise and hardly spend money on traditional marketing. Our company has grown through word of mouth and referrals. Our returns policy is a big part of our growth."[18]

The company's relentless pursuit of the ultimate customer experience is the stuff of legend. Zappos offers extremely fast shipping at no cost and will cover the return shipping if you are dissatisfied for any reason at any time. Hsieh said, employees have to be free to be themselves. That means no-call times or scripts for customer service representatives, regular costume parties, and parades and decorations in each department.[19] Customer service reps are given a lot of leeway to make sure every customer is an enthusiastic customer.[20] When a woman called to return a pair of boots for her deceased husband, Zappos not only accepted the return, they sent flowers.

Zappos' past success comes down to the company's culture and the unusual amount of openness Hsieh encourages among employees, vendors, and other businesses. "If we get the culture right," he says, "most of the other stuff, like the brand and the customer service will just happen. With most companies, as they grow, the culture goes downhill. We want the culture to grow stronger and stronger as we grow."[21]

Now that Zappos is part of Amazon, will it still prosper and grow? Will the company culture and customer service go uphill . . . or down?

Looking Ahead

It seems hard to catch Bezos *not* being upbeat. Even as Amazon's stock values fluctuate, he still believes that customer service, not the stock ticker, defines the Amazon experience. "I think one of the things people don't understand is we can build more shareholder value by lowering product prices than we can by trying to raise margins," he says. "It's a more patient approach, but we think it leads to a stronger, healthier company. It also serves customers much, much better."[14]

In just over a decade, Amazon.com has grown from a one-man operation into a global giant of commerce. By forging alliances to ensure that he has what customers want and making astute purchases, Jeff Bezos has made Amazon the go-to brand for online shopping. But with its significant investments in new media and services, does the company risk spreading itself too thin? Will customers continue to flock to Amazon, the go-to company for their every need?

Discussion Questions

1. In what ways does Bezos's decision to develop and deliver the Kindle show systematic and intuitive thinking?
2. How do you describe the competitive risk in Amazon.com's environment as it leads the market for digital book downloads?
3. Which decision errors and traps are the greatest threats to the success of Bezos's decision making as Amazon's CEO, and why?
4. **FURTHER RESEARCH**—What are the latest initiatives coming out of Amazon? How do they stack up in relation to actual or potential competition? How has the Zappos acquisition turned out? Is Bezos making the right decisions as he guides the firm through today's many business and management challenges?

Case 5: Lands' End: Living the Golden Rule

What's so interesting about a company that just wants to be nice? Longevity and year-after-year success, for starters. From a no-questions-asked return policy to patient, limitless customer support, Lands' End has developed a solid business model around treating customers the way they'd like to be treated. See how this former retailer of sailing products turned good manners into healthy profits.

Customers Come First

Lands' End, a clothing retailer out of Dodgeville, Wisconsin, is known for its generous return policy. But no customer request tested this more than that of a car collector who asked to return a taxicab his wife had purchased for him more than 20 years before. In a novel departure from its normal trade, Lands' End had featured the vintage taxi on the cover of its 1984 holiday catalog and sold it to the woman for $19,000. In 2005, the man contacted Lands' End and inquired about a refund on the car. Cheerfully, Lands' End obliged and returned the woman's full purchase price.

This sort of humble business practice seems unusually generous in today's hypercompetitive retail market. But Lands' End has built a cult following—and consistently strong profits—on the basis of Midwestern kindness and durable, high-quality clothes. When online retail sales top $131 billion, companies need any edge they can get.[1]

Lands' End gets its edge simply by living in accordance with the Golden Rule. All business practices—customer service, phone support, return procedures, employee treatment, and even relationships with suppliers—flow from the company's principled ideals. Lands' End refers to this philosophy in one simple notion: "What is best for our customer is best for all of us."[2]

Lands' End's customer-first policies are necessary to distinguish the company amid such catalog-based competitors as Maine's L.L. Bean, a company that has been around more than fifty years longer and has deeper brand equity. And the firm's inimitable customer experience has long been a shopper's favorite, especially during the holiday season. Though more and more customers order via the company's Web site, many still prefer to work with the well-trained phone staff, who receive 70–80 hours of product, customer service, and computer training when hired. They also respond to e-mails with a personal response, in most cases within three hours.[3]

Jeanne Bliss, author of *Chief Customer Officer* and a 25-year customer service veteran, started her career at Lands' End. She noted, "You've got to do reliability first: 24-hour delivery and answering the phone on the second ring 99.9% of the time. Then you've earned the right to do more." If you're Lands' End, "doing more" means adding fun touches, such as including holiday poems or instructions for turning shipping cartons into barnyard animals.[4]

Born from Boating

Lands' End began in 1963 when founder Gary Comer established the company to sell racing sailboat equipment, along with a handful of sweaters and raincoats. Comer, a 10-year copywriting veteran at the Chicago office of Young & Rubicam,

sought a change of pace after leaving the ad industry and struck up a partnership with like-minded sailing enthusiasts.[5] For several years, the company focused on sailing-related products until it became clear that what had been its peripheral merchandise—clothing, canvas luggage, and shoes—was in fact its most profitable.[6]

As the company's focus shifted to the casual, durable clothing it is known for today, its size and its profits continued to grow. By the spring of 1977, the company discontinued carrying sailing equipment altogether. One year later, Comer moved operations from Chicago to Dodgeville, Wisconsin. "I fell in love with the gently rolling hills and woods and cornfields, and being able to see the changing seasons," Comer said. He also likely fell in love with the substantially lower cost of operations.[7]

Lands' End continued to grow and diversify its clothing line for the next 20 years, culminating in a sale to Sears in 2002 for $1.9 billion. Sears planned to expand on the relatively small number of Lands' End stores (only twelve outlet stores existed at the time) by creating a store-within-a-store concept. Some analysts considered this a brilliant move, especially because Lands' End was the top specialty catalog and top specialty online retailer at the time. But the execution floundered when Sears failed to promote the integration. And when faithful Lands' End customers did come to Sears, they found the stock scattered throughout the store.[8]

Lands' End shops are now distinguished in Sears by navy blue signs and columns and occupy an average of 10,000 square feet per store. According to Sears spokesman Christian Brathwaite, "The idea is to enhance the customer experience and make it easy for customers to shop for Lands' End apparel, coupled with the Lands' End service model. We've seen a very positive customer response."[9]

It's a solid bet for Sears, according to Christopher T. Shannon, managing director at the investment bank, Berkery, Noyes & Co., who perceived that the store-within-a-store model is gaining steam. He noted a "rise in demand from the public for more specialty retailers. I believe the goal is to have more of a one-on-one relationship with the end-buyer and offer as many different ways to make a purchase as possible."[10]

Standing Out from the Crowd

To maintain a competitive presence in the crowded retail clothing market, Lands' End employs a number of creative strategies to stay at the forefront of customers' minds and wallets. Its Web site was the first to offer a feature called "My Virtual Model," a tool that uses customer-supplied measurements to generate a 3-D likeness that can be used to "try on" merchandise. To answer customers' questions as they occur, while maintaining a seamless Web shopping experience, Lands' End installed a chat module called "Lands' End Live."

Banking on the durability and conservative styling of its clothes, Lands'

End branched out of the traditional retail model to market directly to businesses, institutions, and schools. LEBO—the company's business outfitting division—strives to free organizations from the monotony of stuffy, starched uniforms. To attract attention to this program, LEBO provided a free apparel makeover to three companies, partnering to develop new looks that were eventually highlighted in the LEBO catalog.[11]

When the annual holiday shopping season approaches, Lands' End kicks its customer-retention efforts into high gear. In a recent holiday season, one customer service representative from each of the company's three call centers is chosen to serve as Elf of the Day from November 28 to December 18 and given the discretion to offer randomly selected customers complementary upgrades, such as free gift boxing or monogramming. "It's a way to spread a little extra surprise and happiness to customers," said Lands' End spokesperson Amanda Broderick.[12]

But as other clothing retailers follow suit and improve their customer service

skills, Lands' End may begin to find itself with stiff competition and pinched profit margins. Does the company have what it takes to distinguish itself in the crowded apparel marketplace?

Discussion Questions

1. How could the planning process be followed to create a plan for continuous improvements in Lands' End's online customer service?
2. If you were hired by Lands' End to help benchmark its customer service performance, which three companies would you choose and why?
3. How could a clear hierarchy of objectives improve goal alignment and planning within the customer services area?
4. **FURTHER RESEARCH**—Browse the Lands' End Web site and check the business news for updates to learn as much as you can about the company. Do the same for L.L. Bean. Does one firm or the other have any special advantage in respect to planning for future success? Why or why not?

Case 6: Electronic Arts: Inside Fantasy Sports

Electronic Arts is one of the largest and most profitable third-party video game makers. Exclusive contracts with professional sports teams have enabled it to dominate the sports gaming market. Struggling with high development costs and an aging lineup of games, EA's position is beginning to waver and the company would like to acquire a chief competitor to invigorate sales. Can EA maintain the pole position in a crowded and contentious market?

Fantasy Rules

It seems that one company has cornered the market on fantasy. Electronic Arts' customers pay modest prices to make gridiron glory with Super Bowl champions, hunt gangsters with Michael Corleone, and lead a band of elves to save Middle Earth—all from the comfort of their sofas or desks. Call it a dream maker, call it a magician of make-believe, but above all, call Electronic Arts profitable.

The Redwood City, California, video game maker holds some 60% of the sports video gaming market and is well known around the world for its incredibly realistic sports titles.[1] Led by the perpetually successful *Madden NFL* games, Electronic Arts has built an empire around putting gamers shoulder to shoulder with their favorite athletes. At last check, EA posted $4.2 billion in annual sales.[2]

Founded in 1982 by William "Trip" Hawkins, an early director of strategy and marketing for Apple Computer, EA gained quick distinction for its detail-oriented sports titles compatible with the Nintendo and Sega platforms. Although EA has also received good reviews for its strategy and fighting games, it left its heart on the gridiron, diamond, court, or any other playing field long ago. Says EA Sports marketing chief Jeffrey Karp, "We want to be a sports company that makes games."[3]

Ad Revenue In, Ad Revenue Out

Word of mouth may still be the most trusted form of advertising, and EA has always depended on fans to spread its gaming gospel. But in a highly competitive—and lucrative—gaming market, EA knows better than to skimp on brand building. According to TNS Media Intelligence, Electronic Arts spent $34 million in a recent year advertising the EA Sports division and its games.[4] EA knows its audience, and it promotes as heavily to *Game Informer* readers as it does to subscribers of *ESPN The Magazine*.

The realism of EA's graphics set it apart from competitors long ago, but the energy and talent used to depict that realism might be wasted if EA games didn't include the one element fans most want to see: their favorite players. However, top athletes aren't cheap, and neither are their virtual depictions. Players such as Tiger Woods, Donovan McNabb, and Carmelo Anthony expect a tidy sum to promote any product, including video games that use their likenesses. EA spends $100 million annually—three times its ad budget—to license athletes, players' associations, and teams. It's a complex dance: the *FIFA Soccer* game requires 350 different licenses from a total of 18 club leagues, 40 national teams, and 11,000 players.[5] Cheap? Anything but. EA knows that, simply put, players got game.

Locking Down the Gridiron

With such incredible budgets allocated to promotion and locking in players, competing video game makers have found it difficult to challenge EA's pole position—and a recent string of alliances with sports associations might make it next to impossible. Electronic Arts laid out an estimated $300 million for the exclusive rights to publish National Football League (NFL) titles until 2009. EA, whose Madden series is the most commercially successful sports title of all time, faced stiff competition from worldwide competitors seeking NFL exclusivity. The EA team recognized that losing its NFL license—and its star player—was not a feasible play. The NFL saw that the partnership would be mutually beneficial, and it initiated the negotiations with EA. "Because of the deal, we have more access to players, coaches, teams, and other NFL assets than ever before, which allows us to create a more entertaining experience," says Jeff Karp, vice president of marketing for EA Sports.[6]

Securing the likenesses of these major personalities left rival 2K Sports, the sports label of Take-Two Interactive Software, with only one option: to go after retired players. EA rushed to lock up the rights to the most valuable retired players' rights.

But in their effort to score another great deal, EA may have stirred up a lawsuit with angry hall of famers who believe the rights to their likenesses are worth much more than $400,000 per year.[7]

The deal also delivered a crushing blow to competing franchises, such as the otherwise successful *ESPN NFL Football* series from Sega Sports/Visual Concepts. Determined not to be completely outdone, 2K Sports dropped an estimated $90 million to secure a similar deal with Major League Baseball for the next seven years.

But is this what fans really want? Not all fans, it seems. Two gamers have filed a lawsuit in Oakland, California, alleging that EA's exclusive contracts to use the names and likenesses of groups such as the NCAA and the NFL players' association violates U.S. antitrust laws. Not only does this keep other gaming companies from signing similar agreements, thus forcing them out of the market, the suit alleges, but it also allows EA to unfairly raise the price of such games, with no real competition to keep pricing in check.[8]

Paying to Be Seen

Even the most dedicated Madden fans may wonder whether the sports video gaming market has enough muscle to shoulder EA's gargantuan costs. Enter the promotional alliance. Just as EA pays to license the use of NFL logos in its games, big-name sports companies such as Nike and Reebok pay to the tune of $3.5 million a year to get their logos on digital players.[9] One game, *NBA Live*, offers players the opportunity to switch up the color and style of players' logo-friendly footwear. The shoe styles may be virtual, but the value of brand recognition is very real for companies that pony up for sponsorship.

Such brand reinforcement isn't limited to sports games either. EA's *Need for Speed Underground 2*, a fast-paced racing game, takes endorsement beyond the omnipresent billboard ads and vehicle logos found in typical driving simulators. Here players receive "text messages" on the screen suggesting game hints, each bearing the AT&T logo. The significance may be lost on adults, but for a younger generation raised on instant messaging, the placement makes perfect sense.

It makes financial sense, too. A recent poll by Nielsen Entertainment and Activision indicates that this kind of placement may result in notable improvements in both brand recall and favorable brand perception. "I think truly that no other media type can deliver the persuasion that in-game ads can if executed properly," said Michael Dowling, general manager at Nielsen Entertainment, Los Angeles.[10]

Quest for New Blood

In its quest to own the video game market, Electronic Arts made an unsolicited $2 billion cash offer to buy rival Take-Two. EA took the offer public after Take-Two executives privately dismissed the proposal. The offer came at a critical time for both gaming houses: EA's market share had been slowly flagging because of the underperformance of some of its chief titles, and Take-Two was still recovering from having its directors purged by dissident shareholders in a proxy fight.

Corporate consolidation is a fact of life in the cutthroat gaming industry, and EA needs new blood in order to contend with the recent merger of Activision (Guitar Hero III) and the games unit of Vivendi SA (World of Warcraft). EA claims that it can offer Take-Two, whose *Grand Theft Auto* series has sold more than 65 million copies, more extensive foreign distribution networks and the ability to bring Take-Two titles to other formats,

More on Take-Two Interactive

As Electronic Arts was trying to decide how to upgrade and expand its company's portfolio, it took a predatory interest in video game rival Take-Two Interactive Software, Inc. Sometimes referred to as the evil empire for gobbling up smaller development houses to gain their intellectual property, Electronic Arts seemed at it again.

Like "the little engine that could," Take-Two had already fought off a $2 billion hostile acquisition by Electronic Arts—twice! Banking on the future success of games such as its Grand Theft Auto series, the company deemed the new price too low. But many wondered if Take-Two was playing its own high-stakes game by keeping EA's offer at arm's length.[12,13]

Even Ben Feder, Take-Two Chief Executive, said a wave of consolidations in the games business is coming. "The small guys will definitely get either bought up or go away. You'll be left with some large players and I imagine one or two will stay independent and the rest will get swallowed up by media companies."[14]

So, is Take-Two big enough to stay independent? "They're on that cusp right now," said Ben Schachter, an analyst at UBS Securities.[15] Ranked number 28 on the list of largest software companies, Take-Two publishes and develops products through its wholly owned labels Rockstar Games, 2K Games, 2K Sports, and 2K Play; and distributes software, hardware, and accessories in North America through its Jack of All Games subsidiary.[16]

The Company's other proprietary brand franchises include Sid Meier's Civilization® Max Payne, Midnight Club, Manhunt, Red Dead Revolver, BioShock®, Sid Meier's Railroads!®, Sid Meier's Pirates!™, and Top Spin. Licensed brands include the immensely popular sports games Major League Baseball® 2K, NBA® 2K, and NHL® 2K.[17]

Acquiring that kind of lineup would certainly revitalize Electronic Arts. Will EA stop at two unsuccessful attempts to overpower Take-Two? Or will Take-Two thrive as an independent firm?

such as mobile devices. According to analyst Michael Pachter, an acquisition of Take-Two would help EA protect its crucial sports gaming franchises. Because Take-Two is one of the "few credible competitors in sports games," EA could choose to either cherrypick Take-Two's top programmers or simply end production of Take-Two games that rival EA products.[11]

Playing for Keeps

Despite its wild success in the video game market, Electronic Arts faces substantial challenges to its power by competing game companies, the cost of doing business, and even dissatisfied gamers. Can EA overcome these threats and continue producing the sports franchises that brought the company considerable success?

Discussion Questions

1. How can feedforward, concurrent, and feedback controls help Electronic Arts meet its quality goals for video games?
2. What output standards and input standards would be appropriate for the control process as applied to video game production?
3. If you were the head of a project to create and commercialize a new sports video game for teaching math to primary students, how could you use CPM/PERT to assist in project management?
4. **FURTHER RESEARCH**—What is the latest in Electronic Arts' quest to either own or overpower Take-Two Interactive? How well is EA positioned for future competitive advantage? Overall, is EA's executive team still on "top of its game?"

Case 7: Dunkin' Donuts: Betting Dollars on Donuts

Once a niche company operating in the northeast, Dunkin' Donuts is opening hundreds of stores and entering new markets. At the same time, the java giant is broadly expanding both its food and its coffee menus to ride the wave of fresh trends, appealing to a new generation of customers. But is the rest of America ready for Dunkin' Donuts? Can the company keep up with its own rapid growth? With Starbucks rethinking its positioning strategy and McDonald's offering a great tasting coffee at a reasonable price, Dunkin' Donuts is hoping they "Kin Do It."

Serving the Caffeinated Masses

There's a lot more to a coffee shop than just change in the tip jar. Some 400 billion cups of coffee are consumed every year, making it the most popular beverage globally. Estimates indicate that more than 100 million Americans drink a total of 350 million cups of coffee a day.[1] And with Starbucks driving tastes for upscale coffee, some customers may wonder whether any coffee vendors remember the days when drip coffee came in only two varieties—regular and decaf. But Dunkin' Donuts does, and it's betting dollars to donuts that consumers nationwide will

embrace its reputation for value, simplicity, and a superior Boston Kreme donut.

Winning New Customers

Most of America has had an occasional relationship with the Dunkin' Donuts brand through its almost 6,400 domestic outlets, which have their densest cluster in the northeast and a growing presence in the rest of the country.[2] But the brand has also managed to carve out an international niche, not only in expected markets such as Canada and Brazil, but also in some unexpected ones, including Qatar, South Korea, Pakistan, and the Philippines.[3]

If the company has its way, in the future you won't have to go very far to pick up a box of donuts. "We're only represented large-scale in the northeastern market," said Jayne Fitzpatrick, strategy officer for Dunkin' Brands, mentioning plans to expand "as aggressively" as possible. "We're able to do that because we're a franchise system, so access to operators and capital is easier."[4] How aggressively? According to John Fassak, vice president of business development, the company plans to expand to 15,000 outlets by 2020. Sample cities in the Midwest reveal heavy investment: 50 more stores planned in Milwaukee, more than 100 in St. Louis, and 30 in central Ohio.[5]

What Would Consumers Think?

None of Dunkin' Donuts' moves makes much difference unless consumers buy into the notion that the company has the culinary imperative to sell more than its name suggests. If plans prove successful, more customers than ever may flock to indulge in the company's breakfast-to-go menu. If they don't, the

only thing potentially worse for Dunkin' Donuts than diluted coffee could be a diluted brand image. After 60 years, the company has a reputation for doing two things simply and successfully—coffee and donuts. Even when consumers see the line of products expand into what was once solely the realm of the company's competitors, they may be unconvinced that Dunkin' Donuts is *the* shop to go to for breakfast.

For most of its existence, Dunkin' Donuts' main product focus has been implicit in its name: donuts, and coffee in which to dip them. First-time customers acquainted with this simple reputation were often overwhelmed by the wide varieties of donuts stacked end-to-end in neat, mouthwatering rows. Playing catch-up to the rest of the morning market, Dunkin' Donuts has only recently joined the breakfast sandwich game.[6]

According to spokesperson Andrew Mastroangelo, Dunkin' Donuts sells approximately one billion cups of coffee a year, for 62% of the company's annual store revenue.[7] Considering that coffee is the most profitable product on the menu, it's a good bet that those margins give the company room to experiment with its food offerings.

Changing Course to Follow Demand

Faced with the challenge of maintaining a relevant brand image in the face of fierce and innovative competition, Dunkin' Donuts pursued a time-honored business tradition—following the leader. The company now offers a competitive variety of espresso-based drinks complemented with a broad number of sugar-free flavorings, including caramel, vanilla, and Mocha Swirl.[8] Ever-increasing competition in the morning meal market made an update to Dunkin' Donuts' food selection inevitable. The company currently focuses on bagel and croissant-based breakfast sandwiches, as well as its new Oven-Toasted line, including flatbread sandwiches and personal pizzas.

On Every Corner

Starbucks is known for its aggressive dominance of the coffee marketplace. When competitors opened a new store in town, Starbucks didn't worry. It just opened a new store across the street, in a vigorous one-upmanship that conquered new ground and deterred competitors. But many who have struggled to compete with Starbucks have had to do so with limited resources or only a few franchises. Not so with Dunkin' Donuts, whose parent brand, Dunkin' Brands, also owns Baskin-Robbins. Now Starbucks, which is facing slow sales and weak earnings growth as customers cut back on spending, intends to shut down more than 600 U.S. locations as part of a broader plan to revive the company.[9]

Starbucks Goes Instant

Starbucks probably claims the most valuable brand name in its industry. How long can Starbucks keep brewing a better cup of coffee?

"Forever," might answer Howard Schultz, chairman and chief global strategist of the company. When he joined Starbucks in 1982 as director of retail operations, the firm was a small coffee retailer in Seattle. But his vision was much bigger: to have a national chain of stores offering the finest coffee drinks, and "educating consumers everywhere about fine coffee."

Today, Starbucks is found around the world. But it has also become more than just another coffee retailer. Visit a store or go online, and you'll find it selling tea, chocolates,

Simple Food for Simple People

Dunkin Donuts' history of offering simple and straightforward morning snacks has given it the competitive advantage of distinction as *the* anti-Starbucks—earnest and without pretense. Like Craftsman tools and Levi's jeans, the company appeals to simple, modest, and cost-conscious customers.

The Sweet Spot Has a Jelly Center.

Dunkin' Donuts is trying to grow in all directions, reaching more customers in more places with more products. According to Fassak, achieving proper retail placement can be a delicate balance. Although Dunkin' Donuts often partners with a select group of grocery retailers—such as Stop & Shop and Wal-Mart—to create a store-within-a-store concept, the company won't set up shop

ice cream, luncheon sandwiches, specialty apparel, gift cards, a variety of other gift items, and music. It's all part of the global quest for growth. But even a top-notch firm such as Starbucks can't pause and rest on its laurels. Success today is no guarantee of success tomorrow. Businesses must deal with much more demanding customer tastes and markets. Stephen Haeckel, director of strategic studies at IBM's Advanced Business Institute, describes the shift this way: "It's a difference between a bus, which follows a set route, and a taxi which goes where customers tell it to go."[13]

Starbucks Corp., which built a coffee empire on its premium images, wants to convince customers that its drinks aren't that expensive. McDonald's has been taking thinly veiled jabs at Starbucks' prices as it rolls out its own line of lattes, cappuccinos, and mochas. So far, McDonald's local advertising for the drinks has included a billboard in Seattle with the message, "Four bucks is dumb."[14]

"We've also been putting our feet into the shoes of our customers and are responding directly to

in just any grocery store. "We want to be situated in supermarkets that provide a superior overall customer experience," he said. "Of course, we also want to ensure that the supermarket is large enough to allow us to provide the full expression of our brand . . . which includes hot and iced coffee, our line of high-quality espresso beverages, donuts, bagels, muffins, and even our breakfast sandwiches." Furthermore, the outlet's location within the supermarket is critical for a successful relationship. "We want to be accessible and visible to customers, because we feel that gives us the best chance to increase incremental traffic and help the supermarket to enhance their overall performance," Fassak said.

But why stop at grocery stores? Taking this philosophy a step further, Dunkin' Donuts has also entered the lodging market with their first hotel restaurant at the Great Wolf Lodge® in Concord, North

their needs," said Howard Schultz. "Our customers are telling us they want value and quality and we will deliver that in a way that is both meaningful to them and authentic to Starbucks."[15] The newest innovation from Starbucks—Starbucks VIA™ Ready Brew—is now available in more than 200 company-operated Starbucks locations in the greater Seattle area. Additionally, select Target stores in the greater Seattle area have Starbucks VIA™ Ready Brew in the coffee aisle.[16] The idea is to appeal to customers who want a more convenient form of coffee or don't want the waste that comes with brewing an entire pot. Part of the pitch is that it allows customers to have a cup of Starbucks for less than $1.[17] "This is a transformational event in the history of the company," said Schultz in an interview. He served it to guests at his home for months without telling them it's instant and no one detected it, he says.

Is Starbucks on the right path? Or, has its allure peaked and fresher brews will now prosper in the coffee shop marketplace?

Carolina—one of North America's largest indoor water parks. Dunkin' Donuts offers a variety of store models to suit any lodging property, including full retail shops, kiosks, and self-serve hot coffee stations perfect for gift shops and general stores, snack bars, and convention registration areas.[10] Who knows where they'll pop up next?

The launch into the lodging market coincides with Dunkin' Donuts' worldwide expansion program. Steadily and strategically expanding, Dunkin' Donuts unveiled the brand's first-ever theme park restaurant at Hershey Park, new coffee kiosks at sporting venues such as Fenway Park and the TD Banknorth (Boston) Garden, and new stores at airports including Boston, Dallas-Fort Worth, and New York City.[11]

The company is banking on these mutually beneficial partnerships to help it achieve widespread marketplace prominence. Dunkin' Donuts is a nationally known brand with a long reputation for quality, giving the company the benefit of not having to work hard to earn many customers' trust. And if Dunkin' Donuts can find the sweet spot by being within most consumers' reach while falling just short of a Big Brother-like omnipresence,

the company's strategy of expansion may well reward it very handsomely.

But this strategy is not without its risks. In the quest to appeal to new customers, offering too many original products and placements could dilute the essential brand appeal and alienate long-time customers who respect simplicity and authenticity. On the other hand, new customers previously unexposed to Dunkin' Donuts might see it as "yesterday's brand."

If Dunkin' Donuts' executives focus too narrowly on franchising new stores, they might not be aware of issues developing in long-standing or even recently established stores. Some older franchises seem long overdue for a makeover, especially when compared to the Starbucks down the block.

In order to keep up with the latest health concerns, it has reformulated its food and beverages according to its DDSMART criteria so that they meet at least one of these criteria: 25% fewer calories, or 25% less sugar, fat, saturated fat, or sodium than comparable fare.[12] The company has even begun shifting its donut production from individual stores into centralized production facilities designed to serve up to 100 stores apiece.

For the time being, Dunkin' Donuts seems determined in its quest for domination of the coffee and breakfast market. Will Dunkin' Donuts strike the *right* balance of products and placement needed to mount a formidable challenge against competitors?

Discussion Questions:

1. What does a Porter's Five Forces analysis reveal about the industry in which Dunkin' Donuts and Starbuck's compete, and what are its strategic implications for Dunkin' Donuts?

2. In what ways is Dunkin' Donuts presently using strategic alliances, and how could cooperative strategies further assist with its master plan for growth?

3. Which of the globalization strategies will work best in Dunkin' Donuts' global expansion and why?

4. **FURTHER RESEARCH**—Gather information on industry trends, as well as current developments with Dunkin' Donuts and its competitors. Use this information to build an up-to-date SWOT analysis for Dunkin' Donuts. If you were the CEO of the firm, what would you consider to be the strategic management implications of this analysis, and why?

Case 8: Nike: Spreading Out to Stay Together

Nike is indisputably a giant in the athletics industry. But the Portland, Oregon, company has grown large precisely because it knows how to stay small. By focusing on its core competencies—and outsourcing all others—Nike has managed to become a sharply focused industry leader. But can it stay in front?

What Do You Call a Company of Thinkers?

It's not a joke or a Buddhist riddle. Rather, it's a conundrum about one of the most successful companies in the United States—a company known worldwide for its products, none of which it actually makes. This begs two questions: If you don't make anything, what do you

actually do? If you outsource everything, what's left?

A whole lot of brand recognition, for starters. Nike, famous for its trademark Swoosh™, is still among the most recognized brands in the world and is an industry leader in the $79 billion U.S. sports footwear and apparel market.[1] And its 33% market share dominates the global athletic shoe market.[2]

Since captivating the shoe-buying public in the early 1980s with legendary spokesperson Michael Jordan, Nike continues to outpace the athletic shoe competition while spreading its brand through an ever-widening universe of sports equipment, apparel, and paraphernalia. The ever-present Swoosh graces everything from bumper stickers to sunglasses to high school sports uniforms.

Not long after Nike's introduction of Air Jordans, the first strains of the "Just Do It" ad campaign sealed the company's reputation as a megabrand. When Nike made the strategic image shift from simply selling products to embodying a love of sport, discipline, ambition, practice, and all other desirable traits of athleticism, it became among the first in a long line of brands to represent itself as aiding customers in their self-expression as part of its marketing strategy.

Advertising has played a large part in Nike's continued success. Nike recently spent $2.3 billion annually on advertising,[3] with a recent combined total of $220 million in measured media.[4] Portland ad agency Wieden & Kennedy has been instrumental in creating and perpetuating Nike's image—so much so that the agency has a large division in-house at Nike headquarters. This intimate relationship between the two companies allows the agency's creative designers to focus solely on Nike work and gives them unparalleled access to executives, researchers, and anyone else who might provide advertisers with their next inspiration for marketing greatness.

What's Left, Then?

Although Nike has cleverly kept its ad agency nestled close to home, it has relied on outsourcing many nonexecutive responsibilities in order to reduce overhead. It can be argued that Nike, recognizing that its core competency lies in the design—not the manufacturing—of shoes, was wise to transfer production overseas.

But Nike has taken outsourcing to a new level, barely producing any of its products in its own factories. All of its shoes, for instance, are made by subcontractors. Although this allocation of production hasn't hurt the quality of the shoes at all, it has challenged Nike's reputation among fair-trade critics.

After initial allegations of sweatshop labor surfaced at Nike-sponsored factories, the company tried to reach out and reason with its more moderate critics. But this approach failed, and Nike found itself in the unenviable position of trying to defend its outsourcing practices while withholding the location of its favored production shops from the competition.

Boldly, in a move designed to turn critics into converts, Nike posted information on its Web site detailing every one of the approximately 700 factories it uses to make shoes, apparel, and other sporting goods.[5] It released the data in conjunction with a comprehensive new corporate responsibility report summarizing the environmental and labor situations of its contract factories.[6]

"This is a significant step that will blow away the myth that companies can't release their factory names because it's proprietary information," said Charles Kernaghan, executive director of the National Labor Committee, a New York-based anti-sweatshop group that has been no friend to Nike over the years. "If Nike can do it, so can Wal-Mart and all the rest."[7]

Jordan Isn't Forever

Knowing that shoe sales alone wouldn't be enough to sustain continued growth, Nike decided, in a lateral move, to learn more about its customers' interests and involvement in sports, identifying what needs it might be able to fill. Nike's success in the running category, for example, was largely driven by the Apple iPod-linked Nike Plus, which now ranks as the world's largest running club. The technology not only motivates runners with music and tracking their pace, but it also uploads their times and distances into a global community of runners online, creating a social-networking innovation that lets runners race in different countries.[8]

Banking on the star power of its Swoosh, Nike has successfully branded apparel, sporting goods, sunglasses, and even an MP3 player made by Philips. Like many large companies who have found themselves at odds with the possible limitations of their brands, Nike realized that it would have to master the one-two punch: identifying new needs and supplying creative and desirable products to fill those needs.

In fitting with the times, Nike's head designer, John R. Hoke III, is encouraging his designers to develop environmentally sustainable designs.[9] This may come as a surprise to anyone who has ever thought about how much foam and plastic goes into the average Nike sneaker, but a corporate-wide mission called "Considered" has designers rethinking the materials used to put the spring in millions of steps.

The company even launched a line of environmentally sustainable products under the same name, all of them built under the principle established in the Considered program. "I'm very passionate about this idea," Hoke said. "We are going to challenge ourselves to think a little bit differently about the way we create products."[10]

Nipping at Nike's Heels

Despite Nike's success and retention of its market share, things haven't been a bed of roses in the past few years. When CEO Phil Knight decided to step down, he handed the reins to Bill Perez, former CEO of S.C. Johnson and Sons, who became the first outsider recruited for the executive

tier since Nike's founding in 1968. But after barely a year with Perez on the job, Knight, who remained in the inner circle in his position as chairman of the board, decided Perez couldn't "get his arms around the company." Knight accepted Perez's resignation and promoted Mark Parker, a 27-year veteran who was then co-president of the Nike brand, as a replacement.[11]

And pressures are mounting from outside its Beaverton, Oregon, headquarters. German rival Adidas drew a few strides closer to Nike when it purchased Reebok for approximately $3.8 billion.[12] Joining forces will collectively help the brands negotiate shelf space and other sales issues in American stores and will aid the Adidas group in its price discussions with Asian manufacturers. With recent combined global sales of $15 billion,[13] the new supergroup of shoes isn't far off from Nike's $18.6 billion.[14]

According to Jon Hickey, senior vice president of sports and entertainment marketing for the ad agency Mullen, Nike has its "first real, legitimate threat since the '80s. There's no way either one would

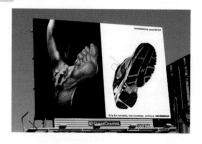

New Balance Runs on Its Own Track

Although New Balance has grown substantially, it has not lost sight of who it is or from where it came. From the beginning, New Balance prided itself on its American roots.[19] To ensure the best fitting, best performing shoes and apparel, it focuses on improving technology and production methods in the good old US of A. Unlike rival Nike, which has outsourced its production overseas, New Balance maintains five manufacturing facilities in the United

States. To this day its headquarters remain in Boston, MA, where its story first began.

It all started in 1906, when a 33-year-old waiter named William J. Riley decided to build arch supports that relieved the pain suffered by people who spent all day working on their feet. His design fit better, and felt better than anything else on the market. Riley designed his first running shoe for the Boston running club, the Boston Brown Bag Harriers, 19 years later. The success of this shoe spread quickly and by 1941 New Balance had taken off, creating custom-made shoes for running, baseball, basketball, tennis, and boxing.[20]

With the introduction of the Trackster in 1960, New Balance began a new direction in shoe manufacturing. The Trackster was the first running shoe available in multiple widths, a feature that would become the standard for New Balance offerings.[21]

Today, New Balance holds onto its history through the numbering system that owes its origins to a man named Arthur Heckler. Instead of naming the different shoe models, Heckler chose to number them because he wanted to place an emphasis on the New Balance philosophy, not any one particular shoe. To this day, that philosophy is upheld as model numbers are advanced to incorporate new technologies and designs.[22] With a core set of values that include integrity, teamwork, and total customer satisfaction, New Balance continues to produce shoes and apparel that meet the standards it has employed for more than 100 years.[23]

Will New Balance make its way further toward the head of the pack? Or will its decision to still employ Americans over cheaper labor overseas mean that it will always be just another smaller player?

even approach Nike, much less overtake them, on their own." But now, adds Hickey, "Nike has to respond. This new, combined entity has a chance to make a run. Now, it's game on."[15]

But when faced with a challenge, Nike simply knocks its bat against its cleats and steps up to the plate. "Our focus is on growing our own business," said Nike spokesman Alan Marks. "Of course we're in a competitive business, but we win by staying focused on our strategies and our consumers. And from that perspective nothing has changed."[16]

Putting It All Together

Nike has balanced its immense size and tremendous pressures to remain successful by leveraging a decentralized corporate structure. Individual business centers—such as research, production, and marketing—are free to focus on their core competencies without worrying about the effects of corporate bloat.

A recent organizational change is part of a wider Nike restructuring that may result in an overall reduction of up to 5% of the company's workforce.[17] "This new model sharpens our consumer focus and will allow us to make faster decisions, with fewer management layers," said Charlie Denson, President of the Nike Brand.[18]

Nike has found continued marketplace success by positioning itself not simply as a sneaker company but as a brand that fulfills the evolving needs of today's athletes. Will Nike continue to profit from its increasingly decentralized business model, or will it spread itself so thin that its competition will overtake it?

Discussion Questions

1. When Nike CEO Phil Knight stepped down and handed the top job to Bill Perez, he stayed on as chairman of the board. In what ways could Knight's continued presence on the board have created an informal structure that prevented Perez from achieving full and complete leadership of Nike?

2. How can Nike utilize both traditional and newer organization structures to support the firm's heavy strategic commitment to outsourcing?

3. Given the problems Nike has had with sweatshop labor being used by some of its foreign contractors, are there subsystems of the firm that need to be run with a mechanistic rather than organic design? Give examples to support your answer.

4. **FURTHER RESEARCH**—Gather information on Nike's recent moves and accomplishments, and those of its rival, Adidas. Are both firms following the same strategies and using the same structures to support them? Or is one doing something quite different from the other? Based on what you learn, what do you predict for the future? Can Nike stay on top, or is Adidas destined to be the next industry leader?

Case 9: Apple Inc.: People and Design Create the Future.

Over a span of more than 30 years, Apple Computer paradoxically existed both as one of America's greatest business successes and as a company that sometimes failed to realize its potential. Apple Inc. ignited the personal computer industry in the 1970s,[1] bringing such behemoths as IBM and Digital Equipment almost to their knees; stagnated when a series of CEOs lost opportunities; and rebounded tremendously since the return of its cofounder and former CEO, Steve Jobs. The firm represents a fascinating microcosm of American business as it continues to leverage its strengths while reinventing itself.

Corporate History

The history of Apple Inc. is a history of passion, whether on the part of its founders, its employees, or its loyal users.[2] It was begun by a pair of Stevens who, from an early age, had an interest in electronics. Steven Wozniak and Steven Jobs initially put their skills to work at Hewlett Packard and Atari,

respectively. But then Wozniak constructed his first personal computer—the Apple I—and, along with Jobs, created Apple Computer on April 1, 1976. Right from the start, Apple exhibited an extreme emphasis on new and innovative styling in its computer offerings. Jobs took a personal interest in the development of new products, including the Lisa and the first, now legendary, Macintosh, or "Mac."

The passion that Apple is so famous for was clearly evident in the design of the Mac. Project teams worked around the clock to develop the machine and its operating system, Mac OS. The use of graphical icons to create simplified user commands was an immensely popular alternative to the command-line structure of DOS found on IBM's first PCs.

When Apple and IBM began to clash head-on in the personal computer market, Jobs recognized the threat and realized that it was time for Apple to "grow up" and be run in a more businesslike fashion. In early 1983, he persuaded John Sculley, at that time president of Pepsi-Cola, to join Apple as president. The two men clashed almost from the start, with Sculley eventually ousting Jobs from the company.

The launch of the Mac reinvigorated Apple's sales. However, by the 1990s, IBM PCs and clones were saturating the personal computer market. Furthermore, Microsoft launched Windows 3.0, a greatly improved version of the Wintel operating system, for use on IBM PCs and clones. Although in 1991 Apple had contemplated licensing its Mac operating system to other computer manufacturers, making it run on Intel-based machines, the idea was nixed by then chief operating officer Michael Spindler in a move that would ultimately give Windows the nod to dominate the market.

Innovative Design to the Rescue

Apple continued to rely on innovative design to remain competitive in the 1990s. It introduced the very popular PowerBook notebook computer line, as well as the unsuccessful Newton personal digital assistant. Sculley was forced out and replaced by Michael Spindler. He oversaw a number of innovations, including the PowerMac family—the first Macs based on the PowerPC chip, an extremely fast processor co-developed with IBM and Motorola. In addition, Apple finally licensed its operating system to a number of Mac-cloners, although never in significant numbers.

After a difficult time in the mid-1990s, Spindler was replaced with Gil Amelio, the former president of National Semiconductor. This set the stage for one of the most famous returns in corporate history.

Jobs's Return

After leaving Apple, Steven Jobs started NeXT computer, which produced an advanced personal computer with a sleek, innovative design. However, the computer, which entered the market late in the game and required proprietary software, never gained a large following. Jobs then cofounded the Pixar computer-animation studio, which coproduced a number of movies with Walt Disney Studios, including the popular *Toy Story*.[3]

In late 1996, Apple purchased NeXT, and Jobs returned to Apple in an unofficial capacity as advisor to the president. When Amelio resigned, Jobs accepted the role of "interim CEO" of Apple Computer and wasted no time in making his return felt. He announced an alliance with Apple's former rival, Microsoft. In exchange for $150 million in Apple stock, Microsoft and Apple would share a five-year patent cross-license for their graphical interface operating systems. He revoked licenses allowing the production of Mac clones and started offering Macs over the Web through the Apple Store.

Beginning with the iMac and the iBook, its laptop cousin, Jobs has continually introduced a series of increasingly popular products that have captured the buying public's imagination. Upon their release, the iPod, MacBook, Apple TV, and iPhone instantly spawned imitators that mimicked the look of these products, but they couldn't duplicate Apple's acute ability to integrate design with usability. Once again, Apple became an industry innovator by introducing certifiably attractive—and powerful— consumer electronics products. Its recent successes have included growing to command approximately 21% of the total computer market[4] and a 66% of the market share for computers priced over $1,000.[5] It also tends to earn more revenue per computer sold than its value-priced competitors.

What Does the Future Hold?

Whenever critics argued that Apple should reinvent itself again, it did just that—and then some. Now it is setting standards with new corporate strategy, taking advantage of the explosion of personal electronic devices. In its first week, iTunes sold 1.5 million songs and captured 80% of the market share of legal music downloads. And now we're into new generation iPhones, wondering just what Apple will next bring to the market.

Casting an ominous shadow on the company was Steve Jobs's announcement in early 2009 of a six-month medical leave. True to his word, Jobs, a pancreatic cancer survivor, officially returned to work over the summer following a liver transplant and months of speculation about his health and his future with the company he co-founded more than 30 years ago. While Jobs was on leave, Chief Operating Officer Tim Cook handled Apple's day-to-day operations. Some analysts think Jobs may transition into an advisory role, focusing on products and strategy and Cook would formally become CEO. Collins Stewart analyst Ashok Kumar said investors will be reassured that Jobs is back at the helm of the company he helped resuscitate over the past decade, with successful products such as the iPod and the iPhone.[6]

For most companies, such information is not crucial because they are not as closely associated with one person. But Apple may be an exception. Since he helped found Apple, Steve Jobs has been inextricably linked to the company and its brand.[7] And there was a lot of concern expressed over Apple's ability to stay on its creative course without Jobs at the helm.

Although able to quietly work miracles, Mr. Cook was not credited with the long-term vision or showmanship of Steve Jobs, who appears capable of peering around corners into the future of technology, and can whip crowds into a frenzy merely by taking something new out of his pocket.[8]

Well, as we all know, Jobs did come back, even though his health remained a concern. The stock markets greeted him with share price rises and consumers eagerly awaited Apple's next new product announcements. The "Job's effect" was positive and well in evidence, and that's his unique reputation.

When Jobs was running Pixar and it was struggling, his co-founder Alny Ray Smith says: "We should have failed, but Steve just wouldn't let it go."[9]

So let's look well into the future. If Steve Jobs is the key to Apple's success, how well can the firm someday do without him? And, what should Jobs himself be doing now to help prepare the firm for this eventuality?

Discussion Questions

1. Apple sells stylish and functional computers as well as a variety of electronic devices, and it operates retail stores. Which type of organization structure would best help Apple keep its creative edge, and why?

2. Should Apple's board of directors be expecting the Jobs to push transformational change or incremental change, or both, at this point in time? Why?

3. How could organization development be used to help the iPhone development teams make sure that they are always working together in the best ways as they pursue the next generations of iPhones and innovative product extensions?

4. **FURTHER RESEARCH**—Review what the analysts are presently saying about Apple. Make a list of all of the praises and criticisms, organize them by themes, and then put them in the priority order you would tackle if taking over from Steve Jobs as Apple's new CEO. In what ways can the praises and criticisms be used to create a leadership agenda for positive change and continuous improvement?

Case 10: Netflix: Making Movie Magic

The Open Secret of Success

What's the most exciting piece of mail you've received lately? Ask more than eight million customers in the United States, and they'll probably reply that it's a little red-and-white envelope from Netflix. More than 46,000 DVD titles are in transit on any given day, requiring the company to stock approximately 55 million DVDs to keep up with customer demand.[1] What accounts for Netflix's success? CEO Reed Hastings believes the key to the sustained growth of

the Los Gatos, California, company is no secret at all—it thrives because of its renowned customer service.[2] Beating out such heavies as Amazon, Apple, and Target, Netflix was crowned Number One in eight straight e-commerce customer satisfaction surveys conducted by ForeSee Results. According to Netflix spokesman Steve Swasey, the company keeps its top place by continuously improving operations—both title selection and customer convenience.[3]

Netflix customers have posted more than two billion movie reviews on its Web site to date; an average customer has posted about two hundred. In return, Netflix recommends movies to customers based on their renting habits. About 60% of its members choose new rentals based on these recommendations.[4]

To improve the tool used to generate these recommendations, Netflix organized a contest to gather its members' ideas. The prize: one million dollars.[5]

Netflix claims that its members rent twice as many movies as they did before joining the service.[6] Given their recent sales figures, it comes as little surprise. At the end of the most recent fiscal year, net income also grew 6% to finish at $67 million, with a 21% growth in revenue that hit $1.2 billion, defying analysts' expectations.[7]

Netflix recently introduced Instant Viewing, which streams any of 12,000 movies and television shows to customers' computers. Within thirty seconds of beginning a download, customers can roll the opening credits. Unlike customers at the Apple's iTunes Store, Netflix customers can wait as long as they want before finishing a streamed movie. Best of all, they don't have to pay extra—the program is built into every membership plan. "It's not branded at all," said Swasey. "It's just part of the service." Since opening up

the service, Netflix has quadrupled its inventory of streaming content.[8]

Taking things a step further—and challenging Apple even more directly—Netflix partnered with the consumer electronics company Roku to produce a palm-sized set-top box that allows customers to view streamed movies on their televisions by using broadband connections.[9] It's a logical move, according to David Cohen, executive vice president and U.S. director of digital communications at Interpublic Group's Universal McCann. "The ability to have thousands, if not millions, of content options delivered to your box is certainly the way of the future," he said.[10]

Some customers even help Netflix expand into markets it has overlooked. A few small libraries are quietly using Netflix to expand their interlibrary loan capabilities.[11] Video stores have caught on, too. One discreet Massachusetts store owner claims to rent ten to fifteen Netflix discs a month, which saves him more than $2,000 in yearly inventory expenses. "It's nice to be able to offer the latest foreign title that no one has heard of," he said.[12]

Slaying the Dragons

Giving customers what they want, Netflix has beaten back competition from some of the biggest names in media. By allowing customers to keep DVDs as long as they like, Netflix undermined the concept of late fees, which had represented a major source of profits for traditional rental companies.[13] And as instant viewing continues to grow in popularity among Netflix customers, the concept is not catching on everywhere—Wal-Mart closed the curtains on its own movie download service.[14]

Putting People Up Front

So, what does the future hold for Netflix? CEO Reed Hastings makes no bones about the business model: "If one thinks about Netflix as a DVD rental business," he says, "one is right to be scared; if one thinks of Netflix as an online movie service with multiple

H ow can the most successful video-delivery company beat its already unbelievable one-day turnaround time? By making a growing portion of its immense catalog available for instant download. Netflix leverages emerging technologies, superior customer service, and an ever-growing subscriber base to transform the traditional video-rental model into a 21st-century on-demand concept.

Blockbuster Isn't in Retreat

Blockbuster Inc., founded in 1985 and headquartered in Dallas, Texas, is another leading global provider of in-home movie and game entertainment, with approximately 8,000 stores throughout the Americas, Europe, Asia, and Australia. The company, once one of the strongest entertainment brands in the world, recently reported worldwide revenues of more than $5.5 billion.[19]

Blockbuster has the largest in-store presence of any company in the movie rental business, a growing online presence, and the capability—currently, the only one in the marketplace to do so—to integrate the physical storefront with its online presence. It is still growing; its share of the store-based rental business continues as a company focus, but Blockbuster is no longer just a chain of video stores. It is an online and an in-store retailer, and becoming more integrated every day.[20] Its Blockbuster Total Access™ movie rental program gives online customers the option of exchanging their DVDs through the mail or returning them to a nearby participating Blockbuster store in exchange for free in-store movie rentals. With this total access, customers no longer have to choose between renting online or renting in-store, and they never have to be without a movie.[21]

As the home entertainment industry has evolved, so, too, has Blockbuster. But has it transformed enough? Blockbuster is facing stiff competition from Netflix on one side and from Redbox on the other. Redbox offers $1 DVD rentals for 24 hours and has more locations than Blockbuster's costly brick and mortar stores. Named one of the "15 Companies That Might Not Survive 2009" in *US News*, Blockbuster isn't giving up yet. Instead, it is inviting consumers to try its service for free, allowing online video game rentals, and offering incentives and deals to drum up business.[22]

Whatever direction the future of home entertainment takes, Blockbuster believes it has the assets that will enable the company to bridge to the future. Do the facts of the market bear out such optimism?

---

different delivery models, then one's a lot less scared. We're only now beginning to deliver the proof points behind that second vision."[15] To "deliver" on this promise, Hastings is now betting as much on people as on his business vision and high technology.

Perks, compensation, and freedom are mainstays of Netflix's commitment to hiring and retaining the best people in the industry. When dealing with competitors such as Apple, Blockbuster, and Amazon, a lot is on the line in the wars for talent. As to salaries, Hastings says: "We're unafraid to pay high."[16] And interestingly, pay isn't linked with performance in the sense of "merit."

Salaries are pegged to job markets to ensure that Netflix pay is always the best around. If you're top talent, you get top salary and are given the freedom to put your talents to work making Netflix's strategy succeed. But if you're something less than a top performer, say, just "average," there isn't room at the company. "At most companies," says Hastings, "average performers get an average raise. At Netflix they get a generous severance package."[17]

Netflix not only hires carefully and well, it offers a unique and highly productive work environment rich in features that appeal to today's high-tech and high-talent workers. Its human resource plan is as creative as its business model: pay higher-than-average salaries; let employees choose how much of their compensation is paid in cash and how much in stock options; encourage each employee to recruit three others they would "love" to work with; let employees take as much time off and vacation as they think they need; limit work rules, maximize work freedom, and make everyone responsible for the choices he or she makes.[18]

Hastings has a lot riding on his human resource strategy. Does Netflix have the right vision for the future?

Discussion Questions

1. What performance appraisal method would you recommend to make sure that only the "best" are kept on the Netflix team?

2. What are the limitations and risks of Hastings' human resource management practices?

3. If Hastings was on the board of a firm such as Procter & Gamble or Home Depot, would his ideas on human resource management work for them? Why or why not?

4. **FURTHER RESEARCH**—Check up on Hastings and Netflix. How is the firm doing right now? How has it changed since the case information was prepared? Are the human resource management practices described here still active at the firm? What else is Netflix doing to create human capital for sustained competitive advantage?

Case 11: Facebook: It's Not Just For Kids.

Social networking web sites are a dime a dozen these days, so how does Facebook stay at the top? By expanding its user base and working with developers and advertisers to create fresh content that keeps users at the site for hours on end. But can Facebook handle the challenges of international expansion and stereotypes about its leadership?

The Perception Counts

Mark Zuckerberg wants you to think differently about Facebook. Unlike most other young Silicon Valley CEOs, he's got experience in managing the kind of changes in perception he hopes to bring about. In 2006 he opened Facebook to users of all ages to convince advertisers—and developers—that social networking was more than kids' stuff. Zuckerberg hopes to persuade these same two groups that Facebook is firmly seated at the top and successfully expanding into global markets.

Although users of Facebook and its social networking rival MySpace might trade barbs over whose site has the best features or the widest selection of friends, there's no denying that Facebook has been a runaway success. It is the sixth-most-trafficked site on the Web, according to Internet research company comScore; it is also the second-most-popular social networking site, trailing only MySpace. Now, more than two-thirds of Facebook users are outside college.[1]

Applications for Every User

Regardless of age or profession, what keeps users coming back to Facebook? The site relies on a host of internally and externally developed applications that integrate directly into the site to keep visitors' eyes glued to Facebook for hours on end. Games and a bevy of trivia contests give users entertaining ways to engage repeatedly with each other.

Commercial marketers are taking note more closely than ever of Facebook's propensity for attracting page views, hoping to benefit from the halo effect surrounding such a successful brand. Companies are integrating their logos and brands into Facebook's built-in culture of sharing and sending. Users can send one another a Wal-Mart–branded ghost, a Ben & Jerry's ice cream cone, virtual birthday bouquets, or even their dream cars. According to Derek Dabrowski, Sunkist brand manager at Dr. Pepper Snapple Group, it's a success. In a promotion to give away 250,000 virtual Sunkist sodas: "We got 130 million brand impressions through that 22-hour time frame. A Super Bowl ad, if you compare it, would have generated somewhere between 6 to 7 million."

Facebook sees the bleak economy as reason to press ahead with its plans for aggressive growth. The company is gearing up for more acquisitions, hiring rapidly, and rolling out new advertising programs. Moving beyond traditional online ads—the text and pictorial banners that show up on most Web sites—they believe that they can stand out among the crowd. Facebook began rolling out "engagement ads" encouraging users to respond to the pitches by commenting, sharing virtual gifts, or becoming fans of the ads themselves. Facebook's online advertising accounts for an estimated $200–225 million in revenue, and its digital goods sell for $1 apiece—generating another $30–40 million.[2]

But the best potential for amassing page views and click-throughs lies in Facebook's ability to integrate applications. The site's photo viewing app, for example—the number-one photo sharing application on the Web—receives more than 850 million photos uploaded to the site each month. Some 6,600,000 developers and entrepreneurs are involved in developing what the company is calling the Facebook Platform. More than 52,000 apps have been developed so far.[3] More than 95% of its members have used at least one application built on the Facebook Platform, and advertisers are betting that they can improve that statistic.[4]

As much as advertisers need Facebook users' page views, Facebook needs those advertisers as loyal customers. Last year, Facebook generated revenues less than one-third what MySpace earned. Facebook ads can sell as inexpensively as 15 cents per 1,000 impressions—compared with an estimated $13 for a similar buy at Yahoo! The pressure is on Facebook to continue to differentiate itself from other social networking sites, according to Jeff Ratner, a managing partner at WPP's MindShare Interaction. If not, "Facebook doesn't look that different," he said. "It just becomes another buy, and there are cheaper, more efficient ways to reach eyes."[5]

Changing Perceptions

On several occasions during his reign at Facebook, the youthful Zuckerberg has fought the common Silicon Valley stereotype of young CEOs who are brash and unripe to lead. His flat rejection of Yahoo!'s $1 billion bid to buy Facebook was criticized by some as a lost opportunity, so he's working to create a professional impression for his company by hiring some experienced Web personalities. Zuckerberg persuaded Sheryl Sandberg to leave Google, where she had developed cash cows Adwords and Adsense, to join Facebook as chief operating officer. Fourteen years older than her boss, Sandberg is charged with bringing a mature personality to the laid-back, collegiate work environment. To do this, she'll integrate performance reviews, refine the recruiting model, and develop a mature, sustainable advertising program that will support Facebook as it evolves. "I'm hopeful that we play a significant role in pushing the envelope [with] awareness building," Sandberg said. "How we get there, I don't think we know yet."[6]

Noting that visitors to the site tripled after Facebook unveiled its international presence, the company is continuing its international growth.[7] In three months, Facebook translated its content into fifteen different languages, with more languages—including Xhosa, Tagalog, and French Canadian—to come soon. This is critical, because

more than 70% of Facebook's 200 million users live outside the United States[8]—double MySpace's percentage. Whereas MySpace specializes in locally themed subsites, Facebook has opted to simply translate its entire site for non-English speakers. "Through the translations we are seeing mass adoption in those markets," said Javier Olivan, an international manager at Facebook, adding that because the site is by its nature a tool for communication, Facebook doesn't need to spend much energy localizing it. "The translation approach allows us to support literally every language in the world," Olivan said.[9]

And to head off the efforts of other social networking sites, Facebook makes data available to users from outside of the site with its Facebook Connect program. Like MySpace's Data Availability (which was announced one day before Facebook's data-sharing concept), Facebook Connect allows users to import their Facebook profiles into other Web sites and synchronize their friend lists.

Changes appear in real time as users modify their Facebook profiles, and users have "total control" of Web site permissions to access Facebook data, according to the company.[10]

With over 87 million visitors to its U.S. site in a recent month, you would think Facebook was worry free. But a rash of unhappy users is stirring up controversy. One even sells "Shut Your Facebook t-shirts." Complaints range from adverse influence—Facebook makes you nosy and limits your social life, to it's just getting to be boring.[11]

What Do You Think?

Despite all of its successes, the management team of Facebook knows that they have serious work ahead in order to change the perception of advertisers, developers, and even some users regarding their ability to lead Facebook successfully and profitably into the future of social networking. Will adding experienced management alter advertisers' stereotypes about youthful Silicon Valley CEOs? Can Facebook

MySpace Makes the Money

Does MySpace have reason to sulk? It was MySpace, after all, that grabbed headlines in 2005 when Rupert Murdoch's News Corp. acquired it for $580 million.[12] In 2006, it was the most popular social networking site in the United States.[13] And it was MySpace that proved social networking could be a mass medium, attracting 10 million users, then 20 million, then 50 million—prompting Murdoch to crow about its "meteoric rise"—back when Facebook was still a college-focused niche player. Yet Facebook has quickly

gained traction and fans. Suddenly, Facebook's worldwide user base surpassed MySpace's in size.[14]

MySpace gives users greater creative freedom by allowing customization of the layout and colors of their profile page with virtually no restrictions—provided that the advertisements are not covered up. So why aren't more users flocking to MySpace?

As many have found, the stylized pages can potentially freeze up Web browsers due to many high bandwidth objects such as videos, graphics, and Flash in their profiles. Sometimes multiple videos and sound files are automatically played at the same time when a profile loads, which is too much for the browser and disconcerting even to the generation accustomed to multi-tasking. While MySpace does block potentially harmful code (such as JavaScript) from profiles, users have occasionally found ways to insert

such code. *PC World* cited this as its main reason for naming MySpace as #1 in its list of twenty-five worst Web sites ever.[15] Continuing problems range from the annoying (spam and service complaints) to the very serious (privacy and child-safety concerns).

But when you peel back the beeping, blinking veneer of its user interface, the MySpace's underlying business model is surprisingly solid. As Facebook appears to focus on expansion and technology first and monetizing second, MySpace is splashing huge portal-like display ads across its site. Although MySpace has fewer users, it generated an estimated $606 million in revenues, according to Goldman Sachs, more than twice Facebook's revenues.[16]

While Facebook is emphasizing expansion, MySpace has scaled back on growth to focus on profits. Will MySpace try to reclaim its number one position, or remain content with being the biggest money maker?

overcome the bad impression being communicated by some disgruntled users?

Discussion Questions

1. Can effective communication be achieved among users of social networking sites such as Facebook?
2. What should Facebook keep in mind as it broadens and diversifies its user base? As users "friend" each other around the globe, do the nuances of cross-cultural communication create problems that Facebook could help address?
3. Sheryl Sandberg is under pressure to bring a mature edge to Facebook. What are the most significant challenges that she most likely faces when communicating with her younger peers at the firm, and how would you advise her to best deal with them?
4. **FURTHER RESEARCH**—Find as much information as you can about Mark Zuckerberg. Does he have what it takes to lead Facebook at this stage in its life? Is he making the right choices in terms of "communicating" himself and his firm to the world? What constructive feedback would you give him as an executive coach?

Case 12: Southwest Airlines: How Herb Kelleher Led the Way

To say that the airline industry has had problems is an understatement. The largest carriers—including American, United, Delta, and USAir—have lost billions of dollars. But Southwest Airlines has weathered the financial storm better than its rivals. How did a little airline get so big and do so well? Its success springs from its core values, developed by Herb Kelleher, cofounder and former CEO, and embraced daily by the company's 35,000 employees: humor, altruism, and "LUV" (the company's NYSE stock ticker symbol).[1]

Unique Character and Success

One thing that makes Southwest Airlines unique is its short-haul focus. The airline does not assign seats; tickets are mostly bought online, with prices varying by how far ahead the flight is booked. The only foods served are snacks, but passengers don't seem to mind. Serving Customers (always written at Southwest with a capital C) is the focus of the company's employees. When Colleen Barrett, until recently Southwest's president and chief operating officer (COO), was the executive vice president for customers, she said, "We will never jump on employees for leaning too far toward the customer, but we come down on them hard for not using common sense."[2] Southwest's core values produce highly motivated employees who care about customers and each other.

At Southwest Airlines, we believe that low costs are crucial, change is inevitable, innovation is necessary, and leadership is essential—particularly during troubling economic times. "Our competitors take drastic/short-sighted measures to compete with us on the price level . . . They make draconian reductions in their employees' salaries, wages, benefits, and pensions. In doing so, they ultimately sacrifice their most important assets—their employees and their employees' goodwill."[3]

Southwest applies this philosophy in an organizational culture that respects employees and their ideas. As executive vice president, Colleen Barrett started a "culture committee" made up of employees from different functional areas and levels. The committee meets quarterly to brainstorm ideas for maintaining Southwest's corporate spirit and image. All managers, officers, and directors are expected to "get out in the field," meeting and talking with employees to understand their jobs. Employees are encouraged to use their creativity and sense of humor to make their jobs, and the customers' experiences, more enjoyable. Gate agents are given books of games to play with passengers waiting for delayed flights. Flight agents might imitate Elvis or Mr. Rogers when making announcements.[4]

The "Luv" Factor

Kelleher, currently chairman emeritus of the board, knows that not everyone would be happy as a Southwest employee: "What we are looking for, first and foremost, is a sense of humor. Then we are looking for people who have to excel to satisfy themselves and who work well in a collegial environment."

To encourage employees to treat one another as well as they treat their customers, departments examine linkages within Southwest to see what their "internal customers" need. The provisioning department, for example, whose responsibility is to provide the snacks and drinks for each flight, selects a flight attendant as "customer of the month." The provisioning department's own board of directors makes the selection decision. Other departments have sent pizza and ice cream to their internal customers. Employees write letters commending the work of other employees or departments that are valued as much as letters from external customers. When problems occur between departments, employees work out solutions in supervised meetings.

Employees exhibit the same attitude of altruism and "luv" (also Southwest's term for its relationship with its customers) toward other groups as well. A significant portion of Southwest employees volunteer at Ronald McDonald Houses throughout Southwest's service territory.[5] When the company purchased a small regional airline, employees sent cards and company T-shirts to their new colleagues to welcome them into the Southwest family.

Profits to Share

Acting in the company's best interests is also directly in the interest of the employees. Southwest has a profit-sharing plan for all eligible employees—and, unlike many of its competitors, Southwest consistently has profits to share. Employees can also purchase Southwest stock at 90% of market value; employees now own about 8% of the total company stock. Although approximately 77% of employees are unionized, the company has a history of good labor relations.[6]

Southwest Airlines is a low-cost operator. But, according to Harvard University professor John Kotter, setting the standard for low costs in the airline industry does not mean Southwest is *cheap*. "Cheap is trying to get your prices down by nibbling costs off everything . . . [Firms such as Southwest Airlines] are thinking 'efficient,' which is very different. . . . They recognize that you don't necessarily have to take a few pennies off of everything. Sometimes you might even spend more."[7] By using only one type of plane in its fleet, Southwest saves on pilot training and aircraft maintenance costs.[8] The *cheap* paradigm would favor used planes, but Southwest's choice for high productivity over lower capital expenditures has given it the youngest fleet of aircraft in the industry.

By using each plane an average of 13 hours daily, Southwest is also able to make more trips with fewer planes than any other airline. It has won the monthly "Triple Crown" distinction—Best On-Time Record, Best Baggage Handling, and Fewest Customer Complaints—more than 30 times.

Sometimes the Voyage Is Better than the Destination.

Despite its impressive record of success, Southwest Airlines has pressing concerns to address. Management worries about the effects that limited promotion opportunities will have on morale. The company has created "job families" with different grade levels so that employees can work their way up within their job. But after five or six years, employees still begin to hit the maximum compensation level for their job.

Another issue is maintaining the culture of caring and fun while expanding rapidly into new markets. Southwest's success has been built with the enthusiasm and hard work of its employees. As Kelleher has said, "The people who work here don't think of Southwest as a business. They think of it as a crusade."[9] Cultivating that atmosphere is a continuing company priority.

From its roots as a regional Texan carrier, Southwest Airlines has grown into one of the most profitable—and most beloved—airlines in American history. The company has created employee satisfaction by focusing on its internal "Customers," who are then positively motivated to show the same degree of concern for external customers. Southwest's perpetual profitability stems not from miserliness but from attention to value and sensible cost savings.

As Colleen Barrett wrote in the company's *Spirit Magazine:* ". . . our steadfast determination remains unbroken to provide the high-spirited Customer Service, low fares, and frequent nonstop flights that Americans want and need."[10] Southwest Airlines continues to be recognized by Fortune magazine as America's most admired airline—one of the most admired companies in America.

When Herb Kelleher relinquished his role as Southwest's CEO, investors worried, because so much of Southwest's success came from Kelleher's unique management and leadership. But events showed that Kelleher's successor Colleen Barrett was well prepared to handle the challenges of maintaining Southwest's culture and success.

Now, Barrett has retired and 22-year employee of the firm, Gary Kelley, has taken the helm. Kelley is navigating Southwest Airlines through one of the industry's most turbulent periods by expanding into new markets, adding flights to heavily trafficked domestic airports, and seeking cross-border alliances with foreign carriers. The airline remains steadfast against charging customers for checking in suitcases and using pillows, as rivals have done. Some analysts question if management has made the right call by not charging for these services, which are generating hundreds of millions of dollars for rivals.[11]

As fuel prices climb and airlines consolidate for security, can Kelley keep Southwest ahead of the airline pack?

Discussion Questions

1. Does the history of Southwest Airlines indicate that Herb Kelleher was a visionary leader, a servant leader, or both? How do you support your answer?
2. What leadership style predominates at Southwest Airlines, and how has this style influenced the firm's culture and management practices.
3. To what extent do Kelleher's and Barrett's leadership approaches show consistency with Drucker's notions of "good old-fashioned leadership?"
4. **FURTHER RESEARCH**—Gary Kelley has had time to bring his personal leadership to Southwest Airlines. But, he has certainly faced some trying times with the economic recession. How well is Kelley doing? Does he have what it takes to keep the airline moving forward in the turbulent environment of the airline industry?

Case 13: Panera Bread Company: Staying Ahead of Long-Term Trends

Panera Bread is in the business of satisfying customers. With fresh-baked breads, gourmet soups, and efficient service, the relatively new franchise has surpassed all expectations for success. But how did a startup food company get so big, so fast? By watching and carefully timing market trends.

French Roots, American Tastes

What's so exciting about bread and soup? For some people, it conjures up images of bland food that soothes an upset stomach. Others think of the kind of simple gruel offered to jailed prisoners in movies. But for Panera Bread, a company able to successfully spot long-term trends in the food industry, artisan-style bread served with deli sandwiches and soups

is a combination proven to please the hungry masses.

Despite its abundance of restaurants, Panera Bread is a relatively new company, known by that name only since 1997. Its roots go back to 1981, when Louis Kane and Ron Shaich founded Au Bon Pain Company Inc., which merged Kane's three existing Au Bon Pain stores with Shaich's Cookie Jar store. The chain of French-style bakeries offered baguettes, coffee, and sandwiches served on either French bread or croissants. It soon became the dominant operator in the bakery-café category on the East Coast. To expand its domestic presence, Au Bon Pain purchased the Saint Louis Bread Company, a Missouri-based chain of about 20 bakery-cafés, in 1993. It renovated the Saint Louis Bread Company stores, renamed them Panera Bread, and their sales skyrocketed.

Executives at Au Bon Pain invested heavily toward building the new brand. In 1999, Panera Bread was spun off as a separate company.[1] Since then, the firm has sought to distinguish itself in the soup-and-sandwich restaurant category. Its offerings have grown to include not only a variety of soups and sandwiches, but also soufflés, salads, panini, breakfast sandwiches, and a variety of pastries and sweets. Most of the menu offerings somehow pay homage to the company name and heritage—bread. Panera takes great pride in noting that its loaves are handmade and baked fresh daily. To conserve valuable real estate in the retail outlets, as well as to reduce the necessary training for new employees, many bread doughs are manufactured off-site at one of the company's 17 manufacturing plants. The dough is then delivered daily by trucks—driving as many

as 9.7 million miles per year—to the stores for shaping and baking.[2] At this point, there are more than 1,260 Panera Bread bakery-cafés in 40 states and in Canada. Franchise stores outnumber company-owned outlets by approximately one-third.[3]

Modern Tastes, Modern Trends

Panera's success has come partly from its ability to predict long-term trends and orient the company toward innovation to fulfill consumers' desires. Its self-perception as a purveyor of artisan bread well predated the current national trend (now rebounded from the brief low-carb craze) for fresh bread and the explosion of artisan bakeries throughout metropolitan America.

Consumers' desire for organic and all-natural foods, once thought to be a marginal market force, has become the norm. Keenly positioning itself at the forefront of retail outlets supporting this trend, Panera recently introduced a children's menu called Panera Kids. Kids can choose from items such as peanut butter and jelly, grilled cheese, and yogurt, and the all-natural and organic foods will please choosy parents.[4]

In addition, Panera proactively responded to unease in the marketplace about the negative impact of trans fats on a healthy diet by voluntarily removing trans fats from its menu. "Panera recognized that trans fat was a growing concern to our customers and the medical community; therefore we made it a priority to eliminate it from our menu," said Tom Gumpel, director of bakery development for Panera Bread. Though reformulating the menu incurred unexpected costs, all Panera menu items are now free from trans fats, except for some small amounts that occur naturally in dairy and meat products, as well as in some condiments.[5]

According to Ron Shaich, chairman and CEO of Panera, "Real success never comes by simply responding to the day-to-day pressures; in fact, most of that is simply noise. The key to leading an organization is understanding the long-term trends at play and getting the organization ready to respond to it."[6]

And let's not forget, we are a coffee nation. For customers who just want to come in, grab a quick cup, and get out, Panera has just the thing. In many stores, coffee customers can avoid the normal line and head straight for the cash register, where they can pick up a cup, drop a small fee into a nearby can, and go directly to the java station. Caffeine-crazed customers can avoid the maddening line during a morning rush and cut the wait for that first steaming sip.

What Makes a Customer Stay?

Panera learned from mega-competitor Starbucks that offering wireless Internet access can make customers linger after their initial purchase, thus increasing the likelihood of a secondary purchase.[7]

Now more than 1,250 of its stores offer customers free Wi-Fi access.[8] According to spokesperson Julie Somers, the decision to offer Wi-Fi began as a way to separate Panera from the competition and to exemplify the company's welcoming atmosphere. "We are the kind of environment where all customers are welcome to hang out," Somers said. "They can get a quick bite or a cup of coffee, read the paper or use a computer, and stay as long as they like. And in the course of staying, people may have a cappuccino and a pastry or a soup." She went on to note that the chief corporate benefit to offering Wi-Fi is that wireless customers tend to help fill out the slow time between main meal segments.[9] Executive Vice President Neal Yanofsky concurred. "We just think it's one more reason to come visit our cafés," he said. And wireless users' tendency to linger is just fine with him. "It leads to food purchases," he concluded.[10] And he's right—the average Panera store has an annualized unit volume of $2 million.[11]

Profits Rise Along with the Dough.

All of Panera's attention to the monitoring of trends has paid off handsomely. Since Panera went public, the company's stock has grown thirteenfold, creating more than $1 billion in shareholder value. *BusinessWeek* recognized Panera as one of its "100 Hot Growth Companies." And even more recently, the *Wall Street Journal* recognized the company as the top performer in the Restaurants and Bars category for one-year returns (63% return), five-year returns (42% return), and ten-year returns (32% return) to shareholders.[12] In addition, a Sandleman & Associates survey of customer satisfaction ranked Panera at the top of the list for four years in a row, beating out 120 other competitors.[13]

Rising to the Top, Then Staying There

Panera Bread plans to take advantage of a weak U.S. real estate market by opening 70–90 new stores in 2009. With a debt-free balance sheet, the company plans to better position itself for the end of the financial crisis.[14]

Panera Bread has demonstrated that sticking to company ideals while successfully forecasting, and then leading the response to long-term industry trends will please customers time and time again. The low-carb craze didn't faze Panera, but can this company continue to navigate the changing dietary trends in today's unstable market?

Discussion Questions

1. How might consumers' perception of Panera's menu and atmosphere affect their dining experience and tendencies to return as customers?

2. Describe how stereotypes about the fast food industry might positively and negatively impact Panera.

3. What are Panera's competitive advantages? Can any of them be deemed "sustainable"?

4. **FURTHER RESEARCH**—Find data reporting on how Panera's sales were affected by the recent economic downturn in the U.S. economy. See if the effects were different in various regions of the country. Does Panera have special strengths that help it deal better than others with challenges such as those posed by a declining economy?

Case 14: Pixar: Animated Geniuses

Pixar has delivered a series of wildly successful animated movies featuring plucky characters and intensely lifelike animation. Yet some of the most memorable ones—Toy Story, Finding Nemo, and The Incredibles—were almost never made. Find out how Apple guru Steve Jobs, whose company struggled to stay alive during its early years, took these upstarts of animation to success.[1]

"The Illusion of Life"

Though the story is far from over, it might seem like a fairytale ending of sorts for John Lasseter, Pixar's creative head, who went from being fired from his position as a Disney animator in the early 80s to running Disney's animation wing with Pixar cohead Edwin Catmull. Lasseter provided the creative direction for Pixar as it grew from an offshoot of Lucasfilm production company into the world's

most successful computer animation company.

Pixar's movies—including *Monsters, Inc.*, *The Incredibles*, *Cars*, *Ratatouille*, and *Up*—have succeeded largely because of Lasseter's focus on employing computer graphics (CG) technology to make the characters, scenery, and minute details as realistic as possible. "Character animation isn't the fact that an object looks like a character or has a face and hands," Lasseter said. "Character animation is when an object moves like it is alive, when it moves like it is thinking and all of its movements are generated by its own thought processes. . . . It is the thinking that gives the illusion of life."[2]

This "illusion of life" is a direct result of the synergy between Pixar's creative teams, who develop the story and characters, and its technical teams who program—and frequently develop—the animation software used to breathe life into each movie. Each forces the other to innovate, and together they successfully balance the latest technology with a back-to-basics focus on interesting characters in compelling stories. "Pixar has such a thoughtful approach, both from a storyline and business perspective," said Ralph Schackart, analyst with William Blair & Co LLC, "I don't think anyone has quite figured out how to do it like them."[3]

In an industry abounding with delight in others' misfortune, some might be surprised that Pixar's old-fashioned approach to moviemaking has succeeded. But Disney CEO Bob Iger believes the opposite. "There is not an ounce of cynicism in Pixar's films," Iger told *Fortune.* "And in a world that is more cynical than it should be, that's pretty refreshing. I think it's a critical ingredient to the success of Pixar's films."[4]

Another unique quality of Pixar is that—unlike competitor Dreamworks Animation SKG—it does not limit its creative products to the animated movies it releases. The studio shares its technical advances with the greater CG community through white papers and technology

partnerships, such as its RenderMan software and hardware.[5]

Perhaps Pixar's closest competitor is Dreamworks, headed by former Disney impresario Jeffrey Katzenberg and backed by media luminaries Steven Spielberg and David Geffen. Other smaller American animation companies such as Orphanage, Wild Brain Inc., and CritterPix Inc. face challenging budgets, limited technology, and tighter deadlines. And in the event these upstarts do manage a theatrical release, they've got a hard act to follow—Pixar grosses an average of $395 million per movie.[6]

An Uphill Battle

Pixar came to life in the early 1980s within a computer graphics division of Lucasfilm, George Lucas's production company.[7] The *Star Wars* director hired the brightest computer programmers he could find to fill the small but growing need in Hollywood for CG graphics. Two of Lucas's programmers, Ed Catmull and Alvy Ray Smith, had developed a number of impressive CG technologies. Enter John Lasseter, just let go by Disney because his intense interest in computer animation wasn't shared by management. At an animation conference, Catmull and Smith tapped Lasseter to work with them on a number of digital animation shorts. One, *The Adventures of André & Wally B.*, was the very first character-animation cartoon done with a computer.[8]

Then came Steve Jobs, who had just left Apple Computer and was looking for a new technology venture. He purchased the division, which he named Pixar, for $5 million, investing another $5 million to make it financially soluble. During Jobs's tenure, Pixar created about one short film a year and slowly broke into producing television commercials. Jobs sought to capitalize on Pixar's inventive sprit by licensing its RenderMan software and selling its Pixar Image Computer. But at $130,000 each, the rendering computers were a difficult sell, even in Hollywood. RenderMan sold only slightly better, earning it a

DreamWorks Delights

DreamWorks Animation SKG began as an ambitious attempt by media moguls Steven Spielberg, Jeffrey Katzenberg, and David Geffen (forming the SKG present on the bottom of the DreamWorks logo) to create a new Hollywood studio. The company was founded after Katzenberg was fired from, you guessed it!, The Walt Disney Company. The Dreamworks studio was officially founded on October 12, 1994, with financial backing of $33 million from each of the three main partners and $500 million from Microsoft co-founder Paul Allen.[18]

DreamWorks Animated SKG is devoted to producing high-quality family entertainment through the use of computer-generated, or CG, animation. With world-class creative talent and technological capabilities, DreamWorks was the first to release two CG animated feature films a year. With each film they strive to tell great stories with a level of sophistication that appeal to both children and adults.[19]

In keeping with the importance of cooperation and teamwork, the open spaces and unique amenities at Dreamworks enhance the collaborative nature of the studio. In fact, the lagoon is a favorite gathering spot for informal meetings. When the fountains are turned off, it doubles as an amphitheater which can hold all employees. To showcase their talents, employees can contribute to on-campus art shows and craft fairs, allowing all to appreciate their fellow employees' abilities.[20]

Its team efforts have paid off. Starting with its first full-length animated feature, *Antz*, DreamWorks has produced more than ten films with box-office grosses totaling more than $100 million each. Its endearing films have included *Bee Movie*, *Monsters vs. Aliens*, and *How to Train Your Dragon*. To date, its most successful release is *Shrek 2*, the third highest grossing film of all time.[21]

Never one to rely on past success, DreamWorks is trying to step it up to three CG animated films a year. It has several in the pipeline. Will DreamWorks' efforts pay off or is it attempting too much too soon?

---

reputation as niche software—especially because the program's primary customer was Disney.[9]

Although Jobs aggressively sought to build Pixar's reputation in the animation industry, it was still an uphill battle. He invested more than $50 million in keeping the company afloat, refusing to concede defeat and even releasing Alvy Smith after repeated personality conflicts. Slowly, Hollywood began to take notice of Pixar. Disney expressed interest in having Pixar develop a feature-length animated movie, and Pixar agreed to animate and produce *Toy Story*. But tired of pouring money into keeping it afloat, Steve Jobs toyed with selling the company. He entertained offers from Oracle, Microsoft, and, curiously enough, the greeting-card company Hallmark.[10] But Jobs held out. "We should have failed," says Smith, "Steve just would not suffer a defeat."[11] The release of *Toy Story* proved his instincts right—the groundbreaking movie earned $362 million worldwide, shattering records for box-office earnings by animated movies.[12] *A Bug's Life* followed, and although the movie did well, especially for an animated feature, it's worth noting that every Pixar release since has done even better.

Acutely aware of a string of failures for its own animated movies, Disney entered into talks to buy Pixar. Lasseter and Catmull were pleasantly surprised when Disney not only purchased Pixar, but also placed the Pixar honchos at the top of Disney's stagnant animation department. The duo moved to dump the top-down development process they say was in place at the studio, favoring instead the collaborative approach at Pixar that famously empowers the creative talent as much as the studio executives. Transplanting some of Pixar's successful processes meant opening up spaces in the mazes of the Disney animation building to allow more chance encounters between employees, and to give animators and other creative types more input in the overall story ideas and the direction of projects.[13]

The sale went through for $7.4 billion, and suddenly Steve Jobs became Disney's single largest shareholder.[14]

Pixar's future looks bright. Never one to rest on its laurels, the company continues to actively invest in software and technology, the tools that have made possible the lifelike rendering that is the hallmark of Pixar movies. But Pixar will have to stay sharp to stave off competition from the junior animation firms that are quickly forging alliances with major production companies to put out feature-length films of their own. Wild Brain, for instance, inked a five-picture deal with Dimension Films, a unit of Miramax (owned by, of all companies, Disney).[15] Questions also remain about Pixar's future within the corporate umbrella of Disney. *BusinessWeek* notes: "Many industry insiders wonder if the company will be able to maintain its string of hits now that it's part of the Magic Kingdom."[16]

But a good part of Pixar's success stems from its ability to generate intriguing stories that warm the hearts of audiences. And according to Ralph Schackart, analyst with William Blair & Co LLC, that's where Pixar has it made: "It all starts with the story. You or I can go buy off-the-shelf software and make an animated film. The barrier to entry for this industry is the story."[17]

Discussion Questions

1. With all of Steve Jobs's wealth and accomplishments, how can the needs theories explain his motivation to make Pixar a success?

2. When Pixar was struggling and Jobs was investing more and more money to keep it afloat, he could have decided to sell and go invest his money and time in other pursuits. But he didn't. How can Jobs's decision to stick with Pixar be explained using Vroom's expectancy theory, and Locke's goal-setting theory?

3. Pixar relies heavily on creative people who are motivated to do their best under production schedules that are often highly stressful. How could a human resource executive embrace the notion of "flexibility" to provide a highly motivating work environment for such people?

4. **FURTHER RESEARCH**—Some predict that Pixar's best days are over and that it will be hard for it to stay creative as a Disney business. What are the facts? In what ways is its current performance consistent with or different from the predictions, and why?

Case 15: NASCAR: Fast Cars, Passion, and Teamwork Create Wins.

By only his second full year of NASCAR Winston Cup Series racing, the young Ryan Newman was rapidly becoming a racing phenomenon. He has since had spectacular consecutive racing seasons, including winning the Daytona 500.[1] What accounts for the success of a top NASCAR driver?

Racing Passion

In a sport that measures victory in hundredths of a second, NASCAR drivers need every competitive edge they can get. And Ryan Newman claims a unique advantage among his racing peers: his education. Ryan graduated from Purdue University with a degree in vehicle structural engineering. He studied part-time while driving race cars. And did it make a difference? The season he graduated, Ryan earned almost $500,000 in NASCAR winnings. One year later, he'd earned nearly ten times as much.

A self-admitted car buff, Ryan Newman loves to drive cars and work on them.[2] His passion for fast cars developed at an early age. Encouraged by his parents, he started racing quarter midgets when he was only four-and-a-half years old. Newman amassed more than 100 midget car victories. Later he raced midget cars and sprint cars, achieving extraordinary success there as well.[3]

When Newman joined the Penske Racing Team, the co-owners hired Buddy

Baker, a former top race car driver, to work with Newman. Being very selective about the drivers he works with, Baker insisted on meeting Newman and his family before accepting the job offer. Baker says: "When I started talking to Ryan, I could feel the energy that he had, and the passion he had for the sport. Then, I met his dad, and right there I knew, OK, he's got a good background. His father's been with him in go-carts, midgets. He turned the wrenches for his son. It was an automatic fit for me."

Baker thinks of Newman as though he were one of his own sons, both of whom briefly tried racing but neither of whom had a passion for it. Baker says that he never wanted to do anything but race, and Newman is just like him. Referring to Newman, Baker says: "From the time he was 5 years old until now, he's never wanted to be anything else."[4]

High Performance Team

About his pre-Winston Cup racing days, Newman says: "I always worked on my own cars and maintained them, did the set-ups, things like that. Obviously, I also drove them so I was always a hands-on, involved, seat of the pants driver." As a Winston Cup driver, Newman acknowledges that he "misses working on the cars, but when you have great guys doing that work, you don't feel like you have to do it yourself."[5]

"For all my life, my family has been my crew," Newman also says. "To come to an organization like Penske, and have so many more people behind you fighting for the same goals, it's like being in a bigger family. When you're with people you like, you have the confidence to do things well."[6] Most of the people who work on Newman's crew are engineers, and all of them are computer whizzes—significant talents for building and maintaining

today's race cars.[7] Newman and the crew try to learn from the problem situations that they encounter so they can "keep the freak things from happening."[8]

Newman asserts that his racing team does the best job it can with what they have. "When there's an opportunity to try and stretch it to the end, we're going to try to stretch to the end," says Newman.[9] He enters every race with the attitude that he can and will win it.[10]

Working together as a team and optimizing every mechanical advantage, Ryan Newman and his team have beat the odds to generate a successful record in the ultracompetitive NASCAR circuit. And though victory brings the loyalty of fans and big prize winnings, it can also create tension among fellow racers, many of whom have been racing decades longer than Newman. What does it take for a young driver with talent, know-how, and commitment to create a NASCAR team that can win over the long haul?

Discussion Questions

1. What are the teamwork and team building challenges that must be mastered to create synergy when a new NASCAR driver joins an established racing team and pit crew?
2. How can a NASCAR owner use insights from the open systems model of team effectiveness to build a true high performance racing team?
3. In what ways can a driver's behavior help with or hinder a crew chief's efforts to build the right norms and a high level of cohesiveness in a pit crew team?
4. **FURTHER RESEARCH**—Pit crews are often in the news. See what you can find out about pit crew performance. Ask: What differentiates the "high performance" pit crews from the "also rans?" If you were to write a class lesson plan on "Pit Crew Insights for Team Success," what would you include in the lesson and why?

Case 16: AFL-CIO: Managing Dissent While Supporting Labor

The AFL-CIO, once America's preeminent labor organization, has been challenged in recent years by dissent within its ranks. But this is nothing new to organized labor. Learn how differing opinions within the labor movement aided the formation of both the AFL and CIO and caused their eventual merger.

A Voice for Labor

Representing nearly 11 million laborers in the United States, the American Federation of Labor and Congress of Industrial Organizations (AFL-CIO) speaks out on behalf of most unionized American workers. The AFL-CIO is not a union itself but a voluntary coalition of 56 national and international labor unions whose members are ultimately represented by local union chapters. Its member unions represent a diverse group of workers, including farm workers, day laborers, musicians and actors, public workers, pilots, transport drivers, medical workers, printers, and many more.[1]

The Roots of the AFL

The American Federation of Labor (AFL) was one of the earliest federations of labor unions in the United States. Founded by

Samuel Gompers in 1886 in Columbus, Ohio, it was originally created as a reorganization of its predecessor, the Federation of Organized Trades and Labor Unions. Gompers's new AFL focused attention on the independence and autonomy of each affiliated trade union. In addition, the AFL limited its membership to workers and their organizations.[2]

When the Knights of Labor, another labor organization, dissolved in the 1890s, the AFL was left as the sole major national union body. To swell its ranks, the AFL widened its scope to include several major unions formed on industrial union lines, including the United Mine Workers, the International Ladies' Garment Workers' Union, and the United Brewery Workers. Despite this, the craft unions of the AFL, who were among its earlier members, still held the balance of power within the organization.[3] To demonstrate its commitment to organizing workers at the local level, the AFL advanced either funds or organizers to a number of budding unions, in some cases actually helping organize unions. The AFL also helped charter "Federal Unions," local unions not affiliated with any national or international union, in industries in which no AFL affiliate member had already claimed jurisdiction.[4]

Bureaucracy Fosters a Split

As the AFL grew in size and scope, so did its bureaucracy. Although strikes were becoming an increasingly powerful tool for addressing what workers perceived

as injustice, its growing size and the scope of concerns made it hard for the AFL to win them. This was especially of concern to steel and auto workers, who found strikes a useful tool with which to gain power. Shortly after the 1934 convention, John L. Lewis of the United Mine Workers of America called together heads of, or representatives from, other unions, including the International Ladies' Garment Workers' Union (ILGWU), to consider forming a new group within the AFL and spearhead industrial organizing. One year later, on November 8, 1935, the creation of the Congress of Industrial Organizations (CIO) was announced.[5]

Although the CIO was announced and intended as simply a group within the AFL gathered to support industrial unionism, the AFL responded with disapproval, refusing to deal with the CIO and demanding that it dissolve. But this only increased the credibility of the burgeoning CIO; many workers were disillusioned by what they saw as the AFL's less-than-credible efforts to support industrial unionizing.[6] Within a year, the CIO effectively organized rubber workers who had gone on strike and formed the Steel Workers Organizing Committee (SWOC). By 1937, the CIO was enjoying considerable momentum. The United Auto Workers, a powerful faction within the CIO, won union recognition from General Motors after a turbulent 43-day sit-down strike, and the SWOC negotiated the signing of a collective bargaining agreement with U.S. Steel, which had until then successfully resisted such efforts.[7]

Coming Full Circle

But the CIO was not without its troubles. Internal tensions limited the CIO's external influence; president John L. Lewis clashed with Philip Murray, his longtime assistant and the head of the SWOC, regarding the organization's activities and its relationship with FDR's administration. In 1941, Lewis resigned and chose Murray to succeed him, and Walter Reuther succeeded Murray in 1952.[8] When William Green, head of the AFL since the 1920s, died, his successor, George Meany, joined Reuther to discuss a merger. Many of the deal-breaking issues that had separated the groups 15 years earlier had faded in importance; in that time, the AFL had embraced both industrial organizing and large industrial unions, such as the Association of Machinists. Thus, in 1955, the AFL-CIO was created by joining the American Federation of Labor and the Congress of Industrial Organizations.[9]

Considerable Challenges to the Present

In the 50-plus years since the joining of the AFL and the CIO, the merged organization has continued to struggle to maintain a unified charter and body of members. In 2003, and after the AFL-CIO internally debated the future direction of the American labor movement, a loose group of some of the AFL-CIO's largest unions came together as a coalition called the New Unity Partnership (NUP). After the 2004 defeat of Democratic presidential candidate John Kerry, who had been heavily supported by labor interests, the NUP's quest for reform began to intensify.[10] In 2005, the NUP dissolved and was replaced in scope by the Change to Win Coalition, whose members threatened to secede from the AFL-CIO if demands for major reorganization were not met.

On the eve of the AFL-CIO's fiftieth anniversary celebration, three of the organization's four largest unions—the Service Employees International Union (SEIU), the International Brotherhood of Teamsters, and the United Food and Commercial Workers International Union (UFCW)—announced their withdrawal.[11]

This split was especially troublesome to the AFL-CIO leadership; SEIU president Andy Stern, an outspoken leader of Change to Win, had previously been considered the protégé of former SEIU president John J. Sweeney.[12] Stern, who has been hailed as being "like no union boss you've ever seen" and "a labor leader who thinks like a CEO," rid the SEIU of old-guard members who spent more time pilfering union dues and guarding their fiefdoms than working to improve working conditions for members. Now the SEIU runs one of the largest political action committees (PACs) in the United States and boasts millions of members.[13]

However divided, the AFL-CIO still stands for the rights of all workers. It even complained to the Office of Trade and Labor Affairs (a division of the Department of Labor) about what it perceived as Guatemala's failure to protect the rights of Guatemalan workers. The petition was the first of its kind to be made under the auspices of the Central American Free Trade Agreement (CAFTA) and was a bold move for the AFL-CIO, which had traditionally been content to focus solely on the rights of American workers.[14] Since then, they've advocated the rights of others around the globe. Policy Director Thea Lee recently told Congress they should not consider a U.S.-Panama trade agreement until Panama implements labor law and tax reforms and the Obama administration lays out a comprehensive, principled trade strategy for the United States.[15] In a separate quest, AFL-CIO demanded that Burma's military release Nobel laureate and democracy activist Aang San Suu Kyi—the legitimate leader of Burma.[16]

Divided We Fall?

Whether united or divided, the component factions of the AFL-CIO have been able to reshape working conditions for millions of industrial workers, laborers, and other tradespersons for more than 100 years. As is common for large, diverse organizations, it has been challenging for the federation to present a consistently unified front, and factions have split off to advance alternative agendas. The split by the Change to Win Coalition severely challenges the AFL-CIO's authority and diminishes the federation's political clout. Will this ultimately spell the end of the AFL-CIO, or will the organization adapt to focus on its remaining membership base? Years from now, might the Change to Win Coalition be reabsorbed, as the CIO was years ago? Millions of hard-working Americans will be waiting to see.

Discussion Questions

1. What have been the primary sources of conflict that affected the working relationships of the AFL and CIO, and the unions that are part of each?
2. Is tension within the AFL-CIO functional or dysfunctional for the accomplishment of its mission? Why?
3. If you were a union negotiator for the United Auto Workers and were leading a delegation that was to negotiate a new three-year contract with Ford Motor Company, what ground rules would you set for your negotiating team to help ensure that the bargaining would be successful?
4. **FURTHER RESEARCH**—Review the Web site of the AFL-CIO. What current issues is the organization tackling on behalf of labor? What are its strategies and with whom does it cooperate in trying to address these issues? Overall, is the AFL-CIO on or off track to be a major voice for labor in the future?

Case 17: Toyota: Looking Far into the Future

By borrowing the best ideas from American brands and innovating the rest itself, Toyota has become a paragon of auto manufacturing efficiency. Its vehicles are widely known for their quality and longevity—and Toyota's sales numbers are the envy of the American Big Three. Here is how Toyota became so efficient at producing high-quality automobiles.

Buy "American"?

"Buy American" used to be a well-known slogan encouraging U.S. car buyers to purchase domestic models assembled in America. Those who still tout the motto have likely done a good bit of head-scratching over how to classify Toyota—a Japanese company sited in rural America that employs American workers to use American-made parts to produce vehicles sold in the United States. What to think when this Japanese brand achieves a product quality far superior to long-known American brands? And Toyota has surged ahead of General Motors to rank number one in global auto sales.[1]

Quality by Design

Toyota's success and growth in the American auto market is no accident. The company has used strategies honed since the 1950s to earn and retain customer satisfaction by producing superior vehicles within a highly efficient production environment. From the home office to factories to showrooms, two core philosophies guide Toyota's business: (1) creating fair, balanced, mutually beneficial relationships with both suppliers and employees, and (2) strictly adhering to a just-in-time (JIT) manufacturing principle.

Collaboration over Competition

Over the decades, American auto manufacturers developed relationships with their suppliers that emphasized tense competition, price-cutting, and the modification of suppliers' production capacities with the changing needs of the domestic market. Year after year, parts suppliers had to bid to renew contracts in a process that valued year-to-year price savings over long-term relationships.

Domestic manufacturers, notorious for changing production demands mid-season to comply with late-breaking market dynamics or customer feedback, forced suppliers to turn to double or triple shifts to keep up with capacity and thus can't avoid the problems—quality slips, recalls, line shutdowns, layoffs—that ultimately slow the final assembly of vehicles. When a carmaker doesn't know what it wants, suppliers have little chance of keeping up. This system of industry dynamics proved susceptible to new approaches from Japanese competitors.

Toyota's model of supply-chain management displays an exclusive commitment to parts suppliers, well-forecast parts orders that are not subject to sways in the market, and genuine concern for the success of suppliers.

In the *Financial Times*, M. Reza Vaghefi noted that supply-chain relationships among Asian manufacturers are based on a complex system of cooperation and equity interests. "Asian values, more so than in [W]estern cultures, traditionally emphasize the collective good over the goals of the individual," he said. "This attitude clearly supports the synergistic approach of supply chain management and has encouraged concern for quality and productivity."[2]

Visiting American auto plants and seeing months' worth of excess parts waiting to be installed taught Toyota the benefit of having only enough supplies on hand to fulfill a given production batch. Toyota plans its production schedules months in advance, dictating regularly scheduled parts shipments from its suppliers. Suppliers benefit by being able to predict long-range demand for products, scheduling production accordingly. This builds mutual loyalty between suppliers and the carmaker—almost as if suppliers are a part of Toyota. The fit and finish in Toyota vehicles is precise because its suppliers can afford to focus on the quality of their parts. And consumers notice: Toyota vehicles consistently earn high marks for customer satisfaction and retain their resale value better than almost any others.[3]

Keep It Lean

Early Toyota presidents Toyoda Kiichiro and Ohno Taiichi are considered the fathers of the Toyota Production System (TPS), known widely by the JIT moniker or as "lean production." Emphasizing quality and efficiency at all levels, it drives nearly all aspects of decision making at Toyota.[4]

Simply put, TPS is "all about producing only what's needed and transferring only what's needed," said Teruyuki Minoura, senior managing director at Toyota. He likened it to a "pull" system—in which workers fetch only that which is immediately needed—as opposed to a traditional "push" system.[5] "Producing what's needed means producing the right quantity of what's needed," he continued. "The answer is a flexible system that allows the line to produce what's necessary when it's necessary. If it takes six people to make a certain quantity of an item and there is a drop in the quantity required, then your system should let one or two of them drop out and get on with something else."[6]

To achieve maximum efficiency, workers at Toyota plants must be exceptionally knowledgeable about all facets of a vehicle's production, able to change responsibilities as needed. "An environment where people have to think brings with it wisdom, and this wisdom brings with it *kaizen* [the notion of continuous improvement]," noted Minoura. "If asked to produce only one unit at a time, to produce according to the flow, a typical line worker is likely to be flummoxed. It's a basic characteristic of human beings that they develop wisdom from being put under pressure."[7]

Keeping Up with the Times

No vehicle represents Toyota's innovation better than the Prius. The Prius has been wildly successful in the United States and has come to represent a coming generation of fuel-sipping cars and the money-conscious consumers who clamor for them.[8] Worldwide, Prius sales recently topped the one-million mark, and the car sells in over 40 countries.[9]

On the other hand, no other Toyota vehicle has come to represent the challenges of adapting to a changing sales landscape as its Tundra pickup truck has. Hoping to make gains over the sales of domestic pickups, Toyota built a Tundra plant in Texas to prove that its trucks were as All-American as those made by the Big Three. But bad became worse when—already 60% over budget—truck sales began to decline as the price of oil rose. Contractors and builders, prime candidates for pickups, began to think twice about new pickup purchases; the San Antonio plant began to run well under capacity.[10]

Despite its best efforts, Toyota is now suffering some of the same ills as General Motors, Ford, and Chrysler. Instead of sending its workers home, as Detroit's Big Three car makers often do, Toyota is keeping them at the plants. Employees spend their days in training sessions designed to sharpen their job skills and find better ways to assemble vehicles.[11]

Toyota is "facing a significant lack of production work for a significant number of workers," said Sean McAlinden, an economist for Automotive Research. He estimates the wage cost of idling the assembly lines at Toyota's two plants at $35 million a month. Still the company has pledged to never lay off any of its full-time employees, who are nonunion. Jim Lentz, president of Toyota U.S. sales unit, said that the company believes keeping employees on the payroll and using the time to improve their capabilities is the best move in the long run. Management expects that the months of downtime spent training will mean better quality and productivity when production resumes.[12]

Gaining the Lead, One Vehicle at a Time

By substituting discipline and efficiency for fanfare, Toyota has quietly earned a long-standing reputation for the reliability and quality of all of its models. Although the company's domestic competitors have taken notice and now use many of Toyota's proven methods, their financial difficulties make it hard to keep up the fight. In such a fierce market, can Toyota maintain the self-control to stay on top?

Discussion Questions

1. How might a cell phone manufacturer, an elementary school, and the local post office each benefit from using Toyota's concept of *kaizen*?

2. Would an employee from Ford or General Motors fit in well if hired by Toyota, or would he or she experience culture shock?

3. Does Toyota value its human resources more than do its U.S. rivals? Is this management approach to people a result of Toyota's business philosophy or its cultural values?

4. **FURTHER RESEARCH**—Toyota isn't alone as a major Asian competitor to the U.S. automakers. Do some investigation; who else is in the picture and what countries are they from? Are the other Asian automakers using operations techniques and values similar to those found at Toyota, or are they bringing new ones into play?

Case 18: Harley-Davidson: Style and Strategy Have Global Reach

Harley-Davidson celebrated a century in business with a year-long International Road Tour. The party culminated in the company's hometown, Milwaukee.[1] Harley is a true American success story. Once near death in the face of global competition, Harley reestablished itself as the dominant maker of big bikes in the United States. However, success breeds imitation and Harley once again faces a mixture of domestic and foreign competitors encroaching on its market. Can it meet the challenge?

Harley-Davidson's Roots

When Harley-Davidson was founded in 1903, it was one of more than 100 firms producing motorcycles in the United States. The U.S. government became an important customer for the company's high-powered, reliable bikes, using them in both world wars. By the 1950s, Harley-Davidson was the only remaining American manufacturer.[2] But by then British competitors were entering the market with faster, lighter-weight bikes. And Honda Motor Company of Japan began marketing lightweight

bikes in the United States, moving into middleweight vehicles in the 1960s. Harley initially tried to compete by manufacturing smaller bikes, but had difficulty making them profitably. The company even purchased an Italian motorcycle firm, Aermacchi, but many of its dealers were reluctant to sell the small Aermacchi Harleys.[3]

Consolidation and Renewal

American Machine and Foundry Co. (AMF) took over Harley in 1969, expanding its portfolio of recreational products. AMF increased production from 14,000 to 50,000 bikes per year. This rapid expansion led to significant problems with quality, and better-built Japanese motorcycles began to take over the market. Harley's share of its major U.S. market—heavyweight motorcycles—was only 23%.[4] A group of 13 managers bought Harley-Davidson back from AMF in 1981 and began to turn the company around with the rallying cry "The Eagle Soars Alone." As Richard Teerlink, former CEO of Harley, explained, "The solution was to get back to detail. The key was to know the business, know the customer, and pay attention to detail."[5] The key elements in this process were increasing quality and improving service to customers and dealers. Management kept the classic Harley style and focused on the company's traditional strength—heavyweight and super heavyweight bikes.

In 1983, the Harley Owners Group (H.O.G.) was formed; H.O.G. membership now exceeds one million members and 1,400 chapters worldwide.[6,7] Also in 1983,

Harley-Davidson asked the International Trade Commission (ITC) for tariff relief on the basis that Japanese manufacturers were stockpiling inventory in the United States and providing unfair competition. The request was granted and a tariff relief for five years was placed on all imported Japanese motorcycles that were 700 cc or larger. By 1987 Harley was confident enough to petition the ITC to have the tariff lifted because the company had improved its ability to compete with foreign imports. Once Harley's image had been restored, the company began to increase production.[8] The firm opened new facilities in Franklin, Milwaukee, and Menomonee Falls, Wisconsin; Kansas City, Missouri; and York, Pennsylvania; and opened a new assembly plant in Manaus, Brazil.[9]

In the 1980s, the average Harley purchaser was in his late thirties, with an average household income of over $40,000. Teerlink didn't like the description of his customers as "aging" baby boomers: "Our customers want the sense of adventure that they get on our bikes. . . . Harley-Davidson doesn't sell transportation, we sell transformation. We sell excitement, a way of life."[10] However, the average age and income of Harley riders has continued to increase. Recently, the median age of a Harley rider was 47, and the median income exceeded $80,000.[11] The company also created a line of Harley accessories available through dealers or by catalog, all adorned with the Harley-Davidson logo. These jackets, caps, T-shirts, and other items became popular with nonbikers as well. In fact, the clothing and parts had a higher profit margin than the motorcycles; nonbike products made up as much as half of sales at some dealerships.

International Efforts

Although the company had been exporting motorcycles ever since it was founded, it was not until the late 1980s that Harley-Davidson management began to think seriously about international markets. Traditionally, the company's ads had been translated word for word into foreign languages. New ads were developed specifically for different markets, and rallies were adapted to fit local customs.[12] The company also began to actively recruit and develop dealers in Europe and Japan. It purchased a Japanese distribution company and built a large parts warehouse in Germany. And Harley learned from its international activities. Recognizing, for example, that German motorcyclists rode at high speeds—often more than 100 mph—the company began studying ways to give Harleys a smoother ride and emphasizing accessories that would give riders more protection.[13]

Harley continues to make inroads in overseas markets. At one time, Harley had 30% of the worldwide market for heavyweight motorcycles—chrome-laden cruisers, aerodynamic rocket bikes mostly produced by the Japanese, and oversize touring motorcycles. In the United States, Harley had the largest market share, 46.4%, followed by Honda with 20.2%. In Europe, Harley ranked sixth, with only 6.6% of the market share behind Honda, Yamaha, BMW, Suzuki, and Kawasaki. However, in the Asia/Pacific market, where one would expect Japanese bikes to dominate, Harley had the largest market shares in the early part of the decade. Harley had 21.3% of the market share, compared to 19.2% for Honda.[14]

Harley motorcycles are among America's fastest-growing exports to Japan. Harley's Japanese subsidiary adapted the company's marketing approach to Japanese tastes, even producing shinier and more complete tool kits than those available in the United States. Harley bikes have long been considered symbols of prestige in Japan; many Japanese enthusiasts see themselves as rebels on wheels.[15]

The company has also made inroads into the previously elusive Chinese market, with the first official Chinese Harley-Davidson dealership opening its doors just outside downtown Beijing. To break into this emerging market, Harley partnered with China's Zongshen Motorcycle Group, which makes more than one million small-engine motorcycles each year.[16] Like other Harley stores, the Chinese outlet stocks bikes, parts and accessories, and branded merchandise, and offers post-sales service. Despite China's growing disposable income, the new store has several hurdles ahead of it, including riding restrictions imposed by the government in urban areas.

The Future

Although its international sales have grown, the domestic market still represents almost 75% of Harley's sales.[17,18] Given the climbing price of gas, Harley is uniquely positioned to take advantage of this economic factor. Many riders report in-town fuel consumption rates in excess of 40 miles per gallon.[19] Analyst Todd Sullivan notes, "I know plenty of F150, Suburban, and Silverado drivers who ride Harleys. They are doubling or even tripling their gas mileage and savings by making the switch."[20]

Executives attribute Harley's success to loyal customers and the Harley-Davidson name. "It is a unique brand that is built on personal relationship and deep connections with customers, unmatched riding experiences, and proud history," says Jim Ziemer, Harley's outgoing president and chief executive.[21]

However, Harley-Davidson has been in a fight not just with the recession and a sharp consumer spending slowdown, but also the aging of its customer base, and a credit crisis that has made it difficult for both the motorcycle maker and its loyal riders to get financing.[22] With 17 consecutive years of increased production, marked with record revenues and earnings, will the future for Harley be bright?[23]

Discussion Questions:

1. If you were CEO of Harley-Davidson, how would you compare the advantages and disadvantages of using exports, joint ventures, and wholly owned subsidiaries as ways of expanding international sales?
2. Given Harley's legacy of quality and craftsmanship, what complications might the Chinese business environment pose for the firm to manufacture there?
3. Harley's positioning, at least in America and Japan, has shifted from providing a product (motorcycles) toward more of providing a service (way of life). How does this positioning affect its potential to succeed in Asia, Africa, and South America?
4. **FURTHER RESEARCH**—Is it accurate to say that Harley is "still on top" of its game? How is the company doing today in both domestic and global markets? Who are its top competitors in other parts of the world, and how is Harley faring against them?

Case 19: Sprinkles: Leading a Sweet Trend

Most people think of cupcakes as either homemade snacks or prepackaged Hostess treats. But Candace Nelson's cupcake-only bakery, Sprinkles, proved that high-end ingredients in a stylish setting could challenge the low-carb craze and inspire food fans to wait in long lines for a bite-sized taste of heaven.

When Oprah Calls . . .

Candace Nelson's big break came courtesy of two of the world's most famous women, 300 cupcakes, and a sleepless red-eye flight. It started when Barbra Streisand bought a dozen cupcakes from Nelson's new bakery, Sprinkles, for her friend Oprah Winfrey. Soon after, Nelson received a 2 PM call

from one of Winfrey's producers with a last-minute order: bring 300 cupcakes to Chicago for an appearance the next morning on *Breakfast with Oprah*.

"You can't say no to Oprah," Nelson jokes. So the investment-banker-turned-baker manned her ovens for six hours before catching an overnight flight to the Windy City. She arrived at Oprah's studios with shopping bags full of her gourmet cupcakes—coconut, red velvet, and Madagascar vanilla, topped with Sprinkles' requisite half-inch-thick sheet of buttercream frosting. Like many before her, Nelson soon benefited from Oprah's magic touch—cupcake sales at the Beverly Hills bakery jumped 50% to 1,500 per day.[1] And at $3.25 per cupcake—nearly as much as a half-dozen Krispy Kreme donuts—it was sweet news for Nelson and her husband, Charles, who co-owns the Sprinkles chain.

Reinventing a Classic

No longer relegated to birthday parties and grade-school classrooms, cupcakes are experiencing a major resurgence as sweet-starved adults rediscover one of childhood's sweetest treats. In a rebound from the low-carb craze that swept calorie-conscious dieters, cupcakes now have their own blogs, baking cups, and presentation stands—Amazon.com even sells a baker's dozen of cookbooks devoted to the bite-sized indulgences.

According to Ruth Reichl, former editor of the now defunct *Gourmet*

magazine, "The rise of the cupcake is very much about going back to our national identity in food, which is all about comfort. In these times fraught with war and a tough economy, people want to think about when they and their country were innocent." When *Gourmet* devoted a cover to cupcakes, impassioned readers sent letters for nearly a year, some reprimanding the magazine for elevating the snack to epicurean standard but others sharing their fondest cupcake moments. "We actually got pictures of people's cupcakes," Reichl fondly reflected. "It's a very emotional dessert."[2]

Not everyone is so philosophical. "Why do I like cupcakes? Wow, a million reasons," said San Francisco cupcake lover Yoli Anyon. "There's less guilt about eating them because they're small. They're also kind of gourmet. And it just feels much more special than eating a candy bar."[3] Model Tyra Banks put her passion about Sprinkles more succinctly. "I'm addicted," she wryly confessed.[4]

At Sprinkles, the line stretches out the door and around the block. Tourists and locals alike often wait well over a half-hour—longer than a cupcake takes to bake and cool—for a taste of one of Sprinkles' 23 custom flavors, only 13 of which are offered each day. Favorites such as dark chocolate and red velvet are available every day, but specialty flavors such as chai latte, carrot cake, and peanut butter chocolate appear sporadically throughout the week. To distinguish her cakes from grocery-store look-alikes capped with piped flowers or blocky writing, Nelson decorates with a minimalist's touch—a sleek buttercream frosting and little decoration.[5]

Though the four Sprinkles locations also sell bottled soda, coffee, and 75-cent frosting shots, cupcakes are their main attraction. If one cupcake isn't enough, Sprinkles will deliver a dozen cupcakes for $46 in a specially designed box, edged with the color band of your choice, to customers who live near a store. Though Sprinkles doesn't yet ship its luscious wares, that didn't stop one fan from taking matters into her own hands. Actress Katie Holmes, whose affinity for Sprinkles has been reported in the popular press, sent hundreds of specially designed boxes of Sprinkles cupcakes to friends and associates as a Christmas gift.[6] But if you're not lucky enough to have famous friends or to live within snacking distance of a Sprinkles, don't fret—Williams-Sonoma stores now sell canisters of Sprinkles cupcake mix for $14.

From Dream to Buttercream

Setting aside two lucrative careers, Candace and Charles Nelson traded long hours of financial-sector work in San Francisco for long hours in the kitchen after Candace concluded a pastry course at top-shelf Bay Area cooking school Tante Marie. "I found the one job where the hours are worse than investment banking," Nelson joked.[7] The couple opened the first Sprinkles location in Beverly Hills in April 2005, believing that an all-cupcake bakery could make it in Los Angeles's fickle "hot or not" environment. "It was time for cupcakes to stop being the backup dancer to cakes," said Candace.[8]

In contrast to the cutesy, bubblegum-pink interiors of other cupcake shops, noted local architect Andrea Lenardin Madden developed a crisp, regimented visual style for Sprinkles. Stores sport custom-made white oak built-in cabinets, strategically located skylights, contemporary and simplified whitewashed walls, a glass-topped bar, and even coordinating benches outside. Each cupcake has its own special location in the display case. "What's distinctive about this store is that it is refined," Nelson noted.[9] Critics agree—Sprinkles Beverly Hills won two Los Angeles restaurant design awards.

It wasn't an easy time to bring the cupcake concept to L.A. With the United States still deep in the throes of the *South Beach Diet Cookbook*-inspired low-carb craze, Nelson faced skepticism from her earliest customers, wedding-shower guests who turned away from her cupcakes in fear of overloading on carbs.[10] Even the Nelsons' landlord doubted, asking, "But what else will you be selling?"[11]

The second Sprinkles outlet opened in the nearby glitzy town of Corona del Mar, a location well suited to its high-end concept. "Because this is purely discretionary spending on food," noted retail consultant Greg Stoffel, "it would require a higher-income area. And in Orange County, you can't get much higher than Corona del Mar."[12]

Cupcake Entrepreneurs

Noted New York bakery Magnolia opened its shutters in 1996, kicking off the cupcake-only trend. *Sex and the City's* Sarah Jessica Parker's love for Magnolia is credited for bringing attention to the palm-sized treat. Fast-forward 10 years, and suddenly a number of aspiring cupcake creators were stepping up to get a taste of sweet success.

Kirk Rossberg, owner of L.A.'s Torrance Bakery and president of the California Retail Bakers Association, found himself overwhelmed with prospective interns; of the 30 he accepted recently, he estimated that 90% had left salaried professions in the hopes of opening bakeries. "Until last year, I never had people asking to work for free," he said. Rebecca Marrs, director of career services at the California School of Culinary Arts in Pasadena, noted a jump in the number of older applicants hoping for a career switch when enrollment in the school's baking program recently grew by nearly a third.[13] Rachel Kramer Bussel, author of the blog *Cupcakes Take the Cake*, receives approximately one e-mail each week from someone hoping to open a new cupcake bakery. She estimates there are about 75 such shops in the United States right now. "I keep waiting for this to die down," she said, "and instead it keeps mushrooming."[14]

Not everyone gets it, though. Georgene Fairbanks, visiting Sprinkles from nearby Mission Viejo on the basis of Oprah's recommendation, couldn't comprehend the fuss. "It's not that I didn't like it," Fairbanks said. "I've just had cupcakes from Betty Crocker that were just as good."[15] And even worse for Sprinkles, there's a very real concern that too many people might get it—with the skyrocketing number of cupcake-only bakeries opening and consumers' fickle food tastes, the cupcake craze might be over before stores have a chance to switch gears and rebrand themselves.

Nonetheless, cupcakes still have their allies. Pulitzer-winning food critic Jonathan Gold observed that "in a town where people say no to you all the time and you rarely have the simple satisfaction of getting something made, being able to make a sweet simple thing that makes people happy is really compelling."[16]

Candace Nelson agreed. "That's why I went into the cupcake business. I'm in this little cupcake bubble where everyone is smiling ear to ear."[17] And with 17 more Sprinkles outlets scheduled to open, Nelson has a lot to smile about.

Discussion Questions

1. What entrepreneurial characteristics did Candace and Charles Nelson display in this case? What other traits and personal characteristics may be necessary for people to succeed as owners of new Sprinkles' franchises?

2. With many stores scheduled to open, what stage in its life-cycle is Sprinkles at, and what are the major management challenges Nelson faces in keeping the firm successful as it grows?

3. What would you include in a business plan for a new venture on your campus called "Sweet Bites," a new cupcake-only eatery?

4. **FURTHER RESEARCH**—How far can a cupcake-only business grow? Gather current information on Sprinkles and do a "venture capitalist" analysis. Looking to the future, what makes the firm attractive to a venture capital investor and what are its downsides? Is Sprinkles a good bet for the future?

TestPrep1

Multiple choice

1. d. 2. c. 3. b. 4. b. 5. b. 6. d. 7. a. 8. d.
9. c. 10. d. 11. c 12. a 13. c 14. c 15. a

Short response

16. Prejudice involves holding a negative stereotype or irrational attitude toward a person who is different from one's self. Discrimination occurs when such prejudice leads to decisions that adversely affect the other person in his or her job or in advancement opportunities at work or in his or her personal lives.

17. The "free agent economy" is one where there is a lot of job-hopping and people work for several different employers over a career, rather than just one. This relates not only to the preferences of the individuals but also the nature of organizational employment practices. As more organizations reduce the hiring of full-time workers in favor of more part-timers and independent contractors, this creates fewer long-term job opportunities for potential employees. Thus they become "free agents" who sell their services to different employers on a part-time and contract basis.

18. You will typically find that top managers are more oriented toward the external environment than the first-level or lower-level managers. This means that top managers must be alert to trends, problems, and opportunities that can affect the performance of the organization as a whole. The first-line or lower manager is most concerned with the performance of his or her immediate work unit, and managing the people and resources of the unit on an operational day-to-day basis. Top management is likely to be more strategic and long term in orientation.

19. Planning sets the objectives or targets that one hopes to accomplish. Controlling measures actual results against the planning objectives or targets, and makes any corrections necessary to better accomplish them. Thus, planning and controlling work together in the management process, with planning setting the stage for controlling.

Integration & application

20. I consider myself "effective" as a manager if I can help my work unit achieve high performance and the persons in it to achieve job satisfaction. In terms of skills and personal development, the framework of essential management skills offered by Katz is a useful starting point. At the first level of management, technical skills are important and I would feel capable in this respect. However, I would expect to learn and refine these skills even more through my work experiences. Human skills, the ability to work well with other people, will also be very important. Given the diversity anticipated for this team, I will need good human skills and I will have to keep improving my capabilities in this area. One area of consideration here is emotional intelligence, or my ability to understand how the emotions of myself and others influence work relationships. I will also have a leadership responsibility to help others on the team develop and utilize these skills so that the team itself can function effectively. Finally, I would expect opportunities to develop my conceptual or analytical skills in anticipation of higher-level appointments. In terms of personal development I should recognize that the conceptual skills will increase in importance relative to the technical skills as I move upward in management responsibility, while the human skills are consistently important.

TestPrep2

Multiple choice

1. a. 2. b. 3. c. 4. a. 5. c. 6. c. 7. d. 8. b.
9. a. 10. a. 11. c 12. a 13. a 14. c 15. a

Short response

16. You can see scientific management principles operating everywhere, from UPS delivery, to fast-food restaurants, to order-fulfillment centers. In each case the workers are trained to perform highly specified job tasks that are carefully engineered to be the most efficient. Their supervisors try to keep the process and workers well supported. In some cases the workers may be paid on the basis of how much work they accomplish in a time period, such as a day or week. The basic principles are to study the job, identify the most efficient job tasks and train the workers, and then support and reward the workers for doing them well.

17. According to the deficit principle, a satisfied need is not a motivator of behavior. The social need, for example, will motivate only if it is deprived or in deficit. According to the progression principle, people move step by step up Maslow's hierarchy as they strive to satisfy their needs. For example, esteem need becomes activated only after the social need is satisfied. Maslow also suggests, however, that the progression principle stops operating at the level of self-actualization; the more this need is satisfied, the stronger it gets.

18. The Hawthorne effect occurs when people singled out for special attention tend to perform as expected. An example would be giving a student a lot of personal attention in class with the result that he or she ends up studying harder and performing better. This is really the same thing as McGregor's notion of the self-fulfilling prophesy with the exception that he identified how it works to both the positive and the negative. When managers, for example, have positive assumptions about people, they tend to treat them well and the people respond in ways that reinforce the original positive thinking. This is a form of the Hawthorne effect. McGregor also pointed out that negative self-fulfilling prophesies result when managers hold negative assumptions about people and behavior accordingly.

19. Contingency thinking takes an "if—then" approach to situations. It seeks to modify or adapt management approaches to fit the needs of each situation. An example would be to give more customer contact responsibility to workers who want to satisfy social needs at work, while giving more supervisory responsibilities to those who want to satisfy their esteem or ego needs.

Integration & application

20. A bureaucracy operates with a strict hierarchy of authority, promotion based on competency and performance, formal rules and procedures, and written documentation. Enrique can do all of these things in his store. However, he must be careful to meet the needs of the workers and not to make the mistake identified by Argyris—failing to treat them as mature adults. While remaining well organized, the store manager has room to help workers meet higher order esteem and self-fulfillment needs, as well as to exercise autonomy under Theory Y assumptions. Enrique must also be alert to the dysfunctions of bureaucracy that appear when changes are needed or when unique problems are posed or when customers want to be treated personally. The demands of these situations are difficult for traditional bureaucracies to handle, due to the fact that they are set up to handle routine work efficiently and impersonally, with an emphasis on rules, procedures, and authority.

TestPrep3

Multiple choice

1. a. **2.** c. **3.** d. **4.** a. **5.** c. **6.** b. **7.** c. **8.** b.
9. a. **10.** a. **11.** b. **12.** b. **13.** b. **14.** d. **15.** d.

Short response

16. Distributive justice means that everyone is treated the same, that there is no discrimination based on things like age, gender, and sexual orientation. An example would be a man and a woman who both apply for the same job. A manager violates distributive justice if he interviews only the man and not the woman as well, or vice versa. Procedural justice means that rules and procedures are fairly followed. For example, a manager violates distributive justice if he or she punishes one person for coming to work late while ignoring late behavior by another person with whom he or she regularly plays golf.

17. The "spotlight questions" for double-checking the ethics of a decision are: "How would I feel if my family finds out?" "How would I feel if this were published in the local newspaper or on the Internet?" "What would the person you know or know of who has the strongest character and best ethical judgment do in this situation?"

18. The rationalizations include believing that (1) the behavior is not really illegal, (2) the behavior is really in everyone's best interests, (3) no one will find out, and (4) the organization will protect you.

19. The "virtuous circle" concept of social responsibility holds that social responsibility practices do not hurt the bottom line and often help it; when socially responsible actions result in improved financial performance, this encourages more of the same actions in the future—a virtuous circle being created.

Integration & application

20. If the manager adopts a position of cultural relativism, there will be no perceived problem in working with the Tanzanian firm. The justification would be that as long as it is operating legally in Tanzania, that makes everything okay. The absolutist position would hold that the contract should not be taken because the factory conditions are unacceptable at home and therefore are unacceptable anywhere. The cultural relativism position can be criticized because it makes it easy to do business in places where people are not treated well; the absolutist position can be criticized as trying to impose one's values on people in a different cultural context.

TestPrep4

Multiple choice

1. b. **2.** c. **3.** a. **4.** c. **5.** d. **6.** a. **7.** b. **8.** c.
9. c. **10.** c. **11.** a. **12.** a. **13.** b. **14.** d. **15.** b.

Short response

16. An optimizing decision represents the absolute "best" choice of alternatives. It is selected from a set of all known alternatives. A satisficing decision selects the first alternative that offers a "satisfactory" choice, not necessarily the absolute best choice. It is selected from a limited or incomplete set of alternatives.

17. A risk environment is one in which things are not known for sure—all of the possible decision alternatives, all of the possible consequences for each alternative—but they can be estimated as probabilities. For example, if I take a new job with a new employer, I can't know for certain that it will turn out as I expect, but I could be 80% sure that I'd like the new responsibilities, or only 60% sure that I might get promoted within a year. In an uncertain environment, things are so speculative that it is hard to even assign such probabilities.

18. A manager using systematic thinking is going to approach problem solving in a logical and rational fashion. The tendency will be to proceed in a linear step-by-step manner, handling one issue at a time. A manager using intuitive thinking will be more spontaneous and open in problem solving. He or she may jump from one stage in the process to the other and deal with many different things at once.

19. Escalating commitment is the tendency of people to keep investing in a previously chosen course of action, continuing to pursue it, even though it is not working. This is a human tendency to try and make things work by trying harder, investing more time, effort, resources, etc. In other words, I have decided in the past to pursue this major in college; I can't be wrong, can I? The feedback from my grades and course satisfaction suggests it isn't working, but I'm doing it now so I just need to make it work, right? I'll just stick with it and see if things eventually turn out okay. In this example, I am making a decision to continue with the major that is most likely an example of escalating commitment.

Integration & application

20. This is what I would say. On the question of whether a group decision is best or an individual decision is best, the appropriate answer is probably: It all depends on the situation. Sometimes one is preferable to the other; each has its potential advantages and disadvantages. If you are in a situation where the problem being addressed is unclear, the information needed to solve it is uncertain, and you don't have a lot of personal expertise, the group approach to decision making is probably best. Group decisions offer advantages like bringing more information and ideas to bear on a problem; they often allow for more creativity; and they tend to build commitments among participants to work hard to implement any decisions reached. On the other hand, groups can be dominated by one or more members, and they can take a lot of time making decisions. Thus, when time is short, the individual decision is sometimes a better choice. However, it is important that you, as this individual, are confident that you have the information needed to solve the problem or can get it before making your decision.

TestPrep 5

Multiple choice

1. d. 2. a. 3. b. 4. d. 5. c. 6. a. 7. d. 8. b.
9. c. 10. a. 11. c. 12. b. 13. d. 14. c. 15. c.

Short response

16. The five steps in the formal planning process are (1) define your objectives, (2) determine where you stand relative to objectives, (3) develop premises about future conditions, (4) identify and choose among action alternatives to accomplish objectives, and (5) implement action plans and evaluate results.

17. Planning facilitates controlling because the planning process sets the objectives and standards that become the basis for the control process. If you don't have objectives and standards, you have nothing to compare actual performance with; consequently, control lacks purpose and specificity.

18. Contingency planning essentially makes available optional plans that can be quickly implemented if things go wrong with the original plan. Scenario planning is a longer-term form of contingency planning that tries to project several future scenarios that might develop over time and to associate each scenario with plans for best dealing with it.

19. Participation is good for the planning process, in part because it brings to the process a lot more information, diverse viewpoints, and potential alternatives than would otherwise be available if just one person or a select group of top managers are doing the planning. Furthermore and very importantly, through participation in the planning process, people develop an understanding of the final plans and the logic used to arrive at them, and they develop personal commitments to trying to follow through and work hard to make implementation of the plans successful.

Integration & application

20. Benchmarking is the use of external standards to help evaluate one's own situation and develop ideas and directions for improvement. Curt and Rich are both right to a certain extent about its potential value for them. Rich is right in suggesting that there is much to learn by looking at what other bookstores are doing really well. The bookstore owner/manager might visit other bookstores in other towns that are known for their success. By observing and studying the operations of those stores and then comparing his store to them, the owner/manager can develop plans for future action. Curt is also right in

suggesting that there is much to be learned potentially from looking outside the bookstore business. They should look at things like inventory management, customer service, and facilities in other settings—not just bookstores; they should also look outside their town as well as within it.

TestPrep6

Multiple choice

1. a. 2. a. 3. d. 4. b. 5. b. 6. c. 7. c. 8. d. 9. a.
10. b. 11. c. 12. a. 13. b. 14. a. 15. c. 16. c.

Short response

17. The Army's "after-action review" takes place after an action or activity has been completed. This makes it a form of "feedback" control. The primary purpose is to critique the action/activity and try to learn from it so that similar things in the future can be done better and so that the people involved can be best trained.

18. Quality circles bring together persons from various parts of the work place with a common commitment to quality improvements. They meet regularly to discuss quality results and options, and to try and maintain a continuous improvement momentum in their work areas. The members may receive special quality training. The members are expected to actively serve as quality champions in their work areas and to work with team members to come up with continuous quality improvements.

19. A progressive discipline system works by adjusting the discipline to fit the severity and frequency of the inappropriate behavior. In the case of a person who comes late to work, for example, progressive discipline might involve a verbal warning after three late arrivals, a written warning after five, and a pay-loss penalty after seven. In the case of a person who steals money from the business, there would be immediate dismissal after the first such infraction.

20. The just-in-time inventory approach reduces the carrying costs of inventories. It does this by trying to have materials arrive at a work station just in time to be used. When this concept works perfectly, there are no inventory carrying costs. However, even if it is imperfect and some inventory ends up being stockpiled, it should still be less than that which would otherwise be the case.

Integration & application

21. I would begin the speech by describing MBO as an integrated planning and control approach. I would also clarify that the key elements in MBO are objectives and participation. Any objectives should be clear, measurable, and time defined. In addition, these objectives should be set with the full involvement and participation of the employees; they should not be set by the manager and then told to the employees. Given this, I would describe how each business manager should jointly set objectives with each of his or her employees and jointly review progress toward their accomplishment. I would suggest that the employees should work on the required activities while staying in communication with their managers. The managers, in turn, should provide any needed support or assistance to their employees. This whole process could be formally recycled at least twice per year.

TestPrep7

Multiple choice

1. a. 2. b. 3. b. 4. c. 5. a. 6. b. 7. c. 8. a.
9. c. 10. d. 11. d. 12. c. 13. a. 14. b. 15. b.

Short response

16. A corporate strategy sets long-term direction for an enterprise as a whole. Functional strategies set directions so that business functions such as marketing and manufacturing support the overall corporate strategy. A corporate strategy sets long-term direction for an enterprise as a whole. Functional strategies set directions so that business functions such as marketing and manufacturing support the overall corporate strategy.

17. If you want to sell at lower prices than competitors and still make a profit, you have to have lower operating costs (profit = revenues − costs). Also, you have to be able to operate at lower costs in ways that are hard for your competitors to copy. This is the point of a cost leadership strategy—always seeking ways to lower costs and operate with greater efficiency than anyone else.

18. A question mark in the BCG matrix has a low market share in a high growth industry. This means that there is a lot of upside potential, but for now it is uncertain whether or not you will be able to capitalize on it. Thus, hard thinking is required. If you are confident, the recommended strategy is growth; if you aren't, it would be retrenchment, to allow resources to be deployed into more promising opportunities.

19. Strategic leadership is the ability to enthuse people to participate in continuous change, performance enhancement, and the implementation of organizational strategies. The special qualities of the successful strategic leader include the ability to make tradeoffs, create a sense of urgency, communicate the strategy, and engage others in continuous learning about the strategy and its performance responsibilities.

Integration & application

20. A SWOT analysis is useful during strategic planning. It involves the analysis of organizational strengths and weaknesses, and of environmental opportunities and threats. Such a SWOT analysis in this case would help frame Kim's thinking about the current and future positioning of her store, particularly in respect to possible core competencies and competitive opportunities and threats. Then she can use Porter's competitive strategy model for further strategic refinements. This involves the possible use of three alternative strategies: differentiation, cost leadership, and focus. In this situation, the larger department store seems better positioned to follow the cost leadership strategy. This means that Kim may want to consider the other two alternatives. A differentiation strategy would involve trying to distinguish Kim's products from those of the larger store. This might involve a "made in America" theme or an emphasis on leather or canvas or some other type of clothing material. A focus strategy might specifically target college students and try to respond to their tastes and needs rather than those of the larger community population. This might involve special orders and other types of individualized service for the college student market.

TestPrep8

Multiple choice

1. b. 2. c. 3. b. 4. a. 5. b. 6. c. 7. b. 8. a.
9. c. 10. d. 11. b. 12. c. 13. b. 14. b. 15. c.

Short response

16. An organization chart depicts the formal structure of the organization. This is the official picture or the way things are supposed to be. However, the likelihood is that an organization chart quickly becomes out of date in today's dynamic environments. So one issue is whether or not the chart one is viewing actually depicts the current official structure. Second, there is a lot more to the way things work in organizations than what is shown in the organization chart. People are involved in a variety of informal networks that create an informal structure. It operates as a shadow lying above or behind the formal structure and also influences operations. Both the formal structure and informal structure must be understood; at best, an organization chart helps with understanding the formal one.

17. There are two major ways that informal structures can be good for organizations. First, they can help get work done efficiently and well. When people know one another in informal relationships, they can and often do use these relationships as part of their jobs. Sometimes an informal contact makes it a lot easier to get something done or learn how to do something than the formal linkages displayed on an organization chart. Second, being part of informal groups is an important source of potential need satisfaction. Being in an informal network or group can satisfy needs in ways that one's job can't sometimes and can add considerably to the potential satisfactions of the work experience.

18. The matrix structure is organized in a traditional functional fashion in the vertical dimension. For example, a business might have marketing, human resources, finance, and manufacturing functions. On the horizontal dimension, however, it is organized divisionally in a product or project fashion, with a manager heading up each special product or project. Members from the functional departments are assigned to permanent cross-functional teams for each product or project. They report vertically to their functional bosses and horizontally to their product/project bosses. This two-boss system is the heart of the matrix organization.

19. An organic design tends to be quicker and more flexible because it is very strong in lateral communication and empowerment. People at all levels are talking to one another and interacting as they gather and process information and solve problems. They don't wait for the vertical structure and "bosses" to do these things for them. This means that as the environment changes they are more likely to be on top of things quickly. It also means that when problems are complex and difficult to solve, they will work with multiple people in various parts of the organization to best deal with them.

Integration & application

20. A network structure often involves one organization "contracting out" aspects of its operations to other organizations that specialize in them. The example used in the text was of a company that contracted out its mailroom services. Through the formation of networks of contracts, the organization is reduced to a core of essential employees whose expertise is concentrated in the primary business areas. The contracts are monitored and maintained in the network to allow the overall operations of the organization to continue even though they are not directly accomplished by full-time employees. There are many possibilities for doing something similar in a university. In one model, the core staff would be the faculty. They would be supported by a few administrators who managed contracts with outsourcing firms for things such as facilities maintenance, mail, technology support, lawns maintenance, food services, housing services, and even things like development, registrar, and student affairs. Another model would have the administrators forming a small core staff who contract out for the above and, in addition, for faculty who would be hired "as needed" and on contracts for specific assignments.

Multiple choice

1. a. 2. c. 3. a. 4. d. 5. b. 6. d. 7. d. 8. b.
9. c 10. b. 11. c. 12. c. 13. c. 14. b. 15. b.

Short response

16. The core values that might be found in high-performance organizational cultures include such things as emphasize performance excellence, innovation, social responsibility, integrity, worker involvement, customer service, and teamwork.

17. Value-based management means that the manager and leader act with a consistent and clear commitment to espoused values. Their values are clear and well communicated. Through their actions they live up to the values of the organization. No one doubts their integrity since there is no inconsistency between what they say and what they do, and their values serve as positive models for others in the organization.

18. Lewin's three phases of planned change are unfreezing, changing, and refreezing. In terms of the change leadership challenges, the major differences in attention would be as follows: unfreezing—preparing a system for change; changing—moving or creating change in a system; and refreezing—stabilizing and reinforcing change once it has occurred.

19. In general, managers can expect that others will be more committed and loyal to changes that are brought about through shared power strategies. Rational persuasion strategies can also create enduring effects if they are accepted. Force-coercion strategies tend to have temporary effects only.

Integration & application

20. In any change situation, it is important to remember that successful planned change occurs only when all three phases of change—unfreezing, changing, and refreezing—have been taken care of. Thus, I would not rush into the changing phase. Rather, I would work with the people involved to develop a felt need for change based on their ideas and inputs as well as mine. Then I would proceed by supporting the changes and helping to stabilize them into everyday routines. I would also be sensitive to any resistance and respect that resistance as a signal that something important is being threatened. By listening to resistance, I would be in a position to better modify the change to achieve a better fit with the people and the situation. Finally, I would want to take maximum advantage of the shared power strategy, supported by rational persuasion, and with limited use of force-coercion (if it is used at all). By doing all of this, I would like my staff to feel empowered and committed to constructive improvement through planned change. Throughout all of this I would strive to perform to the best of my ability and gain trust and credibility with everyone else; in this way I would be a positive role model for change.

Multiple choice

1. a. 2. b. 3. c. 4. b. 5. b. 6. b. 7. a. 8. d.
9. b. 10. d. 11. d. 12. a. 13. a. 14. b. 15. d.

Short response

16. Orientation activities introduce a new employee to the organization and the work environment. This is a time when the individual may develop key attitudes and when performance expectations will also be established. Good orientation communicates positive attitudes and expectations and reinforces the desired organizational culture. It formally introduces the individual to important policies and procedures that everyone is expected to follow.

17. Mentoring is when a senior and experienced individual adopts a newcomer or more junior person with the goal of helping him or her develop into a successful worker. The mentor may or may not be the individual's immediate supervisor. The mentor meets with the individual and discusses problems, shares advice, and generally supports the individual's attempts to grow and perform. Mentors are considered very useful for persons newly appointed to management positions.

18. Any performance assessment approach should be both valid and reliable. To be valid it must measure accurately what it claims to measure—whether that is some aspect of job performance or personal behavior. To be reliable it must deliver the same results consistently—whether applied by different raters to the same person or when measuring the same person over time. Valid and reliable assessments are free from bias and as objective as possible.

19. The graphic rating scale simply asks a supervisor to rate an employee on an established set of criteria, such as quantity of work or attitude toward work. This leaves much room for subjectivity and debate. The behaviorally anchored rating scale asks the supervisor to rate the employee on specific behaviors that had been identified as positively or negatively affecting performance in a given job. This is a more specific appraisal approach and leaves less room for debate and disagreement.

Integration & application

20. As Sy's supervisor, you face a difficult but perhaps expected human resource management problem. Not only is Sy influential as an informal leader, he also has considerable experience on the job and in the company. Even though he is experiencing performance problems using the new computer system, there is no indication

that he doesn't want to work hard and continue to perform for the company. Although retirement is an option, Sy may also be transferred, promoted, or simply terminated. The latter response seems unjustified and may cause legal problems. Transferring Sy, with his agreement, to another position could be a positive move; promoting Sy to a supervisory position in which his experience and networks would be useful is another possibility. The key in this situation seems to be moving Sy out so that a computer-literate person can take over the job, while continuing to utilize Sy in a job that better fits his talents. Transfer and/or promotion should be actively considered both in his and in the company's best interest.

TestPrep11

Multiple choice

1. b. 2. b. 3. a. 4. d. 5. a. 6. c. 7. c. 8. a.
9. a. 10. b. 11. d. 12. d. 13. a. 14. a. 15. a.

Short response

16. Position power is based on reward, coercion or punishment, and legitimacy or formal authority. Managers, however, need to have more power than that made available to them by the position alone. Thus, they have to develop personal power through expertise and reference. This personal power is essential in helping managers get things done beyond the scope of their position power alone.

17. Leadership situations are described by Fiedler according to: Position power—how much power the leader has in terms of rewards, punishments, and legitimacy; Leader-member relations—the quality of relationships between the leader and followers; Task structure—the degree to which the task is clear and well defined, or open ended and more ambiguous. Highly favorable situations are high in position power, have good leader-member relations, and have structured tasks; highly unfavorable situations are low in position power, have poor leader-member relations, and have unstructured tasks.

18. According to House's path-goal theory, the following combinations are consistent with successful leadership. Participative leadership works well, for example, when performance incentives are low and people need to find other sources of need satisfaction. Through participation the leader gains knowledge that can help identify important needs and possible ways of satisfying them other than through the available performance incentives.

Directive leadership works well, for example, when people aren't clear about their jobs or goals. In these cases the leader can step in and provide direction that channels their efforts toward desired activities and outcomes.

19. Servant leadership is basically other-centered and not self-centered. A servant leader is concerned with helping others to perform well so that the organization or group can ultimately do good things for society. The person who accepts the responsibilities of servant leadership is good at empowering others so that they can use their talents while acting independently to do their jobs in the best possible ways.

Integration & application

20. In his new position, Glenn must understand that the transactional aspects of leadership are not sufficient enough to guarantee him long-term leadership effectiveness. He must move beyond the effective use of task-oriented and people-oriented behaviors and demonstrate through his personal qualities the capacity to inspire others. A charismatic leader develops a unique relationship with followers in which they become enthusiastic, highly loyal, and high achievers. Glenn needs to work very hard to develop positive relationships with the team members. He must emphasize in those relationships high aspirations for performance accomplishments, enthusiasm, ethical behavior, integrity and honesty in all dealings, and a clear vision of the future. By working hard with this agenda and by allowing his personality to positively express itself in the team setting, Glenn should make continuous progress as an effective and moral leader.

TestPrep12

Multiple choice

1. a. 2. c. 3. d. 4. b. 5. a. 6. c. 7. b. 8. c.
9. c. 10. b. 11. d. 12. b. 13. a. 14. c. 15. d.

Short response

16. The manager's goal in active listening is to help the subordinate say what he or she really means. To do this, the manager should carefully listen for the content of what someone is saying, paraphrase or reflect back what the person appears to be saying, remain sensitive to nonverbal cues and feelings, and not be evaluative.

17. Well-intentioned managers can make bad decisions when they base decisions on bad information. Because of the manager's position of authority in the organization, those below him or her may be reluctant to communicate upward information that they believe the manager doesn't want to hear. Thus, they may filter the information to make it as agreeable to the manager as possible. As a result of this filtering of upward communication, the manager may end up with poor or incomplete information and subsequently make bad decisions.

18. The four major errors in giving constructive feedback would be (1) being general rather than specific, (2) choosing a poor time, (3) including in the message irrelevant things, and (4) overwhelming the receiver with too much information at once.

19. Ethnocentrism is when a person views his or her own culture as superior to others. It can interfere with cross-cultural communication when the ethnocentrism leads the person to ignore cultural signals that indicate his or her behavior is inappropriate or offensive by local cultural standards. With the ethnocentric attitude of cultural superiority, the individual is inclined not to change personal ways or display the sensitivity to local cultural ways that are necessary to effective communication.

Integration & application

20. Glenn can do a number of things to establish and maintain a system of communication with his employees and for his department store branch. To begin, he should, as much as possible, try to establish a highly interactive style of management based upon credibility and trust. Credibility is earned through building personal power through expertise and reference. With credibility, he might set the tone for the department managers by using MBWA—"managing by wandering around." Once this pattern is established, trust will build between him and other store employees, and he should find that he learns a lot from interacting directly with them. Harold should also set up a formal communication structure, such as bimonthly store meetings, where he communicates store goals, results, and other issues to the staff, and in which he listens to them in return. An e-mail system whereby Glenn and his staff could send messages to one another from their workstation computers would also be beneficial.

TestPrep13

Multiple choice

1. c. **2.** d. **3.** b. **4.** b. **5.** d. **6.** a. **7.** b. **8.** a. **9.** a. **10.** a. **11.** b. **12.** d. **13.** d. **14.** d. **15.** c.

Short response

16. All of the Big Five personality traits are relevant to the workplace. To give some basic examples, consider the following. Extroversion suggests whether or not a person will reach out to relate and work well with others. Agreeableness suggests whether or not a person is open to the ideas of others and willing to go along with group decisions. Conscientiousness suggests whether someone can be depended on to meet commitments and perform agreed-upon tasks. Emotional stability suggests whether or not someone will be relaxed and secure, or uptight and tense, in work situations. Openness suggests whether someone will be open to new ideas or resistant to change.

17. The Type A personality is characteristic of people who bring stress on themselves by virtue of personal characteristics. These tend to be compulsive individuals who are uncomfortable waiting for things to happen, who try to do many things at once, and who generally move fast and have difficulty slowing down. Type A personalities can be stressful for both the individuals and the people around them. Managers must be aware of Type A personality tendencies in their own behavior and among others with whom they work. Ideally, this awareness will help the manager take precautionary steps to best manage the stress caused by this personality type.

18. The halo effect occurs when a single attribute of a person, such as the way he or she dresses, is used to evaluate or form an overall impression of the person. Selective perception occurs when someone focuses in a situation on those aspects that reinforce or are most consistent with his or her existing values, beliefs, or experiences.

19. Job satisfaction is an attitude that reflects how people feel about their jobs, work settings, and the people with whom they work. A typical job satisfaction survey might ask people to respond to questions about their pay, co-worker relationships, quality of supervisor, nature of the work setting, and the type of work they are asked to do. These questions might be framed with a scale ranging from "very satisfied" to "not satisfied at all" for each question or job satisfaction dimension.

Integration & application

20. Scott needs to be careful. Although there is modest research support for the relationship between job satisfaction and performance, there is no guarantee that simply doing things to make people happier at work will cause them to be higher performers. Scott needs to take a broader perspective on this issue and his responsibilities as a manager. He should be interested in job satisfaction for his therapists and do everything he can to help them to experience it. But he should also be performance oriented and understand that performance is achieved through a combination of skills, support, and motivation. He should be helping the therapists to achieve and maintain high levels of job competency. He should also work with them to find out what obstacles they are facing and what support they need—things that perhaps he can deal with in their behalf. All of this relates as well to research indications that performance can be a source of job satisfaction. And finally, Scott should make sure that the therapists believe they are being properly rewarded for their work since rewards are shown by research to have an influence on both job satisfaction and job performance.

Multiple choice

1. b.   2. c.   3. d.   4. d.   5. b.   6. a.   7. b.   8. b.
9. a.   10. d.   11. a.   12. c.   13. c.   14. a.   15. a.

Short response

16. People high in need for achievement will prefer work settings and jobs in which they have (1) challenging but achievable goals, (2) individual responsibility, and (3) performance feedback.

17. MBO is a structured approach to joint goal-setting and performance review by a manager or team leader and subordinates or team members. This offers a direct application of goal-setting theory. Participation of both manager and subordinate in goal setting offers an opportunity to choose goals to which the subordinate will respond and which also will serve the organization. Furthermore, through goal setting, the manager and individual subordinates can identify performance standards or targets. Progress toward these targets can be positively reinforced by the manager. Such reinforcements can serve as indicators of progress to someone with high need for achievement, thus responding to their desires for performance feedback.

18. When perceived inequity exists an individual might (1) quit the job, (2) speak with the boss to try and increase rewards to the point where the inequity no longer exists, or (3) decide to reduce effort to the level that seems consistent with the rewards being received.

19. Shaping encourages the formation of desirable work behaviors by rewarding successive approximations to those behaviors. In this sense, the behavior doesn't have to be perfect to be rewarded—it just has to be moving in the right direction. Over time and with a change of reinforcement scheduling from continuous to intermittent, such rewards can end up drawing forth the desired behavior.

Integration & application

20. The use of Muzak would be considered improvement in a hygiene factor under Herzberg's two-factor theory. Thus it would not be a source of greater work motivation and performance. Herzberg suggests that job content factors are the satisfiers or motivators. Based in the job itself, they represent such things as responsibility, sense of achievement, and feelings of growth. Job context factors are considered sources of dissatisfaction. They are found in the job environment and include such things as base pay, technical quality of supervision, and working conditions. Whereas improvements in job context such as introduction of Muzak make people less dissatisfied, improvements in job content are considered necessary to motivate them to high-performance levels.

Multiple choice

1. d.   2. c.   3. b.   4. d.   5. b.   6. d.   7. a.   8. c.
9. b.   10. a.   11. b.   12. a.   13. a.   14. b.   15. a.

Short response

16. In a task force, members are brought together to work on a specific assignment. The task force usually disbands when the assignment is finished. In an employee involvement group, perhaps a quality circle, members are brought together to work on an issue or task over time. They meet regularly and always deal with the same issue/task. In a self-managing team, the members of a formal work group provide self-direction. They plan, organize, and evaluate their work, share tasks, and help one another develop skills; they may even make hiring decisions. A true self-managing team does not need the traditional "boss" or supervisor, since the team as a whole takes on the supervisory responsibilities.

17. Input factors can have a major impact on group effectiveness. In order to best prepare a group to perform effectively, a manager should make sure that the right people are put in the group (maximize available talents and abilities), that these people are capable of working well together (membership characteristics should promote good relationships), that the tasks are clear, and that the group has the resources and environment needed to perform up to expectations.

18. A group's performance can be analyzed according to the interaction between cohesiveness and performance norms. In a highly cohesive group, members tend to conform to group norms. Thus, when the performance norm is positive and cohesion is high, we can expect everyone to work hard to support the norm—high performance is likely. By the same token, high cohesion and a low performance norm will act similarly—low performance is likely. With other combinations of norms and cohesion, the performance results will be more mixed.

19. The book lists several symptoms of groupthink along with various strategies for avoiding groupthink. For example, a group whose members censure themselves to refrain from contributing "contrary" or "different" opinions and/or whose members keep talking about outsiders as "weak" or the "enemy" may be suffering from groupthink. This may be avoided or corrected, for example, by asking someone to be the "devil's advocate" for a meeting and by inviting in an outside observer to help gather different viewpoints.

Integration & application

20. Mariel is faced with a highly cohesive group whose members conform to a negative or low-performance norm. This is a difficult situation that is ideally resolved by changing the performance norm. In order to gain the group's commitment to a high-performance norm, Mariel should act as a positive role model for the norm. She must communicate the norm clearly and positively to the group. She should not assume that everyone knows what she expects of them. She may also talk to the informal leader and gain his or her commitment to the norm. She might carefully reward high-performance behaviors within the group. She may introduce new members with high-performance records and commitments. And she might hold group meetings in which performance standards and expectations are discussed, with an emphasis on committing to new high-performance directions. If attempts to introduce a high-performance norm fail, Mariel may have to take steps to reduce group cohesiveness so that individual members can pursue higher-performance results without feeling bound by group pressures to restrict their performance.

TestPrep16

Multiple choice

1. d. 2. b. 3. d. 4. c. 5. b. 6. d. 7. a. 8. a.
9. d. 10. a. 11. d. 12. b. 13. b. 14. d. 15. a.

Short response

16. Lose-lose outcomes arise from the conflict management styles of avoiding and accommodating. Win-lose outcomes arise from competing and compromising.

17. Conflict of moderate intensity is often functional because it creates a level of tension or anxiety that causes people to work with greater creativity, to work harder, and to be more persistent. Without any conflict people might become complacent and believe that what they are currently doing or achieving is sufficient, even though things could be done better. When conflict is too high, the anxieties and stresses might overload people and make it difficult for them to stay on task and achieve performance goals.

18. In a negotiation, both substance and relationship goals are important. Substance goals relate to the content of the negotiation. A substance goal, for example, may relate to the final salary agreement between a job candidate and a prospective employer. Relationship goals relate to the quality of the interpersonal relationships among the negotiating parties. Relationship goals are important because the negotiating parties most likely have to work together in the future. For example, if relationships are poor after a labor–management negotiation, the likelihood is that future problems will occur.

19. Arbitration and mediation are both third-party approaches to conflict resolution. However, arbitration involves the third party acting as a judge who actually gives a "ruling" as to how a conflict situation is to be resolved. The mediator, by contrast, works with and listens to the conflicting parties while trying to help them find agreement, but without issuing a binding ruling on the case.

Integration & application

20. This is a typical interpersonal conflict between a person and her boss, one caused by a disagreement over the substance of the work that the person is being assigned. There is no indication that there are any emotional disagreements or issues involved. One possible way to deal with the situation is for the instructor to ask for a meeting with the department head to discuss her teaching assignment. This meeting might be opened by expressing her support for the department's teaching goals and needs, but also expressing concern for her own time and areas of expertise. If the faculty member and/or the department head can get the conversation initially focused on the department's goals and needs, this would provide an overall goal context within which to discuss the problem and hopefully resolve it. By focusing first on the higher-level goal shared in common, it might be possible to find ways to meet the needs of the department while still meeting the needs of the instructor, or at least coming close enough so that she is willing to give her courses her best. This is a form of problem solving in which the two work together to meet their respective individual needs but always referring back to the higher-level goal on which they both agree whenever the discussion gets bogged down.

TestPrep17

Multiple choice

1. c. 2. a. 3. a. 4. b. 5. b. 6. d. 7. a. 8. a.
9. a. 10. d. 11. d. 12. d. 13. c. 14. c. 15. a.

Short response

16. An approach of valuing diversity shows through leadership a commitment to helping people understand their differences, often through education and training programs. An approach of managing diversity, according to Roosevelt Thomas, is a step beyond in that it is where the leadership commits to changing the culture of the organization to empower everyone and create a fully inclusive environment where human resources are respected and fully utilized.

17. There are numbers of subcultures that form in organizations and can become the source of perceived differences

as people work with one another across subculture boundaries. Examples of common organizational subcultures include those based on age, gender, profession, and work function. If younger workers stereotype older workers as uncreative and less ambitious, a team consisting of an age mix of members might experience some difficulties. This illustrates an example of problems among generational subcultures.

18. Organizations are power structures, and the way people view and respond to power differences in organizations can be very significant in how they operate. In a national culture where power distance is high, there would be a tendency in organizations to respect persons of authority—perhaps defer to them, use job titles and formal greetings, and refrain from challenging their views in public meetings. In a low or moderate power distance culture, by contrast, there might be more informality in using first names without job titles and being more casual in relationships and even in public disagreements with views expressed by senior people.

19. The cultural orientation of assertiveness would be important in a corporation's global training because it has a lot to do with how people are likely to handle relationships. A culture that runs high in assertiveness would include societal tendencies toward confrontation and "tough" stances as people in disagreements might deal with one another. In a low assertiveness culture the tendency would be toward modesty and less aggressiveness. When representatives of these different cultures work together, they could have problems dealing with conflict; the high-assertive culture person would appear "pushy" to the other, while the low-assertiveness culture person's behavior might be misinterpreted as a lack of concern. When good problem solving is the goal, these persons might need help understanding one another so that issues are resolved and not just left open.

Integration & application

20. The friend must recognize that the cultural differences between the United States and Japan may affect the success of group-oriented work practices such as quality circles and work teams. The United States was the most individualistic culture in Hofstede's study of national cultures; Japan is much more collectivist. Group practices such as the quality circle and teams are natural and consistent with the Japanese culture. When introduced into a more individualistic culture, these same practices might cause difficulties or require some time for workers to get used to. At the very least, the friend should proceed with caution, discuss ideas for the new practices with the workers before making any changes, and then monitor the changes closely so that adjustments can be made to improve them as the workers gain familiarity with them and have suggestions of their own.

TestPrep18

Multiple choice

1. c. 2. d. 3. d. 4. b. 5. a. 6. b. 7. a. 8. c.
9. d. 10. d. 11. a. 12. b. 13. b. 14. c. 15. a.

Short response

16. In a joint venture the foreign corporation and the local corporation each own a portion of the firm—e.g., 75% and 25%. In a wholly owned subsidiary the foreign firm owns the local subsidiary in its entirety.

17. The relationship between an MNC and a host country should be mutually beneficial. Sometimes, however, host countries complain that MNCs take unfair advantage of them and do not include them in the benefits of their international operations. The complaints against MNCs include taking excessive profits out of the host country, hiring the best local labor, not respecting local laws and customs, and dominating the local economy. Engaging in corrupt practices is another important concern.

18. If a Senator says she favors "protectionism" in international trade, it basically means that she wants to make sure that domestic American firms are protected against foreign competitors. In other words, she doesn't want foreign companies coming into America and destroying through competition the local firms. Thus, she wants to protect them in some ways such as imposing import tariffs on the foreign firms' products or imposing legal restrictions on them setting up businesses in America.

19. Currency risk in international business involves the rise and fall of currencies in relationship with one another. For an American company operating in Japan, currency risk involves the value of the dollar vis-à-vis the yen. When the dollar falls relative to the yen (requiring more of them to buy 1 yen), it means that buying products and making investments in Japan will be more costly; the "risk" of this eventuality needs to be planned for when business relationships are entered in foreign countries. Political risk is the potential loss in one's investments in foreign countries due to wars or political changes that might threaten the assets. An example would be a Socialist government coming into power and deciding to "nationalize" or take over ownership of all foreign companies.

Integration & application

20. This issue of MNC vs. transnational is growing in importance. When a large global company such as Ford or IBM is strongly associated with a national identity, the firm might face risk in international business when foreign consumers or governments are angry at the firm's home country; they might stop buying its products or make it hard for them to operate. When the

MNC has a strong national identity, its home constituents might express anger and create problems when the firm makes investments in creating jobs in other countries. Also, when the leadership of the MNC views itself as having one national home, it might have a more limited and even ethnocentric approach to international operations. When a firm operates as a transnational, by contrast, it becomes a global citizen and, theoretically, at least is freed from some potential problems identified here. Because a transnational views the world as its home, furthermore, its workforce and leadership are more likely to be globally diverse and have broad international perspectives on the company and its opportunities.

TestPrep19

Multiple choice

1. a. 2. a. 3. d. 4. b. 5. b. 6. a. 7. a. 8. b.
9. a. 10. c. 11. c. 12. a. 13. c. 14. b. 15. d.

Short response

16. Entrepreneurship is rich with diversity. It is an avenue for business entry and career success that is pursued by many women and members of minority groups. Data show almost 40% of U.S. businesses are owned by women. Many report leaving other employment because they had limited opportunities. For them, entrepreneurship made available the opportunities for career success that they lacked. Minority-owned businesses are one of the fastest-growing sectors, with the growth rates highest for Hispanic-owned, Asian-owned, and African American-owned businesses in that order.

17. The three stages in the life cycle of an entrepreneurial firm are birth, breakthrough, and maturity. In the birth stage, the leader is challenged to get customers, establish a market, and find the money needed to keep the business going. In the breakthrough stage, the challenges shift to becoming and staying profitable and managing growth. In the maturity stage, a leader is more focused on revising/maintaining a good business strategy and more generally managing the firm for continued success and possibly more future growth.

18. The limited partnership form of small business ownership consists of a general partner and one or more "limited partners." The general partner(s) play an active role in managing and operating the business; the limited partners do not. All contribute resources of some value to the partnership for the conduct of the business. The advantage of any partnership form is that the partners may share in profits, but their potential for losses is limited by the size of their original investments.

19. A venture capitalist is an individual or group of individuals that invests money in new start-up companies and gets a portion of ownership in return. The goal is to sell their ownership stakes in the future for a profit. An angel investor is a type of venture capitalist, but on a smaller and individual scale. This is a person who invests in a new venture, taking a share of ownership, and also hoping to gain profit through a future sale of the ownership.

Integration & application

20. The friend is right—it takes much forethought and planning to prepare the launch of a new business venture. In response to the question of how to ensure that you are really being customer-focused in the new start-up, I would ask and answer the following questions to frame my business model with a strong customer orientation. "Who are my potential customers? What market niche am I shooting for? What do the customers in this market really want? How do these customers make purchase decisions? How much will it cost to produce and distribute my product/service to these customers? How much will it cost to attract and retain customers?" Following an overall executive summary, which includes a commitment to this customer orientation, I would address the following areas in writing up my initial business plan. The plan would address such areas as company description—mission, owners, and legal form—as well as an industry analysis, product and services description, marketing description and strategy, staffing model, financial projections with cash flows, and capital needs.

Glossary

360° feedback 360° feedback includes in the appraisal process superiors, subordinates, peers, and even customers.

A

accommodation Accommodation or smoothing plays down differences and highlights similarities to reduce conflict.

accountability Accountability is the requirement to show performance results to a supervisor.

active listening Active listening helps the source of a message say what he or she really means.

affirmative action Affirmative action is an effort to give preference in employment to women and minority group members.

after-action review An after-action review identifies lessons learned from a completed project, task force assignment, or special operation.

amoral manager An amoral manager fails to consider the ethics of her or his behavior.

anchoring and adjustment heuristic The anchoring and adjustment heuristic adjusts a previously existing value or starting point to make a decision.

angel investor An angel investor is a wealthy individual willing to invest in return for equity in a new venture.

arbitration In arbitration a neutral third party issues a binding decision to resolve a dispute.

assessment center An assessment center examines how job candidates handle simulated work situations.

attitude An attitude is a predisposition to act in a certain way.

attribution Attribution is the process of creating explanations for events.

authoritarianism Authoritarianism is the degree to which a person defers to authority and accepts status differences.

authority decision An authority decision is made by the leader and then communicated to the group.

autocratic style A leader with an autocratic style acts in unilateral command-and-control fashion.

availability heuristic The availability heuristic uses readily available information to assess a current situation.

avoidance Avoidance pretends that a conflict doesn't really exist.

B

B2B business strategy A B2B business strategy uses IT and Web portals to link organizations vertically in supply chains.

B2C business strategy A B2C business strategy uses IT and Web portals to link businesses with customers.

balanced scorecard A balanced scorecard measures performance on financial, customer service, internal process, and innovation and learning goals.

bargaining zone A bargaining zone is the area between one party's minimum reservation point and the other party's maximum reservation point.

BCG Matrix The BCG Matrix analyzes business opportunities according to market growth rate and market share.

behavioral decision model The behavioral decision model describes decision making with limited information and bounded rationality.

behaviorally anchored rating (BARS) A behaviorally anchored rating (BARS) uses specific descriptions of actual behaviors to rate various levels of performance.

benchmarking Benchmarking uses external comparisons to gain insights for planning.

best practices Best practices are methods that lead to superior performance.

biculturalism Biculturalism is when minority members adopt characteristics of majority cultures in order to succeed.

board of directors Members of a board of directors are elected by stockholders to represent their ownership interests.

bona fide occupational qualifications Bona fide occupational qualifications are employment criteria justified by capacity to perform a job.

bonus pay Bonus pay plans provide one-time payments based on performance accomplishments.

brainstorming Brainstorming engages group members in an open, spontaneous discussion of problems and ideas.

budget A budget is a plan that commits resources to projects or activities.

bureaucracy A bureaucracy is a rational and efficient form of organization founded on logic, order, and legitimate authority.

bureaucratic control Bureaucratic control influences behavior through authority, policies, procedures, job descriptions, budgets, and day-to-day supervision.

business model innovations Business model innovations result in ways for firms to make money.

business plan A business plan describes the direction for a new business and the financing needed to operate it.

business strategy A business strategy identifies how a division or strategic business unit will compete in its product or service domain.

C

career development Career development manages how a person grows and progresses in a career.

career planning Career planning is the process of matching career goals and individual capabilities with opportunities for their fulfillment.

centralization With centralization top management keeps the power to make most decisions.

centralized communication network In a centralized communication network, communication flows only between individual members and a hub or center point.

certain environment A certain environment offers complete information on possible action alternatives and their consequences.

change leader A change leader tries to change the behavior of another person or social system.

changing Changing is the phase where a planned change actually takes place.

channel richness Channel richness is the capacity of a communication channel to effectively carry information.

Chapter 11 bankruptcy Chapter 11 bankruptcy protects an insolvent firm from creditors during a period of reorganization to restore profitability.

charismatic leader A charismatic leader develops special leader-follower relationships and inspires followers in extraordinary ways.

child labor Child labor is the full-time employment of children for work ¬otherwise done by adults.

clan control Clan control influences behavior through norms and expectations set by the organizational culture.

classical decision model The classical decision model describes decision making with complete information.

classical view of CSR The classical view of CSR is that business should focus on the pursuit of profits.

coaching Coaching occurs as an experienced person offers performance advice to a less-experienced person.

code of ethics A code of ethics is a formal statement of values and ethical standards.

coercive power Coercive power achieves influence by punishment.

cognitive dissonance Cognitive dissonance is discomfort felt when attitude and behavior are inconsistent.

cohesiveness Cohesiveness is the degree to which members are attracted to and motivated to remain part of a team.

collaboration Collaboration or problem solving involves working through conflict differences and solving problems so everyone wins.

collective bargaining Collective bargaining is the process of negotiating, administering, and interpreting a labor contract.

commercializing innovation Commercializing innovation turns ideas into economic value added.

committee A committee is designated to work on a special task on a continuing basis.

communication Communication is the process of sending and receiving symbols with meanings attached.

communication channel A communication channel is the medium used to carry a message.

comparable worth Comparable worth holds that persons performing jobs of similar importance should receive comparable pay.

competition Competition or authoritative command uses force, superior skill, or domination to win a conflict.

competitive advantage A competitive advantage means operating in successful ways that are difficult to imitate.

compressed workweek A compressed workweek allows a worker to complete a full-time job in less than five days.

compromise Compromise occurs when each party to the conflict gives up something of value to the other.

concentration Growth through concentration means expansion within an existing business area.

conceptual skill A conceptual skill is the ability to think analytically and solve complex problems.

concurrent control Concurrent control focuses on what happens during the work process.

confirmation error Confirmation error is when we attend only to information that confirms a decision already made.

conflict Conflict is a disagreement over issues of substance and/or an emotional antagonism.

conflict resolution Conflict resolution is the removal of the substantial and/or emotional reasons for a conflict.

consensus Consensus is reached when all parties believe they have had their say and been listened to, and agree to support the group's final decision.

constructive stress Constructive stress is a positive influence on effort, creativity, and diligence in work.

consultative decision A consultative decision is made by a leader after receiving information, advice, or opinions from group members.

contingency leadership perspective The contingency leadership perspective suggests that what is successful as a leadership style varies by the situation and the people involved.

contingency planning Contingency planning identifies alternative courses of action to take when things go wrong.

contingency thinking Contingency thinking tries to match management practices with situational demands.

continuous improvement Continuous improvement involves always searching for new ways to improve work quality and performance.

continuous improvement Continuous improvement involves always searching for new ways to improve work quality and performance.

control charts Control charts are graphical ways of displaying trends so that exceptions to quality standards can be identified.

controlling Controlling is the process of measuring performance and taking action to ensure desired results.

co-opetition Co-opetition is the strategy of working with rivals on projects of mutual benefit.

core competency A core competency is a special strength that gives an organization a competitive advantage.

core culture Core culture is found in the underlying values of the organization.

core values Core values are beliefs and values shared by organization members.

corporate governance Corporate governance is oversight of a company's management by a board of directors.

corporate social responsibility Corporate social responsibility is the obligation of an organization to serve its own interests and those of its stakeholders.

corporate strategy A corporate strategy sets long-term direction for the total enterprise.

corporation A corporation is a legal entity that exists separately from its owners.

corruption Corruption involves illegal practices to further one's business interests.

cost leadership strategy A cost leadership strategy seeks to operate with lower costs than competitors.

cost-benefit analysis Cost-benefit analysis involves comparing the costs and benefits of each potential course of action.

CPM/PERT CPM/PERT is a combination of the critical path method and the program evaluation and review technique.

creativity Creativity is the generation of a novel idea or unique approach that solves a problem or crafts an opportunity.

credible communication Credible communication earns trust, respect, and integrity in the eyes of others.

crisis A crisis is an unexpected problem that can lead to disaster if not resolved quickly and appropriately.

critical path The critical path is the pathway from project start to conclusion that involves activities with the longest completion times.

critical-incident technique The critical-incident technique keeps a log of someone's effective and ineffective job behaviors.

cross-functional team A cross-functional team operates with members who come from different functional units of an organization.

cultural etiquette Cultural etiquette is use of appropriate manners and behaviors in cross-cultural situations.

cultural intelligence Cultural intelligence is the ability to adapt to new cultures.

cultural relativism Cultural relativism suggests there is no one right way to behave; cultural context determines ethical behavior.

culture shock Culture shock is the confusion and discomfort that a person experiences when in an unfamiliar culture.

currency risk Currency risk is possible loss because of fluctuating exchange rates.

customer structure A customer structure groups together people and jobs that serve the same customers or clients.

D

debt financing Debt financing involves borrowing money from another person, a bank, or a financial institution.

decentralization With decentralization, top management allows lower levels to help make many decisions.

decentralized communication network A decentralized communication network allows all members to communicate directly with one another.

decision A decision is a choice among possible alternative courses of action.

decision making Decision making is the process of making choices among alternative courses of action.

delegation Delegation is the process of entrusting work to others.

democratic style A leader with a democratic style encourages participation with an emphasis on task and people.

departmentalization Departmentalization is the process of grouping together people and jobs into work units.

destructive stress Destructive stress is a negative influence on one's performance.

differentiation strategy A differentiation strategy offers products that are unique and different from the competition.

discrimination Discrimination occurs when someone is denied a job or job assignment for non-job-relevant reasons.

disruptive behaviors Disruptive behaviors are self-serving and cause problems for team effectiveness.

distributed leadership Distributed leadership is when any and all members contribute helpful task and maintenance activities to the team.

distributive justice Distributive justice focuses on treating people the same regardless of personal characteristics.

distributive negotiation Distributive negotiation focuses on win-lose claims made by each party for certain preferred outcomes.

diversification In diversification, expansion occurs by entering new business areas.

diversity Diversity describes race, gender, age, and other individual differences.

divestiture Divestiture sells off parts of the organization to refocus attention on core business areas.

division of labor The division of labor is people and groups performing different jobs.

divisional structure A divisional structure groups together people working on the same product, in the same area, or with similar customers.

downsizing Downsizing decreases the size of operations.

dysfunctional conflict Dysfunctional conflict is destructive and hurts task performance.

E

e-business strategy An e-business strategy strategically uses the Internet to gain competitive advantage.

ecological fallacy The ecological fallacy assumes that a generalized cultural value applies equally well to all members of the culture.

economic order quantity The economic order quantity method places new orders when inventory levels fall to predetermined points.

effective communication In effective communication the receiver fully understands the intended meaning.

effective manager An effective manager successfully helps others achieve high performance and satisfaction in their work.

effective negotiation Effective negotiation resolves issues of substance while maintaining a positive process.

effective team An effective team achieves high levels of task performance, membership satisfaction, and future viability.

efficient communication Efficient communication occurs at minimum cost to the sender.

electronic grapevine The electronic grapevine uses computer technologies to transmit information around informal networks inside and outside of organizations.

emotional conflict Emotional conflict results from feelings of anger, distrust, dislike, fear, and resentment as well as from personality clashes.

emotional intelligence (EI) Emotional intelligence (EI) is the ability to manage our emotions in social relationships.

emotions Emotions are strong feelings directed toward someone or something.

employee assistance programs Employee assistance programs help employees cope with personal stresses and problems.

employee engagement Employee engagement is a strong sense of belonging and connection with one's work and employer.

employee involvement team An employee involvement team meets on a regular basis to help achieve continuous improvement.

empowerment Empowerment gives people job freedom and power to influence affairs in the organization.

entrepreneur An entrepreneur is willing to pursue opportunities in situations that others view as problems or threats.

entrepreneurship Entrepreneurship is dynamic, risk-taking, creative, growth-oriented behavior.

equal employment opportunity (EEO) Equal employment opportunity (EEO) is the right to employment and advancement without regard to race, sex, religion, color, or national origin.

equity financing Equity financing gives ownership shares to outsiders in return for their financial investments.

escalating commitment Escalating commitment is the continuation of a course of action even though it is not working.

ethical behavior Ethical behavior is "right" or "good" in the context of a governing moral code.

ethical dilemma An ethical dilemma is a situation that although offering potential benefit or gain is also unethical.

ethical frameworks Ethical frameworks are well-thought-out personal rules and strategies for ethical decision making.

ethical imperialism Ethical imperialism is an attempt to impose one's ethical standards on other cultures.

ethical leadership Ethical leadership has integrity and appears to others as "good" or "right" by moral standards.

ethics Ethics set moral standards of what is "good" and "right" behavior in organizations and in our personal lives.

ethics training Ethics training seeks to help people understand the ethical aspects of decision making and to incorporate high ethical standards into their daily behavior.

ethnocentrism Ethnocentrism is the belief that one's membership group or subculture is superior to all others.

evidence-based management Evidence-based management involves making decisions based on hard facts about what really works.

existence needs Existence needs are desires for physiological and material well-being.

expatriate An expatriate lives and works in a foreign country.

expectancy Expectancy is a person's belief that working hard will result in high task performance.

expert power Expert power achieves influence by special knowledge.

exporting In exporting, local products are sold abroad.

external control External control occurs through direct supervision or administrative systems.

extinction Extinction discourages a behavior by making the removal of a desirable consequence contingent on its occurrence.

F

family business feud A family business feud can lead to small business failure.

family businesses Family businesses are owned and financially controlled by family members.

family-friendly benefits Family-friendly benefits help employees achieve better work-life balance.

feedback Feedback is the process of telling someone else how you feel about something that person did or said.

feedback control Feedback control takes place after completing an action.

feedforward control Feedforward control ensures clear directions and needed resources before the work begins.

filtering Filtering is the intentional distortion of information to make it more favorable to the recipient.

first-line managers First-line managers supervise people who perform nonmanagerial duties.

first-mover advantage A first-mover advantage comes from being first to exploit a niche or enter a market.

flexible benefits Flexible benefits programs allow choice to personalize benefits within a set dollar allowance.

flexible working hours Flexible working hours give employees some choice in daily work hours.

focused cost leadership strategy A focused cost leadership strategy seeks the lowest costs of operations within a special market segment.

focused differentiation strategy A focused differentiation strategy offers a unique product to a special market segment.

force-coercion strategy A force-coercion strategy pursues change through formal authority and/or the use of rewards or punishments.

forecasting Forecasting attempts to predict the future.

foreign Corrupt Practices Act The Foreign Corrupt Practices Act makes it illegal for U.S. firms and their representatives to engage in corrupt practices overseas.

foreign subsidiary A foreign subsidiary is a local operation completely owned by a foreign firm.

formal structure Formal structure is the official structure of the organization.

formal team A formal team is officially recognized and supported by the organization.

framing error Framing error is solving a problem in the context perceived.

franchising In franchising, a firm pays a fee for rights to use another company's name and operating methods.

free-agent economy In a free-agent economy, people change jobs more often, and many work on independent contracts with a shifting mix of employers.

fringe benefits Fringe benefits are nonmonetary forms of compensation such as health insurance and retirement plans.

functional chimneys or functional siloes problem The functional chimneys or functional siloes problem is a lack of communication and coordination across functions.

functional conflict Functional conflict is constructive and helps boost task performance.

functional plan A functional plan identifies how different parts of an enterprise will contribute to accomplishing strategic plans.

functional strategy A functional strategy guides activities within one specific area of operations.

functional structure A functional structure groups together people with similar skills who perform similar tasks.

fundamental attribution error Fundamental attribution error overestimates internal factors and underestimates external factors as influences on someone's behavior.

G

gain sharing Gain sharing plans allow employees to share in cost savings or productivity gains realized by their efforts.

gantt chart A Gantt chart graphically displays the scheduling of tasks required to complete a project.

gender similarities hypothesis The gender similarities hypothesis holds that males and females have similar psychological make-ups.

general partnership In a general partnership, owners share management responsibilities.

geographical structure A geographical structure brings together people and jobs performed in the same location.

glass ceiling effect The glass ceiling effect is an invisible barrier limiting career advancement of women and minorities.

global corporation or multinational A global corporation or multinational corporation has extensive international business dealings in many foreign countries.

global economy In the global economy, resources, markets, and competition are worldwide in scope.

global manager A global manager is culturally aware and informed on international affairs.

global outsourcing Global outsourcing involves contracting for work that is performed by workers in other countries.

global sourcing In global sourcing, firms purchase materials or services around the world for local use.

global strategic alliance In a global strategic alliance each partner hopes to achieve through cooperation things they couldn't do alone.

globalization Globalization is the worldwide interdependence of resource flows, product markets, and business competition.

globalization strategy A globalization strategy adopts standardized products and advertising for use worldwide.

governance Governance is oversight of top management by a board of directors or board of trustees.

graphic rating scale A graphic rating scale uses a checklist of traits or characteristics to evaluate performance.

green innovation Green innovation is the process of turning ideas into innovations that reduce the carbon footprint of an organization or its products.

greenfield venture A greenfield venture establishes a foreign subsidiary by building an entirely new operation in a foreign country.

group decision A group decision is made by group members themselves.

groupthink Groupthink is a tendency for highly cohesive teams to lose their evaluative capabilities.

growth needs Growth needs are desires for continued psychological growth and development.

growth strategy A growth strategy involves expansion of the organization's current operations.

H

halo effect A halo effect uses one attribute to develop an overall impression of a person or situation.

Hawthorne effect The Hawthorne effect is the tendency of persons singled out for special attention to perform as expected.

hierarchy of objectives In a hierarchy of objectives, lower-level objectives help to accomplish higher-level ones.

high-context cultures High-context cultures rely on nonverbal and situational cues as well as spoken or written words in communication.

higher-order needs Higher-order needs are esteem and self-actualization needs in Maslow's hierarchy.

high-performance organization A high-performance organization consistently achieves excellence while creating a high-quality work environment.

human capital Human capital is the economic value of people with job-relevant abilities, knowledge, ideas, energies, and commitments.

human relations A leader with a human relations style emphasizes people over tasks.

human resource management (HRM) Human resource management (HRM) is the process of attracting, developing, and maintaining a high-quality workforce.

human resource planning Human resource planning analyzes staffing needs and identifies actions to fill those needs.

human skill A human skill is the ability to work well in cooperation with other people.

hygiene factor A hygiene factor is found in the job context, such as working conditions, interpersonal relations, organizational policies, and salary.

I

immoral manager An immoral manager chooses to behave unethically.

importing Importing is the process of acquiring products abroad and selling them in domestic markets.

impression management Impression management tries to create desired perceptions in the eyes of others.

improvement objectives Improvement objectives document intentions to improve performance in a specific way.

inclusivity Inclusivity is how open the organization is to anyone who can perform a job.

incremental change Incremental change bends and adjusts existing ways to improve performance.

independent contractors Independent contractors are hired on temporary contracts and are not part of the organization's permanent workforce.

individualism view In the individualism view, ethical behavior advances long-term self-interests.

individualism-collectivism Individualism-collectivism is the degree to which a society emphasizes individuals and their self-interests.

informal group An informal group is unofficial and emerges from relationships and shared interests among members.

informal structure Informal structure is the set of unofficial relationships among an organization's members.

information competency Information competency is the ability to gather and use information to solve problems.

initial public offering (IPO) An initial public offering (IPO) is an initial selling of shares of stock to the public at large.

innovation Innovation is the process of taking a new idea and putting it into practice.

input standard An input standard measures work efforts that go into a performance task.

insourcing Insourcing is the creation of domestic jobs by foreign employers.

instrumental values Instrumental values are preferences regarding the means to desired ends.

instrumentality Instrumentality is a person's belief that various outcomes will occur as a result of task performance.

integrative negotiation uses Integrative negotiation uses a win-win orientation to reach solutions acceptable to each party.

integrity Integrity in leadership is honesty, credibility, and consistency in putting values into action.

intellectual capital Intellectual capital is the collective brainpower or shared knowledge of a workforce.

interactional justice Interactional justice is the degree to which others are treated with dignity and respect.

interactive leadership Interactive leadership is strong on motivating, communicating, listening, and relating positively to others.

internal control Internal control occurs through self-discipline and self-control.

international business An international business conducts commercial transactions across national boundaries.

intrapreneurs Intrapreneurs display entrepreneurial behavior as employees of larger firms.

intuitive thinking Intuitive thinking approaches problems in a flexible and spontaneous fashion.

inventory control Inventory control ensures that inventory is only big enough to meet immediate needs.

ISO certification ISO certification indicates conformance with a rigorous set of international quality standards.

J

job burnout Job burnout is physical and mental exhaustion from work stress.

job design Job design is the allocation of specific work tasks to individuals and groups.

job enrichment Job enrichment increases job content by adding work planning and evaluating duties normally performed by the supervisor.

job migration Job migration occurs when global outsourcing shifts from one country to another.

job satisfaction Job satisfaction is the degree to which an individual feels positive about a job and work experience.

job sharing Job sharing splits one job between two people.

joint venture A joint venture operates in a foreign country through co-ownership with local partners.

justice view In the justice view, ethical behavior treats people impartially and fairly.

just-in-time scheduling (JIT) Just-in-time scheduling (JIT) routes materials to workstations just in time for use.

K

knowledge management Knowledge management is the process of using intellectual capital for competitive advantage.

knowledge workers Knowledge workers use their minds and intellects as critical assets to employers.

L

labor contract A labor contract is a formal agreement between a union and an employer about the terms of work for union members.

labor union A labor union is an organization that deals with employers on the workers' collective behalf.

lack-of-participation error Lack-of-participation error is failure to include the right people in the decision-making process.

laissez-faire style A leader with a laissez-faire style is disengaged, showing low task and people concerns.

law of effect The law of effect states that behavior followed by pleasant consequences is likely to be repeated; behavior followed by unpleasant consequences is not.

leadership Leadership is the process of inspiring others to work hard to accomplish important tasks.

leadership style Leadership style is the recurring pattern of behaviors exhibited by a leader.

leading Leading is the process of arousing enthusiasm and inspiring efforts to achieve goals.

learning organization A learning organization continuously changes and improves, using the lessons of experience.

legitimate power Legitimate power achieves influence by formal authority.

licensing In licensing, one firm pays a fee for rights to make or sell another company's products.

lifelong learning Lifelong learning is continuous learning from daily experiences.

Limited Liability Corporation, LLC A limited liability corporation, LLC, combines the advantages of the sole proprietorship, partnership, and corporation.

limited partnership A limited partnership consists of a general partner who manages the business and one or more limited partners.

liquidation Liquidation is where a business closes and sells its assets to pay creditors.

locus of control Locus of control is the extent to which one believes that what happens is within one's control.

long-range plans Long-range plans usually cover three years or more.

lose-lose conflict In lose-lose conflict no one achieves his or her true desires and the underlying reasons for conflict remain unaffected.

low-context cultures Low-context cultures emphasize communication via spoken or written words.

lower-order needs Lower-order needs are physiological, safety, and social needs in Maslow's hierarchy.

M

machiavellianism Machiavellianism is the degree to which someone uses power manipulatively.

maintenance activity A maintenance activity is an action taken by a team member that supports the emotional life of the group.

management by exception Management by exception focuses attention on differences between actual and desired performance.

management process The management process is planning, organizing, leading, and controlling the use of resources to accomplish performance goals.

management science and operations research Management science and operations research apply mathematical techniques to solve management problems.

manager A manager is a person who supports and is responsible for the work of others.

management by objectives Managing by objectives is a process of joint objective setting between a superior and a subordinate.

managing diversity Managing diversity is building an inclusive work environment that allows everyone to reach his or her potential.

market control Market control is essentially the influence of market competition on the behavior of organizations and their members.

masculinity-femininity Masculinity-femininity is the degree to which a society values assertiveness and materialism.

matrix structure A matrix structure combines functional and divisional approaches to emphasize project or program teams.

management by walking around (MBWA) Managers using MBWA spend time out of their offices, meeting and talking with workers at all levels.

mechanistic designs Mechanistic designs are bureaucratic, using a centralized and vertical structure.

mediation In mediation a neutral party tries to help conflicting parties improve communication to resolve their dispute.

membership composition Membership composition is the mix of abilities, skills, backgrounds, and experiences among team members.

mentoring Mentoring assigns early career employees as protégés to more senior ones.

merit pay Merit pay awards pay increases in proportion to performance contributions.

middle managers Middle managers oversee the work of large departments or divisions.

mission The mission is the organization's reason for existence in society.

mixed message A mixed message results when words communicate one message while actions, body language, or appearance communicate something else.

monochronic cultures In monochronic cultures people tend to do one thing at a time.

mood contagion Mood contagion is the spillover of one's positive or negative moods onto others.

moods Moods are generalized positive and negative feelings or states of mind.

moral manager A moral manager makes ethical behavior a personal goal.

moral rights view In the moral rights view, ethical behavior respects and protects fundamental rights.

most favored nation status Most favored nation status gives a trading partner the most favorable treatment for imports and exports.

motivation Motivation accounts for the level, direction, and persistence of effort expended at work.

multicultural organization A multicultural organization is based on pluralism and operates with inclusivity and respect for diversity.

multi-person comparison A multi-person comparison compares one person's performance with that of others.

N

necessity-based entrepreneurship Necessity-based entrepreneurship is when people start new ventures because they have few or no other employment options.

need A need is a physiological or psychological deficiency that a person wants to satisfy.

need for achievement Need for achievement is the desire to do something better, to solve problems, or to master complex tasks.

need for affiliation Need for affiliation is the desire to establish and maintain good relations with people.

need for power Need for power is the desire to control, influence, or be responsible for other people.

negative reinforcement Negative reinforcement strengthens a behavior by making the avoidance of an undesirable consequence contingent on its occurrence.

negotiation Negotiation is the process of making joint decisions when the parties involved have different preferences.

network structure A network structure uses IT to link with networks of outside suppliers and service contractors.

noise Noise is anything that interferes with the communication process.

nominal group technique The nominal group technique structures interaction among team members discussing problems and ideas.

nonprogrammed decision A nonprogrammed decision applies a specific solution that has been crafted to address a unique problem.

Nonverbal communication Nonverbal communication takes place through gestures, expressions, posture, and even use of interpersonal space.

norm A norm is a behavior, rule, or standard expected to be followed by team members.

O

objectives Objectives are specific results that one wishes to achieve.

observable culture The observable culture is what you see and hear when walking around an organization.

open system An open system transforms resource inputs from the environment into product outputs.

operant conditioning Operant conditioning is the control of behavior by manipulating its consequences.

operating objectives Operating objectives are specific results that organizations try to accomplish.

operations management Operations management is the study of how organizations produce goods and services.

optimizing decision An optimizing decision chooses the alternative giving the absolute best solution to a problem.

organic designs Organic designs are adaptive, using a decentralized and horizontal structure.

organization chart An organization chart describes the arrangement of work positions within an organization.

organization structure Organization structure is a system of tasks, reporting relationships, and communication linkages.

organizational citizenship behaviors Organizational citizenship behaviors are the extras people do to go the additional mile in their work.

organizational culture Organizational culture is a system of shared beliefs and values guiding behavior.

organizational design Organizational design is the process of configuring organizations to meet environmental challenges.

organizational subcultures Organizational subcultures are groupings of people based on shared demographic and job identities.

organizing Organizing is the process of assigning tasks, allocating resources, and coordinating work activities.

orientation Orientation familiarizes new employees with jobs, co-workers, and organizational policies and services.

output standard An output standard measures performance results in terms of quantity, quality, cost, or time.

outsourcing Outsourcing shifts local jobs to foreign locations to take advantage of lower-wage labor in other countries.

P

participatory planning Participatory planning includes the persons who will be affected by plans and/or who will be asked to implement them.

partnership A partnership is when two or more people agree to contribute resources to start and operate a business together.

perception Perception is the process through which people receive and interpret information from the environment.

performance appraisal Performance appraisal is the process of formally evaluating performance and providing feedback to a job holder.

performance opportunity A performance opportunity is a situation that offers the possibility of a better future if the right steps are taken.

performance threat A performance threat is a situation where something is wrong or likely to be wrong.

personal development objectives Personal development objectives document intentions to accomplish personal growth, such as expanded job knowledge or skills.

personal wellness Personal wellness is the pursuit of a personal health-promotion program.

personality Personality is the profile of characteristics making a person unique from others.

persuasion Persuasion is presenting a message in a manner that causes others to support it.

persuasive communication Persuasive communication presents a message in a manner that causes others to accept and support it.

plan A plan is a statement of intended means for accomplishing objectives.

planning Planning is the process of setting objectives and determining how to accomplish them.

policy A policy is a standing plan that communicates broad guidelines for decisions and action.

political risk Political risk is the possible loss of investment in or control over a foreign asset because of instability and political changes in the host country.

political-risk analysis Political-risk analysis forecasts how political events may impact foreign investments.

polychronic cultures In polychronic cultures people accomplish many different things at once.

positive reinforcement Positive reinforcement strengthens a behavior by making a desirable consequence contingent on its occurrence.

power Power is the ability to get someone else to do something you want done.

power distance Power distance is the degree to which a society accepts unequal distribution of power.

pregnancy discrimination Pregnancy discrimination penalizes a woman in a job or as a job applicant for being pregnant.

prejudice Prejudice is the display of negative, irrational attitudes toward women or minorities.

problem solving Problem solving involves identifying and taking action to resolve problems.

procedural justice Procedural justice focuses on the fair application of policies and rules.

procedure A procedure or rule precisely describes actions to take in specific situations.

process innovations Process innovations result in better ways of doing things.

product innovations Product innovations result in new or improved goods or services.

product structure A product structure groups together people and jobs working on a single product or service.

profit sharing Profit sharing distributes to employees a proportion of net profits earned by the organization.

programmed decision A programmed decision applies a solution from past experience to a routine problem.

project management Project management makes sure that activities required to complete a project are planned well and accomplished on time.

project team or task force A project team or task force is convened for a specific purpose and disbands after completing its task.

projection Projection assigns personal attributes to other individuals.

projects Projects are one-time activities with many component tasks that must be completed in proper order and according to budget.

protectionism Protectionism is a call for tariffs and favorable treatments to protect domestic firms from foreign competition.

proxemics Proxemics is the study of how people use interpersonal space.

punishment Punishment discourages a behavior by making an unpleasant consequence contingent on its occurrence.

Q

quality circle A quality circle is a team of employees who meet periodically to discuss ways of improving work quality.

quality of work life Quality of work life is the overall quality of human experiences in the workplace.

R

rational persuasion strategy A rational persuasion strategy pursues change through empirical data and rational argument.

realistic job previews Realistic job previews provide job candidates with all pertinent information about a job and organization.

recruitment Recruitment is a set of activities designed to attract a qualified pool of job applicants.

referent power Referent power achieves influence by personal identification.

refreezing Refreezing is the phase at which change is stabilized.

relatedness needs Relatedness needs are desires for satisfying interpersonal relationships.

relationship goals Relationship goals in negotiation focus on people's relationships and interpersonal processes.

reliability Reliability means a selection device gives consistent results over repeated measures.

representativeness heuristic The representativeness heuristic assesses the likelihood of an occurrence using a stereotyped set of similar events.

restricted communication network Subgroups in a restricted communication network contest each others' positions and restrict interactions with one another.

restructuring Restructuring reduces the scale or mix of operations.

retrenchment strategy A retrenchment strategy changes operations to correct weaknesses.

reverse mentoring In reverse mentoring, younger and newly-hired employees mentor senior executives, often on latest developments with digital technologies.

reward power Reward power achieves influence by offering something of value.

risk environment A risk environment lacks complete information but offers probabilities of the likely outcomes for possible action alternatives.

S

Sarbanes-Oxley Act The Sarbanes-Oxley Act requires that top managers properly oversee the financial conduct of their organizations.

satisficing decision A satisficing decision chooses the first satisfactory alternative that presents itself.

satisfier factor A satisfier factor is found in job content, such as a sense of achievement, recognition, responsibility, advancement, or personal growth.

scenario planning Scenario planning identifies alternative future scenarios and makes plans to deal with each.

scientific management Scientific management emphasizes careful selection and training of workers and supervisory support.

selection Selection is choosing whom to hire from a pool of qualified job applicants.

selective perception Selective perception is the tendency to define problems from one's own point of view.

self-fulfilling prophecy A self-fulfilling prophecy occurs when a person acts in ways that confirm another's expectations.

self-management Self-management is the ability to understand oneself, exercise initiative, accept responsibility, and learn from experience.

self-managing team Members of a self-managing team have the authority to make decisions about how they share and complete their work.

self-monitoring Self-monitoring is the degree to which someone is able to adjust behavior in response to external factors.

self-serving bias Self-serving bias underestimates internal factors and overestimates external factors as influences on someone's behavior.

servant leadership Servant leadership means serving others, and helping them use their talents to help organizations best serve society.

shamrock organization A shamrock organization operates with a core group of full-time long-term workers supported by others who work on contracts and part-time.

shaping Shaping is positive reinforcement of successive approximations to the desired behavior.

shared power strategy A shared power strategy pursues change by participation in assessing change needs, values, and goals.

short-range plans Short-range plans usually cover a year or less.

Six Sigma Six Sigma is a quality standard of 3.4 defects or less per million products or service deliveries.

skunkworks Skunkworks are special creative units set free from the normal structure for the purpose of innovation.

small business A small business has fewer than 500 employees, is independently owned and operated, and does not dominate its industry.

social business A social business is one in which the underlying business model directly addresses a social problem.

social entrepreneur A social entrepreneur takes risks to find new ways to solve pressing social problems.

social entrepreneurship Social entrepreneurship pursues creative and innovative ways to solve pressing social problems.

social loafing Social loafing is the tendency of some people to avoid responsibility by free-riding in groups.

social network analysis Social network analysis identifies the informal structures and their embedded social relationships that are active in an organization.

socialization Socialization systematically influences the expectations, behavior, and attitudes of new employees.

socioeconomic view of CSR The socioeconomic view of CSR is that business should focus on contributions to society and not just making profits.

sole proprietorship A sole proprietorship is an individual pursuing business for a profit.

span of control Span of control is the number of persons directly reporting to a manager.

spotlight questions Spotlight Questions highlight the risks from public disclosure of one's actions.

stakeholders Stakeholders are people and institutions most directly affected by an organization's performance.

stereotype A stereotype assigns attributes commonly associated with a group to an individual.

stock options Stock options give the right to purchase shares at a fixed price in the future.

strategic alliance In a strategic alliance, organizations join together in partnership to pursue an area of mutual interest.

strategic control Strategic control makes sure strategies are well implemented and that poor strategies are scrapped or changed.

strategic human resource management Strategic human resource management mobilizes human capital to implement organizational strategies.

strategic intent Strategic intent focuses organizational energies on achieving a compelling goal.

strategic leadership Strategic leadership inspires people to implement organizational strategies.

strategic management Strategic management is the process of formulating and implementing strategies.

strategic plan A strategic plan identifies long-term directions for the organization.

strategy A strategy is a comprehensive plan guiding resource allocation to achieve long-term organization goals.

strategy formulation Strategy formulation is the process of creating strategies.

strategy implementation Strategy implementation is the process of putting strategies into action.

stress Stress is a state of tension experienced by individuals facing extraordinary demands, constraints, or opportunities.

stretch goals Stretch goals are performance targets that we have to work extra hard and stretch to reach.

strong cultures Strong cultures are clear, well defined, and widely shared among members.

substance goals Substance goals in negotiation focus on outcomes.

substantive conflict Substantive conflict involves disagreements over goals, resources, rewards, policies, procedures, and job assignments.

substitutes for leadership Substitutes for leadership are factors in the work setting that direct work efforts without the involvement of a leader.

subsystem A subsystem is a smaller component of a larger system.

succession plan A succession plan describes how the leadership transition and related financial matters will be handled.

succession problem The succession problem is the issue of who will run the business when the current head leaves.

sustainable development Sustainable development meets the needs of the present without hurting future generations.

sweatshops Sweatshops employ workers at very low wages, for long hours, and in poor working conditions.

SWOT analysis A SWOT analysis examines organizational strengths and weaknesses, and environmental opportunities and threats.

symbolic leader A symbolic leader uses symbols to establish and maintain a desired organizational culture.

synergy Synergy is the creation of a whole greater than the sum of its individual parts.

systematic thinking Systematic thinking approaches problems in a rational and analytical fashion.

T

tariffs Tariffs are taxes governments levy on imports from abroad.

tactical plan A tactical plan or operational plan sets out ways to implement a strategic plan.

task activity A task activity is an action taken by a team member that directly contributes to the group's performance purpose.

task force A task force is a team that is convened for a specific purpose and disbands once it is achieved.

team A team is a collection of people who regularly interact to pursue common goals.

team building Team building is a set of collaborative activities to gather and analyze data on a team and make changes to increase its effectiveness.

team process Team process is the way team members work together to accomplish tasks.

team structure A team structure uses permanent and temporary cross-functional teams to improve lateral relations.

teamwork Teamwork is the process of people actively working together to accomplish common goals.

technical skill A technical skill is the ability to use expertise to perform a task with proficiency.

telecommuting Telecommuting involves using IT to work at home or outside the office.

terminal values Terminal values are preferences about desired end states.

theory X Theory X assumes people dislike work, lack ambition, are irresponsible, and prefer to be led.

theory Y Theory Y assumes people are willing to work, accept responsibility, are self-directed, and are creative.

time orientation Time orientation is the degree to which a society emphasizes short-term or long-term goals.

top managers Top managers guide the performance of the organization as a whole or of one of its major parts.

total quality management Total quality management (TQM) commits to quality objectives, continuous improvement, and doing things right the first time.

total quality management Total quality management is managing with an organization-wide commitment to continuous improvement, product quality, and customer needs.

transactional leadership Transactional leadership directs the efforts of others through tasks, rewards, and structures.

transformational change Transformational change results in a major and comprehensive redirection of the organization.

transformational leadership Transformational leadership is inspirational and arouses extraordinary effort and performance.

transnational corporation A transnational corporation is an MNC that operates worldwide on a borderless basis.

triple bottom line The triple bottom line of organizational performance includes financial, social, and environmental criteria.

two-tier wage systems Two-tier wage systems pay new hires less than workers already doing the same jobs with more seniority.

Type A personality A Type A personality is oriented toward extreme achievement, impatience, and perfectionism.

U

uncertain environment An uncertain environment lacks so much information that it is difficult to assign probabilities to the likely outcomes of alternatives.

uncertainty avoidance Uncertainty avoidance is the degree to which a society tolerates risk and uncertainty.

unfreezing Unfreezing is the phase during which a situation is prepared for change.

universalism Universalism suggests ethical standards apply absolutely across all cultures.

utilitarian view In the utilitarian view ethical behavior delivers the greatest good to the most people.

V

valence Valence is the value a person assigns to work-related outcomes.

validity Validity means scores on a selection device have demonstrated links with future job performance.

value-based management Value-based management actively develops, communicates, and enacts shared values.

values Values are broad beliefs about what is appropriate behavior.

venture capitalists Venture capitalists make large investments in new ventures in return for an equity stake in the business.

vertical integration Growth through vertical integration is by acquiring suppliers or distributors.

virtual organization A virtual organization uses information technologies to operate as a shifting network of alliances.

virtual team Members of a virtual team work together and solve problems through computer-based interactions.

virtuous circle The virtuous circle is when corporate social responsibility leads to improved financial performance that leads to more social responsibility.

vision A vision clarifies the purpose of the organization and expresses what it hopes to be in the future.

visionary leadership Visionary leadership brings to the situation a clear sense of the future and an understanding of how to get there.

W

whistleblowers Whistleblowers expose misconduct of organizations and their members.

win-lose conflict In win-lose conflict one party achieves its desires and the other party does not.

win-win conflict In win-win conflict the conflict is resolved to everyone's benefit.

withdrawal behaviors Withdrawal behaviors include absenteeism—not showing up for work, and turnover—quitting one's job.

work sampling Work sampling evaluates applicants as they perform actual work tasks.

workforce diversity Workforce diversity describes differences among workers in gender, race, age, ethnicity, religion, sexual orientation, and able-bodiedness.

work-life balance Work-life balance involves balancing career demands with personal and family needs.

workplace privacy Workplace privacy is the right to privacy while at work.

workplace rage Workplace rage is aggressive behavior toward co-workers or the work setting.

workplace spirituality Workplace spirituality involves practices that create meaning and shared community among organizational members.

world Trade Organization (WTO) The World Trade Organization (WTO) is a global institution established to promote free trade and open markets around the world.

Z

zero-based budget A zero-based budget allocates resources as if each budget was brand new.

Endnotes

Feature Notes 1

The Container Store/Kip Tindell–The founding story of The Container Store is available at www.Containerstore.com. Quotes also from Justin Fox, "Employees First!" *Time* (July 7, 2008), p. 45: "100 Best Companies to Work For," *Fortune* (March, 2009): www.Cnnmoney.com.

Trendsetters–Information and quotes from William M. Bulkeley, "Xerox Names Burns Chief as Mulcahy Retires Early," *The Wall Street Journal* (May 22, 2009), pp. B1, B2; and Nanette Byrnes and Roger O. Crockett, "An Historic Succession at Xerox," *Business Week* (June 9, 2008), pp. 18–21.

News Feed–Information from Alan Murray, "Another Day at the Office," *The Wall Street Journal* (February 23, 2009), p. A13; and Paul Osterman, *The Truth About Middle Managers: Who They Are, How They Work, Why They Matter* (Boston: Harvard Business School Press, 2009).

Stay Tuned–Information from "In CEO Pay, Another Gender Gap," *Business Week* (November 24, 2008), p. 22; "The View from the Kitchen Table," *Newsweek* (January 26, 2009), p. 29; and Del Jones, "Women Slowly Gain on Men," *USA Today* (January 2, 2009), p. 6B; Catalyst research reports at www.Catalyst.org; "Nicking the Glass Ceiling," Business Week (June 9, 2009), p. 18.

Endnotes 1

1 Information from *Wall Street Journal* (September 21, 2005), p. R4.

2 See examples in Carol Hymowitz, "As Managers Climb, They Have to Learn How to Act the Parts," *Wall Street Journal* (November 14, 2005), p. B1.

3 For a perspective on the first-level manager's job, see Leonard A. Schlesinger and Janice A. Klein, "The First-Line Supervisor: Past, Present and Future," pp. 370–82, in Jay W. Lorsch (ed.), *Handbook of Organizational Behavior* (Englewood Cliffs, NJ: Prentice-Hall, 1987). Research reported in "Remember Us?" *Economist* (February 1, 1992), p. 71.

4 For a discussion, see Marcus Buckingham, "What Great Managers Do," *Harvard Business Review* (March, 2005), Reprint R0503D.

5 Ellen Byron, "P&G's Lafley Sees CEOs as Link to World," *The Wall Street Journal* (March 23, 2009), p. B6; and Stefan Stern, "What Exactly Are Chief Executives For?" *Financial Times* (May 15, 2009).

6 6; and Stern, op cit. (2009).

7 John A. Byrne, "Letter from the Editor," *Fast Company* (April, 2005), p. 14.

8 Carol Hymowitz, "Should CEOs Tell Truth About Being in Trouble, Or Is That Foolhardy?" *Wall Street Journal* (February 15, 2005), p. B1; see also Ben Elgin, "Can Anyone Save HP?" *Business Week* (February 21, 2005), pp. 28–35.

9 Stewart D. Friedman, Perry Christensen, and Jessica De Groot, "Work and Life: The End of the Zero-Sum Game," *Harvard Business Review* (November December 1998), pp. 119–29.

10 Alan M. Webber, "Danger: Toxic Company," *Fast Company* (November 1998), pp. 152+.

11 Mintzberg, op cit. (1973/1997), p. 60.

12 Mintzberg, op cit. (1973/1997), p. 30.

13 See, for example, John R. Veiga and Kathleen Dechant, "Wired World Woes: www.Help," *Academy of Management Executive*, vol. 11 (August 1997), pp. 73–79.

14 For research on managerial work, see Morgan W. McCall, Jr., Ann M. Morrison, and Robert L. Hannan, *Studies of Managerial Work: Results and Methods. Technical Report #9* (Greensboro, NC: Center for Creative Leadership, 1978), pp. 7–9. See also John P. Kotter, "What Effective General Managers Really Do," *Harvard Business Review* (November/December 1982), pp. 156–57.

15 For a classic study, see Thomas A. Mahoney, Thomas H. Jerdee, and Stephen J. Carroll, "The Job(s) of Management," *Industrial Relations*, vol. 4 (February 1965), pp. 97–110.

16 This running example is developed from information from "Accountants Have Lives, Too, You Know," *Business Week* (February 23, 1998), pp. 88–90; Silvia Ann Hewlett and Carolyn Buck Luce, "Off-Ramps and On-Ramps: Keeping Talented Women on the Road to Success," *Harvard Business Review* (March, 2005), reprint R0503B; and the Ernst & Young Web site: www.Ey.com.

17 Information on women and men leaving jobs from Hewlett and Luce, op cit.

18 See Mintzberg, op cit. (1973/1997); and Henry Mintzberg, "Covert Leadership: The Art of Managing Professionals," *Harvard Business Review* (November/December 1998), pp. 140–47; and, Jonathan Gosling and Henry Mintzberg, "The Five Minds of a Manager," *Harvard Business Review* (November 2003), pp. 1–9.

19 See Mintzberg, op cit. (1973/1997); and Henry Mintzberg, "Covert Leadership: The Art of Managing Professionals," *Harvard Business Review* (November/December 1998), pp. 140–47; and, Jonathan Gosling and Henry Mintzberg, "The Five Minds of a Manager," *Harvard Business Review* (November 2003), pp. 1–9.

20 This incident is taken from John P. Kotter, "What Effective General Managers Really Do," *Harvard Business Review* (November/December 1982), pp. 156–57.

21 Ibid.

22 Robert L. Katz, "Skills of an Effective Administrator," *Harvard Business Review* (September/October 1974), p. 94.

23 See Daniel Goleman's books *Emotional Intelligence* (New York: Bantam, 1995) and *Working with Emotional Intelligence* (New York: Bantam, 1998); and his articles "What Makes a Leader," *Harvard Business Review* (November/December 1998), pp. 93–102, and "Leadership That Makes a Difference," *Harvard Business Review* (March/April 2000), pp. 79–90, quote from p. 80.

24 Quote from "Insuring Success for the Road," *BizEd* (March/April 2005), p. 19.

25 Henry Mintzberg, "The Manager's Job: Folklore and Fact," *Harvard Business Review*, vol. 53 (July/August 1975), p. 61. See also his book *The Nature of Managerial Work* (New York: Harper & Row, 1973, and HarperCollins, 1997).

26 Kenichi Ohmae's books include *The Borderless World: Power and Strategy in the Interlinked Economy* (New York: Harper, 1989); *The End of the Nation State* (New York: Free Press, 1996); *The Invisible Continent: Four Strategic Imperatives of the New Economy* (New York: Harper, 1999), and *The Next Global Stage: Challenges and Opportunities in Our Borderless World* (Upper Saddle River, N.J.: Wharton School Publishing, 2005).

27 This example is from Friedman, op cit., pp. 208–09.

28 For a discussion of globalization, see Thomas L. Friedman, *The Lexus and the Olive Tree: Understanding Globalization* (New York: Bantam Doubleday Dell, 2000); John Micklethwait and Adrian Woolridge, *A Future Perfect: The Challenges and Hidden Promise of Globalization* (New York: Crown, 2000); and Alfred E. Eckes Jr. and Thomas W. Zeiler, *Globalization and the American Century* (Cambridge, UK: Cambridge University Press, 2003).

29 Christy Lilly, "Rocky Boots CEO Explains Outsourcing," *Connections* (Ohio University College of Business, 2005), p. 6.

30 New for Madoff.

31 Portions adapted from John W. Dienhart and Terry Thomas, "Ethical Leadership: A Primer on Ethical Responsibility in Management," in John R. Schermerhorn, Jr., (ed.), *Management*, 7th ed. (New York: Wiley, 2002).

[32] Daniel Akst, "Room at the Top for Improvement," *The Wall Street Journal* (October 26, 2004), p. D8; and, Herb Baum and Tammy King, *The Transparent Leader* (New York: Collins, 2005).

[33] See Judith Burns, "Everything You Wanted to Know About Corporate Governance . . . But Didn't Know How to Ask," *Wall Street Journal* (October 27, 2003), pp. R1, R7.

[34] *Workforce 2000: Work and Workers for the 21st Century* (Indianapolis: Towers Perrin/Hudson Institute, 1987); Richard W. Judy and Carol D' Amico (eds.), *Work and Workers for the 21st Century* (Indianapolis: Hudson Institute, 1997); See Richard D. Bucher, *Diversity Consciousness: Opening Our Minds to People, Cultures, and Opportunities* (Upper Saddle River, NJ: Prentice-Hall, 2000); R. Roosevelt Thomas, "From Affirmative Action to Affirming Diversity," *Harvard Business Review* (March-April 1990), pp. 107–17; and *Beyond Race and Gender: Unleashing the Power of Your Total Workforce by Managing Diversity* (New York: AMACOM, 1992).

[35] June Dronholz, "Hispanics Gain in Census," *The Wall Street Journal* (May 10, 2006), p. A6; Phillip Toledano, "Demographics: The Population Hourglass," *Fast Company* (March, 2006), p. 56; June Kronholz, "Racial Identity's Gray Area," *The Wall Street Journal* (June 12, 2008), p. A10; "We're Getting Old," *The Wall Street Journal* (March 26, 2009), p. D2; Les Christie, "Hispanic Population Boom Fuels Rising U.S. Diversity," *CnnMoney:* www.cnn.com; and, Betsy Towner, "The New Face of 50+ America," *AARP Bulletin* (June, 2009), p. 31.

[36] Information from "Racism in Hiring Remains, Study Says," *Columbus Dispatch* (January 17, 2003), p. B2.

[37] For discussions of the glass ceiling effect, see Ann M. Morrison, Randall P. White, and Ellen Van Velso, *Breaking the Glass Ceiling* (Reading, MA: Addison-Wesley, 1987); Anne E. Weiss, *The Glass Ceiling: A Look at Women in the Workforce* (New York: Twenty First Century, 1999); and Debra E. Meyerson and Joyce K. Fletcher, "A Modest Manifesto for Shattering the Glass Ceiling," *Harvard Business Review* (January/February 2000).

[38] For background, see Taylor Cox, Jr., "The Multicultural Organization," *Academy of Management Executive*, vol. 5 (1991), pp. 34–47; and *Cultural Diversity in Organizations: Theory, Research and Practice* (San Francisco: Berrett-Koehler, 1993).

[39] See "Women Come on Board," *BusinessWeek* (June 15, 2009), p. 24.

[40] Survey data reported in Sue Shellenbarger, "New Workplact Equalizer: Ambition," *The Wall Street Journal* (March 26, 2009), p. D5.

[41] Judith B. Rosener, "Women Make Good Managers, So What?" *Business Week* (December 11, 2000), p. 24.

[42] *Business Week* (August 8, 1990), p. 50.

[43] Thomas, op cit.

[44] Charles O'Reilly III and Jeffrey Pfeffer, *Hidden Value: How Great Companies Achieve Extraordinary Results with Ordinary People* (Boston: Harvard Business School Press, 2000), p. 2.

[45] See Thomas A. Stewart, *Intellectual Capital: The Wealth of Organizations* (New York: Bantam, 1998).

[46] Dave Ulrich, "Intellectual Capital = Competency × Commitment," *Harvard Business Review* (Winter, 1998), pp. 15–26.

[47] Max DePree's books include *Leadership Is an Art* (New York: Dell, 1990) and *Leadership Jazz* (New York: Dell, 1993). See also Herman Miller's home page at www.Hermanmiller.com.

[48] See Peter F. Drucker, *The Changing World of the Executive* (New York: T.T. Times Books, 1982), and *The Profession of Management* (Cambridge, MA: Harvard Business School Press, 1997); and Francis Horibe, *Managing Knowledge Workers: New Skills and Attitudes to Unlock the Intellectual Capital in Your Organization* (New York: Wiley, 1999).

[49] Daniel Pink, *A Whole New Mind: Moving from the Information Age to the Conceptual Age* (New York: Riverhead Books, 2005).

[50] See Tom Peters, "The Brand Called You," *Fast Company* (August/September 1997), p. 83.

[51] Charles Handy, *The Age of Unreason* (Cambridge, MA: Harvard Business School Press, 1990). See also Michael S. Malone, *The Future Arrived Yesterday: The Rise of the Protean Organization and What It Means for You* (New York: Crown Books, 2009).

[52] See Gareille Monaghan, "Don't Get a Job, Get a Portfolio Career," *The Sunday Times* (April 26, 2009), p. 15.

[53] Peters, op. cit.

[54] Developed from Peters, op cit. (2000).

[55] Originally developed from *Outcome Measurement Project*, Phase I and Phase II Reports (St. Louis: American Assembly of Collegiate Schools of Business, 1986 and 1987).

Feature Notes 2

Life is Good–Information from Leigh Buchanan, "Life Lessons," *Inc.* (June 6, 2006): retrieved from www.inc.com/magazine; "A fortune coined from cheerfulness Entrepreneurship," *Financial Times* (May 20, 2009); and www.lifeisgood.com/about.

Trendsetters–Information from Miguel Helft, "Yahoo's New Chief Makes Decisive Appearance," *The New York Times* (January 16, 2009): www.nytimes.com; and Jessica E. Vascellaro, "Yahoo CEO Set to Install Top-Down Management," *The Wall Street Journal* (February 23, 2009), p. B1; and "A Question of Management," *The Wall Street Journal* (June 2, 2009), p. R4.

News Feed–Information from Catherine Arnst, "10,000 Hours to Greatness," *Business Week* (December 1, 2008), p. 110; and Malcolm Gladwell, *Outliers* (New York: Little, Brown, 2009).

Stay Tuned–Information from "Survey Shows Impact of Downturn on Job Satisfaction," *OH&S: Occupational Health & Safety* (February 7, 2009): www.ohsonline.com/Articles.

Endnotes 2

[1] A thorough review and critique of the history of management thought, including management in ancient civilizations, is provided by Daniel A. Wren, *The Evolution of Management Thought*, 4th ed. (New York: Wiley, 1993).

[2] For a timeline of 20th-century management ideas, see "75 Years of Management Ideas and Practices: 1922–1997," *Harvard Business Review*, supplement (September/October 1997).

[3] For a sample of this work, see Henry L. Gantt, *Industrial Leadership* (Easton, MD: Hive, 1921; Hive edition published in 1974); Henry C. Metcalfe and Lyndall Urwick (eds.), *Dynamic Administration: The Collected Papers of Mary Parker Follett* (New York: Harper & Brothers, 1940); James D. Mooney, *The Principles of Administration*, rev. ed. (New York: Harper & Brothers, 1947); Lyndall Urwick, *The Elements of Administration* (New York: Harper & Brothers, 1943) and *The Golden Book of Management* (London: N. Neame, 1956).

[4] References on Taylor's work are from Frederick W. Taylor, *The Principles of Scientific Management* (New York: W. W. Norton, 1967), originally published by Harper & Brothers in 1911. See Charles W. Wrege and Amedeo G. Perroni, "Taylor's Pig-Tale: A Historical Analysis of Frederick W. Taylor's Pig Iron Experiments," *Academy of Management Journal*, vol. 17 (March 1974), pp. 6–27, for a criticism; see Edwin A. Lock, "The Ideas of Frederick W. Taylor: An Evaluation," *Academy of Management Review*, vol. 7 (1982), p. 14, for an examination of the contemporary significance of Taylor's work. See also the biography, Robert Kanigel, *The One Best Way* (New York: Viking, 1997).

[5] Kanigel, op. cit.

[6] A. M. Henderson and Talcott Parsons (eds. and trans.), *Max Weber: The Theory of Social Economic Organization* (New York: Free Press, 1947).

[7] Ibid., p. 337.

[8] Available in the English language as Henri Fayol, *General and Industrial Administration* (London: Pitman, 1949); subsequent discussion relies on M. B. Brodie, *Fayol on Administration* (London: Pitman, 1949).

[9] M. P. Follett, *Freedom and Coordination* (London: Management Publications Trust, 1949).

[10] Pauline Graham, *Mary Parker Follett—Prophet of Management: A Celebration of Writings from the 1920s* (Boston: Harvard Business School Press, 1995).

[11] Information from "Honesty Top Trait for Chair," *Columbus Dispatch* (January 15, 2003), p. G1.

[12] Peter F. Drucker, "Looking Ahead: Implications of the Present," *Harvard Business Review* (September/October, 1997), pp. 18–32.

[13] The Hawthorne studies are described in detail in F. J. Roethlisberger and William J. Dickson, *Management and the Worker* (Cambridge,

MA: Harvard University Press, 1966); and G. Homans, *Fatigue of Workers* (New York: Reinhold, 1941). For an interview with three of the participants in the relay-assembly test-room studies, see R. G. Greenwood, A. A. Bolton, and R. A. Greenwood, "Hawthorne a Half Century Later: 'Relay Assembly Participants Remember,'" *Journal of Management*, vol. 9 (1983), pp. 217–31.

[14] The criticisms of the Hawthorne studies are detailed in Alex Carey, "The Hawthorne Studies: A Radical Criticism," *American Sociological Review*, vol. 32 (1967), pp. 403–16; H. M. Parsons, "What Happened at Hawthorne?" *Science*, vol. 183 (1974), pp. 922–32; and B. Rice, "The Hawthorne Defect: Persistence of a Flawed Theory," *Psychology Today*, vol. 16 (1982), pp. 70–74. See also Wren, op. cit.

[15] This discussion of Maslow's theory is based on Abraham H. Maslow, *Eupsychian Management* (Homewood, IL: Richard D. Irwin, 1965); and Abraham H. Maslow, *Motivation and Personality*, 2nd ed. (New York: Harper & Row, 1970).

[16] Douglas McGregor, *The Human Side of Enterprise* (New York: McGraw-Hill, 1960).

[17] See Gary Heil, Deborah F. Stevens, and Warren G. Bennis, *Douglas McGregor on Management: Revisiting the Human Side of Enterprise* (New York: Wiley, 2000).

[18] Chris Argyris, *Personality and Organization* (New York: Harper & Row, 1957).

[19] Information on attitude survey in the federal bureaucracy from David E. Rosenbaum, "Study Ranks Homeland Security Dept. Lowest in Morale," *New York Times* (October 16, 2005), p. 17.

[20] Scott Morrison, "Google Searches for Staffing Answers," *The Wall Street Journal* (May 19, 2009), p. B1.

[21] The ideas of Ludwig von Bertalanffy contributed to the emergence of this systems perspective on organizations. See his article, "The History and Status of General Systems Theory," *Academy of Management Journal*, vol. 15 (1972), pp. 407–26. This viewpoint is further developed by Daniel Katz and Robert L. Kahn in their classic book, *The Social Psychology of Organizations* (New York: Wiley, 1978). For an integrated systems view, see Lane Tracy, *The Living Organization* (New York: Quorum Books, 1994). For an overview, see W. Richard Scott, *Organizations: Rational, Natural, and Open Systems*, 4th ed. (Upper Saddle River, NJ: Prentice-Hall, 1998).

[22] See discussion by Scott, op. cit., pp. 66–68.

[23] For an overview, see Scott, op. cit., pp. 95–97.

[24] W. Edwards Deming, *Quality, Productivity, and Competitive Position* (Cambridge, MA: MIT Press, 1982); and, Rafael Aguay, *Dr. Deming: The American Who Taught the Japanese about Quality* (New York: Free Press, 1997).

[25] See Howard S. Gitlow and Shelly J. Gitlow, *The Deming Guide to Quality and Competitive Position* (Englewood Cliffs, NJ: Prentice-Hall, 1987).

[26] See Joseph M. Juran, *Quality Control Handbook*, 3rd ed. (New York: McGraw-Hill, 1979) and "The Quality Trilogy: A Universal Approach to Managing for Quality," in *Total Quality Management*, ed. H. Costin (New York: Dryden, 1994).

[27] Stephen Miller, "Joseph M. Juran: 1904–2008," *The Wall Street Journal* (March 8–9, 2008), p. A7.

[28] See Edward E. Lawler III, Susan Albers Mohrman, and Gerald E. Ledford Jr., *Employee Involvement and Total Quality Management: Practices and Results in Fortune 1000 Companies* (San Francisco: Jossey-Bass, 1992).

[29] See, for example, Thomas H. Davenport and Laurence Prusak, *Working Knowledge: How Organizations Manage What They Know* (Cambridge, MA: Harvard Business School Press, 1997).

[30] Peter Senge, *The Fifth Discipline* (New York: Harper, 1990).

[31] Thomas J. Peters and Robert H. Waterman Jr., *In Search of Excellence: Lessons from America's Best-Run Companies* (New York: Harper-Row, 1982).

[32] For a retrospective on *In Search of Excellence*, see William C. Bogner, "Tom Peters on the Real World of Business" and "Robert Waterman on Being Smart and Lucky," *Academy of Management Executive*, vol. 16 (2002), pp. 40–50.

[33] See Jim Collins and Jerry I. Porras, *Built to Last* (New York: Harper-Collins, 1994); and Jim Collins, *Good to Great* (New York: HarperCollins,

2001). For recent research critical of Collins work, see Bruce G. Resnick and Timothy L. Smunt, "From Good to Great to . . .", *Academy of Management Perspectives* (November, 2008), pp. 6–12; and "Bruce Niendorf and Kristine Beck, "Good to Great, or Just Good?" *Academy of Management Perspectives* (November, 2008), pp. 13-20.

[34] Jeffrey Pfeffer and Robert I. Sutton, *Hard Facts, Dangerous Half-Truths, and Total Nonsense: Profiting from Evidence-Based Management* (Boston: Harvard Business School Press, 2006); Jeffrey Pfeffer and Robert I. Sutton, "Management Half-Truths and Nonsense," *California Management Review*, Vol 48(3), 2006: 77–100; and Jeffrey Pfeffer and Robert I. Sutton, "Evidence-Based Management," *Harvard Business Review* (January, 2006), R0601E.

[35] Jeffrey Pfeffer, The *Human Equation: Building Profits by Putting People First* (Boston: Harvard Business School Press, 1998); and Z. Charles O'Reilly III and Jeffrey Pfeffer, *Hidden Value: How Great Companies Achieve Extraordinary Results with Ordinary People* (Boston: Harvard Business School Press, 2000).

[36] Denise M. Rousseau, "On Organizational Behavior," *BizEd* (May/June, 2008), pp. 30–31.

Feature Notes 3

Grameen Bank/Muhammad Yunus–Information from Jeffrey D. Sachs, *The End of Poverty* (New York: Penguin, 2005); Muhammad Yunus, *Creating a World Without Poverty: Social Business and the Future of Capitalism* (New York: Public Affairs, 2008); "Executive MBA Students Learn About Micro-Lending from Its Founder, Nobel Laureate Muhammad Yunus," *Stern Business* (Spring/Summer, 2008), p. 41; New Steve Hamm, "When the Bottom Line is Ending Poverty," *Business Week* (March 10, 2008), p. 85; Yunus, op. cit.; Daniel Pimlott, "Bangladeshi's Aid for US Poor," *Financial Times* (February 16/17, 2008), p. 4; and Simon Hobbs, "Big Payback," *CNBC European Business* (January/February, 2009), pp. 36–38.

Trendsetters–Information from "Chapter 2," *Kellogg* (Winter, 2004), p. 6; See also *Leaving Microsoft to Change the World* (New York: Harper Collins), 2006.

News Feed–Information and quotes from "Can Business Be Cool?" *The Economist* (June 10, 2006), pp. 59–60; Aubrey Henretty, "A Brighter Day," *Kellogg* (Summer, 2006), pp. 32–34. Quotes from Henretty, op. cit., and Joseph Stiglitz, *Making Globalization Work* (New York: Norton, 2006), p. 172; Jim Phillips, "Business Leaders Say 'Green' Approach Doable," *The Athens News* (March 27, 2008): www.athensnews.com; "The Bottom Line on Business and the Environment," *The Wall Street Journal* (February 12, 2009), p. A7; and Alan G. Robinson and Dean M. Schroeder, "Greener and Cheaper," *The Wall Street Journal* (March 23, 2009), p. R4.

Stay Tuned–Information from Deloitte LLP, "Leadership Counts: 2007 Deloitte & Touche USA Ethics & Workplace Survey Results," *Kiplinger Business Resource Center* (June, 2007): www.kiplinger.com.

Endnotes 3

[1] See the discussion by Terry Thomas, John W. Dienhart, and John R. Schermerhorn Jr., "Leading Toward Ethical Behavior in Business," *Academy of Management Executive*, vol. 18 (May 2004), pp. 56–66.

[2] See the discussion by Lynn Sharpe Paine, "Managing for Organizational Integrity," *Harvard Business Review* (March/April 1994), pp. 106–17.

[3] Desmond Tutu, "Do More Than Win," *Fortune* (December 30, 1991), p. 59.

[4] Ibid.

[5] For an overview, see Linda K. Trevino and Katherine A. Nelson, *Managing Business Ethics*, 3rd ed. (New York: Wiley, 2003).

[6] Information from Sue Shellenbarger, "How and Why We Lie at the Office: From Pilfered Pens to Padded Accounts," *Wall Street Journal* (March 24, 2005), p. D1.

[7] Milton Rokeach, *The Nature of Human Values* (New York: Free Press, 1973). See also W. C. Frederick and J. Weber, "The Values of Corporate Executives and Their Critics: An Empirical Description and Normative Implications," in W. C. Frederick and L. E. Preston (eds.), *Business Ethics: Research Issues and Empirical Studies* (Greenwich, CT: JAI Press, 1990).

[8] Case reported in Michelle Conlin, "Cheating—Or Postmodern Learning?" *Business Week* (May 14, 2007), p. 42.

[9] See Gerald F. Cavanagh, Dennis J. Moberg, and Manuel Velasquez, "The Ethics of Organizational Politics," *Academy of Management Review*, vol. 6 (1981), pp. 363–74; Justin G. Locknecker, Joseph A. McKinney, and Carlos W. Moore, "Egoism and Independence: Entrepreneurial Ethics," *Organizational Dynamics* (Winter 1988), pp. 64–72; and Justin G. Locknecker, Joseph A. McKinney, and Carlos W. Moore, "The Generation Gap in Business Ethics," *Business Horizons* (September/October 1989), pp. 9–14.

[10] Raymond L. Hilgert, "What Ever Happened to Ethics in Business and in Business Schools?". *The Diary of Alpha Kappa Psi* (April 1989), pp. 4–8.

[11] Jerald Greenburg, "Organizational Justice: Yesterday, Today, and Tomorrow," *Journal of Management*, vol. 16 (1990), pp. 399–432; and Mary A. Konovsky, "Understanding Procedural Justice and Its Impact on Business Organizations," *Journal of Management*, vol. 26 (2000), pp. 489–511.

[12] Interactional justice is described by Robert J. Bies, "The Predicament of Injustice: The Management of Moral Outrage," in L. L. Cummings & B. M. Staw (eds.), *Research in Organizational Behavior*, vol. 9 (Greenwich, CT: JAI Press, 1987), pp. 289–319. The example is from Carol T. Kulik & Robert L. Holbrook, "Demographics in Service Encounters: Effects of Racial and Gender Congruence on Perceived Fairness," *Social Justice Research*, vol. 13 (2000), pp. 375–402.

[13] The United Nations' Universal Declaration of Human Rights is available online at: http://www.un.org/Overview/rights.html.

[14] Robert D. Haas, "Ethics—A Global Business Challenge," *Vital Speeches of the Day* (June 1, 1996), pp. 506–9.

[15] This discussion based on Thomas Donaldson, "Values in Tension: Ethics Away from Home," *Harvard Business Review*, vol. 74 (September/October 1996), pp. 48–62.

[16] Ibid; Thomas Donaldson and Thomas W. Dunfee, "Towards a Unified Conception of Business Ethics: Integrative Social Contracts Theory," *Academy of Management Review*, vol. 19 (1994), pp. 252–85.

[17] Developed from Donaldson, op. cit.

[18] Reported in Barbara Ley Toffler, "Tough Choices: Managers Talk Ethics," *New Management*, vol. 4 (1987), pp. 34–39. See also Barbara Ley Toffler, *Tough Choices: Managers Talk Ethics* (New York: Wiley, 1986).

[19] See discussion by Trevino and Nelson, op. cit., pp. 47–62.

[20] Information from Steven N. Brenner and Earl A. Mollander, "Is the Ethics of Business Changing?" *Harvard Business Review*, vol. 55 (January/February 1977).

[21] Deloitte LLP, "Leadership Counts: 2007 Deloitte & Touche USA Ethics & Workplace Survey Results," *Kiplinger Business Resource Center* (June, 2007): www.kiplinger.com.

[22] "Who's to Blame: Washington or Wall Street?" *Newsweek* (March 30, 2009): www.newsweek.com.

[23] This research is summarized by Archie Carroll, "Pressure May Force Ethical Hand," *BGS International Exchange* (Fall 2004), p. 5.

[24] Ibid.

[25] Ibid.

[26] Saul W. Gellerman, "Why 'Good' Managers Make Bad Ethical Choices," *Harvard Business Review*, vol. 64 (July/August, 1986), pp. 85–90.

[27] Survey results from Del Jones, "48% of Workers Admit to Unethical or Illegal Acts," *USA Today* (April 4, 1997), p. A1.

[28] Lawrence Kohlberg, *The Psychology of Moral Development: The Nature and Validity of Moral Stages (Essays in Moral Development, Volume 2)* (New York: Harper Collins, 1984). See also the discussion by Linda K. Trevino, "Moral Reasoning and Business Ethics: Implications for Research, Education, and Management, *Journal of Business Ethics*, Vol. 11 (1992), pp. 445–59.

[29] See, for example, David Bielo, "MBA Programs for Social and Environmental Stewardship," *Business Ethics* (Fall 2005), pp. 22–28.

[30] Alan L. Otten, "Ethics on the Job: Companies Alert Employees to Potential Dilemmas," *Wall Street Journal* (July 14, 1986), p. 17; and "The Business Ethics Debate," *Newsweek* (May 25, 1987), p. 36.

[31] See the Josephson model for ethical decision making: www.josephsoninstitute.org.

[32] Examples from "Whistle-Blowers on Trial," *Business Week* (March 24, 1997), pp. 172–78; and "NLRB Judge Rules for Massachusetts Nurses in Whistle-Blowing Case," *American Nurse* (January/February 1998), p. 7. For a review of whistleblowing, see Marcia P. Micelli and Janet P. Near, *Blowing the Whistle* (Lexington, MA: Lexington Books, 1992; Micelli and Near, "Whistleblowing: Reaping the Benefits," *Academy of Management Executive*, vol. 8 (August 1994), pp. 65–72; and, Cynthia Cooper, *Extraordinary Circumstances* (Hoboken, NJ: John Wiley & Sons, 2009).

[33] Information from Ethics Resource Center, "Major Survey of America's Workers Finds Substantial Improvements in Ethics": www.ethics.org/releas es/nr_20030521_nbes.html.

[34] Information from James A. Waters, "Catch 20.5: Mortality as an Organizational Phenomenon," *Organizational Dynamics*, vol. 6 (Spring 1978), pp. 3–15.

[35] Information from "Gifts of Gab: A Start-up's Social Conscience Pays Off," *Business Week* (February 5, 2001), p. F38.

[36] Developed from recommendations of the Government Accountability Project reported in "Blowing the Whistle without Paying the Piper."

[37] Archie B. Carroll, "In Search of the Moral Manager," *Business Horizons* (March/April, 2001), pp. 7–15.

[38] Kohlberg, op. cit.

[39] See Marc Gunther, "Can Factory Monitoring Ever Really Work?" *Business Ethics* (Fall 2005), p. 12.

[40] Information from corporate Web site: www.gapinc.com/communitysourcing/vendor_conduct.htm.

[41] Information from corporate website: www.gapinc.com/community sourcing/vendor_conduct.htm.

[42] See David Vogel, *The Market for Virtue: The Potential and Limits of Corporate Social Responsibility* (Washington, D.C.: Brookings Institution Press, 2006); and, Thomas et al., op. cit.

[43] Nanett Byrnes, "Heavy Lifting at the Food Bank," *Business Week* (December 17, 2007), pp. SC08–SC09; and Michael E. Porter and Mark R. Kramer, "Strategy & Society: The Link Between Competitive Advantage and Corporate Social Responsibility," *Harvard Business Review* (December, 2006), Reprint R0612D.

[44] Ken Stammen, "Firm Takes Day Off to Give Back to Community," *The Columbus Dispatch* (October 9, 2004), p. E1.

[45] Examples from "Teaching Notes: From IBM Science and Math Teachers," *Business Week* (October 3, 2005); "Googling for Charity," *Business Week Online* (October 28, 2005); "100 Best Corporate Citizens for 2004," www.business-ethics.com (retrieved November 1, 2005).

[46] Information from "The Socially Correct Corporate," *Fortune*, special advertising section (July 24, 2000), pp. S32–S34; Joseph Pereiva, "Doing Good and Doing Well at Timberland," *Wall Street Journal* (September 9, 2003), pp. B1, B10.

[47] The "compliance—conviction" distinction is attributed to Mark Goyder in Martin Waller, "Much Corporate Responsibility Is Box-Ticking," *The Times Business* (July 8, 2003), p. 21.

[48] "University Doesn't Let Up on Being Green for Graduation," *The Columbus Dispatch* (Mary 24, 2009), p. A9.

[49] The historical framework of this discussion is developed from Keith Davis, "The Case For and Against Business Assumption of Social Responsibility," *Academy of Management Journal* (June 1973), pp. 312–22; Keith Davis and William Frederick, *Business and Society: Management: Public Policy, Ethics*, 5th ed. (New York: McGraw-Hill, 1984). This debate is discussed by Joel Makower in *Putting Social Responsibility to Work for Your Business and the World* (New York: Simon & Schuster, 1994), pp. 28–33. See also "Civics 101," *Economist* (May 11, 1996), p. 61.

[50] The Friedman quotation is from Milton Friedman, *Capitalism and Freedom* (Chicago: University of Chicago Press, 1962); the Samuelson quotation is from Paul A. Samuelson, "Love That Corporation," *Mountain Bell Magazine* (Spring 1971). Both are cited in Davis, op. cit.

[51] See James K. Glassman, "When Ethics Meet Earnings," *International Herald Tribune* (May 24–25, 2003), p. 15; Simon Zaydek, "The

Path to Corporate Social Responsibility," *Harvard Business Review* (December 2004), pp. 125–32.

⁵² See Makower, op. cit. (1994), pp. 71–75; and Sandra A. Waddock and Samuel B. Graves, "The Corporate Social Performance–Financial Performance Link," *Strategic Management Journal* (1997), pp. 303–19; and, Vogel, op. cit. (2006).

⁵³ See Alan G. Robinson and Dean M. Schroeder, "Greener and Cheaper," *The Wall Street Journal* (March 23, 2009), p. R4.

⁵⁴ Chip Fleiss, "Social Enterprise—the Fiegling Fourth Sector Soapbox," *Financial Times* (June 15, 2009).

⁵⁵ David Bornstein, *How to Change the World—Social Entrepreneurs and the Power of New Ideas* (Oxford, UK: Oxford University Press, 2004).

⁵⁶ See Laura D' Andrea Tyson, "Good Works—With a Business Plan," *Business Week* (May 3, 2004), retrieved from Business Week Online (November 14, 2005) at www.Businessweek.com.

⁵⁷ Judith Burns, "Everything You Wanted to Know About Corporate Governance . . . But Didn't Know to Ask," *Wall Street Journal* (October 27, 2003), p. R6.

⁵⁸ "Warming to Corporate Reform," *Wall Street Journal* (October 25, 2005), p. R2.

⁵⁹ Adapted from James Weber, "Management Value Orientations: A Typology and Assessment," *International Journal of Value Based Management,* vol. 3, no. 2 (1990), pp. 37–54.

Feature Notes 4

Monster.com – See Bridget Carey, "Old Resume Just the Start These Days," *The Columbus Dispatch* (March 16, 2008), p. D3; Joseph De Avila, "CEO Reorganizes Job-Search Pioneer, *The Wall Street Journal* (May 12, 2008), p. B1; Sarah E. Needleman, "Recruiters Use Search Engiines to Lure Job Hunters," *The Wall Street Journal* (March 9, 2009), p. B4; and www.monster.com.

Trendsetters–Information from Kate Klonick, "Pepsi's CEO a Refreshing Change" (August 15, 2006): www.abcnews.com; Diane Brady, "Indra Nooyi: Keeping Cool in Hot Water," *Business Week* (June 11, 2007), special report; Indra Nooyi, "The Best Advice I Ever Got," CNNMoney (April 30, 2008), www.Cnnnmoney.com; and "Indra Nooyi," *The Wall Street Journal* (November 10, 2008), p. R3.

News Feed–Information and quotes from Craig Karmin, "Shareholders Push to Regulate Executive Pay," *The Wall Street Journal* (February 13, 2009), p. C1; "N.Y. Subpoenas Thain Over Merrill Bonuses," *The Charlotte Observer* (January 27, 2009): www.Investing.businessweek.com; Joann S. Lublin, Phred Dvorak, and Cari Tuna, "Motorola Co-CEO Tops Pay Survey," *The Wall Street Journal* (April 3, 2009), pp. B1, B4; Joann S. Lublin, "CEO Pay Sinks Along with Profits," *The Wall Street Journal* (April 3, 2009), p. A1.

Stay Tuned–Information from "Six Products, Six Carbon Footprints," *The Wall Street Journal* (October 6, 2008), p. R3. Data reported are 2006 figures.

Tips to Remember–Developed from Anna Muoio, "Where There's Smoke It Helps to Have a Smoke Jumper," *Fast Company*, vol. 33, p. 290.

Endnotes 4

¹ Paul Ingrassia, "How GM Lost Its Way," *The Wall Street Journal* (June 2, 2009), p. A21. See also Paul Ingrassia, *Crash Course: The American Automobile Industry's Road from Glory to Ruin* (New York: Random House, 2010).

² Peter F. Drucker, "Looking Ahead: Implications of the Present," *Harvard Business Review* (September/October 1997), pp. 18–32. See also Shaker A. Zahra, "An Interview with Peter Drucker," *Academy of Management Executive*, vol. 17 (August 2003), pp. 9–12.

³ Henry Mintzberg, *The Nature of Managerial Work* (New York: HarperCollins, 1997).

⁴ "Why Drucker Still Matters," *Business Week* (November 28, 2005), p. 100.

⁵ For a good discussion, see Watson H. Agor, *Intuition in Organizations: Leading and Managing Productively* (Newbury Park, CA: Sage, 1989); Herbert A. Simon, "Making Management Decisions: The Role of Intuition and Emotion," *Academy of Management Executive*, vol. 1

(1987), pp. 57–64; Orlando Behling and Norman L. Eckel, "Making Sense Out of Intuition," *Academy of Management Executive,* vol. 1 (1987), pp. 57–64; Orlando Behling and Norman L. Eckel, "Making Sense Out of Intuition," *Academy of Management Executive,* vol. 5 (1991), pp. 46–54.

⁶ Alan Deutschman, "Inside the Mind of Jeff Bezos," *Fast Company,* Issue 85 (August, 2004); www.fastcompany.com.

⁷ Quote from Susan Carey, "Pilot 'in shock' as He Landed Jet in River," *The Wall Street Journal* (February 9, 2009), p. A6.

⁸ Based on Carl Jung's typology, as described in Donald Bowen, "Learning and Problem-Solving: You're Never Too Jung," in Donald D. Bowen, Roy J. Lewicki, Donald T. Hall, and Francine S. Hall, eds., *Experiences in Management and Organizational Behavior,* 4th ed. (New York: Wiley, 1997), pp. 7–13; and John W. Slocum Jr., "Cognitive Style in Learning and Problem Solving," ibid., pp. 349–53.

⁹ See Hugh Courtney, Jane Kirkland, and Patrick Viguerie, "Strategy Under Uncertainty," *Harvard Business Review* (November/December 1997), pp. 67–79.

¹⁰ See George P. Huber, *Managerial Decision Making* (Glenview, IL: Scott, Foresman 1975). For a comparison, see the steps in Xerox's problem-solving process, as described in David A. Garvin, "Building a Learning Organization," *Harvard Business Review* (July/August 1993), pp. 78–91, and the Josephson model for ethical decision making described at www.josephsoninstitute.org/MED/MED-4sevensteppath.htm.

¹¹ Joseph B. White and Lee Hawkins Jr., "GM Cuts Deeper in North America," *Wall Street Journal* (November 22, 2005), p. A3. See also Rick Wagoner, "A Portrait of My Industry," *Wall Street Journal* (December 6, 2005), p. A20.

¹² For a sample of Simon's work, see Herbert A. Simon, *Administrative Behavior* (New York: Free Press, 1947); James G. March and Herbert A. Simon, *Organizations* (New York: Wiley, 1958); Herbert A. Simon, *The New Science of Management Decision* (New York: Harper, 1960).

¹³ This figure and the related discussion is developed from conversations with Dr. Alma Acevedo of the University of Puerto Rico at Rio Piedras, and her articles "Of Fallacies and Curricula: A Case of Business Ethics," *Teaching Business Ethics,* Vol. 5 (2001), pp. 157–170; and, "Business Ethics: An Introduction," working paper (2009).

¹⁴ Based on Gerald F. Cavanagh, American Business Values, 4th ed. (Upper Saddle River, NJ: Prentice-Hall, 1998).

¹⁵ The third spotlight question is based on the Josephson model for ethical decision making: www.josephsoninstitute.org/MED/MED-4sevensteppath.htm.

¹⁶ Information from "Lonnie Johnson," *USAA Magazine* (Fall, 2007), p. 38; and www.johnsonrd.com.

¹⁷ See, for example, Roger von Oech, *A Whack on the Side of the Head* (New York: Warner Books, 1983) and *A Kick in the Seat of the Pants* (New York: Harper & Row, 1986).

¹⁸ Teresa M. Amabile, "Motivating Creativity in Organizations," *California Management Review,* vol. 40 (Fall, 1997), pp. 39–58.

¹⁹ Developed from discussions by Edward DeBono, *Lateral Thinking: Creativity Step-by-Step* (New York: Harper-Collins, 1970); John S. Dacey and Kathleen H. Lennon, *Understanding Creativity* (San Francisco: Jossey-Bass, 1998); and Bettina von Stamm, *Managing Innovation, Design & Creativity* (Chichester, England: John Wiley & Sons, 2003).

²⁰ Ibid.

²¹ The classic work is Norman R. Maier, "Assets and Liabilities in Group Problem Solving," *Psychological Review,* vol. 74 (1967), pp. 239–49.

²² This presentation is based on the work of R. H. Hogarth, D. Kahneman, A. Tversky, and others, as discussed in Max H. Bazerman, *Judgment in Managerial Decision Making,* 3rd ed. (New York: Wiley, 1994).

²³ Barry M. Staw, "The Escalation of Commitment to a Course of Action," *Academy of Management Review,* vol. 6 (1981), pp. 577–87; and Barry M. Staw and Jerry Ross, "Knowing When to Pull the Plug," *Harvard Business Review,* vol. 65 (March/April 1987), pp. 68–74.

²⁴ For scholarly reviews, see Dean Tjosvold, "Effects of Crisis Orientation on Managers' Approach to Controversy in Decision Making," *Academy of Management Journal,* vol. 27 (1984), pp. 130–38; and Ian I. Mitroff, Paul Shrivastava, and Firdaus E. Udwadia, "Effective Crisis Management," *Academy of Management Executive,* vol. 1 (1987), pp. 283–92.

[25] Anna Muoio, "Where There's Smoke It Helps to Have a Smoke Jumper," *Fast Company,* vol. 33, p. 290.

[26] AIM Survey (El Paso, TX: ENFP Enterprises, 1989). Copyright ©1989 by Weston H. Agor. Used by permission.

Feature Notes 5

Oprah's Leadership Academy–Information and quotes from *The Associated Press,* "Oprah Opens School for Girls. In S. Africa Lavish Leadership Academy Aims to Give Impoverished Chance To Succeed," www.MSNBC.com (January 2, 2007); "Oprah Winfrey Leadership Academy for Girls–South Africa Celebrates Its Official Opening," www. oprah.com/about; and Jed Dreben, "Oprah Winfrey: 'I Don't Regret' Opening School," www.people.com (December 12, 2007).

Trendsetters–Information from Julie Bennett, "Don Thompson Engineers Winning Role as McDonald's President," *Franchise Times* (February, 2008): www.franchisetimes.com.

News Feed–Information from Ben Worthen, "Shifting Priorities," *The Wall Street Journal* (February 17, 2009), p. R8.

Stay Tuned–Information from Phred Dvorak, Baob Davis, and Louise Radnofsky, "Firms Confront Boss-Subordinate Love Affairs," *The Wall Street Journal* (October 27, 2008), p. B5. Survey data from Society for Human Resource Management.

Endnotes 5

[1] *Eaton Corporation Annual Report,* 1985.

[2] See Paul Ingrassia, "The Right Stuff," *Wall Street Journal* (April 8, 2005), p. D5.

[3] Henry Mintzberg, "The Manager's Job: Folklore and Fact," *Harvard Business Review,* vol. 53 (July/August 1975), pp. 54–67; and Henry Mintzberg, "Planning on the Left Side and Managing on the Right," *Harvard Business Review,* vol. 54 (July/August 1976), pp. 46–55.

[4] For a classic study, see Stanley Thune and Robert House, "Where Long-Range Planning Pays Off," *Business Horizons,* vol. 13 (1970), pp. 81–87. For a critical review of the literature, see Milton Leontiades and Ahmet Teel, "Planning Perceptions and Planning Results," *Strategic Management Journal,* vol. 1 (1980), pp. 65–75; and J. Scott Armstrong, "The Value of Formal Planning for Strategic Decisions," *Strategic Management Journal,* vol. 3 (1982), pp. 197–211. For special attention to the small business setting, see Richard B. Robinson Jr., John A. Pearce II, George S. Vozikis, and Timothy S. Mescon, "The Relationship between Stage of Development and Small Firm Planning and Performance," *Journal of Small Business Management,* vol. 22 (1984), pp. 45–52; and Christopher Orphen, "The Effects of Long-Range Planning on Small Business Performance: A Further Examination," *Journal of Small Business Management,* vol. 23 (1985), pp. 16–23. For an empirical study of large corporations, see Vasudevan Ramanujam and N. Venkatraman, "Planning and Performance: A New Look at an Old Question," *Business Horizons,* vol. 30 (1987), pp. 19–25.

[5] Quote from Stephen Covey and Roger Merrill, "New Ways to Get Organized at Work," *USA Weekend* (February 6/8, 1998), p. 18. Books by Stephen R. Covey include: *The 7 Habits of Highly Effective People: Powerful Lessons in Personal Change* (New York: Fireside, 1990), and Stephen R. Covey and Sandra Merril Covey, *The 7 Habits of Highly Effective Families: Building a Beautiful Family Culture in a Turbulent World* (New York: Golden Books, 1996).

[6] "McDonald's Tech Turnaround," *Harvard Business Review* (November 2004), p. 128.

[7] Information from Carol Hymowitz, "Packed Calendars Rule Over Executives," *The Wall Street Journal* (June 16, 2008), p. B1.

[8] Quotes from *Business Week* (August 8, 1994), pp. 78–86.

[9] See William Oncken Jr., and Donald L. Wass, "Management Time: Who's Got the Monkey?" *Harvard Business Review,* vol. 52 (September/October 1974), pp. 75–80, and featured as an HBR classic, *Harvard Business Review* (November/December 1999).

[10] For more on the long term, see Danny Miller and Isabelle Le Breton-Miller, *Managing for the Long Run* (Cambridge, MA: Harvard Business School Press, 2005).

[11] See Elliot Jaques, *The Form of Time* (New York: Russak & Co., 1982). For an executive commentary on his research, see Walter Kiechel III, "How Executives Think," *Fortune* (December 21, 1987), pp. 139–44.

[12] See Henry Mintzberg, "Rounding Out the Manager's Job," *Sloan Management Review* (Fall 1994), pp. 1–25.

[13] Excerpts in sample sexual harassment policy from American Express's advice to small businesses at www.americanexpress.com (retrieved November 21, 2005).

[14] Information from "Avoiding a Time Bomb: Sexual Harassment," *Business Week,* Enterprise issue (October 13, 1997), pp. ENT20–21.

[15] For a thorough review of forecasting, see J. Scott Armstrong, *Long-Range Forecasting,* 2nd ed. (New York: Wiley, 1985).

[16] Forecasts in Stay Informed from "Long-Term Forecasts on EIU Country Data and Market Indicators & Forecasts," *The Economist Intelligence Unit,* www.eiu.com (retrieved November 21, 2005).

[17] Information from *Associated Press,* "Cola Jihad Bubbling in Europe," *Columbus Dispatch* (February 11, 2003), pp. C1, C2.

[18] The scenario-planning approach is described in Peter Schwartz, *The Art of the Long View* (New York: Doubleday/Currency, 1991); and Arie de Geus, *The Living Company: Habits for Survival in a Turbulent Business Environment* (Boston, MA: Harvard Business School Press, 1997).

[19] Ibid.

[20] See, for example, Robert C. Camp, *Business Process Benchmarking* (Milwaukee: ASQ Quality Press 1994); Michael J. Spendolini, *The Benchmarking Book* (New York: AMACOM, 1992); and Christopher E. Bogan and Michael J. English, *Benchmarking for Best Practices: Winning Through Innovative Adaptation* (New York: McGraw-Hill, 1994).

[21] "How Classy Can 7-Eleven Get?" *Business Week* (September 1, 1997), pp. 74–75; and Kellie B. Gormly, "7-Eleven Moving Up a Grade," *Columbus Dispatch* (August 3, 2000), pp. C1–C2.

[21] David Kiley, "One Ford for the Whole World," *Business Week* (June 15, 2009), pp. 58–59.

[22] T. J. Rodgers, with William Taylor and Rick Foreman, "No Excuses Management," *World Executive's Digest* (May 1994), pp. 26–30.

[23] Suggested by a discussion in Robert Quimm, Sue R. Faerman, Michael P. Thompson, and Michael R. McGrath, *Becoming a Master Manager: A Contemporary Framework* (New York: Wiley, 1990), pp. 75–76.

Feature Notes 6

Chick-fil-A–Information and quotes from Daniel Yee, "Chick—Fill—A Recipe Winning Customers," *The Columbus Dispatch* (September 9, 2006), p. D1; Tom Murphy, "Chick-fil-A plans aggressive product rollout initiatives," *Rocky Mount Telegram* (May 28, 2008): www.rockymount-telegram.com; and, "Chick-fil-A Reaches 20,000th Scholarship Milestone" (July 28, 2005), Chick-fil-A press release: www.csrwire.com.

Trendsetters–Information and quotes from Stacy Perman, "Scones and Social Responsibility," *BusinessWeek* (August 21/28, 2006), p. 38; and www.dancingdeer.com.

News Feed–Information from Dalton Conley, "Welcome to Elsewhere," *Newsweek* (January 26, 2009), pp. 25–26.

Stay Tuned–Information from Sarah E. Needleman, "Businesses Say Theft by Their Workers Is Up," *The Wall Street Journal* (December 11, 2008), p. B8; Michelle Conlin, "To Catch a Corporate Thief," *Business Week* (February 16, 2009), p. 52; and Simona Covel, "Small Businesses Face More Fraud in Downturn," *The Wall Street Journal* (February 19, 2009), p. B5.

Endnotes 6

[1] "The Renewal Factor: Friendly Fact, Congenial Controls," *Business Week* (September 14, 1987), p. 105.

[2] Rob Cross and Lloyd Baird, "Technology Is Not Enough: Improving Performance by Building Institutional Memory," *Sloan Management Review* (spring 2000), p. 73.

[3] Information from Pep Sappal, "Integrated Inclusion Initiative," *The Wall Street Journal* (October 3, 2006), p. A2.

[4] Example from George Anders, "Management Guru Turns Focus to Orchestras, Hospitals," *Wall Street Journal* (November 21, 2005), pp. B1, B5.

[5] Information from Leon E. Wynter, "Allstate Rates Managers on Handling Diversity," *Wall Street Journal* (October 1, 1997), p. B1.

[6] Information from Kathryn Kranhold, "U.S. Firms Raise Ethics Focus," *Wall Street Journal* (November 28, 2005), p. B4.

[7] Information from Raju Narisetti, "For IBM, a Groundbreaking Sales Chief," *Wall Street Journal* (January 19, 1998), pp. B1, B5.

[8] Based on discussion by Harold Koontz and Cyril O'Donnell, *Essentials of Management* (New York: McGraw-Hill, 1974), pp. 362–65; see also Cross and Baird, op. cit.

[9] Information from Louis Lee, "I'm Proud of What I've Made Myself Into—What I've Created," *Wall Street Journal* (August 27, 1997), pp. B1, B5; and Jim Collins, "Bigger, Better, Faster," *Fast Company*, vol. 71 (June 2003), p. 74.

[10] Douglas McGregor, *The Human Side of Enterprise* (New York: McGraw-Hill, 1960).

[11] This distinction is made in William G. Ouchi, "Markets, Bureaucracies and Clans," *Administrative Science Quarterly*, vol. 25 (1980), pp. 129–41.

[12] Martin LaMonica, "Wal-Mart Readies Long-Term Move into Solar Power," *CNET News.com* (January 3, 2007).

[13] See Dale D. McConkey, *How to Manage by Results*, 3rd ed. (New York: AMACOM, 1976); Stephen J. Carroll Jr., and Henry J. Tosi Jr., *Management by Objectives: Applications and Research* (New York: Macmillan, 1973); and Anthony P. Raia, *Managing by Objectives* (Glenview, IL: Scott, Foresman, 1974).

[14] For a discussion of research on MBO, see Carroll and Tosi, op. cit.; Raia, op. cit; and Steven Kerr, "Overcoming the Dysfunctions of MBO," *Management by Objectives*, vol. 5, no. 1 (1976). Information in part from Dylan Loeb McClain, "Job Forecast: Internet's Still Hot," *New York Times* (January 30, 2001), p. 9.

[15] McGregor, op. cit.

[16] The work on goal setting and motivation is summarized in Edwin A. Locke and Gary P. Latham, *Goal Setting: A Motivational Technique That Works!* (Englewood Cliffs, NJ: Prentice-Hall, 1984).

[17] The "hot stove rules" are developed from R. Bruce McAfee and William Poffenberger, *Productivity Strategies: Enhancing Employee Job Performance* (Englewood Cliffs, NJ: Prentice-Hall, 1982), pp. 54–55. They are originally attributed to Douglas McGregor, "Hot Stove Rules of Discipline," in G. Strauss and L. Sayles (eds), *Personnel: The Human Problems of Management* (Englewood Cliffs, NJ: Prentice-Hall, 1967).

[18] For basic readings on quality control, see Joseph M. Juran, *Quality Control Handbook*, 3rd ed. (New York: McGraw-Hill, 1979) and "The Quality Trilogy: A Universal Approach to Managing for Quality," in H. Costin (ed.), *Total Quality Management* (New York: Dryden, 1994); W. Edwards Deming, *Out of Crisis* (Cambridge, MA: MIT Press, 1986) and "Deming's Quality Manifesto," *Best of Business Quarterly*, vol. 12 (Winter 1990–1991), pp. 6–101; Howard S. Gitlow and Shelly J. Gitlow, *The Deming Guide to Quality and Competitive Position* (Englewood Cliffs, NJ: Prentice-Hall, 1987); Juran, op. cit. (1993); and Rafael Aguay, *Dr. Deming: The American Who Taught the Japanese About Quality* (New York: Free Press, 1997).

[19] Rafael Aguay, *Dr. Deming: The American Who Taught the Japanese about Quality* (New York: Free Press, 1997); W. Edwards Deming, op. cit. (1986).

[20] "Gauging the Wal-Mart Effect," *Wall Street Journal* (December 3–4, 2005), p. 1 A9.

[21] Information from Karen Carney, "Successful Performance Measurement: A Checklist," *Harvard Management Update* (No. U9911B), 1999.

[22] Robert S. Kaplan and David P. Norton, "The Balanced Scorecard: Measures that Drive Performance," *Harvard Business Review* (July–August, 2005); see also Robert S. Kaplan and David P. Norton, *The Balanced Scorecard* (Cambridge, MA: Harvard Business School Press, 1996).

[23] Julian P. Rotter, "External Control and Internal Control," *Psychology Today* (June, 1971), p. 42. Used by permission.

Feature Notes 7

Patagonia/Yvon Chouinard–Information and quotes from Yvon Chouinard, *Let My People Go Surfing: The Education of a Reluctant Businessman* (New York: Penguin Press HC, 2005); Steve Hamm, "A Passion for the Plan," *Business Week* (August 21/28, 2006), pp. 92–94; and www.patagonia.com/web/us/patagonia.go?assetid=2047&ln=24.

Trendsetters–Information and quotes from "Who's Who on Obama's New Economic Advisory Board," LATimesBlog (February 6, 2009): www.latimesblogs.latimes.com; "'Diversify' Isn't Just Smart Financial Advice," *BlackMBA* (Winter, 2008/2009), p. 54; "*Black Enterprise* Announces 100 Most Powerful African Americans in Corporate America," Press Release (February 5, 2009): www.biz.yahoo.com/bw; and www.blackentrepreneurprofile.com/fortune-500-ceos (February 23, 2009).

News Feed–Information from Leila Abboud, "Faded Green: A Car Maker's Woes," *The Wall Street Journal* (January 26, 2009): www.wsj.com; and "Clean Energy," *Financial Times* (March 6, 2009).

Stay Tuned–Information from Sarah E. Needleman, "Layoffs Are Just One Threat," *The Wall Street Journal* (February 26, 2009), p. D4.

Endnotes 7

[1] Information and quotes from Marcia Stepanek, "How Fast Is Net Fast?" *Business Week E-Biz* (November 1, 1999), pp. EB52–EB54.

[2] Keith H. Hammond, "Michael Porter's Big Ideas," *Fast Company* (March 2001), pp. 150–156.

[3] Gary Hamel and C. K. Prahalad, "Strategic Intent," *Harvard Business Review* (May/June 1989), pp. 63–76.

[4] See "Gauging the Wal-Mart Effect," *Wall Street Journal* (December 3–4, 2005), p. A9; and, Matthew Boyle, "Wal-Mart's Magic Moment," *Business Week* (June 15, 2009), pp. 58–59.

[5] The four grand strategies were originally described by William F. Glueck, *Business Policy: Strategy Formulation and Management Action*, 2nd ed. (New York: McGraw-Hill, 1976).

[6] Michael A. Hitt, R. Duane Ireland, and Robert E. Hoskisson, *Strategic Management: Competitiveness and Globalization* (Minneapolis: West, 1997), p. 197.

[7] See William McKinley, Carol M. Sanchez, and A. G. Schick, "Organizational Downsizing: Constraining, Cloning, Learning," *Academy of Management Executive*, vol. 9 (August 1995), pp. 32–44.

[8] Kim S. Cameron, Sara J. Freeman, and A. K. Mishra, "Best Practices in White-Collar Downsizing: Managing Contradictions," *Academy of Management Executive*, vol. 4 (August 1991), pp. 57–73.

[9] "Overheard," *The Wall Street Journal* (April 16, 2009), p. C10; and, Geoffrey A. Fowler and Evan Ramstad," EBay Looks Abroad for Growth," *The Wall Street Journal* (April 16, 2009), p. B2.

[10] This strategy classification is found in Hitt et al., op. cit.; the attitudes are from a discussion by Howard V. Perlmutter, "The Tortuous Evolution of the Multinational Corporation," *Columbia Journal of World Business*, vol. 4 (January/February 1969).

[11] Fowler and Ramstand, op. cit., 2009.

[12] Adam M. Brandenburger and Barry J. Nalebuff, *Co-Opetition: A Revolution Mindset that Combines Competition and Cooperation* (New York: Bantam, 1996).

[13] Peter Coy, "Sleeping with the Enemy," *Business Week* (August 21/28, 2006), pp. 96–97.

[14] See Michael E. Porter, "Strategy and the Internet," *Harvard Business Review* (March 2001), pp. 63–78.

[15] See Michael Rappa, *Business Models on the Web* (www.ecommerce.ncsu.edu/business_models.html. February 6, 2001).

[16] Peter F. Drucker, *Management: Tasks, Responsibilities, Practices* (New York: Harper & Row, 1973), p. 122.

[17] See Laura Nash, "Mission Statements—Mirrors and Windows," *Harvard Business Review* (March/April 1988), pp. 155–56; James C. Collins and Jerry I. Porras, "Building Your Company's Vision," *Harvard Business Review* (September/October 1996), pp. 65–77; and James C. Collins and Jerry I. Porras, *Built to Last: Successful Habits of Visionary Companies* (New York: Harper Business, 1997).

[18] Gary Hamel, *Leading the Revolution* (Boston, MA: Harvard Business School Press, 2000), pp. 72–73.

[19] Collins and Porras, op. cit.

[20] See Peter F. Drucker's views on organizational objectives in his classic books: *The Practice of Management* (New York: Harper & Row, 1954), and *Management: Tasks, Responsibilities, Practices* (New York: Harper & Row, 1973). For a more recent commentary, see his article, "Management: The Problems of Success," *Academy of Management Executive*, vol. 1 (1987), pp. 13–19.

[21] C. K. Prahalad and Gary Hamel, "The Core Competencies of the Corporation," *Harvard Business Review* (May/June 1990), pp. 79–91; see also Hitt et al., op. cit., pp. 99–103.

[22] For a discussion of Michael Porter's approach to strategic planning, see his books, *Competitive Strategy* and *Competitive Advantage*, and his article, "What Is Strategy? *Harvard Business Review* (November/December, 1996), pp. 61–78; and Richard M. Hodgetts' interview "A Conversation with Michael E. Porter: A Significant Extension Toward Operational Improvement and Positioning," *Organizational Dynamics* (Summer 1999), pp. 24–33.

[23] See Michael E. Porter, *Competitive Strategy: Techniques for Analyzing Industries and Competitors* (New York: Free Press, 1980), and *Competitive Advantage: Creating and Sustaining Superior Performance* (New York: Free Press, 1986).

[24] Information from www.polo.com.

[25] www.vanguard.com.

[26] Bruce Einhorn, "Acer's Game-Changing PC Offensive," *Business Week* (April 20, 2009), p. 65.

[27] For more on GE and Jeffrey Immelt, see "The Immelt Revolution," *Business Week* (March 28, 2005), pp. 64–73.

[28] Richard G. Hammermesh, "Making Planning Strategic," *Harvard Business Review*, vol. 64 (July/August 1986), pp. 115–20; and Richard G. Hammermesh, *Making Strategy Work* (New York: Wiley, 1986).

[29] See Gerald B. Allan, "A Note on the Boston Consulting Group Concept of Competitive Analysis and Corporate Strategy," Harvard Business School, Intercollegiate Case Clearing House, ICCH9-175-175 (Boston: Harvard Business School, June 1976).

[30] www.patagonia.com/web/us/patagonia.go?assetid=3351.

[31] R. Duane Ireland and Michael A. Hitt, "Achieving and Maintaining Strategic Competitiveness in the 21st Century," *Academy of Management Executive*, vol. 13 (1999), pp. 43–57.

[32] Hammond, op. cit.

[33] Joseph A. Devito, *Messages: Building Interpersonal Communication Skills,* 3rd ed. (New York: HarperCollins, 1996), referencing William Haney, *Communicational Behavior: Text and Cases,* 3rd ed. (Homewood, IL: Irwin, 1973). Reprinted by permission.

Feature Notes 8

Build-A-Bear/Maxine Clark–Information and quotes from "Build-A-Bear Workshop, Inc., Funding Universe": www.fundinguniverse.com/company-histories/BuildABear-Workshop-Inc (accessed March 9, 2009); and www.buildabear.com. See also Maxine Clark and Amy Joyner, *The Bear Necessities of Business: Building a Company with Heart* (Hoboken, NJ: John Wiley & Sons, 2007).

Trendsetters–Information and quotes from David Kiley, "Ford's Savior?" *Business Week* (March 16, 2009), pp. 31–34; and, Alex Taylor III, "Fixing up Ford," *Fortune* (May 14, 2009).

News Feed–Information from Dana Mattioli, "Job Fears Make Offices All Ears," *The Wall Street Journal* (January 20, 2009): www.wsj.com.

Stay Tuned–Information from Heather Bousley, "Job Losses Continue at Accelerated Pace," Center for American Progress (February 6, 2009): www.americanprogress.org/issues/2009.

Endnotes 8

[1] Henry Mintzberg and Ludo Van der Heyden, "Organigraphs: Drawing How Companies Really Work," *Harvard Business Review* (September/October 1999), pp. 87–94.

[2] Ibid.

[3] The classic work is Alfred D. Chandler, *Strategy and Structure* (Cambridge, MA: MIT Press, 1962).

[4] See Alfred D. Chandler, Jr., "Origins of the Organization Chart," *Harvard Business Review* (March/April 1988), pp. 156–57.

[5] "A Question of Management," *The Wall Street Journal* (June 2, 2009), p. R4.

[6] Joann S. Lublin, "Chairman-CEO Split Gains Allies," *The Wall Street Journal* (March 30, 2009), p. B4.

[7] See David Krackhardt and Jeffrey R. Hanson, "Informal Networks: The Company Behind the Chart," *Harvard Business Review* (July/August 1993), pp. 104–11.

[8] Information from Jena McGregor, "The Office Chart that Really Counts," *Business Week* (February 27, 2006), pp. 48–49.

[9] See Phred Dvorak, "Engineering Firm Charts Ties," *The Wall Street Journal* (January 26, 2009): www.wsj.com.

[10] See Kenneth Noble, "A Clash of Styles: Japanese Companies in the U.S.," *New York Times* (January 25, 1988), p. 7.

[11] For a discussion of departmentalization, see H. I. Ansoff and R. G. Bradenburg, "A Language for Organization Design," *Management Science*, vol. 17 (August 1971), pp. B705–B731; Mariann Jelinek, "Organization Structure: The Basic Conformations," in Mariann Jelinek, Joseph A. Litterer, and Raymond E. Miles (eds.), *Organizations by Design: Theory and Practice* (Plano, TX: Business Publications, 1981), pp. 293–302; Henry Mintzberg, "The Structuring of Organizations," in James Brian Quinn, Henry Mintzberg, and Robert M. James (eds.), *The Strategy Process: Concepts, Contexts, and Cases* (Englewood Cliffs, NJ: Prentice-Hall, 1988), pp. 276–304.

[12] "A Question of Management," op. cit.

[13] Example reported in "Top Business Teams: A Lesson Straight from Mars," *Time* (February 9, 2009), p. 40; and Howard M. Guttman, *Great Business Teams* (Hoboken, NJ: John Wiley & Sons, 2009).

[14] These alternatives are well described by Mintzberg, op. cit.

[15] Norihiko Shirouzu, "Toyota Plans a Major Overhaul in U. S.," *The Wall Street Journal* (April 10, 2009), p. B3.

[16] Information and quotes from "Management Shake-Up to Create 'Leaner Structure'," *Financial Times* (June 11, 2009).

[17] Information and quote from "Revamped GM Updates Image of Core Brands," *Financial Times* (June 18, 2009).

[18] Excellent reviews of matrix concepts are found in Stanley M. Davis and Paul R. Lawrence, *Matrix* (Reading, MA: Addison-Wesley, 1977); Paul R. Lawrence, Harvey F. Kolodny, and Stanley M. Davis, "The Human Side of the Matrix," *Organizational Dynamics*, vol. 6 (1977), pp. 43–61; and Harvey F. Kolodny, "Evolution to a Matrix Organization," *Academy of Management Review*, vol. 4 (1979), pp. 543–53.

[19] Davis and Lawrence, op. cit.

[20] Susan Albers Mohrman, Susan G. Cohen, and Allan M. Mohrman, Jr., *Designing Team-Based Organizations* (San Francisco: Jossey-Bass, 1996).

[21] See Glenn M. Parker, *Cross-Functional Teams* (San Francisco: Jossey-Bass, 1995).

[22] Information from William Bridges, "The End of the Job," *Fortune* (September 19, 1994), pp. 62–74; Alan Deutschman, "The Managing Wisdom of High-Tech Superstars," *Fortune* (October 17, 1994), pp. 197–206.

[23] See the discussion by Jay R. Galbraith, "Designing the Networked Organization: Leveraging Size and Competencies," in Susan Albers Mohrman, Jay R. Galbraith, Edward E. Lawler III, and Associates, *Tomorrow's Organizations: Crafting Winning Strategies in a Dynamic World* (San Francisco: Jossey-Bass, 1998), pp. 76–102. See also Rupert F. Chisholm, *Developing Network Organizations: Learning from Practice and Theory* (Reading, MA: Addison-Wesley, 1998); and, Michael S. Malone, The Future Arrived Yesterday: The Rise of the Protean Corporation and What it Means for You (New York: Crown Books, 2009).

[24] See Jerome Barthelemy, "The Seven Deadly Sins of Outsourcing," *Academy of Management Executive*, vol. 17 (2003), pp. 87–98; and, Paulo Prada and Jiraj Sheth, "Delta Air Ends Use of India Call Centers," *The Wall Street Journal* (April 18–19, 2009), pp. B1, B5.

[25] See the collection of articles by Cary L. Cooper and Denise M. Rousseau (eds.), *The Virtual Organization: Vol. 6, Trends in Organizational Behavior* (New York: Wiley, 2000).

[26] For a discussion of organization theory, see W. Richard Scott, *Organizations: Rational, Natural, and Open Systems*, 4th ed. (Upper Saddle River, NJ: Prentice-Hall, 1998).

[27] For a classic work, see Jay R. Galbraith, *Organizational Design* (Reading, MA: Addison Wesley, 1977).

[28] David Van Fleet, "Span of Management Research and Issues," *Academy of Management Journal*, vol. 26 (1983), pp. 546–52.

[29] Information and quotes from Ellen Byron and Joann S. Lublin, "Appointment of New P&G Chief Sends Ripples Through Ranks," *The Wall Street Journal* (June 11, 2009), P. B3.

[30] Information for Stay Informed from Tim Stevens, "Winning the World Over," *Industry Week* (November 15, 1999).

31 See George P. Huber, "A Theory of Effects of Advanced Information Technologies on Organizational Design, Intelligence, and Decision Making," *Academy of Management Review*, vol. 15 (1990), pp. 67–71.

32 Developed from Roger Fritz, *Rate Your Executive Potential* (New York: Wiley, 1988), pp. 185–86; Roy J. Lewicki, Donald D. Bowen, Douglas T. Hall, and Francine S. Hall, *Experiences in Management and Organizational Behavior*, 3rd ed. (New York: Wiley, 1988), p. 144.

33 Max Weber, *The Theory of Social and Economic Organization*, A. M. Henderson, trans., and H. T. Parsons (New York: Free Press, 1947). For classic treatments of bureaucracy, see also Alvin Gouldner, *Patterns of Industrial Bureaucracy* (New York: Free Press, 1954); and Robert K. Merton, *Social Theory and Social Structure* (New York: Free Press, 1957).

34 Tom Burns and George M. Stalker, *The Management of Innovation* (London: Tavistock, 1961), republished (London: Oxford University Press, 1994). See also Wesley D. Sine, Hitoshi Mitsuhashi, and David A. Kirsch, "Revisiting Burns and Stalker: Formal Structure and New Venture Performance in Emerging Economic Sectors," *Academy of Management Journal*, vol. 49 (2006), pp. 121–32. The Burns and Stalker study was later extended by Paul R. Lawrence and Jay W. Lorsch, *Organizations and Environment* (Boston: Division of Research, Graduate School of Business Administration, Harvard University, 1967).

35 See Henry Mintzberg, *Structure in Fives: Designing Effective Organizations* (Englewood Cliffs, NJ: Prentice-Hall, 1983).

36 "What Ails Microsoft?" *Business Week* (September 26, 2005), p. 101.

37 "Should Microsoft Break Up, on Its Own?" *Wall Street Journal* (November 26–27, 2005), p. B16.

38 See, for example, Jay R. Galbraith, Edward E. Lawler III, and Associates, *Organizing for the Future* (San Francisco: Jossey-Bass, 1993); and Susan Albers Mohrman, Jay R. Galbraith, Edward E. Lawler III, and Associates, *Tomorrow's Organizations: Crafting Winning Strategies in a Dynamic World* (San Francisco: Jossey-Bass, 1998).

39 Peter Senge, *The Fifth Discipline: The Art and Practice of the Learning Organization* (New York: Doubleday, 1994).

40 See Rosabeth Moss Kanter, *The Changing Masters* (New York: Simon & Schuster, 1983). Quotation from Rosabeth Moss Kanter and John D. Buck, "Reorganizing Part of Honeywell: From Strategy to Structure," *Organizational Dynamics*, vol. 13 (Winter 1985), p. 6.

41 Barney Olmsted and Suzanne Smith, *Creating a Flexible Workplace: How to Select and Manage Alternative Work Options* (New York: American Management Association, 1989).

42 See Allen R. Cohen and Herman Gadon, *Alternative Work Schedules: Integrating Individual and Organizational Needs* (Reading, MA: Addison-Wesley, 1978), p. 125; Simcha Ronen and Sophia B. Primps, "The Compressed Work Week as Organizational Change: Behavioral and Attitudinal Outcomes," *Academy of Management Review*, vol. 6 (1981), pp. 61–74.

43 Information from Lesli Hicks, "Workers, Employers Praise Their Four-Day Workweek," *Columbus Dispatch* (August 22, 1994), p. 6.

44 Business for Social Responsibility Resource Center: www.bsr.org/resourcecenter (January 24, 2001); Anusha Shrivastava, "Flextime is Now Key Benefit for Mom-Friendly Employers," *Columbus Dispatch* (September 23, 2003), p. C2; Sue Shellenbarger, "Number of Women Managers Rises," *Wall Street Journal* (September 30, 2003), p. D2.

45 "Networked Workers," *Business Week* (October 6, 1997), p. 8; and Diane E. Lewis, "Flexible Work Arrangements as Important as Salary to Some," *Columbus Dispatch* (May 25, 1998), p. 8.

46 Christopher Rhoads and Sara Silver, "Working at Home Gets Easier," *Wall Street Journal* (December 29, 2005), p. B4.

47 For a review, see Wayne F. Cascio, "Managing a Virtual Workplace," *Academy of Management Executive*, vol. 14 (2000), pp. 81–90.

48 Quote from Phil Porter, "Telecommuting Mom Is Part of a National Trend," *Columbus Dispatch* (November 29, 2000), pp. H1, H2.

49 These guidelines are collected from a variety of sources, including: The Southern California Telecommuting Partnership: www.socalcommute.org/telecom.htm; ISDN Group; www.isdnzone.com/telcom/tips.

50 John F. Veiga and John N. Yanouzas, *The Dynamics of Organization Theory: Gaining a Macro Perspective* (St. Paul, MN: West, 1979), pp. 158-160. Used by permission.

Feature Notes 9

IDEO Inc.–Information and quotes from Phred Dvorak, "Businesses Take a Page from Design Firms," *The Wall Street Journal* (November, 10, 2008), p. B4; Tim Brown, "Design Thinking," *Harvard Business Review* (June, 2008); www.adsoftheworld.comand, www.ideo.com/culture; and, Tim Brown, "Change by Design," Business Week (Oct 5, 2009), pp. 54–56. See also Tim Brown, *Change by Design; How Design Thinking Tranforms Organizations and Inspires Innovation* (New York: Harper Business, 2009).

Trendsetters–Information from David A. Price, "From Dorm Room to Wal-Mart," *The Wall Street Journal* (March 11, 2009), p. A13; "Huddler.com Interview with CEO and Founder Tom Szaky," www.greenhome.huddler.com/wiki/terracycle; and Tom Szaky, *Revolution in a Bottle* (Knoxville, TN: Portfolio Trade, 2009).

News Feed–Information from Ellen Byron, "A New Odd Couple: Google, P&G Swap Workers to Spur Innovation," *The Wall Street Journal* (November 19, 2008), pp. A1, A18.

Stay Tuned–Information from Knowledge@Wharton, "A World Transformed: What Are the Top 30 Innovations of the Last 30 Years?" (February, 19, 2009): www.knowledge.wharton.upenn.edu.

Endnotes 9

1 See the discussion of Antropologie in William C. Taylor and Polly LaBarre, *Mavericks at Work: Why the Most Original Minds in Business Win* (New York: William Morrow, 2006).

2 Edgar H. Schein, "Organizational Culture," *American Psychologist*, vol. 45 (1990), pp. 109–19. See also Schein's *Organizational Culture and Leadership*, 2nd ed. (San Francisco: Jossey-Bass, 1997); and *The Corporate Culture Survival Guide* (San Francisco: Jossey-Bass, 1999).

3 Jena McGregor, "Zappos' Secret: It's an Open Book," *Business Week* (March 23 & 30, 2009), p. 62.

4 Rajiv Dutta, "eBay's Meg Whitman on Building a Company's Culture," *Business Week* (March 27, 2009): www.businessweek.com.

5 James Collins and Jerry Porras, *Built to Last* (New York: Harper Business, 1994).

6 Schein, op. cit. (1997); Terrence E. Deal and Alan A. Kennedy, *Corporate Cultures: The Rites and Rituals of Corporate Life* (Reading, MA: Addison-Wesley, 1982); and Ralph Kilmann, *Beyond the Quick Fix* (San Francisco: Jossey-Bass, 1984).

7 In their book *Corporate Culture and Performance* (New York: Macmillan, 1992), John P. Kotter and James L. Heskett make the point that strong cultures have the desired effects over the long term only if they encourage adaptation to a changing environment. See also Collins and Porras, op. cit. (1994).

8 Steve Hamm, "Big Blue Goes for the Big Win," *Business Week* (March 10, 2008), pp. 63–65.

9 In their book Corporate Culture and Performance (New York: Macmillan, 1992), John P. Kotter and James L. Heskett make the point that strong cultures have the desired effects over the long term only if they encourage adaptation to a changing environment. See also Collins and Porras, op. cit. (1994).

10 John P. Wanous, *Organizational Entry*, 2nd ed. (New York: Addison-Wesley, 1992).

11 Scott Madison Patton, "Service Quality, Disney Style" (Lake Buena Vista, FL: Disney Institute, 1997).

12 This is a simplified model developed from Schein, op. cit. (1997).

13 James C. Collins and Jerry I. Porras, "Building Your Company's Vision," *Harvard Business Review* (September/October 1996), pp. 65–77.

14 David Rocks, "Reinventing Herman Miller," *Business Week* eBiz (April 2, 2000), pp. E88–E96; www.hermanmiller.com

15 The prior list of criteria is from Ralph H. Kilmann, Mary J. Saxton, and Roy Serpa, "Issues in Understanding and Changing Corporate Culture," *California Management Review*, vol. 28 (1986), pp. 87–94. The Tom's of Maine example is from Jenny C. McCune, "Making Lemonade," *Management Review* (June 1997), pp. 49–53.

16 See Robert A. Giacalone and Carol L. Jurkiewicz (Eds.), *Handbook of Workplace Spirituality and Organizational Performance* (Armonk, NY: M. E. Sharpe, 2003).

[17] See Mary Kay Ash, *Mary Kay: You Can Have It All* (New York: Roseville, CA: Prima Publishing, 1995).

[18] Information from "On the Road to Innovation," in special advertising section, "Charting the Course: Global Business Sets Its Goals," *Fortune* (August 4, 1997).

[19] Information from "'Mosh Pits' of Creativity," *Business Week* (November 7, 2005), pp. 98–99.

[20] See Peter F. Drucker, "The Discipline of Innovation," *Harvard Business Review* (November/December 1998), pp. 3–8.

[21] Peter F. Drucker, *Management: Tasks, Responsibilities, and Practices* (New York: Harper & Row, 1973), p. 797.

[22] See Cortis R. Carlson and William W. Wilmont, *Getting to "Aha"* (New York: Crown Business, 2006).

[23] Information from Jena McGregor, "The World's Most Innovative Companies," *Business Week* (April 24, 2006), pp. 63–74; and Jena McGregor, "Most Innovative Companies: Smart Ideas for Tough Times," *Business Week* (April 28, 2008), pp. 61–63.

[24] See "Green Business Innovations" and "New Life for Old Threads," both in *Business Week* (April 28, 2008), special advertising section.

[25] Information and quote from "$5 Solar Oven Wins $75,000 Green Innovation Award," www.solarfeeds.com (April 18, 2009), and Saeed Rahmed, "Inventor turns cardboard boxes into eco-friendly oven," www.cnn.com (April 9, 2009).

[26] David Bornstein, *How to Change the World: Social Entrepreneurs and the Power of New Ideas* (Oxford, U.K.: Oxford University Press, 2004).

[27] Example from Aubrey Henvetty "Seeds of Change," *Kellogg* (Summer, 2006), p. 13; and "Amid Turmoil, One Acre Fund Sows Hope in Africa," *Kellogg* (Spring, 2008), p. 7.

[28] This discussion is stimulated by James Brian Quinn, "Managing Innovation Controlled Chaos," *Harvard Business Review,* vol. 63 (May-June 1985).

[29] Based on Edward B. Roberts, "Managing Invention and Innovation," *Research Technology Management* (January-February 1988), pp. 1–19, and, Gary Hamel, *Leading the Revolution* (Boston, MA: Harvard Business School Press, 2000).

[30] Robert Berner, "How P&G Pampers New Thinking," *Business Week* (April 14, 2008), pp. 73–74.

[31] "How P&G Plans to Clean Up," *Business Week* (April 13, 2009), pp. 44–45.

[32] Information and quotes from Nancy Gohring, "Microsoft: Stodgy or Innovative? It's All About Perception," *PC World* (July 25, 2008).

[33] This discussion is stimulated by James Brian Quinn, "Managing Innovation Controlled Chaos," *Harvard Business Review,* vol. 63 (May/June 1985).

[34] Quote from www.ideo.com/culture/ (retrieved: March 11, 2009).

[35] Information and quotes from Yukari Iwatani Kane, "Sony CEO Urges Managers to Get 'Mad'," *The Wall Street Journal* (May 23, 2008), p. B8.

[36] Jessica E. Vascellaro, "Google Searches for Ways to Keep Big Ideas at Home," *The Wall Street Journal* (June 18, 2009), pp. B1,B5.

[37] "'Mosh Pits' of Creativity," *Business Week* (November 7, 2005), p. 99.

[38] Reena Jana, "Brickhouse: Yahoo's Hot Little Incubator," *Business Week* (November, 2007), p. IN 14.

[39] "How Google Fuels Its Idea Factory," *Business Week* (May 12, 2008), pp. 54–55.

[40] Kenneth Labich "The Innovators," *Fortune* (June 6, 1988), pp. 49–64.

[41] Quote from Brad Stone, "Amid the Gloom, an E-Commerce War," *The New York Times* (October 12, 2008): www.nytimes.com.

[42] Reported in Carol Hymowitz, "Task of Managing Changes in Workplace Takes a Careful Hand," *Wall Street Journal* (July 1, 1997), p. B1.

[43] For an overview, see W. Warner Burke, *Organization Change: Theory and Practice* (Thousand Oaks, CA: Sage, 2002).

[44] For a discussion of alternative types of change, see David A. Nadler and Michael L. Tushman, *Strategic Organizational Design* (Glenview, Il: Scott, Foresman, 1988); John P. Kotter, "Leading Change: Why Transformations Efforts Fail," *Harvard Business Review* (March/April 1995), pp. 59–67; and W. Warner Burke, *Organization Change* (Thousand Oaks, CA: Sage, 2002).

[45] Beer and Nohria, op. cit.; and "Change Management, An Inside Job," *Economist* (July 15, 2000), p. 61.

[46] Beer and Nohria, op. cit.; and "Change Management, An Inside Job," *Economist* (July 15, 2000), p. 61.

[47] Based on Kotter, op. cit.

[48] Beer & Nohria, op. cit.

[49] Kurt Lewin, "Group Decision and Social Change," in G. E. Swanson, T. M. Newcomb, and E. L. Hartley (eds.), *Readings in Social Psychology* (New York: Holt, Rinehart, 1952), pp. 459–73.

[50] Criteria in box based on Everett C. Rogers, *Communication of Innovations*, 3rd ed. (New York: Free Press, 1993).

[51] This discussion is based on Robert Chin and Kenneth D. Benne, "General Strategies for Effecting Changes in Human Systems," in Warren G. Bennis, Kenneth D. Benne, Robert Chin, and Kenneth E. Corey (eds.), *The Planning of Change*, 3rd ed. (New York: Holt, Rinehart, 1969), pp. 22–45.

[52] The change agent descriptions here and following are developed from an exercise reported in J. William Pfeiffer and John E. Jones, *A Handbook of Structured Experiences for Human Relations Training*, vol. 2 (LaJolla, CA: University Associates, 1973).

[53] Ram N. Aditya, Robert J. House, and Steven Kerr, "Theory and Practice of Leadership: Into the New Millennium," Chapter 6 in Cary L. Cooper and Edwin A. Locke, *Industrial and Organizational Psychology: Linking Theory with Practice* (Malden, MA: Blackwell, 2000).

[54] Information from Mike Schneider, "Disney Teaching Execs Magic of Customer Service," *Columbus Dispatch* (December 17, 2000), p. G9.

[55] Teresa M. Amabile, "How to Kill Creativity," *Harvard Business Review* (September/October 1998), pp. 77–87.

[56] See Jeffrey D. Ford and Laurie W. Ford, "Decoding Resistance to Change," *Harvard Business Review* (April, 2009), pp. 99–103.

[57] John P. Kotter and Leonard A. Schlesinger, "Choosing Strategies for Change," *Harvard Business Review*, vol. 57 (March/April 1979), pp. 109–12.

[58] Based on Budner, S. "Intolerance of Ambiguity as a Personality Variable," *Journal of Personality*, vol. 30, No. 1, (1962), pp. 29–50.

Feature Notes 10

Working Mother Media–Information and quote from Information from workingmother.com (retrieved September 29, 2006 and August 1, 2008); see also workingmother.com.

Trendsetters–Information and quotes from Joann S. Lublin and Ellen Byron, "Arnold Likely to be Wooed for Top Post," *The Wall Street Journal* (March 10, 2009), p. B5; www.cnn.money.com and, www.topix.com/forum/news.

News Feed–Information and quotes from Jennifer Levitz and Philip Shiskin, "More Workers Cite Age Bias After Layoffs," *The Wall Street Journal* (March 11, 2009), pp. D1, D2.

Stay Tuned–Information from "Negative Attitudes to Labor Unions Show Little Change in Last Decade" Harris Poll #68 (August 31, 2005): www.harrisinteractive.com; and *DPA NewsLine* (February, 2009): www.dpeaflcio.org; and, www.afl-cio.org.

Endnotes 10

[1] See Jeffrey Pfeffer, *The Human Equation: Building Profits by Putting People First* (Boston: Harvard University Press, 1998).

[2] Jeffrey Pfeffer and John F. Veiga, "Putting People First for Organizational Success," *Academy of Management Executive*, vol. 13 (May 1999), pp. 37–48.

[3] Ibid.; and Pfeffer, op. cit. See also James N. Baron and David M. Kreps, *Strategic Human Resources: Frameworks for General Managers* (New York: Wiley, 1999).

[4] Information from "New Face at Facebook Hopes to Map Out a Road to Growth," *The Wall Street Journal* (April 15, 2008), pp. B1, B5.

[5] James N. Baron and David M. Kreps, *Strategic Human Resources: Framework for General Managers* (New York: Wiley, 1999).

[6] Quotes from Kris Maher, "Human-Resources Directors Are Assuming Strategic Roles," *Wall Street Journal* (June 17, 2003), p. B8.

[7] Ibid.

8 See also R. Roosevelt Thomas Jr. 's books, *Beyond Race and Gender* (New York: AMACOM, 1999); and (with Marjorie I. Woodruff) *Building a House for Diversity* (New York: AMACOM, 1999); and Richard D. Bucher, *Diversity Consciousness* (Englewood Cliffs, NJ: Prentice-Hall, 2000).

9 For a discussion of affirmative action, see R. Roosevelt Thomas, Jr., "From 'Affirmative Action' to 'Affirming Diversity,'" *Harvard Business Review* (November/December 1990), pp. 107–117.

10 See the discussion by David A. DeCenzo and Stephen P. Robbins, *Human Resource Management*, 6th ed. (New York: Wiley, 1999) pp. 66–68 and 81–83.

11 Ibid., pp. 77–79.

12 See, for example, Randall Smith, "African-American Broker Sues Alleging Bias at Merrill Lynch," *Wall Street Journal* (December 1, 2005), p. C3.

13 Case reported in Sue Shellenbarger, "Work & Family Mailbox," *The Wall Street Journal* (March 11, 2009), p. D6.

14 Information and quotes here and in photo from Sheryl Gay Stolberg, "Obama Signs Equal-Pay Legislation," *The New York Times* (January 30, 2009): www.nytimes.com.

15 "What to Expect When You're Expecting," *Business Week* (May 26, 2008), p. 17.

16 Ibid; and Madeline Heilman and Tyhler G. Okimoto, "Motherhood: A Potential Source of Bias in Employment Decisions," *Journal of Applied Psychology*, vol. 93, no. 1 (2008), pp. 189–98.

17 See Frederick S. Lane, *The Naked Employee: How Technology Is Compromising Workplace Privacy* (New York: Amacon, 2003).

18 Quote from George Myers, "Bookshelf," *Columbus Dispatch* (June 9, 2003), p. E6.

19 Quote from William Bridges, "The End of the Job," *Fortune* (September 19, 1994), p. 68.

20 Mina Kimes, "P&G's Leadership Machine," *Fortune* (April 14, 2009).

21 See Sarah E. Needleman, "Initial Phone Interviews Do Count," *The Wall Street Journal* (February 7, 2006), p. 29; Needleman, op. cit.

22 Information and quote from Sarah E. Needleman, "The New Trouble on the Line," *The Wall Street Journal* (June 2, 2009): www.wsj.com.

23 See John P. Wanous, *Organizational Entry: Recruitment, Selection, and Socialization of Newcomers* (Reading, MA: Addison-Wesley, 1980), pp. 34–44.

24 Josey Puliyenthuruthel, "How Google Searches for Talent," *Business Week* (April 11, 2005), p. 52.

25 Quote from Ronald Henkoff, "Finding, Training, and Keeping the Best Service Workers," *Fortune* (October 3, 1994), pp. 110–122.

26 Kimes, op. cit.

27 See Harry J. Martin, "Lessons Learned," *The Wall Street Journal* (December 15, 2008), p. R11.

28 "A to Z of Generation Y Attitudes," *Financial Times* (June 18, 2009) "When Three Generations Can Work Better than One," *Financial Times* (September 16, 2009).

29 Dick Grote, "Performance Appraisal Reappraised," *Harvard Business Review Best Practice* (1999), Reprint F00105.

30 See Larry L. Cummings and Donald P. Schwab, *Performance in Organizations: Determinants and Appraisal* (Glenview, IL: Scott, Foresman, 1973).

31 For a good review, see Gary P. Latham, Joan Almost, Sara Mann, and Celia Moore, "New Developments in Performance Management," *Organizational Dynamics*, vol. 34, no. 1 (2005), pp. 77–87.

32 See Mark R. Edwards and Ann J. Ewen, *360-Degree Feedback: The Powerful New Tool for Employee Feedback and Performance Improvement* (New York: AMACOM, 1996).

33 Examples are from Jena McGregor, "Job Review in 140 Keystrokes," *Business Week* (March 23 & 30, 2009), p. 58.

34 Kimes, op. cit., 2009.

35 Timothy Butler and James Waldroop, "Job Sculpting: The Art of Retaining Your Best People," *Harvard Business Review* (September-October 1999), pp. 144–52.

36 Information from "What Are the Most Effective Retention Tools?" *Fortune* (October 9, 2000), p. S7.

37 See Betty Friedan, *Beyond Gender: The New Politics of Work and the Family* (Washington, DC: Woodrow Wilson Center Press, 1997); and James A. Levine, *Working Fathers: New Strategies for Balancing Work and Family* (Reading, MA: Addison-Wesley, 1997).

38 Data reported in "A Saner Workplace," *Business Week* (June 1, 2009), pp. 66–69, and based on excerpt from Claire Shipman and Katty Kay, *Womenomics: Write Your Own Rules for Success* (New York: Harper Business, 2009).

39 Data from Ibid, and "A to Z of Generation Y Attitudes," *Financial Times* (June 18, 2009).

40 Study reported in Ann Belser, "Employers Using less-Costly Ways to Retain Workers," *The Columbus Disptach* (June 1, 2008), p. D3.

41 Information from Sue Shellenbarger, "What Makes a Company a Great Place to Work Today," *The Wall Street Journal* (October 4, 2007), p. D1.

42 Information from Sue Shellenbarger, "What Makes a Company a Great Place to Work Today," *The Wall Street Journal* (October 4, 2007), p. D1.

43 Examples from Amy Saunders, "A Creative Approach to Work," *The Columbus Dispatch* (May 2, 2008), pp. C1, C9; Shellenbarger, op. cit.; and Michelle Conlin and Jay Greene, "How to Make a Microserf Smile," *Business Week* (September 10, 2007), pp. 57–59.

44 "A Saner Workplace," op. cit.

45 See Kaja Whitehouse, "More Companies Offer Packages Linking Pay Plans to Performance," *Wall Street Journal* (December 13, 2005), p. B6.

46 Ibid.

47 Erin White, "How to Reduce Turnover," *Wall Street Journal* (November 21, 2005), p. B5.

48 Ibid.

49 Information from Susan Pulliam, "New Dot-Com Mantra: 'Just Pay Me in Cash, Please,'" *Wall Street Journal* (November 28, 2000), p. C1.

50 Opdyke, op. cit.

51 Nanette Byrnes, "Pain, but no Layoffs at Nucor," *Business Week* (March 26, 2009): www.businessweek.com.

52 Jeffrey Pfeffer and John F. Veiga, "Putting People First for Organizational Success," *Academy of Management Executive*, vol. 13 (May 1999), pp. 37–48.

53 Information from www.intel.com and "Stock Ownership for Everyone," *Hewitt Associates* (November 27, 2000), www.hewitt.com/hewitt/business/talent/subtalent/con_bckg_global.htm.

54 A good overview is found in the special section on "Employee Benefits," *The Wall Street Journal* (April 22, 2008), pp. A11–A17.

55 "Benefits: For Companies, the Runaway Train is Slowing Down," *Business Week* (February 16, 2009), p. 15.

56 For reviews see Richard B. Freeman and James L. Medoff, *What Do Unions Do?* (New York: Basic Books, 1984); Charles C. Heckscher, *The New Unionism* (New York: Basic Books, 1988); and Barry T. Hirsch, *Labor Unions and the Economic Performance of Firms* (Kalamazoo, MI: W.E. Upjohn Institute for Employment Research, 1991).

57 Paul Glover, "Will Workers Unionize During the Recession?" *Fast Company* (March 19, 2009); www.fastcompany.com.

58 Example from Timothy Aeppel, "Pay Scales Divide Factory Floors," *The Wall Street Journal* (April 9, 2008), p. B4.

59 "Southwest Reaches Tentative Deal with Attendants," *The Associated Press* (March 26, 2009): www.businessweek.com.

60 See Jeff Bennett and Sharon Terlep, "Concessions to Even Ford's Labor Costs with Toyota's," *The Wall Street Journal* (March 12, 2009), p. B1.

61 Developed in part from Robert E. Quinn, Sue R. Faermon, Michael P. Thompson, and Michael R. McGrath, *Becoming a Master Manager! A Contemporary Framework* (New York: John Wiley & Sons, 1990), p. 187. Used by permission.

Feature Notes 11

Southwest Airlines–Information from Sharon Shinn, "Luv, Colleen," *BizEd* (March–April 2003), pp. 18–23; "Southwest Airlines and the MBTI® : Creating a Culture that Soars," www.cpp.com/Pr/southwest_airlines; corporate Web site: www.southwestairlines.com; and "Southwest's Kelleher Hands Reins to Gary Kelly," *Dallas Business Journal* (May 21, 2008): www.dallas.bizjournals.com.

Trendsetters–Information and quotes from Lorraine Monroe, "Leadership Is About Making Vision Happen—What I Call 'Vision Acts,'" *Fast Company* (March 2001), p. 98; Lorraine Monroe Leadership Institute Web site: www.lorrainemonroe.com. See also Lorraine Monroe, *Nothing's Impossible: Leadership Lessons from Inside and Outside The Classroom* (New York: PublicAffairs Books, 1999), and *The Monroe Doctrine: An ABC Guide To What Great Bosses Do* (New York: PublicAffairs Books, 2003).

News Feed–Information and quotes from "An American Sage," *Wall Street Journal* (November 14, 2005), p. A22; Scott Thurm and Joann S. Lublin, "Peter Drucker's Legacy Includes Simple Advice: It's All About People," *Wall Street Journal* (November 14, 2005), pp. B1, B3; and John A. Byrne, "The Man Who Invented Management," *Business Week* (November 28, 2005), pp. 96–106.

Stay Tuned–Information from "Many U.S. Employees Have Negative Attitudes to Their Jobs, Employers and Top Managers," Harris Poll #38 (May 6, 2005), retrieved from www.harrisinteractive.com.

Endnotes 11

[1] Abraham Zaleznick, "Leaders and Managers: Are They Different?" *Harvard Business Review* (May/June 1977), pp. 67–78.

[2] Tom Peters, "Rule #3: Leadership Is Confusing as Hell," *Fast Company* (March 2001), pp. 124–40.

[3] Quotations from Marshall Loeb, "Where Leaders Come From," *Fortune* (September 19, 1994), pp. 241–42; Genevieve Capowski, "Anatomy of a Leader: Where Are the Leaders of Tomorrow?" *Management Review* (March 1994), pp. 10–17. For additional thoughts, see Warren Bennis, *Why Leaders Can't Lead* (San Francisco: Jossey-Bass, 1996).

[4] See Jean Lipman-Blumen, *Connective Leadership: Managing in a Changing World* (New York: Oxford University Press, 1996), pp. 3–11.

[5] Rosabeth Moss Kanter, "Power Failure in Management Circuits," *Harvard Business Review* (July/August 1979), pp. 65–75.

[6] The classic treatment of these power bases is John R. P. French Jr. and Bertram Raven, "The Bases of Social Power," in Darwin Cartwright (ed.), *Group Dynamics: Research and Theory* (Evanson, IL: Row, Peterson, 1962), pp. 607–13.

[7] For managerial applications of this basic framework, see Gary Yukl and Tom Taber, "The Effective Use of Managerial Power," *Personnel,* vol. 60 (1983), pp. 37–49; and Robert C. Benfari, Harry E. Wilkinson, and Charles D. Orth, "The Effective Use of Power," *Business Horizons,* vol. 29 (1986), pp. 12–16. Gary A. Yukl, *Leadership in Organizations,* 4th ed. (Englewood Cliffs, NJ: Prentice-Hall, 1998), includes "information" as a separate, but related, power source.

[8] James M. Kouzes and Barry Z. Posner, "The Leadership Challenge," *Success* (April 1988), p. 68. See also their books *Credibility: How Leaders Gain and Lose It; Why People Demand It* (San Francisco: Jossey-Bass, 1996); *Encouraging the Heart: A Leader's Guide to Rewarding and Recognizing Others* (San Francisco: Jossey-Bass, 1999); and *The Leadership Challenge: How to Get Extraordinary Things Done in Organizations,* 3rd ed. (San Francisco: Jossey-Bass, 2002).

[9] Quote from Andy Serwer, "Game Changers: Legendary Basketball Coach John Wooden and Starbucks' Howard Schultz Talk about a Common Interest—Leadership," *Fortune* (August 11, 2008): www.cnnmoney.com.

[10] Burt Nanus, *Visionary Leadership: Creating a Compelling Sense of Vision for Your Organization* (San Francisco: Jossey-Bass, 1992).

[11] The early work on leader traits is well represented in Ralph M. Stogdill, "Personal Factors Associated with Leadership: A Survey of the Literature," *Journal of Psychology,* vol. 25 (1948), pp. 35–71. See also Edwin E. Ghiselli, *Explorations in Management Talent* (Santa Monica, CA: Goodyear, 1971); and Shirley A. Kirkpatrick and Edwin A. Locke, "Leadership: Do Traits Really Matter?" *Academy of Management Executive* (1991), pp. 48–60.

[12] See also John W. Gardner's article, "The Context and Attributes of Leadership," *New Management,* vol. 5 (1988), pp. 18–22; John P. Kotter, *The Leadership Factor* (New York: Free Press, 1988); and Bernard M. Bass, *Stogdill's Handbook of Leadership* (New York: Free Press, 1990).

[13] Kirkpatrick and Locke, op. cit. (1991).

[14] This terminology comes from the classic studies by Kurt Lewin and his associates at the University of Iowa. See, for example, K. Lewin and R. Lippitt, "An Experimental Approach to the Study of Autocracy and Democracy: A Preliminary Note," *Sociometry,* vol. 1 (1938), pp. 292–300; K. Lewin, "Field Theory and Experiment in Social Psychology: Concepts and Methods," *American Journal of Sociology,* vol. 44 (1939); and K. Lewin, R. Lippitt, and R. K. White, "Patterns of Aggressive Behavior in Experimentally Created Social Climates," *Journal of Social Psychology,* vol. 10 (1939), pp. 271–301.

[15] Robert R. Blake and Jane Srygley Mouton, *The New Managerial Grid III* (Houston: Gulf Publishing, 1985).

[16] For a good discussion of this theory, see Fred E. Fiedler, Martin M. Chemers, and Linda Mahar, *The Leadership Match Concept* (New York: Wiley, 1978); Fiedler's current contingency research with the cognitive resource theory is summarized in Fred E. Fiedler and Joseph E. Garcia, *New Approaches to Effective Leadership* (New York: Wiley, 1987).

[17] Paul Hersey and Kenneth H. Blanchard, *Management and Organizational Behavior* (Englewood Cliffs, NJ: Prentice-Hall, 1988). For an interview with Paul Hersey on the origins of the model, see John R. Schermerhorn Jr., "Situational Leadership: Conversations with Paul Hersey," *Mid-American Journal of Business* (fall 1997), pp. 5–12.

[18] See Claude L. Graeff, "The Situational Leadership Theory: A Critical View," *Academy of Management Review,* vol. 8 (1983), pp. 285–91; and, Carmen F. Fenandez and Robert P. Vecchio, "Situational Leadership Theory Revisited: A Test of an Across-Jobs Perspective," *Leadership Quarterly,* vol. 8 (summer 1997), pp. 67–84.

[19] See, for example, Robert J. House, "A Path-Goal Theory of Leader Effectiveness," *Administrative Sciences Quarterly,* vol. 16 (1971), pp. 321–38; Robert J. House and Terrence R. Mitchell, "Path-Goal Theory of Leadership," *Journal of Contemporary Business* (Autumn 1974), pp. 81–97; the path-goal theory is reviewed by Bass, op. cit., and Yukl, op. cit. A supportive review of research is offered in Julie Indvik, "Path-Goal Theory of Leadership. A Meta-Analysis," in John A. Pearce II and Richard B. Robinson Jr. (eds.), *Academy of Management Best Paper Proceedings* (1986), pp. 189–92.

[20] See the discussions of path-goal theory in Yukl, op. cit.; and Bernard M. Bass, "Leadership: Good, Better, Best," *Organizational Dynamics* (Winter 1985), pp. 26–40.

[21] See Steven Kerr and John Jermier, "Substitutes for Leadership: Their Meaning and Measurement," *Organizational Behavior and Human Performance,* vol. 22 (1978), pp. 375–403; Jon P. Howell and Peter W. Dorfman, "Leadership and Substitutes for Leadership among Professional and Nonprofessional Workers," *Journal of Applied Behavioral Science,* vol. 22 (1986), pp. 29–46.

[22] An early presentation of the theory is F. Dansereau Jr., G. Graen, and W. J. Haga, "A Vertical Dyad Linkage Approach to Leadership Within Formal Organizations: A Longitudinal Investigation of the Role Making Process," *Organizational Behavior and Human Performance,* vol. 13, pp. 46–78.

[23] This discussion is based on Yukl, op. cit., pp. 117–22.

[24] Ibid.

[25] Victor H. Vroom and Arthur G. Jago, *The New Leadership: Managing Participation in Organizations* (Englewood Cliffs, NJ: Prentice-Hall, 1988). This is based on earlier work by Victor H. Vroom, "A New Look in Managerial Decision-Making," *Organizational Dynamics* (spring 1973), pp. 66–80; and Victor H. Vroom and Phillip Yetton, *Leadership and Decision-Making* (Pittsburgh: University of Pittsburgh Press, 1973).

[26] Vroom and Jago, op. cit.

[27] For a related discussion, see Edgar H. Schein, *Process Consultation Revisited: Building the Helping Relationship* (Reading, MA: Addison-Wesley, 1999).

[28] For a review see Yukl, op. cit.

[29] See the discussion by Victor H. Vroom, "Leadership and the Decision Making Process," *Organizational Dynamics,* vol. 28 (2000), pp. 82–94.

[30] Survey data in Stay Informed box from Gallup Leadership Institute, *Briefings Report 2005-01* (Lincoln, NE: University of Nebraska-Lincoln); "The Stat," *Business Week* (September 12, 2005), p. 16; and "U.S. Job Satisfaction Keeps Falling, the Conference Board Reports Today," The

Conference Board (February 28, 2005), retrieved from www.conference-board.org.

[31] Among the popular books addressing this point of view are Warren Bennis and Burt Nanus, *Leaders: The Strategies for Taking Charge* (New York: Harper Business 1997); Max DePree, *Leadership Is an Art,* op. cit.; Kotter, *The Leadership Factor,* op. cit.; Kouzes and Posner, *The Leadership Challenge,* op. cit.

[32] The distinction was originally made by James McGregor Burns, *Leadership* (New York: Harper & Row, 1978) and was further developed by Bernard Bass, *Leadership and Performance Beyond Expectations* (New York: Free Press, 1985) and Bernard M. Bass, "Leadership: Good, Better, Best," *Organizational Dynamics* (Winter 1985), pp. 26–40. See also Bernard M. Bass, "Does the Transactional-Transformational Leadership Paradigm Transcend Organizational and National Boundaries?" *American Psychologist,* vol. 52 (February 1997), pp. 130–39.

[33] See the discussion in Bass, op. cit., 1997.

[34] This list is based on Kouzes and Posner, op. cit.; Gardner, op. cit.

[35] Daniel Goleman, "Leadership That Gets Results," *Harvard Business Review* (March/April 2000), pp. 78–90. See also his books *Emotional Intelligence* (New York: Bantam Books, 1995) and *Working with Emotional Intelligence* (New York: Bantam Books, 1998).

[36] Daniel Goleman, Annie McKee, and Richard E. Boyatsis, *Primal Leadership: Realizing the Power of Emotional Intelligence* (Boston, MA: Harvard Business School Press, 2002), p. 3.

[37] Daniel Goleman, "What Makes a Leader?" *Harvard Business Review* (November/December 1998), pp. 93–102.

[38] Goleman, op. cit. (1998).

[39] Information from "Women and Men, Work and Power," *Fast Company,* issue 13 (1998), p. 71.

[40] Jane Shibley Hyde, "The Gender Similarities Hypothesis," *American Psychologist,* vol. 60, no. 6 (2005), pp. 581–92.

[41] A. H. Eagley, S. J. Daran, and M. G. Makhijani, "Gender and the Effectiveness of Leaders: A Meta-Analysis," *Psychological Bulletin,* vol. 117(1995), pp. 125–45.

[42] Research on gender issues in leadership is reported in Sally Helgesen, *The Female Advantage: Women's Ways of Leadership* (New York: Doubleday, 1990); Judith B. Rosener, "Ways Women Lead," *Harvard Business Review* (November/December 1990), pp. 119–25; and Alice H. Eagley, Steven J. Karau, and Blair T. Johnson, "Gender and Leadership Style Among School Principals: A Meta Analysis," *Administrative Science Quarterly,* vol. 27 (1992), pp. 76–102; Jean Lipman-Blumen, *Connective Leadership: Managing in a Changing World* (New York: Oxford University Press, 1996); Alice H. Eagley, Mary C. Johannesen-Smith, and Marloes L. van Engen, "Transformational, Transactional and Laissez-Faire Leadership: A Meta-Analysis of Women and Men," *Psychological Bulletin,* vol. 124, no. 4 (2003), pp. 569–591; and Carol Hymowitz, "Too Many Women Fall for Stereotypes of Selves, Study Says," *Wall Street Journal* (October 24, 2005), p. B.1.

[43] Data reported by Rochelle Sharpe, "As Women Rule," *Business Week* (November 20, 2000), p. 75.

[44] Herminia Ibarra and Otilia Obodaru, "Women and the Vision Thing," *Harvard Business Review* (January, 2009): Reprint R0901E.

[45] Eagley et al., op. cit.; Hymowitz, op. cit.; Rosener, op. cit.; Vroom, op. cit.; and, Ibarra and Obodaru, op. cit.

[46] Rosener, op. cit. (1990).

[47] See research summarized by Stephanie Armour, "Do Women Compete in Unhealthy Ways at Work?" *USA Today* (December 30, 2005), pp. B1–B2.

[48] Quote from "As Leaders, Women Rule," *Business Week* (November 20, 2000), pp. 75–84. Rosabeth Moss Kanter is the author of *Men and Women of the Corporation,* 2nd ed. (New York: Basic Books, 1993).

[49] Del Jones, "Women CEOs Slowly Gain on Corporate America," *USA Today* (January 1, 2009): www.usatoday.com; and Morice Mendoza, "Davos 2009: Where Are the Women?" *Business Week* (January 26, 2009): www.businessweek.com.

[50] Hyde, op. cit.; Hymowitz, op. cit.

[51] For debate on whether some transformational leadership qualities tend to be associated more with female than male leaders, see "Debate: Ways Women and Men Lead," *Harvard Business Review* (January/February 1991), pp. 150–60.

[52] "Many U.S. Employees Have Negative Attitudes to Their Jobs, Employers and Top Managers," Harris Poll #38 (May 6, 2005), retrieved from www.harrisinteractive.com.

[53] Information from "The Stat," *Business Week* (September 12, 2005), p. 16.

[54] See Terry Thomas, John R. Schermerhorn Jr., and John W. Dienhart, "Strategic Leadership of Ethical Behavior in Business," *Academy of Management Executive,* vol. 18 (May 2004), pp. 56–66.

[55] Doug May, Adrian Chan, Timothy Hodges, and Bruce Avolio, "Developing the Moral Component of Authentic Leadership," *Organizational Dynamics,* vol. 32 (2003), pp. 247–60.

[56] Peter F. Drucker, "Leadership: More Doing than Dash," *The Wall Street Journal* (January 6, 1988), p. 16.

[57] "Information from Southwest CEO Puts Emphasis on Character," *USA Today* (September 26, 2004), retrieved from www.usatoday/money/companies/management on December 12, 2005.

[58] Robert K. Greenleaf and Larry C. Spears, *The Power of Servant Leadership: Essays* (San Francisco: Berrett-Koehler, 1996).

[59] Jay A. Conger, "Leadership: The Art of Empowering Others," *Academy of Management Executive,* vol. 3 (1989), pp. 17–24.

[60] Max DePree, "An Old Pro's Wisdom: It Begins with a Belief in People," *New York Times* (September 10, 1989), p. F2; Max DePree, *Leadership Is an Art* (New York: Doubleday, 1989); David Woodruff, "Herman Miller: How Green Is My Factory," *Business Week* (September 16, 1991), pp. 54–56; and Max DePree, *Leadership Jazz* (New York: Doubleday, 1992).

[61] Lorraine Monroe, "Leadership Is About Making Vision Happen— What I Call 'Vision Acts,'" *Fast Company* (March 2001), p. 98; School Leadership Academy Web site: www.lorrainemonroe.com.

[62] Greenleaf and Spears, op. cit., p. 78.

[63] Fred E. Fiedler and Martin M. Chemers, *Improving Leadership Effectiveness: The Leader Match Concept,* 2nd ed. (New York: Wiley, 1984). Used by permission.

Feature Notes 12

Center for Creative Leadership–Examples and quotes from *Business Week* (July 8, 1991), pp. 60–61; and www.ccl.org/leadership/programs/profiles/lisaDitullio.aspx (retrieved August 12, 2008).

Trendsetters–Information from Erica Noonan, *Boston Globe* (January 4, 2009): www.boston.com/bostonglobe; "Six Million Users: Nothing to Twitter At," *Business Week* (March 16, 2009), pp. 51–52; wikipedia.com; and Michael S. Malone, "The Twitter Revolution," *The Wall Street Journal* (April 18–19, 2009), p. A11; and Jessica E. Vascellaro, "Twitter Trips on Rapid Growth," *The Wall Street Journal* (May 26, 2009), p. B1.

News Feed–Information and quotes from "The 'Millennials' Are Coming," CBS *60 Minutes* (November 11.2007); Brittany Hite, "Employers Rethink How they Give Feedback," *The Wall Street Journal* (October 13, 2008), p. B5; Shelly Banjo, "A Perfect Match?" *The Wall Street Journal* (October 13, 2009), p. R9; Olga Kharif, "Raised on the Web and Ready for Business," *Business Week* (December 8, 2008), pp. 77–78; and, Emma Jacobs, "Reality Check for Gen Y and Its Managers," *Financial Times* (May 14, 2009). See also Ron Alsop, *The Trophy Kids Grow Up* (New York: Dow Jones, 2008) and Sylvia Ann Hewlett, Maggie Jackson, Laura Sherbin, Peggy Shiller, Eytan Sosnovich, and Karen Sumberg, *Bookend Generations: Leveraging Talent and Finding Common Ground* (New York: Center for Work-Life Policy, 2009).

Stay Tuned–Information from American Management Association, "Electronic Monitoring & Surveillance Survey" (February 8, 2008): www.press.amanet.org/press-releases; and Liz Wolgemuth, "Why Web Surfing is a Noproblem," *U.S. News & World Report* (August 22, 2008): www.usnews.com/blogs.

Endnotes 12

[1] See Mintzberg, op. cit.; Kotter, op. cit.

[2] Henry Mintzberg, *The Nature of Managerial Work* (New York: Harper & Row, 1973).

3 John P. Kotter, "What Effective General Managers Really Do," *Harvard Business Review*, vol. 60 (November/December 1982), pp. 156–57; and *The General Managers* (New York: Macmillan, 1986).

4 "Relationships Are the Most Powerful Form of Media," *Fast Company* (March 2001), p. 100.

5 Information from American Management Association, "The Passionate Organization Fast-Response Survey" (September 25–29, 2000), and organization Web site: http://www.amanet.org/aboutama/index.htm.

6 Survey information from "What Do Recruiters Want?" *BizEd* (November/December 2002), p. 9; "Much to Learn, Professors Say," *USA Today* (July 5, 2001), p. 8D; and AMA Fast-Response Survey, "The Passionate Organization" (September 26–29, 2000).

7 Jay A. Conger, *Winning 'Em Over: A New Model for Managing in the Age of Persuasion* (New York: Simon & Schuster, 1998), pp. 24–79.

8 This discussion developed from ibid.

9 Quotations from John Huey, "America's Most Successful Merchant," *Fortune* (September 23, 1991), pp. 46–59; see also Sam Walton and John Huey, *Sam Walton: Made in America: My Story* (New York: Bantam Books, 1993).

10 *Business Week* (February 10, 1992), pp. 102–08.

11 See Robert H. Lengel and Richard L. Daft, "The Selection of Communication Media as an Executive Skill," *Academy of Management Executive*, vol. 2 (August 1988), pp. 225–32.

12 See Ibid.

13 See Eric Matson, "Now That We Have Your Complete Attention," *Fast Company* (February/March 1997), pp. 124–32.

14 Information from Sam Dillon, "What Corporate America Can't Build: A Sentence," *The New York Times* (December 7, 2004).

15 David McNeill, *Hand and Mind: What Gestures Reveal about Thought* (Chicago: University of Chicago Press, 1992).

16 Martin J. Gannon, *Paradoxes of Culture and Globalization* (Los Angeles: Sage, 2008), p. 76.

17 McNeill, op. cit.

18 Adapted from Richard V. Farace, Peter R. Monge, and Hamish M. Russell, *Communicating and Organizing* (Reading, MA: Addison-Wesley, 1977), pp. 97–98.

19 Tom Peters and Nancy Austin, *A Passion for Excellence* (New York: Random House, 1985).

20 Quote from Andy Serwer, "Game Changers: Legendary Basketball Coach John Wooden and Starbucks' Howard Schultz Talk about a Common Interest–Leadership," *Fortune* (August 11, 2008): www.cnnmoney.com.

21 This discussion is based on Carl R. Rogers and Richard E. Farson, "Active Listening" (Chicago: Industrial Relations Center of the University of Chicago, n.d.); see also Carl R. Rogers and Fritz J. Roethlisberger, "Barriers and Gateways to Communication," *Harvard Business Review* (November-December, 1001), Reprint 91610.

22 Ibid.

23 Information from Carol Hymowitz, "Managers See Feedback from Their Staffers as Most Valuable," *Wall Street Journal* (August 22, 2000), p. B1.

24 A useful source of guidelines is John J. Gabarro and Linda A. Hill, "Managing Performance," Note 9-96-022 (Boston, MA: Harvard Business School Publishing, n.d.).

25 Nanette Byrnes, "A Steely Resolve," *Business Week* (April 6, 2009), p. 54.

26 Information and quotes from "Undercover Boss Gets the Communication Message," *Financial Times* (June 9, 2009).

27 Information and quote from Jack Ewing, "Nokia: Bring on the Employee Rants," *Business Week* (June 22, 2009), p. 50.

28 A classic work on proxemics is Edward T. Hall's book, *The Hidden Dimension* (Garden City, NY: Doubleday, 1986).

29 Information from Rachel Metz, Office Décor First Change by New AOI Executive," *The Columbus Dispatch* (May 25, 2009), p. A7.

30 Mirand Ewell, "Alternative Spaces Spawning Desk-Free Zones," *Columbus Dispatch* (May 18, 1998), pp. 10–11.

31 "Tread: Rethinking the Workplace," *Business Week* (September 25, 2006), p. IN.

32 Amy Saunders, "A Creative Approach to Work," *The Columbus Dispatch* (May 2, 2008), pp. C1, C9.

33 Information and quotes from Sarah E. Needleman, "Thnx for the IView! I Wud Luv to Work 4 U!!;)," *The Wall Street Journal Online* (July 31, 2008).

34 Ibid.

35 Stephanie Clifford, "Video Prank at Domino's Taints Brand," *The New York Times* (April 16, 2009): www.nytimes.com; and, Deborah Stead, "An Unwelcome Delivery," *Business Week* (May 4, 2009), p. 15.

36 Information and quotes form Michelle Conlin and Douglas MacMillan, "Managing the Tweets," *Business Week* (June 1, 2009), pp. 20–21.

37 Data in Stay Informed from "Privacy Special Report," *PC Computing* (March 2000), p. 88.

38 Ibid.

39 Information from Carol Hymowitz, "More American Chiefs Are Taking Top Posts at Overseas Concerns," *Wall Street Journal* (October 17, 2005), p. B1.

40 Examples reported in Martin J. Gannon, *Paradoxes of Culture and Globalization* (Los Angeles: Sage Publications, 2008), p. 80.

41 Ibid.

42 Information from Ben Brown, "Atlanta Out to Mind Its Manners," *USA Today* (March 14, 1996), p. 7.

43 Douglas T. Hall, Donald D. Bowen, Roy J. Lewicki, and Francine S. Hall, *Experiences in Management and Organizational Behavior*, 2nd ed. (New York: Wiley, 1985). Used by permission.

Feature Notes 13

Spanx–Information from Andrew Ward, "Spanx Queen Firms up the Bottom Line," *Financial Times* (November 30, 2006), p. 7; and, Simona Covel, "A Dated Industry Gets a Modern Makeover," *The Wall Street Journal* (August 7, 2008), p. B9.

Trendsetters–Information and quotes the corporate Web sites and from The Entrepreneur's Hall of Fame: www.1tbn.com/halloffame.html; Knowledge@Wharton, "The Importance of Being Richard Branson," *Wharton School Publishing* (June 3, 2005): www.whartonsp.com.

News Feed–Information and quotes from "Racial Bias and Leadership," *BizEd* (November/December 2008), pp. 58–59; see also Ashleigh Shelby Rosette, Geoffrey Leonardelli, and Katherine Phillips, "The White Standard: Racial Bias in Leader Categorization," *Journal of Applied Psychology*, vol. 93, no. 4 (2008), pp. 758–77.

Stay Tuned–See Linda Grant, "Happy Workers, High Returns," *Fortune* (January 12, 1998), p. 81; Timothy A. Judge, "Promote Job Satisfaction Through Mental Challenge," Chapter 6 in Edwin A. Locke, ed., *The Blackwell Handbook of Organizational Behavior* (Malden, MA: Blackwell, 2004); "U.S. Employees More Dissatisfied with Their Jobs," *Associated Press* (February 28, 2005), retrieved from: www.msnbc.com; and "U.S. Job Satisfaction Keeps Falling, The Conference Board Reports Today," *The Conference Board* (February 28, 2005): www.conference-board.org.

Endnotes 13

1 See H. R. Schiffman, *Sensation and Perception: An Integrated Approach*, 3rd ed. (New York: Wiley, 1990).

2 Information from "Misconceptions About Women in the Global Arena Keep Their Numbers Low," Catalyst study: www.catalystwomen.org/home.html.

3 The classic work is Dewitt C. Dearborn and Herbert A. Simon, "Selective Perception: A Note on the Departmental Identification of Executives," *Sociometry*, vol. 21 (1958), pp. 140–44. See also J. P. Walsh, "Selectivity and Selective Perception: Belief Structures and Information Processing," *Academy of Management Journal*, vol. 24 (1988), pp. 453–70.

4 Quote from Sheila O'Flanagan, "Underestimate Casual Dressers at Your Peril," *The Irish Times* (July 22, 2005).

5 See William L. Gardner and Mark J. Martinko, "Impression Management in Organizations," *Journal of Management* (June 1988), pp. 332–43.

6 Sandy Wayne and Robert Liden, "Effects of Impression Management on Performance Ratings," *Academy of Management Journal* (February 2005), pp. 232–52.

[7] See M. R. Barrick and M. K. Mount, "The Big Five Personality Dimensions and Job Performance: A Meta-Analysis," *Personnel Psychology*, vol. 44 (1991), pp. 1–26.

[8] For a sample of research, see G. M. Hurtz and J. J. Donovan, "Personality and Job Performance: The Big Five Revisited," *Journal of Applied Psychology*, vol. 85 (2000), pp. 869–79; and T. A. Judge and R. Ilies, "Relationship of Personality to Performance Motivation: A Meta-Analytic Review," *Journal of Applied Psychology*, vol. 87 (2002), pp. 797–807.

[9] Carl G. Jung, *Psychological Types*, H. G. Baynes trans. (Princeton, NJ: Princeton University Press, 1971).

[10] I. Briggs-Myers, *Introduction to Type* (Palo Alto, CA: Consulting Psychologists Press, 1980).

[11] See, for example, William L. Gardner and Mark J. Martinko, "Using the Myers-Briggs Type Indicator to Study Managers: A Literature Review and Research Agenda," *Journal of Management,* vol. 22 (1996), pp. 45–83; Naomi L. Quenk, Essentials of Myers-Briggs Type Indicator Assessment (New York: Wiley, 2000).

[12] This discussion based in part on John R. Schermerhorn Jr., James G. Hunt, and Richard N. Osborn, *Organizational Behavior*, 9th ed. (New York: John Wiley & Sons, 2005), pp. 54–60.

[13] J. B. Rotter, "Generalized Expectancies for Internal versus External Control of Reinforcement," *Psychological Monographs*, vol. 80 (1966), pp. 1–28.

[14] T. W. Adorno, E. Frenkel-Brunswick, D. J. Levinson, and R. N. Sanford, *The Authoritarian Personality* (New York: Harper & Row, 1950).

[15] Niccolo Machiavelli, *The Prince*, trans. George Bull (Middlesex, UK: Penguin, 1961).

[16] See M. Snyder, *Public Appearances/Private Realities: The Psychology of Self-Monitoring* (New York: Freeman, 1987).

[17] See Arthur P. Brief, Randall S. Schuler, and Mary Van Sell, *Managing Job Stress* (Boston: Little, Brown, 1981), pp. 7, 8.

[18] The classic work is Meyer Friedman and Ray Roseman, *Type A Behavior and Your Heart* (New York: Knopf, 1974).

[19] Sue Shellenbarger, "Do We Work More or Not? Either Way, We Feel Frazzled," *Wall Street Journal* (July 30, 1997), p. B1.

[20] See, for example, "Desk Rage," *Business Week* (November 27, 2000), p. 12.

[21] See Hans Selye, *Stress in Health and Disease* (Boston: Butterworth, 1976).

[22] Carol Hymowitz, "Can Workplace Stress Get *Worse?*" *Wall Street Journal* (January 16, 2001), pp. B1, B3.

[23] See Steve M. Jex, *Stress and Job Performance* (San Francisco: Jossey-Bass, 1998).

[24] The extreme case of "workplace violence" is discussed by Richard V. Denenberg and Mark Braverman, *The Violence-Prone Workplace* (Ithaca, NY: Cornell University Press, 1999).

[25] David Gauthier-Villars and Leila Abboud, "In France, CEOs Can Become Hostages," *The Wall Street Journal* (April 3, 2009), pp. B1, B4.

[26] See Daniel C. Ganster and Larry Murphy, "Workplace Interventions to Prevent Stress-Related Illness: Lessons from Research and Practice," Chapter 2 in Cooper and Locke (eds.), *Industrial and Organizational Psychology: Linking Theory with Practice* (Malden, MA: Blackwell Business, 2000); Jonathan D. Quick, Amy B. Henley, and James Campbell Quick, "The Balancing Act—At Work and at Home," *Organizational Dynamics*, vol. 33 (2004), pp. 426–37.

[27] Data in Stay Informed from "Michael Mandel, "The Real Reasons You're Working So Hard," *Business Week* (October 3, 2005), pp. 60–70; "Many U.S. Employees Have Negative Attitudes to Their Jobs, Employers and Top Managers," *The Harris Poll #38* (May 6, 2005), retrieved from www.harrisinteractive.com; Sue Shellenberger, "If You Need to Work Better, Maybe Try Working Less," *The Wall Street Journal* (September 23, 2009), pp. D1, D2.

[28] See Melinda Beck, "Stress So Bad It Hurts—Really," *Wall Street Journal* (March 17, 2009), pp. D1, D6.

[29] Information and quote from Joann S. Lublin, "How One Black Woman Lands Her Top Jobs: Risks and Networking," *Wall Street Journal* (March 4, 2003), p. B1.

[30] Martin Fishbein and Icek Ajzen, *Belief, Attitude, Intention and Behavior: An Introduction to Theory and Research* (Reading, MA: Addison-Wesley, 1973).

[31] See Leon Festinger, *A Theory of Cognitive Dissonance* (Palo Alto, CA: Stanford University Press, 1957).

[32] For an overview, see Paul E. Spector, *Job Satisfaction* (Thousand Oaks, CA: Sage, 1997); Timothy A. Judge and Allan H. Church, "Job Satisfaction: Research and Practice," Chapter 7 in Cary L. Cooper and Edwin A. Locke (eds.), op. cit.(2000); Timothy A. Judge, "Promote Job Satisfaction Through Mental Challenge," Chapter 6 in Edwin A. Locke (ed.), *The Blackwell Handbook of Principles of Organizational Behavior* (Malden, MA: Blackwell, 2004).

[33] Information in Stay Informed from Linda Grant, "Happy Workers, High Returns," *Fortune* (January 12, 1998), p. 81; Judge, op. cit. (2002); "U.S. Employees More Dissatisfied With Their Jobs," *Associated Press* (February 28, 2005), retrieved from www.msnbc.com; "U.S. Job Satisfaction Keeps Falling, The Conference Board Reports Today," *The Conference Board* (February 28, 2005), retrieved from www.conference-board.org; and Salary.com, "Survey Shows Impact of Downturn on Job Satisfaction," *OH&S: Occupational Health and Safety* (February 7, 2009): www.ohsonline.com.

[34] *What Workers Want: A Worldwide Study of Attitudes to Work and Work-Life Balance* (London: FDS International, 2007).

[35] Data reported in "When Loyalty Erodes, So Do Profits," *Business Week* (August 13, 2001), p. 8.

[36] Dennis W. Organ, *Organizational Citizenship Behavior: The Good Soldier Syndrome* (Lexington, MA: Lexington Books, 1988).

[37] See Mark C. Bolino and William H. Turnley, "Going the Extra Mile: Cultivating and Managing Employee Citizenship Behavior," *Academy of Management Executive*, vol. 17 (August 2003), pp. 60–67.

[38] Tony DiRomualdo, "The High Cost of Employee Disengagement" (July 7, 2004): www.wistechnology.com.

[39] These relationships are discussed in Charles N. Greene, "The Satisfaction-Performance Controversy," *Business Horizons*, vol. 15 (1982), pp. 31; Michelle T. Iaffaldano and Paul M. Muchinsky, "Job Satisfaction and Job Performance: A Meta Analysis," *Psychological Bulletin*, vol. 97 (1985), pp. 251–73.

[40] This discussion follows conclusions in Judge, op. cit. (2004). For a summary of the early research, see Iaffaldano and Muchinsky, op. cit. Self Assessment: Adapted from R. W. Bortner, "A Short Rating scale as a Potential Measure of Type A Behavior," *Journal of Chronic Diseases*, vol. 22 (1966), pp. 87–91. Used by permission.

[41] Daniel Goleman, "Leadership That Gets Results," *Harvard Business Review* (March–April 2000), pp. 78–90. See also his books, *Emotional Intelligence* (New York: Bantam Books, 1995) and *Working with Emotional Intelligence* (New York: Bantam Books, 1998).

[42] See Robert G. Lord, Richard J. Klimoski, and Ruth Knafer (eds.), *Emotions in the Workplace; Understanding the Structure and Role of Emotions in Organizational Behavior* (San Francisco: Jossey-Bass, 2002); Roy L. Payne and Cary L. Cooper (eds.), *Emotions at Work: Theory Research and Applications for Management* (Chichester, UK: John Wiley & Sons, 2004); and Daniel Goleman and Richard Boyatzis, "Social Intelligence and the Biology of Leadership," *Harvard Business Review* (September 2008), Reprint R0809E.

[43] Joyce E. Bono and Remus Ilies, "Charisma, Positive Emotions and Mood Contagion," *Leadership Quarterly,* vol. 17 (2006), pp. 317–34; and Goleman and Boyatzis, op. cit.

[44] Adapted from R.W. Bortner, "A Short Rating Scale as a Potential Measure of Type A Behavior, "*Journal of Chronic Diseases,* vol. 22 (1966), pp. 87–91. Used by permission.

Feature Notes 14

Butcher Company/Charlie Butcher–Information from information and quotes from Julie Flaherty, "A Parting Gift from the Boss Who Cared," *New York Times* (September 28, 2000), pp. C1, C25; Business Wire Press Release, "Employees of the Butcher Company Share over $18 Million as Owner Shares Benefits of Success" (September 21, 2000); and "Butcher, Charles," *The New York Times* (June 20, 2004): www.nytimes.com.

Trendsetters–Information from "HopeLab Video Games for Health," *Fast Company* (December, 2008/January, 2009), p. 116; and www.hopelab.org.

News Feed–Information and quotes from Jane Hodges, "A Virtual Matchmaker for Volunteers," *The Wall Street Journal* (February 12, 2009), p. D3; Dana Mattioli, "The Laid-Off Can Do Well Doing Good," *The Wall Street Journal* (March 17, 2009), p. D1; Elizabeth Garone, "Paying It Forward is a Full-Time Job," *The Wall Street Journal* (March 17, 2009), p. D4.

Stay Tuned–Information from Del Jones, "Women Slowly Gain on Corporate America," *USA Today* (January 2, 2009), p. 6B; "Catalyst 2008 Census of the Fortune 500 Reveals Women Gained Little Ground Advancing to Business Leadership Positions," *Catalyst Press Release* (December 8, 2008): www.catalyst.org/press_release.

Endnotes 14

[1] Information from Melinda Beck, "If at First You Don't Succeed, You're in Excellent Company," *The Wall Street Journal* (April 29, 2008), p. D1.

[2] See Abraham H. Maslow, *Eupsychian Management* (Homewood, IL: Richard D. Irwin, 1965); Abraham H. Maslow, *Motivation and Personality*, 2nd ed. (New York: Harper & Row, 1970). For a research perspective, see Mahmoud A. Wahba and Lawrence G. Bridwell, "Maslow Reconsidered: A Review of Research on the Need Hierarchy," *Organizational Behavior and Human Performance*, vol. 16 (1976), pp. 212–40.

[3] Clayton P. Alderfer, *Existence, Relatedness, and Growth* (New York: Free Press, 1972).

[4] Developed originally from a discussion in Edward E. Lawler III, *Motivation in Work Organizations* (Monterey, CA: Brooks/Cole Publishing, 1973), pp. 30–36.

[5] For a collection of McClelland's work, see David C. McClelland, *The Achieving Society* (New York: Van Nostrand, 1961); "Business Drive and National Achievement," *Harvard Business Review*, vol. 40 (July/August 1962), pp. 99–112; David C. McClelland, *Human Motivation* (Glenview, IL: Scott, Foresman, 1985); David C. McClelland and Richard E. Boyatsis, "The Leadership Motive Pattern and Long-Term Success in Management," *Journal of Applied Psychology*, vol. 67 (1982), pp. 737–43.

[6] David C. McClelland and David H. Burnham, "Power Is the Great Motivator," *Harvard Business Review* (March/April 1976), pp. 100–10.

[7] The complete two-factor theory is in Frederick Herzberg, Bernard Mausner, and Barbara Block Synderman, *The Motivation to Work*, 2nd ed. (New York: Wiley, 1967); Frederick Herzberg, "One More Time: How Do You Motivate Employees?" *Harvard Business Review* (January/February 1968), pp. 53–62, and reprinted as an *HBR classic* (September/October 1987), pp. 109–20.

[8] Critical reviews are provided by Robert J. House and Lawrence A. Wigdor, "Herzberg's Dual-Factor Theory of Job Satisfaction and Motivation: A Review of the Evidence and a Criticism," *Personnel Psychology*, vol. 20 (Winter 1967), pp. 369–89; Steven Kerr, Anne Harlan, and Ralph Stogdill, "Preference for Motivator and Hygiene Factors in a Hypothetical Interview Situation," *Personnel Psychology*, vol. 27 (Winter 1974), pp. 109–24. See also Frederick Herzberg, "Workers' Needs: The Same around the World," *Industry Week* (September 21, 1987), pp. 29–32.

[9] See Frederick Herzberg, Bernard Mausner, and Barbara Block Synderman, *The Motivation to Work*, 2nd ed. (New York: Wiley, 1967). The quotation is from Frederick Herzberg, "One More Time: Employees?" *Harvard Business Review* (January/February 1968), pp. 53–62, and reprinted as an HBR Classic in (September/October 1987), pp. 109–120.

[10] For a complete description of the core characteristics model, see J. Richard Hackman and Greg R. Oldham, *Work Redesign* (Reading, MA: Addison—Wesley, 1980).

[11] Information in "Stay Informed" from "CEO Pay: Sky High Gets Even Higher," *CNN Money* (August 30, 2005), retrieved from www.money.cnn.com. Suggested by Victoria Richebacher.

[12] See, for example, J. Stacy Adams, "Toward an Understanding of Inequity," *Journal of Abnormal and Social Psychology*, vol. 67 (1963), pp. 422–36; J. Stacy Adams, "Inequity in Social Exchange," in vol. 2, L. Berkowitz (ed.), *Advances in Experimental Social Psychology* (New York: Academic Press, 1965), pp. 267–300.

[13] See, for example, J. W. Harder, "Play for Pay: Effects of Inequity in a Pay-for-Performance Context," *Administrative Science Quarterly*, vol. 37 (1992), pp. 321–35.

[14] Information and quotes from Alistair Barr, "A Look at Some of the Most Luxurious Executive Perks," *The Columbus Dispatch* (May 24, 2009), p. D1.

[15] Victor H. Vroom, *Work and Motivation* (New York: Wiley, 1964; republished by Jossey-Bass, 1994).

[16] The work on goal-setting theory is well summarized in Edwin A. Locke and Gary P. Latham, *Goal Setting: A Motivational Technique That Works!* (Englewood Cliffs, NJ: Prentice Hall, 1984). See also Edwin A. Locke, Kenneth N. Shaw, Lisa A. Saari, and Gary P. Latham, "Goal Setting and Task Performance 1969–1980," *Psychological Bulletin*, vol. 90 (1981), pp. 125–52; Mark E. Tubbs, "Goal Setting: A Meta-Analytic Examination of the Empirical Evidence," *Journal of Applied Psychology*, vol. 71 (1986), pp. 474–83; and Terence R. Mitchell, Kenneth R. Thompson, and Jane George-Falvy, "Goal Setting: Theory and Practice," Chapter 9 in Cary L. Cooper and Edwin A. Locke (eds.), *Industrial and Organizational Psychology: Linking Theory with Practice* (Malden, MA: Blackwell Business, 2000), pp. 211–49.

[17] For a recent critical discussion of goal-setting theory, see Lisa D. Ordonez, Maurice E. Schweitzer, Adam D. Galinsky, and Max H. Bazerman, "Goals Gone Wild: The Systematic Side Effects of Overprescribing Goal Setting," *Academy of Management Perspectives*, vol. 23 (February, 2009), pp. 6–16; and Edwin A. Locke and Gary P. Latham, "Has Goal Setting Gone Wild, or Have Its Attackers Abandoned Good Scholarship?" *Academy of Management Perspectives*, vol. 23 (February, 2009), pp. 17–23.

[18] "The Boss: Goal by Goal," *The New York Times* (August 31, 2008), p. 10.

[19] Gary P. Latham and Edwin A. Locke, "Self-Regulation Through Goal Setting," *Organizational Behavior and Human Decision Processes*, vol. 50 (1991), pp. 212–47.

[20] Edwin A. Locke, "Guest Editor's Introduction: Goal-Setting Theory and Its Applications to the World of Business," *Academy of Management Executive*, vol. 18, no. 4 (2004), pp. 124–25.

[21] E. L. Thorndike, *Animal Intelligence* (New York: Macmillan, 1911), p. 244.

[22] B. F. Skinner, *Walden Two* (New York: Macmillan, 1948); *Science and Human Behavior* (New York: Macmillan, 1953); *Contingencies of Reinforcement* (New York: Appleton-Century-Crofts, 1969).

[23] Knowledge@Wharton, "The Importance of Being Richard Branson," *Wharton School Publishing* (June 3, 2005): www.whartonsp.com.

[24] Richard Gibson, "Pitchman in the Corner Office," *The Wall Street Journal* (October 24, 2007), p. D10. See also David Novak, *The Education of an Accidental CEO: Lessons Learned from the Trailer Park to the Corner Office* (New York: Crown Business, 2007).

[25] For a good review, see Lee W. Frederickson (ed.), *Handbook of Organizational Behavior Management* (New York: Wiley-Interscience, 1982); Fred Luthans and Robert Kreitner, *Organizational Behavior Modification* (Glenview, IL: Scott-Foresman, 1985); and Andrew D. Stajkovic and Fred Luthans, "A Meta-Analysis of the Effects of Organizational Behavior Modification on Task Performance 1975–95," *Academy of Management Journal*, vol. 40 (1997), pp. 1122–49.

[26] Edwin A. Locke, "The Myths of Behavior Mod in Organizations," *Academy of Management Review*, vol. 2 (October 1977), pp. 543–53.

Feature Notes 15

NASCAR Pit Crews–Information and quotes from Allen St. John, "Racing's Fastest Pit Crew," *The Wall Street Journal* (May 9, 2008), p. W4; see also "High-Octane Business Training," *BizEd* (July/August, 2008), p. 72.

Trendsetters–Information and quotes from Robert D. Hof, "Amazon's Risky Bet," *Business Week* (November 13, 2006), p. 52; Jon Neale, "Jeff Bezos," *BusinessWings* (February 16, 2007): www.businesswings.co.uk; Alan Deutschman, "Inside the Mind of Jeff Bezos," *Fast Company* (December 19, 2007); www.fastcompany.com/magazine/85; and http://en.wikipedia.org/wiki/Jeff_Bezos.

News Feed–Information from Reena Jana, "Real Life Imitates *Real World*," *BusinessWeek* (March 23 & 30, 2009), p. 42.

Stay Tuned–Information from "Two Wasted Days at Work," *CNNMoney.com* (March 16, 2005): www.cnnmoney.com.

Endnotes 15

1 See, for example, Edward E. Lawler III, Susan Albers Mohrman, and Gerald E. Ledford Jr., *Employee Involvement and Total Quality Management: Practices and Results in Fortune 1000 Companies* (San Francisco: Jossey-Bass, 1992); Susan A. Mohrman, Susan A. Cohen, and Monty A. Mohrman, *Designing Team-based Organizations: New Forms for Knowledge Work* (San Francisco: Jossey-Bass, 1995).

2 Jon R. Katzenbach and Douglas K. Smith, *The Wisdom of Teams: Creating the High Performance Organization* (Boston: Harvard Business School Press, 1993).

3 See Edward E. Lawler III, *From the Ground Up: Six Principles for Building the New Logic Corporation* (San Francisco: Jossey-Bass, 1996), p. 131.

4 Data from Lynda C. McDermott, Nolan Brawley, and William A. Waite, *World-Class Teams: Working Across Borders* (New York: Wiley, 1998), p. 5; Survey reported in "Meetings Among Top Ten Time Wasters," *San Francisco Business Times* (April 7, 2003); www.bizjournals.com/sanfrancisco/stories/2003/04/07/daily21.html.

5 Information from Scott Thurm, "Teamwork Raises Everyone's Game," *Wall Street Journal* (November 7, 2005), p. B7.

6 Harold J. Leavitt, "Suppose We Took Groups More Seriously," in Eugene L. Cass and Frederick G. Zimmer (eds.), *Man and Work in Society* (New York: Van Nostrand Reinhold, 1975), pp. 67–77.

7 See Marvin E. Shaw, *Group Dynamics: The Psychology of Small Group Behavior*, 2nd ed. (New York: McGraw-Hill, 1976); Leavitt, op. cit.

8 A classic work is Bib Latane, Kipling Williams, and Stephen Harkins, "Many Hands Make Light the Work: The Causes and Consequences of Social Loafing," *Journal of Personality and Social Psychology*, vol. 37 (1978), pp. 822–32. See also John M. George, "Extrinsic and Intrinsic Origins of Perceived Social Loafing in Organizations," *Academy of Management Journal* (March 1992), pp. 191–202; and W. Jack Duncan, "Why Some People Loaf in Groups While Others Loaf Alone," *Academy of Management Executive*, vol. 8 (1994), pp. 79–80.

9 The "linking pin" concept is introduced in Rensis Likert, *New Patterns of Management* (New York: McGraw-Hill, 1962).

10 See discussion by Susan G. Cohen and Don Mankin, "The Changing Nature of Work," in Susan Albers Mohrman, Jay R. Galbraith, Edward E. Lawler III, and Associates, *Tomorrow's Organization: Crafting Winning Capabilities in a Dynamic World* (San Francisco: Jossey-Bass, 1998), pp. 154–78.

11 Information from "Diversity: America's Strength," special advertising section, *Fortune* (June 23, 1997); American Express corporate communication (1998).

12 See Susan D. Van Raalte, "Preparing the Task Force to Get Good Results," *S.A.M. Advanced Management Journal*, vol. 47 (Winter 1982), pp. 11–16; Walter Kiechel III, "The Art of the Corporate Task Force," *Fortune* (January 28, 1991), pp. 104–06.

13 Developed from Eric Matson, "The Seven Sins of Deadly Meetings," *Fast Company* (April/May 1996), p. 122.

14 Mohrman et al., op. cit.

15 Information from Jenny C. McCune, "Making Lemonade," *Management Review* (June 1997), pp. 49–53.

16 For a good discussion of quality circles, see Edward E. Lawler III and Susan A. Mohrman, "Quality Circles After the Fad," *Harvard Business Review*, vol. 63 (January/February 1985), pp. 65–71; Edward E. Lawler III and Susan Albers Mohrman, "Employee Involvement, Reengineering, and TQM: Focusing on Capability Development," in Mohrman et al. (1998), pp. 179–208.

17 William M. Bulkeley, "Computerizing Dull Meetings Is Touted as an Antidote to the Mouth That Bored," *Wall Street Journal* (January 28, 1992), pp. B1, B2.

18 See Wayne F. Cascio, "Managing a Virtual Workplace," *Academy of Management Executive*, vol. 14 (2000), pp. 81–90.

19 Robert D. Hof, "Teamwork, Supercharged," *Business Week* (November 21, 2005), pp. 90–92.

20 See Sheila Simsarian Webber, "Virtual Teams: A Meta-Analysis," http://www.shrm.org/foundation/findings.asp.

21 See Stacie A. Furst, Martha Reeves, Benson Rosen, and Richard S. Blackburn, "Managing the Life Cycle of Virtual Teams," *Academy of Management Executive*, vol. 18, no. 2 (2004), pp. 6–11.

22 R. Brent Gallupe and William H. Cooper, "Brainstorming Electronically," *Sloan Management Review* (Winter 1997), pp. 11–21; Cascio, op. cit.

23 Cascio, op. cit.; Furst, et al., op. cit.

24 See, for example, Paul S. Goodman, Rukmini Devadas, and Terri L. Griffith Hughson, "Groups and Productivity: Analyzing the Effectiveness of Self-Managing Teams," Chapter 11 in John R. Campbell and Richard J. Campbell, *Productivity in Organizations* (San Francisco: Jossey-Bass, 1988); Jack Orsbrun, Linda Moran, Ed Musslewhite, and John H. Zenger, with Craig Perrin, *Self-Directed Work Teams: The New American Challenge* (Homewood, IL: Business One Irwin, 1990); Dale E. Yeatts and Cloyd Hyten, High *Performing Self-Managed Work Teams* (Thousand Oaks, CA: Sage, 1997).

25 Ibid.; Lawler et al., op. cit., 1998.

26 For a review of research on group effectiveness, see J. Richard Hackman, "The Design of Work Teams," in Jay W. Lorsch (ed.), *Handbook of Organizational Behavior* (Englewood Cliffs, NJ: Prentice-Hall, 1987), pp. 315–42; and J. Richard Hackman, Ruth Wageman, Thomas M. Ruddy, and Charles L. Ray, "Team Effectiveness in Theory and Practice," Chapter 5 in Cary L. Cooper and Edwin A. Locke, *Industrial and Organizational Psychology: Linking Theory with Practice* (Malden, MA: Blackwell, 2000).

27 For a discussion of effectiveness in the context of top management teams, see Edward E. Lawler III, David Finegold, and Jay A. Conger, "Corporate Boards: Developing Effectiveness at the Top," in Mohrman, op. cit. (1998), pp. 23–50.

28 Quote from Alex Markels, "Money & Business," *U. S. News online* (October 22, 2006).

29 "Dream Teams," *Northwestern* (Winter 2005), p. 10; Matt Golosinski, "Teamwork Takes Center Stage," *Northwestern* (Winter 2005), p. 39.

30 Golosinski, op. cit., p. 39.

31 Information from Susan Carey, "Racing to Improve," *The Wall Street Journal* (March 24, 2006), pp. B1, B6.

32 Robert D. Hof, "Amazon's Risky Bet," *Business Week* (November 13, 2006), p. 52.

33 J. Steven Heinen and Eugene Jacobson, "A Model of Task Group Development in Complex Organizations and a Strategy of Implementation," *Academy of Management Review*, vol. 1 (1976), pp. 98–111; Bruce W. Tuckman, "Developmental Sequence in Small Groups," *Psychological Bulletin*, vol. 63 (1965), pp. 384–99; Bruce W. Tuckman and Mary Ann C. Jensen, "Stages of Small-Group Development Revisited," *Group & Organization Studies*, vol. 2 (1977), pp. 419–27.

34 See Warren Watson, "Cultural Diversity's Impact on Interaction Process and Performance," *Academy of Management Journal*, vol. 16 (1993); Christopher Earley and Elaine Mosakowski, "Creating Hybrid Team Structures: An Empirical Test of Transnational Team Functioning," *Academy of Management Journal*, vol. 5 (February 2000), pp. 26–49; Eric Kearney, Diether Gebert, and Sven C. Voilpel, "When and How Diversity Benefits Teams: The Importance of Team Members' Need for Cognition," *Academy of Management Journal,* vol. 52 (2009), pp. 582–598; and, Aparna Joshi and Hyuntak Roh, "The Role of Context in Work Team Diversity Research: A Meta-analytic Approach," *Academy of Management Journal,* vol. 52 (2009), pp. 599–628.

35 See, for example, Edgar Schein, *Process Consultation* (Reading, MA: Addison-Wesley, 1988); and Linda C. McDermott, Nolan Brawley, and William A. Waite, *World-Class Teams: Working Across Borders* (New York: Wiley, 1998).

36 For a good discussion, see Robert F. Allen and Saul Pilnick, "Confronting the Shadow Organization: How to Detect and Defeat Negative Norms," *Organizational Dynamics* (Spring 1973), pp. 13–16.

37 See Schein, op. cit., pp. 76–79.

38 Marvin E. Shaw, *Group Dynamics: The Psychology of Small Group Behavior* (New York: McGraw-Hill, 1976).

39 A classic work in this area is K. Benne and P. Sheets, *Journal of Social Issues*, vol. 2 (1948), pp. 42–47; see also Likert, op. cit., pp. 166–69; Schein, op. cit. pp. 49–56.

40 Based on John R. Schermerhorn Jr., James G. Hunt, and Richard N. Osborn, *Organizational Behavior*, 7th ed. (New York: Wiley, 2000), pp. 345–46.

41 Schein, op. cit., pp. 69–75.

[42] A good overview is William D. Dyer, *Team-Building* (Reading MA: Addison-Wesley, 1977).

[43] Dennis Berman, "Zap! Pow! Splat!" *Business Week,* Enterprise issue (February 9, 1998), p. ENT22.

[44] Victor H. Vroom and Arthur G. Jago, *The New Leadership: Managing Participation in Organizations* (Englewood Cliffs, NJ: Prentice Hall, 1988); Victor H. Vroom, "A New Look in Managerial Decision-Making," *Organizational Dynamics* (Spring 1973), pp. 66–80; Victor H. Vroom and Phillip Yetton, *Leadership and Decision-Making* (Pittsburgh: University of Pittsburgh Press, 1973).

[45] Schein, op. cit., pp. 69–75.

[46] See Kathleen M. Eisenhardt, Jean L. Kahwajy, and L. J. Bourgeois III, "How Management Teams Can Have a Good Fight," *Harvard Business Review* (July/August 1997), pp. 77–85.

[47] Michael A. Roberto, "Why Making the Decisions the Right Way Is More Important Than Making the Right Decisions," *Ivey Business Journal* (September/October 2005), pp. 1–7.

[48] See Irving L. Janis, "Groupthink," *Psychology Today* (November 1971), pp. 43–46; and *Victims of Groupthink,* 2nd ed. (Boston: Houghton Mifflin, 1982).

[49] See also Michael Harvey, M. Ronald Buckley, Milorad M. Novicevic, and Jonathon R. B. Halbesleben, "The Abilene Paradox After Thirty Years: A Global Perspective," *Organizational Dynamics,* vol. 33 (2004), pp. 215–26.

[50] These techniques are well described in Andre L. Delbecq, Andrew H. Van de Ven, and David H. Gustafson, *Group Techniques for Program Planning* (Glenview, IL: Scott, Foresman, 1975).

[51] Developed from Lynda McDermott, Nolan Brawley, and William Waite, *World-Class Teams: Working across Borders* (New York: Wiley, 1998).

Feature Notes 16

*NPR–Vivian Schiller–*Information and quotes from Anya Kamenetz, "Will NPR Save the News?" *Fast Company* (March 18, 2009): www.Fastcompany.com.

*Trendsetters–*Information and quotes from "Secretary General–My Priorities for a Better World," www.un.org/sg/priority.

*Tips to Remember–*Modified by permission from John R. Schermerhorn Jr., James G. Hunt, and Richard N. Osborn, *Organizational Behavior 10e* (Hoboken, NJ: John Wiley & Sons, 2008), p. 354, with information from Robert Moskowitz, "How to Negotiate an Increase," www.worktree.com (retrieved March 8, 2007); Mark Gordon, "Negotiating What You're Worth," *Harvard Management Communication Letter,* vol. 2, no. 1 (Winter, 2005); and Dona DeZube, "Salary Negotiation Know-How," www.monster.com (retrieved March 8, 2007).

News Feed–"Bridget Jones, Blogger Fire Fury," *CNN.com* (July 19, 2006).

*Stay Tuned–*Information and quotes from Sue Shellenbarger, "New Workplace Equalizer," *The Wall Street Journal* (March 26, 2009), p. D5. See also www.familiesandwork.org.

Endnotes 16

[1] Richard E. Walton, *Interpersonal Peacemaking: Confrontations and Third-Party Consultation* (Reading, MA: Addison-Wesley, 1969), p. 2.

[2] Case from "Top Business Teams: A Lesson Straight from Mars," *Time* (February 9, 2009), p. 40; and Howard M. Guttman, *Great Business Teams* (Hoboken, NJ: John Wiley & Sons, 2009).

[3] See Kenneth W. Thomas, "Conflict and Conflict Management," in M. D. Dunnett (ed.), *Handbook of Industrial and Organizational Behavior* (Chicago: Rand McNally, 1976), pp. 889–935.

[4] See Robert R. Blake and Jane Strygley Mouton, "The Fifth Achievement," *Journal of Applied Behavioral Science,* vol. 6 (1970), pp. 413–27; and Alan C. Filley, *Interpersonal Conflict Resolution* (Glenview, IL: Scott, Foresman, 1975); and L. David Brown, *Managing Conflict at Organizational Interfaces* (Reading, MA: Addison-Wesley, 1983).

[5] Filley, op. cit.

[6] See Bert Spector, "An Interview with Roger Fisher and William Ury," *Academy of Management Executive,* vol. 18 (2004), pp. 101–12.

[7] See Roger Fisher and William Ury, *Getting to Yes: Negotiating Agreement Without Giving In* (New York: Penguin, 1983); James A. Wall Jr., *Negotiation: Theory and Practice* (Glenview, IL: Scott, Foresman, 1985); and William L. Ury, Jeanne M. Brett, and Stephen B. Goldberg, *Getting Disputes Resolved* (San Francisco: Jossey-Bass, 1997).

[8] Danny Ertel, "Getting Past Yes: Negotiating as if Implementation Mattered," *Harvard Business Review* (November 2004), pp. 60–68.

[9] Fisher and Ury, op. cit.; Ury, Brett, and Goldberg, op. cit.

[10] Fisher and Ury, op. cit.

[11] Example from Spector, op. cit., p. 105.

[12] Ibid.; see also Spector, op. cit.

[13] Developed from Max H. Bazerman, *Judgment in Managerial Decision Making,* 4th ed. (New York: Wiley, 1998), chapter 7.

[14] Roy J. Lewicki and Joseph A. Litterer, *Negotiation* (Homewood, IL: Irwin, 1985).

[15] Fisher and Ury, op. cit.

[16] "A classes grapher's care," *Kellogg* (Summer, 2006), p. 40.

[17] This instrument is described in Carsten K. W. De Drew, Arne Evers, Bianca Beersma, Esther S. Kluwer, and Aukje Nauta, "A Theory-Based Measure of Conflict Management Strategies in the Workplace," *Journal of Organizational Behavior,* vol. 22 (2001), pp. 645–668. Used by permission.

Feature Notes 17

*Tata Nano–*Information and quotes from Jessie Scanlon, "What Can Tata's Nano Teach Detroit?" *Business Week* (March 18, 2009): www.businessweek.com; Santanu Choudhury, "Tata Hopes Tiny Car is Big Hit," *The Wall Street Journal* (March 21–22, 2009), p. B5; and "Tata Motors Delivers Its First Nano to First-time Car Owner in Mumbai," *The Irish Times Motors* (July 22, 2009), p. 10.

*Trendsetter–*Information and quotes from Joshua Molina, "A Vision for Change: Tech Innovator and Entrepreneur David Segura," *HispanicBusiness.com* (December 3, 2008): www.hispanicbusiness.com; "2008 Ernst & Young Entrepreneur of the Year: David Segura," *Smart Business Detroit* (July, 2008); and "David Segura Hispanic Business Entrepreneur of the Year," press release, Michigan Minority Business Council (November 13, 2008): www.mmbdc.com.

*News Feed–*Information and quotes from Jane Spencer and Kevin J. Delaney, "YouTube Unplugged," *The Wall Street Journal* (March 31, 2008), pp. B1–B2; "Skype's China Practices Draw Ire," *The Wall Street Journal* (October 2, 2008), p. B2; and Maggie Shiels, "China Criticized Over YouTube," *BBC News* (March 25, 2009): www.newsvote.bbc.com.

*Stay Tuned–*Information from *What Workers Want: A Worldwide Study of Attitudes to Work and Work-Life Balance* (London: FDS International Limited, 2007).

Endnotes 17

[1] Lee Gardenswartz and Anita Rowe, *Managing Diversity: A Complete Desk Reference and Planning Guide* (Chicago: Irwin, 1993).

[2] R. Roosevelt Thomas Jr., *Beyond Race and Gender* (New York: AMACOM, 1992), p. 10; see also R. Roosevelt Thomas Jr., "From 'Affirmative Action' to 'Affirming Diversity,'" *Harvard Business Review* (November/December 1990), pp. 107–17; R. Roosevelt Thomas Jr., with Marjorie I. Woodruff, *Building a House for Diversity* (New York: AMACOM, 1999).

[3] "The Conundrum of the Glass Ceiling," *The Economist* (July 23, 2005), p. 64.

[4] Information from Hymowitz, op. cit., p. R3.

[5] Carol Stephenson, "Leveraging Diversity to Maximum Advantage: The Business Case for Appointing More Women to Boards," *Ivey Business Journal* (September/October 2004), Reprint # 9B04TE03, pp. 1–8.

[6] Survey reported in "The Most Inclusive Workplaces Generate the Most Loyal Employees," *Gallup Management Journal* (December 2001), retrieved from http://gmj.gallup.com/press_room/release.asp?i=117.

[7] Points in the business case box are from Donald H. Oliver, "Achieving Results Through Diversity: A Strategy for Success," *Ivey Business Journal* (March/April, 2005), Reprint #9B05TB09, pp. 1–6.

[8] Thomas Kochan, Katerina Bezrukova, Robin Ely, Susan Jackson, Aparna Joshi, Karen Jehn, Jonathan Leonard, David Levine, and David Thomas, "The Effects of Diversity on Business Performance: Report of the Diversity Research Network," reported in *SHRM Foundation*

Research Findings (retrieved from www.shrm.org/foundation/findings. asp). Full article published in *Human Resource Management* (2003).

⁹ Oliver, op. cit.

¹⁰ Gardenswartz and Rowe, op. cit., p. 220.

¹¹ Taylor Cox Jr., *Cultural Diversity in Organizations* (San Francisco: Berrett Koehler, 1994).

¹² Nanette Byrnes and Roger O. Crockett, "An Historic Succession at Xerox," *Business Week* (June 9, 2008), pp. 18–21.

¹³ See Anthony Robbins and Joseph McClendon III, *Unlimited Power: A Black Choice* (New York: Free Press, 1997), and Augusto Failde and William Doyle, *Latino Success: Insights from America's Most Powerful Latino Executives* (New York: Free Press, 1996).

¹⁴ Barbara Benedict Bunker, "Appreciating Diversity and Modifying Organizational Cultures: Men and Women at Work," Chapter 5 in Suresh Srivastava and David L. Cooperrider, *Appreciative Management and Leadership* (San Francisco: Jossey-Bass, 1990).

¹⁵ See Gary N. Powell, *Women-Men in Management* (Thousand Oaks, CA: Sage, 1993), and Cliff Cheng (ed.), *Masculinities in Organizations* (Thousand Oaks, CA: Sage, 1996). For added background, see also Sally Helgesen, *Everyday Revolutionaries: Working Women and the Transformation of American Life* (New York: Doubleday, 1998).

¹⁶ Information from "Demographics: The Young and the Restful," *Harvard Business Review* (November 2004), p. 25.

¹⁷ "Many U.S. Employees Have Negative Attitudes to their Jobs, Employers and Top Managers," *The Harris Poll #38* (May 6, 2005), available from www.harrisinteractive.com; and "U. S. Job Satisfaction Keeps Falling," *The Conference Board Reports Today* (February 25, 2005; retrieved from www.conference-board.org).

¹⁸ Mayo Clinic, "Workplace Generation Gap: Understand Differences Among Colleagues" (July 6, 2005; retrieved from http://www.cnn.com/HEALTH/library/WL/00045.html).

¹⁹ Developed from ibid.

²⁰ Information in "Stay Informed" based on "The Conundrum of the Glass Ceiling," *The Economist* (July 23, 2005), pp. 63–65.

²¹ Stephanie N. Mehta, "What Minority Employees Really Want," *Fortune* (July 10, 2000), pp. 181–86.

²² "Bias Cases by Workers Increase 9%," *The Wall Street Journal* (March 6, 2008), p. D6; and, Ibid. See also "The 50 Women to Watch: 2005," *Wall Street Journal* (October 31, 2005), pp. R1–R11.

²³ Thomas, op. cit. Minifigure developed op. cit. 1992, p. 28.

²⁴ Amy Chozick, "Beyond the Numbers," *Wall Street Journal* (November 14, 2005), p. R4.

²⁵ Thomas, op. cit. (1992), p. 17.

²⁶ Information from "100 Best Corporate Citizens," *Business Ethics* online (retrieved from www.business-ethics.com, November 1, 2005).

²⁷ Thomas, op. cit. (1992), p. 17.

²⁸ Thomas and Woodruff, op. cit. (1999), pp. 211–26.

²⁹ "Diversity Today: Corporate Recruiting Practices in Inclusive Workplaces," *Fortune* (June 12, 2000), p. S4.

³⁰ For a good overview, see Richard D. Lewis, *The Cultural Imperative: Global Trends in the 21st Century* (Yarmouth, ME: Intercultural Press, 2002); and Martin J. Gannon, *Understanding Global Cultures* (Thousand Oaks, CA: Sage, 1994).

³¹ Based on Barbara Benedict Bunker, "Appreciating Diversity and Modifying Organizational Cultures: Men and Women at Work," in Suresh Srivastava and David L. Cooperrider (eds.), *Appreciative Management and Leadership: The Power of Positive Thought and Action in Organizations* (San Francisco: Jossey-Bass, 1990), pp. 127–49.

³² Examples reported in Neil Chesanow, *The World-Class Executive* (New York: Rawson Associates, 1985).

³³ P. Christopher Earley and Elaine Mosakowski, "Toward Cultural Intelligence: Turning Cultural Differences Into Workplace Advantage," *Academy of Management Executive*, vol. 18 (2004), pp. 151–57.

³⁴ Example from Fong, op. cit.

³⁵ Information from Emily Parker, "The Roots of Chinese Nationalism," *The Wall Street Journal* (April 1, 2008), p. A17.

³⁶ See Gary P. Ferraro, "The Need for Linguistic Proficiency in Global Business," *Business Horizons* (May/June 1996), pp. 39–46; quote from Carol Hymowitz, "Companies Go Global, but Many Managers Just

Don't Travel Well," *Wall Street Journal* (August 15, 2000), p. B1. See also Edward T. Hall, *The Silent Language* (New York: Anchor Books, 1959).

³⁷ Edward T. Hall, *Beyond Culture* (New York: Doubleday, 1976).

³⁸ Edward T. Hall, *Hidden Differences* (New York: Doubleday, 1990).

³⁹ Geert Hofstede, *Culture's Consequences* (Beverly Hills, CA: Sage, 1984), and *Culture's Consequences: Comparing Values, Behaviors, Institutions and Organizations Across Nations*, 2nd ed. (Thousand Oaks, CA: Sage, 2001). See also Michael H. Hoppe, "An Interview with Geert Hofstede," *Academy of Management Executive*, vol. 18 (2004), pp. 75–79.

⁴⁰ Geert Hofstede and Michael H. Bond, "The Confucius Connection: From Cultural Roots to Economic Growth," *Organizational Dynamics*, vol. 16 (1988), pp. 4–21.

⁴¹ This dimension is explained more thoroughly by Geert Hofstede et al., *Masculinity and Femininty: The Taboo Dimension of National Cultures* (Thousand Oaks, CA.: Sage, 1998).

⁴² Information for "Stay Informed" from "The Conundrum of the Glass Ceiling," *The Economist* (July 23, 2005), p. 634, and "Japan's Diversity Problem," *The Wall Street Journal* (October 24, 2005), pp. B1, B5.

⁴³ "Japan's Diversity Problem," op. cit.

⁴⁴ See Hofstede and Bond, op. cit.

⁴⁵ See Geert Hofstede, *Culture and Organizations: Software of the Mind* (London: McGraw-Hill, 1991).

⁴⁶ Robert J, House, Paul J. Hanges, Mansour Javidan, Peter W. Dorfman, and Vipin Gupta (eds.), *Culture, Leadership and Organizations: The GLOBE Study of 62 Societies* (Thousand Oaks, CA: Sage Publications, Inc., 2004).

⁴⁷ This summary is based on ibid, and Mansour Javidan, P. Dorfman, Mary Sully de Luque, and Robert J. House, "In the Eye of the Beholder: Cross Cultural Lessons in Leadership from Project GLOBE," *Academy of Management Perspectives* (February, 2006), pp. 67–90.

⁴⁸ For additional cultural models and research, see the summary in House, op. cit., as well as Fons Trompenaars, *Riding the Waves of Culture: Understanding Cultural Diversity in Business* (London: Nicholas Brealey Publishing, 1993); Harry C. Triandis, *Culture and Social Behavior* (New York: McGraw-Hill, 1994); Steven H. Schwartz, "A Theory of Cultural Values and Some Implications for Work," *Applied Psychology: An International Review*, vol. 48 (1999), pp. 23–47; Martin J. Gannon, *Understanding Global Cultures*, 3rd ed. (Thousand Oaks, CA: Sage, 2004).

⁴⁹ Items selected from "WV Cultural Awareness Quiz," James P. Morgan, Jr., published by University Associates, 1987. Used by permission.

Feature Notes 18

Limted/Les Wexner–Information and quotes from www.limited.com/feature.jsp and www.limited.com/who/index.jsp. See also Les Wexner, "How I Conquered the Women's Retail Clothing Industry (and an Ulcer), *Fortune Small Business* (September 2003), pp. 40–43.

Trendsetters–Information and quotes from Matthew Saltmarsh, "A Staunch Advocate of Globalization and Trade," *International Herald Tribune* (March 20, 2009): www.iht.com; and Anne Lee, "2009 Fast 50: The Most Innovative Companies in China," *Fast Company* (February 11, 2009): www.fastcompany.com/fast_50; and, Bruce Emhorn, "How Not to Sweat The Retail Deals," *Business Week* (May 25, 2009), pp. 52–59.

News Feed–Information from Peter Burrows, "Stalking High-Tech Sweatshops" *Business Week* (June 19, 2006), pp. 62–63.

Stay Tuned–Information from Transparency International, "Corruption Perceptions Index 2008," and "Bribe Payers Index" (December 9, 2008), both available from: www.transparency.org.

Endnotes 18

¹ Sample articles include "Globalization Bites Boeing," *Business Week* (March 24, 2008), p. 32; "One World, One Cr, One Name," *Business Week* (March 24, 2008), p. 32; Eric Bellman and Jackie Range, "Indian-Style Mergers: Buy a Brand, Leave it Alone," *The Wall Street Journal* (March 22–23, 2008), pp. A9, A14; and David Kiley, "One Ford for the Whole Wide World," *Business Week* (June 15, 2009), pp. 58–59.

² Kenichi Ohmae's books include *The Borderless World: Power and Strategy in the Interlinked Economy* (New York: Harper, 1989); *The*

End of the Nation State (New York: Free Press, 1996); and *The Invisible Continent: Four Strategic Imperatives of the New Economy* (New York: Harper, 1999); and *The Next Global Stage: Challenges and Opportunities in Our Borderless World* (Philadelphia: Wharton School Publishing, 2006).

[3] For a discussion of globalization, see Thomas L. Friedman, *The Lexus and the Olive Tree: Understanding Globalization* (New York: Bantam Doubleday Dell, 2000); John Micklethwait and Adrian Woodridge, *A Future Perfect: The Challenges and Hidden Promise of Globalization* (New York: Crown, 2000); and Thomas L. Friedman, *The World is Flat: A Brief History of the Twenty-First Century* (New York: Farrar, Straus and Giroux, 2005).

[4] Rosabeth Moss Kanter, *World Class: Thinking Locally in the Global Economy* (New York: Simon-Schuster, 1995), preface.

[5] Paul Wilson, "Foreign Companies Big Employers in Ohio," *Columbus Dispatch* (December 26, 2005), p. F6.

[6] Information from Mark Niquette, "Honda's 'Bold Move' Paid Off," *Columbus Dispatch* (November 16, 2002), pp. C1, C2.

[7] Quote from John A. Byrne, "Visionary vs. Visionary," *Business Week* (August 28, 2000), p. 210.

[8] Information from newbalance.com/corporate.

[9] See Mauro F. Guillén and Esteban García-Canal, "The American Model of the Multinational Firm and the "New' Multinationals from Emerging Economies," *Academy of Management Perspectives,* Vol. 23 (2009), pp. 23–35.

[10] Steve Hamm, "Into Africa: Capitalism from the Ground Up," *Business Week* (May 4, 2009), pp. 60–61.

[11] Information in box from "Factory to the World," *National Geographic* (May, 2008), p. 170. For how Chinese firms are being affected by the global economic slowdown, see Dexter Roberts, "China's Factory Blues," *Business Week* (April 7, 2008), pp. 78–82.

[12] Reported in *Business Week* (February 29, 1988), pp. 63–66; further information on corporate Web site: www.falconproducts.com/.

[13] "Survey: Intellectual Property Theft now accounts for 31% of Global Counterfeiting." *Gieschen Consultancy,* February 25, 2005.

[14] Information from "Not Exactly Counterfeit," *Fortune* (April 26, 2006): oney.cnn.com/magazines/fortune.

[15] Criteria for choosing joint venture partners developed from Anthony J. F. O'Reilly, "Establishing Successful Joint Ventures in Developing Nations: A CEO's Perspective," *Columbia Journal of World Business* (Spring 1988), pp. 65–71; and "Best Practices for Global Competitiveness," *Fortune* (March 30, 1998), pp. S1–S3, special advertising section.

[16] Karby Leggett, "U.S. Auto Makers Find Promise—and Peril—in China," *Wall Street Journal* (June 19, 2003), p. B1; "Did Spark Spark a Copycat?" *Business Week* (February 7, 2005), p. 64.

[17] Quote from Charles Forelle and Don Clark, "Intel Fine Jolts Tech Sector," *The Wall Street Journal* (May 14, 2009), pp. A1, A14.

[18] "Starbucks Wins Trademark Case," *The Economic Times*, Bangalore (January 3, 2006), p. 8.

[19] See Cliff Edwards, "HP Declares War on Counterfeiters," *Business Week* (June 8, 2009), pp. 44–45.

[20] The WTO website for the quote is www.wto.org (accessed March 25, 2008) See also "WTO takes up US complaint against China patent regime," *AFP* (September 7, 2007): afp.google.com/article/ALeqM5hASBbePC8gtbmtfzExtmfkdNDvKQ.

[21] This index is reported in the *Economist.* Data in table are from "Big Mac Index," economist.com (February 4, 2009).

[22] Many newspapers and magazines publish annual lists of the world's largest multinational coporations. *Fortune*'s annual listing is available from www.fortune.com.

[23] See Fortune.com and Ftimes.com.

[24] Information from Steve Hamm, "IBM vs. TATA: Which is More American?" *Business Week* (May 5, 2008), p. 28.

[25] See Peter F. Drucker, "The Global Economy and the Nation-State," *Foreign Affairs*, vol. 76 (September/October 1997), pp. 159–71.

[26] Michael Mandel, "Multinationals: Are they Good for America?," *Business Week* (February 28, 2008): businessweek.com.

[27] Ibid.

[28] "Count: Really Big Business," *Fast Company* (December, 2008/January, 2009), p. 46.

[29] Adapted from R. Hall Mason, "Conflicts between Host Countries and Multinational Enterprise," *California Management Review*, vol. 17 (1974), pp. 6, 7.

[30] Devon Maylie, "Alcoa Invests Near Planned Mines," *The Wall Street Journal* (March 24, 2008), p. B4; Tom Wright, "Indonesia's Commodity Boom Is a Mixed Bag," *The Wall Street Journal* (March 24, 2008), p. A8; and James T. Areddy, "Tibet Unrest May Deter Foreign Investors," *The Wall Street Journal* (March 24, 2008), p. A3.

[31] See Dionne Searcey, "U.S. Cracks Down on Corporate Bribes," *The Wall Street Journal* (May 26, 2009), pp. A1–A4.

[32] Ibid.

[33] Marc Gunther, "Can Factory Monitoring Ever Really Work?" *Business Ethics* (Fall 2005), p. 12.

[34] "An Industry Monitors Child Labor," *New York Times* (October 16, 1997), pp. B1, B9; and Rugmark International Web site: www.rugmark.de.

[35] See Simon Zadek, "The Path to Corporate Responsibility," *Harvard Business Review* (December 2004), pp. 125–30; and information at corporate Web site: www.nikeBiz.com/labor/toc_monitoring.html.

[36] "Endgame: Hypocrisy, Blindness, and the Doomsday Scenario," op. cit.

[37] Definition from *World Commission on Environment and Development, Our Common Future* (Oxford: Oxford University Press, 1987); reported on International Institute for Sustainable Development Web site: www.iisdl.iisd.ca

[38] Ibid.

[39] www.global100.org.

[40] See, for example, Peter Marsh, "The Country Prince Comes of Age," *Business Life* (August 9, 2005), p. 9.

[41] For a perspective on the role of women in expatriate managerial assignments, see Marianne Jelinek and Nancy J. Adler, "Women: World-Class Managers for Global Competition," *Academy of Management Executive* (February 1988), pp. 11–19.

[42] See J. Stewart Black and Hal B. Gregersen, "The Right Way to Manage Expats," *Harvard Business Review* (March/April 1999), Reprint #99201.

[43] Information from Mark Niquette, "Honda's 'Bold Move' Paid Off," Columbus Dispatch (November 16, 2002), pp. C1, C2; and, Mei Fong, "Chinese Refrigerator Maker Finds U.S. Chilly," *The Wall Street Journal* (March 18, 2008), pp. B1, B2.

[44] See Robert B. Reich, "Who Is Them?" *Harvard Business Review* (March/April 1991), pp. 77–88.

[45] Carol Hymowitz, "The New Diversity," *Wall Street Journal* (November 14, 2005), p. R1.

[46] This summary is based on Mansour Javidan, P. Dorfman, Mary Sully de Luque, and Robert J. House, "In the Eye of the Beholder: Cross Cultural Lessons in Leadership from Project GLOBE," *Academy of Management Perspectives* (February 2006), pp. 67–90; and, Martin J. Gannon, *Paradoxes of Culture and Globalization* (Thousand Oaks, CA: Sage, 2008), p. 52.

[47] Developed from "Is Your Company Really Global?" *Business Week* (December 1, 1997).

Feature Notes 19

Anita Santiago/Count-Me-In–Information from "Got Spanish?" *Business Week Frontier* (August 14, 2000), p. F12; "Cultivating Creativity," Interview by National Association of Female Executives (August 2000): www.nafe.com; www.anitasantiago.com/who; "Women Business Owners Receive First-Ever Micro Loans Via the Internet," *Business Wire* (August 9, 2000); Jim Hopkins, "Non-Profit Loan Group Takes Risks on Women in Business," *USA Today* (August 9, 2000), p. 2B; www.ethnicedibles.com and www.makemineamillion.org.

Stay Tuned–Data reported by Karen E. Klein, "Minority Start Ups: A Measure of Progress," *Business Week* (August 25, 2005), retrieved from www.businessweekonline.com; and press release, Minority Business Development Agency (March 5, 2009): www.mbda.gov.

News Feed–Information from "Husk Power Systems: Rice-Fired Electricity," "Mercy Corps: The Bank of Banks," and "DataDyne EpiSurveyor," *Fast Company* (December, 2008/January, 2009), pp. 112–16.

Trendsetters–Information and quotes from Aina Hunter, "Making the Men of Iraq Listen," *The Village Voice* (March 9, 2005): www.villagevoice.com; *Women for Women International Annual Report* (Washington: Women for Women International, 2007); "Zainab Salbi, Founder and CEO, Women for Women International," www.womenforwomen.org: accessed March 25, 2009. See also Zainab Salbi and Laurie Becklund, *Between Two Worlds: Escape from Tyranny: Growing Up in the Shadow of Saddam* (New York: Gotham, 2006).

Endnotes 19

[1] Examples from "America's Best Young Entrepreneurs 2008," *Business Week* (September 8, 2009): www.businessweek.com.

[2] Speech at the Lloyd Greif Center for Entrepreneurial Studies, Marshall School of Business, University of Southern California, 1996.

[3] This list is developed from Jeffry A. Timmons, *New Venture Creation: Entrepreneurship for the 21st Century* (New York: Irwin/McGraw-Hill, 1999), pp. 47–48; and Robert D. Hisrich and Michael P. Peters, *Entrepreneurship*, 4th ed. (New York: Irwin/McGraw-Hill, 1998), pp. 67–70.

[4] Information from these profiles from the corporate Web sites, The Entrepreneur's Hall of Fame: www.ltbn.com/halloffame.html and, http://people.forbes.com.

[5] For the top selling franchises, see "Top 10 Franchises for 2009," *Entrepreneur Magazine* (January, 2009): www.entrepreneur.com.

[6] For a review and discussion of the entrepreneurial mind, see Timmons, op. cit., pp. 219–225.

[7] Timothy Butler and James Waldroop, "Job Sculpting: The Art of Retaining Your Best People," *Harvard Business Review* (September/October 1999), pp. 144–52.

[8] Based on research summarized by Hisrich and Peters, op. cit., pp. 70–74.

[9] Information and quote from Jim Hopkins, "Serial Entrepreneur Strikes Again at Age 70," USA Today (August 15, 2000).

[10] See the review by Hisrich and Peters, op. cit.; and Paulette Thomas, "Entrepreneurs' Biggest Problems and How They Solve Them," *Wall Street Journal Reports* (March 17, 2003), pp. R1, R2.

[11] See the review by Robert D. Hisrich and Michael P. Peters, *Entrepreneurship*, 4th ed. (New York: Irwin/McGraw-Hill, 1998), pp. 67–70; and Paulette Thomas. "Entrepreneurs' Biggest Problems and How They Solve Them," *Wall Street Journal Reports* (March 17, 2003), pp. R1, R2.

[12] This list is developed from Timmons, op. cit, pp. 47–48; and Hisrich and Peters, op. cit., pp. 67–70.

[13] "Smart Talk: Start-Ups and Schooling," *Wall Street Journal* (September 7, 2004), p. B4.

[14] Data from *Paths to Entrepreneurship: New Directions for Women in Business* (New York: Catalyst, 1998) as summarized on the National Foundation for Women Business Owners Web site: www.nfwbo.org/key.html.

[15] National Foundation for Women Business Owners, *Women Business Owners of Color: Challenges and Accomplishments* (1998).

[16] David Bornstein, *How to Change the World: Social Entrepreneurs and the Power of New Ideas* (Oxford, U.K.: Oxford University Press, 2004).

[17] See Laura D'Andrea Tyson, "Good Works—With a Business Plan," *Business Week* (May 3, 2004), retrieved from *Business Week Online* (November 14, 2005) at www.businessweek.com.

[18] "Women Business Owners Receive First-Ever Micro Loans Via the Internet," *Business Wire* (August 9, 2000); Jim Hopkins, "Non-Profit Loan Group Takes Risks on Women in Business," *USA Today* (August 9, 2000), p. 2B; www.ethnicedibles.com and www.makemineamillion.org.

[19] Examples are from Byrnes and "Growing Green Business," *Northwestern* (Winter, 2007), p. 19; and Byrnes, op. cit.; and Regina McEnery, "Cancer Patients Getting the White-Glove Treatment," *The Columbus Dispatch* (March 1, 2008).

[20] *The Facts About Small Business 1999* (Washington, DC: U.S. Small Business Administration, Office of Advocacy).

[21] Reported by Sue Shellenbarger, "Plumbing for Joy? Be Your Own Boss," *The Wall Street Journal* (September 16, 2009), pp. D1, D2.

[22] Ibid.

[23] See U.S. Small Business Administration Web site: www.sba.gov; and *Statistical Abstract of the United States* (Washington, DC: U.S. Census Bureau, 1999).

[24] "Small Business Expansions in Electronic Commerce," U.S. Small Business Administration, Office of Advocacy (June 2000).

[25] Information from Will Christensen, "Rod Spencer's Sports-Card Business Has Migrated Cyberspace Marketplace," *Columbus Dispatch* (July 24, 2000), p. F1.

[26] Discussion based on "The Life Cycle of Entrepreneurial Firms," in Ricky Griffin (ed.), *Management*, 6th ed. (New York: Houghton Mifflin, 1999), pp. 309–10; and Neil C. Churchill and Virginia L. Lewis, "The Five Stages of Small Business Growth," *Harvard Business Review* (May/June 1993), pp. 30–50.

[27] Information reported in "The Rewards," *Inc. State of Small Business* (May 20–21, 2001), pp. 50–51.

[28] Data reported by The Family Firm Institute: www.ffi.org/looking/factsfb.html.

[29] Conversation from the case "Am I My Uncle's Keeper?" by Paul I. Karofsky (Northeastern University Center for Family Business) and published at www.fambiz.com/contprov.cfm? ContProvCode=NECFB&ID=140.

[30] *Survey of Small and Mid-Sized Businesses: Trends for 2000* (Arthur Andersen, 2000).

[31] Ibid.

[32] See U.S. Small Business Administration Web site: www.sba.gov.

[33] George Gendron, "The Failure Myth," *Inc.* (January 2001), p. 13. Information and quotes from Dana Mattioli, "Recession 'spells End for Many Family Enterprises," *The Wall Street Journal* (October 6, 2009), p. B6.

[34] Based on Norman M. Scarborough and Thomas W. Zimmerer, *Effective Small Business Management* (Englewood Cliffs, NJ: Prentice-Hall, 2000), pp. 25–30; and Scott Clark, "Most Small-Business Failures Tied to Poor Management," *Business Journal* (April 10, 2000).

[35] Developed from William S. Sahlman, "How to Write a Great Business Plan," *Harvard Business Review* (July/August 1997), pp. 98–108.

[36] Marcia H. Pounds, "Business Plan Sets Course for Growth," *Columbus Dispatch* (March 16, 1998), p. 9; see also firm Web site: www.calcustoms.com.

[37] Standard components of business plans are described in many text sources, such as Linda Pinson and Jerry Jinnett, *Anatomy of a Business Plan: A Step-by-Step Guide to Starting Smart, Building the Business, and Securing Your Company's Future*, 4th ed. (Dearborn Trade, 1999), and Scarborough and Zimmerer, op. cit.; and on Web sites such as American Express Small Business Services, Business Town.com., and BizplanIt.com.

[38] "You've Come a Long Way Baby," *Business Week Frontier* (July 10, 2000).

[39] Instrument adapted from Norman M. Scarborough and Thomas W. Zimmerer, *Effective Small Business Management*, 3rd ed. (Columbus: Merrill, 1991), pp. 26–27. Used by permission.

Case 1 Endnotes

[1] www.traderjoes.com/history.html.

[2] Deborah Orr, "The Cheap Gourmet," *Forbes* (April 10, 2006).

[3] *Business Week Online* (February 21, 2008).

[4] Kerry Hannon, "Let Them Eat Ahi Jerky," *U.S. News & World Report* (July 7, 1997).

[5] Marianne Wilson, "When Less is More," *Chain Store Age* (November 2006).

[6] Orr.

[7] Hannon.

[8] Supermarket News's Top 75 Retailers (January 12, 2009).

[9] Hannon.

[10] www.traderjoes.com/value.html.

[11] www.traderjoes.com/how_we_do_biz.html.

[12] "Win at the Grocery Game," *Consumer Reports* (October 2006), p. 10.

[13] Orr.

[14] www.traderjoes.com/tjs_faqs.asp#DiscontinueProducts.

15 www.latimes.com/business/la-fi-tj12feb12,1,1079460.story.

16 Jena McGregor, "2004 Customer 1st," *Fast Company* (October 2004).

17 Orr.

18 Irwin Speizer, "The Grocery Chain That Shouldn't Be," *Fast Company* (February 2004).

19 Heidi Brown, "Buy German," *Forbes* (January 12, 2004).

20 www.traderjoes.com/benefits.html.

21 Irwin Speizer, "Shopper's Special," *Workforce Management* (September 2004).

22 Ibid.

23 "Retailer Spotlight," *Gourmet Retailer* (June 2006).

24 http://www.wholefoodsmarket.com/company/index.php.

25 "Downturn Could Burn Whole Foods," *The Walls Street Journal* (November 3, 2008), pp. B1.

26 "Employees First!" *Time* (July 7, 2008), p. 4.

27 http://www.wholefoodsmarket.com/company/index.php.

28 "Employees First!" *Time* (July 7, 2008), p. 4.

29 "Downturn Could Burn Whole Foods," *The Wall Street Journal* (November 3, 2008), pp. B1, B9.

30 Matt Andrejczak, "Have Investors Whet Their Appetite on Whole Foods?" *MarketWatch* (May 19, 2009).

31 "Downturn Could Burn Whole Foods."

Case 2 Endnotes

1 Inditex Press Dossier: www.inditex.com/en/press/information/press_kit (accessed May 17, 2009).

2 "Zara Grows as Retail Rivals Struggle," *Wall Street Journal* (March 26, 2009).

3 "Zara, A Spanish Success Story," CNN (June 15, 2001).

4 Inditex Press Dossier.

5 Cecile Rohwedder and Keith Johnson, "Pace-setting Zara Seeks More Speed to Fight Its Rising Cheap-Chic Rivals," *Wall Street Journal* (February, 20, 2008), p. B1.

6 "The Future of Fast Fashion."

7 "Zara: Taking the Lead in Fast-Fashion," *Business Week* (April 4, 2006).

8 Rohwedder and Johnson.

9 Ibid.

10 "Zara Grows as Retail Rivals Struggle," *Wall Street Journal* (March 26, 2009).

11 "Zara Grows as Retail Rivals Struggle."

12 Ibid.

13 Diana Middleton, "Fashion for the Frugal," *The Florida Times-Union* (October 1, 2006).

14 Inditex Press Dossier.

15 "Our Group," www.inditex.com/en/who_we_are/timeline (accessed May 18, 2008).

16 "Who We Are," www.inditex.com/en/who_we_are/timeline (accessed May 18, 2008).

17 Inditex Press Dossier.

18 "Our Group."

19 Inditex Press Dossier.

20 Ibid.

21 Ibid.

22 "Shining Examples," *Economist* (June 17, 2006).

23 Inditex Press Dossier.

24 "The Future of Fast Fashion."

25 "Westfield Looks to Zara for Fuller Figure of $1bn Australian," *The Australian* (September 3, 2007), p. 3.

26 Inditex Press Dossier.

27 "Ortega's Empire Showed Rivals New Style of Retailing," *The Times* (United Kingdom) (June 14, 2007).

28 "The Future of Fast Fashion."

29 Rohwedder and Johnson.

30 "Zara Grows as Retail Rivals Struggle," *Wall Street Journal* (March 26, 2009).

31 "The Future of Fast Fashion."

Case 3 Endnotes

1 Laura Zinn, "Tom Chappell: Sweet Success From Unsweetened Toothpaste," *BusinessWeek* (September 2, 1991), p. 52.

2 Janet Bamford, "Changing Business as Usual," *Working Women*, vol. 18 (November 1993), p. 106.

3 Judy Quinn, "Tom's of Maine," *Incentive* (December 1993), p. A4.

4 Ibid.

5 Craig Cox, "Interview: Tom Chappell, Minister of Commerce," *Business Ethics*, vol. 8 (January 1994), p. 42.

6 Mary Martin, "Toothpaste and Technology," *Boston Globe* (October 10, 1993), p. A4.

7 Cox.

8 Mary Martin, "A 'Nuisance' to Rivals," *Boston Globe* (October 1993), p. A4.

9 Cox.

10 Ibid.

11 "The Tom's of Maine Mission": at www.tomsofmaine.com/about/mission.asp.

12 Quinn.

13 Ellyn E. Spagins, "Paying Employees to Work Elsewhere," *Inc.* (February 1993), p. 29.

14 Quinn.

15 Ibid.

16 Martin Everett, "Profiles in Marketing: Katie Shisler," *Sales and Marketing Management* (March 1993), p. 12.

17 Quinn.

18 Cox.

19 Ibid.

20 Ibid.

21 www.cosmeticsdesign.com/news/ng.asp?n=84131-tom-s-of-maine-toothpaste-natural-glycyrrhisin.

22 www.tomsofmaine.com/about/Colgate.asp.

23 www.oregonlive.com/business/oregonian/index.ssf?/base/business/1191637537264110.xml&coll=7.

24 Tom's of Maine home page: www.tomsofmaine.com.

25 Louise Story, "Can Burt's Bees Turn Clorox Green?" *The New York Times* (January 6, 2008).

26 http://www.burtsbees.com/webapp/wcs/stores/servlet/ContentView?storeId=10001&langId=-1&catalogId=10051&contentPageId=27.

27 http://www.burtsbees.com/wcsstore/Bee2C/upload/pdf/Climate%20Leaders.pdf.

28 http://www.nytimes.com/2008/01/06/business/06bees.html?pagewanted=1&_r=1.

29 Story.

30 Ibid.

Case 4 Endnotes

1 www.amazon.com.

2 http://www.amazon.com/Locations-Careers/b?ie=UTF8&node=239366011.

3 www.jumpstart-it.com/jumpstart-it-on-amazon.html.

4 Sean O'Neill, "Indulge Your Literary Urge," *Kiplinger's Personal Finance*, vol. 59, no. 8 (August 2005).

5 "Amazon CEO Takes Long View," *USA Today* (July 6, 2005).

6 David Meerman Scott, "The Flip Side of Free," *eContent*, vol. 28, no. 10 October 2005.

7 "New Amazon MP3 Clips Widget Ads to Suite of Digital Product Widgets?" (accessed at http://top10-charts.com/news.php?nid=40273 May 29, 2008).

8 Thomas Ricker, "Amazon Adds Audible to its Digital Empire" (accessed at http://www.engadget.com/2008/01/31/amazon-adds-audible-to-its-digital-empire/ May 28, 2008).

9 "Amazon Unbox on TiVo" (accessed at http://www.amazon.com/gp/video/tivo May 29, 2008).

10 Steven Levy, "The Future of Reading," *Newsweek* (November 26. 2007).

[11] Tim O''Reilly, "Why Kindle Should Be an Open Book," *Forbes* (accessed at http://www.forbes.com/2009/02/22/kindle-oreilly-ebooks-technology-breakthroughs_oreilly.html).

[12] http://www.applelinks.com/index.php/more/amazon_launches_optimized_kindle_store_seamlessly_integrated_with_kindle_fo/. Accessed March 4, 2009.

[13] "10 Questions."

[14] "Amazon CEO Takes Long View."

[15] Brad Stone, "The Zappos Way of Managing," *The New York Times* (March 28, 2009).

[16] http://about.zappos.com/zappos-story/looking-ahead-let-there-be-anything-and-everything.

[17] http://about.zappos.com/press-center/zappos-finds-perfect-fit Zappos finds a perfect fit.

[18] Gene Marks, "Many Happy Returns" (accessed at http://www.forbes.com/2009/01/05/zappos-retail-return-ent-manage-cx_gm_0105genemarksreturns.html).

[19] http://www.businessweek.com/smallbiz/content/sep2008/sb20080916_288698.htm).

[20] http://about.zappos.com/press-center/workplace-fun-shoe-fits-zappos.

[21] "Zappos Secret: It's an Open Book," *Business Week* (March 23 & 30, 2009).

Case 5 Endnotes

[1] Barry Silverstein, "Lands' End: Hard Landing?" *Brand Profile* (October 7, 2007).

[2] "The Lands' End Principles of Doing Business" at www.landsend.com (accessed May 26, 2008).

[3] "About Lands' End" at www.landsend.com (accessed May 26, 2008).

[4] David Lidsky. "Basic Training," *Fast Company,* issue 108 (September 2006).

[5] "History" at www.landsend.com (accessed May 26, 2008).

[6] www.fundinguniverse.com/company-histories/Lands-End-Inc-Company-History.html (accessed May 27, 2008).

[7] Ibid.

[8] Kelly Nolan. "Sears Gives Lands' End New Beginning," *Retailing Today,* vol. 45, no. 18 (October 9, 2006).

[9] Jim Tierney, "Sears Stores Find a Fit for Lands' End," *Multichannel Merchant* (October 2007).

[10] "Dressed for Success?" *Uniforms* (May/June 2007), p. 50.

[11] "Lands' End Elfs It Up," *Multichannel Merchant* (February 2006), p. 44.

[12] *Multichannel Merchant.*

Case 6 Endnotes

[1] "EA Reports Fourth Quarter and Fiscal Year 2008 Results" (accessed July 9, 2008, at media.corporate-ir.net/media_files/IROL/88/88189/Q4Release.pdf).

[2] "EA Reports Fourth Quarter and Fiscal Year 2009 Results," http://news.ea.com/news/ea/20090505006595/en (accessed May 23, 2009).

[3] David Whelan, "Name Recognition," *Forbes* (June 20, 2005).

[4] Ibid.

[5] Ibid

[6] Martin McEachern, "The Only Game in Town," *Computer Graphics World* (October 2005).

[7] Owen Good, "Lawsuit: Retired NFLers Cheated by EA, Union" (accessed May 23, 2009, at http://kotaku.com/5059011/lawsuit-retired-nflers-cheated-by-ea-union).

[8] "Anti-trust lawsuit over exclusive license contract" (accessed July 9, 2008, at http://www.aolcdn.com/tmz_socumetns/0611_nfl_ea_wm.pdf).

[9] Whelan.

[10] Kenneth Hein, "Gaming Product Placement Gets Good Scores in Study," *Brandweek* (December 5, 2005).

[11] Nick Wingfield, "Electronic Arts Offers $2 Billion for Take-Two," *Wall Street Journal* (February 25, 2008).

[12] Nick Wingfield, "Take-Two's Earnings Report May Be a Coda to EA Offer," *Wall Street Journal* (December 15, 2008).

[13] http://www.nytimes.com/2008/04/19/technology/19taketwo.html.

[14] Wingfield. "Take-Two's Earnings Report . . ."

[15] *Software Top 100*: "The World's Largest Software Companies" (accessed May 23, 2009, at http://www.softwaretop100.org/).

[16] "Take 2 Interactive Corporate Overview" (accessed at http://ir.take2games.com/).

[17] Ibid.

Case 7 Endnotes

[1] dunkindonuts.com/aboutus/company/products/CoffeeConsFacts.aspx?Section=company.

[2] www.dunkindonuts.com/aboutus/company.

[3] www.dunkindonuts.comaboutus/company/Global.aspx.

[4] Susan Spielberg, "For Snack Chains, Coffee Drinks the Best Way to Sweeten Profits," *Nation's Restaurant News* (June 27, 2005).

[5] www.bizjournals.ocm/boston/gen/company.html?gcode=3AF1302DF8B5463AA3EA890B32D5B9C2.

[6] dunkindonuts.com/aboutus/company/products/BreakfastSandFacts.aspx?Section=company.

[7] Kara Kridler, "Dunkin Donuts to Add 150 Stores in Baltimore-Washington Area," *Daily Record* (Baltimore) (May 6, 2005).

[8] dunkindonuts.com/aboutus/products/HotCoffee.aspx.

[9] Janet Adamy, "As Starbucks Pares Stores, Tension Rises Over Leases," *The Wall Street Journal* (October 13, 2008), p. B1.

[10] https://www.dunkindonuts.com/aboutus/press/PressRelease.aspx?viewtype=current&id=100140.

[11] http://www.reuters.com/article/pressRelease/idUS133273+14-Apr-2009+PRN20090414.

[12] https://www.dunkindonuts.com/downloads/pdf/DD_Press_Kit.pdf.

[13] http://leadership.wharton.upenn.edu/digest/attachments/BW-EBIZ_How-Fast.pdf.

[14] Janet Adamy, "Starbucks Plays Common Joe," *The Wall Street Journal* (February 9, 2009), p. B3.

[15] http://investor.starbucks.com/phoenix.zhtml?c=99518&p=irol-newsArticle&ID=1267447&highlight.

[16] http://news.starbucks.com/article_display.cfm?article_id=180.

[17] Janet Adamy, "Starbucks Takes Plunge into Instant Coffee," *The Wall Street Journal* (February 13, 2009), p. B8.

Case 8 Endnotes

[1] www.apparelandfootwear.org/Statistics.asp.

[2] NKE 2008 10-K, p. 20. http://sec.gov/Archives/edgar/data/320187/000119312508159004/d10k.htm.

[3] NKE 2008 10-K, p. 53. http://sec.gov/Archives/edgar/data/320187/000119312508159004/d10k.htm#tx16266_23.

[4] articles moneycentral.msn.com/Investigating/CNBC/TVReports/NikeStarEndorsements.aspx.

[5] nikeresponsibility.com/#workers-facotries/active_factories.

[6] Aaron Bernstein, "Nike Names Names," *BusinessWeek Online* (April 13, 2005).

[7] Ibid.

[8] http://adage.com/moy2008/article?article_id=131755.

[9] http://www.nikebiz.com/responsibility/.

[10] Stanley Holmes, "Green Foot Forward," *BusinessWeek* (November 28, 2005).

[11] "Nike Replaces CEO After 13 months," *USA Today* (January 24, 2006).

[12] "Just Doing It," *Economist*, vol. 376, no. 8438 (August 6, 2005).

[13] findarticles.com/p/articles/mi_mOEIN/is_2008_March_5/ai_n24363712.

[14] Nike 2008 Annual Report. http://media.corporate-ir.net/media_files/irol/10/100529/ar_08/nike_ar_2008/docs/Nike_AR_2008.pdf downloaded May 28, 2009.

[15] "Deal Sets Stage."

[16] "Adidas-Reebok Merger."

17 http://www.nikebiz.com/media/pr/2009/05/14_NikeRestructuring Statement.html.

18 "Adidas-Reebok Merger."

19 http://www.newbalance.com/corporate/aboutus/corporate_about_ourcompany.php.

20 http://www.newbalance.com/corporate/aboutus/corporate_about_ourheritage.php.

21 Ibid.

22 Ibid.

23 http://www.newbalance.com/corporate/aboutus/corporate_about.php.

Case 9 Endnotes

1 Apple Inc. home page: http://www.apple.com.

2 Ibid.

3 Pixar home page: http://www.pixar.com.

4 apple20.blogs.fortune.cnn.com/2008/04/01/analyst-apples-us-consumer-market-share-now-21-percent/.

5 apple20.blogs.fortune.cnn.com/2008/05/19/report-apples-market-share-of-pcs-over-1000-hits-66/.

6 Brad Stone, "Apple's Chief Takes a Medical Leave."

7 Ibid.

8 Ibid.

9 Peter Burrows, "The Improbable Heroes of Toontown," *Business-Week* (May 26, 2008), pp. 81–82.

Case 10 Endnotes

1 Netflix Consumer Press Kit, at http:cdn-0.nflximg.com/us/pdf/Consumer_Press_Kit.pdf (accessed May 27, 2009).

2 Jennifer Netherby, "Netflix Builds Profit, Subs," *Video Business* (January 21, 2008).

3 Susanne Ault, "Netflix No. 1 in Online Customer Service," *Video Business* (May 19, 2008).

4 Netflix Consumer Press Kit.

5 Mary Brandel, "The 'In' Crowd," *Computerworld* (March 3, 2008).

6 Netflix Consumer Press Kit.

7 "Netflix Builds Profit, Subs."

8 Danny King, "Netflix Now," *Video Business* (May 1, 2008).

9 Josh Quittner, "The Idiot Box Gets Smart," *Time*, vol. 171, no. 22 (June 2, 2008).

10 Brian Steinberg, "Transforming the Movie-Rental Model," *Advertising Age*, vol. 79, no. 1 (January 7, 2008).

11 Lynn Blumenstein, "Small Libraries Start Using Netflix," *Library Journal*, vol. 133, no. 7 (April 15, 2008).

12 Daniel McGinn, "Sure, We've Got That!" *Newsweek*, vol. 151, no. 10 (March 10, 2008).

13 Nancy MacDonald, "Blockbuster Proves It's Not Dead Yet," *Maclean's*, vol. 121, no. 11 (March 24, 2008).

14 Samantha Murphy, "Movies Made Easy," *Chain Store Age*, vol. 84, no. 2 (February 2008).

15 Nick Wingfield, "Netflix vs. Naysayers," *Wall Street Journal* (March 27, 2008), pp. B1, B2.

16 Michelle Conlin, "Netflix: Flex to the Max," *BusinessWeek* (September 4, 2007), p. 72.

17 Ibid.

18 Ibid.

19 Blockbuster Corporate Overview (accessed May 23, 2009 at http://www.blockbuster.com/corporate/companyOverview).

20 Ibid.

21 Ibid.

22 Jeff Leins, "Blockbuster Going Under Trying Anything," *News In Film* (May 28, 2009) (accessed at http://newsinfilm.com/?p=15421).

Case 11 Endnotes

1 Facebook Press Room, Statistics, at http://www.facebook.com/press/info.php?statistics (accessed May 31, 2009).

2 Spencer E. Ante, "Facebook's Land Grab in the Face of a Downturn," *BusinessWeek* (December 1, 2008).

3 Ibid.

4 Facebook Press Room, Statistics, at http://www.facebook.com/press/info.php?statistics (accessed June 27, 2008).

5 Jessi Hempel, "Finding Cracks in Facebook," *Fortune*, vol. 157, no. 11 (May 26, 2008).

6 Ibid.

7 Ibid.

8 Facebook Press Room, Statistics (accessed May 31, 2009).

9 Catherine Holahan, "Facebook's New Friends Abroad," *BusinessWeek Online* (May 14, 2008).

10 Bill Greenwood, "MySpace, Facebook, Google Integrate Data Portability," *Information Today*, vol. 25, no. 6 (June 2008).

11 "Facebook Exodus," nytimes.com/2009/08/30 (accessed September 3, 2008).

12 Dan Tynan, "The 25 Worst Web Sites," *PC World* (accessed at http://www.fastcompany.com/magazine/128/myspace-the-sequel.html?page=0%2C1).

13 http://mashable.com/2006/07/11/myspace-americas-number-one/.

14 fast company

15 Ibid. http://www.pcworld.com/article/127116-7/the_25_worst_web_sites.html.

16 Ante.

Case 12 Endnotes

1 Southwest Airlines Corporate Fact Sheet, at www.swamedia.com/swamedia/fact_sheet.pdf (accessed May 25, 2009). See also James Campbell Quick, "Crafting and Organizational Culture: Herb's Hand at Southwest Airlines," *Organizational Dynamics*, vol. 21 (August 1992), p. 47.

2 Richard S. Teitelbaum, "Where Service Flies Right," *Fortune* (August 24, 1992), p. 115.

3 http://www.swamedia.com/swamedia/speeches/fred_taylor_speech.pdf.

4 Colleen Barrett, "Pampering Customers on a Budget," *Working Woman* (April 1993), pp. 19–22.

5 Southwest Airlines Corporate Fact Sheet, op. cit.

6 Ibid.

7 "Did We Say Cheap?" *Inc.* (October 1997), p. 60.

8 Southwest Airlines Corporate Fact Sheet, op. cit.

9 Teitelbaum, op. cit., p. 116.

10 Colleen's Corner" (June 27, 2003), www.southwest.com.

11 Adapted from Mike Esterl, "Southwest Airlines CEO Flies Unchartered Skies," *The Wall Street Journal* (March 25, 2009), p. B1.

Case 13 Endnotes

1 http://www.panerabread.com/about/company/.

2 www.bakingbusiness.com/bs/channel.asp?ArticleID=73003 (accessed August 2, 2006).

3 www.panerabread.com/about/press/kit/#faqs (accessed May 25, 2009).

4 www.panerabread.com/menu/cafe/kids.php (accessed May 25, 2009).

5 "Panera Bread Removes Trans Fat from Menu," Panera Bread press release (February 23, 2006).

6 Ron Shaich, speech at Annual Meeting 2006, Temple Israel (June 28, 2006).

7 www.starbucks.com/retail/wireless.asp (accessed May 18, 2008).

8 www.panerabread.com/cafes/wifi.php (accessed May 25, 2009).

9 Ron Miller, "Wi Fi Continues Its Extended Coffee Break," *Information Week* (January 4, 2006). Accessed August 2, 2006.

10 Jefferson Graham, "As Wi-Fi Spreads, More Free Locations Popping Up," *USA Today* (December 8, 2005) (accessed August 2, 2006, at usatoday.com/tech/wireless/2005-12-08-wi-fi-free_x.htm).

11 www.panerabread.com/about/press/kit/#financial (accessed May 25, 2009).

12 "Panera Bread Recognized as Top Performer in Restaurant Category for One-, Five-, Ten-Year Returns to Shareholders," Panera Bread press release (May 4, 2006).

13 www.panerabread.com/about/press/kit/#leadership (accessed May 18, 2008).

14 http://www.bloomberg.com/apps/news?pid=20601087&sid=aFA7bcdaRgL4&refer=home.

Case 14 Endnotes

[1] See David A. Price, *The Pixar Touch* (New York: Knopf, 2008); and Ed Catmull, "How Pixar Fosters Collective Creativity," *Harvard Business Review* (September 2008), Reprint R0809D.

[2] Doug Childers, "Pixar's success is more than just pixel-deep," in *Rich.com* (June 1, 2008).

[3] Greg Sandoval, "New Competitors Challenge Pixar's Animation Domination," *The Sacramento Union* (December 2, 2005).

[4] "How Disney Knew it Needed Pixar," *Fortune*, vol. 153, no. 10 (May 29, 2006).

[5] Pixar corporate Overview at http://www.pixar.com/companyinfo/about_us/overview.htm. Accessed June 8, 2008.

[6] www.worstpreviews.com/review.php?id=758&section=preview.

[7] See Price, op. cit.; Peter Burrow, "The Improbable Heroes of Toontown," *BusinessWeek* (May 26, 2008), p. 82; and Paul Boutin, "An Industry Gets Animated," *Wall Street Journal* (May 14, 2008), p. A19.

[8] Brent Schlender and Christopher Tkaczyk, "Pixar's Magic Man," *Fortune*, vol. 153, no. 10 (May 29, 2006).

[9] David Price, "How Pixar Cheated Death," *Inc.*, vol. 28, no. 6 (June 2006).

[10] Jia Lynn Yang, "How Disney Picked Up Pixar," *Fortune*, vol. 157, no. 9 (May 5, 2008).

[11] Quote from Burrows, op. cit.

[12] Childers, op. cit.

[13] Peter Sanders, "Disney Learns Lessons from Pixar," *Wall Street Journal* (October 27, 2008).

[14] Peter Cohen, "Disney Buys Pixar," *Macworld* vol. 23, no. 4 (April 2006).

[15] Sandovar, op. cit.

[16] Quote from Burrows, op. cit.

[17] Sandovar, op. cit.

[18–21] Adapted from http://dreamworks-skg.com/.

Case 15 Endnotes

[1] "Ryan Newman Biography" http://www.nascar.com/news/headlines/cup/newman.bio/ (accessed September 4, 2009).

[2] Ibid.

[3] Ibid.

[4] Harris, Mike. "Baker: Newman the Perfect Protégé," http://www.nascar.com/2003/news/headlines/wc/04/10/rnewman_bbaker.ap/index.html (accessed September 4, 2009).

[5] Rodman, Dave. "Conversation: Ryan Newman." http://cgi.nascar.com/2003/news/features/conversation/06/09/rnewman_pocono/index.html (accessed September 4, 2009).

[6] Ryan Newman Biography, op. cit.

[7] Harris, op. cit.

[8] Rodman, op. cit.

[9] Bresidine, Steve. "Critics Don't Deter Newman: Accusation of Cheating Fuel Driver's Inner Fire," *Associated Press:* October 10, 2003.

[10] "Newman Looking Forward to Speedweeks Experience," http://ww.nascar.com.

Case 16 Endnotes

[1] "AFL-CIO, About Us" (accessed May 31, 2009, at http://www.aflcio.org/aboutus/).

[2] "This Is the AFL-CIO" (accessed August 15, 2006, at aflcio.com/aboutus/thisistheaflcio).

[3] Ibid.

[4] nwlaborerstraining.org/birth%2520of%2520a%2520union.pdf.

[5] Ibid.

[6] Ibid.

[7] Ibid.

[8] dicitonary.laborlawtalk.com/Congress_of_Industrial_Organizations.

[9] Ibid.

[10] Steven Greenhouse, "Unions Resume Debate over Merging and Power," *New York Times* (November 18, 2004) at http://www.labornotes.org/archives/2004/12/articles/ghtml (accessed September 14, 2006).

[11] www.changetowin.org/about-us/who-we-are.html.

[12] experts.about.com/e/j/jo/John_Sweeney_(labor_leader).htm.

[13] Bradford Plumer, "Labor's Love Lost," *New Republic* (April 23, 2008).

[14] Liza Casabona, "AFL-CIO Tests Free Trade Pacts," *Women's Wear Daily* (April 24, 2008).

[15] http://blog.aflcio.org/2009/05/21/afl-cio-opposes-panama-deal-calls-for-trade-policy-review/.

[16] http://blog.aflcio.org/2009/05/15/afl-cio-calls-for-release-of-burmas-aung-san-suu-kyi/.

Case 17 Endnotes

[1] "Toyota Outsells GM, Ford Posts Eye-Popping Loss," *US News & World Reports* (posted online July 24, 2008), wsj.com/mdc/public/page/2_3022-autosales.html.

[2] M. Reza Vaghefi, "Creating Sustainable Competitive Advantage: The Toyota Philosophy and Its Effects," *Mastering Management Online* (October 2001) (accessed January 13, 2006, at www.ftmastering.com/mmo/index.htm).

[3] "Top 10 SUVs, Pickups and Minivans with the Best Residual Value for 2005," *Edmunds.com* (accessed January 14, 2006, at www.edmunds.com/reviews/list/top10/103633/article.html).

[4] "Making Things: The Essence and Evolution of the Toyota Production System," Toyota Motor Corporation (www.toyota.com).

[5] "The 'Thinking' Production System: TPS as a Winning Strategy for Developing People in the Global Manufacturing Environment," Toyota Motor Corporation (www.toyota.com).

[6] Ibid.

[7] Ibid.

[8] money.cnn.com/magazines/fortune/fortune_archive/2006/03/06/8370702/index.htm.

[9] www.toyota.com/about/our_news/product.html.

[10] Rick Newman, "Toyota's Next Turn," *US News & World Report* (posted online June 16, 2008).

[11] Kate Linebaugh, "Idle Workers Busy at Toyota," *Wall Street Journal* (October 13, 2008).

[12] Ibid.

Case 18 Endnotes

[1] http://www.harley-davidson.com/wcm/Content/Pages/Events/100th_anniversary.jsp?locale=en_US (accessed May 25, 2009).

[2] Malia Boyd, "Harley-Davidson Motor Company," *Incentive* (September 1993), pp. 26–27.

[3] Shrader et al., "Harley-Davidson, Inc.—1991," In Fred David, ed., *Strategic Management*, 4th ed. (New York: Macmillan, 1993), p. 655.

[4] Ibid.

[5] Marktha H. Peak, "Harley-Davidson: Going Whole Hog to Provide Stakeholder Satisfaction," *Management Review*, vol. 82 (June 1993), p. 53.

[6] http://www.harley-davidson.com/wcm/Content/Pages/HOG/about_hog.jsp?locale=en_US. Accessed May 18, 2008.

[7] http://www.motorcyclistonline.com/calendar/122_0709_hog_members_adirondacks/index.html (accessed May 18, 2009).

[8] Harley-Davidson, 1992 Form 10K, p. 33.

[9] Harley-Davidson home page.

[10] Peak.

[11] http://www.harley-davidson.com/wcm/Content/Pages/Student_Center/student_center.jsp?locale=en_US&request_key=-126553922&bmLocale=en_US#demographics.

[12] Kevin Kelly and Karen Miller, "The Rumble Heard Round the World: Harley's," *Business Week* (May 24, 1993), p. 60.

[13] Ibid.

[14] Harley-Davidson home page.

[15] Sandra Dallas and Emily Thornton, "Japan's Bikers: The Tame Ones," *BusinessWeek* (October 20, 1997), p. 159.

[16] http://www.motorcyclistonline.com/newsandupdates/harley_davidson_chinese_motorcycle_market/index.html.

[17] "H-D Cautiously Upbeat over Beijing Dealer," *Dealer News* (May 2006), p. 67.

[18] Harley-Davidson Motorcycles and Customer Data: Registrations (accessed May 20, 2008, at http://investor.harley-davidson.com/registrations.cfm?locale=en_US&bmLocale=en_US).

[19] http://www.cyclespot.com/forums/showthread.php?t=10328 (accessed May 21, 2008).

[20] http://seekingalpha.com/article/75695-high-gas-prices-may-help-harley-davidson-more-evidence (accessed May 21. 2008).

[21] http://www.businessweek.com/investor/content/apr2009/pi20090416_239475_page_2.htm.

[22] http://www.businessweek.com/investor/content/apr2009/pi20090416_239475.htm?chan=rss_topEmailedStories_ssi_5.

[23] Harley-Davidson home page.

Case 19 Endnotes

[1] Nancy Luna, "Sprinkles Bakery to Open in Corona del Mar," *The Orange County Register* (May 18, 2006).

[2] Morco R. della Cava, "Cupcake Bakeries Cater to the Kid in Us," *USA Today* (September 18, 2007).

[3] Ibid.

[4] "Cupcake Crazy!" *People in Touch* (July 31, 2006).

[5] http://www.sprinkles.com/flavors.html.

[6] TomKat's Tasty Holiday Treats," *OK Magazine* (December 21, 2007).

[7] Audrey Davidow, "So, Sweetie, I Quit to Bake Cupcakes," *The New York Times* (June 3, 2007).

[8] "Cupcake Bakeries," *USA Today*, op. cit.

[9] "Sprinkles Cupcake Bakery" (accessed May 25, 2008, at www.dmagazine.com).

[10] "So, Sweetie," *The New York Times*, op. cit.

[11] "Cupcake Bakeries," *USA Today*, op. cit.

[12] "Sprinkles Bakery," *The Orange County Register*, op. cit.

[13] "So, Sweetie," *The New York Times*, op. cit.

[14] "Cupcake Bakeries," *USA Today*, op. cit.

[15] "Sprinkles Bakery," *The Orange County Register*, op. cit.

[16] "So, Sweetie," *The New York Times*, op. cit.

[17] Joel Stein, "Cupcake Nation," *Time* (August 28, 2006).

[Photo Credits]

Chapter 1

Page 3: Melanie Stetson Freeman/Getty Images, Inc. **Page 5:** Al Behrman/©AP/Wide World Photos **Page 12:** Landov **Page 16:** NewsCom **Page 17:** Reprinted by permission of Harvard Business School Press. THE TRUTH ABOUT MIDDLE MANAGERS by Paul Osterman. Copyright ©2008 by the Harvard Business School Publishing Corporation; all rights reserved. **Page 18:** iStockphoto **Page 21:** iStockphoto **Page 24:** Michael Nagle/Getty Images, Inc.

Chapter 2

Page 27: Michael Dwyer/©AP/Wide World Photos **Page 29 (top):** Paul Sakuma/©AP/Wide World Photos **Page 29 (center):** Jack Wackerhausen/iStockphoto **Page 33:** Jacob Wackerhausen/iStockphoto **Page 36:** Outliers: The Story of Success by Malcolm Gladwell. Copyright 2008. Reproduced with permission of Little Brown and Company **Page 41:** Landov LLC **Page 42:** Ethan Miller/Getty Images, Inc. **Page 47:** SERGIO PEREZ/Reuters/Landov LLC

Chapter 3

Page 49: ©Haley/Sipa/AP/Wide World Photos **Page 51:** Monika Wisniewska/iStockphoto **Page 53:** ©AP/Wide World Photos **Page 55:** e Stock Photo/Alamy **Page 58:** iStockphoto **Page 59:** Photo by Judy Beedle, courtesy of Mad Gab's **Page 60:** Dana White/PhotoEdit **Page 63 (top):** Xinhua /Landov LLC **Page 63 (center):** John Moore/Getty Images, Inc. **Page 64:** Andy Kropa/Redux Pictures **Page 65:** AFP/NewsCom **Page 70:** GLEN ARGOV/Landov

Chapter 4

Page 73: KRT/NewsCom **Page 76:** Steven Day/©AP/Wide World Photos **Page 83:** Manish Swarup/©AP/Wide World Photos **Page 85:** ©AP/Wide World Photos: **Page 86:** Kin Cheung/©AP/Wide World Photos **Page 88:** Torbjorn Lagerwall/iStockphoto **Page 89:** iStockphoto **Page 93:** Brad Swonetz/Redux Pictures

Chapter 5

Page 95: Rajesh Jantila/AFP/Getty Images, Inc. **Page 99:** iStockphoto **Page 102:** Used with permission from McDonald's Corporation **Page 103:** iStockphoto **Page 105:** Jonathan Nourok/PhotoEdit **Page 106 (top):** KPA Hackenberg/NewsCom **Page 106 (bottom):** Pat Wellenbach/©AP/Wide World Photos **Page 112:** Nam Y. Huh/©AP/Wide World Photos

Chapter 6

Page 115: Zumaphotos/NewsCom **Page 119 (top):** Michael Tercha/Chicago Tribune/NewsCom **Page 118 (top):** Stockbyte/Getty Images, Inc. **Page 118 (bottom):** Courtesy Linda S. Sanford, SVP, IBM Corporation. **Page 119 (top): Page 121:** ©Caro/Alamy **Page 122:** Jupiter Images/Brand X/Alamy **Page 124:** iStockphoto **Page 130:** Jaime Lopez/Jam Media/LatinContent/Getty Images, Inc. **Page 134:** MARIO ANZUONI/Reuters/Landov LLC

Chapter 7

Page 137: David Young-Woff/PhotoEdit **Page 139:** Mark Lennihan/©AP/Wide World Photos **Page 141:** Oleksiy Maksymenko/Alamy **Page 145:** iStockphoto **Page 150:** iStockphoto **Page 154:** Lisa Poole/©AP/Wide World Photos

Chapter 8

Page 157: David Sherman/NBAE/Getty Images, Inc. **Page 161:** Masterfile **Page 166:** MARVIN FONG/The Plain Dealer/Landov LLC **Page 171:** Bill Pugliano/Getty Images, Inc. **Page 174:** Masterfile **Page 175:** Masterfile **Page 179:** STEPHEN HILGER/Landov LLC

Chapter 9

Page 181: AFP/Getty Images, Inc. **Page 182:** Jeff Greenberg/PhotoEdit **Page 183 (top):** Masterfile **Page 183 (bottom):** JAYANTA SHAW/Reuters/Landov **Page 186:** David Mclain/Aurora Photos Inc. **Page 189:** Anders Pettersson/Liaison/Getty Images, Inc. **Page 190:** ANDREW WINNING/Reuters/Landov **Page 191:** Mark Lennihan/©AP/Wide World Photos **Page 193:** Mark Lennihan/©AP/Wide World Photos **Page 192:** ©IDEO **Page 196:** Image Source/Getty Images, Inc. **Page 199:** Photo by Dara Seabridge, Courtesy TerraCycle, Inc. **Page 204:** AFP/Getty Images, Inc.

Chapter 10

Page 207: Courtesy Working Mother magazine **Page 210:** ©Yuri Arcurs/Shutterstock **Page 211:** Ron Edmonds/©AP/Wide World Photos **Page 214:** iStockphoto **Page 215:** Chris Ryan/Getty Images, Inc. **Page 216:** Sheer Photo, Inc./Getty Images, Inc. **Page 218 (top):** iStockphoto **Page 219:** Ben Baker/Redux Pictures **Page 221:** Stockbyte/Alamy **Page 222:** Jeff Greenberg/PhotoEdit **Page 224:** iStockphoto **Page 229:** Paul Sakuma/©AP/Wide World Photos

Chapter 11

Page 231: William Thomas Cain/Getty Images, Inc. **Page 234 (top):** Sports Illustrated/Getty Images/Getty Images, Inc. **Page 234 (center):** Copyright © 2003 by Lorraine Monroe, Reprinted by permission of PUBLICAFFAIRS, a member of Perseus Books Group. All rights reserved. **Page 244 (top):** Rolls Press/Popperfoto/Getty Images, Inc. **Page 244 (bottom):** iStockphoto **Page 246 (top):** Bettmann/©Corbis-Bettmann **Page 246 (bottom):** Angelo Cavalli/Getty Images, Inc. **Page 247:** NewsCom **Page 251:** Glen Stubbe/Star Tribune/Zuma Press

Chapter 12

Page 253: Courtesy The Center For Creative Leadership **Page 256:** Peter DaSilva/The New York Times/Redux Pictures **Page 257:** Gilles Mingasson/Getty Images, Inc. **Page 261:** Dimitri Vervits/Getty Images, Inc. **Page 262:** iStockphoto **Page 264:** Photodisc/Getty Images **Page 265:** John Fedele/Getty Images, Inc. **Page 268:** Troy Aossey/Getty Images, Inc. **Page 273:** KIMBERLY WHITE/Reuters/Landov LLC

Chapter 13

Page 275: Courtesy Spanx, Inc. www.spanx.com, http://www.spanx.com **Page 277:** Matthias Clamer/Getty Images, Inc. **Page 279:** Rosie Greenway/Getty Images **Page 283 (top):** iStockphoto **Page 283 (bottom):** Emma Innocenti/Getty Images, Inc. **Page 284:** Stockbyte/Getty Images **Page 287:** Tommy Flynn/Getty Images, Inc. **Page 293:** Jesse Grant/Getty Images, Inc.

Chapter 14

Page 295: iStockphoto **Page 296:** Bettmann/©Corbis **Page 298:** ©AP/Wide World Photos **Page 300:** Henny Ray Abrams/©AP/Wide World Photos **Page 304:** iStockphoto **Page 306:** George C. Anderson. Courtesy Bob Evans Farms, Inc. **Page 309:** Photo by Liz Song, courtesy of HopeLab **Page 314:** Paul Sakuma/©AP/Wide World Photos

Chapter 15

Page 317: Robert Lesieur/Reuters/Landov LLC **Page 319:** Allstair Berg/Digital Vision/Getty Images **Page 320:** Christopher Robbins/Getty Images, Inc. **Page 321 (top):** Masterfile **Page 321 (bottom):** Jose Luiis Pelaez/Getty Images, Inc. **Page 325:** Ted S. Warren/©AP/Wide World Photos **Page 327:** VEER Florian Franke/Getty Images, Inc. **Page 332:** Ruth Fremson/The New York Times/Redux Pictures **Page 333:** THE VOTE: BUSH, GORE & THE SUPREME COURT by Cass R. Sunstein and Richard A. Epstein, reprinted with permission of University of Chicago Press. © 2001 by The University of Chicago, All rights reserved. **Page 338:** John Raoux/©AP/Wide World Photos

Chapter 16

Page 341: GARY O'BRIEN/MCT/Landov LLC **Page 342:** Medioimages/Photodisc/Getty Images, Inc. **Page 344:** Christoph Martin/Getty Images, Inc. **Page 349:** iStockphoto **Page 352 (top):** Seth Perlman/©AP/Wide World Photos **Page 352 (center):** Filip Horvat/©AP/Wide World Photos **Page 353:** Gallo Images/Getty Images, Inc. **Page 357:** Ron Edmonds/©AP/Wide World Photos

Chapter 17

Page 359: NewsCom **Page 360:** Courtesy of VisionIT **Page 362:** Ricky John Molloy/Getty Images, Inc. **Page 367:** iStockphoto **Page 368 (top):** ©Trip/Alamy **Page 368 (bottom):** MIKE CLARKE/AFP/Getty Images, Inc. **Page 369:** iStockphoto **Page 371:** Greg Wood/AFP/Getty Images, Inc. **Page 377:** YOSHIKAZU TSUNO/AFP/Getty Images, Inc.

Chapter 18

Page 379: Jeff Greenberg/Alamy **Page 380:** Erich Schlegel/The New York Times/Redux Pictures **Page 381:** ©AP/Wide World Photos **Page 382:** AFP/Getty Images, Inc. **Page 383:** Ian Hayhurst/Getty Images, Inc. **Page 384:** Forrest Anderson//Time Life Pictures/Getty Images, Inc. **Page 389:** iStockphoto **Page 390:** Per-Anders Pettersson/Getty Images, Inc. **Page 391:** COLLAPSE by Jared Diamond. Copyright Penguin Group USA. **Page 397:** Chuck Burton/©AP/Wide World Photos

Chapter 19

Page 399: Getty Images, Inc. **Page 400:** ©AP/Wide World Photos **Page 401 (top):** ©AP/Wide World Photos **Page 401 (center):** ©AP/Wide World Photos **Page 403:** iStockphoto **Page 404:** Cassandra Nelson/Mercy Corps **Page 407:** Jeff Greenberg/PhotoEdit **Page 409:** Alamy **Page 410:** Michael Buckner/Getty Images, Inc. **Page 415:** Marissa Roth/The New York Times/Redux Pictures

Cases

Page 416: Michael Nagle/Getty Images, Inc. **Page 417:** Justin Sullivan/Getty Images, Inc. **Page 419:** REUTERS/Susana Vera /Landov LLC **Page 421:** Joe Raedle/Getty Images, Inc. **Page 422:** NewsCom **Page 424:** Dan Lamont/©Corbis **Page 425:** Brad Swonetz/Redux Pictures **Page 427:** John Gress/Reuters/Landov LLC **Page 429:** Peter Steffen/dpa/Landov LLC **Page 430:** The New York Times/Redux Pictures **Page 432:** Francis Dean/NewsCom **Page 433:** JIM BRYANT/UPI/Landov LLC **Page 435:** ©AP/Wide World Photos **Page 436:** Bill Aron/PhotoEdit **Page 438:** Tony Avelar/AFP/Getty Images, Inc. **Page 440:** ©AP/Wide World Photos **Page 441:** Hans Edinger/©AP/Wide World Photos **Page 442:** Chris Jackson/Getty Images **Page 443:** NewsCom **Page 445:** William Thomas Cain/Getty Images **Page 447:** ©AP/Wide World Photos **Page 449:** Randi Lynn Beach/©AP/Wide World Photos **Page 450:** ANDREA ROSSI/Maxppp/Landov LLC **Page 452:** REUTERS/Pierre Ducharme /Landov LLC **Page 453:** ©AP/Wide World Photos **Page 455:** Bryan Mitchell/Getty Images, Inc. **Page 457:** ©AP/Wide World Photos **Page 459:** NewsCom

Name Index

[Subject Index]

Conflict resolution, 346
Conflicts
    approach-approach, 344
    approach-avoidance, 344
    avoidance-avoidance, 344
    defined, 342
    functional *vs.* dysfunctional, 343–344
    intergroup, 344–345
    interorganizational, 344–345
    interpersonal, 344, 345–346
    lose-lose, 346
    management styles in handling, 345–346
    organizational sources, 344–345
    resource-driven, 346
    role of UN Secretary General, 352
    structural approaches to handling, 346–347
    substantive *vs.* emotional, 342–343
    types, 344–345
    win-lose, 346
    win-win, 346
Conscientiousness, as Big Five personality
    trait, 281
Consensus, 333
Constructive feedback, giving, 265
Constructive stress, 284
Consultative decisions, 241, 242
Contingency leadership perspective, 238
Contingency planning, 106
Contingency thinking, 41
Continuous improvement, 42, 126
Control charts, 126
Control equation, 118–119
Controlling
    defined, 10, 116
    in global corporations, 391
    integrating with planning, 123–124
    as one of four functions of management,
        10, 96, 98, 116–117
    steps in process, 117–119
    types of controls, 121–124
Co-opetition, 141
Core competencies, 146
Core culture, 184–185
Core values, 184–185
Corporate governance
    defined, 18, 65
    and ethical issues, 18
    need for strengthening, 65–66
    when CEO same person as Chairman
        of the Board, 159
Corporate greens, 63
Corporate social responsibility
    arguments for and against, 63–64
    classival view *vs.* socioeconomic view,
        63–64
    defined, 62
    examples, 63
    and social businesses, 64–65
Corporate strategy, 138–139
Corporations, defined, 410. *See also* Global
    corporations
Corruption, 389
Cost cutting, 150
Cost leadership strategies, 147
Cost-benefit analysis, 81
CPM/PERT, 127–128
Creativity, 85–86
Credible communication, 257
Crisis, 89

Critical path, 128
Critical thinking, as "must have" managerial
    skill, 14
Critical-incident technique, 218
Cross-cultural communication, 268–269,
    367, 368
Cross-functional teams, 167, 320
Cultural comfort, premature, 352–353
Cultural etiquette, 269
Cultural intelligence, 368, 393
Cultural relativism, 53
Culture clusters, 371–373
Culture shock, 367, 368
Cultures. *See also* Organizational cultures
    Hofstede's five dimensions of national
        value differences, 369–371
    project GLOBE clusters, 371–373
    silent languages in, 369
Cupcakes, 459–460
Currency risk, 391
Customer structures, 165–166
Customers
    as reason for businesses to go
        international, 381
    treating employees as, 230–231

D

Debt financing, 410
Decentralization, 172
Decentralized communication networks,
    329–330
Decision making. *See also* Problem solving
    by authority rule, 333
    behavioral model, 82
    causes of errors, 87–88
    classical model, 81
    by consensus, 333
    creativity in, 85–86
    in crisis, 89
    defined, 333
    in groups, 87
    groupthink problem, 333–334
    increasing team creativity, 334
    leader's choice of method, 241–242
    by majority rule, 333
    by minority rule, 333
    need for ethical reasoning, 83
    steps in process, 80–83
    team methods, 333
    types of environments for, 76–77
    by unanimity, 333
Decision-making process
    identifying problem, 80–81
    defining problem, 80–81
    evaluating alternative courses of action, 81
    deciding on preferred course of action,
        81–82
    implementing decisions, 82
    evaluating results, 82–83
    Ajax case, 80–83
    defined, 80
    steps in, 80–83
Decisions, defined, 78
Deficit principle, 34
Delegation, 172
Democratic leadership style, 236
Departmentalization, 163
Departments, as teams, 319
Destructive stress, 284

Differentiation strategies, 147
Disabilities. *See* Americans with Disabilities Act
Discrimination, 19, 209, 210–211, 363–364
Disruptive behaviors, 329
Distributive justice, 52
Distributive negotiation, 350
Diversification, 139, 140
Diversity
    among global cultures, 367–373
    business case for, 360–361
    defined, 18–19, 360, 361
    as potential competitive advantage, 360–361
    uneven distribution, 363–364
    valuing, 364, 365
Divestiture, 140
Division of labor, 159
Divisional structures, 164–165
Divisions, as teams, 319
Downsizing, 140
Dysfunctional conflicts, 343–344

E

EBM. *See* Evidence-based management (EBM)
E-business strategies, 142
Ecological fallacy, 371
Economic crisis of 2008
    corporate governance issue, 65–66
    effect on informal organizational
        structures, 161
    employer cost-cutting strategies, 150
    maintaining strategic control, 150
    as planning opportunity, 105
Economic development, as reason for
    businesses to go international, 381
Economic order quantity, 128
Effective communication, 255–256
Effective managers, 6
Effective negotiation, 349–350
Effective teams, 324
Efficient communication, 256
EI. *See* Emotional intelligence
Electronic grapevine, 267
Electronic meetings, 321
E-mail, 267, 268
Emotional conflicts, 342
Emotional intelligence
    defined, 13, 244, 288–289
    as leadership trait, 244–245
    and self-management, 21
Emotional stability, as Big Five personality
    trait, 281
Emotions, defined, 288
Employee assistance programs, 223
Employee engagement, 286–287
Employee involvement teams, 320
Employees
    alternative work schedules, 174–175
    bloggers in workplace, 342
    informal talk of job loss, 161
    maintaining open communication
        channels with, 265–266
    morale, ranked by country, 367
    role of human resource management,
        208–209
    roles in innovative organizations, 193
    satisfaction and retention survey, 33
    stock options, 223
    training, 216
    treating as important customers, 230–231

Employment discrimination, 19, 209, 210–211, 363–364
Empowerment, 172, 247
Entrepreneurs. *See also* Small businesses
common myths, 400
defined, 400
necessity-based, 403
personal characteristics, 401–403
as risk-takers, 400, 402
social, 404
women and minorities as, 398–399, 403
Entrepreneurship
defined, 400
Hispanic Entrepreneur of the Year, 360
social, 65
women in, 398–399, 403
Environment
green economy, 63, 141
green innovation, 189
greenhouse-gas emissions, 88
Equal employment opportunity (EEO), 209–210
Equal Employment Opportunity Commission (EEOC), 210
Equal Pay Act of 1963, 209, 211
Equity financing, 410–411
Equity theory of motivation, 303–304
ERG theory, 296–297
Escalating commitments, 88
Esteem, as need, 34, 35
Ethical behavior
cultural context, 53
defined, 50
individualism view, 52
in international business, 53–54
justice view, 52
managers as positive role models, 59–60
and moral leadership, 246
moral reasoning approaches, 51–53
moral rights view, 52
role of ethics training, 58
utilitarian view, 51–52
as values driven, 50–51
Ethical dilemmas
"bad boss" behaviors, 54–55
defined, 54
spotlight questions, 58
tips for dealing with, 58
in the workplace, 54–55
Ethical frameworks, 57
Ethical imperialism, 53
Ethical leadership, 246
Ethics. *See also* Corporate social responsibility; Ethical behavior
and corporate governance, 18
in decision making, 83
defined, 17, 50
failures, 17–18
formal codes, 60
maintaining high standards in organizations, 57–60
in negotiation, 351–352
protecting whistleblowers, 59
rationalizing unethical behaviors, 55
workplace dilemmas, 54–55
Ethics training, 58
Ethnic subcultures, 362
Ethnocentrism, 268–269, 362, 368
Etiquette, cultural, 269

Evidence-based management (EBM), 43
Existence needs, 297, 298
Expatriate workers, 392
Expectancy, defined, 304
Expectancy theory, 304–306
Expert power, 234
Exporting, 382
External controls, 122
Extinction, 309
Extroversion, as Big Five personality trait, 281

F

Facilities plans, 102
Family and Medical Leave Act, 211
Family business feuds, 407
Family businesses, 407–408
Family-friendly benefits, 223
Feedback, in communication, 265
Feedback controls, 121–122
Feedforward controls, 121
Female leaders, 245–246. *See also* Women, in workplace
Fiedler contingency model, 238–239
The Fifth Discipline (Senge), 42
Filtering, 262
Financial budgets, 103
Financial plans, 102
Financial ratios, 129
First-line managers, 4
First-mover advantage, 400
Fixed budgets, 103
"Fixed pie," 352
Flexible benefits, 223
Flexible budgets, 103
Flexible working hours, 175
Flextime, 175
Focused cost leadership strategy, 147
Focused differentiation strategy, 147
Force-coercion change strategy, 198–199
Forecasting, 105
Foreign Corrupt Practices Act, 389
Foreign exchange rates, 391
Foreign subsidiaries, 383
Formal structures, 159
Formal teams, 319
Framing errors, 88
Franchising, 383
Free-agent economy, 20
Friendship groups, 320
Fringe benefits, 223
Functional chimneys problem, 164
Functional conflicts, 343
Functional plans, 102
Functional siloes problem, 164
Functional strategies, 139
Functional structures, 163–164
Fundamental attribution error, 278
Future orientation, as project GLOBE dimension, 372–373

G

Gain sharing, 222
Gantt charts, 38, 127
Gender. *See also* Women, in workplace
egalitarianism as project GLOBE dimension, 372
and international job stereotype, 277
and leadership differences, 245–246
organizational subculture differences, 362

Gender similarities hypothesis, 245
General partnerships, 409–410
Generational subcultures, 362. *See also* Baby boomers; Millennials
Geographical structures, 165
Glass ceiling, 18, 363
Global area structure, 391, 392
Global corporations
compared with international businesses, 387
as controversial, 387–388
defined, 387
ethical challenges, 388–389
leadership challenges, 393
organizing in, 391–392
planning and controlling in, 391
staffing international operations, 392
and sustainable development issue, 390
Global economy, 380
Global managers, 393
Global outsourcing, 16
Global product structure, 391, 392
Global recession, 16–17
Global sourcing
as common form of international business, 382
defined, 382
Limited Brands example, 378–379
Global strategic alliances, 383
Globalization
defined, 16, 380
gap between large multinationals and everyone else, 388
impact on international businesses, 380–385
Limited Brands example, 378–379
Globalization strategy, 140–141
Goal setting, 108, 306
Good to Great (Collins), 43
Governance, 5, 17–18. *See also* Corporate governance
Graphic rating scale, 217
Green economy, 63, 141
Green innovation, 189
Greenfield ventures, 383
Greenhouse-gas emissions, 88
Group decisions, 87, 241, 242
Group dynamics, 326
Group meetings, 266
Groups. *See* Teams
Groupthink, 333, 334
Growth needs, 297
Growth strategies, 139

H

Halo effect, 277
Hawthorne effect, 34
Hersey-Blanchard situational leadership model, 239–240
Heuristics
anchoring and adjustment, 87–88
availability, 87
representativeness, 87
Hierarchy of needs, 34–35, 296, 297
Hierarchy of objectives, 98
High-context cultures, 369
Higher-order needs, 296, 297, 298
High-performance organizations, 43
Human capital, 208–209
Human relations leadership style, 236

Management by objectives. *See* Managing by objectives
Management by wandering around (MBWA), 265
Management process, 9–10, 11
Management science, 38
Managers
    accountability, 5–6
    agenda setting, 11
    as decision makers, 74–78
    decisional roles, 11
    defined, 4
    and delegation, 172
    effective, 6
    essential skills, 12–13
    as ethical role models, 59–60
    expectations of, 6–7
    first-line, 4
    foundations for effective leadership, 232–236
    global, need for, 393
    informational roles, 11
    interpersonal roles, 11
    leading organizational change process, 195–200
    learning from experience, 13–14
    maintaining open communication channels with employees, 265–266
    middle, 4–5
    Mintzberg's view of roles, 11
    "must have" skills list, 14
    as problem solvers, 74–78
    role in upside-down pyramid, 7
    sources of power, 233–234
    top, 5
    types and levels, 4–5
    what they do, 8–15
Managing by objectives (MBO), 123–124, 306
Managing diversity, 364–365, 365
Market controls, 123
Marketing plans, 102
Masculinity-femininity, 371, 372
Matrix structures, 166–167
MBO. *See* Managing by objectives (MBO)
MBWA (management by wandering around), 265
Means-ends chain, 98
Mechanistic design, 173
Mediation, 353
Meetings
    electronic, 321
    group, 266
    online, 321
    unproductive, 320
Membership composition, 325
Mentoring, 216
Merit pay, 222
Micro-finance, 404, 410
Middle managers
    defined, 4
    essential skills, 13
    examples, 5
    Osterman's views, 17
Millennials, 262, 267, 362
Mining industry, and sustainable development, 390
Minorities, 363–364. *See also* Diversity
Minority-owned businesses, 403
Mission, 144–145

Mixed messages, 261
Monochronic cultures, 369
Mood contagion, 289
Moods, 289
Moral development, Kohlberg's three stages, 57–58
Moral managers, 60
Moral rights view of ethical behavior, 52
Most favored nation status, 385
Motivation
    Alderfer's ERG theory, 296–297
    core characteristics model, 299–300
    deficit principle, 296
    defined, 296
    equity theory, 303–304
    expectancy theory, 304–306
    goal-setting theory, 306
    Herzberg's two-factor theory, 298–299
    hygiene factors, 299
    and job design, 299–300, 301
    Maslow's hierarchy of needs, 296, 297
    McClelland's acquired needs, 297–298
    progression principle, 296
    role of reinforcement, 308–310
    satisfier factors, 298–299
Multicultural organizations, 361
Multinational corporations (MNCs), 381, 387, 388, 392. *See also* Global corporations
Multinational organizations, 387
Multi-person comparisons, 218
Myers-Briggs Type Indicator, 281–282
Myth of the "fixed pie," 352

N

Nano (automobile), 188, 358–359
National cultures, Hofstede's five dimensions of value differences, 369–371
National subcultures, 362
Necessity-based entrepreneurs, 403
Need for achievement, 298
Need for affiliation, 298
Need for power, 298
Needs, Maslow's hierarchy, 34–35, 296
Negative reinforcement, 308
Negotiation
    bargaining zone, 351
    common pitfalls, 352–353
    defined, 349
    distributive *vs.* integrative, 350
    effective, 349–350
    ethics in, 351–352
    over salaries, 349
    between parties from different cultures, 352–353
    role of UN Secretary General, 352
    third-party, 353
Network structures, 168–169
Networks, 12, 329–330. *See also* Social networking
Noise, in communication, 259
Nominal group technique, 334
Non-monetary budgets, 103
Nonprofit organizations, 4
Nonprogrammed decisions, 78
Nonverbal communication, 261
Norms, 328

O

Objectives
    defined, 96

defining, 96–97
    hierarchy, 98
    improvement, 124
    managing by, 123–124, 306
    as means-ends chain, 98
    operating, 145
    personal development, 124
    writing, 124
Observable culture, 183
Occupational Health and Safety Act, 209
Occupational qualifications, 209–210
Occupational subcultures, 362
Office romances, 103
Office spaces, designing to encourage communication, 266–267
Online meetings, 321
Open systems, 39–40
Openness to experience, as Big Five personality trait, 281
Operant conditioning, 308
Operating budgets, 103
Operating objectives, 145
Operational plans, 101
Operations management, 39
Operations research, 38
Opportunities. *See* SWOT analysis
Optimizing decisions, 81
Organic designs, 173
Organization charts, 159
Organization structures
    customer, 165–166
    decentralized, 172
    defined, 159
    designing, 171–175
    divisional, 164–165
    formal *vs.* informal, 159–160
    functional, 163–164
    geographic, 165
    matrix, 166–167
    network, 168–169
    product, 165
    support for innovation, 192
    team, 167–168
    types, 163–169
Organizational citizenship behaviors, 286
Organizational cultures
    defined, 182
    impact on performance, 182–183
    inclusive, 361
    observable, 183–184
    subcultures as challenge, 361–362
    support for diversity, 361
    support for innovation, 192
    tips on understanding, 183
Organizational design, 171
Organizational subcultures, 361–362
Organizations. *See also* Organization structures
    high-performance, 43
    innovative, 188–193
    leadership of change process, 195–200
    mechanistic *vs.* organic designs, 173–174
    as networks of subsystems, 40
    as open systems, 39–40
    phases of planned change, 196–198
    social network analysis, 160
    stakeholders, 62
    transformational *vs.* incremental change, 195–196

Organizing
    defined, 9, 10, 158
    in global corporations, 391–392
    as one of four functions of management,
        9, 10, 96, 158
Orientation, 215
Output standards, 117
Outsourcing, 16, 141, 168–169, 381

P

Participatory planning, 107
Partnerships, 409–410
Path-goal theory, 240
Perceived negative inequity, 303
Perceived positive inequity, 303
Perceptions
    as cause of attribution errors, 278
    defined, 276
    influence on individual behavior, 276–279
    and racial bias, 277
    selective, 277
Performance appraisal
    critical-incident technique, 218
    defined, 217
    rating scales, 217
Performance objectives. See Objectives
Performance opportunities, 74–75
Performance orientation, as project GLOBE
        dimension, 372, 373
Performance threats, 74
Permatemps, 212
Personal development objectives, 124
Personal integrity, 246
Personal power, 298
Personal wellness, 284
Personality
    Big Five traits, 281
    defined, 281
    and Myers-Briggs Type Indicator, 281–282
    traits that influence work behavior,
        281–283
Persuasion. See Rational persuasion change
        strategy
Persuasive communication, 257
Physiological needs, 34, 35
Pit crews, 316–317, 325
Planned change, 196–198, 199
Planning
    contingency, 105–106
    defined, 9, 10, 96
    forecasting for, 105
    in global corporations, 391
    impact on performance, 97–99
    integrating with controlling, 123–124
    as one of four functions of management,
        9, 10, 96
    participatory, 107
    role of staff planners, 107
    scenario, 106
    steps in process, 96–97
Plans
    budgets as, 103
    defined, 97
    functional, 102
    and goal setting, 108
    long-range, 101
    operational, 101
    policies and procedures as, 102–103
    short-range, 101

    strategic, 101
    tactical, 101
    types, 101–102
Policies, 102
Political risk, 391
Political-risk analysis, 391
Polychronic cultures, 369
Portfolio planning, 148–149
Positive reinforcement, 308
Post-It Notes, 190
Power
    defined, 233
    need for, 298
    personal, 234
    personal vs. social, 298
    position, 233–234
Power distance, 370, 372
Pregnancy discrimination, 212
Pregnancy Discrimination Act, 209, 211
Prejudice, 19
Presentations, tips for making, 260
Problem solving. See also Decision making
    defined, 73
    performance opportunities, 74–75
    performance threats, 74
    programmed vs. nonprogrammed
        decisions, 78
Procedural justice, 52
Procedures, 102–103
Process innovation, 188
Product innovation, 188
Product structures, 165
Production plans, 102
Professionalism, as "must have" managerial
        skill, 14
Profit sharing, 222
Profitability, 129
Profits, as reason for businesses to go
        international, 381
Programmed decisions, 78
Progression principle, 34
Project GLOBE (Global Leadership and
        Organizational Behavior Effectiveness),
        371–372
Project management, 127–128
Project teams, 320
Projection, 277
Projects, 127
Protectionism, 384, 385
Proxemics, 267, 369
Punishment, 309, 310

Q

Quality circles, 320
Quality control, 126–127
Quality of work life (QWL), 6
QWL. See Quality of work life (QWL)

R

Racial subcultures, 362
Rating scales, for performance appraisal, 217
Rational persuasion change strategy, 199
Rationalization, 55
Realistic job previews, 215
Reality team building, 332
Recession, 16–17
Recruitment, 214
Referent power, 234
Refreezing phase of planned change, 197–198

Reinforcement
    continuous schedule, 310
    intermittent schedule, 310
    positive vs. negative, 308–310
Relatedness needs, 297
Relationship goals, 349
Reliability, in employment tests, 215
Representativeness heuristic, 87
Restricted communication networks, 330
Retrenchment strategies, 140
Reverse discrimination, 210
Reverse mentoring, 216
Reward power, 233
Risk, as reason for businesses to go
        international, 381
Risk environments, 77
Roman Empire, 28
Rules. See Procedures

S

Safety needs, 34, 35
Salaries, negotiating, 349
Sarbanes-Oxley Act, 65
Satisficing decisions, 82
Satisfier factors, 298, 299
Scenario planning, 106
Scientific management, 28–29
Selection, 214
Selective perception, 277
Self-actualization, as need, 34, 35, 296
Self-fulfilling prophecies, 35–36
Self-management, 14, 21
Self-managing teams, 321–322
Self-monitoring, 283
Self-serving bias, 278
Sensation feelers, 76
Sensation thinkers, 76
Servant leadership, 247
Sexual harassment, 363–364
Shamrock organizations, 20
Shaping, 309–310
Shared power change strategy, 199–200
Short-range plans, 101
Silent languages, 369
Siloes. See Functional siloes problem
Situational leadership model, 239–240
Six Signs, 127
Skunkworks, 192
Small businesses
    defined, 406
    failure rate, 408
    family-owned, 407–408
    life cycle stages, 406–407
    need for sound business plan, 409
    reasons for failure, 408
    types of ownership, 409–410
    ways to finance, 410–411
Social businesses, 49, 64
Social entrepreneurs, 404
Social entrepreneurship, 65, 189–190
Social loafing, 319
Social needs, 34, 35
Social network analysis, 160
Social networking, 265–266, 267, 268. See
        also Facebook in Organizations Index
Social power, 298
Social responsibility. See Corporate social
        responsibility
Socialization, 183, 215

Socioeconomic view of CSR, 64
Sole proprietorships, 409
Span of control, 171
Spirituality, workplace, 185
Spotlight questions, 58, 83
Staff planners, 107
Stakeholders, 62
Standard operating procedures (SOPs), 102–103
Stereotypes, 276
Stock options, 223
Strategic alliances, 141, 168–169
Strategic control, 150
Strategic human resource management, 209
Strategic intent, 138
Strategic leadership, 150
Strategic management
    defined, 144
    portfolio planning, 148–149
    steps in process, 144–146
    SWOT analysis, 145–146
Strategic plans, 101
Strategies
    cooperative, 141–142
    defined, 138
    for e-business, 142
    formulating and implementing, 144–150
    functional, 139
    global, 140–141
    growth, 139
    for retrenchment, 140
    types, 138–142
Strategy formulation, 144
Strategy implementation, 144
Strengths. *See* SWOT analysis
Stress
    consequences, 283–284
    constructive, 284
    defined, 283
    destructive, 284
Stretch goals, 97
Strong cultures, 182
Subcultures, organizational, 361–362
Substance goals, 349
Substantive conflicts, 342
Substitutes for leadership, 240
Subsystems, 40
Succession plans, for family businesses, 408
Succession problem, in family businesses, 407–408
Supplier alliances, 141
Suppliers, as reason for businesses to go international, 381
Support groups, 320
Sustainable development, 390
Sweatshops, 389, 390
SWOT analysis, defined, 145–146
Symbolic leaders, 186
Synergy, 318
Systematic thinking, 75

T

Tactical plans, 101
Take Our Daughters to Work Day, 399
Tariffs, 385
TARP (Troubled Asset Relief Program), 78
Task activities, 329
Task forces, 320. *See also* Teams
TAT (Thematic Apperception Test), 297–298

Team building, 332–333
Team process, 326
Team structures, 167
Teams
    assessing process maturity, 327
    benefits for organizations, 318
    cohesiveness, 328, 329
    creating and leading, 332–334
    cross-functional, 167, 320
    decision-making methods, 333
    defined, 318
    distributed leadership, 329
    diversity factor, 326
    effect of communication networks on performance, 329–330
    effect of task and maintenance roles on performance, 329
    effective, 324–330
    formal, 318–319
    free-riding by some members, 319
    and group norms, 328, 329
    high-performance characteristics, 332–334
    impact of disruptive behaviors, 329
    increasing decision-making creativity, 334
    life cycle, 326–328
    manager's role, 319–320
    measuring effectiveness, 324
    membership composition, 325
    organizational support, 325–326
    organizations as networks of, 319–320
    performance problems, 318–319
    self-managing, 321–322
    size considerations, 326
    stages of development, 326–328
    types, 320
    virtual, 321
Teamwork
    building blocks, 324–330
    defined, 318
    as "must have" managerial skill, 14
Technical skills, 12
Telecommuting, 175
Telephone interviews, 214, 215
Terminal values, 51
Text messaging, 267
Thematic Apperception Test (TAT), 297–298
Theory X, 35, 36
Theory Y, 35, 36, 122
Thievery, corporate, 118
Threats. *See* SWOT analysis, defined
Time management, 98–99
Time orientation, 371, 373
Top managers, 5, 13
Total quality management (TQM), 42, 126
TQM (total quality management), 42, 126
Trade barriers, 385
Training, 216
Transactional leadership, 244
Transformational change, 195–196
Transformational leadership, 244
Transnational corporations, 387. *See also* Global corporations
Triple bottom line, 63
Troubled Asset Relief Program (TARP), 78
Turnover, 287
Two-tier wage systems, 224
Type A personality, 283

U

Uncertain environments, defined, 77
Uncertainty avoidance, 370, 372
Unfreezing phase of planned change, 196–197
Unions, labor, 223–224, 225, 253, 454
Universal Declaration of Human Rights, 53
Universalism, 53
Unproductive meetings, 320
Unrelated diversification, 140
Upside-down pyramid, 7
U.S. auto industry, 171, 225, 383, 455–456.
    See also Ford Motor Co. *and* General Motors *in Organizations Index*
Utilitarian view of ethical behavior, 51

V

Valence, 304, 305
Validity, in employment tests, 215
Value-based management, 185–186
Values, 50–51
Venture capitalists, 411
Vertical integration, 140
Video game therapy, 309
Videoconferencing, 266
Virtual organizations, 169
Virtual teams, 321
Virtuous circle, 64
Vision, 235
Visionary leadership, 235
Volunteering, 300
Vroom-Jago model, 241–242

W

Weaknesses. *See* SWOT analysis
Web 2.0, 273
Wellness, personal, 284
Whistleblowers, 59
Wi-Fi, 448
Winfrey, Oprah, 459
Win-lose conflicts, 346
Win-win conflicts, 346
Withdrawal behaviors, 286
Women, in workplace. *See also* Diversity
    best employers for working mothers, 206
    and diversity bias, 363–364
    as entrepreneurs, 398–399, 403
    and glass ceiling, 363
    and international job stereotype, 277
    as leaders, 245–246
    organizational subculture differences, 362
Work sampling, 215
Work units, as teams, 319
Workforce. *See* Diversity; Employees
Working mothers, best employers for, 206
Work-life balance, 221
Workplace privacy, 212
Workplace rage, 284
Workplace spirituality, 185
World trade. *See* Globalization; International businesses
World Trade Organization (WTO), 385

Y

YouTube videos, 267, 268, 371

Z

Zero-based budgets, 103
Zero-sum game. *See* Myth of the "fixed pie"

Organization Index

EXPLORING MANAGEMENT, 2E SPECIAL FEATURES

TRENDSETTERS

Ursula Burns, Xerox
Carol Bartz, Yahoo
John Wood, Room to Read
Indra Nooyi, Pepsi
Don Thompson, McDonalds USA
Patricia Karter, Dancing Deer
Roger W. Ferguson, TIAA-CREF
Alan Mulally, Ford
Tom Szaky, TerraCycle
Susan Arnold, Procter & Gamble
Lorraine Monroe, Leadership Institute
Evan Williams & Biz Stone, Twitter
Richard Branson, Virgin Group
Pat Christen, HopeLab
Jeff Bezos, Amazon.com
Ban Ki-Moon, UN
David Segura, VisionIT
Victor Fung, Li & Fung
Zainab Salbi, Women for Women
    International

STAY TUNED

Employment Contradictions in
    Workforce Diversity
Employee Satisfaction and Retention
Behavior of Managers Key to Ethical
    Workplace
Greenhouse-Gas Emissions Join
    List of Executive Priorities
Policies on Office Romances
    Vary Widely
Bad Economy Brings Out More
    Corporate Thieves
Cost-Cutting Abounds When
    Times Get Tough
What Recession Means in Job Losses
Union Membership Declines in U.S.
U.S. Workers Report Concerns
    about Leaders
Employees Have Cause to Worry
    about Electronic Monitoring
Job Satisfaction Trends
Women Still Behind in Pay and Top Jobs
Unproductive Meetings Are Major
    Time Wasters
Work-Family Conflict Rises for Men,
    Falls for Women
Employee Morale Varies Around
    the World
Corruption and Bribes Haunt
    International Business
Minority Entrepreneurs Lead the Way

NEWS FEED

Good and Bad News for Middle
    Managers
Practice Beats Intelligence among
    Super Achievers
Welcome Corporate Greens and the
    New ECOnomics
Shareholders Push to Regulate
    Executive Pay
Recession Is a Good Time for
    Setting Priorities
Elsewhere Class Struggles to Balance
    Work and Leisure
Clean Energy Hurt by Financial Crisis
Job Fears the Talk of Informal Structure
Google and Procter & Gamble Swap
    Workers to Fuel Innovation
Age Bias Complaints Are on the Rise
Why Peter Drucker's Leadership
    Advice Still Matters
Millenials May Need Special Handling
Racial Bias Embedded in the
    Perception of Many
Volunteers Find They Do Well
    by Doing Good
Reality TV Rubs Off on Reality Team
    Building
Blogger's Rights a Growing Point of
    Conflict
Internet Censorship Fuels Global
    Debate
More Global Firms Employ Sweatshop
    Hunters
Social Entrepreneurs Turn Dreams
    into Progress

SPECIAL RESOURCES

CASES

Trader Joe's
Zara International
Tom's of Maine
Amazon.com
Land's End
Electronic Arts
Dunkin' Donuts
Nike
Apple
Netflix
Southwest Airlines
Facebook
Panera Bread
Pixar
NASCAR
AFL-CIO
Toyota
Harley-Davidson
Sprinkles

SELF-ASSESSMENTS

Personal Management Foundations
Managerial Assumptions
Terminal Values Survey
Intuitive Ability
Time Management Profile
Internal/External Control
Facts and Inferences
Organizational Design Preferences
Tolerance for Ambiguity
Performance Appraisal Assumptions
Least Preferred Co-Worker Scale
Feedback and Assertiveness
Stress Test
Two-Factor Profile
Team Leaders Skills
Conflict Management Strategies
Diversity Awareness
Global Readiness
Entrepreneurship Orientation